ASPECTS OF EDUCATIONAL TECHNOLOGY

Aspects of Educational Technology

Volume XI
The Spread of Educational
Technology

*Edited for the Association for
Programmed Learning
and Educational Technology by*
Philip Hills and John Gilbert

General Editor:
R E B Budgett *Department of Teaching Media,
University of Southampton*

Kogan Page

First published 1977
by Kogan Page Limited,
120 Pentonville Road, London N1 9JN

Copyright © Association for Programmed Learning
and Educational Technology, 1977
Printed in Great Britain by
Anchor Press Ltd, Tiptree, Essex

ISBN 0 85038 093 6

Distributed in the USA by Nichols Publishing Co
PO Box 96, New York NY 10024

Contents

Section 10: Schools

Section 11: Curriculum

Reviews of Workshops, Post-Deadline Papers and Delegates Forum

Editorial Comment

P J Hills, J K Gilbert

ETIC 77 was a successful conference both in terms of numbers attending, the quality and quantity of the papers and the reactions of participants. A total of 264 attended the conference, 194 from the UK and 70 from overseas, representing an extremely broad interpretation of 'educational technology'. The quantity of papers presented (68 in the formal sessions plus many in the informal sessions), together with the number of workshops (11), represents a high level of activity in a broad range of subjects.

This volume of the Proceedings is organized in the same way as the conference itself, ie as a series of sections containing papers which were grouped under these headings on the basis of authors' abstracts. The section 'Educational Technology Abroad', which includes a review of theoretical developments, contains papers on the application of ideas in the developing countries (Romiszowsky, Vari) as well as in the newly-rich countries (El-Araby). The 'Tertiary' section deals mainly with application in physical science courses. The 'Systems' section is dominated by CAL, reflecting perhaps the recent level of expenditure in the field, although the overall theme of 'implementational problems' comes through in all contributions. The existence of a medical section is itself welcome, the papers being mainly concerned to present the application of the educational technology approach to solve problems presented by large numbers of students. The 'Educational Management' section was difficult to assemble, reflecting perhaps a relative neglect of this vital area, but the papers cover a broad area from schools to industry. The section 'Educational Technology: Today and Tomorrow' produced some futurology (Elton), together with interesting papers on problem solving and communication (Cowan, Percival) and distance learning (Butts and Megarry). In 'Evaluation' the conclusions of a broader set of interpretations of this activity, as applied to a diverse set of subject areas, were presented. 'Skills' consists of a wide range of well organized practical schemes, from schools to industry. 'Dissemination', the section perhaps most closely related to the theme of the conference, discusses mechanisms, both within particular kinds of institutions and for particular kinds of innovations, as well as generalized strategies. The papers concerning 'Schools' were very diverse in character, with the principles and practice of curriculum design broadly represented in the 'Curriculum' section.

Overall, a number of general issues stand out from the conference. The tendency for educational technology, as a field of practice and research, to splinter progressively into subsidiary areas has, as far as it concerns ETIC 77, been avoided. Thus it was particularly gratifying to see the 'medical' and 'computer' orientated areas fully represented, and the development of systems considered together with their management. The insidious effects of fashion, ie the tendency to treat a subject superficially before moving on, were often resisted: Elizabeth Bingham's paper on 'Free-Format Timetabling Revisited' is of a type to be encouraged.

Although a good number of papers were presented on the theme of the conference, a high proportion represented general and continuing concerns. The implication of this, for the organization of future conferences, must be considered. The limitations to the 'paper' method of presentation, touched upon by Geoffrey Hubbard, should be given more thought, and ways of facilitating a broader range of professional contents, within the confines of the conference, should be considered.

Acknowledgements

The Conference Organizers wish to acknowledge the support and assistance given by the following who, through their generosity and provision, contributed so greatly to the success of the Conference:

The Vice-Chancellor and Staff of the University of Surrey
Hunt & Broadhurst Ltd
Thomas Tait and Sons Ltd
General Binding Co Ltd
International Computers Ltd
The Department of Education and Science.
Cover Design by H K Teh, AVA Unit, University of Surrey.

Case Study in the Implementation of Innovation. A New Model for Developmental Testing. Fig 2. *E S Henderson, M B Nathenson*

Is Educational Technology Infectious? Figs 1 & 4. *I Townsend, J Heath*

Evaluation of Chemical Card Games as Learning Aids *K Vaughan*

Sir Walter Perry, The Open University.

General Nursing Council for England and Wales, 23 Portland Place, London W1A 1BA. Nursing Times, 4 Little Essex Street, London WC2R 2LF.

Heyden & Son Ltd, Spectrum House, Alderton Crescent, London NW4 3XX.

List of Contributors

Anderson, J S A	CAMOL Project, New University of Ulster, Coleraine, N Ireland
Bateson, Major C M	RAEC RET DT Brompton Barracks, Chatham, Kent
Behling, Dr B	West Virginia University, Morgantown, USA.
Bellamy, J A	Loughborough University of Technology, Loughborough, Leicestershire
Bingham, Mrs E G	Heriot-Watt University, Riccarton, Currie EH14 4HS
Blithe, T M	Dept of Mathematics, Victoria University of Wellington, Wellington, New Zealand
Bond, Lt Cdr J P	Royal Naval School of Educational Training and Technology, HMS Nelson, Portsmouth, Hants
Boyd, Dr G M	Concordia University Education Dept, 1445 de Maisonneuve Blvd West, Montreal, Quebec H3G 1M8, Canada
Branthwaite, A	University of Keele, Keele, Staffs
Buter, Dr E M	University of Amsterdam, Stadionweg 222^2, Amsterdam, Holland
Butts, D C	Jordanhill College of Education, Glasgow G13 1PP
Sinha R del Canto, S	Universidad de los Andes, PO Box 128, Venezuela
Cartwright, Dr G F	Faculty of Education, McGill University, 3700 McTavish Street, Montreal, Quebec, Canada
Chan, Dr Geok Oon	Centre for Educational Studies, Universiti Sains Malaysia, Minden, Penang, Malaysia
Chaudhri, M M	National Council for Educational Research & Training, 10B Ring Road, New Delhi, India
Chaves, Dr O E	Universidad de los Andes, PO Box 128, Merida, Venezuela
Christensen, S H B	Brigham Young University, Provo, Utah, USA
Clark, Ms M J	Victoria University of Wellington, Wellington, New Zealand
Clarke, J	West Virginia University, Morgantown, USA
Clifford, D M	British Gas, 5 Grosvenor Crescent, London SW1X 7EE
Coldevin, Dr G O	Concordia University, 1455 de Maisonneuve Blvd West, Montreal, Quebec H3G 1M8, Canada
Coles, C R	Department of Teaching Media, The University, Southampton SO9 5NH
Cowan, J	Department of Civil Engineering, Learning Unit, Heriot-Watt University, Riccarton, Currie EH14 4AF
Coutts-Clay, Mrs J	Sales Training Manager, British Airways, West London Terminal, Cromwell Road, London SW7

13

Cuneo, P	Universidad de los Andes, PO Box 128, Merida, Venezuela
Davies, W J K	County Programmed Learning Centre at St Albans College, Hatfield Road, St Albans, Herts
Derevensky, Dr J L	Faculty of Education, McGill University, 3700 McTavish Street, Montreal, Quebec, Canada
Dorman, W	Universidad de los Andes, PO Box 128, Merida, Venezuela
Dowdeswell, Professor W H	University of Bath School of Education, Claverton Down, Bath BA2 7AY
Edwards, Miss S	Institute for Educational Technology, University of Surrey, Guildford, Surrey
El-Araby, Dr S A	The Arab States Centre for Educational Media, Kuwait
Ellington, Dr H I	Educational Technology Unit, Robert Gordon's Institute of Technology, St Andrews Street, Aberdeen
Elton, Professor L R B	Institute for Educational Technology, University of Surrey, Guildford, Surrey
Evans, C	Fulham Chest Clinic, at Western Hospital, Seagrave Road, London SW6
Evans, L F	The City University, St John Street, London EC1V 4PB
Evers, V H C	Philips Research Laboratories, Willem Alexanderlaan 76, Geldrop, The Netherlands
Fisher, Dr B C	Department of Mechanical Engineering, Loughborough University of Technology, Loughborough, Leics LE11 3TU
Fjällbrant, Dr N	Chalmers University of Technology Library, Fack S-40220, Gothenburg, Sweden
Frazer, Professor M J	School of Chemical Sciences, University of East Anglia, Norwich, Norfolk
Gilbert, Dr J K	Institute for Educational Technology, University of Surrey, Guildford, Surrey
Govinda, R	Centre for Advanced Study in Education, Faculty of Education & Psychology, University of Baroda, Lokmanya, Tilak Road, Baroda 2, India
Green, Dr E E	Brigham Young University, Provo, Utah, USA
Green, Dr J	Learning Systems Unit, Middlesex Polytechnic, Queensway, Enfield, Middlesex EN3 4SF
Hall, L	West Virginia University, Morgantown, USA
Hall, Dr W C	Advisory Centre for University Education, The University of Adelaide, Adelaide, S Australia 5001
Hammond, R	Centre for Educational Technology, University College, PO Box 78, Cardiff, South Wales
Harris, N D C	University of Bath, Claverton Down, Bath BA2 7AY
Hartley, Dr J	Dept of Psychology, University of Keele, Keele, Staffs
Hazewindus, N	Philips Research Laboratories, Willem Alexanderlaan 76, Geldrop, The Netherlands
Heath, Mrs J	NHS Learning Resources Unit, 13 Grove Road, Totley Rise, Sheffield
Henderson, Dr E S	Institute for Educational Technology, Open University, Walton Hall, Milton Keynes MK7 6AA
Herbert, D F	School of Chemical Sciences, University of East Anglia, Norwich, Norfolk

Hills, Dr P J	Institute for Educational Technology, University of Surrey, Guildford, Surrey
Hooper, R	Directorate, National Development Programme in Computer Assisted Learning, 37-41 Mortimer Street, London W1A 2JL
Howard, M	West Virginia University, Morgantown, USA
Hubbard, G	Director, Council for Educational Technology, 3 Devonshire Street, London W1N 2BA
Hunter, Mrs E	Avery Hill College of Education, Bexley Road, Eltham SE9 2PQ
Imrie, B W	Victoria University of Wellington, Wellington, New Zealand
Jaknowitz, L	West Virginia University, Morgantown, USA
Johnston, L C	Department of Mathematics, Victoria University of Wellington, Wellington, New Zealand
Kasipar, C	Thai-German TTC, PO Box 8/17, Bangkok 8, Thailand
Kirkhope, Ms S	University of Bath, Claverton Down, Bath BA2 7AY
Langton, N H	Educational Technology Unit, Robert Gordon's Institute of Technology, St Andrews Street, Aberdeen
Laurillard, Miss D	Institute for Educational Technology, University of Surrey, Guildford, Surrey
Leedham, Dr J	48 Swithland Lane, Rothley, Leics LE7 7SE
Leevers, S	County Programmed Learning Centre at St Albans College, Hatfield Road, St Albans, Herts
Leiblum, Dr M	CAI Project, Katholieke Universitet, URC Toernooiveld, Nigmegen, The Netherlands
Lewis, P G J	Royal School of Military Engineering, Chatham, Kent
Logan, A	Dumfries & Galloway College of Technology, Heathall, Dumfries DG1 3QZ
Malcolm, W G	Victoria University of Wellington, Wellington, New Zealand
Matthews, Dr J C	Department of Physics, The University of Nottingham, University Park, Nottingham NG7 2RD
McCavitt, Professor W E	School of Communication, Clarion State College, Clarion, Pennsylvania 16214, USA
McHugh, Dr C R	School of Chemistry, Thames Polytechnic, Wellington Street, London SE18 6PF
McKay, O O	Brigham Young University, Provo, Utah, USA
McMahon, H F	The New University of Ulster, Coleraine, County Londonderry, Northern Ireland BT52 1SA
McQuade, E	Plymouth Polytechnic, Drake Circus, Plymouth, Devon PL4 8AA
Megarry, Dr J	Jordanhill College of Education, Southbrae Drive, Glasgow G13 1PP
Metcalf, N F	Department of Anatomy, University of Nebraska Medical Centre, 42nd & Dewey, Omaha, Nebraska 68105, USA
Metcalf, Professor W K	Department of Anatomy, University of Nebraska Medical Centre, 42nd & Dewey, Omaha, Nebraska 68105, USA
Mitchell, Professor P D	Concordia University, 1455 de Maisonneuve Blvd West, Montreal, Quebec H3G 1M8, Canada

Moore, J D S	Royal Naval School of Educational Training and Technology, HMS Nelson, Portsmouth, Hants
Morris, R	The Beeches, 249 Bramhall Moore Lane, Hazel Grove, Cheshire SK7 5JL
Moss, Dr G D	Centre for Educational Technology, University College, Cardiff, South Wales
Moult, G	British Airways, West London Terminal, Cromwell Road, London SW7
Moyes, Dr R B	University of Hull, Hull
Murza, G	Institut für Dokumentation und Information, 48 Bielefeld 1, Westerfeldstrasse 15, West Germany
Needham, Ms M	County Programmed Learning Centre at St Albans College, Hatfield Road, St Albans, Herts
Novak, M	West Virginia University, Morgantown, USA
Parsonage, J R	Thames Polytechnic, Wellington Street, London SE18 6PF
Pastor, H V	Department of Supervision, Instituto Radio Diffusao Educativa da Bahia, Agencia Barra Mar Ques de Caravelas, CP 409S, Salvador 40,000, Bahia, Brazil
Percival, Dr F	Educational Technology Unit, Robert Gordon's Institute of Technology, St Andrew Street, Aberdeen
Perez, L O	Universidad de los Andes, PO Box 128, Merida, Venezuela
Portnoy, E	West Virginia University, Morgantown, USA
Prentice, E D	Department of Anatomy, University of Nebraska Medical Centre, 42nd & Dewey, Omaha, Nebraska 68105, USA
Price, Dr H C	Fulham Chest Clinic at Western Hospital, Seagrave Road, London SW6
Roach, D K	Centre for Educational Technology, University College, Cardiff, South Wales
Romiszowski, Dr A J	Middlesex Polytechnic, Queensway, Enfield, Middlesex
Rushby, N J	CAMOL Co-ordinator, National Development Programme in Computer-Assisted Learning, 37-41 Mortimer Street, London W1N 7RJ
Smith, B	Stronlonag, Glenmassan, By Dunoon, Argyll PA23 8RA
Smith, C	West Virginia University, Morgantown, USA
Smith, J	British Gas, 5 Grosvenor Crescent, London SW1X 7EE
Smythe, M	Educational Technology Unit, Robert Gordon's Institute of Technology, St Andrews Street, Aberdeen
Stitzel, Dr J	West Virginia University, Morgantown, USA
Thaitrong, S	Thai-German TTC, PO Box 8/17, Bangkok 8, Thailand
Townsend, I	NHS Learning Resources Unit, 13 Grove Road, Totley Rise, Sheffield
Trott, A J	School of In-Service Education & Research, Bulmershe College of Higher Education, Earley, Reading, Berks
Vargo, R	West Virginia University, Morgantown, USA
Vari, P	National Centre for Educational Technology, 1093, Budapest, Zsil, v 2/4, Hungary
Vaughan, B W	Glenrowan, Priory Road, Bradford-upon-Avon, Wilts
Vaughan, Dr K	Department of Pharmacy, University of Aston, Birmingham

Waterhouse, P	Resources for Learning Development Unit, County of Avon, Red Cross Street, Bristol BS2 0BA
Webb, Dr F J	Harwell Education Centre, AERE, Didcot, Oxfordshire
Wild, R	Plymouth Polytechnic, Drake Circus, Plymouth, Devon PL4 8AA
Wild, Dr S	Department of Systems Science, The City University, St John Street, London EC1V 4PB
Winfield, I J	North Staffordshire Polytechnic, Stoke-on-Trent, Staffs
Winterburn, N R	The City University, St John Street, London EC1V 4PB
Wolf, J	West Virginia University, Morgantown, USA
Wroot, R E	Program Development Officer, Research & Academic Development, North Alberta Institute of Technology, Edmonton, Alberta, Canada
Wyant, T G	Thai-German TTC, PO Box 8/17, Bangkok 8, Thailand
Yadav, M S	Centre of Advanced Study in Education, Faculty of Education & Psychology, University of Baroda, Lokmanya Tilak Road, Baroda 2, India

Summation of the Conference

G Hubbard

'A cold coming we had of it, just the worst time of the year . . .' I shall not continue the quotation to the evident discomfiture of Nick Rushby and his colleagues — 'The Camels galled, sore-footed, refractory' — but simply say that at the beginning of the week it was cold enough to freeze the wings of a Golden Angel.

That was one notable feature of ETIC 77. Another — one of those memorable moments one will recall when old and sitting by the fire and dreaming dreams — was the vigorous young Treasurer of APLET leaping on to the table during the magnificent Elizabethan Conference Dinner, his white locks tossing as he joined the lusty serving wench in her dancing.

But I do not think I am here to recall simply the highlights — and I am certainly not going to attempt to summarize a conference of 80 or more presentations in three days, a conference of which, since by reason of some personal defect or weakness of character I can only be in one place at any one time, I have experienced at best only one-sixth.

Instead, I am going to conduct a brief inquiry into the objectives of the conference, and thus attempt a rough and ready evaluation. It is, I hope, a formative evaluation, because I hope we are still searching for better and better ways of using this annual opportunity.

We — who are we? Define, in the jargon of the trade, the target population.

Well, we are a good sample of the members of APLET; a good sample therefore of those who are prepared to be called educational technologists. And educational technologists are those who are concerned one way and another with a systematic approach to the problems of teaching and learning.

Now, the second question, it seems to me, is: what are we here for? What, if it is not an improper term to use in such a gathering, are our objectives? I detect three principal objectives:

1. Meeting our friends (very successful).
2. Developing our perception of the subject.
3. Presenting the work done.

If 1 is successful, what about 2 and 3?

I have been aware of some developments in perception surfacing:

1. The re-establishment of CAL as an aspect of educational technology — some protests from CAL 77 participants but a number of CAL presentations have come naturally and unasked into the programme — not a matter of metaphysics, just of report. (After NDPCAL what?)
2. Some voices, notably Professor Elton's, emphasizing that educational technology is not, and may not become, a respectable academic discipline, but is craft-based: in my own mind I see it as a kit of tools.
3. A concern with educational technology as an infection, an epidemic — perhaps as a side-effect of having a medical session. I am not sure about this;

there are interesting extensions of the analogy to include immunization and the change from epidemic to endemic, but the same data could, I suspect, equally well support an analogy with wildlife populations, their explosions and subsequent collapse.

But, unless I was somewhere else at the time (and inevitably this was usually the case), we have not discussed either the urgent issue of the time or the long-term development of the subject. Well, that is not quite true. The small seminar convened at the request of Dr Matkhanov of UNESCO did talk about the long-term development of learning theory, and Andrew Trott and Jon Green's workshop was concerned with mapping what educational technology is about.

But as for the urgent issues — the contribution of educational technology to the problems being aired in the Great Debate, the upheaval (to use a fairly neutral word) in teacher education, the effects of economic stringency, and the potentially catalysing impact of TEC and BEC — are all these subjects too traumatic to contemplate? (Richard Hooper probably said the most significant things for the ETIC audience, in discussing how to be a successful innovator.)

The third purpose is to report work. This we have done; comprehensively, almost overwhelmingly. But half an hour is not very long, and all too often the speaker found it impossible to cover the ground and still leave time for even a minimal question-time.

I commented on this problem in a review of Aspects VII and observed that I was in the fortunate position of not being at a suitable institution and therefore not being liable to be invited to organize an ETIC conference. So I can toss ideas about in the happy certainty that I will not have to implement them.

In the light of ETIC 77 — which will be *Aspects XI* — the printed volume being, so to speak, the conference preserved in aspic — it seems to me that the one thing we must try to preserve is the annual opportunity to see each other.

I still feel that the need to report progress would be best met by calling for papers, not to be presented, but to be printed in the proceedings. And by offering facilities for demonstration — an extension of the workshop idea or of the members' exhibition, concentrating on giving opportunities for trying out each other's systems and developments undistracted by presented papers competing in parallel sessions, but with groups of authors on cognate subjects gathering in seminars now and then to give an opportunity for discussing their particular interest area. At the same time, I hope, we might have thought-provoking and entertaining speakers (which APLET seems particularly skilled in finding) to prod us to further exploration of our subject.

I hope ideas along these lines may already be active in the minds of those planning future conferences. We need the opportunities to meet and discuss our common interests which the conferences provide; we need the facility for publishing papers which advance the theory and practice of educational technology which *Aspects* represents. Other disciplines can reasonably accept the customary conference and conference report format in dignified conservative calm; those whose business is with new methods in learning have a particular responsibility to think about their own methods and to consider whether they cannot make a good thing rather better.

And, finally, let me turn to those who organized this conference. Let me say first that I have not been conscious of any difficulties; and of course the essence of good organization is that you do not notice it is there. As you probably know, in the last crucial weeks the students were sitting-in and messages had to be conveyed to the beleaguered organizers by carrier pigeon or Montgolfier hot-air balloon. How fortunate that Lewis Elton is a physicist in disguise!

But you would never have guessed this from the unruffled demeanour of Phil

Hills, who, having survived that as Organizing Secretary, would, I think, be equally unruffled if Cathedral Hill turned out to be an active volcano.

Nevertheless, I do wonder it is is quite fair, or absolutely necessary, to put this load on the host institution. The volunteers come forward — we shall all be at the Polytechnic of Wales next year — but I wonder whether there could not be a measure of support for the Chairman and the Organizing Secretary: a conference organizer, say, who might move on year by year, so that, at that level, the experience (hard-won experience) was carried on from year to year.

I have used my opportunity today to make comments which I trust are constructive, and are certainly meant in that sense. Conferences such as this are of great value anyway; in these times of economic stringency we need to see, as in all our activity, whether we can squeeze a little more value still out of them.

I have mentioned Lewis Elton and Phil Hills; it has been very much their conference. I raise my glass (metaphorically for me since it would be filled with pineapple juice) to Leo Evans. I thank on your behalf the Vice-Chancellor and the staff of the University of Surrey, and particularly those who recalled for us an earlier Elizabethan age. I thank all those who have given papers, run workshops, acted as chairmen, put on displays, or worked so unobtrusively behind the scenes. Oh, and Mrs Frances Hills and her helpers at the desk — continuous problem-solving!

Finally — thank you. A conference is only as good as its participants. This has been a good conference; next year to the Principality.

The Dissemination and Assimilation of Educational Innovation

R Hooper

Introduction

In January 1973, a few days after the launching of the good ship NDPCAL (National Development Programme in Computer-Assisted Learning), from the Government dry dock on its five-year, £2.5 million odyssey, two aims — ASSimilation and DISSemination — were pinned firmly to the mast-head. These twin aims, assimilation (NDPCAL jargon: 'institutionalization') and dissemination ('transferability') are crucial to any understanding of the National Programme's activities over the past five years. Now, in the closing months of the five-year odyssey, it seems appropriate to review:

1. the reasons for choosing the aims of ASS and DISS;
2. the strategies adopted to achieve ASS and DISS; and
3. a tentative, brief evaluation of the success of the ASS and DISS policy.

Assimilation

Definition

The term 'assimilation' (which I will regard for the purposes of this paper to be synonymous with NDPCAL's term 'institutionalization') is defined within the National Programme as the successful take-over of an innovation on to local budgets on a permanent basis after the period of external funding runs out.

Reason for Selecting ASS

The reason for selecting ASS as the main aim of the National Programme is probably obvious — growing concern in the educational technology community at the lack of success in the assimilation of innovation over the past 20 years on both sides of the Atlantic. The influential US Carnegie Commission on Higher Education wrote in its 1972 report, *The Fourth Revolution*, 'One of the great disappointments of the national effort to date is that for all the funds and effort thus far expended on the advancement of instructional technology, penetration of new learning materials and media into higher education has thus far been shallow' (The Carnegie Commission on Higher Education, 1972, p 47).

Surprisingly, given the obviousness of this aim of assimilation, very few educational technology or curriculum development projects on either side of the Atlantic have adopted it explicitly. The large schools curriculum development projects, funded in the UK and the USA, have tended to have as their aim the development of high quality teaching materials, based on appropriate definition of educational objectives and a sound curriculum design. In higher education, many of the educational technology projects have had what I would describe as research aims — to demonstrate the value of, for example, computer-assisted learning (CAL), to identify its cost effectiveness and to elaborate its theoretical bases.

Many of these schools and higher education projects have assumed, and on occasions claimed, that the existence of high quality teaching materials, positive research data, or elegant theoretical explications will ensure the assimilation of the particular innovation. History would suggest that such an assumption is quite unwarranted. Indeed, I believe that, in many cases, the research project syndrome 'here today, gone tomorrow' clearly militates against successful assimilation. Educational decision-making is, in fact, to the chagrin of those who inhabit the Age of Reason, 'incremental and disjointed . . . polycentral' and not all that rational (Kogan, 1976, p 2).

Thus, within the National Programme, assimilation has been seen above all as a political process, involving a whole range of factors that go far beyond the existence of good software or positive research results.

ASS Strategies

NDPCAL's view of ASSimilation is best understood by examining the strategies adopted to pursue it. The main ASS strategies can be listed as follows:

1. the choice of location of projects;
2. organizational structure and the choice of project director;
3. matched funding;
4. critical mass;
5. curriculum integration;
6. 'riding the educational wave';
7. closing the programme.

1. LOCATION OF PROJECTS

The first major strategic decision in pursuit of ASS concerned the choice of location of projects. The original National Council for Educational Technology reports of 1969, which led to the setting up of NDPCAL, recommended the development work to be carried out at a few research centres attached to universities (Hooper, 1974). Given ASS as an aim, this would have been, in my view, a totally unproductive strategy.

For computer-assisted learning (CAL) or computer-managed learning (CML) to survive in the longer-term future, projects had to be based close to the sources of institutional power, and that power in the British system of education is highly distributed. Two things followed from this. First, the Programme used its funds to encourage as many growth points across the UK (around 80 in 1975/6) as were compatible with money available and the requirements of critical mass. Second, the majority of higher education projects, for example, were located not in educational technology or educational research departments, which are, whether we like it or not, on the periphery of institutional power, but in the mainstream teaching departments — physics, chemistry, mathematics. At schools level, for the same reasons, projects (with one exception) have been located directly in local education authorities, and not in universities, which has been the Schools Council pattern.

2. ORGANIZATIONAL STRUCTURE

Following on from the location of projects, there were particular concerns about the choice of project director and organizational structure of the project. Who reports to whom, and who is on which committee, are highly relevant considerations for projects aiming at assimilation. The choice of project director is also crucial. Does the project director have academic credibility? Can he or she manage? Can he or she present results in a convincing way to colleagues and to decision-makers? Does the director know the way around the corridors of power in the particular institution or local authority?

3. MATCHED FUNDING
'Matched funding' was a specific strategy used to strengthen the chances of future assimilation. Unlike many research funding agencies, the National Programme did not pay overheads to project institutions. On the contrary, project institutions were expected to contribute resources alongside NDPCAL funding. The existence of matched funding ensured the involvement of decision-makers at the project's inception, thus preparing the ground well in advance for the vital assimilation decisions later on. Another strength of 'matched funding' is that it softens the financial transition to assimilation at the end of external funding, since parts of the project are already being paid for locally.

4. CRITICAL MASS
The strategy of 'critical mass', called somewhat mischievously 'The Numbers Game' within the National Programme, is premised on the belief that an innovation which is in widespread use across an institution or authority will acquire the broad base of support and visibility that is difficult to stop. By contrast, the CAL research experiment with a handful of students on alternate Fridays can be closed down without much trouble. In one recent assimilation negotiation in one of our higher education projects, the project director pointed out to the university that if the CAL work were not continued someone else would need to provide 3,000 hours of student teaching from October 1977.

5. CURRICULUM INTEGRATION
The strategy of curriculum integration tries to ensure that CAL or CML developments happen within a framework of broader curriculum and course redesign. This is to avoid the innovation remaining an optional extra, which can be discarded at a time of financial squeeze. At Imperial College, for example, a group of third-year courses in heat transfer and fluid flow have been totally redesigned around a computing core. If CAL were to be discarded, then the courses themselves would also have to go.

6. 'RIDING THE EDUCATIONAL WAVE'
The penultimate ASS strategy can be termed, to continue the nautical metaphor, 'riding the educational wave'. This relates to the need to develop innovations that reinforce existing trends within the educational system. Test-marking by computer, for example, has quickly found favour because it has ridden in on top of the existing wave of objective testing and continuous assessment. But of course, as with surfing, choosing the right wave is important. Some waves look all right but are, in Australian surfing parlance, 'dumpers'.

7. CLOSING THE PROGRAMME
The final — in every sense of the word — ASS strategy was the decision taken to close the Programme down at the end of its five-year term. This concentrates the mind on assimilation wonderfully!

Dissemination

Definition

Turning from ASS to DISS, the landscape is immediately more familiar. Many educational technology and curriculum development projects have stressed the importance of dissemination. For the purposes of this paper I will regard the term 'dissemination' as synonymous with the NDPCAL term 'transferability'. Dissemination is defined here as the systematic attempt to promote the spread and adoption of new ideas or practices.

Reasons for Selecting DISS

NDPCAL selected DISS as a twin aim alongside ASS for two reasons. First of all, dissemination was essential to spread the high costs of developing CAL and CML, in the accepted tradition of economies of scale. Secondly, dissemination was a useful mechanism for testing the resilience and worthwhileness of the innovation, and I shall return to this topic at the end of the paper.

The 'ideological' approach to DISS that gradually emerged within NDPCAL needs to be identified. In essence, we came to question the conventional wisdom that the dissemination problem is just a communication problem and that dissemination failure can be attributed solely to failures of communication.

> 'The problem of communication is a product of the rhetoric of curriculum development rather than of the reality. The rhetoric is premised on an unexamined assumption: that all of us concerned with the education of pupils — teachers, administrators, advisers, researchers, theorists — basically share the same educational values and have overlapping visions of curriculum excellence. A confirmation of the argument is the proposition that if there are major discrepancies between the advocacies of the support groups and the behaviour of the practitioner groups ... then there is prima facie a problem of communication ... All this is not to say that there are no problems of transmission which can be accounted for in terms of poor presentation: of course there are. But curriculum innovators face a much more significant problem which needs to be distinguished from this but is often confused with it: the issue of whether people want to hear what they have to say. The answer does not necessarily lie in saying it more clearly.' *(MacDonald and Walker, 1976, p 44)*

DISS Strategies

The following list of strategies to achieve DISSemination has been used by the National Programme:

1. inter-institutional projects;
2. personal contact;
3. existing communications channels;
4. presentational skills;
5. technical portability;
6. program exchange centres.

1. INTER-INSTITUTIONAL PROJECTS

The first, and key, DISS strategy was the funding of inter-institutional projects. By contrast, most higher education research and development funding has tended to go to single institutions. Funding of inter-institutional projects encourages the idea of dissemination being seen as part of development, not an afterthought. In the design of teaching material, decisions of an educational and technical nature can take into account the differing requirements of a spectrum of potential users, thus making the end product more easy to disseminate. Inter-institutional funding is a departure from the tradition of 'centres of excellence' and 'centre-periphery' models of curriculum development. Inter-institutional projects multiply the number of participating teachers and therefore the likelihood of future assimilation via critical mass. Inter-institutional projects, designed as cooperative federal networks, grow organically as interest grows. They are based on the belief that teachers will more readily adopt an innovation if they have participated in its development. This reduces the power of the NIH (not invented here) syndrome. It also, finally, enables the conflicting, non-consensual values of the participants to be voiced early on, thus reducing the so-called 'communications problem'.

2. PERSONAL CONTACT

House, in his book *The Politics of Educational Innovation*, wrote:

> 'To control the flow of personal contact is to control innovation. As the flow of blood is essential to human life, so direct personal contact is essential to the propagation of innovation . . . Who knows whom and who talks to whom are powerful indicators of where and when an innovation is accepted, or if it is accepted at all.' *(House, 1974, p 6)*

Personal contact has been a central DISS strategy. By comparison with many research-funding agencies, NDPCAL has always, for example, been generous with travel and subsistence monies. Inter-project visits, overseas visits, intra-project meetings, meetings with prospective adopters, conferences, have all been directly encouraged.

Professor Peter Ayscough, the director of the large CALCHEM project, based at Leeds University and Sheffield Polytechnic, has summarized the NDPCAL view perfectly:

> 'We are, after all, trying to address ourselves to practising teachers who are not particularly interested in educational research as such . . . the (CALCHEM) project has expanded very satisfactorily without the support of weighty analysis and impressive publications. Our conclusion is that those who have pursued their investigations of CAL to the point at which they have a reasonable grasp of what we are doing, recognise that the real evidence they seek can only be obtained by observing the system in action . . . dissemination of this particular innovation has occurred almost entirely on a person-to-person basis and by direct observation, not by evangelical contribution to seminars and journals.' *(Ayscough, 1976, p 6)*

3. EXISTING COMMUNICATION CHANNELS

Personal contact has been strengthened by exploiting the existing communications channels used by practising teachers, for example the Chemical Society or the Geographical Association. NDPCAL has worked directly with these professional associations, setting up workshops, journal articles and special publications, to accelerate dissemination. By and large, in initial encounters with CAL, chemistry teachers, for example, will listen to other chemists and not to educational technologists or computing specialists. There is one disadvantage of this subject discipline-based strategy — it reduces opportunities for inter-disciplinary work and cross-disciplinary transfer.

4. PRESENTATIONAL SKILL

The presentational skill of project staff was emphasized early on in the National Programme as an important, yet often overlooked, component of dissemination strategy. Presentational skill is not synonymous with slick, professional presentation. Indeed, in educational circles, slick presentations can be counterproductive. In the military training environment, by contrast, it is essential.

The educational evaluation team, UNCAL, alerted us to the need to consider the varying requirements of different audiences. Choice of language used is all-important. Computing and educational technology jargon may put off the customer, whereas a few scrawled equations on the blackboard may seduce him. In addition to the usual conferences, various other mechanisms have been used to encourage projects to pay attention to presentation. The midterm evaluations of projects, two-day site visits which lead to discussions to continue or suspend further funding, have been particularly useful in this respect.

5. TECHNICAL PORTABILITY

It is, I hope, clear from the DISS strategies outlined so far that, within NDPCAL, the major problems surrounding dissemination are seen to be human and psychological, rather than technical. In the USA, the cultural tendency is to be concerned with the technical considerations of CAL at the expense of human factors. To stress human factors is, of course, not to deny the existence of a number of significant technical obstacles. Because of the way that the world computing industry has developed, the 'portability' of software from one machine to another, even within the same manufacturer's range, is often difficult. In brief, the main components of NDPCAL's strategy in relation to technical portability concerned choice of programming languages ('standardizing' on BASIC, FORTRAN and COBOL), emphasis on good documentation, and good program design (for example, ease of modification and modularization).

6. PROGRAM EXCHANGE CENTRES

The final DISS strategy used by NDPCAL involved the funding of subject discipline-affiliated program exchange centres. Activities of these centres include the maintenance of a catalogue and library operation, 'standards' setting, teacher-training, consultancy, salesmanship and the encouragement of a new software development.

Tensions between ASS and DISS

Before reviewing the success of the ASS and DISS strategies outlined, one further point about them needs to be made. When ASS and DISS were pinned to the masthead, it was not realized that, in some senses, the two aims were mutually incompatible. Within, for example, a university, the cultural and financial incentives tend to favour ASS at the expense of DISS. The parent institution, especially at times of economic stringency, will tend to question the extra resources that are necessary to make a product, that is working well locally, transferable. By and large it is our experience that ASS is a necessary precondition and launch platform for DISS, but DISS is not usually a necessary precondition for ASS. (DISS within an institution is likely to speed ASS, however.) As a result, DISS needs special attention from funding agencies both now and in the future, unless there is a radical change in reward structures for innovators.

Evaluating the Success of ASS and DISS

The ASS, and to a lesser extent the DISS, aims of the National Programme cannot by their very nature be properly evaluated until after NDPCAL has closed down. On the evidence to date, sprinkled with appropriate dashes of salt, it would seem likely that 70% of the projects will achieve satisfactory levels of assimilation and dissemination. The presence of independent financial and educational evaluators in the National Programme will serve, I hope, to counterbalance any undue optimism on the part of myself and project staff now that the 'season of claims and mellow fruitfulness' is nigh.

In general, the ASS and DISS strategies adopted by NDPCAL have been more successful in the higher education and military training sectors than in schools and in industrial training. In the higher education projects, for example, we may achieve close to a 100% success rate with assimilation of CAL and CML activity.

Evidence to support the claims for ASS success will be set out in detail in my final report to be published in December 1977 (Hooper, 1977). A sample of that evidence would be the recent decision by the Senate of the University of Leeds to make three tenured appointments for the Computer-Based Learning Project; the Computer Board's approval of a prime computer and support staff at the University of Surrey dedicated to a university-wide CAL service (with a matched funding: NDPCAL funding ratio of 8 : 1); the purchase in 1976 of a dedicated CAL machine at the University of Glasgow for use in five teaching departments; the decision at the turn of this last year by Hertfordshire County Council to continue to support the schools' computer-managed mathematics project after 1977; in military training, the recent purchase with Army funds of an ICL 2903 Educational System dedicated to CAMOL (Computer-Assisted Management of Learning) at Catterick Camp. A Federal Committee in Canada on Computer Communications in Education has written about NDPCAL in a survey of international developments '. . . initial results indicate a high probability of the Programme successfully achieving its objective of "assimilation of computer-assisted learning on a regular institutional basis at reasonable cost" ' (Dept of Communication, 1975, p 13).

A sample of the evidence to support the claims for DISS success is as follows. The Engineering Sciences Project, for example, based at Queen Mary College, London, began in 1973/4 in five engineering departments in three institutions, grew to 10 engineering departments in six institutions by September 1976, involving 29 academic staff and some 750 students and had transferred CAL packages to 21 other institutions in the UK and abroad. The CAMOL project, a joint development between NDPCAL and International Computers Ltd (ICL), involved by 1976/7 one university, two polytechnics, a grammar school, an FE college and the trade training school at Catterick. In addition, a large local authority was preparing to purchase CAMOL for use in its secondary schools, and a pilot operation with Open University students in Northern Ireland was starting. At Glasgow University, the 'content-free' computer software produced and in use for medical teaching, has been transferred successfully for use in the training of guidance counsellors, and in police training.

ASS + DISS + Evaluation

The story of ASS and DISS cannot end neatly here. Success in achieving ASS and DISS is a very useful, practical, credible criterion for measuring the worthwhileness of computer-assisted learning, but is not a sufficient criterion. Both ASS and DISS have been used within the National Programme as 'obstacle courses' to test the resilience of the various innovations, and the claims of project staff. The achievement of ASS by itself, particularly when money is tight, is indeed good evidence of the value of CAL or CML. The achievement of ASS + DISS by a project is better evidence still because it increases the size of the test-bed. The achievement of ASS + DISS + ASS (ie the innovation that has been assimilated in the originating institution is successfully imported and assimilated in a new institution) is better evidence still — but again not sufficient. We need evaluation — preferably independent evaluation — to enter and hold the ring, for one simple reason: unworthwhile ideas in education can and do get assimilated and disseminated. Only one example of this is needed (and we can all think of more than one) to make ASS and DISS indicative but never sufficient criteria for measuring worthwhileness.

The arrival of evaluation brings with it new tensions to the story of ASS and DISS, and new conflicts for the funding agency. Does the good ship NDPCAL, as it nears its final port of call, continue to support a project which looks like achieving the assimilation of a poor computer application? Will, on the other hand, when December 1977 comes, the worthwhile and the imaginative computer application necessarily be assimilated and disseminated?

References

Ayscough, P (1976) 'Academic Reactions to Educational Innovation. Studies in Higher Education' 1, 1.

Carnegie Commission on Higher Education (1972) 'The Fourth Revolution, a Report and Recommendations of the Carnegie Commission on Higher Education' McGraw-Hill, New York.

Department of Communications (1975) 'Federal Working Committee on Computer Communications in Education: Final Report' Department of Communications, Educational Technology Branch, Ottawa.

Hooper, R (1974) 'The National Development Programme in Computer Assisted Learning – Origins and Starting Point' 'Programmed Learning' 11, 2.

Hooper, R (1977) 'The National Development Programme in Computer Assisted Learning – final report of the Director's Council for Educational Technology, London. In press.

House, E (1974) 'The Politics of Educational Innovation' McCutchan Publishing Corporation, Berkeley, California.

Kogan, M (1976) 'The Next Ten Years — a Speculative Essay on Educational Futures' Commissioned paper for NDPCAL future study on computers in education and training in the 1980s.

MacDonald, B and Waler, R (1976) 'Changing the curriculum' Open Books, London.

Illustrations, Adjuncts and Alternatives: An Account of Experiences in Faculty Development Workshops in West Virginia

L F Evans, B Behling, J Clarke, L Hall, M Howard, L Jaknowitz,
M Novak, E Portnoy, C Smith, J Stitzel, R Vargo, J Wolf

In May 1976 the first named author directed three 'Workshops for the Improvement of Instruction' in West Virginia University, Morgantown, West Virginia, USA. These were based on workshops and other staff training activities of the Centre for Educational Technology of the City University, London, adapted to the North American ambience. They had the two-fold purpose of providing a development opportunity to academic staff in West Virginia University and neighbouring colleges, and of training staff in West Virginia University to take over the provision and direction of similar workshops. Participation in the first workshop was limited to 12 members of academic staff from West Virginia University. In the second and third, the number of participants was increased to 24, including state colleges in the area.

The workshops were publicized in a circular letter to staff in the university and colleges. Applications greatly exceeded places, and participants were selected primarily on a 'first come' basis, but also to provide a range of disciplines and experiences in the workshops. When informed of their acceptance and arrangements for joining, they also received the following:

Professor Evans has asked that you come to the workshop prepared with the following:

1. A short 5–7 minute 'lecturette' which can be either specially prepared for this occasion or, if it is a single entity, an excerpt from a standard lecture you give.
2. A 30-minute lecture, including any visual material, support material, hand-outs and other ancillary material you may use for that lecture.
3. A piece of continuous prose, between 200-400 words in length from a text-book, part of an essay, etc relating to your subject.
4. A passage from a text-book, used by you or your students, which presents some difficulty in comprehension, between 300-600 words in length.
5. Any part of your course which is 'bugging' you — to work on and perhaps discuss during the workshop.

I hope you are looking forward to these three days as much as I am.

Cordially,

Martha Howard

Figure 1.

Those from 'out of town' were lodged in a university residence, where all participants and staff gathered on the Sunday evening before the formal start of the workshop, for a meal and an informal 'get together'. Work started at 08.30 hrs on Monday morning, with the programme shown in Figure 2.

Monday			
May 10	08.30	Workshop assemblies	Room 512
	08.35—09.00	Introduction to workshop	
	09.00—10.00	'A dozen do's'	Room 512
	10.00—10.30	Coffee break	
	10.30—12.00	Lecturette recording	Room 512
		see roster	
	12.00—13.30	Luncheon	
	13.30—14.30	Individual video review	Rooms 402, 403, 404A, 404B
		see roster	
	14.30—15.00	Individual discussions	Rooms 507 A, B, C, D, D plus 403, 404A, 405
		see roster	
	15.00—15.30	Tea break	
	15.30—16.30	Individual discussions	Rooms as above
		see roster	
	16.30—17.00	Plenary session	Room 512
Tuesday			
May 11	08.30—09.00	'Illustrations, adjuncts, and alternatives'	Room 512
	09.00—12.30	Media workshop	Room 407
	14.00—17.00	Voice workshop	Rooms 403, 512
		'Explaining workshop'	Room 404A
	see roster	'Lecture workshop'	Room 402
		'Debugging'	Room 404B
Wednesday			
May 12	08.30—10.00	Lecturette preparation	
	10.00—10.30	Coffee break	
	10.30—12.00	Lecturette recording	Room 512
	13.30—15.30	Small group video replay and discussion	Rooms 402, 403, 404A, 404B
	15.30—16.00	Coffee break	
	16.00—16.30	Plenary discussion	Room 512
	16.30—17.00	Workshop evaluation	Room 512
	17.00	Workshop ends	
	18.00	'Happy hour' for dinner at 19.00	

Figure 2.

The activities listed are described below.

Introduction to Workshop

The participants were asked, on arrival, to 'write on the badge provided one name —
eg Fred, Ann, Ma'am — by which you are willing to be addressed during the
workshop'. They were then reminded of the request to bring with them their
prepared lecturette, 'explaining material', a full-length lecture, ideas for
visualization, and problems in their classroom teaching that were 'bugging' them.
They were given their rosters for the various group and individual activities and
consultations, and provided with an opportunity to ask questions of the staff, or, if

they felt that the programme outlined was not for them, 'to make an excuse and leave'. Evaluation forms were distributed and their use and purpose explained.

EVALUATION OF COURSE

Please complete this form, in order to assist in the evaluation of this course, and to use the information in planning future activities.

Ring round the response which most nearly corresponds to your opinion, using the scale +3 to −3 given, 0 indicating 'no opinion' and inserting further comment in the space provided.

Session	Interest + + + − − − 3 2 1 0 1 2 3	Usefulness + + + − − − 3 2 1 0 1 2 3	Effectiveness + + + − − − 3 2 1 0 1 2 3

Further comments on session

	Interest + + + − − − 3 2 1 0 1 2 3	Usefulness + + + − − − 3 2 1 0 1 2 3	Effectiveness + + + − − − 3 2 1 0 1 2 3
The course as a whole			

Comments on course organization

Comments on 'ambience' ie rooms, facilities, meals, accommodation

Any other comments or suggestions

Figure 3.

A Dozen Do's

This exercise was conceived with the dual purpose of acting as an 'ice-breaker' and also establishing some consensus as to what was perceived as 'good' practice. The work sheet shown in Figure 4 was distributed, and individuals asked to rate the items on a five-point scale for their importance in effective lecture presentation, or to rate '0' if considered irrelevant or inapplicable. Five minutes were allowed for this individual rating, after which time participants were asked to form 'free-choice' groups of three or four, to compare their individual ratings, then discuss and agree a 'group' rating, and devise one further 'do' which the group would rate 4-5. Fifteen minutes was suggested as a sufficient time for this stage, with an extension if required by the majority. In practice, this stage took at least 20 minutes. The ratings of each group were then displayed on a previously prepared grid and their additional 'statement' written on an acetate slip and displayed, using an overhead

33

	a	b	c
1. Speaks clearly	—	—	—
2. Paces presentation to listeners' needs	—	—	—
3. States, clarifies, and confirms purpose	—	—	—
4. Maintains contact with listeners	—	—	—
5. Supports oral presentation with visual material	—	—	—
6. Provides a comprehensible structure	—	—	—
7. Plans breaks and pauses	—	—	—
8. Avoids jargon	—	—	—
9. Encourages questions	—	—	—
10. Links with past and future	—	—	—
11. Monitors 'ambience'	—	—	—
12. Generates excitement	—	—	—

Rate each item on a scale 1-5, for its importance in effective lecture presentation: 1, least important; 5, most important; or '0' if considered irrelevant or inapplicable. Do not 'grade' items. Write your answers in column (a)

Figure 4. *A Dozen 'Do's'*

projector. The workshop director then attempted to reach a consensus view for each statement, including those produced by the participants, as the basis for the assessment of performance in classroom presentation.

Lecturette Recording

The participants presented their 'lecturettes' in a conventional classroom, provided with chalk-boards and a full range of audio-visual equipment. The 'class' consisted of the other participants and the workshop staff, all of whom were provided with 'lecture feedback' forms (shown in Figure 5) which they were asked to complete for each presentation as it was made. The presentations were video-recorded, using a single camera with operator, placed near the back of the classroom. A 'two-minute' warning and a 'finish' sign were displayed when appropriate at eight and 10 minutes of presentation time. The camera operator had been previously briefed to avoid 'camera comment'. The quality and the veracity of the recordings made were of a very high standard.

At the conclusion of the session, the feedback forms were collected and collated ready to pass on to the individual participants.

Individual Video Review

The video-recording had been so arranged as to facilitate replay of individual presentations at a number of locations. In groups of three, in four separate rooms, the participants reviewed their performance. After the first review, they were asked to complete a feedback form in the same way that the 'class members' had done. After this, they were given all the feedback forms for their presentation, and after studying these, were able to review their recording again, replaying any incidents at will if they so desired.

Individual Discussion

Following the 'isolated' review, the participants in this session discussed their presentation and the feedback they had received with three different workshop

LECTURE FEEDBACK

Underline the statements that most nearly represent your opinion of the presentation.

The Lecturer

Speed of speech	Much too fast	Fast	Just right	Slow	Much too slow
Clarity of diction		Clear	Difficult to understand	Very difficult to understand	
Voice volume	Inaudible	Too quiet	Clearly audible	Too loud	Deafening
Contact with audience	Nil	Intermittent	Continuous and strong	Continuous and weak	
'Manner'	Very pleasant	Pleasant	Acceptable	Rather disagreeable	Unpleasant

The Material

Organization of information	Totally disordered	Confused	Very effective	Effective	Adequate
Rate of presentation	Much too fast	Fast	Correct	Slow	Much too slow
'Interest'	Very great	Great	Good	Moderate	None
Clarity of exposition	Just compre-hensible	Clear	Very clear	Unclear	Incompre-hensible
Visual illustration	Excessive	Effective	Adequate	Inadequate	Absent

Any other comments:

Figure 5.

staff members. One of these was an experienced teacher recognized by her/his peers for teaching ability, one an experienced teacher specializing in the fields of oral communication, voice, public speaking and/or drama, and the third was an undergraduate student of West Virginia University. Participants had 30-minute sessions, singly or in pairs, with each type of 'tutor' in turn.

Plenary Session

This was devoted to ensuring that everyone had survived the long hard day, was effectively briefed for the morrow, to recreate the unity of the opening session, and to give an opportunity for critical or commendatory comment from particpants.

Illustrations, Adjuncts and Alternatives

This was an interactive lecture presentation with these main aims:

1. To place the participants in a typical 'classroom students' role, to enable them to appreciate the situation and 'sufferings' of their students.
2. To illustrate the range of visual and auditory support which could be available in classroom teaching, and to encourage its use.
3. To demonstrate the need for structure, timing and definition of purpose.
4. To demonstrate that 'you, too, can use any of this'.
5. 'Hopefully' to motivate participants to analyze their teaching and to make appropriate and effective use of 'illustrations, adjuncts and alternatives' in their own teaching.

During the course of the presentation, the following were used: chalk-board, flip-chart, wall chart, overhead projector, slide projector, audio-cassette, 16mm film with sound, synchronized tape/slide, off-air, live and recorded video.

Media Workshop

Participants worked in a purposely arranged 'media laboratory', staffed by professionally expert tutors, in which they were able to adopt a 'hands-on' approach to the preparation of teaching media. They made OHP transparencies, 2" x 2" slides, charts and, in some cases, models. They used still and movie cameras, draughting and reprographic equipment, and studio and portable video equipment.

Voice Workshop

In classrooms of differing sizes and acoustic properties, participants worked with the 'speech specialists' mentioned above to improve their 'total' presentation, using audio-recording and playback, exercises and practice, to identify deficiencies and improve abilities.

Explaining Workshop

Triggered by George Brown's postulate that a major purpose of the lecture is to 'explain' difficult concepts, the participant in this session was required to 'explain' a concept, or a text-book passage, to a group comprising a fellow participant, a 'tutor student' and a 'tutor teacher'. The explanation was discussed, feedback given, and continued until the participant had ensured that her/his 'explanation' was understood.

Lecture Workshop

Participants were given the opportunity of presenting a full-length 'lecture' to a small audience including a 'tutor-student' and a 'tutor teacher', and to discuss their planning, preparation and presentation.

De-bugging

Nothing to do with Watergate, but a one-to-one discussion with the workshop director of particular problems in classroom teaching that were of concern to the participant.

Lecturette Preparation

Participants were required to make a second presentation for analysis, and were free to decide whether they modified and repeated their original, or prepared an entirely new lecturette. During this session, they were able to use any of the media workshop facilities they required, and/or to work with any of the workshop staff in adapting their original or preparing a new presentation.

Lecturette Recording

The 'modified' presentations were made by participants in a session similar to that previously described, including the completion of feedback forms.

Small Group Video Replay and Discussion

Groups comprising three to six participants with two to four staff were formed, and the recorded lecturettes of the participants in the group replayed to the entire group, feedback provided to the presenters, followed by an analytical discussion involving the whole group.

Plenary Discussion

A general discussion session, in which learning points of interest generally were elucidated by participants, and in which 'staff' comment on observable general changes in performances was made.

Workshop Evaluation

Participants were given an opportunity to complete their evaluation forms, particularly the sections dealing with 'the course as a whole', following which 'full, frank and free' comment was invited by the staff, and given by participants.

Happy Hour

A euphemism for the consumption, in a convivial atmosphere, by most of the staff and participants, of not inconsiderable quantities of highly alcoholic beverages.

Résumé

Before starting the first workshop, the staff spent two working days in briefing, discussion and preparation, which involved the agreement of a common and 'helping' approach to participants, and a mutual decoding of unfamiliar usages of English on the two sides of the Atlantic. This was followed by a half-day 'walk-through' including the provision of video-recording and playback of 'lecturettes' by staff.

During the initial stages of the scheme and prior to the author's arrival at West Virginia University, two members of academic staff had been selected and designated as potential workshop directors. These colleagues, Dr Judith Stitzel and Dr Robert Behling, took part in the preparatory briefing sessions, and had further extended discussions with the author, both prior to the first workshop and between each of the others.

During the first workshop, these two acted as 'tutor teachers'; in the second, took over responsibility for the video-recording sessions; and in addition, for the third workshop, led the two plenary discussions, and took over responsibility for the overall 'continuity' of the activities. In the morning following each workshop, all the staff met to read the evaluation forms, to make known their own views on the experience, and to consider any requisite adaptations or changes.

The two 'co-directors' then met with the author to implement any agreed changes for the next workshop.

Following the last of the three workshops, a more extended 'de-briefing' was held, to facilitate the planning of the first projected 'All West Virginia' workshop, to be held some months later, in anticipation of which the author also spent further time in individual discussion with Dr Stitzel and Dr Behling, who were jointly to direct that workshop.

For this projected workshop, it was agreed that, in the light of comments made by staff and participants, and information gained from the evaluation forms, the general structure of the workshop should remain unchanged. Some modification of detail was needed, and was made as follows:

1. The initial Sunday evening 'get together' would be formalized as part of the programme, and the 'dozen do's' exercise worked during that evening.
2. The 'de-bugging' session, which had in part been included to give participants an opportunity for 'trans-Atlantic' contact, should be transposed to provide opportunity for open-ended discussion after the 'mini-workshops' and the first lecturette review, and before making the second presentation.
3. Some of the hand-outs should be modified to render them more comprehensible/acceptable in the West Virginia context.
4. The information on material to be prepared and provided should be modified.

Those applicants accepted for the 'All American' workshop to be held in August thus received the following request:

The following materials should be prepared by you for this workshop:

1. A short 5-7 minute 'lecturette'. This mini-lecture will be presented during a microteach session. It may be specially prepared for the workshop or it may be an excerpt (a single concept, perhaps) from one of your own lectures.

2. A 20-30 minute lecture, including any visual materials, hand-outs, or other ancillary items you may use for that lecture.

3. One of the following:
   (a) a passage from a text-book (or hand-out) used by you or your students, which presents some difficulty in comprehension. (One or two pages are more than sufficient.)
   (b) a concept, theory, or explanation you must present to your students.

4. Any part of any course you teach which is 'bugging' you . . . we will work on and discuss such bugs during the workshop.

5. A piece of continuous prose, between 200-300 words in length, from a text-book, essay, etc relating to your subject. (This could be the same as in 3(a) above.)

Figure 6.

The programme given in Figure 7 was then followed. The 'dozen do's' now appeared in the form given in Figure 8, and lecture feedback was given using the format shown in Figure 9.

An analysis and commentary on the evaluation of the four workshops provided by the participants will be the subject of a future communication in *Programmed Learning & Educational Technology*, the journal of APLET, the purpose of this paper being to recount and to discuss the workshop activity described. It may, however, be not inapposite to conclude with the information that the continuance of such workshops is recommended as an essential part of future faculty

AUGUST 1976
WEST VIRGINIA UNIVERSITY

Sunday
August 15

5.00— 6.00	Registration	Holiday Inn
6.00— 7.15	Dinner	WVU Room
7.30— 9.00	Introduction to workshop 'A dozen do's'	Monongahela Room

Monday
August 16

8.30	Workshop assemblies	Room 512, Allen Hall
8.35— 9.15	Introduction to workshop facilities at Allen Hall	
9.15— 9.45	Coffee break and orientation to facilities	Fourth floor
9.45—12.00	Lecturette recording see roster	Rooms 511, 512
12.00— 1.00	Lunch (on your own)	
1.00— 2.30	Individual video review see roster	Fourth floor
2.30— 2.45	Coffee break	Fourth floor
2.45— 4.45	Individual discussions see roster	Rooms 507 A, B, C, D, E, plus rooms on fourth floor
4.45— 5.00	Plenary session	Room 512

Tuesday
August 17

8.30— 9.20	'Illustrations, adjuncts and alternatives'	Room 512
9.30—11.00	A carrousel of four workshops:	
11.00—12.30	Media	Room 407
1.30— 3.00	Voice	Rooms 507 A, B etc
3.00— 4.30	Lecture (20-30 mins) Explaining see roster	Rooms 511, 512 Rooms to be announced
4.45— 5.00	Plenary session	Room 512

Wednesday
August 18

8.30—10.00	Individual attention help with lecturette Media assistance 'De-bugging'	Rooms 511, 512 Room 407 Rooms 507 A, B etc
10.00—10.15	Coffee break	
10.15—12.00	Lecturette recording	Rooms 511, 512
12.00— 1.00	Lunch (on your own)	
1.00— 2.45	Small group video replay and discussion	Rooms on fourth floor
2.45— 3.00	Coffee break	
3.00— 4.30	Plenary session and workshop evaluation	Room 512
6.00— 7.00	'Happy hour'	Holiday Inn
7.00— 8.00	Prime rib buffet	Executive Club

Figure 7.

A DOZEN DO'S

SPEAKS CLEARLY
PACES PRESENTATION TO LISTENERS' NEEDS
STATES, CLARIFIES, AND CONFIRMS PURPOSE
MAINTAINS CONTACT WITH LISTENERS
SUPPORTS ORAL PRESENTATION WITH VISUAL MATERIAL
PROVIDES A COMPREHENSIBLE STRUCTURE
RECOGNIZES IMPORTANCE OF BREAKS AND PAUSES
AVOIDS JARGON
ENCOURAGES QUESTIONS
PROVIDES TRANSITION BETWEEN LECTURES
REMAINS SENSITIVE TO CLASSROOM ENVIRONMENT
GENERATES EXCITEMENT IN SUBJECT MATTER

Figure 8.

LECTURE FEEDBACK

Circle the number that most nearly represents your opinion of the presentation.

Note: Possible statements corresponding to your feedback are included based on comments from previous participants.

	1	2	3	4	5
Speed of speech	Much too fast		Just right		Much too slow
Voice volume	Too loud		Just right		Inaudible
Rate of presentation	Much too fast		Correct		Much too slow
Clarity of diction	Very difficult to understand		Average		Very clear
Contact with audience	None		Intermittent		Continuous and strong
'Manner'	Unpleasant		Acceptable		Very pleasant
Organization of information	Totally disordered		Adequate		Very effective
Clarity of exposition	Incomprehensible		Adequate		Very effective
Visual illustration	1 Absent / 1 Excessive	2	3 / Adequate	4	5 / Excellent
'Interest'	None		Good		Very great

	Yes	No
Content was a problem for me		
The content problem affected my feedback		

For additional comments, please use other side.

Figure 9.

development in West Virginia, it being reported in the official submission for the State program that:

> 'The success of his (Professor L F Evans) efforts was unparalleled in any previous program in the State. Its proven suitability for a West Virginia clientele established, Professor Evans' program was examined by Glenville State College and it was determined that it met the needs of the consortium better than any other program currently available'.

The transfer between the disparate environments of the City University, London, and West Virginia University, Morgantown, was only made possible by the willingness, ability and heartening co-operation of the West Virginia University staff, whose contribution is acknowledged in the title page of this paper, and Mrs W F Ghouse and Mr P Brown of the Centre for Educational Technology, who helped to prepare so much material 'for export'.

Multi-Media Packages in Teacher Training

P Vari

The dissemination of educational technology over all the country is the basic task of the National Centre for Educational Technology (OOK).*

One of the strategies which can lead to the accomplishment of the objective mentioned above lies in providing training for teacher candidates and in-service teachers in the field of educational technology in which we rely basically on multi-media teaching packages.

In our present training system, in accordance with the central curriculum, teacher candidates attend compulsory courses on educational technology and they also have the opportunity to take part in optional courses in the same subject. In-service training courses — in which all our teachers are supposed to take part — are also organized on a regular basis and educational technology is one of the subjects that can be chosen.

Since the resources of the OOK are not sufficient for satisfying all the needs of this kind of training, teaching materials must be developed, with the help of which it can be assured that training and in-service training of teachers is carried out on a uniform basis all over the country. Teaching and learning packages seem to be the most appropriate form of media for meeting this requirement.

Teaching Packages on Educational Technology in Teacher Training

We have developed teaching packages on different topics of educational technology like programmed learning, the application of still pictures and films in teaching, microteaching, media selection. These packages are composed of modules, a solution which enables course organizers to draw up the programme taking into consideration the time available, the target population, background and similar factors and to choose the modules accordingly.

In order to illustrate the structure of teaching packages, allow me to give you some examples.

The package on programmed learning consists of 28 modules from which several courses can be set up. Let us take one of our most frequently used course structures which consists of three courses built on each other.

The first one is about the background of programmed learning, the different styles of programming, the aids of present programmes and the new tendencies in programmed learning. The seven modules from which this course can be set up contains series of OHP transparencies, slide-tape presentations, films and printed programmed materials. The modules include materials that are suitable for individual and/or group work, ie the course can be learned either individually with

*OOK is the abbreviation of the Hungarian name for the National Centre for Educational Technology.

42

the teacher's guidance or in a traditional organized way.

The second course which can be set up from 19 modules of the package trains program writers. With the help of AV and printed materials, participants first analyse programmed materials and second, study the process of programming — from specifying objectives to the trial of programs. By the end of the course participants are supposed to prepare their own programmed materials and in this way all the theoretical knowledge they have acquired during the course is put into practice.

The third course enables participants to design multi-media teaching packages.

The package on still pictures and their application in teaching also uses modules. As far as their contents are concerned they can be grouped into the following categories:

- modules for presenting the technical characteristics and location of the different kinds of still picture projectors, and for practising their operation;
- modules dealing with the types and design of different media that can be shown by still picture projectors;
- modules illustrating the application of different still picture projectors in teaching.

The 33 modules of the still picture package can be used for organizing different courses for technicians, teachers and school managers, eg 'The design and preparation of OHP transparencies'; 'The operation and location of the OHP'; 'The types, analysis and evaluation of still pictures', etc.

The main advantage of developing teaching packages on a modular basis lies in the possibility of further developing the modules and inserting new ones to meet needs without disruption. In this way package development can be made flexible enough to reflect the development of the discipline and to follow the field of interest and knowledge of the given target population.

An Indirect Way of Training in Educational Technology

Although the courses described above contribute considerably to the spread of educational technology, they cannot ensure in themselves its large-scale practical application in schools. This can mainly be attributed to the fact that, getting back to their 'everyday' circumstances after finishing the course, teachers are faced with several unfavourable factors hindering them from putting into practice the knowledge acquired as a result of the course.

The discussion with teachers who participated in one of our experiments contributed to better understanding of the above problem. Ten schools were involved in the experiment which investigated the effectiveness of using AV aids in teaching reading. The teachers were trained in operating AV equipment, instructed how to use the AV materials in the teaching-learning process, and provided with a list of available AV media (including educational radio and television programmes) which can be used in teaching reading. At the end of the academic year we made an assessment of reading skills and of the children's attitude to teaching. The discussion mentioned above was held at the end of the experiment.

We learned that during the first period of the experiment teachers had a lot of difficulty in using the experiment, since they were uncertain about handling it, but an even greater problem for them was how to fit AV materials into the teaching-learning process. They said had they not been asked to participate in this experiment, they would have given it up and would have slipped back to their 'good' old ways. But as time passed they began to feel that AV materials in fact provide greater possibilities, particularly in activating their pupils. It was a turning-point after which they simply could not do without educational aids and AV materials became integral parts of their teaching.

This conversation convinced us that there is a need for the 'after treatment' of teachers who attended our courses, in order to help them get over their initial difficulties. But how can we do it? Keeping in touch with all our previous students, helping them with advice and encouraging them would seem to be a natural but hardly feasible solution. On the other hand, a material way of doing this would be a practical solution, ie providing these teachers right after finishing the course with teaching aids which help them to use educational technology in their everyday work. As is borne out by experience, teaching packages developed for classroom use would be suitable for accomplishing the above-mentioned functions, besides containing useful materials for compulsory education. These packages usually embrace approximately 10-20 hour teaching units. The most important element of the package is the teachers' guide which assists and directs teachers by making suggestions as to how to proceed with lessons. It contains the precise objectives the students have to achieve, the methods which seem to be best suited for working up the unit, gives the possible ways of using printed and non-printed materials and, finally, it also provides the teacher with the methods and means of evaluation. When using this kind of package, teachers meet the essential elements of educational design in their materialized form. The elements of educational design, ie the precise specification of objectives, the selection of the appropriate methods and media, working out the means of evaluation, are implicitly touched upon in the teachers' guide. With encouraging the teachers to use these packages — which they are ready to do quite willingly — our aim is to prove that efficiency can be raised if the design is based on educational technology. It can be expected that teaching with the help of packages will get teachers over the above-mentioned 'deadlock', and stimulate them to follow similar guidelines in teaching units where there are no packages. To promote this 'transfer' it is highly advisable to furnish teachers with an annotated list of teaching aids available in their particular subjects and provide them with a selection of case studies on methods of fitting teaching aids into the teaching-learning process.

In this case teaching packages serve the purpose of training teachers in educational technology in an indirect way, as opposed to the types of packages on educational technology described in the first part of the paper which are the means of direct training.

In recent years several teaching packages on different subjects have been developed at the OOK. As it was shown by the try-out of some packages (eg 'The Noun' for children of 12, 'Sets of Points' for children of 15) their use has a considerable influence on teachers. It goes without saying that our hypothesis, according to which teaching packages promote the transfer effect, ie putting into practice educational technology in the classroom, has to be supported by further scientific research.

As a result of it we expect to find answers to the following questions: How do teaching packages, as the materialized forms of educational design, affect everyday teaching practice? How many teaching packages should be provided for a given course, and in which sequence, so that the desired transfer effect appears in the teaching activity?

Educational Media for the Arab World—The Arab States Educational Media Centre

S A El-Araby

This paper begins by outlining the highlights of the changing conditions in the Arab world that have left their fingerprints on the social, economic, political and educational scene. These influences are bound to change attitudes towards the application of technology in the educational process. The paper then proceeds to explain the needs, objectives and organizational structure of the Arab States Educational Media Centre stressing its functions and activities as processes designed to realize the basic objectives. The presentation ends with a request to all institutions, local, regional or international, to supply the organizers of this pioneer project with information about conferences, training courses, research studies, resource persons, hardware, software and any other data that would help the Centre start on the right track.

The Changing Scene in the Arab World

Many Arab States have justifiably challenged their inclusion in the category of developing nations. Oil-rich countries like Saudi Arabia, Iraq, Kuwait, Algieria and Libya are already pushing their way to the forefront of the international scene, affecting world economy and playing a key role in influencing the decisions of the major political powers of the 1970s. Kuwait, for example, has the highest per capita income in the world according to 1976 UN statistics. In terms of the kilowatt consumption of electricity, the mileage of well-paved roads, the adoption of computerized systems in industry, the proportion of schools, cinema theatres, telephones, motor cars, TV sets (coloured) to the population, Kuwait is far ahead of many so-called fully developed countries. Similar material progress pertains in other oil-rich countries. Among the rest of the Arab States, some do suffer from the usual pains of overpopulation and industrial underdevelopment, but they are comparatively rich in agricultural and human resources.

The dynamics of social relations in the oil-rich countries is passing through a unique stage. The problems of material progress coming too soon to a society not fully prepared for them are rubbing shoulders with the inhibiting influences of strictly traditional semi-tribal attitudes. Although some modern young Arabs enjoy loud western music, frequently visit first-class tourist resorts in Europe, drive expensive sports cars and engage in multi-million business deals, they still pray five times a day, fast during the lunar month of Ramadan, obey their parents, respect their elders and observe all other time-honoured traditions of Islam. In these cases, material progress has not affected the basic spiritual values which the Arab heritage has established throughout the ages. In other cases, material prosperity has acted against positive values to the extent of destroying them without offering suitable substitutes. On the other hand, very few Arab groups still believe in long-lasting feuds among families, fanatic, blind allegiance to their clan, and in rejecting

45

technological progress as an evil to be avoided at all costs.

In order to deal with some of these conflicting trends as they affect the application of technology to education, the Arab League Educational, Cultural and Scientific Organization (ALECSO, or Arab UNESCO) established the Arab States Educational Media Centre in Kuwait. This pioneer project was launched in 1976 to serve the audio-visual needs of 20 Arab countries of similar cultural and language backgrounds.

Need for the Centre

In order to deal with some of the common problems of applying technology to education, it was deemed necessary to establish one central institution to offer services, disseminate information and send consultants to all Arab countries which request assistance. Specialization in the educational media field is still rare in this part of the world. Some of those who have PhD-level specialization in this field have either emigrated to better jobs abroad or occupied higher administrative positions at home which are not remotely related to educational technology. The picture is further complicated by the different nature of administrative structures of AV services. In some cases, the audio-visual department is part of the central ministry of education. In others, educational radio and TV in particular, are affiliates of ministries of culture and information. In a few cases educational media are dispensed with as academic luxuries to be considered in the unforeseeable future after more basic educational needs have been met. A central organization is needed to help realize meaningful communication among these different agencies.

On the positive side, some national audio-visual centres have successfully produced educational media according to international standards. Jordan boasts one of the best educational TV programmes which has won international prizes. Kuwait and Saudi Arabia have the most updated software and hardware which serve the needs of instruction at all levels. Egypt is rich in human expertise in technical, theoretical and applied aspects of educational technology. The Arab States Centre was therefore established to pool all these Arab resources with a view to consolidating and co-ordinating professional services among national centres and agencies in the sister Arab countries.

Organizational Structure

Starting a new centre is both a challenging and a rewarding experience. It is challenging in that no previous model exists that can be expanded, modified or improved. According to UNESCO/ICEM report (Jongbloed, ed, 1976a) no formal structures exist for the establishment of international services among countries with similar problems or of regional services between countries of similar cultural and language backgrounds. The only attempt quoted in the same report is the initial design for the present centre which was conceived by 17 Arab countries in 1969 to be finally carried out in 1976. Moreover, the report mentions four administrative set-ups for the management of AV resources (Jongbloed, ed, 1976b) international, regional, national and local/institutional. The Arab States Centre does not seem to fit comfortably into any of these classifications. It is not international in the sense of offering membership to any country outside the Arab world which seeks to join. Nor is it regional in terms of a group of states which have geographic proximity as the determining factor for attempting concerted educational media activity. As the line drawing shows, its organizational structure seems to lie in between the international and regional category.

```
INTERNATIONAL
SEMI-INTERNATIONAL      — The Arab Centre
REGIONAL
NATIONAL
LOCAL/INSTITUTIONAL
```

Hierarchy of AV services with the Arab Centre as semi-international

Common cultural features and language background, Arabic in this case, are the two most important factors for pooling Arab efforts in this area of specialization. The difficulty therefore lies in the absence of blueprints to copy or previous models to follow. All regulations, procedures and relations with international, regional or other agencies have to be created and conducted on an experimental, trial and error basis.

This apparent disadvantage, considered from another point of view, can be the main strength of this pioneer endeavour. Problems may arise when well-established operations, with many years invested in their development, have to redirect or reform their services in terms of new trends in educational technology. A brand new operation has the advantage of being free to fashion its own rules, functions and activities without being cramped by traditional, deeply entrenched attitudes that tend to resist any change, even for the better. For example, the Centre can assume leadership in promoting the changing role of the media specialist from that of a hardware man or distributor of media to that of the instructional designer who has the right to make far-reaching educational decisions. It can also disseminate information about new trends in educational media such as trait-treatment interaction, instructional systems design and computer-assisted learning. The Centre will have the flexibility of adapting its objectives to changing needs.

Present Objectives

Since educational media are playing an increasingly key role in the instructional process, and as schools in many Arab countries suffer from a shortage of specialists, materials and equipment, the Arab Centre has been established to help alleviate these problems.

Perhaps the primary and most important objective is to develop awareness of the contribution of educational media to the improvement of the educational process. As has been mentioned elsewhere (El-Araby, 1974) many teachers shy away from using even the simplest aids on the outdated assumption that teachers should teach the way they were taught. If they are convinced that judicial use of media should save them time and effort, they may consider these aids in a totally different light.

The second objective is concerned with the most efficient use of all media resources available in the Arab world. Some national centres produce excellent graphics, others are experienced in audio or video production, a third group of centres has varied expertise and highly qualified technicians, program designers and media-oriented teachers. Co-ordination and integration of human and material resources among Arab countries are badly needed to make the best use of available talent, equipment and locally-made aids.

In an effort to solve the problem of the shortage of qualified personnel in the media field, the Arab Centre plans to provide consultants who explore the needs of each country and suggest ways of improving services and resources. This third objective can be realized through sending experts from the Arab Centres to these countries, or through contracting Arab or foreign agencies to carry out these responsibilities.

The fourth objective aims at providing each Arab country with a national media centre within two years. Many Arab countries have had for a long time well-established centres whose impact on the educational scene is clearly felt. A few countries are still hesitant about the feasibility of assigning funds and qualified personnel for the purpose. When the first objective of the Centre is fully realized, awareness of the value of educational media will gradually convince decision-makers of the importance of having at least one central authority to co-ordinate the use of technological aids.

The fifth objective is concerned with upgrading the efficiency of Arab media practitioners and keeping them up-to-date with regard to what goes on in other national centres in the Arab world. Communication among specialists and educators through conferences, symposia and meetings is planned to provide opportunities for exchanging information and reaching criteria for the evaluation of programs, hardware and software.

Finally, the sixth objective is to create a central clearing-house agency which examines all relevant information and the most recent findings in the field of educational media. Experts at the Centre survey these data, condense information pertinent to the Arab scene and disseminate summaries to the centres which would make the best use of them.

Functions and Activities

Headed by experts in the theory and practice of educational media, five professional divisions have been established to carry out functions and activities aimed at realizing the Centre's objectives. Being Arab nationals who have spent most of their professional career in the Arab countries, these experts have lived in the changing conditions in this part of the world. They are knowledgeable about the educational philosophies of Arab authorities and the administrative channels necessary to convert plans into action. The general attitudes of these experts reflect, more or less, what Brown and others (Brown *et al*, 1972) have stated:

'Media resources (are to) be viewed . . . as integral elements of curriculum development and instruction and there should be direct and continuous involvement of media professionals with teachers, curriculum and subject matter specialists, students and others in designing, testing and implementing such programs.'

Although the five divisions of the Centre — information, training, research, production and international — have not been fully staffed, the following functions and activities are already under way.

The information division has contacted all sources listed in library catalogues to provide the centre's library with the most recent references on software, hardware and educational media programmes. Plans are made to secure samples of films, transparencies, video programmes and other materials representative of novel trends in the field. Articles have been prepared for the quarterly newsletter *Educational Media* to be published by the Centre next month.

The training and consultation division has already conducted one training course for leaders in the AV field held in Cairo during November 1976. The division is currently engaged in administering two other training courses, one in Cairo for the construction and utilization of simple teaching aids, and one in Kuwait for improving the skills of AV technical personnel. Its future activities will include offering professional consultation to national centres, establishing criteria for training programmes and co-ordinating training activities among Arab centres.

The research division is currently engaged in surveying all research in the educational media field with a view to focusing on studies of most benefit to Arab countries. AV technical terminology has been compiled in order to reach standardized translation of terms for future use by all Arab media experts. Among the short-term future plans of the division is the encouragement of the translation and publication of original works in the area of educational media. It has also planned to design and conduct experimental research with the help of other Arab and foreign resource persons. An AV text-book for trainers of teachers is also being planned as one of the division's future activities.

The production division has started its functions by sending questionnaires to all national centres inquiring about their local production of media in order to exchange these materials and avoid unnecessary duplication of effort. Future plans include co-ordinating Arab production of media, offering consultation on the production and utilization of materials and providing national centres with standard specifications for AV software and hardware.

The fifth and last is the international division which has already made inquiries of all known educational media associations, especially non-profit ones, in Europe and North America, seeking information about their activities. Among the current interests of the division is following up on new findings in materials and equipment and collecting data on suitable software and hardware produced by foreign companies. Future plans call for full participation in international and regional symposia, conferences and exhibitions as well as editing and adapting foreign educational media to suit Arab culture.

How Can APLET Help?

The previous presentation shows that the new Arab States Educational Media Centre is concerned with promoting the use of new media in Arab curriculum programmes, in stimulating media research, in informing national centres in 20 Arab countries of appropriate application of available studies and experiments, in publishing descriptions of promising new media practices and in establishing standards which will help national centres in evaluating new media needs and in selecting media equipment and materials. Such an ambitious programme needs help from more established educational media agencies and associations to give it the initial push it needs to realize its objectives. To start with, there is a need for collecting information on programmes, new trends in instructional technology, recent discoveries in material and equipment. Representatives of APLET and similar international associations are kindly requested to put the address of the Centre, PO Box 24017, Safat, Kuwait, on their mailing lists to keep us informed of all activities, conferences, publications and research in the various specializations of the educational media field.

References

Brown, J, Norberg, K and Srygley, S (1972) 'Administering Educational Media' McGraw-Hill, New York, p 15.

El-Araby, S (1974) 'Audio-Visual Aids in Teaching English: an Introduction to Materials and Methods' Longman Group, London.

Jongbloed, H (ed, 1976) 'Guidelines for the Establishment and Management of Audio-Visual Services in Advanced and Developing Countries' UNESCO/ICEM, The Hague, (a) p 50, (b) p 15.

An Examination of Developments in Programmed Learning since 1968: Reflections on the UNESCO Conference, Tbilisi, USSR 1976

J Leedham

UNESCO convened a symposium of high-level experts in July 1976. The conference was serviced jointly by the USSR and UNESCO; it was attended by participants from 20 countries, with many more observing. This paper attempts to outline the intention of UNESCO, and the contributions on behalf of America, the Soviet Union and Western Europe.

The symposium itself was related to one held in 1968, 'The Varna Conference' which dealt with the same topic. In 1976 attention was directed towards developments which had occurred since 1968 in the psychological bases of programmed learning. Orientation papers were prepared on behalf of the UNESCO Secretariat, the USA, Western Europe and the Soviet Union. Whilst other very important papers were submitted from India and Africa, this presentation of detail is confined to the UNESCO, USA, Western Europe and USSR contributions.

UNESCO (UNESCO: Tbilisi Symposium 1976)

UNESCO appreciated that programmed learning had outgrown its original behaviouristic parameters both as to theory and application. They considered that its 'self-correcting, continuous exposure to testing and its affinity with systems methodology' should enable experts to determine whether there had been any true development towards a global theory of learning.

UNESCO's views on this had been strengthened by intervening smaller conferences in Paris and Geneva. The minimum hope expressed was that there would be a possibility of 'identifying a general mode of learning activity, both cognitive and professional, so as to elaborate programming strategies'.

The optimal aim was that sufficient information would emerge for a 'universally applicable theory of learning science to be arrived at'. As a personal comment it appeared to me that the expectancy of a 'single universal approach to the learning process' was optimistic. This was particularly the case after reviewing the diverse approaches made across Europe. Nevertheless, it was appreciated that the role of UNESCO was to 'set the sights'.

The USA (UNESCO: Tbilisi Conference 1976)

In 1974, reviewing the Brighton Conference (Leedham, 1974), I wrote of the contribution by Professor R Glaser that he outlined a future for learning theory which described quite exactly the practices in English primary schooling. It was Professor Glaser who gave the paper *Developments in the American Region* at Tbilisi. During the conference, Professor Glaser did not extend his arguments fully but the following is a fair summary.

'A new concept is emerging which is concerned with the psychological analysis of the instructional process. A theory of instruction is being developed in an attempt to link psychology and instruction for the design of optimal instructional conditions . . . Certain components of such a theory have become more clearly defined in terms of new theories of cognitive performance. These components are:

(a) analysis of competence (the state of knowledge or skill to be achieved);
(b) description of initial state with which learning begins;
(c) conditions which can be implemented to change state (b) to state (a);
(d) assessment of immediate and long-term outcome.'

The paper discussed theory design and illustrative research reflecting current activity. It was not clear to me that this represented any fundamental development in learning theory as applied to programmed learning. The detail that was quoted appeared a reformulation of criteria that have for long been identified with the practice of programmed learning as systems methodology.

It could indeed be a question of emphasis. Point (a) would often come before point (b) in most prescriptive systems, but otherwise the value of Professor Glaser's submission lay in the written extension of his outline which was thorough and authoritative. Nevertheless, seen from the limited view of a pedagogic researcher, the developments are in depth, not in breadth. The psychological territory is being 'reworked'.

Western Europe (UNESCO Western Europe 1976)

APLET were called upon to provide a study within a short time limit. Most of the material was drawn from the many publications of the Association since 1968 and it was acknowledged that the review was perfunctory in some respects. It was much easier to find accounts of empirical pragmatic developments in the field of programmed learning than to find any ascription to fields of relevant psychological theory. This is particularly true in the UK. Hartley (1974) has often been definite on this issue. He points to the complexity of the task, the lack of knowledge of the required techniques, the cultural inertia as reasons why little progress can be discerned in the development of psychological bases for programmed learning.

In an attempted analysis, country by country, in Western Europe it appeared that there was no fundamental progress. Sweden could point to depth analysis of specifics in task structure, Germany could stress the values of cybernetically orientated approaches. But the hierarchies of Gagné and the strategies of Bruner appeared still to be the bases on which programmed learning progressed. Very significant statements were contributed by Hooper (Hooper, 1974) and the Open University (Hawkridge, 1976) which suggested that the precepts of instruction so far derived from educational technology (programmed learning) were of little help to practitioners. The contributions from linguists — Chomsky for example — did not appear to have made any significant contribution to the bases of programmed learning. Such progress as was reported appeared to rely upon systems methodology and information theory.

It was in the presentation of this paper that it became clear that the many representatives from the socialist countries and the USSR believed very firmly that they had isolated new psychological bases for programmed learning which had proved highly successful. These bases were regarded as most likely to provide indicators for future progress. Listening to translation it appeared to me that the psychologists from the University of Soviet Georgia disagreed about this but the presentation of the main Soviet case was by Professor Talyzina identifying the Gal Perin School of Psychology.

51

USSR (UNESCO Tbilisi USSR 1976)

Professor Talyzina, supported by eminent Eastern Bloc psychologists, stated that the socialist countries had always doubted the efficacy of behaviourism. Since the Varna Conference developments had taken place related to Marxist psychology which stressed the activity function of study.

There was a necessity to discover a preliminary basis for action, then to create an operational structure which included a functional system for learning. The Soviet view was that cognitive training was imperative. This would lead to habits of independence, speed and ability to plan. Experience had shown that problem-orientated learning was especially successful. For example, senior classes had a complete year's work given to them in problem form. Their individual solutions were compared, the best commended. Such research work had indicated the need for studying the motivation and personal factors arising in learning situations. These studies and experiences suggested two ways of creating learning situations:

1. By organizing material to lead to achievement.
2. By teaching students to be able to transfer general concepts and strategies to specific learning tasks.

To achieve the second, much preferred, learning situation the Gal Perin School of Psychology provided suitable psychological bases which were universally applicable in learning situations.

A preliminary tenet was that knowledge is activity and if it is not applied it cannot be discerned. Material which is to be learned needs rational analysis to exclude the non-essential. For example, Gal Perin experimentation had reduced the 400 punctuation conventions of the Russian language to three for the purpose of instruction.

One way of producing a model for instructional procedure is to analyse the behaviour pattern of a successful group. A model based on analysis of problem, group and function can then serve future situations.

Within Gal Perin theory it is considered that too specific subject content can inhibit cognitive activity. More generalized content aids cognitive activity. The rational analysis of material to identify its 'root' or 'essence' together with controlled student activity related to the material leads to highly successful achievement. In the sphere of cognitive activity the following occur:

1. Forms of action: first material — exteriorized
                     second vocal — part interiorized
                     third mental — interiorized
2. Particularized
   Integrability: the elimination of inessential data or activity.
3. Assimilation: leading to automatic response

The control components of learning involve:

1. Stage one (material)
   Complete control of external operations
2. Stage two (vocal level)
   Systematic control
3. Subsequent stages
   Control episodic and at student request.

The application of such instructional patterns produces generalized forms of cognitive behaviour which ensure learning and transfer of concepts in relation to new phenomena. Such a theoretical base has global application.

Summary Content

This account represents what I understood of the Gal Perin case. I could not readily identify points of psychological principle which have not been examined in depth in APLET literature. Because of this the UNESCO summary covering this part of the conference was very brief acknowledging systems procedures and the Gal Perin arguments.

References

Hawkridge, D *et al* (1976) 'Open University' 'Journal of Educational Technology 7' 1 March.
Hooper, R (1974) 'Computers and Sacred Cows' in 'Aspects of Educational Technology VIII', (ed) J Leedham.
Leedham, J (1974, 1975, 1976) 'Aspects of Educational Technology VII, VIII, IX, X'.
UNESCO Tbilisi Symposium, July 1976 Ed 76/806/4.
UNESCO Tbilisi Symposium, USA Ed 76/806/5.
UNESCO Tbilisi Symposium, W Europe Ed 76/806/6.
UNESCO Tbilisi Symposium, USSR Ed 76/806/7.

The In-Service Training of Educational and Para-Educational Staff in Educational Technology Projects in Brazil

A J Romiszowski, H V Pastor

Introduction

Although the size of a typical Brazilian state is akin to a typical country in Europe, the population of a typical state is akin to that of a local authority. Thus the State of Rio Grande do Norte is about the size of Scotland and has a population smaller than Glasgow's. Bahia is bigger than France but has less than four million inhabitants.

But also states are poor or rich, and the educational systems reflect this very much. So in Sao Paulo, which is a highly industrialized city conglomeration, about as large as London, the educational system runs on very traditional lines and, for example, turning to educational technology, we find that ETV is used in much the same way as it is used in Britain and the United States: as 'icing on the cake' that some teachers choose to use, others do not. They have, for instance, a Brazilian version of 'Sesame Street'.

In other parts of the country, the situation is very different indeed. There are very underdeveloped educational systems in some states, and we shall be concentrating mainly on these states in the projects to be discussed.

The Maranhao Project

We shall start with the State of Maranhao, which in 1969 launched a project of TV-based secondary education.

In 1968 only three per cent of the 11-15 age group were in any sort of full-time education, almost all of those in private schools, convent schools, and so on. In 1969 a pilot project was installed, with the result that by the end of that year over 20 per cent of that age-band were participating in higher secondary education based on meeting in a church hall with a television, and with group organizers. These group leaders, or 'orientators' had several weeks of training on how to run the groups (mainly training in group dynamics techniques), but were not subject-matter experts. The television programmes and supporting printed materials were the instruments of instruction. The orientators' role was more one of 'control'.

Initially the project had various drawbacks. It was rapidly put together. Domestic televisions were installed and broke down in large numbers. Most of the programmes in the initial stages were a man with a piece of chalk in front of a television camera.

But this does not alter the fact that within one year there was an educational system where previously there had been none at all. And this system is running more or less on the same lines, with some technical improvements, to this date.

That is a sad state of affairs from some points of view because the system could have been improved a lot more. Turning to the question of teacher-training, for instance, one 'negative' aspect has recently appeared. I read in the paper that 'we are getting a sort of revolutionary atmosphere among our orientators' because they are trying to take over the teaching from the television and written support materials. They are trying to impose their own personality and their own techniques on the pre-prepared, pre-programmed presentations. 'And this must be stopped!'

Of course, it need not be stopped. It could very well be a way of training a body of teachers, where before teachers have not existed, on an entirely in-service basis.

Could we not, through a process of controlled supervision coupled to a teacher-education programme also distributed via mass media, gradually delegate progressively greater responsibilities to our orientators as they prove themselves capable of accepting and executing them? Could one not utilize the group encounters as a 'teaching laboratory' for staff development?

The fourth project that we shall be presenting is a federal government project, which is in fact trying to implement this sort of teacher training in Maranhao and other states.

Project SACI

The second project is Project SACI which is linked to the 'educational television by satellite' programme of Brazil.

Like several other countries, including notably India, Brazil has for some years been researching into the use of satellite transmissions for educational purposes. These researches have been the subject of many published papers. Pilot projects have been run and project SACI is one of these. However, large-scale, nationwide transmissions of educational programmes via satellite have not yet commenced, and it appears increasingly less likely that they ever will.

Be that as it may, there have been some useful 'spin-off' results so far. Project SACI was very concerned with the production of the 'software' (TV programmes, radio programmes and supporting texts), as well as the 'hardware' to transmit them. Table 1 shows the materials produced by the project — the group A+D materials covering the curriculum of the first four years of schooling, and group B+C materials specifically for teacher training.

		Radio Lessons	TV Lessons
(A)	Mathematics	106	106
	Portuguese	104	104
	Sciences	90	90
	Social Studies	90	90
	'Citizenship'	30	30
(B)	Education	30	30
	Teaching Method	30	30
(C)	PI Texts for the teachers to supplement all of Group A		
(D)	Classroom support material, tests, texts, etc for all of Group A		

Table 1. *Project SACI Materials Produced*

So far these materials have been implemented in only one state — Rio Grande do Norte — in the poor north-eastern part of Brazil. Rio Grande do Norte is a very small state with about one and a half million inhabitants only, and it was chosen as being a manageable pilot project area.

Of all the teachers operating in the first four years of primary education in Brazil, about 80 per cent are non-trained. In this project, 1000+ teachers were involved who had just completed the first four years of elementary education (or who had not even completed that).

These 1000 or so teachers were given teacher-training, and this training consisted of putting them through the course materials. Thus the first validation of the course was on the teachers who were going to use it. The teacher course was supported by a range of programmed texts. The project produced a set of programmed texts in all subjects for four years of a primary school curriculum.

Thus we see two radically different approaches to the teacher shortage, exemplified by the projects in Maranhao and Rio Grande do Norte. In the former state, the teacher's functions have been largely taken over by 'high technology' systems. The staff employed in the system are rapidly trained 'para-educational' staff, their responsibility restricted to the 'maintenance of the system's operation'. In the latter state, the teachers' functions remain much as in a traditional system enhanced by educational technology. The radio and TV broadcasts form only a small part of all teaching time. Very many classroom activities are performed by the teacher. However, he receives training in the performance of these activities, on a totally in-service basis, and almost entirely via educational technology.

The Projects of IRDEB

We shall now move on to the IRDEB project, which is in the adult education field. The State of Bahia published the statistics shown in Table 2 in 1976.

In primary education (first 4 years)	56,800
Over 14 years old with first 4 years incomplete	67,100

Table 2.*1976 Date — State of Bahia*

This was the justification for launching a radio-based (plus group orientators) adult education system within the state. The State of Bahia is quite big, and it has taken quite a long time to launch the project fully. It started in 1973, and by 1973/74 it was running with two major areas of curriculum: language skills and social studies. Only later were the science and mathematics content also programmed. It has now been running fully since 1975, with about 8000 students per year.

It operates through a network of study centres which are called *telepostos* (distance education centres). At the moment there are 30 study centres in the capital area and 76 more in the interior. Most of the study centres run either a maths and science semester, or a language skills semester, and then the next half-year they run the other one, and the next half-year the third, so it takes a year and a half to complete the equivalent, more or less, of a four-year elementary education.

One should observe here that the daily radio transmission is of 15 to 25 minutes' duration for each of the three subject areas. Thus the group leaders, or orientators, have a considerable teaching task to perform. Typically, a daily session would be structured as follows:

1. 45 minutes — revision of previous work, comments on previous exercises, preparation for the transmission. (This is planned in the leader's notes, pre-circulated to all the leaders.)
2. 15 minutes — radio transmission.
3. Two hours — follow-up work, from the printed support materials. The overall structure of this session is planned and pre-circulated in the leader's notes, but

the control of the session, individual help to students in difficulties, occasional addition to the plan and modifications to local conditions are very much at the discretion of the leader.

Thus the orientators employed in Bahia have more responsibility (and therefore need more training) than those used in Maranhao. They have received this by attending central training courses and by in-service training based on circulated materials and a team of visiting supervisors.

By much supervision, carried out by fully trained and qualified staff, IRDEB has attempted to strike a middle path between the approaches described in the two other projects. Like Maranhao, the system in Bahia uses rapidly trained para-educational staff, effective in the field after only a few weeks or months of initial training. Unlike Maranhao, the group leaders in Bahia have more responsibility and more flexibility of action. However, the extent to which they assume such responsibility and exercise such flexibility is controlled by a more highly qualified supervisory staff.

Project LOGOS

In the light of the previous three projects and others like them, the federal ministry has recently launched a programme called LOGOS, which is a correspondence-based, in-service teacher-training course, which has components as shown in Table 3.

(Correspondence; Media; Groups; Visits)
Characteristics
1. Self-study modules
2. Self-paced progress
3. Continuous assessment — mastery model
4. Microteaching
5. Classroom as teaching laboratory
6. Group work in centres
7. Regular supervision in school
8. Use of radio mainly for orientation and motivation
9. Occasional use of radio/TV when the objectives justify the media.

Table 3. *LOGOS 1 + 11 (Federal Ministry of Education) In-Service Teacher-Training*

It looks somewhat like an Open University mix. The influence here was direct. However, the objective is not to provide an alternative, general education, like the Open University in Britain, but to satisfy a very important need for improved teacher-training. It is being run in five very scattered states, Rio Grande do Norte, Paraiba, Piaui, Rondonia and Parana. The pilot project, LOGOS I, involved 1900 teachers, during the 1973/74 years. The overall results are shown in Table 4.

The course is master-learning oriented; there is no time limit and everyone works at their own pace. The cost per student, in order to teach a high level of mastery on well-designed instructional materials, appears very reasonable.

On the basis of this pilot project, the second stage, LOGOS II, was launched in 1975. This now has a complete set of teacher-training materials, estimated to give a course length of about 27 months for the average student. Naturally, the course continues to follow a mastery-oriented, student-paced model.

It is estimated that in the five states involved in the project there are over 300,000 untrained teachers. The objective of LOGOS II is to qualify 15 per cent of these by 1979 — that means upwards of 45,000 teachers to be fully trained by means of a distance education system coupled to in-service training.

(12-month, part course)	
1900 teachers in 5 states	
Passed	90%
Failed/drop out	10%
Average score on evaluations (80% minimum)	88%
Cost/student qualified	£25

Table 4.*LOGOS I Pilot Project 1973/74*

The objectives are detailed in Table 5 below.

(Teacher-Training at a Distance)			
State	Teachers to be qualified	School children who will benefit directly	Self-study modules to be distributed
Paraiba	10,000	400,000	2,000,000
Parana	18,000	720,000	3,600,000
Piaui	7,000	280,000	1,400,000
Rio Grande do Norte	10,000	400,000	2,000,000
Rondonia	900	36,000	180,000
Total	45,900	1,836,000	9,180,000

Table 5.*Proposed Impact of LOGOS II 1975-79*

Further spin-off benefits are expected, as the 45,900 teachers participating are from more than 30,000 separate schools, where they can involve other teachers in participation in later stages of the project, or even in informal study of the self-study modules which are being circulated. This spin-off use is being encouraged. Although the project has at present only sufficient resources to attend to the needs of the 45,000-odd students already registered, any teacher who wishes to may subscribe to the self-study modules. Several thousand non-supervised students, from nearly all the states of Brazil, are subscribing in this way. As greater resources become available, these independent students could possibly get some sort of correspondence service.

The budget for LOGOS II, based on the experiences with the pilot project LOGOS I, is not very high. The figures published by the Federal Ministry of Education are shown (translated approximately into pounds sterling) in Table 6.

Year	Quantity
1975	£1,277,000
1976	594,000
1977	340,000
1978	480,000
1979	481,000
Total	£3,172,000

Table 6.*Budget for LOGOS II*

This works out at about £70 per trainee which, for a course averaging two to two and a half years to complete, totally 'packaged' in self-study modules and broadcasts, supported by visiting supervisors/trainers, offering a correspondence service and incorporating group meetings, seems a very reasonable cost indeed.

Two side benefits: one of course is that due to the in-service training aspect you are not going to lose your teachers out of your schools during the course. The other is that you do not lose them afterwards either because they never leave their little village during training. These are two very important points which recommend the in-service approach to teacher-training in a country with a still-developing educational system, as is Brazil.

Conclusion

The four approaches described in this paper have highlighted several approaches to an acute shortage of well-trained, qualified teachers. These have ranged from the elimination of the teacher from the system, substituting in his place a para-educational 'operative' trained rapidly to administer a mass media-based instructional system (Maranhao) to a media-based, mastery learning-oriented, self-paced in-service training system designed to train and qualify teachers to perform what may be termed a 'traditional' teaching function, (LOGOS).

These are the two extremes: using educational technology to replace the teacher and using it to train the teacher. The other two projects described have illustrated possible intermediate paths. One (SACI) has the 'traditional' teacher supplemented by a highly structured media-based course. The teacher receives in-service training in parallel with his work as a teacher. At the end of the process we have a fully trained teacher with some experience in the 'non-traditional' skills of teaching a highly structured media-based course, but the teacher remains quite 'traditional' in terms of his authority and control of the process.

The other project (IRDEB) used para-educational staff to administer a media-based distance education system, but gives them much greater, teacher-like responsibilities, developed by a system of in-service supervision/guidance and regular refresher training. We identified the germs of a competency-based promotional hierarchy in this system.

Which of these various approaches to solving the teacher shortage in Brazil is the best? Probably not any one of them. The very fact that so many approaches can be tried in such a short span of years, all of them giving promising (initial) results suggests that no one approach can be applied to the variety of local (geographical, economical and historical) problems which exist in a rapidly developing country of such a size.

Experiences with the Maranhao project suggest that it would be unwise to attempt to do without teachers altogether, or even to limit rigidly the roles of less qualified, para-educational staff. On the other hand, the Maranhao project created a working educational system almost overnight, whilst even the LOGOS project will take some decades to reach all untrained teachers in the country.

All four projects have one factor in common, a factor which underlies their viability. This is the extensive use of educational technology in all its forms. But how best to use this technology is still under study. The one thing that is obvious so far is that systems must be allowed to evolve. We need adaptive systems of education at all levels, including teacher-training. This seems more likely to be achieved through in-service training rather than through college-based training.

The Great Shift—a Perspective on the Change of System-Resistance to the Spread of Educational Technology

E M Buter

About the Resistance to the Spread of Educational Technology

There seems to be some truth in the observation that people are reluctant to use teaching aids, and in all probability they are often right. However, could it not be that they are right for the wrong reason? Let us look at some of those reasons.

There are many schools where a lot of teaching aids are used. Many teaching institutions, for example the Open University, have introduced expert planning. Some teaching systems, like the Montessori, give an indication of the possibilities offered by the integration of teaching aids and a systematic organization of the learning environment. At the same time, such teachers or such systems indicate reasons for resistance to the introduction of educational technology. It is essential for such systems to have very intensive supportive management.

I very often meet teachers who, within the realm of their own classroom, try to realize an educational technology approach. However they soon meet a kind of invisible wall. There are no hours available for developmental tasks. The school management has no insight into the necessary organizational structures to support such efforts. Media specialists lack insight into the didactical performance required. Some educational specialists lack insight into problems related to small-scale management. Often the enthusiastic teacher becomes a 'do-it-yourselfer' on a large scale. Later he relapses into the relative safety of traditional teaching.

Other teachers often start ventures like project work, sometimes with the minimum of supportive material and administrative backing and very often with a maximum of improvization. This is personally very rewarding, but such effects are incidental, because they are not part of the system. However they can create an unfavourable image of educational technology.

What Do We Really Want?

It is very easy to imagine a society where formal education is only available at a very low level of organization. But in our society we want to progress to the delegation of education to formal institutions. We want a longer learning time for the individual. We want a larger slice of the population to make use of teaching facilities. More variety is needed in teaching/learning situations. It also seems that much more attention must be given to a greater variety of needs.

We must come to the inescapable conclusion, already often made before: the amount of lifehours of any population spent on formal education (LH_{fe}) will gradually grow to a very substantial part of the total amount of lifehours (LH_{tot}) available in that population. (See Figure 1.) Our wishful thinking might easily lead to the conclusion that we want this proportion to be equal to one. However, without drastic changes in the system, realization of this fantasy would certainly

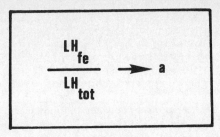

Figure 1 . . . *some of us seem to want a to become equal to 1* . . .

lead to a breakdown of that system.

Let us analyse this a little more. What kind of tasks which already have their place in teaching are not really integrated in the system? In big classrooms we often come across exercises to encourage individualization. In large, often very inhomogenous groups we try to create different teaching/learning situations at the same time. New methods of teaching are often needed which are totally unfit for use with the traditional frontal-lecturing mode.

Some of us have to cope, within the same lecture period, with pupils of very different backgrounds and entrance behaviour. Others take on administrative and technical jobs or work hard in committees or working parties. These are just some of the developments one can observe in schools. To me, they are signs of the times.

The quest for less students per teacher does not help very much. Only if we lower the ratio drastically, let us say to five students per teacher, would we get some relief of teaching pressure.

More generally we can say that new educational concepts require new tasks and functions, and these cannot be fulfilled easily by traditionally trained personnel. The traditional school system has no room for such functions.

It is my opinion that these issues are very relevant to the spread of educational technology in schools.

Some conclusions seem inevitable.

The first conclusion might well be that we must quantitatively re-allocate students to alternative teaching/learning situations, those that are not yet systematically created in the prevailing school system.

The second conclusion is that we must systematically restructure the teaching profession. The result should be that a whole range of new tasks can be performed within the school system as an integral part of that system.

Let us not jump to the conclusion that this is merely a question of manpower. A little bit more here and a little bit less there will not do the trick at all. The introduction of full-scale television in schools will not do the trick either. If we really want to reduce the ratio of students to teachers to, let us say, one quarter of what is now normal, we must have three times the qualified teaching personnel — or the delegation of teaching to other teaching/learning situations becomes a very serious issue indeed. (We have very good examples of this in institutions like the Open University, where sometimes about 70 per cent of the teaching is taken over by written texts.)

Some Possibilities, Judged from an Educational Management Viewpoint

We are in a very lucky position in that we have many different lines of development at our fingertips. It is possible to create flexible alternatives to traditional modes of teaching.

Many movements paved the way for new integrative developments: programmed learning in the late fifties; media use during the second half of this century; discussions about methods and objectives in educational management; and attention to personalized and experimental learning. These are only a few examples from a very long list.

And the integration of fact and fancy in this western world, as well as the integration of scientifictiory (!) and visionary approaches, shows us the way. It seems that there is a direct relationship between taxonomies of objectives and optimal learning situations. And this seems to hold, notwithstanding the many variations in interpretation of this terminology.

I will use the term response range to indicate the variety of responses to a given stimulus (−situation) in a given teaching sequence. If we ask a student to indicate on a map the capital of his country, the probability that he will be wrong is very small. We say that the response range is very small. If we ask a student to give a definition of democracy, the chance that he will give the definition we have in mind will be very small indeed. The response range is now very great. If we ask 100 students to mark the three differences in the definition of democracy, as given in a sentence by writers A and B, the chance that they will come up with approximately the same items will be relatively great. The response range is relatively small. This concept of response range is at the same time an expression of what we know of learning processes and an indication for the management of learning situations.

Now let us look at the diagram. (See Figure 2.) In this diagram there are two co-ordinates. The horizontal indicates the levels or clusters of objectives in the cognitive domain. The vertical does the same for the affective domain.

I choose the Bloom approach because it is comparatively easy to interpret and is very useful for management purposes. It is thus a very suitable approximation.

On the diagonal the relevant teaching/learning situations are indicated. In reality such teaching/learning situations form a continuum. One of the variables we can use to define the teaching/learning situation appears to be the response range. In the diagram we have indicated the response range by a double-pointed arrow. It will be clear that many forms of instruction, such as classroom instruction, CAI, programmed teaching, will be found in the lower left-hand corner of the diagram. Teaching/learning situations with a high degree of student autonomy, like project work or self-study, are in the right-hand upper corner. Through this approach we define many teaching/learning situations in an operational way. In the diagram the step from closed loop to open loop situations is important.

In many teaching/learning situations we constantly jump from the open loop system to the closed loop system and back again. This happens even in the most advanced and free learning situations. (It is a very healthy exercise to study the work of Paolo Freire with this observation in mind.) The further we move up along the diagonal the more we meet teaching/learning situations which lack external control and allow for more freedom for the student. Control and evaluation are shifted to the student. In all probability there is an inverse relationship between the response range aimed at and the amount of external control possible.

This model is a very productive aid to the design of teaching/learning situations. It is not a descriptive model, but a productive model.

Most teachers I know seem to have no systematic approach to the decisions necessary for facilitating specific teaching/learning situations. It seems to be thus quite understandable that many teachers tend to translate the use of teaching/learning materials to the monoculture of the frontal lecture approach. A diagram like this could help to make decisions more varied and more flexible, thereby focusing on a polyculture of many interlocking teaching/learning situations.

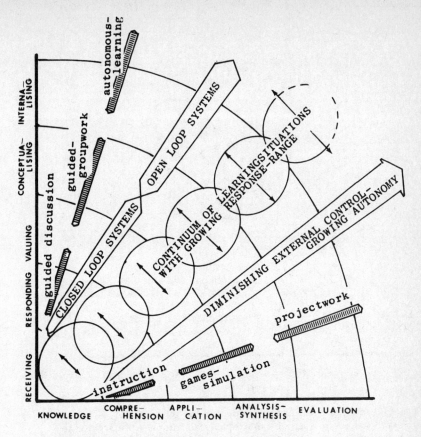

Figure 2. *Relation between objective-domains, response-range
and teaching-learning situations*

The 1 : 1 : 1 Hypothesis

As mentioned earlier, the pressure is great to allocate students to other teaching/
learning situations, like tele-tv or distance learning. It is regrettable that at the
moment this leads to a reduction of teaching/learning situations to the lower
cognitive and affective levels. In the following diagram I have indicated the areas of
teaching and learning that seem in many instances neglected, if not totally
overlooked. See the arrows in the diagram in Figure 3.

However, it is just those neglected areas that are of the greatest importance for
the management of educational technology and its spread to schools in general.

The lowest areas in the diagram can probably be delegated to teaching/learning
situations which are characterized by a narrow response range and high external
control. Such situations are still allocated to teachers who spend many hours in
frontal teaching, often robot-fashion. Many teaching devices could very easily be
used in such cases.

For the development of supporting materials, however, an intensive retraining of
teaching personnel is needed, away from frontal lecturing and into the
developmental and controlling mode. In doing this we will discover many

63

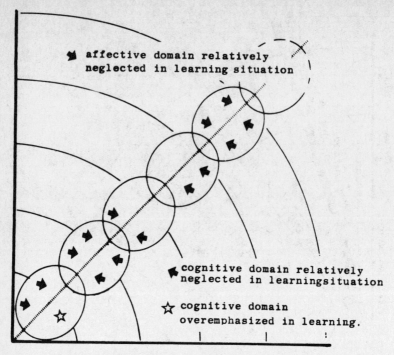

Figure 3. *Areas of teaching possibilities often neglected in contemporary education*

subdivisions in tasks, some already known, some very new.

The top part of the diagram can probably be completely delegated to autonomous students. These are characterized by a very wide response range and by the absence of external control. In fact we depend here on the development of internal control. The materials needed are more of the resource and do-it-yourself type of student activity.

For the development of such supporting materials in many cases we need content specialists, persons who are able to write and design, and a blend of journalism. Again, within this area, we will discover that there are many new tasks to be done, some developmental, some managerial.

For the teacher function the middle area is very important. In this area we find those teaching/learning situations in which students are trained to link the facts and rules learned with their application in much more complex situations. This is the area with a response range that is medium, characterized by small groups and where it is still possible to use external control in an optimal way. It is here that the teacher has his highest applicability.

And again, here we need new developments, eg teachers need to be trained for these highly skilled tasks, which at the same time require very much of their personality.

From long experience and observation I assess that it is possible to allocate learning to the mentioned areas on a 1 : 1 : 1 basis. However, when teaching/learning is developed along these lines educational technology will enter the schools, wanted or not. Let us be very clear about statements of this kind.

The human being, on the one hand, is very creative. To care for his varying needs it is necessary to facilitate access to a variety of learning processes with more variation than we now offer, on a systematic basis. There is not a shred of proof that we need specific training for every specific need. It is thus a very sound observation that all management of teaching/learning has a high degree of arbitrariness. The decision to opt for variety in teaching/learning depends more on external criteria, and less on the characteristics of learning processes.

However, if we can realize great variety in teaching and learning, this makes room for a spectrum of response ranges and seems very sound management.

The model makes the following conclusion clear: it is possible to reallocate learning to different teaching/learning situations, systematically and intensively.

This of course ties in very neatly with the already stated need for a fundamental reallocation based on the constantly growing need for personalized education.

The Great Shift

Throughout the rest of this paper I intend to refer to these reallocations as the great shift. Let me repeat:

1. There is a need for intensive reallocation of students to very different teaching situations, to cater for the growing needs of teaching.
2. It is possible to reallocate learning to a variety of teaching situations, related to, eg, taxonomies of objectives, and very different from the frontal lecturing mode.

These two points however bring with them a third aspect which falls under the same heading. It has to do with the reshuffle of personnel.

Even if we allow for a slight growth of personnel in the teaching sector, this alone cannot perceptibly lessen the burden of teaching. If we want to facilitate the realization of both the quantitative and qualitative aspects mentioned, we must reallocate personnel within the system, based on the many tasks that must be incorporated.

We need more writers, more analysers of subject matter, more developers of teaching devices, more managers, more network planners, more programmers and, what seems very important to me, more functionaries who are able to translate abstract needs into practical procedures, processes and money. We need specially trained architects, technicians and media specialists who understand educational specialists and vice versa.

So there is this third aspect of the great shift:

3. To realize a workable teaching system which facilitates more teaching hours for a growing variety of needs and a growing quantity of students, it is necessary to reshuffle teaching personnel and probably train or retrain them for their tasks.

The Great Shift and the Empty Meso-Level

Most functions mentioned are supporting functions. In the teaching structure it is convenient to recognize three levels as a model for consideration: the micro-level, that is where the actual teaching takes place; the meso-level, where supporting tasks are done; and the macro-level, where general, often political, decisions are made and where the money comes from.

Now we could say that, apart from directors and some co-ordinators, typists and technicians, the meso-level generally is a very empty area indeed. Those who find in some places a number of people in this level, still will agree that this is not overcrowded. And many who could be recognized as belonging to the meso-level are

65

not an integrated part of the teaching system. When we ask why teachers do not use educational technology the answer is that the level where educational technology must get its developmental background is missing. For general frontal lessons educational technology is not a great necessity. For all other kinds of teaching there is no systematic support structure.

To spread educational technology to teaching, we must recognize that we must fill the meso-level adequately, and in relation to the other aspects of the great shift.

Professionalization and Conditioning Research

Let us round this off with a few observations before we come to the final summing up.

First: there is a very low level of professionalism as far as the meso-level functions are concerned, especially when dealing with knowledge about applied didactics, learning psychology and other fundamental disciplines. There is, secondly, an even greater hiatus in professionalism in those working in teaching concerning operational disciplines, like management or quantifying organizational routines.

Thus the realization of the great shift asks for an intensive programme of professionalization focused on meso-level functions. It might well be that in the drive to attain this, institutes for teacher-training might have to change their names to 'institutes for applied educational sciences', to be more in line with their intentions.

Within such institutes we see not only the training of a much greater variety of personnel engaged in teaching (instead of training teacher personnel). We also see people who spend a great deal of their time on developmental research directed at the meso-level functions. It might well be that educational technology as it is now developing finds its optimalization right there: in the meso-level area.

To Sum Up

There seems to be a need of, and a distinct possibility of attaining, greater flexibility in our teaching systems to cater for growing individualization — based on more freedom in the level of objectives and more freedom in modes of teaching. Fundamental changes in the system are, in this article, called the great shift.

1. The overall situation in our society indicates that we must use all the means we have to find ways of allocating students to a range of alternative teaching/ learning situations. If this cannot be done we end up with a very inflexible teaching system based on traditional patterns, or, in trying to lay down the burden of the individualization on traditional teaching systems, we create very unfavourable conditions for teaching.
2. It is very fortunate that analyses of objectives, like, eg, those of Bloom, can be linked up with analyses of teaching/learning situations in which those learning processes needing to reach specific kinds of objectives can be optimalized. An analysis of this linkage indicates that probably two-thirds of teaching/learning situations can be made independent to a very large degree of the presence of professional teachers.
3. However, to realize alternative teaching/learning situations it is very necessary to change existing schooling systems intensively. The basis of this change leans heavily on the assumption that a relatively wide shift of personnel to meso-level functions is necessary. Otherwise a wide variety of supportive tasks, mainly of management and developmental character, cannot be fulfilled systematically. Professionalization for such tasks is an immediate necessity.

4. It is highly probable that realization of the great shift, and the development of a full meso-level, is fundamental to the development of educational technology, and its systematic spread to the teaching arena.

References

Buter, E M (1974) 'A Spectrum of Potential Learning Situations, Related to a Taxonomy of Objectives' (Translation from the Dutch) 'Educational Technology II' p 325.
Lindblad, S (1976) 'Experiences and paradigms in educational technology' Educational Technology Theory and Policy Workshop II in Strasbourg, 8-10 December 1976.
Williams, F E (1969) 'Models for encouraging creativity in the classroom by integrating cognitive-affective behaviours' 'Educational Technology' 9, pp 7-13.

Free Format Timetabling Revisited

E G Bingham

Introduction

The gist of this paper is an admission of a change of mind — a phenomenon normally associated with the female prerogative. The writer hastens to add, however, that this change was the systematic result of an iterative process in an ongoing free format timetabling experiment, and modifies a view expressed and published (Morton, *et al*, 1975) at an early experimental stage.

In 1974, the writer assisted two colleagues in presenting an enthusiastic report of their first-year study of a system of administering learning resources which they had called 'Free Format Timetabling'. This term was a shorthand description of a scheme whereby students, following individualized learning schemes, could reserve study places and resource materials, subject only to their availability. Offering the students freedom was felt to have several attractions both real and apparent, and so it was felt to merit an extended trial run in the writers' department.

The year-long experiment seemed fairly successful but was not repeated in the following session — for two reasons: the return to more 'conventional' teaching of the most enthusiastic exponent of the free format scheme, and the promise (or threat?) of an impending move to a new campus, where facilities were likely to be acutely restricted. But the synthesis of the 1973/74 experiment and of a smaller scale version since 1975 highlighted the factors which surround and influence such an innovation, and whose corollary is the demand for a complex balancing of priorities.

Since the original report was presented at an APLET conference, it is felt appropriate to choose a later ETIC conference to modify, retract or even perhaps to denounce the views expressed earlier, with the support of the remaining co-author.

The Argument for Free Format Timetabling

The reader may wish to be reminded of the arguments in favour of free format timetabling. These are certainly not difficult to find; for instance, it could be seen as a positive advantage for the divergent student who rejects a 'school-type' regime and disagrees with a particular kind of order (Hudson, 1968). But whatever their personality, it is surely accepted generally that students in every discipline, past and present, have their own personal study preferences and are usually quite conscious of them. Naturally every individual is inclined to believe that his own distinct pattern of studying is the 'best' method for him, and that the success of his learning would be seriously impaired if he were constrained to adopt any other scheme of study. No matter how valid such beliefs may be, their existence and popularity probably explain the current widespread support for learning systems in which the student is offered autonomy of pace, method and even of content. These in their turn presuppose the creation of a learning environment in which each individual learner can indulge his preferences, and may then follow differing routes through varying subject matter, at a pace which is independent of external constraints.

Thus can be argued the case for a system of resource-based learning which will offer the user all of the freedoms which he desires and, in particular, the ability to 'book-in' at times of his own choice. It is this latter characteristic which has been called 'free format' timetabling, although when the writer joined with Morton and Cowan (Morton, *et al*, 1975) to describe their joint experience in this field, they were quick to point out that their experiment was several stages removed from the ideal.

The Problem of Demand in a Completely Free Format Scheme

Mathematical arguments often make for tedious reading, so the writer will restrict herself to a simple example. Let us consider the case of a resource centre which is open to a certain class for w hours/week. We will assume that the class contains N students, each of whom will wish to attend the centre, or use a particular facility in it, for h hours per week.

In these circumstances the minimum capacity required to cope steadily with the average demand is Nh/w places. This capacity could be sufficient, provided the students were told when to attend, or were required to queue for a place in the centre until it became available.

In contrast, if it has been decided that complete freedom of format is to be permitted, then it is conceivable that all the class members might just choose to use the facilities at the same time. In this case the requirement is for a centre with N study places; and the difference between this and the minimum possible provision (Nh/w places) will decrease as the ratio h/w increases. But, even for a class which spends eight hours out of a 40-hour week in its resource centre, the ratio of the two values is still 5 : 1. In other words, the highest possible overall utilization for a centre which is genuinely offering completely free format booking (without delays) would be 20 per cent, in that case. Such a value for the utilization of university accommodation would be quite unacceptable according to current UGC practice. It is obvious that the economic climate which recently led the new University College, Buckingham, to reorganize their academic year in order to make better and more sustained use of their capital resources (Watson, 1976), will also discourage low utilization in other sectors of education in this country.

It is freely and immediately admitted that the writer has arrived at the above figures by considering extreme and perhaps unlikely figures. So it is of interest to consider immediately the evidence which is available from our own unit, covering occasions when the students have had some freedom to indicate their booking preferences outwith the two experimental courses. Their partial freedom has mainly arisen because a few spare places were available to those who preferred to work at that time rather than as booked.

All the figures were obtained from partially constrained situations; peak demands were reduced by the presence of booking systems or by timetabled commitments elsewhere, and by the fact that the maximum demand was sometimes still unsatisfied at the capacity quoted. Since the figures relate to everyday learning situations, they infer that, in these circumstances, even a system containing approximately 3 x Nh/w places will on occasions be unable to cope with peak demands. It may be estimated that a completely free format arrangement for any of these courses would call for the provision of specialist facilities at the rate of approximately four times the average demand, with a limit of about N/2; whereas a provision of N/6 (being the average demand plus 30 per cent) has been found to be sufficient to cater for a (basically) timetabled fixed format class which regularly spends five hours in one eight-hour day per week in the unit, using prerecorded instruction in one form or another (Cowan, *et al*, 1974).

The penalty for making a change from fixed to free format timetabling, in circumstances where resource-based learning takes up a minor part of the students' time, can therefore be seen as the application of a multiplying factor of the order of three or four, which will increase the costs of equipment, software, accommodation and storage. Where resources are used for a higher proportion of the standard working week, the increase in costs for equipment and accommodation will be less, but the same order of multiplying factor is likely to apply to the software provision. The increase in the provision of supporting staff would perhaps be rather less than this in both cases, but the change in the pattern of demand for academic staff in their role as 'resource persons' is quite serious. For the fixed format (or semi-fixed format) scheme rather tidily spreads the demand on the lecturers (Hudson, 1968) during the academic day, thereby making them more accessible to the students (Cowan, *et al*, 1974). But the free format equivalent tends to create high values of peak demand for tutorial assistance during the relatively short 'popular study periods'. Inevitably these peaks are likely to be satisfied in practice by reducing either the duration or the quality of the tutorial contact; both seem distinctly undesirable outcomes, since the demand will not be satisfied in the full meaning of the word.

Independent Learning with Fixed Format Timetabling

In a fixed format timetable the student is presented with a set of firm bookings for all the activities in his course, at times of day and in a sequence which have been chosen for him by the organizing authority. Unless the class is ideally matched to the capacity of the resource centre, there will be some slack capacity in the system and this will presumably be made available for use by students who are progressing slowly, who encounter problems, who sleep in, or who prefer to avoid their original booking for some other reason. But clearly the success of the fixed format arrangement depends on the correctness of the assumption that the majority of students will adhere to the bookings which have been made for them.

The fixed format student has therefore relatively little control over his study times, or over the order in which he encounters the activities in his programme. But when he is involved in any small group learning, he can (and should) take an active part in directing the progress of his group. And when he is placed in an individual learning situation, he should then have a high measure of independence of both pace and method, provided a range of learning materials is made available to him at that time.

The writer would therefore maintain that, although independence is far from complete in a fixed format timetable, the extent to which the students are offered autonomy can nevertheless be appreciable. This compromise may even bring positive benefits, since the offer of complete freedom can only be responsibly made when students are able and willing to make meaningful choices and decisions (Bingham, 1976). Thus a measure of guidance is provided in a fixed format scheme which caters for both the convergent students, whom Kirk (Kirk, unpublished thesis) saw as being distrustful of the unfamiliar, and the divergers, who are flexible and welcome new situations.

The learning unit now offers a first-year course in structures (a subject of a problem-solving nature) in which the initial (introduction) teaching is on group-paced tape-overhead sequences. These sequences have an uninterrupted run-time of about 35 minutes; but it is found that the groups generally spend almost an hour on a sequence. This suggests a measure of autonomy during the group-based learning, even before they move on to the learning lab, where a range of four or five types of follow-up tapes and a demonstrator are available to them. Given that the subject matter is chosen by the syllabus, and not by the students, a high degree of independence in both pace and method is open again, despite the fact that study appointment times are predetermined by the timetable. And a few students can, and do, take advantage of the slack in the system to adjust their times for one reason or another.

The variation in the study profiles is felt to be sufficient to demonstrate that striking variations are possible, both between individuals and, for one individual, between one week's topic and the next. They also confirm that control of study time need not necessarily entail control of study method or pace.

A Further Experiment with Free Format

In their 1974 paper the writers concluded (Morton, *et al*, 1975) that the case for free format timetabling was best described in the words of the Scottish verdict 'not proven'. It has already been reported here that, with the departure of Morton, his two colleagues reverted to a fixed format timetable. Lest this be seen as a complete rejection of free format, it is now felt important to report and discuss a further use of free format which was attempted, in good faith and with high hopes of success, in session 1975/76.

A new experimental course was being offered on an alternative syllabus (Watson, 1976) for a group of 12 students drawn from a first-year class of 81 students. The experimental course was intended to offer freedom, not only of pace and method, but also of content. It hoped to do so by providing, in an order to be chosen by the student, resource materials which would 'set the scene', by establishing, so to speak, the chapter headings and introductory paragraphs in the student's notes, leaving the student to extract and collate the remaining subject matter on his own. Clearly such freedom could only be offered in a relatively constraint-free situation: and it was for that reason that a small-scale return to free format was planned.

The students were offered a fair measure of participation in their course planning, considerable control of pace and extensive freedom from restraints on studying. The more able students could move more quickly through the subject matter, after a training period in the use of the new study methods had led on to the finally desired situation.

It was hoped that the attendant booking problems would be minimal, but in the event that hope was to prove unfounded. There was a marked congestion, because all the students tended to favour the same study pattern. The provision of study places was very high (N/2); but although the average utilization was quite low (17 per cent), peak demands were noticeably unsatisfied. Consequently the unit has not dared to envisage extension of this scheme to a complete class, without previously arranging some simple constraints in the form of an equitable booking system to allocate equipment and resources to students. Indeed such a booking system had to be provided in the experimental course. And so the logical conclusion of this experiment is seen as a preordained and permuted scheme of adequate, or preferably over-adequate, bookings for equipment and study places, which each student may (or may not) take up as he wishes or requires — in other words, a fixed format system in regard to the allocation of facilities, but a free format use of resources within that framework.

Student Opinion

The writer tends to be suspicious of the results obtained from questionnaires, and makes no exception in the case of our own results, despite the fact that the opinions appear to confirm the writer's own view. We issued a questionnaire to the 'rump' of the class advancing to the third year from the original first-year free format experiment (Morton, *et al*, 1975). This questionnaire was issued by the lecturer concerned at mid-session, with the genuine explanation that the answers would be used to determine the timetabling policy for the remainder of the session. It was hoped that this approach would ensure sincere responses, rather than elicit replies influenced by wishful thinking. The responses were to some extent verified by the writer, who had informally interviewed almost half of the class at various times prior to the issue of the questionnaire, and had recorded the findings privately.

The favourable reaction to fixed format timetabling is felt to be especially significant, since this was the class which had strongly favoured the free format scheme when it was introduced in session 1973/74 (Morton, *et al*, 1975). Their change of opinion was perhaps explained in the words of one student, who pointed out that in the first year they had been asked to compare what they considered a good scheme (on the basis of their experience of it), with a hypothetical alternative which was no more than a vague idea to most of them. But now, in their third year, he explained that they were choosing between two options, having experienced both.

Conclusion

As with any educational innovation the variety of factors to be considered in reaching a judgement will hinge, to a large extent, on the criteria favoured by the particular school, college or university. In our experience the free format scheme called for careful consideration of four main variables:

1. The degree of freedom in learning which was considered desirable;
2. The learning effectiveness of that freedom;
3. The social and psychological implications of the offer of autonomy;
4. The cost of implementation of free format timetabling.

The priority given to one or any combination of the first three factors will almost always be tempered by the fourth element, unless the innovators are fortunate enough to be in a position to disregard expense. But if they wish to remain cost viable, then the degree of free format which can be offered must decrease as the cost of the necessary resources increases. No matter how many other variables are then considered, it will be a complex decision based on the degree to which each factor is judged to be important.

The experience and chosen solution at Heriot-Watt arose from the recognition of a compromise as the only possible course. It was not considered a second-best choice; for a carefully planned fixed format system can cater for diverse personalities and can give them a high degree of independence to the benefit of their learning, while yet, and above all, remaining cost effective.

References

Bingham, E G (1976) 'Skills for the Occasion' 'Aspects of Educational Technology X' Kogan Page.
Cowan, J, Morton, J and Bingham, E G (1974) 'An Intermediate Assessment of a Developing Learning Unit' 'Aspects of Educational Technology VII' Methuen.

Hudson, L (1968) 'Frames of Mind' Methuen.

Kirk, G 'An Investigation of the Factor which Influences G S Pupils to Prefer Science Subjects' unpublished MA (Educ) thesis, University of London.

Morton, J, Bingham, E G and Cowan, J (1975) 'A Free-Format Course Based on Pre-Recorded Learning Materials' 'Aspects of Educational Technology VIII' Pitman.

Watson, L J (1976) 'Buckinghamshire's Second Open University' 'Education and Training' 18, 10, Nov-Dec 1976.

Teaching Developments in a First-Year Mechanical Engineering Course

B C Fisher

The Need for Innovation in Engineering Teaching

Engineering education is more concerned with ensuring that the undergraduate acquires knowledge and technical skills than with educational processes which might contribute towards his individual development. Perhaps this partly explains why noticeable characteristics of engineering graduates are poor inter-personal and communicative skills; need of close supervision; a lack of flexibility, breadth of vision and creativity in problem-solving; and poor personal motivation (Confederation of British Industry, 1975). Certainly the strongly convergent thought processes involved in assimilating technical knowledge run counter to the development of such qualities, although it would be naïve to assume that higher education is the only shaping influence on future professional engineering manpower. The currently recognized *malaise* in the higher education of engineers is a complex compound of political, social, industrial and educational factors (Select Committee on Science and Technology, 1976).

Some fundamental ideas for developing the creative abilities of science and technology undergraduates were stated almost 20 years ago (Land, 1957). The Undergraduate Research Opportunities Program (Cohen and MacVicar, 1976) and the Engineering Innovation Centre (Innovation Centre, 1975) at the Massachusetts Institute of Technology, are outstandingly successful applications of these ideas. Such educational innovations give students help where it is most needed. Students need to experience activities which integrate knowledge taught in separate subjects, and they need help in understanding the purpose and value of their knowledge and how it will be used in engineering situations.

And future engineering is likely to require engineers who are more flexible and adaptable to cope quickly with changing technology, new products, new techniques; and teaching methods must prepare undergraduate engineers for this role (Tribus, 1977). The educational process needs to encourage students to take responsibility for their own education. Problem-solving should not be so concerned with 'given this — find that'. The engineering world does not have well-organized problems — often the biggest problem is finding out what the problem is!

But such demands conflict with the style most engineering lecturers use in teaching a discipline, and the influence of discipline affects the way universities are organized and who is promoted. Promotion criteria encourage the academic approach, and consequently teaching methods emphasize the analytical, scientific and logical presentation of knowledge. By contrast the engineering world emphasizes activities such as managing, designing, manufacturing, etc, which have to meet the needs of society — transportation, communication, energy distribution, etc (Tribus, 1976).

New teaching methods (eg, Grayson and Biedenbach, 1974) have to be placed in perspective against this background of future engineering need. They do involve students more actively in the learning process, a necessary prerequisite for one of higher education's major aims — to develop independence of learning. But it would be wrong to assume that there is one most effective method. Students benefit from a variety of approaches (Taylor, 1976). More importantly though, it is still not clear how we go about meeting some of the fundamental educational psychology issues which are crucial to innovation in teaching. How do students learn? (Entwistle and Hounsell, 1975). How do we develop problem-solving ability? (Larkin, 1976).

But clearly there is a need for innovation in engineering teaching, and there are areas where significant contributions can be made towards improving the undergraduate's problem-solving and communication skills. One strategy is to develop a project laboratory approach where the student is given a feel for the engineering application of theoretical knowledge as he progresses through the undergraduate course. An integral part of such an approach is that he discusses and communicates his ideas, his difficulties and his solutions. The following sections describe the introduction of such a strategy in the first year of an undergraduate mechanical engineering course.

First-Year Teaching Developments

First-year engineering undergraduates need preparatory teaching before becoming involved in realistic laboratory projects. There are the needs to teach new skills and to cater for the variety in student laboratory experience. For example, most students need help with instrumentation and in determining the accuracy of experimental work. Also, the analysis of results and the presentation and writing of technical reports are areas where student skills generally do not meet the standards required for engineering project work. Thus the immediate need is for two distinct teaching efforts — one to teach experimental method and the other to improve technical writing ability.

But writing technical reports is only one aspect of communication. The process of communication involves the strategies and tactics of sending and obtaining information in many different situations. That professional engineers need communication skills is clear (Venning, 1975), but the full scope of an engineering laboratory course in providing opportunities for developing some of these skills is not often exploited. The technical report is only one form of communication. Time-limited oral presentation and space-limited write-ups are valuable in stimulating the student to present his ideas concisely and accurately. Group project work which gives students the responsibility for defining experimental objectives introduces at a low level the problems of group communication and project management.

From these considerations it was natural that two subjects should be developed which should be closely linked through parts of their syllabuses. One subject is engineering experimentation and the other is communication studies.

Engineering Experimentation

Between 80 and 90 mechanical engineering undergraduates take the course. Although the subject is not designed to a list of aims ranked by importance, the philosophy of approach does mean that some aims naturally assume more importance than others. For example, a student should readily perceive that the subject aims to develop his abilities to formulate experimental objectives, to understand the principles and limitations of engineering equipment, and to communicate the nature and findings of experimental investigations.

The subject is in two parts. The first part concerns the fundamentals of experimental method. The approach is based around a self-study booklet, (Fisher, 1976). Study aims and objectives are given in the booklet by four structured scripts which students complete in the laboratory. The scripts are marked and discussed at tutorials.

A study guide outlines a schedule of six supporting lectures and the work which students are expected to complete by themselves. Also described are several tape-slide audio tutorial packages which provide reinforcement, and information on instrument use and techniques. These packages are available in a learning unit, which has 12 study booths and two tape-slide replay units. Each study booth has tape replay and headphones.

The laboratory projects of the second part are based in other studied subject areas, but they are not necessarily linked directly to that subject material. Topics fall into two categories. One tends to emphasize instrumentation and measurement. The other category covers multiparameter situations which may be described by empirically derived equations.

The style of laboratory supervision is very important with this work. A student group is given a statement of the particular problem to be investigated and then encouraged to work independently to solve it. The work spans two weeks (two three-hour periods), and between laboratory sessions students can consolidate their ideas, look through literature and plan for the final part of the work. A student will write one project as a technical report (after discussing a draft at an editorial meeting with a lecturer) and the other three in a laboratory notebook. There are fixed dates for submitting work and collecting it after marking. Assessment includes laboratory discussion as well as written work, and students have complete assessment details.

Communication Studies

The subject places particular emphasis on improving basic communication skills and the major part of the work is concerned with technical writing and speaking, particularly to cover the communication activities of both the academic and industrial parts of the mechanical engineering sandwich course. Subjects in later years of the course deal with other aspects of communication.

The starting point for communication studies is to develop an attitude and an awareness of the process of putting information over to other people, that the student is not a free agent when writing and speaking. He must consider carefully the readers and listeners, decide what needs and expectations arise from the communication situation and how they might effectively be met.

These principles are then applied to technical writing and speaking. Firstly in dealing with writing, and especially in the light of recent work (Bullock, 1975), it is necessary to ensure that students understand the fundamentals which are used in subordinating ideas, and structuring sentences and paragraphs. The approach is not to teach grammar *per se* but to work from the standpoint that the difficulty of communicating complex technical material should not be made more difficult by using complex grammatical structures.

It is then possible to talk about writing style (verbosity, accuracy of meaning, choice of vocabulary and ease of readability), the need for clear information structures, and aspects of the presentation and layout of reports. Writing summaries, introductions and discussions gives most students difficulty, and few appreciate the potential of graphic illustrations. An early failing is for students to present a wealth of information in prose form without regard for the reader's need to visualize.

Oral communication aspects of the subject concentrate on informative speaking

— basically the planning, preparation and presentation of technical talks. Distinctions are made between writing and speaking as communication processes, possibly the most important being that speaking operates as a closed-loop system with some feedback between audience and speaker, whereas writing has no immediate feedback.

The subject is assessed by coursework over two terms and is taught by mechanical engineering departmental staff. It is important not to use traditional essay-type questions in assessment. A clear definition of assessment aims and objectives is necessary to play down the subjective element and concentrate on testing, for example, the student's ability to organize written information (Kirkman, 1974).

A student will have approximately three hours of tutorial work. This includes discussion of the tactics and approaches to specific writing tasks, and one video-taped speaking exercise with critique. The video-taped exercises are popular. Students appear to have no difficulty in realizing the advantages of being able to give a good technical speech.

Evaluations of First-Year Teaching Developments

Several evaluations have been run during the three-year period of the two new subjects. These have concentrated on laboratory work and associated methods. They have followed three basic patterns, and the following sections present the findings.

Communication studies has not been evaluated directly, but there is some feedback from the laboratory work evaluations and informal staff/student discussions. The general impression is that although students might initially take the subject seriously because it carries an assessment weighting equal to other technical subjects, they later realize the immediate and long-term benefits of being able to communicate well and make genuine efforts to master the subject.

Attitudes to Laboratory Work of Final-Year Students

Two surveys (Robertson, 1974 and 1975) commissioned internally but conducted from outside the university clarified considerably the situation of student attitudes towards laboratory work and associated report writing. A one-third random selection from two final-year student groups were given open-ended semi-structured interviews. Appendix 1 shows the nine questions.

At the time of the surveys, laboratory work was organized by subject and tended to follow the traditional pattern of directly reinforcing theory presented during lectures.

The findings left no doubt that students have strong opinions on laboratory work, and the same major points emerged from both surveys. Students felt that laboratory work occupied too much time. Often the work was unnecessarily difficult because it preceded the lecture theory, and consequently the real issues and intended outcomes were not clear. In some cases students were spending considerable amounts of time writing reports. On average short reports took three to six hours, and full technical reports at least seven or eight.

These pressures of time and difficulties with theory created impasses which could only be broken by copying. About 50% of students appeared to be using old reports either completely or in part. This was a source of annoyance to those students who did not copy. It also inhibited staff/student discussion of the work.

The interest and enthusiasm for laboratory work varied widely. There was a similar variation in the opinions about the usefulness of report writing. Certainly a major reason for such conflicting student opinions was that the aims of laboratory work were not fully understood.

In both surveys students stated that more project work should be introduced. In particular the project laboratory approach of one final-year subject was very popular, but also demanding. The approach uses student groups to investigate a broadly defined area. Such a situation is very much under student control and requires considerable independence of thought to formulate the overall experimental programme. Important criteria for the success of the approach are thorough student supervision, explicit descriptions of student tasks, and quick marking and performance feedback.

The surveys highlighted the importance of quick and thorough feedback to students on their laboratory work, and that same principle must be followed with evaluation work. The two surveys aroused curiosity in so many students that it would have been a psychological mistake to leave it unsatisfied. Consequently there was feedback to students on the ideas, the results and the modifications which sprang from the surveys.

The two surveys were part of a total effort of laboratory work discussion and review which spanned about two years. The effort included the ideas of industry and other university departments. Two major effects of this process on the style of first-year laboratory work have been the deliberate attempt to teach the method of engineering project work and to ensure that students are completely clear about what we are doing and what is reasonably expected of them.

Evaluation of Engineering Experimentation

An aims questionnaire was completed by two complete groups of first-year students. One evaluation was for the traditional approach to laboratory work (in 1974) and the other for the new subject engineering experimentation (in 1975). The form of the questionnaire follows previous work (Boud, 1973).

A complete discussion of the evaluation is available (Fisher, 1977). That work also evaluates separately student response to using structured scripts during the first part of this subject. But the four main points arising from the complete subject evaluation are:

1. Students have their own set of ideal aims for laboratory work which are not met by a traditional approach.
2. Students taking engineering experimentation had a higher set of ideal aims for laboratory work.
3. Engineering experimentation came closer to meeting these ideal aims; and
4. Engineering experimentation achieved the course aims more closely than a traditional approach.

It was encouraging to have these results for engineering experimentation after the first year of the new subject. Perhaps part of the success could be attributed to staff enthusiasm for the new subject, but the results were not without student suggestions for improvement. These suggestions mainly came from students who felt handicapped because they were not mastering experimental method fundamentals in the lecture situation.

The subject has remained substantially unaltered since the evaluation, and because of the close staff/student contact it is not difficult to get feedback. New projects are introduced each year, which keeps staff interest and cuts down the student copying element. Laboratory discussions are valuable for assessing individual student ability.

Evaluation of Teaching Methods

The initial approach was to present the experimental method fundamentals for engineering experimentation as a course of six lectures. This was not entirely satisfactory since a significant number of students had difficulty in using the fundamentals when they came to tackle their projects. Probably there are two main reasons. Firstly, the lecture does not actively involve the student in the comprehension and application levels of cognitive behaviour, thus limiting the mastery with which he can use knowledge in the laboratory situation. Secondly it is not possible to adapt lecture content and presentation to accommodate the wide range of first-year student laboratory experience.

A teaching approach based on individualized study appeared to offer certain advantages in this situation. In the second year, the experimental method fundamentals were presented as a set of self-study written units, audio-tutorials and tape-slide packages. Consequently students had some choice over studied material and pace of study. A study guide linked this individualized study material to a recommended text-book (Penny, 1974), which most students bought.

One lecture introduced the subject and explained the teaching approach. Seminar sessions were held to clear up difficulties over studied material. Also the four structured scripts completed in the laboratory during this first part of the subject were marked and discussed at a tutorial, as before. This assessment indicated that student cognitive ability (up to and including the knowledge application level) was not significantly different from that of the previous year — although it is perhaps premature to make judgements about the effectiveness of teaching methods from comparisons of only two student groups!

But students were asked how effective they thought a lecture course presentation of the fundamentals would have been compared with the individualized study approach, using their experience of other first-year lectured subjects as a basis for comparison. The questionnaire in Appendix 2 was given to 85 students.

Most students who preferred the individualized study approach thought that they understood the material better than they would have done by traditional lecture methods. An improved retention of knowledge was one stated advantage. Students liked the active response and the facility for repeating material to improve understanding. Some students felt that lectures were boring and that too many subjects relied totally on lectures without using films or slides.

Some students were undecided about their preference. They felt that a variety of teaching methods was desirable.

On the other hand, a group of students thought that individualized study was no improvement on lecture presentation. They considered that they learned more from lectures. They liked the lecture presentation of information, especially when worked examples were given.

These results and comments gave the general picture that students respond favourably to the individualized approach, but that a significant number like variety in teaching methods, including the traditional lecture presentation. (In addition, the individualized teaching approach did stretch departmental resources to the limit, especially the use of the learning unit.)

These factors led to the present teaching approach being based around a self-study booklet. The lectures aim mainly to give perspective, and students who wish to study only the booklet may do so. Although this teaching method has not been evaluated, it does seem at the moment to have been the most successful out of the three methods tried.

Concluding Remarks

It is important to realize that the philosophies of both engineering experimentation and communication studies involve attempts to change student attitudes as well as to develop cognitive skills. Essentially we are saying that an independent self-motivated approach is required in the laboratory, and that there are certain preferred styles of communication. The successful implementation of these philosophies probably involves two main factors.

Firstly, attempts at developing student abilities in both subjects must be realistic. It is not practical to try and completely develop professional competence in first-year students. The maturity of students, their reasoning powers, their scientific knowledge and many other qualities are involved. Ideally the development of the ideas presented in this paper should continue throughout the engineering course.

Secondly, since the philosophies of both subjects work towards the development of necessary professional engineering abilities, it is easy for staff to be enthusiastic and enthuse a class of students the first time round. But enthusiasm and interest must be maintained for subsequent years. Particularly with laboratory work this requires fresh ideas for projects — to spring the surprise — so as not to let the subjects remain static. Evaluation of how students are seeing the subjects is necessary.

We have also found that to run these subjects is probably more time- and energy-consuming than running those taught by traditional methods, and especially so with engineering experimentation. Student supervision is more demanding, and since communication and problem-solving abilities are mainly improved by practice, prompt and thorough feedback on students' written work and discussion is very important.

References

Boud, D J (1973) 'The Laboratory Aims Questionnaire — A New Method for Course Improvement?' 'Higher Education', Vol 2, pp 81-94.

Bullock, Sir Alan (1975) 'A Language for Life' HMSO.

Cohen, S A and MacVicar, M L A (1976) 'Establishing an Undergraduate Research Program in Physics: How it was done' 'American Journal of Physics', Vol 44, No 3, pp 199-203.

Confederation of British Industry (1976) 'Qualified Scientists and Engineers — Industry's Requirements from the Higher Education System' 'CBI Education and Training Bulletin' May 1976.

Entwistle, N and Hounsell, D (eds) (1975) 'How Students Learn' Institute for Post-Compulsory Education, University of Lancaster.

Fisher, B C (1976) 'Engineering Experimentation' (unpublished).

Fisher, B C (1977) 'Evaluating Mechanical Engineering Laboratory Work' 'International Journal of Mechanical Engineering Education', April, Vol 5, No 2.

Grayson, L P and Biedenbach, J M (eds) (1974) 'Individualized Instruction in Engineering Education' American Society for Engineering Education, Washington, DC.

Innovation Centre (1975) A booklet available from Innovation Center, Massachusetts Institute of Technology, Cambridge, MA 02139.

Kirkman, J (1974) 'Compiling Objective Tests on Technical Writing Ability' 'Technical Communication', Vol 21, No 2, pp 9-14.

Land, E H (1957) 'Generation of Greatness' Ninth Annual Arthur Dehon Little Memorial Lecture at Massachusetts Institute of Technology (available from Polaroid Corporation, 740 Main Street, Cambridge, MA 02139).

Larkin, Jill (1976) 'Cognitive Structures and Problem Solving Ability' Report JL 060176, Group in Science and Mathematics Education, University of California, Berkeley.

Penny, R K (ed) (1974) 'The Experimental Method' Longman, London.

Robertson, M F (1974 and 1975) 'Survey of the Attitudes to Laboratory Work of Final Year Undergraduates' Internal Confidential Reports, Department of Mechanical Engineering, Loughborough University of Technology.

Select Committee on Science and Technology (1976) Third Report on University-Industry Relations. HMSO.

Taylor, E F (1976) 'Some Significant Difference' 'American Journal of Physics', Vol 44, No 11.

Tribus, M (1976) 'Along the Corridors of Power — Where are the Engineers?' 'Mechanical Engineer', April pp 24-27.

Tribus, M (1977) 'The Challenge of Continuous Education — Will the Universities be Part of the Solution, or Part of the Problem?' Text of a lecture presented at University of California, Berkeley, January.

Venning, M (1975) 'Professional Engineers, Scientists and Technologists in the Engineering Industry' Engineering Industry Training Board, Research Report No 4.

Appendix 1

1. *How do you feel about laboratory work?*

   Easy   Difficult   Interesting   A Bore   Varies

2. *Is laboratory work out of balance in terms of time?*

   Too much   About right   Too little   Don't know

3. *How do you regard report writing?*

   Useful   A chore

4. *What is the purpose of writing reports?*

5. *How do you set about report writing?*

   Follow instructions   Copy old reports

6. *On average, how long do you spend writing up a laboratory report?*

   Shorter reports   Longer reports

7. *From your experience of laboratory work at Loughborough, what do you think have been the aims of this work?*

8. *Do you think that the structure of any laboratory subject in Parts A, B and C stands out as trying to achieve all the aims? If yes, state the subject. If no, state, None. (Students were shown a comprehensive list of laboratory work aims.)*

   Yes — subject   Nearest   None

9. *Are there any other comments you would like to make?*

Appendix 2

1. How do you think your understanding of the subject would rate against that obtained only from a lecture course?	Much less		More		Much more
	1	2	3	4	5
2. How efficiently do you think your time was used compared with that in a lecture course?	Much less		More		Much more
	1	2	3	4	5
3. In terms of helping you learn, how useful was the follow-up seminar?	No use		Useful		Very useful
	1	2	3	4	5
4. Would you prefer a conventional lecture course?	Yes		Undecided		No
5. Outside of timetabled study periods, how much time did you spend on the study material of this course compared with other lecture courses?	More time		Same		Less time
6. How well do you think you have learned from the total course of study plus laboratory scripts compared with other courses you are taking?	Better		Same		Worse

Introductory Statistics: a Simplified Approach

E E Green, S H B Christensen

'Statistical thinking,' declared H G Wells, 'will one day be as necessary for efficient citizenship as the ability to read and write.' All things being equal, the next generation will no doubt live to see the fulfilment of this once dubious prediction. Already, in this age of unisex, oil shortages, environmentalism, and urban crisis, statisticians are plying their trade in numerous areas that critically affect the life of every world citizen, from estimating population growth to forecasting economic cycles, measuring dosage levels of medicines, studying environmental conditions, predicting the migration habits of animals, and even connecting deathdays and birthdays. And true to the Wellsian prophecy, the application of statistics is already becoming nearly as varied and widespread as that of language itself.

As a result, there is an ever-increasing demand by academic departments in colleges and universities for better quality introductory courses in statistics. In order to meet this demand at Brigham Young University, the department of statistics offered for several years an elementary statistics course that consisted of three one-hour lecture periods and one one-hour lab period each week. The lectures were given to present new concepts, while the labs were used to clarify, explain and apply the theory learned in class. Texts for the class included *Elements of Statistical Inference* by Huntsberger and *Introduction to Probability and Statistics* by Mendenhall. The lab manual developed at BYU was used to help direct student activity in statistical applications. Furthermore, two films available from the McGraw-Hill Company were used when feasible to stimulate interest and to help students struggling to understand the concepts of 'mean, median, and mode,' and 'probability'.

Notwithstanding the efforts made to meet the demand for a high quality statistics course, dissatisfaction from three sources indicated a need for a new type of presentation. The three sources of dissatisfaction were (1) the students enrolled in the course, (2) the Statistics Department, and (3) the administration of the college and university.

The student dissatisfaction manifested itself rather predictably. There were complaints that the mathematical concepts being taught were too difficult, that they were too abstract, that the course consisted of nothing but problems, problems, and more problems that had no bearing or relation to subjects in which students were majoring. In time, the course got a bad name altogether, and students were passing on negative comments to their colleagues. As a result, students would put off taking the course until their junior or senior years — even though the class was meant for under-classmen.

The bad reputation of the course troubled the Statistics Department; however, no action was taken to remedy the situation until a number of other departments in other colleges began offering their own statistical courses in order to adapt the materials better to the subject-matter needs of their majors.

At this point the university administration began to be concerned because the duplication of effort was not in keeping with the general policy of conserving cost, space, and faculty time.

With general administration involvement, a proposal was soon forthcoming that outlined a complete restructuring of the elementary statistics course so that it would better serve the university community, and simultaneously make the course reasonably popular with the student body. By the fall of 1972, BYU began the development of Statistics 221 through the cooperative effort of the Statistics Department and the Department of Instructional Development (DID), the development arm of the Division of Instructional Research, Development, and Evaluation (now a part of the David D McKay Institute of Education).

After a preliminary study, the following seven problem areas were identified:

1. Other departments had not felt that the Statistics Department was making its elementary statistics course relevant to the peculiar problems commonly met by majors in sociology, psychology, education, physical education or business.
2. Practical application of most statistical concepts was not apparent to the students, causing them to be bored and negative about the course.
3. The reputation of the course was such that the students delayed taking it until their junior and senior years, although it was originally conceived as a sophomore-level course.
4. So many different instructors were teaching the course that great variability existed among the sections of the course being taught.
5. Many lecture sections were not being taught by full-time faculty members, but by inexperienced graduate assistants.
6. Lab space was inadequate.
7. The lab manual was not coordinated with problems in the lecture, the text, or the examinations.

The DID was to act as a facilitator to the project and to be specifically responsible for course and materials design, materials searches, production of prototypes, revisions; and to function as a coordinator for the evaluation and packaging of the final product. Final decisions concerning the content and the design of the course and materials were the responsibility of the senior author, who was selected from the statistics faculty, and the chairman of the Statistics Department.

The course director and DID had as their goals the resolution of the seven problems listed above. Their goals, which correlate with the seven problems, were as follows:

1. To provide students with a broad range of examples and practice problems that showed the application of statistical principles to sociology, psychology, physical education, education, and business. It was hoped that with the assistance of the respective departments these examples could be completed.
2. To provide students with an explanation of how the various statistical concepts can be and are applied in actual workaday settings.
3. To evaluate the student's response to the new course in order to measure the level of interest and determine whether students still procrastinate over taking the course until their junior or senior year.
4. To coordinate the development of the content so it would fit the needs of students majoring in other areas.
5. To assign one instructor for all students taking the course in order to eliminate variability in teaching approaches and variance in subject matter

covered. Graduate assistants will be assigned to assist as tutors or to teach small help sections.

6. To eliminate the required lab and allow students to attend the help sections on a 'come when you want to' basis.
7. To create a self-instructional text that will permit the student to pace himself through the course. By providing problems of graded difficulty, the disabled learners will be able to resort to especially prepared materials developed to assist them to understand the subject matter.

Work on the text and management system started in earnest during the summer of 1973 and experimental sections began that Fall under the management system that had been developed. During the first year the course was highly unstructured, with no deadlines set and class time used only for questions and answers. A crude testing centre was in operation and multiple parallel forms of the same exam were available for takes and retakes. Incompletes were given to all who did not finish the course.

The text was revised twice that year with both revisions representing a substantial effort to remove typing errors and to improve the style and readability of the text. The format, however, remained unchanged.

During 1974/75 the entire testing procedures and implementation was moved to the BYU Testing Centre. Tests were revised, a comprehensive final was prepared, and practice exams were made available to students. The programme was expanded to include all sections of Stat 221 which was comprised of four large lecture sections which attended one lecture and one quiz section per week. Deadlines were implemented and further refinements were made in the management system.

During 1975/76 a third revision was undertaken based upon expert reviews from members of the statistics profession. The basic format of the text remained unchanged but other sequences and more accurate content were provided. This revision will be implemented during the Fall semester of 1977 in a published text version entitled *Statistics: Step by Step.*

In the winter of 1976 an optional experimental programme was utilized in two of the four lecture sections, in which students were introduced to the use of the computer as a supplement to the course. In addition, during the spring and summer of 1976 a series of 14 one-hour lectures and demonstrations was implemented so that special applications of statistics to business problems could be presented. This was necessary since approximately 73% of all students taking State 221 were from the Business Department. The present system, which is the result of four and a half years of experimentation, now has these elements:

1. The basic text;
2. A revised management system;
3. A revised testing and grading scheme.

Here is a brief description of each of these elements:

The overall structure of the text consists of units and lessons. A unit consists of a logical set of related concepts while a lesson consists of a single or small set of closely related concepts. We found that so many concepts were closely associated that it was much easier to explain them by relating them to each other. For example, it was much easier to explain the concepts 'sample', 'population', and 'inference' together rather than separately. Clusters of concepts rather than isolated concepts emerged as the content was developed and further refined.

The organization of units is standard throughout the text. The following diagram (Figure 1) illustrates the special features of each unit. The unit map is a diagram which shows the relationship between concepts covered in the particular unit.

It is a typical hierarchy which shows dependent and non-dependent relationships between the concepts covered. The unit introduction and vocabulary ties together all of the concepts that are defined and clarified within the lesson and presents a listing of the most important concepts. Each lesson has the following components:

1. A task definition which explains to the student exactly what he should be able to do when he finishes the particular lesson of study.
2. A discussion which gives a definition of each concept included in the lesson. Occasionally these definitions are closely inter-related and are explained in the context of each other as explained above.
3. A simplified discussion puts the concept definitions into a more concrete form by relating relevant information with which the student is most likely to be familiar already.
4. The example problems give examples in the light of the previous discussion and task definitions. Answers are given and keyed to the previous discussion as well.
5. Practice problems enable the student to practise on his own an extension of the example file which he has previously encountered. It will enable him to check whether or not he understands the concepts and will prepare him for the unit exams which he will take in the Testing Centre.

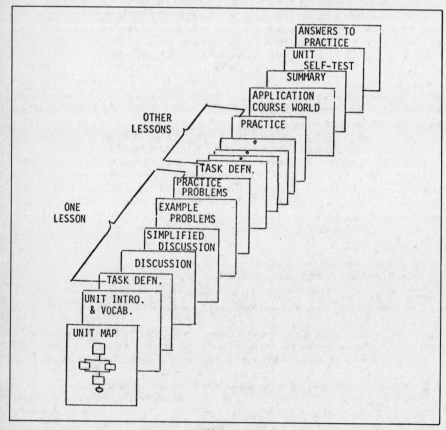

Figure 1.

Other lessons follow in a similar manner throughout the text thereby enabling the student to follow the same structure and to follow his own learning style. He may, for example, wish to examine example problems which will either refresh his memory of things with which he is already familiar, or which will present new information to him. He could merely look at the discussion or the simplified discussion and then refer to a sample set of practice problems. In other words, he may use the files of information which are given to him at the lesson level for study at his own discretion. He may, in effect, determine his own learning style as he proceeds through the course and the materials.

At the end of each unit he is given an explanation of the application of the materials to the course and to the real world. He is then given a summary of all of the units and the purpose for which he has studied the particular concepts. At this time he may then take a practice unit test before he enters the testing system within the Testing Centre. If he is not satisfied with the score which he is given immediately after taking the test, then he may rechallenge it and pay for that test to cover the Testing Centre Facility cost of administration.

Specific examples of the files which have been explained can be found in the text which was on display during this conference.

Instructional Management System

Currently, approximately 600 students per semester enrol in the course which is taught by four PhD faculty members and no graduate assistants. The following diagram (Figure 2) outlines the system as a whole. The student enters the course and attends the orientation lecture. It is explained to him at this time that he will attend one lecture and one quiz section per week. The student then interacts with the unit and lesson materials on the pre-determined schedule which is given to him. The experiences that lie ahead are ultimately to prepare each student for the unit exams. He might use the text materials, lectures, homework centre, media aids, and/or instructor tutors to assist him in the mastery of these materials and tasks as outlined in the text. When he feels that he is ready for the exam (no later than the end deadline given in the course schedule) he enters the Testing Centre to take the exam. He is given immediate feedback and if his score is satisfactory, he proceeds to the next unit. If it is not satisfactory to either himself or to his instructor he will be given test feedback for rechallenging the exam and/or extra credit options which are given in the form of extra reading assignments and extra practical work which is appropriate to his particular subject matter. He continues working in this way until he finishes the course.

Summary

The last four and a half years have provided a rich experience in the area of instructional design as well as in the content definition of an introductory statistics course. The experience has benefited both author and developer in that the author now feels more secure in meeting the needs of students who enter from individual disciplines. He also has reported to his department chairman and the vice-president of the university the evaluation data which shows that all seven objectives that he set out to accomplish are well on the road to accomplishment. In addition, the things that have been learned concerning procedures for the developer-client relationship, for determining content, and for instructional design have been considerable. Techniques and processes have been applied in other areas such as law, medicine, elementary education, and other general education courses at Brigham

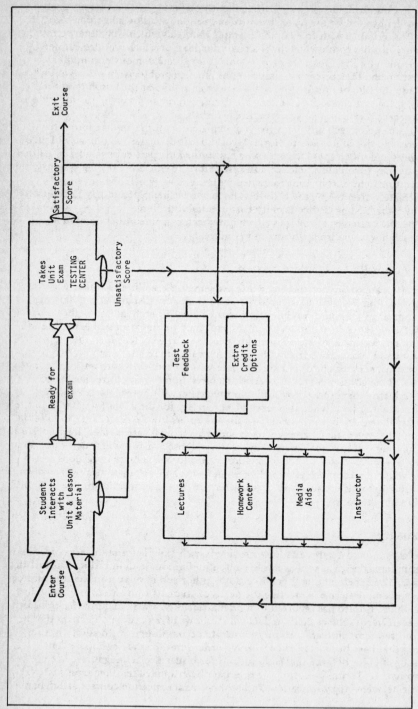

Figure 2. *Instruction and Management System*

Young University and within the Church Education System, reaching faraway places such as the LDS Fiji Technical College and literacy programmes sponsored by the Church Education System in Central and South America. Documentation has been kept for all phases of the development work, and hopefully the continuation of the development model as it has been refined during this work will have a further impact upon future work within the development services of the David D McKay Institute as it influences world-wide educational and training systems.

A Case Study in the Design and Evaluation of a Unit on Waveform Analysis

R Wild, E McQuade

Introduction

This paper describes the design, implementation and evaluation of a course unit on
waveform analysis. The unit is multi-media in nature, comprising a video recording,
a slide-tape sequence, some printed notes and two computer-assisted learning (CAL)
packages, and was designed for use with first or second-year degree students at the
School of Electrical Engineering, Plymouth Polytechnic. The work is also a
contribution to the Engineering Science Project of the National Development
Programme in Computer-Assisted Learning (NDPCAL) of which the School is a
member (Hooper, 1973).

CAL at Plymouth Polytechnic began several years ago, since when increasing
amounts of CAL material have been assimilated into the curriculum. Generally,
packages are of the laboratory/simulator type (Hooper, 1975) using the computer
as a high-speed calculator. Computer graphics and interactive use are considered to
be very important. In the 1975/76 session, the CAL packages for the waveform
analysis unit were run on an overworked PDP 8/L based system. The problems of
catering for large student numbers and frequent equipment breakdowns had the
effect of clouding some of the educational issues. In the spring of 1976 the school
acquired a PDP 11/10 complete with 28 K of core, dual floppy discs and a
Tektronix 4010 alphanumeric/graphics terminal. The two CAL packages, called
PEEP 31 and PEEP 33, were hurriedly transferred to the new system for use with a
group of students in the summer term. Since then, the course unit has been run
with two more groups during the current 1976/77 session, giving a total of five
groups, about 100 students, who have worked through the unit. The new, reliable
equipment has removed many of the problems encountered in that first year.

Despite the inadequacies of the early equipment, the use of such a small
computer helped to mould CAL philosophy at Plymouth (Broadhurst, 1974;
Broadhurst *et al*, 1975). It encouraged a trend to small efficient programs — the
first package, PEEP 31, used less than 750 words of core. Wordy dialogue between
computer and user is avoided and the computer is used only when it provides the
best tool for the job, often giving way to cheaper, more flexible media where
appropriate.

The Course Content

Concepts concerned with the analysis, synthesis and manipulation of periodic
waveforms and the parameters and methods of representing them are of
fundamental importance throughout electrical engineering. The topic is virtually
technology-independent and unlikely to go out of date quickly, an important
consideration in developing a unit of this type since development is expensive on

staff time and other resources. High initial costs can be justified if the material can be used for several years.

Traditionally, waveform analysis has tended to receive a rather abstract, often purely mathematical, treatment (Lahti, 1965; Barker, 1972), namely the presentation of Fourier series and Fourier Analysis. While mathematics is of utmost importance to the electrical engineer — it is the language which helps him communicate — the concept of electrical signals is for him a very visual and intuitive one. After all, two of his most useful instruments are the oscilloscope and the spectrum analyser. These enable him to study physical events, summarized in a convenient graphical form.

In developing this unit, an attempt was made to present this visual topic in a visual way, developing the mathematical representations at the same time but keeping their importance in perspective. Students are encouraged to develop a sound physical appreciation of periodic waveforms and to familiarize themselves with the various ways of representing them, both graphically in time and frequency domain and mathematically as trigonometric functions. Instrumental in achieving these aims is the student's capability to manipulate waveforms by varying the parameters describing them, using the computer to perform the waveform synthesis. Hopefully, developing a sounder physical appreciation at this stage will enable students to accept more readily more advanced and abstract concepts at a later stage, topics such as linear systems theory, frequency transform methods, modulation, correlation, noise and information transmission.

CAL as a medium for the presentation of this unit involves an element of what Hooper calls 'a qualitative shift in content' (Hooper, 1975). Fourier analysis can be performed analytically only if the equation of the waveform is known. Otherwise a numerical method must be employed (Noakes, 1956). A numerical analysis, even with the aid of a calculator, is either of limited accuracy or very tedious. So, traditionally, numerical analyses were hardly possible but now, with the aid of the computer, they are. Even the labour of plotting waveforms by hand is eliminated by using computer graphics. In evaluating the course unit no attempt was made to compare this with a traditional presentation because by using CAL and other media the very nature of the course had changed.

The Course Unit — an Outline Description

Figure 1 summarizes the structure of the unit. A 20-minute video recording is used to revise or introduce important concepts, state conventions used in the unit and demonstrate a worked example of the first package, PEEP 31. Summary notes are then given to the students. The video is shown in normal lecture time and serves to a large extent as a lecture replacement. Originally, the medium was chosen so that identical lectures could be presented to different classes at different times — an important evaluation requirement. However, the video proved an excellent way of presenting a large amount of graphical material quickly and conveniently and could also be used by individual students for remedial work.

Using PEEP 31, students work through the first tutorial problem sheet. They book the computer and work through the problems in their own time. An assessment of the learner's performance in solving the problems is used to provide his course-work marks. The package was designed to take about two hours working at the terminal. Some students prefer to work alone and others in groups, the maximum group size allowed being three. Some groups try to complete their problems in a single session and others prefer to break this up into two smaller ones. Staff involvement is kept to a minimum at this stage, but usually there is someone available for consultation should problems arise.

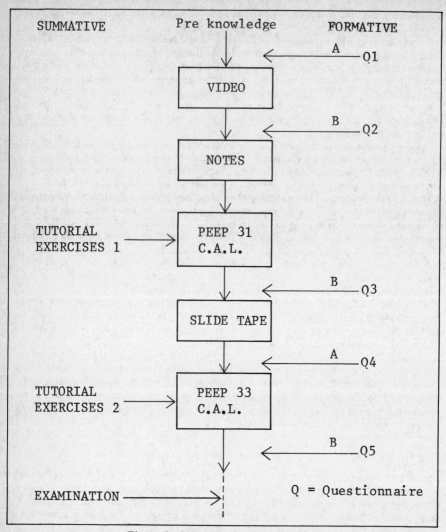

Figure 1. *Course evaluation 1975-76*

Students are asked to synthesize waveforms by specifying their harmonic content. They can add harmonics, remove harmonics or modify any harmonic contained in the waveform. They can build up quite complex waveforms term by term, making observations as they do so. For this exercise a selection of reference waveforms is supplied. Students are asked to estimate the harmonic content of each of these and check their estimates by synthesizing a matching waveform. By performing these tasks, students are able to deduce for themselves rules relating the shape and symmetry of waveforms to their harmonic content. Visual analysis, although very important, has its limitations and students soon discover these when they try to match more complicated waveforms, realizing the need for a more convenient and precise method.

The slide tape is presented following the first CAL package. This is used to summarize the most important outcome of the package and to introduce the second CAL package.

PEEP 33 provides the learner with a reasonably accurate Fourier analyser with which he can analyze another set of reference waveforms given in the second tutorial problem sheet. Some of these waveforms are quite complex and would be extremely difficult to analyze using the matching method. The steps in the analysis are specified by the student and performed numerically by the computer and are exactly the same steps that would be necessary using an analytical method. The student performs the analysis but does not get involved with the details of each step. Again, he needs to make visual estimates from waveform displays which are checked by the computer. Poor estimates cause him to be lead back through the problem and he is assured of the correct answer eventually. So, he becomes familiar with the steps involved in a Fourier analysis, he sees many of the intermediate results displayed graphically and most of all he sees that the method does work. The student is then required to interpret the result of his analysis. He has to plot the amplitude and phase spectra himself and describe the waveform mathematically. If the waveform is described by an infinite series, he is expected to spot the series and note the relationship between consecutive terms.

Evaluation

This unit was used as a case study (MacDonald and Walker, 1974), a step towards quantifying the contributions of CAL to electrical engineering education at Plymouth Polytechnic. Generally, educational evaluation can be regarded as a process of picture building whereby information is gathered from many different sources, interpreted and conclusions drawn by a process of triangulation (MacDonald *et al*, 1975). This picture was built up using information gathered from several sources: student comments, observations of student behaviour, the tutorial, problem sheets, examination results and a set of pre- and post-tests (questionnaires). The whole evaluation can be regarded as a mixture of formal and informal and formative and summative components (Bloom *et al*, 1971). Tutorial problems, examinations and the questionnaires comprised the formal element, student comments and observations the informal. The examinations were summative, their primary role being to grade student performance and to judge the end products of the course of instructions. Conversely, the formative evaluation, the informal elements and the questionnaires, assess relatively small numbers of objectives at many points in the unit. The questionnaires were used to find out at which points in the course particular objectives were being met and to discover where the unit could be improved.

Examinations and tutorial problems are a normal part of any course, as in the informal evaluation, and therefore had little disruptive effect on the course. This was not so with the pre- and post-tests. These tended to add an artificial element. They became part of the course itself, shifting its emphasis slightly but providing much useful information.

Pre- and Post-Tests — the Questionnaire

Two matched objective tests (A and B) were designed, each comprising over 50 multiple-choice items. These were to measure the objectives of each of the major elements of the unit: the video, PEEP 31, the slide tape and PEEP 33. The questionnaire was administered five times, Q1 to Q5 in Figure 1. To prevent students from becoming too familiar with the same test, the questionnaires were given in the order A, B, B, A and B.

Test items were presented on 35 mm slides, providing several advantages. Items could be re-used, the questionnaires could be modified easily, the use of a large volume of paper was avoided and the method allowed the control of pacing. Each item provided four possible choices: a, b, c or d. A fifth choice e indicated a 'don't know'. Answers were graded and analysed using a batch FORTRAN program.

While multiple-choice testing has not escaped criticism (Ebel, 1965), this style of question was chosen because the tests were easy to administer, they were of a form familiar to students, they have widespread acceptance and they could be marked by computer. They can be used to test all the important educational outcomes of knowledge, understanding, judgement and problem-solving ability.

The results were analysed in three main ways. The average number of correct responses and the standard deviations are given in Figure 2. The progress of individual students through the questionnaires is shown in Figure 3. Also, an item analysis was performed whereby each item was considered in turn, from which it was possible to tell where and how well each specific objective was being met.

1975-76		Q1	Q2	Q3	Q4	Q5	
P.D.2	Mean	27.7	42.9	43.1	49.8	53.1	%
	S.D.	5.9	6.6	8.0	10.1	8.7	
B.Sc.2	Mean	39.5	48.2	47.1	57.2	63.2	%
	S.D.	8.8	12.6	11.9	12.1	13.2	
Both	Mean	35.8	46.6	45.9	54.9	60.0	%
	S.D.	9.7	11.4	11.0	12.0	12.9	

Figure 2. *Average scores and mean deviations for correct answers*

From the analysis of the 1975/76 results several important conclusions were drawn both regarding the course unit itself and the method evaluation. It was recommended that the tutorial problem sheets should be improved. They would be more structured, contain simple instructions on how to get started at the terminal, begin with simple examples to help the students build up confidence and include a model answer which would eliminate the need for the worked example in the video. The questionnaires showed that generally the video and the slide-tape were performing well despite their poor quality production. Questionnaire performance seemed to be susceptible to the time delays. Whereas Q1 and Q2 were administered in the same one-hour session, a period of two or three weeks passed before Q3 and Q4 were given. Students seemed enthusiastic about the CAL packages and worked hard at them, producing good answers to the tutorial problems, but the questionnaires showed little about the learning from using the packages. It was considered that the questionnaire was too long, it needed to be administered too many times and for some items the matching was poor.

For the 1976/77 session the unit was modified, the main alterations being in the form of the tutorial sheets. These alterations were easily made. Although it was desirable to improve the quality of the video, time did not permit this. The new computer system proved to be faster and more convenient to use, so it was possible to include a greater variety of examples in the problem sheets. A new, modified questionnaire was designed with only 40 questions. This was presented four instead of five times and more care had been taken when matching items of the two sets. Re-examination of the previous year's questionnaire had revealed that few questions were really appropriate to the PEEP 31 and the PEEP 33 areas. This was partly due to the difficulty of specifying good operational objectives for the CAL packages. About 20 items from the old questionnaire were retained, making it

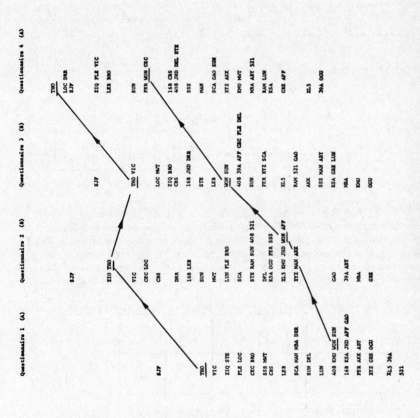

Figure 3. Rank Order Table B.Sc.2/P.D.2 1975-76

possible to compare the performances of the two years, and about 20 new items were designed, testing mainly the objectives of PEEP 31. This had the effect of making the instrument more sensitive to the PEEP 31 area.

In addition, a simple control experimental was run, as shown in Figure 4. The whole class was given Q1, shown the video and then presented with Q2. The class was then split into its two existing tutorial groups (X and Y). Group X worked

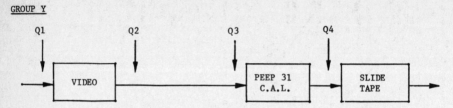

Figure 4. *A control experiment 1976-77*

through PEEP 31 and then the whole class was re-tested using Q3. Group Y were then allowed their turn at PEEP 31, after which both groups were tested again using Q4. By comparing the two groups, it was possible to study the effect of PEEP 31 and also examine the effect of delays between tests. Figure 5 is a summary of the scores of the two groups, expressed as percentages. The performances of the two groups are close, indicating that they are reasonably matched. Both groups

	Q1	Q2	Q3	Q4	
GROUP X	25.3	42.6	51.5	49.3	%
GROUP Y	21.4	42.9	38.6	52.5	%

Figure 5. *B.Sc.2 correct answers 1976-77*

show a gain of about 10 per cent on working through PEEP 31. The performance of each group decreases slightly owing to the delays, Group Y is between Q2 and Q3 and Group X is between Q3 and Q4. The scores did indicate that PEEP 31 was having a measurable effect which could be studied in more detail by performing-student-and-item analyses as in the previous year.

Some Conclusions

At this stage analysis of the collected data is still in progress, but it is possible to make some comments.

The item analysis in both years showed that the video was working quite well, in general, although points were identified which were not covered in enough detail or were laboured unnecessarily. It was difficult to tell whether the success of the video was partly due to the questionnaires. By presenting students with a pre-test, points covered in the video were highlighted and so students tended to pay special attention to these.

PEEP 31 seemed to work well when it was used as a reinforcement tool, but did not seem to work well when used as a medium for discovery learning, yet this is claimed to be one of the strong points of this style of CAL (Hooper, 1975). Students tended to miss the deeper and more subtle facets of the exercise. The technique of allowing students to deduce rules for themselves should perhaps be abandoned in favour of the alternative approach of presenting them with the rules and allowing them to gain confidence by applying them.

The slide tape, as with the video, seemed to be fairly effective and few changes are recommended.

The questionnaires showed little of the effect of PEEP 33 in the first year and in the second year this area was not covered. However, evidence from other sources indicates that again the inductive approach adopted did not appear to be very successful. Perhaps to use Fourier Analysis before the topic was covered in formal mathematics lectures was too great a step for students to take. Perhaps discovery learning at this stage is inappropriate; maybe students are not used to such an approach; perhaps they require more time for the technique to be successful; or maybe the approach is more successful than is apparent and its beneficial effects will show up only in the long term.

This evaluation exercise has resulted in isolating many possible improvements to this particular course unit. It has provided a deeper insight into the contributions of this style of computer-assisted learning in electrical engineering courses at Plymouth and has provided many guidelines which should help the development of future packages. The unit will continue to be used, although the rather disruptive pre- and post-tests will be omitted. Possibly some of the items will be built into the tutorial sheets at appropriate points. Evaluation will continue, but on a more informal basis. Even now improvements are possible and it is important to see the effects of removing the rather cumbersome components of the evaluation.

Acknowledgements

We are particularly grateful to David Tawney, formerly of UNCAL at the University of East Anglia, for some very useful and constructive discussions of the problems of educational evaluation. In addition, we received much encouragement from the members of the Engineering Science Project of the National Development Program in Computer Assisted Learning. We are especially indebted to our colleague Sid Broadhurst for his constant guidance and assistance throughout this case study.

References

Barker, K (1971) 'Visual Presentation in the Teaching and Learning of Fourier Series' International Journal of Electrical Engineering Education 10, p 62-65 Manchester University Press.

Bloom, B S, Hastings, J T and Madaus, G F (1971) 'Handbook of Formative and Summative Evaluation of Student Learning', p 10 McGraw-Hill Inc.

Broadhurst, S, McQuade, E, Roberts, A and Yeats, R (1975) 'A Multimedia Approach to the Teaching and Learning of Continuous Variable System Theory' In Computers in Education. Proceedings of the IFIP 2nd World Conference, p 873-876.

Broadhurst, S and Webster, B (1974) 'Contributions of Computer and CCTV to the Teaching and Learning of Circuit Analysis' In Conference on Frontiers in Education. Institute of Electrical Engineers Conference Publication 115, p 223.

Ebel, R L (1965) 'Measuring Educational Achievement', p 149-151 Prentice Hall Inc.

Hooper, R (1973) 'The National Development Programme in Computer Assisted Learning' Published by the Council for Educational Technology.

Hooper, R (1975) 'Two Years on, the National Development Program in Computer Assisted Learning', p 13. Published by the Council for Educational Technology.

Hooper, R (1975) 'Making Claims for Computers' International Journal of Mathematics, Education, Science and Technology 5, p 364.

Keller, F S (1968) 'Goodbye Teacher' Journal of Applied Behaviour Analysis, p 79-89.

Lahti, B P (1965) 'Signals, Systems and Communications, Preface' John Wiley and Sons.

MacDonald, B, Jenkins, D, Kemmis, S and Tawney, D (1975) 'The Programme at Two' Centre for Applied Research in Education, University of East Anglia.

MacDonald, B and Walker, R 'Case Study and the Social Philosophy of Educational Research' Ford SAFARI project. Centre for Applied Research in Education, University of East Anglia.

Noakes, G R (1956) 'Electrical Fundamentals' The Services Textbook of Radio 1 HMSO.

The Need for Library User Orientation and the Design and Development of Material and Methods to Meet This Need

N Fjällbrant

Introduction

This paper will describe studies of the needs of student library users at Chalmers University of Technology as seen by different groups — students, teachers and library staff. One of these needs was for orientation in the use of the library. Goals and objectives were formulated for library orientation. A choice of suitable methods was made, based on a study of teaching methods and media. These methods and material have come into gradual use over the last two years, and a discussion based on observations and interviews is given on the effectiveness of the material so far provided, and the need for further work.

Background

Chalmers University of Technology is situated in Gothenburg, Sweden. The university has approximately 4000 undergraduates and some 600 postgraduates who study in one of the six Schools of Engineering:

1. School of Engineering Physics
2. School of Mechanical Engineering
3. School of Electrical Engineering
4. School of Civil Engineering
5. School of Chemical Engineering
6. School of Architecture

The undergraduate programme takes four to five years and leads to the degree of 'civilingenjör' — equivalent to MSc or MEng. Further details of courses within the different Schools of Engineering can be obtained from the 1976 edition of *Some facts about Chalmers University of Technology* published by the university authorities.

Chalmers University is served by a main library plus a number of smaller section and departmental libraries. The main library has a collection of some 270,000 volumes. The number of currently held periodicals is 5300. Most of the collection is placed in a closed book magazine or 'book-tower' to which users do not have direct access. Material to be borrowed must be ordered on special order forms which contain information on the unit to be borrowed and on the borrower. The material requested, if available, is then taken out of the store and brought to the borrowing desk. This takes an average of about five minutes. At present, one of the main aims of the library staff is to convert the existing closed-access system to open-access, thereby increasing the availability of the resources.

The Needs of the Student Library User as Seen by Different Groups

User studies showed that very few (6%) of the undergraduates used the library as a place for optional studies, and that the majority (92%) considered that they bought most of the literature required for their studies. As so few of the undergraduates made use of the library for traditional purposes of study or for borrowing material in connection with their studies, it was asked how much did they know of the information resources available at their university library. It was shown that while 31% of the undergraduates were aware that the library possessed a subject catalogue, only 25% were aware of the existence of abstracts, 32% of the existence of indexes and 36% of interlibrary loan services. Of the undergraduates who knew of the existence of the subject catalogue, about half said that they either did not use it or that they experienced difficulties in its use. Students could hardly be said to make active use of the library, or to be aware of the information resources available there. Yet students commented, when being interviewed, that they were interested in finding out more about the library and how to use it in connection with definite projects such as seminars or their undergraduate research project. (Fjällbrant, 1976).

In connection with descriptive observations and interviews carried out as a part of the evaluation of introductory courses in information retrieval at Chalmers Library, students described their initial reaction to the library:

S: 'So you come into the library and it's like a jungle, lots of books and so many of them in English.'

The jungle parallel seemed popular, as can be seen from another interview:

S: 'Well you can say that when we came here, one hadn't a clue about how to start, knew nothing, like a jungle.'

Students thought that an early introduction course would have been useful:

S: 'The fear if you know what I mean of going into the library would be reduced.
"Yes that's right, I didn't dare to go in there to borrow a book.'
Interviewer asked, 'You mean you really didn't dare to go in to borrow a book?'
Student, 'Well you know what I mean, one didn't want to try these things, because, well you'd heard that it was such a difficult business to borrow a book there, so one tried to avoid it as long as possible and borrowed books from the public library instead.'

Some of the students interviewed had tried to carry out literature searches prior to taking part in the introductory course in information retrieval. Their experiences can be illustrated by the following interviews:

One students said that he had visited the library a month previous to the course, and tried a search on his own:

S: 'I didn't get anywhere.'
I: 'You didn't get anywhere? What did you do then?'
S: 'First I came in there and saw some books, and I thought they don't have many books. Then I found out that they were just a lot of lists, that you could use to look up books. Then somebody helped me, so I found a book, and I went home and read it.'
I: 'Did you ask at the Information Desk?'
S: 'Mm, and she helped me to find a book.'
I: 'Just one book?'

S: 'Well, she looked in a card catalogue, and then I looked there.'
I: 'Was it the subject catalogue?'
S: 'Yes that's right.'
I: 'Didn't you borrow any more books?'
S: 'No, it seemed so meaningless.'

These interviews illustrate that students often experience difficulties in their attempts to use the academic libraries. Previous experience is based on the use of school libraries and public libraries. The interviews given were typical of students at Chalmers University and they indicated the need for some form of early library orientation and a systematic instruction in the obtaining of information.

The needs of the student library user as perceived by other groups — academic staff, library staff, administrative staff and industrial engineers were also studied. These findings are summarized in Table 1. It can be observed that there were considerable differences between the perceived needs for student use of the library,

Group	Theory	Practice
Undergraduates	Not much reason to use library in first two years. Library — useful as source of material for study projects — literature seminars & undergrad. project.	Little use of library for optional studies or borrowing. Unaware of tools for information retrieval. Library used in connection with study projects.
Academic staff	Student use of library 'desirable' as source of information. Prepared to encourage library use (but not at expense of own courses).	Few teachers actively promote the use of the library in connection with studies. Lack of time for additional material.
Library staff	Library information resources should be of great value for the students. Students should learn how to use the tools at the library.	Lack of contact with academic staff. Difficulties in knowing what courses are planned & therefore what information students are likely to require.
Administrative staff	Library resources should be maximally utilized.	No money provided for instruction in how to use. (This changed to — money provided for instruction.)
Industrial engineers & librarians in industrial concerns	Library and instruction in use should be project-linked.	(Use library in connection with industrial projects themselves.)

Table 1. *The use of the library by students — as perceived by different groups*

between the different groups, and that there were considerable differences between theory and practice. Academic staff stressed the students' need to obtain information in connection with their academic studies, as an aid to independent thinking and problem-solving activities. Students wished to be able to find information that would be useful for their actual study projects. Librarians, on the other hand, were concerned with the utilization of resources possessed by the

101

library, and the use of library tools such as the card catalogue, rather than on the method of information retrieval in connection with the students' academic courses.

A pilot study of the needs of the library user, as seen by academic staff, library staff and students, has been carried out, as part of an OSTI research project, at the Institute for Educational Technology, University of Surrey, England (Roy, 1974). In this descriptive study, Roy showed that the students viewed the library as a tool to be used in response to stimuli such as essays, projects and exams, whereas the ideal of 'most of the academic staff and all library staff' was that the library should be 'the centre for information, sources of constant references, and stimulus to the course'. Studies of a similar type have been carried out in the USA by Taylor (Taylor, 1971).

Goals for the Programme of User Education at Chalmers University

The goals or main objectives for a course of library instruction must be in accordance with the goals expressed by the students and academic staff. As Watkins pointed out, in 1970,

> 'It is now, and always will be, the classroom and its ideals which by and large determine the activity at our loan desk.' (Watkins, 1970.)

There is a need for cooperation between library staff, academic staff and students, in order to decide on the main goals for library education (see Figure 1).

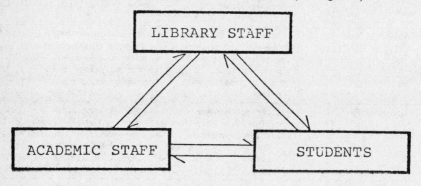

Figure 1.

The goals and objectives for the programme of library user education at Chalmers University were based on an attempt to integrate the views of students, academic staff and library staff. In formulating the main goals, particular attention was paid to the views of the students and academic staff, as the library instruction courses had to form part of the total education programme at the university. The specific objectives suggested by the library staff were useful in the detailed design of how to implement these goals.

The following main goals were formulated for the programme of library user education at Chalmers University:

After completing the user education programme the student should have obtained:

1. The ability to apply the principles of scientific communication to problems of information retrieval.
2. The ability to use the various tools available in the university library (and other libraries) in order to obtain information useful in connection with studies and later work, as and when required.
3. A sense of enjoyment in information searching.

The first of these goals can be described as cognitive, the second as mixed cognitive and affective and the third as affective (Bloom *et al*, 1971).

Library Orientation and Library Instruction

Having formulated the broad general goals for the programme of user education, it was possible to draw up a number of specific and limited objectives within this framework. A distinction was made between library orientation and library instruction.

Library orientation is concerned with enabling the student to become aware of the existence of the university library and the services available there (WHAT is available) and enabling the student to learn about the general use of the library:

1. WHEN the library is open
2. WHERE specific items are to be found
3. HOW to actually obtain/borrow the material required.

Library instruction is concerned with enabling the student to obtain information required for a specific purpose by making full use of the resources and materials available at the library. It is concerned with problems of information retrieval.

A three stage programme of library user education was drawn up based on the main goals formulated above:

1. Orientation for new users.
2. An introductory course in information retrieval for undergraduates.
3. An advanced course in information retrieval for postgraduates.

Detailed lists of specific objectives were drawn up for each part of the programme (Fjällbrant, 1976). The specific objectives for library orientation were formulated as follows:

After library orientation, the student should:

1. Be aware of the existence of the university library, what it contains, and when it is open.
2. Have the ability to locate handbooks, encyclopedias, periodicals (on open shelves), dictionaries, the reprocentre.
3. Be able to distinguish between the use of the author catalogue and the subject catalogue.
4. Have the ability to use a closed-access library and be able to fill in a requisition form for the three most common types of loan (books, journals, and parts of a series).
5. Want to use, and actually be able to use, the university library with confidence, in connection with studies.

Teaching Method	Factors Affecting Learning				Sensory Input			Interaction	
	M	A	U	F	Au	V	R	T-S	S-S
Lecture	±	±	±	−	+	+	−	+	−
Seminar/ demonstration	±	±	±	+	+	+	+	+	±
Guided tour	∓	−	∓	−	+	+	−	+	−
Film/video, tape/slide for group instruction	±	−	±	−	+	+	−	−	−
Tape/slide for individual instruction	+	+	±	−	+	+	+	−	−
Book/printed media	+	+	±	−	−	+	+	−	−
Practical exercises	+	+	±	+	+	+	+	+	+
Programmed instruction	+	+	±	+	+	+	+	−	−
Self-instruction	+	+	−	+	−	+	+	−	−
Individual help	+	±	−	+	+	+	±	+	−

+	=	presence (of a factor etc)	Au	=	auditory sensory input
−	=	absence	V	=	visual sensory input
M	=	the need for a student to be sufficiently motivated (motivation)	R	=	possibility for learner to control the rate of flow of information
A	=	the need for a student to be actively involved (active work)	T-S	=	teacher-student interaction
			S-S	=	student-student interaction
U	=	the need to relate new work to existing knowledge (understanding)			
F	=	the need for a student to evaluate his progress continuously (feedback)			

Table 2. *Learning methods — a summary of factors affecting learning, sensory inputs and student-teacher interaction.*

The Choice of Teaching Methods and Media

Teaching methods and media were then chosen for the implementation of the three different stages (Fjällbrant, 1976). Traditional library orientation has made considerable use of the lecture method for large groups, the guided or 'herded' tour for smaller groups, and individual help for students who ask for this at the information desk. In Table 2 an attempt is made to consider these and other methods with respect to factors affecting the learning process (Hills, 1974), the number of sensory inputs involved and interaction between students, and students and teachers.

The Guided Tour

The traditional approach to library orientation is the so called guided tour (or 'herded' tour), in which students are given a short tour of the library during their first weeks as university students. Harlan has described a guided tour as follows:

'Batches of students — I have seen as many as thirty in a group — are herded through a dozen or so stations. The guide is not always a librarian, nor is he always well-prepared. "This", he says with a wave of his hand, "is the Periodicals Room. That", with a nod, "is CBI, a universal English language bibliography, dictionary arrangement, with author, title and subject entries: You must remember that the main entry is author" ... Small wonder that at the third and fourth station, most of the students stop listening. Libraries and librarians, they conclude, are as bad as anticipated. Obviously one's efforts are best applied in finding ways of avoiding, not utilizing, the library.' (Harland, 1970.)

The type of orientation described above is often given when students have little or no motivation to actually use the library. The students themselves take little active part in the teaching/learning process, but tend to follow passively round the various stations. From the point of view of the library administration, the guided tour type of library orientation makes heavy demands on library staff time. There is also the problem, common to courses with high-recurrent frequency, of remembering exactly what has been said to each particular group.

The Lecture

The lecture, as a form of communication in higher education, has been strongly criticized, not least by the students themselves (McLeish, 1968). With regard to orientation in library use, Ford stated in 1973 that:

'The lecture commonly given to freshmen students at the beginning of their first sessions, must surely be a waste of time. The library with its vague connection with academic work, can hold little attraction for a student struggling to adjust to university life.' (Ford, 1975.)

Individual Instruction

The assumption is generally made that the best form of library instruction can be given by the personalized service at the reference desk. This is because the student asks a question about the use of some part of the library when he/she is motivated to learn about that particular point. The student is actively involved in the learning process, and is receiving tuition from an expert. However, this idealized picture takes little account of reality. The reference librarian may be harassed by several enquiries, telephones ringing and so on. Many students are shy, and, if they see that the librarian is busy, do not like to explain that they did not really understand what was being said. The student numbers have increased, but there has been no corresponding increase in the number of librarians.

Self-Instructional Material

As can be seen from Table 1, guided tours and lectures do not seem to be particularly suitable for library orientation. It was therefore decided to make use of mainly self-instructional methods for this part of the programme. The first part of the information was sent out in the form of a single sheet, handwritten and reproduced by offset printing. This paper contained information likely to be of interest to the new student.

'At Chalmers University there is a Library, where you can read Yachting News (and 4700 other periodicals).'

It continued with the information that there were study places for student use, and a reference collection of dictionaries, encyclopedias, handbooks and tables available for consultation, and that there was a reserve book collection of set course literature. It also contained information about the hours of opening of the library, and the vital information that there was a pleasant cafeteria.

The second printed handout was intended for students during their first term, and took the form of a 16-page A5 *Guide to the Use of Chalmers Library*. This guide described the services and resource available, the hours of opening, the location of the material, and how to obtain the literature required. This guide was written with the user in mind. Technical jargon was avoided throughout. It was produced in a size that would fit into a pocket or handbag, and there were a number of illustrations produced by two architects who had just completed their studies at Chalmers University.

A self-guiding colour-shape coding system was designed for the location of material available for direct access to the library. Schemes of colour-coding/shape-coding have been developed at a number of libraries. One place where such a scheme has been developed in detail, is at Hatfield Polytechnic Library in England (Carey 1971 and Carey 1974). The colour scheme at Chalmers utilized the different colours used by the six Schools of Engineering. With this scheme, material pertaining to the School of Electrical Engineering is coded with yellow symbols — the colour used by that School of Engineering. Differently shaped symbols have also been chosen to represent different types of material to be found in the library (see Figure 2).

In addition to the location signs, other signs were made and put up, for example a sign showing how to complete a loan-request form for the three most common types of material to be borrowed — books, periodicals, and series. This sign was hung over the author catalogues.

A tape-slide guide to the use of Chalmers University Library was made. This presentation lasted for five minutes. This tape-slide guide describes the library and the material it contains and explains that as the main part of this material is kept in a closed-access book store, it is necessary to fill in a loan requisition form on which the store location number is marked, in order to obtain material. The tape-slide guide was designed to meet both the cognitive goals for library orientation, which have been described above, and to meet the affective goals — realization that the library could be a pleasant place in which to work, and removal of the fear caused by a new, strange environment and new borrowing procedures. This tape-slide guide has been used as part of a very short general introduction for freshers, and as introductory material for various groups visiting the library.

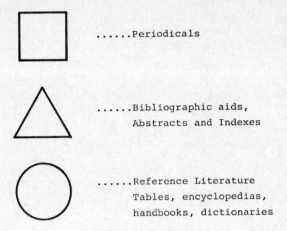

Figure 2. *Symbols representing the different types of material to be found in the library*

Discussion

Preliminary observational studies on the use of the self-guiding material provided for library orientation have been carried out, and from these it could be concluded that the orientation material so far provided for students was of help in the actual use of the library. However, this material alone did not supply adequate motivation to encourage new students to come to the library. The material so far provided did not provide new users with an adequate explanation as to why they should use certain catalogues or other resources. It had been seen that students at Chalmers made little use of the library's reading-room facilities, nor did they borrow material in connection with their university studies.

Motivation to visit the library can be provided in a number of ways — by arousing curiosity and interest, for example, by providing handouts and Library Guides, or by introductory lectures, or by stressing the availability of other services such as the café. Motivation to visit the library can be provided in this way, and this may result in the students gradually becoming aware of the resources available there, but this may not necessarily result in motivation to use the library.

During the first year at Chalmers many of the students, particularly those in the large Schools of Engineering — Electrical and Mechanical Engineering — work in traditional large-group lecture environments, with compulsory laboratory work. A considerable amount of time is spent on theoretical introductory studies such as mathematics. Against this background, students suggested that first-year students could work in small groups on practical projects, where they would have to look up a certain amount of information. This would enable students to get to know a number of their fellow students, provide study motivation in the form of a practical engineering problem, and provide the students with motivation to use the library to look up information. Since 1975/76 students at the School of Architecture at Chalmers University have taken part in project-based courses, from their first year at the university. This has resulted in a considerable increase in the use of the Architecture Section Library.

Plans have now been made for the introduction of small-group, project-based studies for the 200 first-year students in the School of Mechanical Engineering, from the academic year 1977/78. Library orientation and use will form part of this project work. Discussions have also been held in the School of Electrical Engineering, as to the possibility of starting project work at the beginning of university studies. It is hoped that in the future, library orientation can be provided as an integrated part of the normal course of studies at the university.

References

Bloom, B S, Hastings, J T and Madaus, G F (1971) 'Handbook on Formative and Summative Evaluation of Student Learning, McGraw-Hill, New York. (Chapter 1 A view of education.)

Carey, R J P (1971) 'Making Libraries Easy to Use: a Systems Approach.' In Library Association Record, Vol 73, pp 132-135.

Carey, R J P (1974) 'Library Guiding. A Programme for Exploiting Library Resources.' Bingley, London.

Fjällbrant, N (1976a) 'The Development of a Programme of User Education at Chalmers University of Technology Library.' PhD thesis, University of Surrey, 499 pp.

Fjällbrant, N (1976b) 'Teaching Methods for the Education of the Library User' In Libri, Vol 26, No 4, pp 252-267.

Ford, G (1973) 'Research in User Behaviour in University Libraries' Journal of Documentation, Vol 29, pp 85-106.

Harlan, R (1970) 'Welcoming Notes' In Instruction in the Use of the College and University Library — Selected Conference Papers, p 2. University of California School of Librarianship, Berkeley.

Hills, P J (1974) 'Library Instruction and the Development of the Individual' in Journal of Librarianship, Vol 6, no 4, pp 255-263.

McLeish, J (1968) 'The Lecture Method' Cambridge Institute of Education.

Roy, B (1974) 'The Needs of the Student Library User as Seen by Academic Staff, Library Staff and Students' — a report of the pilot study at the University of Surrey, Guildford, Institute for Educational Technology, University of Surrey.

'Some facts about Chalmers University of Technology' (1976) Chalmers tekniska högskola, Gothenburg 74 pp.

Taylor, R S (1971) 'Orienting the Library to the User at Hampshire College' In Drexel Library Quarterly, Vol 7, pp 357-64.

Watkins, D R (1970) 'Some notes on "orienting the library to the user"' In 'Use, Mis-use and Non-use of Academic Libraries' pp 43-45. New York Library Association College and University Libraries Section.

PIP — a Tape-Film System

J C Matthews

Introduction

About two years ago, with the permission of a colleague, I attended an undergraduate lecture course on Mathematical Physics given to our second-year Honours Physics students. While listening to the lectures I realized that many of the ideas that were being presented along with some of the abstract and fundamental concepts involved in Quantum Mechanics could be usefully illustrated by animated diagrams. I decided to look for a do-it-yourself system that would allow such programs to be made.

There were two principal constraints on such a system:

1. Production of animated sequences would have to be simple and inexpensive.
2. The programs should be convenient for use by individual students in an unsupervised self-instruction room.

The three media available in the Physics Department at the time were tape-slide, 16mm film and television.

Tape-slide is an attractive medium for do-it-yourself producers but it is impossible to introduce animation due to the long pull-down time.

We had a 16mm Beaulieu cine-camera which was not being used. However, the time involved in detailed planning and then shooting 20,000 frames for a 15-minute animated film was daunting to say the least, and an estimate of the cost of film stock needed for such a short film, assuming zero wastage, suggested a figure of at least £80. Furthermore, although we had a 16mm projector which was used in lecture rooms, it would have been necessary to buy an additional 'student-proof' projector costing in the region of £700.

Although it is possible to record animated programs on television (usually via 16mm film) the equipment available was quite inadequate and additional costs would have been prohibitive.

The Phillips PIP System

In 1972 the Phillips PIP cassettescope was introduced in the UK and this was the first tape-film system to be made available commercially. More recently the Beseler Cue See has appeared and this operates in the same way. Tape-film seemed to be the ideal medium for simple animation.

The system is not well known and the aim of this paper is to demonstrate the ease with which tape-film programs can be made. Before doing so a brief description of the projector may be useful.

The cassettescope is a small-screen super-8 back projector suited to the needs of the single student. The principle of operation is the same as tape-slide. Super-8 film is advanced one frame at a time by pulses on track 4 of an audio-cassette which also carry the commentary on tracks 1 and 2. The film may be advanced at any speed up to 24 frames per second so that still frames, animation or live action may be mixed in a single program by recording an appropriate set of pulses. The pull-down time is so short that it is impossible to detect any flicker during a frame change. A full length of 50 feet of super-8 film consists of 3600 frames and several useful 15-minute programs may be recorded on it. In the example to be shown six programs, each lasting about 15 minutes, are held in a single Phillips film cassette and since the cost of the film is only £2 the average cost of film stock for each program is less than 35p. The psychological cost barrier is completely removed.

In the following, only program production will be explained. There will be no discussion of the effectiveness of the system in terms of program objectives, etc.

Production of Tape-Film Software

The final software product consists of:

1. A set of images recorded on super-8 colour film and stored in a Phillips film cassette;
2. A commentary recorded on tracks 1 and 2 of an audio-cassette; and
3. A set of pulses recorded on track 4 of the same audio-cassette.

Production follows the same pattern as in the case of tape-slide, viz:

1. Planning
2. Shooting the film
3. Transferring film to cassette
4. Writing the commentary
5. Recording the commentary
6. Writing the pulse cues
7. Recording the pulse cues
8. Checking the recording
9. Transferring the signals to audio-cassette
10. Operation of the program.

1. Planning

The only planning that is necessary is the production of rough layouts of completed diagrams. As in tape-slide, it is unnecessary to predetermine the timing of particular sequences since the pulses ensure that the film moves with the commentary, and this is at a later stage. This contrasts strongly with ordinary film animation where every sequence must be preplanned in time so that the correct number of frames may be shot to fit each section of commentary. In fact in tape-film there is no need to count frames during production.

2. Shooting the Film

Super-8 is the popular 'domestic' format and a good camera may be bought for about £100, which is very much less than the price of a good 16mm camera. The camera must have single shot capability and good focus and aperture control. Any additional features are luxuries.

The program must commence with a distinctive and progressive sequence of about 40 count-down frames leading to a synchronising frame so that a search for

110

1. Planning

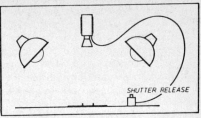

2. Shooting the film

3. Transferring film to cassette

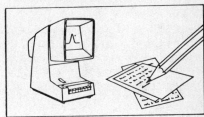

4. Writing the commentary

5. Recording the commentary

6. Writing the pulse cues

7. Recording the pulse cues

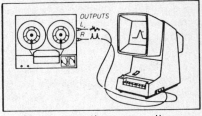

8. Checking the recording

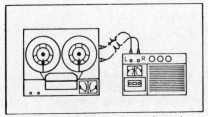

9. Transferring the signals to audio cassette

10. Operation of the program

the latter can be made at high speed (60 frames/second).

This is followed by the titles and then the program is shot frame by frame. It consists of building up diagrams or using computer-generated curves and then moving small pieces of paper over the drawings to simulate movement. A typical sequence might consist of about 30 frames. However, there are as many different styles of software production as there are in any other medium and it will not be elaborated here. It is useful to complete the program with an END frame so that the student knows that the film has in fact finished.

3. Transferring Film to Cassette

The super-8 film is processed by the manufacturer, taking as little as 4 days in the slack season and is returned on a small 50 foot spool. It then has to be transferred to a Phillips film-cassette. This is similar to a compact sound-cassette and has a spring-loaded cover which is easily removed. The film is threaded into the cassette, hooked on to the take-up spool and wound in. The other end of the film is threaded back and hooked on to the feed spool and finally the cover is replaced.

4. Writing the Commentary

The film now may be viewed frame by frame in the cassette-scope and it has been found to be most convenient to write the detailed commentary at this stage.

5. Recording the Commentary

The commentary is recorded on one track of a reel-to-reel stereo recorder. It would be quite impossible to record the pulses and the commentary simultaneously. (NB An AV cassette-recorder could be used here but this was not available in the present work.)

6. Writing the Pulse Cues

Again viewing the film frame by frame, pulse cues are written into the script at appropriate points. Where animated sequences are required, a single pulse is replaced by a train of pulses and it is only necessary to indicate their number, eg [20].
　　For example:

'Now consider [1] this potential function. Here a particle [20] is approaching a region where potential is large. Its velocity decreases and is finally reversed. If the particle approaches with greater energy [30] it may be able to pass over the region of high potential and continue in its original direction.'

7. Recording the Pulse Cues

The pulses are recorded alongside the commentary on the other track of the reel-to-reel recorder. Each pulse consists of a 25 ms burst of 1 Khz and in an animated sequence of, say, 30 frames it would be tedious if not impossible to record manually the required train of pulses. In order to do this it is necessary to use a pulse generator, which can not only deliver the pulses at any desired rate, but which also can be preset to stop after the correct number has been produced. This requirement is responsible for the general lack of interest in the tape-film system, since the pulse generators made by Phillips and Beseler each now (1977) cost more

112

than £1000. However, by making use of integrated circuits it is not difficult to build an inexpensive generator which has all the functions required to produce the synchronising pulses (Matthews, 1975).

In order to record the pulses the commentary track is set to 'read' and the pulse track to 'record'. Following the script it is easy to insert the pulses at the cueing points and if the outputs of both tracks are fed to the input socket of the cassettescope the timing of the pulses may be checked as they are being recorded. After a set of pulses has been recorded the recorder may be paused and the pulse generator reset to the next cueing requirement. If any train of pulses appears to be too fast, too slow or wrong in number it is easy to backtrack and re-record them.

8. Checking the Recording

After completing the reel-to-reel recording of commentary and pulses the program is viewed on the cassettescope driven by the audio and pulse signals from the reel-to-reel recorder and any necessary changes are made at this stage.

9. Transferring the Signals to Audio-Cassette

Using a stereo cassette deck the commentary and pulses are finally transferred from reel-to-reel on to a compact audio-cassette. Commentary is recorded on tracks 1 and 2 and pulses on track 4 so it is necessary to fit an AV cassette head (Phillips type 249/100/28) to the deck.

10. Operation of the Program

Finally the cassette is inserted in the cassettescope and, if there are no errors, the program is complete.

The Programs in Use

Two PIP cassettescopes along with copies of the software relating to 'Contour Integration', 1-4, and 'Wave Mechanics', 1-6, have been placed in booths in a 'self-instruction room' and are available at all times to students. During the appropriate part of the lecture course and again shortly before examinations the programs are in heavy demand, but this falls off at other times. Their use is completely unsupervised, the students simply being told of their availability. After explaining in detail to a few students how to use the projectors it has been found unnecessary to demonstrate it to the whole class, since they are quite capable of asking for help from their colleagues. In fact, visiting sixth-form pupils 'play' with the programs and find no difficulty in operating them.

During the last year the programs have been used perhaps 150 times and no damage of any kind has occurred to either film or audio-cassettes. There have been minor problems associated with the projector itself (bulb replacement, cassette cover jamming, etc) but these have been quite easy to rectify.

For the non-professional do-it-yourself academic the tape-film system has been found to be an ideal medium for the production and presentation of short animated programs to be used by individual students in a self-instruction room.

References

Matthews, J C (1975) 'A Pulse Generator for PIP' Journal Educational Television 3.

Case Study in the Implementation of Innovation: a New Model for Developmental Testing

E S Henderson, M B Nathenson

The Problem

In developing any instructional material, course designers sooner or later face, or are faced with the question: 'Will the students be able to learn from our course material?'. However much care has gone into the development of the course, and however many experts have critically reviewed the materials, problems may still exist.

Some course teams at the Open University* have crossed their fingers and hoped for the best. The results of this have sometimes been frustrated students, high drop-out, low pass-rate, abusive letters, and consequent heavy expenditure of time and money to patch things up during the first year of the course's run or, worse still, later. Sometimes, of course, there have been no problems: or rather, no problems have been detected.

Educational technology has for many years had a better answer in its tool-kit, variously called developmental testing, piloting, rehearsal, dry run, pretest, try-out, formative evaluation, or more recently, learner verification and revision (LVR). When the Open University's course design process was conceived in 1969/70, developmental testing was recognised as an important stage (Lewis, 1971). Vigorous efforts were made to pretest the first four foundation courses in 1970 (Rowntree, 1971), but execution fell far short of expectation.

The problems were multiple (Nathenson and Henderson, 1977). For example, the drop-out rate amongst individuals participating in developmental testing programmes was unacceptably high and the quality of feedback was very low. It was apparent that testers were not motivated to the same extent as real students. There was little understanding of the process of transforming feedback into revisions. Even when testing data pointed firmly to an inadequacy in the teaching material, it only very rarely gave a positive indication of how the instruction might be changed to obviate the problem. There were also operational difficulties. As a result, only about half of the correspondence units** for each of the four foundation courses were tested, and not always in the correct sequence. In addition, processing of the data could not always be completed in time to revise teaching materials prior to publishing deadlines.

---

* A course team at the Open University is comprised of a number of subject matter experts and other specialists (BBC producers, educational technologists, editors, graphic designers, etc). All aspects of course production are the team's collective responsibility (Riley, 1976).
** The term 'unit' is used to describe one week's work (average 10-14 hours) on a full-credit Open University course, or a fortnight's work on a half-credit course. The core of each unit is a specially-written correspondence text, which may be associated with a variety of other components — radio, television, readings from set books, assignments, supplementary materials of various kinds, etc. A full-credit course has 32 units and a half-credit 16.

These problems led to searching questions being raised about the value of developmental testing. Are courses which are tested any better than courses which are not? Can a model for developmental testing be designed which is operationally feasible?

Educational technologists could not answer these questions. Like so many of the tools of educational technology, developmental testing lacks a firm empirical base. We have not been able to find a single research study in the area of higher education which demonstrates that developmental testing can significantly improve a course of instruction. We also noticed a marked 'lack of reality' in implementing developmental testing programmes. Again, like so many of the educational technologist's tools, developmental testing has usually been carried out in artificial situations. Typically, testers, often not representative of the target population, are paid a nominal sum of money to comment on a sample of the learning materials. In our opinion, such lack of reality breeds failure.

Design of a Solution

To overcome the problems that had been experienced at the Open University and elsewhere, we designed a twofold solution:

Stage I We generated a new developmental testing model that would operate within the real constraints of the Open University system; and
Stage II We demonstrated that the model significantly improves the 'learnability' of Open University courses.

The system was evolved and has been described elsewhere (Henderson and Nathenson, 1976, 1977). Its five main features can be summarized briefly as follows:

(a) We recognized the importance of selecting a sample of testers from the intended target population. Although this should be a self-evident principle, it is one that has often been violated. In addition, since the Open University's student population is extremely heterogeneous, any sample of testers must be stratified with respect to entry behaviour by means of pre-tests on a course's objectives.
(b) We were convinced by our study of reports of earlier developmental testing projects that paid testers do not behave like real students. So we rejected financial incentives and looked for a way to motivate testers in the same way as the target population. In the Open University context, this meant that testers must be eligible to obtain a course credit if they reach the required standard in their assignments and examination.
(c) We consider it essential that the learning environment for testers should simulate the learning environment of the target population as closely as possible. For example, testers must work at home and study the whole course in the correct sequence.
(d) We devised an integrated feedback system to collect data. Frequent open and closed-ended questions are interpolated into the text as critical points, to seek immediate responses to small sections of the text.
(e) We designed a data-processing algorithm which enabled us systematically to search for and discover both learning problems and potential solutions.

Stage I: Operational Feasibility

In implementing our model, we faced an organization in which developmental testing, of a kind, had been tried, found wanting, and rejected. We needed to demonstrate that our new approach to developmental testing was operationally feasible: a pilot run was clearly required. The first step was to select a course which would lend itself to developmental testing in 1976. There was no shortage of potential candidates, with 13 new courses scheduled for first presentation in 1977. All were at a point in the production cycle where academics should have been asking themselves the question: 'Will the students be able to learn from our course material?' In selecting one of these candidates, we had two considerations in mind:

(a) Were members of the course team already asking themselves the crucial question about the 'learnability' of their material? Was learnability a real problem for them?
(b) Was the course team sufficiently advanced in its work schedule to allow developmental testing to proceed through its various stages of feedback and revision?

Investigation revealed that the half-credit course Elements of Music most closely met our requirements. This course aims to 'familiarize students thoroughly with the elements of music, develop aural perception, teach score reading, and give them the technical knowledge to practise harmonic and stylistic analysis of the period between about 1730 and 1900' (Open University, 1976). Early drafts of course materials had already been intensively read and commented upon by various members of the course team, including an educational technologist, and modified accordingly by their authors. But teaching the technical aspects of music at a distance was a new venture, both at the Open University and, so far as we are aware, elsewhere and the course team expressed real concern about the effectiveness of the teaching strategies. More particularly, the course is intended for students with no previous musical expertise and the course team was by no means certain that the pace of the instruction had been correctly judged, especially in the earlier units.

The pilot run began in January 1976 with a stratified sample of 28 testers. These testers worked through the 16 units in sequence, submitted assignments to a tutor, sat in examination, and provided detailed written feedback on all components of the course. After processing the data the educational technologist on the course team prepared a report on each unit, summarizing problems experienced by the testers and indicating, where appropriate, possible alternative teaching strategies which had been suggested by the testers. On the basis of these reports, the course team made alterations before handing over the units for publication. The pilot run ended in December 1976, with all 16 units revised in the light of tester feedback. Stage I of the twofold solution had been accomplished. The new developmental testing model had been shown to operate smoothly within the real world of the Open University course production system.

Stage II: Proof of the Efficacy of Developmental Testing

To show that our system was capable of producing significant improvements in the course, we designed a research study. We selected a second sample of testers, from the same population, who also worked through Elements of Music. Like the first group, they completed written feedback, submitted assignments to the same tutor, and sat the same examination. Unlike the first group, they began two months later (to allow time for revision) and studied the units modified in the light of developmental testing. The group studying the original version (Group O) began with 28 testers, while the group studying the version revised in the light of developmental testing (Group R) began with 20. The comparability of Groups O and R was investigated by three measures: previous educational experience, musical background, and entry-level pretests. On none of these measures did the two groups differ significantly.

Data from Group R came too late for further modification of the course: its sole function was to enable comparisons to be made to determine whether the revisions arising from the developmental testing run with the first group had resulted in more effective learning (ie increased performance), more efficient learning (ie decreased study time), and/or fewer learning difficulties. The findings of this study have been described in some detail elsewhere (Henderson, Hodgson and Nathenson, 1977); there is space here only for a brief summary:

(a) The performance differences were dramatic. The two groups submitted the same eight continuous assessment assignments during the course, which were graded on the University's five point scale by the tutor. Group R, which studied the course material modified in the light of developmental testing, submitted significantly better assignments in all but one case. On the first two assignments Group R scored on average about one and a half grades higher than Group O, and on assignments 3, 4, 6, 7 and 8 Group R scored on average about a half to one grade higher than Group O. Only on the fifth assignment was there no statistically significant difference between the average grades of the two groups. This assignment was based on the two units of the course in which developmental testing had revealed fewest problems. The second group therefore studied these two units in a form differing relatively little from the original version.

(b) It was immediately obvious that the effect of the revisions arising from developmental testing had been to reduce study time on a majority of units. The overall mean study time per unit fell by almost 15%. There were a number of other interesting effects on study time. For example, in three of the 16 units the text was lengthened considerably following developmental testing. This resulted from the addition of new worked examples, and the elaboration of existing worked examples, at the suggestion of some testers. Yet on none of these three units did the study time increase, and in one case an increase in text length of over 25% resulted in a decrease in mean study time of about 15% — a particularly clear case of increased learning efficiency.

(c) The changes that were made as a result of developmental testing often eliminated, or at least reduced, the occurrence of learning difficulties encountered by Group O (Henderson and Nathenson, 1976; Henderson, Hodgson and Nathenson, 1977). There is not space in this paper to describe specific instances, but it is certainly the case that the changes made as a result of developmental testing had a marked effect on the quality of learning experienced by Group R.

Thus Stage II had been successful. Our research study had demonstrated that Elements of Music had become a better course as a result of developmental testing.

Dissemination

The pilot run of our model was successful in demonstrating that it was operationally feasible to conduct developmental testing in a way which closely simulated the learning environment of Open University students, and that there were significant academic advantages in terms of substantive improvements to a course. But we were also anxious to reawaken interest in developmental testing throughout the University. We therefore attempted to generate the maximum dissemination of information about our activities during the year in which the pilot run was being conducted. Dissemination occurred within two contexts, on the micro-scale within the course team, and on the micro-scale within the University.

The course team were receiving continuously, throughout 1976, data from both the developmental testing group and the research group. The effect of this, both for the individual authors of units, and for the course team as a whole, was a marked increase in enthusiasm. At the end of 1975, when developmental testing was proposed, members of the team had certainly welcomed it, seeing it as a possible solution to their uncertainties about the potential success of their course. As the year progressed, and they saw the fruits of their (and our) labours, they became increasingly enthusiastic, to the point where they were convinced that without developmental testing the course might well have proved a new disaster and that, in the words of the course team chairman: 'this developmental testing is the greatest invention since the wheel'. There is no doubt that the enthusiasm generated within the course team made an important contribution towards dissemination.

The Open University, like many organizations, operates through a network of committees, which has grown up partly to assist the smooth running of the organization. Several of the innovative elements of our developmental testing system required modifications or additions to the normal practices of the University and thus had to be argued before, and approved by, the relevant committees. Without involving these committees, developmental testing would not have been possible. There were three elements in our model which involved us with the University's committee structure: the need for funds, our desire to use applicants as testers, and our wish to make our testers eligible for credit. Figure 1 illustrates the Open University's committee structure (adapted from Perry, 1976) and will help to clarify the extent of our involvement.

(a) Our need for funds required a special submission to the Course Resources Committee, where we successfully argued that our system offered sufficient potential benefits to justify such expenditure. This decision required reporting to the Planning Board.
(b) In order to select our testers from applicants to the University and to admit them as students, we needed permission from the Admissions Committee. As this idea was an original one, the Admissions Committee had to refer back to the Student Affairs Board. The issue proved, however, not to be seriously contentious.
(c) The idea of permitting developmental testers to be eligible for credit on the course they were testing was a very radical change for the University. We first approached the Examinations Committee, who raised no objections in principle, but who considered that the precedent was of such importance that it should be referred upwards through the Academic Board and the Student Affairs Board to the Senate. Before making submissions to these Boards, in both of which we were aware that there would probably be significant opposition, we prepared the ground carefully. We organized a seminar, to which we invited a number of the University's key academic staff. We also published a paper in *Teaching at a Distance*, the Open University's own journal which is distributed to all central and regional staff (Nathenson and Henderson, 1976). Perhaps as a result of this preparatory work (which included a great deal of lobbying), the proposal passed through both Boards fairly easily, and the Senate subsequently endorsed their recommendations.

118

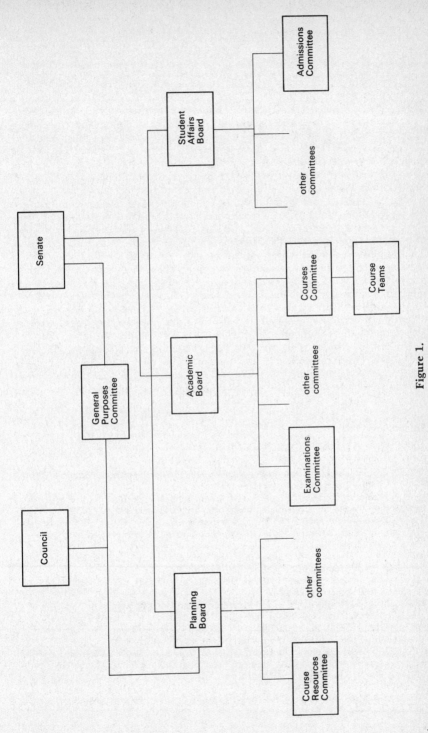

Figure 1.

119

The exposure that this necessary committee work gave to our activities made, without doubt, a very significant contribution to dissemination.

Epilogue

What has happened to developmental testing at the Open University since the pilot run in 1976? A new foundation course, scheduled for first presentation to students in 1978, embarked on comprehensive developmental testing in 1977. At least five more course teams preparing 1979 courses have decided to implement our model in 1978. The administration has restored flexibility into the course production cycle to allow course teams the option of developmental testing. A very much simplified procedure has been established for approving developmental testing schemes where eligibility of testers for credit is involved, requiring a single submission to Course Committee (see Figure 1). We attribute this success to two factors.

Firstly, we insisted that the pilot run be conducted under realistic conditions, ie in a typical Open University course team and within the real constraints of the University's course production schedules. This established operational feasibility and at the same time generated a dissemination process that was intrinsic to the design and piloting of the innovation. It is far more common for the tools of educational technology to be developed and piloted in such a way as to cause the minimum perturbation to the organization, with two adverse consequences. Compromises have often to be made which result in the tool being piloted under artificial conditions, so that its viability in the real world is open to question. Also, the dissemination process becomes a separate exercise, as described by Havelock's (1971) 'research, development and diffusion' (RD & D) model. Our case study suggests that there are considerable advantages in deliberately creating a dynamic relationship between research and development on the one hand, and diffusion on the other.

Secondly, we proved to doubting academics that at least one tool in the educational technologist's tool-kit actually worked.

References

Havelock, R G (1971) 'The Utilisation of Educational Research and Development' British Journal of Educational Technology 2,2 p 84-98.

Henderson, E S, Hodgson, B K and Nathenson, M B (1977) 'Developmental Testing: the Proof of the Pudding' Teaching at a Distance 10 (in press).

Henderson, E S and Nathenson, M B (1976) 'Developmental Testing: an Empirical Approach to Course Improvement' Programmed Learning and Educational Technology 13,4 p 31-42.

Henderson, E S and Nathenson, M B (1977) 'Developmental Testing: Collecting Feedback and Transforming it into Revisions' Journal of the National Society for Performance and Instruction 16,2 p 6-10.

Lewis, B N (1971) 'Course Production at the Open University II: Activities and Activity Networks' British Journal of Educational Technology 2,2 p 111-23.

Nathenson, M B and Henderson, E S (1976) 'Developmental Testing: a New Beginning' Teaching at a Distance 7 p 28-41.

Nathenson, M B and Henderson, E S (1977) 'Problems and Issues in Developmental Testing' Journal of the National Society for Performance and Instruction 16,1 p 9-10.

Open University (1976) 'Courses Handbook 1976' Open University Press, Milton Keynes.

Perry, W (1976) 'Open University' Open University Press, Milton Keynes.

Riley, J (1976) 'Course Teams at the Open University' Studies in Higher Education 1,1 p 57-61. (Also in Squires, G [Ed] 'Course Teams: Four Studies and a Commentary' Nuffield Foundation, London, 1975)

Rowntree, D G F (1971) 'The Open University — A Case Study in Educational Technology V: Course Production' In Packham, D et al (Eds) Aspects of Educational Technology V p 64-75 Pitman, London.

Some Criteria for an Instructional System for Professional Training

G Murza

This article describes a procedure which enables Idis* to train new employees individually.

From the retrospective view there were five problems that had to be solved:

— analysis of structure	planning
— criteria for a training system	condition
— instructional system	development
— production/application of learning packages	realization
— extension of utilization	modification

As you will find elsewhere (Murza, 1975a) a more detailed description of the basic training concept which is geared to social medicine and documentation, I intend to explain only general conditions and stages of planning.

Analysis of Structure

The first phase, analysis of structure, had to be tackled after the decision had been made to train new employees audio-visually. In other words, the determination of the educational objectives was the prerequisite for further activities.

There are several procedures. A known method that surpasses Mager's operational concept is proposed by Tyler; it is based on an arrangement of the subject matter in two dimensions: the behavioural aspect and the content aspect.

An example of such a determination of the objectives for a high school course in biological science can be seen in the Table overleaf.

Klauer (1974) points out that in the category of the behavioural aspect the 'taxonomy of the cognitive domain' by Bloom can be integrated; it is divided into:

knowledge
understanding
application
analysis
synthesis
evaluation

According to Klauer, Gagné's six types of learning could also be integrated: these are:

signal learning
stimulus response learning
training
verbal association

* Idis: Institut für Dokumentation und Information über Sozialmedizin und öffentliches Gesundheitswesen, Bielefeld.

OBJECTIVES FOR A HIGH SCHOOL COURSE IN BIOLOGICAL SCIENCE

Content Aspect of the Objectives	Behavioural Aspect of the Objectives						
	1. Understanding of important facts and principles	2. Familiarity with dependable sources of information	3. Ability to interpret data	4. Ability to apply principles	5. Ability to study and report results of study	6. Broad and mature interests	7. Social attitudes
A. Functions of Human Organisms							
1. Nutrition	X	X	X	X	X	X	X
2. Digestion	X		X	X	X	X	
3. Circulation	X		X	X	X	X	
4. Respiration	X		X	X	X	X	X
5. Reproduction	X	X	X	X	X	X	X
B. Use of Plant and Animal Resources							
1. Energy relationships	X		X	X	X	X	X
2. Environmental factors conditioning plant and animal growth	X	X	X	X	X	X	X
3. Heredity and genetics	X	X	X	X	X	X	X
4. Land utilization	X	X	X	X	X	X	X
C. Evolution and Development	X	X	X		X	X	X

(Tyler, 1950)

discrimination learning
concept learning

In several aspects such an analysis is successful and useful:

- it guarantees an explicit and controllable formulation of educational goals;
- it facilitates planning for the production of learning packages, especially with regard to time, costs, extent and number of packages;
- it is the base for the development of the programmed instruction itself;
- it can be the base for the production of criterion-orientated test items;
- it facilitates the formulation of the conditions the technical system should have.

However, this last-mentioned aspect is often neglected because the range offered in instructional systems is very limited. The control of performance is restricted through the facilities a system has. The consequence is that there are restrictions on information transmission as well as on controlling the achievement of educational goals.

Therefore, we have analyzed charts of educational objectives on our subject matter under consideration of the characteristics of learner groups, in order to ascertain which requirements the system should fulfil.

In the following we would like to explain the prerequisites such a system should have.

Criteria for an Instructional System

Training System for Individual Instruction

As a rule, instructional systems are planned either for individual or for group instruction; the application of learning packages to groups is of course useful from the economic point of view. On the other hand, in the case of group instruction many advantages of programmed instruction cannot be used, such as individual reinforcement, individual times of learning and individual instructing strategies.

As you know, there has been much discussion about the effectiveness of programmed instruction when compared with conventional instruction.

Generally speaking, programmed instruction is a matter of individual learning and only under this condition are improved results to be expected.

Furthermore, a decision about individualized instruction versus group instruction must be made after consideration of the number of trained employees per time-unit as well as of the number of learning packages to be passed.

However such reflections concerning cost-benefit relations are not yet available.

Economical and Technical Uncomplicated Program Production

Program conception and program production should exclusively be determined by aspects of subject matter, pedagogics and psychology. Experience, however, has shown that costs may influence program development. A technical, complicated system might involve expensive program production; in practice this often results in developments that are not solely determined by the above-mentioned aspects.

Program Branching

In a lot of instructional situations there are many learners who differ in their intellectual flexibility, but who take part in the same lessons; that means different learner groups with different pre-knowledge and different education have partly to learn the same lessons. The earlier principle of programmed instruction consisted of constructing frames which ought to involve a positive reinforcement. The implication was: the frames were small and the standard of difficulty was such that the majority of learners (80 − 90%) succeeded. On the other hand, we know the different point of view represented by Crowder. He argued for attending to each kind of mistake individually and supplied thereby the basis of program branching.

The program frames promoted by Crowder seldom correspond to the degree of difficulty laid down by Skinner. The results of recent research into motivation point out that the principles formulated by Skinner are only valid under restrictions. The successful completion of tasks with a moderate degree of difficulty has a greater influence on motivation. The necessity for program branching would seem to be reinforced from the motivational aspect.

In order to avoid a permanent confrontation with too difficult or too easy frames it is recommended constructing parallel passages with varying degrees of difficulty.

Audio-Visual Presentation

Many subject matters in professional training call for the correct handling of materials, in order to acquire the requested performance. In most training situations it is not possible to confront the learner directly with these materials for organizational, technical, financial and other reasons.

Instead of this we made use of simulation; if this is the case it is necessary to use a medium which allows the projection of objects, illustrations and drawings. In our case the individual should learn how to handle properly books, files, signatures and so on which are also simulated for audio-visual training.

High Fidelity of Visual Reproduction

Especially in visual reproduction the quality of projection demands high standards. On the other hand, many audio-visual systems put restrictions on the fidelity of reproduction. Slide projection guarantees a presentation true to nature; the screen of a terminal, however, allows no detailed illustration.

In our case the demonstration of medical subject matters as well as the projection of illustrations which partly contain rather small letters, requires technical equipment of high quality.

Constructed (Free) Responses

Most instructional systems control knowledge only by one kind of questioning: the learner is asked to respond to alternatives. Apart from the fact that this multiple-choice principle might bring statistical problems, not all kinds of achievement can be checked by such a procedure.

In many instructional situations you can make sure of perfect performance only by activating the learner, which means it is necessary to induce the learner to formulate answers himself. If we want to know whether the individual has learned the correct performance, for example with rules on bibliographic registration, it is not sufficient that the learner is able to identify all correct registrations, manual abilities must also be controlled.

Easy Production of Software and Easy Program Modifications

It is well known that in practice it is always necessary to revise or supplement program parts. However, even slight modifications often imply great financial or time-spending strains, so that hardly any instructional system fulfils these requirements. In consequence, packages remain unmodified and become obsolete. For this reason the claim for easy software production/modification must not be neglected.

The Instructional System

The training system used in Idis is explained in detail elsewhere (Murza, 1975b). It is based on two slide-projectors which project on the same surface, therefore soft and hard cross-fading as well as blending-in is possible. Each slide of the magazine has its own label and may be chosen in a few seconds. As these impulses may be stored on a cassette-tape, a synchronized presentation is guaranteed at any time.

By setting code-marks, which are counted on another track of the tape, it is possible to jump to any mark. Thereby program branching may be achieved.

The system involves not only multiple-choice questions but also free responses which may be controlled on a paper-strip that moves under a glass cover allowing the learner to compare his own answer with the solution. At this stage the learner can no longer alter his answer.

Modifications of a program are no problem, because slides may easily be exchanged; the impulses of slide labels can also be selectively extinguished and renewed: procedures familiar to us from manual tape-recording.

Production of Learning Packages

We have already produced the following instructional units:

Medical terminology (6);
Introduction to the handling of the Dewey Decimal Classification (7);
Rules on bibliographic storage of literature (4);
Introduction to law: questions on public health and social medicine (4).

The numbers in brackets represent the lessons. The learning time of each lesson is individual: the average is about 30 minutes.

Extension of Utilization

The described instructional system fulfils the above-mentioned criteria. In looking forward to further possible instructional systems we would like to point to another medium which is, regarding the quality of projection, comparable to slides; this medium also has additional advantages. Microfiche is a film of 105 x 148 mm — the size of a postcard. The capacity of this film is variable and dependent on the reducing factor by which the information/illustration is stored: a factor of 24 implies a capacity of 98 pages in A4.

To make use of microfiche, a reader must be at one's disposal. Microfiche is not a revolutionary thing: it is a well-known medium for documentary purpose; up to now, however, it has not been used for instruction because films were available only in black and white.

In the meantime we have found methods of producing colour microfiches of high quality (Murza, G; Nacke, O; Strate, KH; 1976) and there is no longer any reason not to use it for instructional purposes. The advantage of microfiche is evident; it is an economical and manageable medium of high capacity that facilitates straightforward and decentralized training.

As we know, there exists at present no system that is comparable to the described instructing machine; however, in the meantime there are readers which allow a tape-controlled, automized adjustment of microfiche pictures.

In Germany an advanced technical system is not expected to be available before 1978.

References

Bloom, B S (1956) 'Taxonomy of Education Objectives' New York.

Frank, H (1969) 'Kybernetische Grundlagen der Pädagogik' Bd II, 2, Auflage, Baden-Baden.

Hofer, M, Simons, H, Weinert, F E , Zielinski, W (1976) 'Lehren und Instruktionsoptimierung' Pädogogische Psychologie, Bd 4, Weinheim.

Klauer, K J (1974) 'Methodik der Lehrzieldefinition und Lehrstoffanalyse' Düsseldorf.

Mager, R F (1965) 'Lernziele und Programmierter Unterricht' Weinheim.

Murza, G (1975a) 'Das Ausbildungskonzept des Idis' Nachrichten für Dokumentation 26, 2, S 63-67.

Murza, G (1975b) 'Durch Selbsthilfe ein Zweckentsprechendes Lehrsystem' Aula 8, 3, S 273-276.

Murza, G, Nacke, O, Strate, K H (1976) 'Ein Einfaches Verfahren zum Herstellen von Colour- und Halbton- Mikrofiches' Nachrichten für Dokumentation 27, 4/5, S 163-164.

Tyler, R W (1950) 'Basic Principles of Curriculum and Instruction' Chicago.

Computerized System of Integral Student and Teaching Evaluation

O E Chaves, L O Perez, P Cuneo, W Dorman, S Sinha, R del Canto

Foreword

It is a commonly accepted fact that the evaluation forms an extremely important part of the whole teaching-learning process. This has given us a permanent reason to try to produce or improve a system which can enable us not only to know and measure student ability and academic performance, but also to achieve the objectives set out in our teaching programmes, which are concerned with the informative and personality-formation aspects, as well as with methods and resources with which the actual teaching is accomplished.

For this reason, the Department of Biochemistry of the Faculty of Medicine in collaboration with the Computer Center and the Institute of Statistics of the University of Los Andes, has been systematically applying for the last three years objective tests of multiple-choice-question (MCQ) type in the final, end-of-term and mid-term examinations. These tests were subjected to an extensive statistical analysis and to another special analysis of each separate question, as is specified in the evaluation programme called CORREX (Chaves, 1974) for which we have now substituted this present study which we refer to as SEIAULA (Sistema de Evaluacion Integral Automizado ULA) which directly resulted from our experience with CORREX, its study and its critical analysis.

Thus, in this paper, we omit the aspects relating to concepts, criteria and methods of evaluation, and limit our discussion to the characteristics, implementation and application of SEIAULA.

SEIAULA

The system is subdivided into six sections:

- ☐ Computerization of question bank
- ☐ Production and format of exam papers
- ☐ Evaluation of exams
- ☐ General statistical analysis
- ☐ Analysis of questions
- ☐ Historical archive

With the existence of a question bank, one can computerize the evaluation by using objective tests of the MCQ type with only one correct answer possible. Also, one can produce a complete analysis of the questions themselves and obtain additional statistical information of their quality and of other aspects related to the teaching-learning process.

Computerization of Question Bank

This sub-system consists of four programmes for organization of storage (historical archive) of the question bank of each subject.

1. Verification. The programme consists of special coding of each question and its respective answer options. The input data is in the form of cards containing questions on one particular subject, for one school of one faculty. The output lists the questions and their answer options and indicates errors in the coding. When the lists are ready, the question wording is checked.
2. Formation of question bank. This programme reads the corrected cards, puts them in proper order and forms a sequential index storage together with the question bank. What is more it creates a storage with direct access to the question coding classified by weight within the unit.
3. Up-dating. This consists of four options:
   L = Listing of all the questions in the storage
   E = Elimination of questions
   I = Additions to the questions
   C = Change or replacements of questions.
   During elimination or change of questions, care must be taken that this information is also passed on to the main storage (historical archive).
4. Information transfer from disc to tape. This is used to establish a reference library for question banks on different subjects.

Production and Format of Exam Papers

This sub-system contains two programmes:

1. Transfer of tape information to disc from the questions and coding storage for a particular subject.
2. Preparation of exam. This programme can fabricate exams by any combination of the 10 following options:
   - Number of questions taken from all the units.
   - Unit number of questions.
   - Unit, type, number of questions.
   - Unit, weight, number of questions.
   - Coding of specific questions.
   - Question-test.
   - Weight, number of questions.
   - Type, number of questions.
   - Type-weight, number of questions.

To make this possible the planning of the exam was done in accordance with the following points:

1. Define exam purpose.
2. Identify the groups for which the exam is being prepared.
3. Decide on subject matter.
4. Prepare specification table (example, Table 1).
5. Contrive problems based on specific objectives of the subject programme.
6. Decide on the type of questions to be used, which have to fulful the conditions we have established for accepting a good question.
7. Select the reference material which can be used if need arises.
8. Decide the degree of difficulty of the questions.
9. Group questions according to alphabet, logic or any other order.

10. Select the correct answers.
11. Decide the length of test and answer time to be allowed.

The input date is in the form of cards containing indications as to the exam type and the following information: exam data, subject, faculty, school, section, professor's name, number and number of different exams.

This programme supplies the exam list and forms the special storage protected by a special key, including keys to alterations.

Specific Objective / Subject Content	Comprehension and Interpretation	Generalization analysis and synthesis	Memorization	Total
Theme	%	%	%	
I	15	10	5	30
II	20	15	15	50
III	10	5	5	20
Total	45	30	25	100

Table 1. *Exam preparation, specification table, example*

Evaluation of Exams

This sub-system tabulates the marks gained by students in the exams, together with the questions, answers and statistical analysis. Also, it guards in the main storage (historical archive) the past exams which can be used for post-analysis and research purposes.

The correction of tests is centred around four aspects:

1. Listing of correct answers.
2. Tabulation of marks: proportional distribution of information to each of the corrected tests in the following way:
   — Number of correct answers.
   — Number of incorrect answers.
   — Number of unanswered questions.
   — Transformed mark, according to the maximum indicated.
   — Absolute mark (0—20 range).
3. Correction factor: if need be, the programme has a correction factor in order to eliminate from the marks the random factor which can exist in the selection of correct answers. This factor adjusts the absolute mark obtained by the student according to the number of correct answers in the following way: each (NALT-1) incorrect answer eliminates a correct one, where NALT is the number of answer options for each question.
   Example: In an exam of n answer options (true-false), one incorrect answer eliminates a correct one. In three answer options, two incorrect answers will eliminate one correct one and so on.
   Correction factor is calculated from the following formula:

$$NA = \frac{(RL - RI)}{NALT-1} \frac{20}{NP}$$

where
$$NA = \text{absolute mark}$$
$$RL = \text{number of correct answers}$$
$$RI = \text{number of incorrect answers}$$
$$NALT = \text{number of options for each question}$$
$$NP = \text{number of questions.}$$

4. Recorrection. If needed, this programme contemplates the possibility of amending exam marking when one or more questions are declared void according to the statistical analysis.

General Statistical Analysis

Consists basically of calculations of the following:

1. Number of students.
2. Number of passes. This corresponds to the number of students whose absolute mark was higher or equal to 9.50.
3. Number of failures. This corresponds to the number of students whose absolute mark was lower than 9.50.
4. % of passes (as % of total number of students).
5. % of failures (as % of the total number of students).
6. Maximum number of correct answers, corresponding to the highest mark.
7. Minimum number of correct answers, corresponding to the lowest mark.
8. Average mark.
9. Standard deviation.
10. Reliability (estimation of the correlation which can be obtained when the same exam is applied to the same group, but at a certain interval so that the group will not remember the questions, nor be able to study the subject to a greater extent).

Number 20 Kuder-Richardson formula is used for calculation.
In general, it is accepted as good if the index of reliability is greater than 0.9. Nevertheless, in practice, an index greater than 0.6 is also acceptable.

Analysis of Questions

Analysis of each question according to the three main criteria.

1. Difficulty Index: This simply represents the proportion of students who answered incorrectly. If the majority did not answer correctly we would assume that the question was difficult. On the other hand, if only a minority answered incorrectly, then the question was easy.
2. Discrimination Index: At the same time the exam as a whole and each individual question is considered. It is said that the exam or question discriminates if it is correctly answered by the better students only, and incorrectly by the worse students. This is clearly shown by *Point Biserial Correlation Coefficient*, which can range between −1 and +1. Direct correlation occurs between 0 and +1, and reverse correlation between 0 and −1. The correlation is significant if greater than +0.3, when we say the exam or the question is really discriminating.
   We used this formula for the *Point Biserial Correlation Coefficient Calculation:*

$$CB = \frac{\overline{x}_p - \overline{x}_n}{s} \sqrt{pq}$$

where:
S = standard deviation of mark distribution
$\bar{x}_p$ = average of marks obtained by the better students
$\bar{x}_q$ = average of marks obtained by the worse students
P = proportion of better students
p = proportion of worse students

The P B C C must always be proved statistically by the t-test.

$$t_v = CB \left(\frac{n-2}{1-CB^2} \right)$$

where:
$V = N-2$ degrees of freedom
N = total number of students

3. Effectiveness of options: Through this analysis we can study the function of different options of each question. It is obvious that if the question has been constructed well and the examinees form a normal group of mixed ability there will be a certain proportion of students who answer correctly and others incorrectly, using one of the distractors. If the question is discriminating, it is certain that the group which answers correctly will also obtain the highest exam marks.

This analysis is based on three factors:

(a) Number of students who choose the same option for the same question.
(b) % of students who choose the same option for the same question.
(c) Average mark for students who choose the same option for the same question.

Historical Archive

General storage of all the exams and analyses are taped and stored.

Conclusions

Experimental application of this programme in Biochemistry II has proved to be of invaluable help to the teaching staff, and was acceptable to the students who considered it more fair (advantageous to them). The Difficulty and Discrimination Index, as well as the Effectiveness of Questions had been successfully used to correct the wording of the questions and to streamline the teaching methods. Now, SEIAULA is implemented on a regular basis in the Biochemistry II exams, and when its full value has been assessed and proved it will be extended to the other departments and schools of the University of Los Andes. In the next paper (in process of preparation) we will present all the results and conclusions drawn from the experimental and regular application of SEIAULA, showing the degree of achievement of all the objectives, set out for this particular system.

References

Adkins Wood, Dorothy (1961) 'Test Construction' Charles Merril Books, Ing Columbus, Ohio, 3rd ed.

Aguilera Camacho, Bernado (1965) 'El Test' Technicas para la Construccion de Pruebas Objectivas Editorial Pacifico, Cali, Colombia, 2nd ed.

Anderson, J, Pettingale, K W and Tomlinson, R W S (1970) 'Evaluation of Topic Teaching using Computer Marked Objective Tests' British Journal of Medical Education, 4, 216-218.

Beard, Ruth M and Pole, Kay (1971) 'Content and Purpose of Biochemistry Examinations' British Journal of Medical Education, 5, 13-21.

Charvat, J, McGuire, C and Parsons, V (1969) 'Caracteristicas y Aplicaciones de los Examenes en la Ensenanza de la Medicina' Cuadernos de Salud Publica No 36 Organizacion Mundial de la Salud.

Chaves, O E y Sljussar, A (1974) 'Intento de Evaluacion como Proceso Auxiliar de Ensenanza de Bioquimica II en la Facultad de Medicina de las Universidad de Los Andes' Resumenes de la V Conferencia Panamericana de Educacion Medica, Caraballeda, Noviembre.

Dobles, Margarita (1967) 'Criterio Operacional en la Evaluacion del Plan de Estudios' 'Laboratorio de Trabajo' Consejo Nacional de Universidades, Facultad de Odontologia, Universidad del Zulia.

Facultad de Humanidades (1967) 'El aprendizaje en la evaluacion' Boletin del Departamento de Pedagogia, Escuela de Educacion, ULA.

Farga, Victorino (1964) 'Algunas observaciones sobre Educacion Mexica' Documentos Universitarios, Revista Medica de Chile No 6 Ano (vol) 92, 470-47, Santiago de Chile.

Fraenkel, J R (1967) 'Formula la pregunta adecuada' Revista del Centre Regional 4, No 6 1971 UNESCO.

Hebel, Richard (1974) 'The Number of Questions Needed for Discriminatory Power on Multiple-Choice Examinations' British Journal of Medical Education, 49, 787-789.

Hullinger, Ronald L, Moon, Charles E and Render, Gary F (1973) 'Evaluation in Support of Learning' British Journal of Medical Education, 7, 182-185.

Lennox, Bernard and Lever, Rosemary (1970) 'Seminar of the Machine Marking of Medical Multiple-Choice Question Papers' British Journal of Medical Education, 4, 219-227.

Lipton, A and Huxman, G J (1970) 'Comparison of Multiple-Choice and Essay Testing in Preclinical Physiology' British Journal of Medical Education, 4, 228-238.

Man Pang Lau (1972) 'A Theory of Multiple-Choice Examination' British Journal of Medical Education, 6, 61-67.

Mattson, Dale E (1971) 'Criterio-Related Measures in Education' British Journal of Medical Education, 46, 185-189.

Mizrahi Harary, Clements (1967) 'Evaluacion en Educacion' VIII Congreso Venezolano de Ciencias Basicas, Academia Nacional de Medicina.

Nedelsky, Leo (1968) 'Ensenanza y Evaluacion en Educacion Dental' traduccion, Facultad de Odontologia, Universidad del Zulia, Maracaibo, Marzo 21.

Rommers, H H and Gage, N L (1943) 'Education Measurement and Evaluation' Harper & Brothers, New York.

Sanchez Hidalgo, Efrain (1963) 'Psicologia Educativa' Editorial Universitaria, Rio Piedra, Puerto Rica, 3rd ed.

'Seminario Sobre la Docencia de Ciencias Basicas en la Escuela de Medicina Jose Maria Vargas' (1969) Publicacion de la Oficina de Orientacion y Educacion Medica, Universidad Central de Venezuela.

Sharp, Buckley and Harris, F T C (1971) 'The Scoring of Multiple-Choice Questions' British Journal of Medical Education, 5, 279-288.

Velasco Martin, D Alfonso (1972) 'Evaluacion y Calificacion de los Estudiantes' Archivos de la Faculdad de Medicina de Madrid, Vol XXII, No 5, 267-287.

Villarroel, Cesar A 'Criterios y Escalas de Calificacion en la Educacion Superior' Revista de Pedagogia, No 3, Escuela de Pedagogia, Universidad Central de Venezuela.

Young, Stuart and Gillespie, Gordon (1972) 'Experience with the Multiple-Choice Paper in the Primary Fellowship Examination in Glasgow' British Journal of Medical Education, 6, 44-52.

Managing with Computers— Simulations in Management Education

R Morris

Introduction

Imagine yourself to be a supervisor who, six weeks ago, was given a new operator. Imagine that on at least one day each week, that man has turned up late, or has not been in at all. What would you do? Would you recommend him for dismissal? Would you harangue him? Would you find out from his previous employers if he had a record for absenteeism? Would you ask him what was wrong?

The position described here ('Joe Bailey' Action Maze) is typical of the simulation exercises used in modern management education. Such simulations allow trainee managers to investigate their natural management styles and find out how they work on idealized subjects. Other, more complex, situations allow the trainees to find out how their style works on real people — but that requires role-playing and contains some degree of personal risk. Using 'real people' also means that the motivation of everyone concerned must be maintained at a high level to be certain of good role-playing, and this is frequently attempted by staging an incident over a short period of time (say two hours). This incident may be an intellectual one (eg negotiating a wage increase, with some trainees playing the management, others the unions and the remainder watching), or one which uses mechanical aids (eg building a tower out of Lego!). Provided that everyone concerned is fully committed to a three-foot pile of Lego bricks, or can happily play the role of someone they have probably never seen (the union official), such simulations can be most helpful.

As school leavers and graduates become increasingly worldly wise, one might expect their acceptance of such unrealities to become less total. And this would seem to be the case. Established managers being subjected to a dose of reorientation are also demonstrably unenthusiastic about such activities. Management training is, therefore, in need of some new approaches, one of which is the computer-based business simulation.

Computer-Based Simulations

Although it has just been said that *new* techniques are needed, and that a computer-based simulation is one of them, it should be said that the history of such simulations stretches back over 20 years (Zoll, 1966). But industry has not yet generally recognised the role and application of them. To be honest, the simulations themselves have often left much to be desired, both in terms of fidelity and flexibility. For example, how can anyone become committed to a game in which the rules take longer to learn than the game takes to play? Such was the state of some of the early business games (Zoll, 1966). Now, with new computer technologies, it is possible to create simulations — not games — which are true to life, flexible and, above all, interesting.

It is the interest which a computer-based business simulation (henceforth called a COMSIM, to save space!) generates which makes it so valuable as a learning resource. Many of the lessons which managers need to learn are fairly simple ones to state — truisms one might say — but much more difficult to carry out. After all, to stay in business one only has to sell one's products for more than they cost to make. So keep your expenditure down, or your prices up! And getting people to do things for you is essentially a matter of asking them nicely.

Somehow, it doesn't always work as neatly as that in real life — though it can be made to do so in a standard management simulation. When people have pressures on them to meet deadlines, produce results, make decisions, communicate with their bosses, some of these universal truths get lost in the pursuit of lesser goals.

Comsims can be so engrossing — and that is a statement based on years of observing people immersed in them — that the participants almost accept them as real life. Practising the universal truths is a genuine learning experience which stays with the participants after they have left the learning environment. The Comsim, properly used, then becomes a vehicle for conveying any learning material which the tutors wish to load on it. That is not to say that a Comsim will always be successful. It must be well designed, have high business fidelity, be easy to use (for both tutors and participants), and must be contained within a good training design.

In short, if you decide to run a business game as a 'topic' within a course, do not expect anyone to learn anything. Think of it for what it is — a bit of light relief. However, if you design a course around a good simulation, you can expect a high degree of learning.

Categories of Learning

There are three categories which may be covered by a Comsim; in fact, some areas within these categories are necessary to the operation of the simulation; and part of the skill in designing a good course lies in establishing the required set of priorities and emphases in the mind of the trainee. Using some of the work of the London Business School (whose staff have recently been working along similar lines to those described here), one can look at learning under three categories:

1. Technical
2. Human (Relationships)
3. Conceptual (Business).

Traditional training methods may try to treat each of these separately using 'part-learning' methods. It is then hoped that the parts will come together to produce a whole — but the 'coming together' is largely left to chance. More often than not, single bits of each area are treated and then left to coalesce. (For example, learning about discounted cash flows or capital requisitions may be covered in two different 'lessons'.) Not surprisingly, they often do not come together, and the learner does not get an understanding of the concepts under-lying the techniques.

'Different managers operate with multiple and different frames of reference. A fluency in switching between their own frames of reference and in comprehending those used by others is a crucial skill ...'. *(See Information Leaflet DP4/01 — 'Management Decision-Making', National Development Programme in Computer-Assisted Learning.)*

In order to gain this skill rather special learning media are needed. It is fortuitous that Comsims will provide just such a medium.

The remainder of this paper will look at the development of one particular computer-based business simulation and its uses in the training of management and supervisory staff.

Technical

In 1970 when the idea of a Comsim to allow managers to practise 'switching between their frames of reference' was conceived within ICI Petrochemicals Division by Philip Youle and Jeff Farr, there were three large stumbling blocks to be overcome.

Firstly, most of the computers which were around only ran in 'batch' mode, that is, the user had to wait in a queue for anything from half an hour to one day! Data entry was via punched cards, and errors (due to rushing) were many. The result was that decisions often had to be processed overnight, with long 'fill in' lectures or exercises to disguise the delay. Of course, no one was fooled, and the Game became a game.

Secondly, computers had not been big enough to accommodate the large programs needed to give adequate fidelity. The result was low-fi models in which delegates were typically restricted to one product, three markets, and draconian restrictions on reducing prices or production. In particular, the games had to contain arbitrary rules which would prevent a division by zero. Delegates could see if one had occurred by looking for signs of hysteria in the tutors!

Finally, the cost of a week's rented computer time was generally in excess of a Training Department's annual budget. Trying to get time on an in-house machine, overloaded as they always were with the accounting suites, turned activities like looking for needles in haystacks, squeezing blood from stones or lassoing the moon into relatively trivial tasks.

Fortunately, time-shared computing was slowly becoming available, and through the RTS service the Division's computer specialists were able to produce a program which allowed up to four teams to sell three products into four markets. The teams could merge, lend each other money, go bankrupt and pursue any purchasing or selling policies they please (ethical or otherwise) without causing too much tutor-hysteria.

The program was given the name 'Counterpoint' ('Counterpoint' is an ICI Registered Trade Mark) and put to work in the Division's management development programme.

The course prepared around Counterpoint relied totally on the commitment generated by the experience of the simulation, with minimum tutor intervention. In the next two to three years most of the Division's management suffered at the hands of Counterpoint, with remarkably few dissidents (Morris, 1971).

A basic structure ensured that teams produced budgets and objectives, and reviewed these 'annually'. It insisted on external approval for expansion, and in doing so encouraged teams to investigate project-planning and financial forecasting techniques (though it must be said that the computer facilities were not able to cope with these aspects, which had to be done by hand). In this way, the technical category of learning was incorporated. There is, of course, the point that only those delegates who were unfamiliar with the technical elements needed to learn them — others just applied them. If a team contained a mix of talents and experience, people could — and did — learn from each other. As said earlier, this learning was taking place in parallel with a host of other activities.

'Running in parallel was the normal in-company running of a business. Each company was preparing budgets, balance sheets, expenditure proposals and flow-charting its information, decision-making and control systems for the course tutors to monitor. Each company was still making the same sets of decisions on price, marketing, research and development, production, loans, dividends, etc. They were also submitting to the course tutors records of their variance from predicted values of both income and expenditure as well as any changes in their system of operation, or their objectives. They were controlling most aspects of a modern business.'

Human Relationships

It has been argued that using a Comsim to deal with Human Relationships training is like taking a sledge-hammer to crack a nut. Apart from the fact that such an argument devalues the importance of the human touch in business, the impact of human problems on a technically-oriented group is wonderful to see and the learning is considerable.

Within a simulation context, relationships take three very distinct forms. That between team-members (intra-group); that between teams (inter-group); and external relations with the tutors, technical advisors, and any of the learning materials provided (programmed texts, tape-slide presentations etc).

Perhaps one of the most significant observations on the Counterpoint course was the team's progression from technical, to intra-group, inter-group and finally to external relationships (Bloom *et al*, 1956).

But what is it that people gain from a computer-based simulation such as Counterpoint which they cannot gain from the more traditional management exercises? Some of the shortcomings of the usual exercise have been mentioned earlier — piece-meal learning, motivation and commitment problems — and it must be admitted that the gain is more by using technology to overcome these shortcomings than through new features. What the simulation adds is a complexity which allows for 'parallel learning', and a computational facility which allows delegates to concentrate on the things which are important to them.

So far, we have been looking at group behaviour and attitudes, but what is said of the group is equally true of individuals. Many of the interactive skills techniques which have been developed in the past few years have suffered from the relatively weak situation dramas used to provide practice. The fact that people seem to believe (if only briefly) in their Comsim environment makes it a much more potent learning vehicle, as has been demonstrated many times.

Concepts

Finally we have the Conceptual category. In this category one can put learning such as 'understanding the role of money in a business'. That may not be a good behavioural objective, but it describes the need of those who believe that a company's annual profits are shared out between its directors! (True — there are people who believe that!) In some way, it also describes the transition from knowing that profits are only possible if sales income is greater than expenditures, to actually doing it.

' "We found out how important cash is in a business"; "We discovered that you have to make a lot of profit just to pay the taxman"; "We did not take (sufficient) account of depreciation". These were some of the more common comments which were received when participants were asked what they had got out of (it).' (Holman and Morris, 1976.)

The acceptance of a Conceptual basis for business operations depends on your views on 'insight' and 'judgement', but an article in the *Harvard Business Review* (Harvard Business Review, 1976) provides an interesting hypothesis to support the view that forms of 'insight' activity occur. Whatever one's view, there can be little doubt that there is more to business success than the sum of the parts, and perhaps — just perhaps — the use of a Comsim will help to establish some of the 'charisma' needed to be successful in modern business.

Recent Developments

When the original Counterpoint simulation was fully operational some three to four years ago, the facilities of the computers then available were being stretched to the limit — and sometimes beyond it. By 1975, however, there had been such advances in hardware technology that it seemed the right time to reappraise the program to see how these advances could be used to improve the learning experiences for trainees.

During the 1970s, the role of the computer in business had also altered. When Counterpoint was devised, most computers were seen by 'user' management as the plaything of the Data Processing Department, and 'user' management had to use the Reports given to them by the DP Department. Requests for changes to Reports were treated with a mixture of horror and cynicism, and barriers grew between departments. By 1975 data-base techniques were well developed, and some of the country's more enlightened companies were starting to use them as 'Management Information Systems'. Clearly some training was needed for user management to add this dimension to existing frames of reference. This view was supported by the National Computer Centre which said:

'The major problem in providing practical training for managers is to produce a suitable vehicle ... Experience has shown that the only satisfactory way to ensure an appreciation of the overall problem of information processing and retrieval is to use a large scale case-study or game. Individual exercises are useful for the appreciation of particular techniques, but often result in the student not being able to see the wood for the trees.

'The large-scale study, on the other hand, requires more time for initial appreciation of the situation, time which managers can ill-afford. Hence the problem is to provide some vehicle which is sufficiently complex to provide a near approach to a real life management situation, while at the same time being simple enough to enable the student to comprehend it within a matter of hours.

'Additional problems arise when the vehicle involves the hands-on use of a computer. The student must be taught some sort of language with which he can communicate with the machine. It must be simple, enabling him to get the information he wants without having to worry about the detail and idiosyncracies of the particular system being used. Ideally he should be able to get something useful out of the machine within an hour or two.

'However, it must not be made to appear too easy. The student must not go away with the idea that he can get all he wants by pressing a couple of buttons. He must be given an awareness that getting the right information out of the system depends upon, firstly, collecting, validating and organising all the necessary data, and secondly, having a well designed system using a lot of complex hardware and software.' (Morton, 1976.)

A joint venture between NCC and CAP/ITB emerged, with the original Counterpoint program (with the agreement of ICI) to meet the aims expressed in Ray Morton's article.

Thus a new suite of programs was developed during 1975/76 which gave participants direct access to a data-base. The original Reports (printed by a computer terminal) went, and teams were allowed to ask for the information they wanted. Decisions, previously entered by the long-suffering tutors, were put in directly by team-members using a terminal. More important, the suite of programs used to check the decisions produced a speculative profit and loss account. Teams which did not like the look of the results the computer expected them to achieve could change their decisions — time and again if they so wished — until the time came to run to main simulation program. (The entire system as presently envisaged is shown in Figure 1.)

The Simulation

The NCC/CAPITB simulation has extended the range of variables in the original Counterpoint programs by introducing various raw materials (again an indefinite number, restricted only by computer capacity) any or all of which may be needed for more than one product. In this way the technical aspects of resource allocation can be investigated, or co-operation between 'Production Managers' can be encouraged. A maintenance budget, which significantly affects production costs, has also been added.

The most significant enhancement from the user's viewpoint is, however, the introduction of on-linework. Every interaction between teams and the computer is initiated by the team through the suite of programs enclosing the simulation.

Tutor intervention only occurs if the environment is to be changed (economic conditions, minimum lending rate, tariff barriers, strikes etc) or to initiate the simulation run.

Since the simulation compares the decisions of each team before calculating orders and sales, every team must have a valid set of decisions on its file. Each team has its own file which cannot be reached by other teams — and enough have tried for us to be sure that the protection is secure. When the simulation run is started, it first computes the total orders available in the market then, by looking at the past and present marketing policies of each team, allocates those orders. At this stage the simulation appears (to the participants) to be behaving heuristically, or at least probabilistically. In fact there are no probability factors in the simulation which performs its allocations according to sets of equations which relate each team's decisions to the others.

Once orders are determined, production gets under way, completely deterministically. Each product is produced in an order of priority, to the extent that raw materials are available. Thus, a raw material shortage will result in a loss of production. Each loss of production carries penalties over and above those of potential loss of earnings. Other production costs include labour and overheads.

Sales are made to each market in proportion until orders are achieved, or finished goods stock runs out. In this latter case, the team loses orders in the following period!

Finally, interest on loans from the bank is calculated, and new loan potentials computed on the strength of each company's performance in relation to the performance of the others. Results are transferred by the simulation to the data-bases ready for interrogation by the competing teams. With a good computer system the complete process, from the initiation of the simulation run to the updating of the data-base should not take more than a couple of minutes — five at the most.

The complete system is designed to be controlled from teletype terminals via

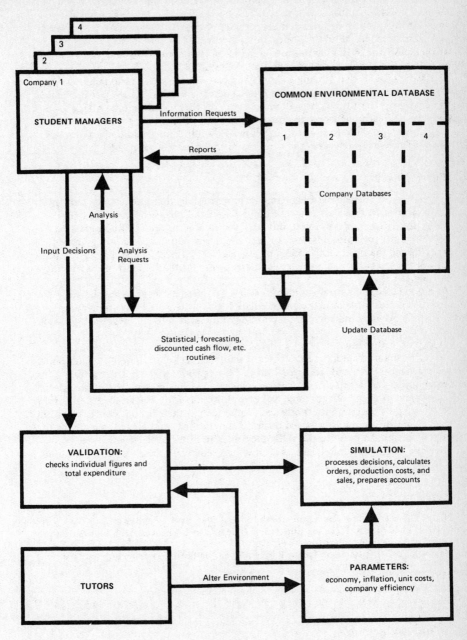

Figure 1.

GPO lines to the central processer. At the present, this means linking to the NCC ICL 1905F, but it is intended to make it available through DEC 10 and Sigma 9 computers, both of which have very sophisticated time-sharing interfaces. In this way any obligation on the part of tutors to learn about computers can be minimized. Mind you, they should expect to be able to use one, since one of the aims of introducing on-line facilities to a company is so that everyone will be able to use the tool, rather than be used by it.

Having said all that, the new simulation can be operated in the same way as Counterpoint if on-line experience is not one of your aims. That is, teams make the decisions, the tutors enter them and process them, and report-writing programs, already incorporated into the suite, produce paper for teams to read.

It is even possible to run it in batch mode — but that would be bad practice, since it necessarily relegates the Comsim to the level of a game.

Where Next?

Technology in all fields is advancing far more rapidly than the average person can conceive. In those areas where immediate benefits can be measured, and where specialists are employed, industry is well able to turn technological developments into practical use. In the computer field, LSI technology has transformed main-frame thinking, produced calculators for 'under a fiver', and turned the television set into games of electronic football, tennis, motor-racing and the OK Corral.

Regrettably, industrial training does not yet have its share of specialists — and it can seldom demonstrate immediate benefits. It is unlikely, therefore, that the hardware and software technology now available will become out-dated quickly.

Rather, effort must now be diverted to helping industry make use of the educational and training technologies available to it. Programmed learning came — and went — but needs to be revived to fill its proper place in the training regime (and that is not as a universal panacea). Various ed tech methodologies known and used in colleges need to be established within the armoury of training officers, and simulation methods need to be seen in their proper context. Within this framework, computer-based business simulations can be used as a means of helping people to practise the skills they need in order to be effective in business. Through pilot studies we know that, correctly used by skilled training staff, they are effective.

References

Bloom, B S et al (1956) 'Taxonomy of Educational Objectives' Longmans.
Holman, J and Morris, R (1976) 'Simulation Training Part 5 Uncovering Business Talent' Industrial Training International, September.
Morris, R (1971) 'Turning on Latent Business Talent' Industrial Training International, November.
Morton, R (1976) 'Courses to Match Advancing Technology' January.
Zoll, A A (1966) 'Dynamic Management Education' Addison Wesley.
'Planning on the Left Side, Managing on the Right' Harvard Business Review, July 1976.

Acknowledgements

The idea for the 'Counterpoint' business simulation, from which everything else followed, came from Jeff Farr of ICI (Petrochemicals) to whom I offer my thanks for his efforts during the development phase, support in application, and permission to use his brain-child with other people and applications.

I would also like to acknowledge the work of Ray Morton and his colleagues at the National Computing Centre in developing the 'Counterpoint' concept into a new form for the new conditions in which we are operating.

Willing Horse, Camel and Committee—
a Description of Innovation
in a College of Technology

A Logan

Introduction

It must be emphasized at the start that 'the refreshing definition of a camel: a horse planned by a committee' (Adams 1969) is not relevant to this paper. Max Black in his book *Models and Metaphors* (Black 1962) warns of the dangers inherent in the use of analogies and so it might be useful for the words 'willing horse', 'camel' and 'committee' to be defined for the purposes of this paper.

The willing horse is the teacher who wishes to use alternative techniques (there are ways of doing and thinking which do not necessarily conform to a traditional view of teaching). This teacher has 'horse sense — or put another way, is a stable thinker' (Levinson 1970).

The camel has been defined as an animal that ruined its shape trying to get through the eye of a needle (Levinson 1970). In this case the camel is the willing horse, who, unable to pursue its inclinations because of organizational and social inhibitions within and around the institution in which it works, takes the 'hump'.

A committee has been described as a group that keeps minutes and wastes hours (Levinson 1970). The committee concept which is to be preferred is a committee which does keep minutes in order that information be made freely available to all interested parties. It does not waste hours but saves *ours*, 'ours' being the resources available to an institution, and the committee conceived in this paper endeavours to maximize and improve efficiency in the use of resources. Charles Lamb wrote 'A pun is a pistol let off at the ear, not a feather to tickle the intellect' (Adams 1969) and so having cleared the air it is now possible, perhaps even advisable, to move to the main purpose of this paper.

In 1973 Dumfries Technical College was situated in the centre of the town of Dumfries, and was housed in old school premises. At that time the first phase of a new college (The Dumfries and Galloway College of Technology) was in the process of completion.

On the 13th February 1973 the first meeting of the College Educational Technology Committee took place. As a direct result of that meeting and subsequent meetings of the committee, students at the college are not only better accommodated, but are being taught by lecturers using a variety of techniques and aids which were not used before. Since this paper describes all the factors which were taken into account in the innovative process at the college, two pertinent points arise from the previous statements. The first that should be noted is that there was a mood of change among the lecturers, arising from the move to new premises and to what extent this influenced the innovative process is not known, but it is a variable which cannot be excluded. The second factor was the College Educational Technology Committee. This is a much more important factor and will be expanded later.

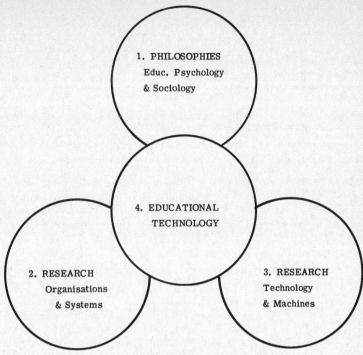

Figure 1. *Rationale*

Other factors which were and still are being taken into account, since the process is ongoing, are listed below:

1. The innovation — educational technology
2. The existing college authority
3. The lecturers as individuals (personality profiles etc)
4. The lecturers in social and working groups
5. The innovator
6. The original college organizational structure
7. The organizational structure which the innovator would attempt to obtain.

Factors 1 and 5 are related since the term educational technology can mean different things to different people. Factors 2 and 6 might appear to be synonymous, but it will be submitted that they are not necessarily as closely connected as would appear initially.

Each of the above factors (which are not in a hierarchy of priorities) can only be briefly explained in a paper such as this and it is hoped that the brevity of explanation will not derogate the importance of their study in relation to an innovative exercise.

Educational Technology

1. Philosophies which accentuate the importance of the individual are represented here. Educational psychology and sociology are also

included here.

2. Organization and methods, systems approach etc, in fact any technique which endeavours to optimize the efficient working of any system, is represented here.

3. New machines and equipment, and adaptations of equipment which can be incorporated into the above systems and which can be shown to increase the efficiency of a system, are represented here.

4. Established principles and research findings which have stood up to contemporary re-examination are exemplified, and their importance re-affirmed by the new technology.

The College Authority

The principal is the ultimate authority within the college. He delegates areas of authority to the Depute Principal. For example, the Depute Principal represents 'authority' on the College Educational Technology Committee. The Principal is also aided by the Principal's Management Committee which consists of the Principal, Depute Principal, Heads of Department and College Registrar.

The Lecturers (Individuals)

It seems important for the innovator to realize that teachers were taught by teachers and they believe they owe their present success to the fact that they accepted the methods used to teach them. All they are and all they own proves the validity and reliability of their present methods. It is almost as if the innovator, in suggesting change, is denying them their birthright. This could apply particularly to promoted staff. To use an Americanism, 'How can you change the ball game when these guys have reached first, second or third base?' A resistance to change from promoted staff is almost inevitable (MaClure 1975).

The Lecturers (Social and Working Groups)

The behaviour and attitude exhibited by people in groups may have a completely different set of determinants from that which they would or might exhibit as individuals (Musgrove 1972, Biddle and Ellena 1964, Sayles and Strauss 1966, Hargreaves 1972). Most lecturers at the College endorsed the idea of educational technology when they responded to questions in a post-test given after a series of dissemination sessions. Although there was still a fairly positive vote at a subsequent public meeting, the positive vote was not as high as had been obtained by the summation of individual post-test results.

The Innovator

The writer of this paper realizes that, as a reporter of events in which he was a participant, this part of the paper might be more subjective than others. There are, however, certain facts which appear salient. The first is the definition of the term 'innovator' in respect of this study. Some writers use the term change agents (Gross et al 1971). Reddin uses the same term and defines a background of training for such an agent (Reddin 1970). Brembreck and Howell conceptualize a persuader and include trust or ethos as an important character trait along with a high reputation. They couple the persuader with an opinion leader who by showing he accepts the ideas of the persuader, influences others to do the same (Brembreck and Howell 1976).

144

The writer was unable to reconcile completely these ideas with the 'innovator'. Greiner analyzed the reports on a study of a number of organizational change efforts and selected a set of common characteristics pertaining to all the successful change efforts which were not present in the less successful ones.

Here is the list:

1. There is pressure on the top management which induces some arousal to action.
2. There is some form of intervention at the top, either a new member of the organization, or a consultant, or a new staff head in organization development. This induces some reorientation in looking at internal problems.
3. There is a diagnosis of the problem areas and this induces an analysis of specific problems.
4. There is an invention of some new solutions to problems and this produces some commitment to new courses of action.
5. There is some experimentation with new solutions and this produces a search for results with the experiments.
6. There is reinforcement in the system from positive results and this produces acceptance of the new practices (Greiner 1967).

The characteristic number 2 on the list appears relevant and as the writer took up a post as a consultant in the College, this seems appropriate.

Lawrence and Lorsch call a change agent an organizational development specialist (Lawrence and Lorsch 1969). Speaking of OD specialists they say that top decision-making must have confidence in the OD specialist. It would appear that the 'innovator' could be a combination of two people, a specialist, and someone in authority who can make decisions about implementation. In this case the writer supplied the ideas and the Depute Principal refined them and provided the necessary authority for their implementation.

If innovation is seen as only the initial acts of a continuing process then the Depute Principal and the educational technologist are the 'innovator'. If, however, innovation is seen as a continuing process then the 'innovator' in the College would now be the Educational Technology Committee.

One further fact would appear important. Shipman states:

'The spread of an innovation involves increasing numbers of teachers who lack the skills and enthusiasm of the pioneers. The promotion prospects of involvement in an innovation are rapidly exhausted and the ambitious look to the next bandwagon. The result is that an apparently successful innovation in the hands of a few can fail when generally adopted and diluted.' (Shipman 1974.)

In the light of the above quotation it should be noted that the writer remained in the College as College Educational Technologist and a major part of his work is to prevent entropy.

The Original College Organizational Structure

The ultimate authority in the College is vested in the Principal and the diagram (Figure 2) shows the original College structure.

The Organizational Structure (Innovative)

The organizational structure which replaced the one above is shown in Figure 3. Here the Educational Technology Committee make direct representation to the Principal.

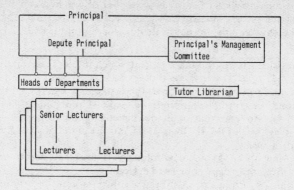

Figure 2.

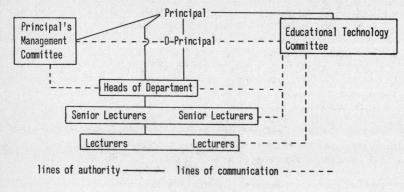

lines of authority ————— lines of communication — — — — —

Figure 3.

The composition of the Educational Technology Committee is as follows: one elected representative from each department, plus one elected member from senior staff representing heads of departments and senior lecturers. The remainder of the Committee is made up of the Depute Principal, the Head of Learning Resource Centre and the educational technologist. The Educational Technology Committee is primarily concerned with teaching methods, but can as part of its remit point out where it thinks administrative constraints are inhibiting progress. Another prime function of the Committee is to ensure that the College assimilates the innovation at a rate it can comfortably sustain. It will be appreciated from this remark that it is not necessarily desirable that all members of the Committee avidly endorse educational technology.

Factors Involved in Innovation

The factors involved in the innovative process have been outlined and are shown in a schematic diagram below.

The numbers in brackets relate to the factors described earlier. Areas F, D and G, have no factor numbers. Area G represents a facet or stage of the innovation

146

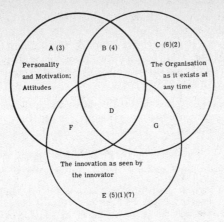

Figure 4. *Factors in innovation*

under consideration. It is not possible to implement the whole innovation at one stroke using the technique described in this paper. Area F denotes the relationship between other lecturers and the writer, who retrained as an educational technologist, moving from a peripheral position in the College structure to a more centralized one. The writer as a researcher caused little reaction in area F, but as developments took place change occurred in this area, particularly when the writer adopted a change of role in the organization from being merely a disseminator of information (on educational technology) to that of educational technologist. The problems inherent in such role changes are complex and can cause problems (Hardgreaves 1972, Levy 1970, Biddle, BJ 1961).

Area D represents the area of decision. Decisions can be made with greater confidence when the other areas are studied, researched and hypotheses developed and tested.

Before the formation of the Educational Technology Committee decisions in area D were made by the writer with approval of the College Principal and Depute Principal. The Committee now operates in area D and decisions affecting the College organization are passed to the Principal as recommendations.

The obvious fulcrum on which innovation in the College now turns is the Educational Technology Committee.

The study of innovation and subsequent planning commenced a number of years before the inception of educational technology in the College. The decision, for example, to offer the staff the opportunity to form an Educational Technology Committee was not arbitrary. It evolved from the study of prevailing conditions. The idea was that the innovation should grow from the initiative of individual staff members and not be something overlaid in the hope that it might permeate down through the organization. It seemed appropriate that the teacher in the classroom should be given some say and a committee appeared the best way of achieving this.

The sequence of events which preceded the formation of the Committee are important and are briefly described below.

Stage I Secondment of the writer to qualify as an educational technologist.

Stage II A one-year study of the factors or variables involved in the innovative process with particular reference to Dumfries Technical College.

147

Stage III Every member of the teaching staff (including promoted staff) attended compulsory sessions consisting of lecture and discussion. Each person attended as part of a group of between five and eight members. The dissemination periods were used to (a) clear up misconceptions about educational technology and (b) pose questions during the discussion sessions which, by way of cognitive dissonance, might promote action (Logan 1972).

Stage IV A post-test was given and the results showed that the majority of lecturers endorsed the innovation with the qualification that they had some control over its implementation.

Stage V A full staff meeting confirmed the results of the post-test.

The following quotation by Katz and Kahn, 1966, is particularly relevant:

'The major error in dealing with problems of organizational change both at the practical and theoretical level is to disregard the systematic properties of the organization and to confuse individual change with modifications in organizational variables, behaviour related to such things as role relationships.... The confusion between individual and organizational change is due in part of lack of precise terminology for distinguishing between behaviour determined largely by structured roles within a system and behaviour determined more directly by personality needs and values. The behaviour of people in organizations is still the behaviour of individuals, but it has a different set of determinants.......... scientists and practitioners have assumed too often that an individual change will produce a corresponding organizational change. This assumption seems to us indefensible.' (Gross *et al,* 1971).

It must be stressed that individual change, in the writer's opinion, precedes organizational change and the individual change should occur as a result of persuasion (Brembeck and Howell 1976).

Persuasion implies choice. Persons must be given the opportunity to choose whether to accept or reject the innovation. In the situation described by this paper each lecturer can choose whether or not to adopt new techniques and also decide the degree of use.

The Committee ensures that facilities are freely available to those who wish to use them. The Committee would also feel obliged to act where a lecturer was being coerced into using a system or technique which he could not ethically or practically endorse.

Innovation demands a change of attitude and the means whereby a change of attitude can be transmitted into action.

The fact is, old attitudes take time to change and if the attitude is fundamental and basic then it takes a long time, longer than most innovators can afford, and so the innovation falls into a stage of discontinuance (Rogers 1962).

Innovation and attitude change take time. Those who wish to innovate must appreciate how the interaction of one variable upon another affects the situation prevailing at any one time. The situation is never static, so decisions made previously may need modification. New decisions, however, will be based on a re-appraisal of all relevant variables.

The decision-making machinery in an organization must be sensitive to change. It must also be flexible so that it can make modifications and thus keep an innovation on course.

References

Adams, A K (1969) 'Cassell's Book of Humorous Quotations' Cassell, London, pp 24-1, 174-6.
Bembreck, W L and Howell, W S (1976) 'Persuasion a Means of Social Influence', 2nd Ed,

Prentice Hall Inc, Englewood Cliffs, New Jersey, pp260,261.

Biddle, B J (1961) 'The Present Status of Role Theory', University of Missouri, USA.

Biddle, B J and Ellena, W J (1964) 'Contemporary Research on Teacher Effectiveness' Holt Rinehart and Winston Inc, USA, p39.

Black, M (1962) 'Models and Metaphors' Ithea Cornell University Press, Chapter 13.

Greiner, L E (1967) 'Patterns of Organizations Change' Harvard Business Review 45, No 3, May/June 1967.

Gross, N et al (1971) 'Implementing Organizational Innovations' Harper International Edition, Harper Row Publishers, London, pp23, 15.

Hardgreaves, D H (1972) 'Interpersonal Relations and Education' Routledge Kegan Paul, London, Chapters 9, 4.

Lawrence, P R and Lorsch, J W (1969) 'Developing Organizations, Diagnosis and Action' Adison-Wesley Publishing Co, London, p95.

Levinson, L L (1970) 'The Left-Handed Dictionary' Collier Books, Collier-MacMillan Ltd, London, pp107,37,48.

Levy, H L (1970) 'Conceptions of Personality, Theories and Research' Random House, New York, pp309,354.

Logan, A (1972) 'Cognitive Dissonance a Tool for Innovation' Unpublished Dissertation, DPLET, Birmingham University.

MaClure, S (1975) 'British Journal of Educational Technology' No 2, Vol 6, May 1975.

Musgrove, P W (1972) 'The Sociology of Education' 2nd edition, Methuen and Co Ltd, London, pp231,223.

Rogers, E M (1962) 'Diffusion of Innovations' New York, The Free Press of Glencoe.

Reddin, W J (1970) 'Industrial Training International' March 1970, No 3, Vol 5, pp132-4.

Sayles, R S and Strauss, G (1966) 'Human Behaviour in Organizations, Prentice Hall International, USA, pp305-307.

Shipman, M (1974) 'Inside a Curriculum Project' London, Methuen, p36.

Implementing a CML System— the Tutor's Role in Course Development and Teaching

H F McMahon, J S A Anderson

Introduction

The work at the Education Centre of the New University of Ulster, in association with the National Development Programme in Computer-Assisted Learning, has involved the development of a content-free computer-managed learning (CML) system called CAMOL and its implementation in a semester-long course in Curriculum Design and Development, offered to a large and heterogeneous group of pre-service teaching trainees and staffed by a single academic tutor.

We examine, firstly, the tutor's role as course developer during the run-up to course commencement and secondly, as teacher during the course itself, as he uses the CML to overcome the burdens of this teaching situation without diminishing the quality of teaching and learning (McMahon and Jenkins, 1976; McConnellogue, McMahon and Anderson, in press).

Course Establishment — the Tutor as Developer

The development of any new course requires considerable investment of time and expertise, and much has been written on the various development strategies which could or should be employed. A similar analysis, touching on the problems of specifying objectives, selecting content, media and assessment procedures could be made here, for many if not most of the problems facing the developer of a CML course are much the same as those facing the developer of any multi-media individualized course. We will concentrate our attention on those development functions which arise directly from the impact of the functions of the computer as manager of learning.

The starting point for a course developer in CML can be a statement of course objectives, an exploration of the needs of students, an epistemological analysis of the course content, a catalogue of learning resources or whatever, but sooner or later he comes up against the design characteristics of the CML system, in our case CAMOL (Rushby *et al*, 1976). These may well have been established with a view to the provision of maximum flexibility and adaptability (Rushby and McMahon, 1977) but like a two-edged sword they can be wielded to constrain or to liberate, or both. Lest the reader assumes otherwise, we have quite deliberately used both sides of the sword.

The design characteristics of CAMOL, notionally described as a content and context-free computer management system, are such as to provide these facilities:

— a test marking program;
— a test analysis program (handling both objective computer-marked questions and subjective tutor-marked questions);

- a routing program;
- a record-keeping program;
- a report production for staff;
- report production for students.

An early decision for the tutor as course developer is the level of operation of the CML system. If the lower of the levels is chosen, then development time is cut dramatically, for at this level the computer is used only to mark tests, to record and to report. The test marking, recording and straight reporting facilities are used in a manner synonymous with data processing and 'number crunching'. Such a computer facility is in itself a clerical boon to the time-consuming need of universities and other awarding institutions to process and mark large numbers of end-of-course and final examinations where the only output required is a score or grade. Development cost is relatively low because the only major educational input not otherwise involved is the development of objective tests for computer marking. Indeed, the system could operate at this level without reliance on such tests, if so desired. Alternatively the course designer may choose, as we did, to implement CML at a higher, more sophisticated, level where in addition the comment generation and routing facilities are deployed to make possible:

- the use of tests as learning and study aids;
- the rapid provision to students of information on their own levels or performance *vis-à-vis* the study material upon which further study, review or revision decisions can be made;
- variation on an individual basis and for a large number of students of the type and amount of tutorial assistance provided in support of student learning;
- management of the extent to which the study programme of an individual student is prescribed by the tutor or controlled by the student.

Through three cycles of development and teaching in the years 1974/75, 1975/76 and 1976/77 we have evolved, and evaluated in use, a CML system which exhibits these features.

The system as it operated over a twelve-week course in the autumn of 1976/77 was underpinned by a management-of-learning model which operates upon a basic dimension of prescription of curricular elements and control of progression within the course, where control can reside at a range of positions between the teacher and the student for any individual, dependent upon a variety of educational factors which can be recognized by the computer's routing programs. For us, 'management' does not equate with 'tutor prescription' of learning. It equates with management of learning in an environment containing a number of learning tasks or situations each containing in turn different levels of balance between student and tutor control — and varying individually for large heterogeneous learning groups. These tasks are differentiated by the concept of control, and so concepts of 'control' reside at the centre of both our course development and evaluation analytic frameworks.

The major design feature which has emerged during course development is the distinction between what we call 'independent study' and 'guided study'. In independent study the student has freedom of choice of study material and is left to make his own decisions on the pace and sequence of his study and the use of computer-marked diagnostic tests. In contrast, students who either opt for or are directed to guided study can expect a high degree of tutor control. Acting as course developer the tutor is able in advance to prescribe a structure of study routes, through which the student on guided study is directed on a lock-step basis. The precise route he takes and the extent to which extra tutorial resources are brought to bear in support of his learning depends largely on the student's declared preferences for learning via face-to-face staff-student contact.

Upon entering the course students embark on a four-week study period, supported by lectures, during which all students are deemed to be on independent study. However, at this early stage of the course the control of sequence and pace of learning lie largely with the tutor as he operates through the lecture system. During this four-week period students are induced into the use of the CAMOL-marked diagnostic tests and, depending on their performance and on their response to an invitation to see their tutor to discuss progress to date, may or may not be invited or directed to seminars and/or tutorials. This four-week introduction culminates with an in-course assessment test which adds further information upon which the tutor is able to 'sort' students into those who are directed into guided study and those who are given the opportunity of opting into guided study or of remaining on independent study.

This division of students into two cycles, one obtaining structure and support on a tutor-regulated basis with the other allowing independence and student self-reliance, characterize the management routine of the rest of the course. However, implicit in the management model is a set of objectives which are a reflection of an ideology of teacher education at NUU. In addition to the cognitive objectives of performance and attainment which the two learning styles aim to support, there are the additional social learning objectives of providing student teachers with situations in which they are required to make their own learning decisions, and to take responsibility for success and failure and to face the ambiguities which that implies. The tutor can valuably spend his time, not only in fostering students' cognitive learning while on guided study, but in easing and 'weaning' them into a decision-taking mode, removing direction gradually but leaving support available for those who need it.

The major formal mechanism for identifying student needs is our application of CML in the diagnostic test. It is on the evidence of these test results that students are, for example, encouraged to diversify their study, advised to carry out revision, invited to a seminar or directed to attend an individual tutorial after revising a particular topic. The design and implementation of these tests raises development problems, some of which are unique to computer-managed learning.

Typically, a diagnostic test would be taken by a student on an individual basis some time during the study of a course module, which would on average occupy about two weeks of the student's time on the computer-managed course — which in turn is designed to be one-third of the student's total work load. Aiming for such a norm is in itself a major design decision. Fewer tests would on average be farther apart in time, would cover substantially more content and thus involve less compartmentalization of knowledge, would be larger and therefore more reliable, would place less demand on computer usage; but would give both students and tutor less rapid feedback on progress, and might also cause severe resource provision problems if students were to leave much of their study to the end of an extended cycle of work, as the research evidence suggests they often do.

Taking the development decision to go for more frequent tests would lead to more rapid feedback to users and would spread the load on resources more evenly; but at the probable cost of loss of synthesis of knowledge, lower reliability in smaller tests, increased demand on computer time, data preparation services and the like.

Our experience in designing diagnostic tests for computer managed learning in Curriculum Design and Development has resulted in what we would accept as an uneasy compromise between the two approaches of criterion and norm-referenced testing. Without question the computer analysis of a student's performance on the total test and sub-sections of the test, upon which routing decisions are based, reflects the ideology of criterion-referenced testing. For example, in a test with two content sub-sections the student's score on objective test items in each of the sub-sections would be measured against criterion scores, and the student routed to revision in either or both sections or to new study depending on whether or not he has reached the criterion score. However, we have moved some distance away from implementing the mastery learning model by introducing criterion scores at several levels — not just at the so-called mastery level — and by drawing back from the claim that on each test item the student is either entirely right or entirely wrong, and that if right his score on that item contributes uniquely to a measure of the mastery or non-mastery of a specified learning objective.

Both these decisions, to use multiple-level criteria for routing and to write 'soft-edged' objective test items have followed from our intention to manage the extent to which the study programme of an individual student is prescribed by the tutor or controlled by the student.

We can best illustrate the outcome of using multiple-level criteria by giving examples of the general comments appearing on the computer print-out which a student receives after taking his diagnostic test. Depending on the level of his performance on sub-sections of the test the student, whether on independent or guided study, receives one or other of anything up to 16 so-called 'assessment' comments which lie on a spectrum running from high student performance and low tutor control to low student performance and increased tutor control. The purpose of the assessment comment is to give feedback to the student on his test performance and to suggest a broadening of study or consolidation through specific revision. In general, the student is left in control of the content, pace and sequencing of further study, and only in cases of very poor performance is the individual tutorial suggested or required. For example, in a test on curriculum development in the United Kingdom there are 16 possible assessment comments, two of which are illustrated below:

'This is an excellent performance, though perhaps you should look again at the few questions you missed on N Ireland. If your performance on the rest of Unit 7 reaches this level, why not consider broadening your study by looking at either Unit 5 or 6 as well?'

'You seem to have gone for all the "wrong" answers. It seems to me that we should go through the questions together as soon as possible, so please call at B114 straight away.'

In addition to the appropriate assessment comment, students on guided study also receive one of a spectrum of 'assignment' comments which again reflect a dimension running from routing by student decision to routing by tutor prescription. The purpose of the assignment comment is to direct the student to his next study on a lock-step basis and to deploy the resources available in the person of the tutor in support of those students who have both opted for this kind of support and shown that they need it. For the same test, 16 such additional comments are possible. Here are two:

'Perhaps you should consider returning to independent study so that you can continue to work under your own steam? If you decide to stay on guided study your next deadline is to complete diagnostic test 121 by Friday 26th November at the latest.'

'And I would strongly recommend that you attend the seminar on "Setting the Scene" on Tuesday 23rd November at 9.15 in LT1. Your deadline for completing the next diagnostic test 121 is Friday 26th November.'

When an assessment and an assignment comment are printed out for a student on guided study they appear as a single extended comment. A major problem is that of predicting the 'live' performance of the tests and, in particular, students' responses to the assessment and assignment comments they receive. The frightening thought which eats away in the sub-conscious mind of the course designer is that if the performance criteria are set at too high a level, if the test items have too low a facility, and if the students respond unpredictably by rapidly obeying directive comments, then he could have, as tutor, 200 students lining up outside his door, baying either for an individual tutorial or the computer's blood.

We have found that the only realistic way to design and implement such tests in an ongoing development situation is to consider carefully what one would say in a face-to-face situation to a student who had performed in the test in a particular way, to trust one's intuitive judgement as to the probability of the student following through the suggestion or direction when he receives it via the computer, to implement and hope for the best.

The style to use in the so-called 'corrective' comments which are related to each item within the test has been a key development decision in our implementation of CML. The use of the term 'corrective' suggests that the prime purpose of these comments is to tell the student if he is right or wrong. We have them in this mode:

'Yes: Phil McConnellogue's research indicates that primary school teachers in N Ireland in general want and expect control of the curriculum via syllabusses and programme guides.'

But increasingly, we find ourselves moving into a more speculative style which attempts to indicate to the student the problematic nature of the knowledge under analysis, and the personal interpretation of the tutor. Hence:

'For me, "E" is the best answer at the moment. There are exceptions, but on the whole curriculum development is not based firmly on research. With luck, in the future the best answer will be "D".'

Some idea of the size of the development task involved in comment writing can be indicated by the fact that for a one-semester course we have generated approximately 240 of the general assessment and assignment comments which are used for routing and about 1000 corrective comments for diagnostic test items.

At the very heart of the computer-managed learning system lie the so-called decision tables. These are the technical devices which are used by the computer to select the appropriate routing comments for individual students at different points in the course. The task of the tutor as developer is to design these decision tables so that all possible combinations of levels of student performance on each sub-section of the diagnostic test are identified, and each associated with a particular assessment or assignment comment. This is an exercise which in its technical aspects is not unlike filling in the football pools, but in terms of its educational implications it is the linchpin of decision-making at the design stage. The identification of points in the course where routing decisions must be made; the design of diagnostic tests; the specification of criteria at multiple levels within sub-sections of the tests; the possible use of criteria for routing other than the student's test performance, for example, his request for a tutorial; the generation of all possible permutations of satisfied and unsatisfied criteria and the writing of the associated assignment and assessment comments for each of them: the output from these development tasks are the essential ingredients in the decision table. Just as in baking, the act of cooking up a decision table is as much an art as a science, and is best learnt in the kitchen, where it does get hot from time to time.

Course Implementation — the Tutor as Teacher

Ideally, all the development tasks outlined above would be out of the way before course commencement, and the tutor freed to take on a teaching role which complements the provision made via computer-managed learning. We still entertain the hope that some year we might achieve this ideal. During the first four weeks of our course the tutor provides eight lectures which act as a pacing device for all students, and provide a sense of conventional security while students become familiar with the diagnostic testing system and independent study. This period is also crucial in establishing the credibility of open-tutor access; an open-door policy only becomes a reality when students, choosing themselves to seek out the tutor, or directed or invited to see him through computer print-out, actually find him available as promised.

Once students are 'sorted' during the fifth week into independent and guided study modes the tutor's contact time with students is largely devoted to regular lock-step seminars and individual tutorials for the students on guided study who respond positively to any invitations or directions they receive in the form of assignment comments from the computer. This is not to say that a student in independent study cannot attend the seminars or arrange a tutorial. Nevertheless, if he has chosen to remain on independent study, the initiative for making use of these teaching resources rests firmly with him and not with his tutor.

In general, we find that students attending these seminars and tutorials come well prepared. Rapid progress can be made in a face-to-face situation where both tutor and students have clear expectations of the issues and problems to be considered. However, we are still ironing out some problems, for example, how to suppress the invitation to a seminar which has already taken place; or how to get students to realize that if they have been invited to a tutorial because they have asked specially for it, in response to a diagnostic test item, then it is up to them to initiate discussion of the problems they are facing.

As a complement to the student's independent or guided study, the course also includes a student-led workshop activity in which the only function of the computer is to record the tutor's subjective assessment marks. In this activity the tutor's function is more intuitive and spontaneous, since the major characteristic of these groups is their spontaneity and complexity; the groups form freely, determine their own objectives, methods and content and the main problem for the tutor is making decisions on the levels of support, direction or challenge which he issues to each group.

Thus, the computer-managed learning system which we have implemented at the New Univeristy of Ulster has resulted in a shift of the tutor's role into the complementary teaching activities outlined above. The tutor has now much more face-to-face contact with small self-selected or tutor-selected groups of students who want or need help, but much less contact of this type with students who have shown that they can stand on their own feet and take control of their own learning.

Back to Development — or is it Research?

The yearly cycle of development-teaching-development has implicit within it those activities which might fall under the role of the tutor as researcher. An evaluation study of the student's behaviour and attitudes during the 1976/77 course now under analysis seems to indicate that the student's tolerance of ambiguity is a good indicator of his capacity to succeed on independent study (McMahon H F, Anderson J S A, Barton J S). The key development decision for 1977/78 could well be whether or not we write the student's score on a tolerance-of-ambiguity scale into the decision table, within which the student's choice or tutor's requirement of independent study or guided study is processed.

References

McConnellogue, P, McMahon, H F and Anderson, J S A (in press) 'The Development of CAMOL in Northern Ireland' The Northern Teacher.

McMahon, H F, Anderson, J S A and Barton, J C (1977) 'Student Responses to Differentiated Learning Tasks in CML' Journal of APLET, Vol 14, No 2.

McMahon, H F and Jenkins, D (1976) 'Computer Managed Learning at NUU' IMTEC (INTTI) Training for Educational Change Seminar, Norway.

Rushby, N J et al (1976) 'Computer Assisted Management of Learning — the CAMOL Project' in 'Aspects of Educational Technology' Vol X, Clarke, J and Leedham, J (eds), Kogan Page, London.

Rushby, N J and McMahon, H F (1977) 'Institutional Transfer and Adaptation of a Content-Free CML System' In 'Aspects of Educational Technology' Vol X, Hills, P J and Gilbert, J F (eds), Kogan Page, London.

Course Designing: Some Suggestions Following Observations of Undergraduate Medical Courses

C R Coles

Sometimes it seems as though, traditionally, courses were not designed, they just happened. Perhaps a few members of staff put their heads together and worked out some sort of programme, often reflecting their research interests. The innovators involved junior staff. The radicals even invited the opinion of students! Ultimately the course was allocated to individual members of staff to be taught.

Now, either because of greater numbers, or because of the increased need for accountability or perhaps through a desire for efficiency, course design has become big business. The classic approach has given way to the rational approach and the rational has become 'objective' (see for example Engel [1972], and WHO Technical Report 521 [1973]).

Now it is not the intention here to rekindle the smouldering fires of the 'objectives' debate. Not only has it been well documented elsewhere (see, in particular, Stenhouse [1975] Chs 5&6, MacDonald-Ross [1973] Ch 3) but, more important, it is something of a red herring: it forces course designers to focus on less crucial issues, indeed, inappropriate ones. This paper proposes that course design be looked at from a somewhat different perspective — that of the evaluation of teaching and learning: such an approach raises issues not faced up to conventionally by course designers.

The methodology of this form of evaluation needs some explanation. Traditionally it was felt necessary for educational research to emulate scientific inquiry by undertaking comparative studies. This inevitably necessitated experimental and control groups with identified and isolated variables. Large samples were taken to minimize chance effects and statistical techniques employed to represent the results with some objectivity.

But education is not like this. It is very often small-scale, local and transient. Frequently, it needs to adapt to unforeseen changes in the immediate conditions which may not be repeated or repeatable. Indeed, attempts to rationalize education in order to make it more predictable in terms of its 'outcomes' ignores a most important attribute: it is a more or less unique interaction between a teacher and a class.

Comparative research, then, applies a framework into which the nature of educational practice will not fit. The quest for objectivity has lead to artificiality. Is it small wonder that academics view the outcome of this sort of research with what amounts to suspicion.

Recently, it has been suggested that a more descriptive and analytic approach would be of more value in studying educational situations by focussing on the views held by those involved in it. Its major 'weakness' — subjectivity — becomes its greatest strength: the researcher and the researched both come to understand the situation because of their interaction. Any bias or presupposition (neither, incidentally, absent in so-called objective research) is minimized by the neutrality of an evaluator who is constantly aware of and accounts for his own attitudes, assumptions and values. Such a methodology attempts to get underneath the surface of courses. Essentially, it employs the methods of participant observation, following courses through and interviewing staff and students both formally and informally. Above all it is 'action research': it aims to provide feedback which may help to improve the course whilst it is in progress rather than after it has finished. This approach, which might be termed 'interactive', has been well documented and a number of recent works serve both as an orientation and bibliography (see in particular Stenhouse [1975], Hamilton [1976] and Becker [1961]).

The classic study by Howard Becker *Boys in White,* was based on this approach and heralded a turning-point in the understanding of medical curricula. Becker was not concerned with comparing observed outcomes with defined objectives, he looked more fundamentally at how staff and students were coping with their courses. Fifteen years ago he was suggesting that very early on in their courses, medical students realise that the subject is too broad to encompass: they quickly decide to study what their teacher appears to want them to study which frequently means concentrating on passing the next examination in an attempt to reduce the 'overload'.

How much has this situation been alleviated over the last two decades by some of the new types of courses that have emerged? From evidence of some more recent evaluative studies based on an interactive methodology, it seems that there has been little change. More particularly, it is suggested here that such developments as there have been in the medical undergraduate curriculum have continued to confine themselves to re-ordering the content of the courses rather than focussing on the processes which make for more effective teaching and learning. Indeed, as a driving force behind some recent changes, the 'objectives' approach has a lot to answer for. Three such broad trends may serve as illustrations of the apparent inability of course designers to 'see the wood for the trees'.

The first might be called epistemological — that is, changes in the nature of the subject itself — and can be seen in attempts to integrate hitherto watertight subject disciplines on perhaps a topic or thematic basis. It is also apparent where there has been the emergence of whole new areas of study such as in microbiology, medical physics or rehabilitation. A second trend might be termed pedagogic, that is, modes of teaching and learning. Here, there have been a number of developments, but one in particular has been almost universally popular — the move towards individualized instruction. A third trend is in the vexed and often controversial area of assessment procedures. Recently, there has been a marked shift towards what has been described as 'objective' testing: the adoption of multiple-choice questions (MCQs) for examination purposes. Recently the writer has made an all too brief sortie into each of these areas and has found little comfort for Becker. The 'evidence' given here is by no means exhaustive nor is it more than representative of the data collected. Neither does the argument presented do justice to the issues: of necessity it is starkly truncated. It is, as it were, circumstantial evidence indicating the need to take a different perspective in course designing. The thesis here is that these innovations have been like new wine in old bottles.

One evaluation (Coles 1976a) looked at a situation where there was an interdisciplinary approach to the study of basic medical science by focussing on bodily system, (cardiovascular, respiratory, reproductive, renal, gastro-intestinal and nervous); each course being 'designed' by a team representing the various contributing 'disciplines' (physiology, pathology, anatomy, clinical medicine etc) and lead by a course co-ordinator. Courses ran consecutively and were intensive — lasting between four and eight weeks and virtually filling the available time.

In one particular course, about half of the students appeared to be coping quite well. They were achieving the intended integration and spoke quite freely about acquiring their own 'model' of the system and seeing the relationships between the various 'discipline-orientated' contributions to the course. They even indicated links between different courses running both concurrently and consecutively. These students, who might be called 'the integrators', were characterized by 'going it alone', rather than strictly following the pattern of the course. One student said:

'I don't go to lectures, I plan my day, I can't work for an hour or so, it has to be half a day at least.'

Whilst another said:

'I didn't got to all the lectures — I concentrated on the ones that I thought were going to be of some use. Lectures help to tie things in, but you have to do a lot of work on your own as well.'

It was as though the 'integrators' were 'creating space' for themselves in which to integrate.

The remaining students did not speak in terms of having a 'picture' of the bodily system. For them integration was not taking place although they clearly 'understood' the various parts of the course. These 'non-integrators' appeared to adhere much more closely to the form and format of the course even though they became critical of it. One remarked:

'This whole course is lecture-dominated, even the lecturers say so.'

and another reported:

'Sometimes we have lectures all morning or all afternoon, with only a 10-minute break. Once we went from 2 till 5 with no break at all. Beyond a certain point you just switch off, and that is after about 40 minutes. People do wonder how much they are going to remember of it all when you are say a 40-year-old doctor.'

It was these students who were complaining of being overloaded. Perhaps the 'integrators' were more able to fit the knowledge into their model of the system and so reduce the complexity of the learning task. The 'non-integrators' had no such 'pigeon-holes' and, as it were, constantly had to handle an enormous pile of 'unsorted mail'. In a sense these students reduced this complexity by 'putting blinkers on' — they concentrated on passing the examination. What this course lacked was not more relevance or a clearer statement of its goals — it had these. At face value it was well designed. What it seemed to need was some way of helping students towards an appropriate way of handling the information — integration — rather than relying on chance which understandably led most students to an inappropriate strategy — how to pass the examination. The major problem facing the course designer, then, is to identify and incorporate this sort of 'help' — a theme we shall return to later.

Another course evaluated (Coles 1976b) was early on in the students' introduction to clinical medicine. Again, this course was well organised and carefully thought out by the department running it: on paper it was laudible. The innovation, in this case, was pedagogic.

Teaching the course raised a number of problems because of its particular constraints. In this area of clinical medicine tutors frequently were not available or were called away at short notice. Moreover, the staff attended several hospitals and clinics and the students were allocated to these different locations, so that the staff were faced with either repeating themselves or reassembling the students for teaching purposes. It was decided that these problems would be overcome by adopting some form of individualized instruction. Tape-slide programmes were produced and students were encouraged to work through them in preparation for a seminar, during which the topic would be discussed.

However, again, most of the students felt overloaded and focussed on the end of attachment test. One said:

'Well it's just a matter of getting through the year isn't it. All you have to do is to pass the exam anyway.'

They appeared to accept the overload as inevitable and settled for rather less than the staff might have hoped for. The remainder, less than half, were characterized by one student who said:

'Well if I am going to be a doctor, now is the time for me to learn all I can.'

These students returned to the unit on their half day and at weekends to follow through interesting cases. It seemed as though these students were looking beyond the confines of this particular course and anticipating the future.

What was going wrong here? The staff were trying hard to make the course a success. They met frequently to discuss its objectives, they identified the knowledge and skills needed for this area of medicine, they produced learning packages containing a digest of that knowledge and they planned each student's ward-based experience to illuminate that knowledge. Perhaps it was that the course appeared to the students as facts to be learnt, rather than principles to be acquired — content rather than processes.

The third area of innovation in medical education is not a 'course', but exerts an indirect and somewhat insiduous influence on a great deal of teaching and learning: the nature of the assessment procedures. It was suggested above that overloaded students frequently seem to reduce the complexity of their task by concentrating on passing the next examination. The question that needs to be asked is whether recent trends in examining are consistent with developments in the course they claim to assess. Multiple-choice questions have been widely adopted to minimize marker discrepancy and to optimize marker efficiency. Moves towards continuous assessment have meant more occasions on which the student is assessed, and hence more marking for tutors. However, reliability and efficiency are not the same as validity, and continuous assessment by MCQs is perhaps not the educational panacea it was heralded to be (see, in particular, Miller [1976]). The purpose of this paper is not to enter this debate but to examine students' reactions. One spoke for many when she said:

'We used to be assessed at the end of the course and it was a big swot. Now it's a big swot all the time.'

another suggested:

'MCQs are simply testing what we don't know.'

whilst a tutor was more guarded:

'I'm not sure that MCQs are assessing the right things.'

Most of the opinion sampled about this form of assessment indicated that it was testing knowledge of facts — hardly innovatory.

It seems that these examples reflect two major problem areas in education: the first is perhaps self-evident, the second not readily so. Firstly, there is frequently a 'mis-match' between the view of knowledge presented by the course, the way it is taught and the mechanism of assessment. In the case of the integrated course, radical epistemological changes were introduced without a corresponding review of the pedagogy and its examinations. The course was aiming at integration whilst it was being taught on a conventional lecture format and assessed by MCQs. Surely it is paradoxical to suggest that one can teach 'integration' and illogical to suggest that one can infer its acquisition from a 'memory of fact' test. In the case of the clinical course, pedagogic changes were introduced without a corresponding review of the epistemology. The teaching methods — individualized learning packages — were encouraging the student to work on his own, but because the information was, as it were, predigested, it was making him more dependent upon the teacher for the organization of the knowledge. Individualized instruction is not the same as independent learning. The assessment pattern in general encouraged students to learn factual information, rather than its application or underlying principles. As the mis-matches became more confusing and overload built up, so many of the students focussed their attention on the only certainty — swotting for the examination.

The second problem area is less obvious but, perhaps, more crucial. Both of the courses presented here were attempting to derive certain principles out of the knowledge that the students were expected to learn. In the first case it was an integration of difference subject areas, in the second an understanding of the process of diagnosis in a particular area of clinical medicine. The hope was (and in many similar situations it is an unrecognised hope) that the students' learning would proceed from the specific to the general.

For many students the 'general' never materialized even though they acquired a considerable amount of 'specifics' — some students obtaining 'good' exam grades in the process! It is suggested here that this basis for teaching and learning — moving from the specific to the general — results from conventional course planning (including approaches such as the accurate definition of terminal learning behaviour) because it concentrates on content: knowledge is seens as facts to be learnt. However, knowledge is more than this. All knowledge is encapsulated within a structure, but we generate the structures. Sometimes we call the structures a 'subject' and we can identify its boundaries, its methodologies, its philosophical, theoretical and empirical nature. Sometimes the structure is a topic or theme which inputs from different subject areas. Sometimes the structure is a set of guiding principles such as 'scientific method' or 'clinical diagnosis'. Course designers might attempt first to identify the nature of the structure of knowledge to be taught and then to teach the structure rather than examples of the structure: that is, consider a move from the general to the specific.

One reason why this does not happen naturally is that it is rare for courses to be designed *ab initio*. Even in new medical schools there are often established departments of basic medical science and frequently there are flourishing postgraduate medical centres. (No doubt their existence influences the choice of location for new schools.) Moreover, staff appointed to teaching posts frequently come from a teaching background, but in any case all members of staff were themselves students and bring with them valued judgements about their role as teachers and assumptions about the nature of their subject as they see it. Frequently, staff are unaware of these, such that even before courses are designed, there are strong covert influences on the curriculum: in a sense, courses are never designed — they are re-designed. During the studies reported here staff frequently said:

'I never thought about it like that before',

or

'Nobody has ever asked me my opinion about teaching'.

Often staff accept at face value, for example, an integrated approach or a change-over to individualized instruction, without working out for themselves the implications.

In order to achieve this 'self awareness', there is a strong case for medical teachers undertaking research into their own activities in an attempt to identify the principles under which they operate professionally. In a study at McMaster University Medical School, Barrows and his associates (Barrows 1976, Barrows & Tamblyn) recorded colleagues undertaking clinical interviews. After the interview the clinicians were asked to identify what they had been thinking as well as doing. Frequently this was a difficult task: a professional operates in a highly specific and idiosyncratic manner of which he is generally unaware. Barrows found that often the cognitive processes were inconsistent with the overt behaviour — a situation that makes medicine appear more of an art than a science to the outsider and which must surely lead to confusion in the student's mind. Conventional clinical courses appear to concentrate on the overt knowledge and skills rather than the 'hidden' cognitive processes. At McMaster, problem-based learning units are developed in an attempt to teach the general principles of clinical medicine. The hope is (and here it is a recognised hope) that whilst these are developing, relevant knowledge and skills will be acquired. The 'course' — if such it can be called — begins at the general, moves to the specific, and then, as it were, oscillates between the two with the tutor occupying the middle ground. The approach to course design, then, first required an identification of the fundamental structure of clinical diagnosis, and then the devising of a scheme which 'taught' that structure.

The question is how to get at the nature of this fundamental structure. The theory is well documented, (Bruner [1960], Sockett [1976] Chs 4&5). In practice there are a number of ways. It might be possible to use an 'outside' evaluator acting in a neutral monitoring role employing an interactive methodology as is suggested here. However, this is not always possible and, quite understandably, not always considered desirable by those involved with the course.

Another approach might be for staff to talk more with students, not by proliferating staff/student liaison committees nor by appointing more student representatives on faculty boards and working parties, byt by staff getting to know the nature of students' learning difficulties and finding how they are coping with the course (GRIHE 1976).

A further suggestion might be for staff to talk more with each other, again not just in departmental meetings where much of the business is administrative, the organization formal and 'reputations' to be won or lost. Departmental seminars might be organized on the lines of research reports or CPCs, but orientated educationally. One member of staff might undertake some research into an aspect of teaching and learning which interests him and report his findings for general discussion.

Perhaps more fundamentally, course co-ordinators — assuming they exist at all — might undertake a review of the course. This might commence with an attempt to make an accurate description of the course: when, how and for whom it runs; what it follows and builds upon; what it precedes and becomes a prerequisite for, etc (frequently this is a much more difficult exercise than might be expected but proves to be invaluable in identifying the precise 'nature' of the course). The review body might then move on to identify and discuss the underlying assumptions, values and attitudes embodied within the course and its contributors. This might be set against, as it were, a 'conceptual spectrum' taking as the starting point a series of questions. These might include:

1. What is the nature of the subject of the course? Is it essential knowledge, is it a method of inquiry, is it a set of principles, etc?
2. What are the teaching methods employed? Are they consistant with the nature of the subject? Do they encourage dependence or independence?
3. What are the 'process' features of the course? How are students (and staff) coping? Is it possible to suggest appropriate strategies that might be adopted by those in difficulty? Where are the links between subjects and topics? How might they be formed?
4. What is the role of the examination in the course? Is it testing factual knowledge — if so, is this appropriate? Are objective tests such as MCQs being employed to facilitate marking rather than to test understanding?

As answers are generated to these questions a number of differing perspectives will no doubt emerge, leading to a continuing debate. Of all the educational enterprises, curriculum development must surely be curriculum negotiation.

References

Barrows, H S (1976) 'Problem-Based Learning in Medicine', in Clarke, J and Leedham, J (eds) 'Aspects of Educational Technology X: Individualised Learning' Kogan Page, London.
Barrows, H S and Tamblyn, R M 'Monograph 1, Guide to the Development of Skills in Problem-Based Learning and Clinical (Diagnosis) Reasoning' McMaster, Ontario Project for Learning, Resources Design, McMaster University, Faculty of Medicine.
Becker, H S, Geer, B and Hughes, E C (1961) 'Boys in White: Student Culture in Medical School' University of Chicago Press.
Bruner, J S (1960) 'The Process of Education' Cambridge, Mass, Harvard University Press.
Coles, C R (1976a) 'Integration and Concentration: an Evaluation of the Cardio-Vascular Systems Course at the University of Southampton' (abs) Medical Education, 10, 6.
Coles, C R (1976b) 'Developing Professionalism: an Evaluation of Teaching and Learning in Clinical Medicine' University of Sussex MA thesis (part) unpublished.
Engel, C E (1972) 'Educational Technology in Medical Education' Proceedings of the Royal Society of Medicine, 65, 9.
Group for Research and Innovation in Higher Education (1976) 'Learning From Learners: a Study of the Student's Experience of Academic Life' by Parlett, M and Simons, H with Simmonds, R and Hewton, E London, Nuffield Foundation.
Hamilton, D (1976) 'Curriculum Evaluation' London, Open Books.
MacDonald-Ross, M (1973) 'Behavioural Objectives: a Critical Review' reprinted in Golby, M, Greenwald, J and West, R (eds), 'Curriculum Design' London, Croom Helm, (1975).
Miller, G E (1976) 'Continuous Assessment' Medical Education, 10, 2.
Sockett, H (1976) 'Designing the Curriculum' London, Open Books.
Stenhouse, L (1975) 'An Introduction to Curriculum Research and Development' London, Heinemann.
World Health Organisation (1973) 'Training and Preparation of Teachers for Schools of Medicine and Allied Health Science' Report of a WHO study group, Technical Report Series No 521, Geneva, WHO.

The Development of Self-Instructing Materials for Diagnostic Radiology

E E Green

A proposal written by Dr Anne G Osborn of the University of Utah Medical Center and Medical School was accepted for funding by the James Picker foundation.

Dr Osborn received a grant to explore new and better ways of instructing practising medical doctors in diagnostic radiology as it deals directly with studies of the brain. The Development Services programme within the David O McKay Institute of Brigham Young University was asked to participate as the design, production and evaluation facilitator for the project and work began in the spring of 1973. A team comprised of a subject matter expert (Dr Osborn), an instructional designer, a technical writer, message designers and an evaluator was formed to work on the project.

The evaluator and instructional designer worked with Dr Osborn initially to determine methods of writing objectives and ways of determining their appropriateness and accuracy. It was decided at this time that the development team would be responsible for producing one unit of instruction out of a possible 10 units which were ultimately to be produced. After the development team had formed the design, evaluation and revision work it was to be submitted to a medical publisher to follow the design and complete the remaining nine units.

The 10 units which were to be developed are listed below:

Unit 1. Principles and Techniques of Cerebral Angiography.
Unit 2. The Aortic Arch and its Branches.
Unit 3. The External Carotid Artery.
Unit 4. The Internal Carotid Artery.
Unit 5. The Anterior Cerebral Artery.
Unit 6. The Middle Cerebral Artery.
Unit 7. The Subratentorial Venous System.
Unit 8. Arterial Anatomy of the Posterior Fossa.
Unit 9. Venous Drainage of the Posterior Fossa.
Unit 10. The Circle of Willis.

We chose Unit 5, the Anterior Cerebral Artery, as the prototype unit of instruction which would be developed by the development team.

The development of the text and slide-tape versions of the products associated with the introduction to the Cerebral Angiography course consisted of four major phases: (1) analysis, (2) production, (3) evaluation, and (4) revision.

Analysis

Analysis refers to the development of the subject matter content and the examination of the needs of the audience for whom the materials are intended. In the first step of this phase the subject matter had to be determined and arranged

164

into major topical categories. These categories, or units, were then subdivided into manageable instructional components, called sections, that were subsequently put into order of priority and sequenced to facilitate the self-study process.

At both the unit and the section levels, there were formulated learning objectives that set forth the skill or concept the student was expected to master by the conclusion of the section. These section objectives were written in sufficient detail so that they also provided the students with a preview of the material they were about to encounter. The unit level objectives pulled together the various section objectives into a concise statement of the unit's purpose, thus giving learners a clearer picture of the relation of the parts to the whole of the instructional packet. Here is a sample set of a unit objective and its accompanying section objectives:

Unit Objective: When you have completed this unit, you should be able to recognize normal and pathological states of the anterior cerebral artery.

Section 1 Objectives: (1) Identify the anterior cerebral artery (ACA) and name its relationship to adjacent structures at any given point. (2) Identify the major branches of the ACA including the anterior communicating artery.

Section 2 Objectives: (1) Identify the ACA and its major branches on various normal anteroposterior (AP) and lateral internal carotid angiograms. (2) Identify the anterior communicating artery on oblique views.

Section 3 Objective: Recognize common normal variations of the ACA.

Section 4 Objective: On an AP internal carotid angiogram, construct a midline measurement for the ACA and then identify any deviations from that midline.

Section 5 Objectives: (1) Identify the type of shift (deviation from the midline) of the ACA appearing on any abnormal AP internal carotid angiogram. (2) Predict the most likely location(s) of the mass lesion which produced that particular type of shift.

Section 6 Objective: Recognize a displacement of the ACA due to a supracellular mass.

Section 7 Objectives: (1) Correctly identify aneurysms of anterior cerebral and anterior communicating arteries, and (2) select those cases for which additional projections are necessary in order to demonstrate completely the presence of an aneurysm.

Section 8 Objectives: Given a group of radiographs in which anterior communicating artery aneurysms appear, (1) identify those aneurysms that are likely to have ruptured, and (2) provide an explanation for your decision.

Section 9 Objectives: Given AP and lateral views of a carotid antiogram, explain the procedure required to verify the presence of an occlusion of the anterior cerebral artery.

Section 10 Objective: Given an AP or a lateral carotid antiogram, arterial phase, determine if hydrocephalus is present.

Note that the objectives progress from a simple level of learning tasks (identify, recognize) to a more complex level (explain reasons for, diagnosis).

Production

Once the objectives were formulated, the subject-matter text, along with illustrations and examples, practice, and actual text problems, was written. The production phase also included the selection of graphic materials to illustrate the diagnostic principles and techniques under consideration. These illustrations were of three types: anatomic sketches, routine X-ray prints and subtraction prints. The photosketching technique allowed us to use low-cost graphics personnel and also allowed comparison between real X-rays and sketches isolating important characteristics of the visuals. With both the learning objectives and the illustrations at hand, it was then possible to write and verify a text to explain the concepts and skills the student was to master.

The subject matter was presented in a step-by-step manner so that the student was required to demonstrate his mastery of one objective before proceeding on to another on a more advanced instructional level. Message design personnel were able to sequence the various levels of difficulty and to ensure that information presented was not only technically accurate, but was expressed in as simple and straightforward a style as possible. Special attention was given to proper labelling of each illustration, with complete identifying information included in the captions. Furthermore, material was extensively rewritten so that the graphic illustrations and the textual material would be presented as a clear, readable, cogent and unified whole. Occasionally, supplementary examples and important non-examples were provided to facilitate learning.

In addition, graphics personnel were able to create all the visual aids in both versions of the materials. They planned layouts, provided audio support and produced all the visual cues, such as arrows, labels, shadings, colour-coding, sketches and other mnemonic devices.

Throughout the production process, formative evaluations were conducted which disclosed areas where improvements in the materials could be made before final evaluation of the materials could begin. The text, the illustrations, and the learning objectives were the core of the instructional materials for the course.

At the end of each section, a self-check quiz was included to help the student ascertain if he had actually mastered the learning objectives set forth at the beginning of each instructional component. It was felt that additional examples and practice tests could be included to further clarify concepts to those students who may have trouble mastering them after just one or two exposures to the material.

Answers to the question and other feedback were provided for the student after each section quiz and after the concluding test at the end of the unit. This feedback is intended to assist the student as he corrects his misinterpretations and misconceptions. Also, by parcelling the materials into small, manageable components, students could more easily identify problem areas and correct them by reviewing materials in a minimal amount of time.

Evaluation and Revision

Evaluation of the materials, their implementation and the students' response to them is now taking place by Harper and Row, a publisher of medical texts. Results of this summative evaluation will be the basis for the revision of the materials that will take place before a final, validated, and instructionally sound version of the instructional packet is produced for commercial distribution. This distribution is intended to occur in January, 1978.

The Evaluation of
a Self-Instructional Zoology Course

G D Moss, D K Roach, R Hammond

In the summer of 1974, the Department of Zoology and the Centre for Educational Technology at University College, Cardiff, began a collaborative project to redesign the zoology first-year course and present it as a self-instructional course.

The reasons for the change in the course are given in detail elsewhere (Roach and Hammond, 1976) but they were based on the need to accommodate more students in a limited space. Biological sciences in general have experienced an increase in the number of applications received and this solution was the only one open to the College.

The course is presented in a modified teaching laboratory with 32 study carrels (each containing a microscope, a Phillips PIP machine and a work area), and a central display/experimental area (Hammond and Roach, 1976). At one end of the laboratory is a student library and at the other end a technical service area. The course can manage up to 150 students a week, assuming six hours of contact time in the teaching area, and the system is based, with some major modifications, on the audio-tutorial system devised by Postlethwaite (1972).

The course itself consists of 20 self-instructional units, presented as structured teaching texts, and ultimately each text will have integrated with it a series of audio-visual support materials in the form of 8 mm film loops for the PIP system. In addition, the laboratory in any week contains experiments and demonstrations referred to in the text, and each week the students have a general review session which they may attend. All students are members of tutorial groups. Thus the major course activity is self-instructional and there are no formal lectures. Assessment is split 50:50 between continuous assessment (made up of multiple-choice tests and tutor-marked work in the form of laboratory reports and structured essays) and a final three-hour written examination and a practical examination.

The course has been in operation since October 1975, when materials were produced mainly in a developmental form. Since the summer of 1974 the course has been evaluated in terms of its teaching effectiveness, the attitudes of the first-year students to this approach (particularly important since in the first year at Cardiff students study three subjects, so the zoology course is seen in direct comparison with two other courses of equal weight) and the attitudes of the staff involved in the production of the new course.

The information presented in the paper attempts to summarize the results of this evaluation and to make a series of observations on the results which we hope are relevant and potentially useful to other departments and other institutions who are contemplating similar developments.

The Reactions of the Teaching Staff

Much of this information has been accumulated by questionnaire and discussion. Since the number of teaching staff is relatively small and not all of them have been involved in the part one course, there is no virtue in attempting any kind of statistical analyses on the results.

The staff were asked for their overall reaction to the course at three points in time with the following results:

	Summer 1974	October 1975	December 1976*
Very favourable	0	2	1
Favourable	7	7	5
Neutral	3	1	3
Slightly unfavourable	2	2	1
Very unfavourable	1	0	0

*The lower numbers in 1976 reflect those staff members actually involved (except one who refused to respond to any questionnaire).

It is important to emphasize at the outset that the expectations of the staff have largely been realized. Any critical comments which follow should be seen in this overall context.

Asked how they felt the teaching effectiveness of the part one course would be affected (1975) or had been affected (1976) by the new course, the responses were:

	October 1975	December 1976
Is/would be improved	8	6
Is/would be unchanged	0	0
Is/would be worse	0	1
Cannot say	4	3

In 1975 the staff were asked if they had any reservations about the way in which the course was developing. At that time, six were happy and six had some kind of reservation, mainly on the preparation time required. In 1976 they were asked a similar question in two parts, one relating to the texts, the other to the A/V material. With the texts, four were happy and six had reservations, mainly on the length of the text and what they regarded as 'too much introductory material'. With the A/V material the split was 5/5 and the reservations were almost entirely justifiable technical criticisms on colour quality, legibility of captions, etc.

The texts have been produced by 'unit teams' made up of Dr R Hammond, Dr K Roach, the author(s) and other academic advisers. Of the nine major authors, only one has been dissatisfied with this arrangement. However, in 1975 two-thirds of the 10 potential authors felt that they were inadequately briefed concerning the design of self-instructional material. It may be that in being anxious to go ahead with the course, the need for an adequate briefing of participants was overlooked. This has certainly had repercussions, in that frequently authors have not appreciated the technical problems involved in making film loops and texts available to students. Original material handed over late, through ignorance of the consequences, has led to several periods of overtime in the technical areas to regain a schedule and occasionally texts have had to be duplicated when they might otherwise have been printed.

One other general point to emerge is that authors generally criticize the texts as being too long and containing too much introductory or transitional material (transitional, that is, from A level to university). It may be that in previous courses they have 'assumed' this to be covered before moving to a higher level and now they find it difficult to cover the material briefly in textual form. While the students (see below) agree that there is too much material in the course, there is no evidence of criticisms that the academic level of the material is too low. In fact, evaluation studies reveal that most of the material is new to most students.

The final criticisms of the staff are that they are concerned that there is too little practical work in the new course compared to previous courses and that the continuous assessment (which they themselves devise) is too easy. However, it must be said that neither of these criticisms stand up to examination. The practical work which is retained is essential and relevant to the objectives of the course and a great deal of non-essential practical work has been discarded, some of it being replaced by analytical exercises in the texts, etc. The criticism of the continuous assessment may mean that inadequate training in the design, especially of multiple-choice items, has been given. However, despite this lack of training, many of the multiple-choice items show good item analysis characteristics although some have very high facility indices. The reactions of the staff also reflect a natural hostility towards non-essay assessment which is apparent in discussions with one or two members of staff. In fact when analyses of the multiple-choice tests are made they are each seen to give mean scores of around 12-14 out of 20 (60-70%) which is quite acceptable for a test in a continuous assessment sequence. It may be that the department will have to revise its concept of a pass/fail at 40% and have more regard for the actual distribution of the scores in the various components of the assessment.

The Reactions of the Students

Apart from their more detailed comments on specific units and the subject matter of those units, students were also asked their general reactions to the course and the method of teaching. It is these more general reactions which are presented here. The results are taken from questionnaires returned by over 90 students from a class of about 120.

Content:

Q. What is your opinion of the overall course content, its significance and relevance to the needs of Part 1 courses?

Very good	16%
Good	70%
Moderate	14%
Rather inadequate	0
Poor	0

Q. How does the overall quantity of information and the ground covered compare with other Part 1 courses?

Much more material in zoology	62%
Rather more material in zoology	38%
The same material in zoology	0
Rather less material in zoology	0
Much less material in zoology	0

Q. What aspects of the course content would you like to see omitted or modified?
NB   This was an open-ended question and the responses have been analyzed into the following categories:

Comment	Student Response
1. Reduce the overall amount of material	20%

Comment	Student Response
2. Concentrate less on taxonomy and classification	15%
3. Have fewer detailed examples and spend more time on scientific principles and concepts	15%
4. More illustrations needed	10%
5. Less statistics or simpler statistics	8%
6. Better guidance on practical work	5%

In these results we see that the students are happy with the course content but not with the amount of material. There is a clear guide to the authors over which areas of the course to reduce, namely classification and taxonomy.

Method:

Q. Do you prefer the self-study method of zoology to the more conventional course methods?

Yes	82%
No	18%

Q. Have you found learning to be more effective with the zoology system?

Yes	66%
No	28%
Don't know	6%

Q. Which components of the present course do you particularly like?
NB   Students were told that if they wished they could leave all the response cells blank for this question, or fill in as many as they wished.

The audio-visual programmes	82%
The self-instructional texts	
The continuous assessment	68%
The self-assessment questions	
The integrated practicals	44%
The tutorials	32%
The general session	20%

Q. Which of these components do you not like, and why?
The response to this question was open-ended. The commonest analyzed responses are as follows:

Tutorials should be better organized and conducted	30%
General sessions should be improved	28%
Continuous assessment causes pressure	12%

Q. How would you like to see the general sessions used?

For general background work, films, etc.	58%
For remedial work on the units	48%
To discuss applications of ideas introduced in the unit	16%

Q. How helpful were the unit objectives?

1. Helpful in initial reading of the unit	12%
2. Helpful in organizing study time	20%
3. Helpful in preparing for tests	16%
4. Helpful in revising exams	54%
5. Very little help	14%
6. Useless	6%

Q. Which type of A/V component did you find most useful?

Slide-tape	2%
Film loop	8%
PIP	86%
No difference	6%

Q. If you go on to study zoology, what proportion of higher level courses would you like to see presented in a manner similar to the Part 1 course?

A small proportion	38%
About half	36%
A large proportion	18%
All of it	2%

It is significant that when asked to compare different aspects of the course, the self-instructional features performed well leaving the general sessions and tutorial sessions under most criticism. However, a specific aspect of the self-instructional course, the objectives, are seen to be most helpful in a revision context rather than in a study context.

In more general terms, the students were asked to comment on the work load of this course compared to that of other first-year courses (with a notional six hours per week of contact time plus a further three hours of independent study). It can be seen that, as with many self-instructional programmes, overloading is a problem.

Q. How does your time spent on zoology compare with time spent on other subjects?

Much more on zoology	88%
The same	12%
Much less on zoology	0%

Q. How long should a one-week unit of study last?

Less than six hours	0%
Six hours	4%
Seven hours	14%
Eight hours	24%
Nine hours	14%
Ten hours	38%
More than ten hours	6%

Student Attainment

One of the commonest criticisms levelled by the staff in 1976 is that the continuous assessment is 'too easy'. In fact the students indicated that the tests tend to be fairly difficult and they are in favour of retaining a continuous assessment element of about 50%. It may be that two factors are at work here:

1. The inexperience of the staff in designing valid multiple-choice tests.
2. The expectations of the staff in terms of student performance are related to traditional style, norm-referenced exams while the continuous assessment on the course is essentially criterion referenced.

It is worth looking more closely at student attainment to assess the role and influence of each component in the assessment system.

In 1975/76 the overall results looked like this: *(see following page)*

	Mean Score	Standard Deviation
Multiple-Choice Tests	68.2	7.25
Tutor-Marked Tests	64.4	5.13
Written Exam	45.9	8.25
Practical Exam	56.5	11.35

Each student had his score for each component added and the total divided by four to give an overall percentage.

The result was twofold:

1. There were no failures since the final score for all students was above the traditional 40% pass/fail line.
2. The continuous assessment components heavily influenced the final scores since their score distributions were much higher than those from the exams.

The result of this was that while the students were happy, the staff in general had misgivings resulting in the reactions indicated in an earlier section. Since that time, however, the scores involved have been subjected to normalizing procedures which have the effect of giving equal weight to the four components of the assessment. The results of this are very interesting. First of all, about 3% of all students now fall below the traditional 40% pass/fail line (although in Cardiff a student is not failed in his first year until the scores for all three first-year subjects are considered together) and the new, more familiar distribution of scores has acted as a reassurance to the staff. However, the results are more interesting when considered from the point of view of the predictive value of the various assessment components. Here are the correlation coefficients between the component part score distributions and the final, normalized score distributions.

	Correlation with overall normalized score
Multiple-Choice Tests	.805
Tutor-Marked Tests	.804
Written Exam	.702
Practical Exam	.805

We can see that the multiple-choice tests are the best predictor of overall student performance and the written exam the worst predictor. This is confirmed when student rankings are examined. Only two of the top six students overall are in the top six in the written exam while the other assessment components have at least four of the top six in common. Similarly, only three of the bottom six students overall are in the bottom six of the exam, while the other components each again have at least four in common. Naturally this is due in part to the different types of skill being tested by the four components and it suggests that perhaps grade profiles might be more appropriate then overall scores in situations like this.

As a general point it is reassuring to find that the score distributions of the four components each have relatively high correlations with the overall normalized score, since this supports the claim by the course organizers that the continuous assessment component of the overall assessment is as valid as the exam component. It also shows that, provided normalizing procedures are adopted, students can be permitted to take 50% of their marks as continuous assessment (which they prefer to do) without invalidating the assessment system.

Summary

The Part 1 Zoology course is now in its second full year of operation and clearly it is an evolving system. It seems that the expectations of the staff have, in the main, been realized but both staff and students are concerned about the overloading of the course. The students are very much in favour of the self-instructional methods being used, tending to criticize the more traditional elements within the course.

There is some evidence that certain aspects of the course and some of the production problems encountered could have been overcome by more adequate briefing of the staff during the early design stages of the course.

Student performance on the course is good as measured in terms of continuous assessment scores and examination scores. There is no evidence to suggest that continuous assessment techniques reduce the reliability or validity of the assessment system.

References

Hammond, R A and Roach, D K (1976) 'The Phillips PIP System on a Self-Instructional First-Year Zoology Course' Medical and Biology, III, 26, p87-90.

Postlethwaite, S N, Novak, J and Murray, H T (1972) 'The Audio-Tutorial Approach to Learning' (3rd Ed) Minneapolis, Burgess.

Roach, D K and Hammond, R (1976) 'Zoology by Self-Instruction' Studies in Higher Education, 1, 2, p179-196.

Development and Evaluation
of Individual Learning Systems
in the Anatomical Sciences

E D Prentice, W K Metcalf, N F Metcalf

During the last decade, a number of medical schools have experienced a progressive decrease in the number of hours allotted to the basic medical sciences. This has obviously created instructional problems, which are often compounded by increased class sizes, faculty shortages and a general knowledge 'explosion'. The stimulus-response result has been a renewed emphasis on quality teaching and the development of more effective instructional techniques. To this end, the Department of Anatomy at the University of Nebraska Medical Center is making an intensive effort to develop and apply the most efficient and effective teaching techniques possible in human anatomy instruction.

With respect to the technique of auto-instruction, the literature is replete with reports supporting its effectiveness. Indeed, auto-instruction is now used to teach a wide range of basic and clinical sciences that require the student to master both cognitive objectives and psychomotor skills. It therefore seems reasonable to suggest that auto-instruction can be effectively used to teach selected aspects of anatomy to medical students. With this objective in mind, the anatomy faculty at Nebraska embarked upon an extensive project involving the development and evaluation of a number of different auto-instructional programs applied to the anatomical sciences.

Development

Development of all Nebraska auto-instructional programs begins with identification of the objectives the student is expected to accomplish upon successful completion of the program. The next stage of development is concerned with program design, ie the number and length of units or modules per program, the nature of the instructional material, the sequencing of learning steps and the employment of feedback mechanisms. In the final phase of development, all instructional materials are produced and the complete auto-instructional program is assembled and duplicated.

In order to provide students with auto-instructional programs that have common educational characteristics, all Nebraska programs are designed to conform to a master learning strategy (Bloom, 1971) which specifies a high level of student achievement (90%). To facilitate mastery learning, each unit within an auto-instructional program incorporates the features of: (1) defined objectives written in behavioural terms; (2) established student entry-level via a pre-test; (3) self-pacing; (4) sequential learning steps; (5) opportunities for student response and immediate feedback; (6) final student assessment via a post-test; and (7) an attitudinal questionnaire designed to help identify instructional deficiencies.

Description

The following is a description of the major auto-instructional programs in human anatomy which are at present used at Nebraska. All individualized learning programs are considered instructional components of a total anatomy teaching system called the Multi-Media Approach (Prentice, 1974). In addition to auto-instruction, this approach includes lectures, laboratories, tutorial discussions, films, video-tapes and closed circuit television.

The Stereoscopic Anatomy Auto-Instructional Program

The Stereoscopic Anatomy Auto-Instructional Program (Prentice, 1975; Prentice, 1976) was designed to provide students with a viable alternative and/or supplement to anatomical dissection. The complete program consists of 70 units which are organized anatomically on a regional basis. Instructional material in each unit consists of 8 to 10 stereoscopic slides (35mm) taken of sequential anatomical dissections. Prior to photography, important anatomical structures were labelled and all arteries, veins, nerves, and lymphatics were coloured in accordance with the standard anatomical colour code. Each unit also contains a 15 to 25-minute script in written and audio-cassette forms.

Auto-Instructional Program in Radiological Anatomy

Historically, radiological anatomy has been taught as an adjunct to gross anatomy by inspection of radiographs placed in the dissecting room. To improve the efficiency and effectiveness of this part of anatomy education, a series of self-instructional units in radiological anatomy (Sharp, 1975) are available which teach basic radiation protection, physics of radiology and nuclear medicine and all aspects of radiological anatomy. Instructional material in each unit consists of high quality transparencies of selected radiographs or radio-nucleide scans, and illustrative line drawings. All units employ written and cassette tape commentaries 20 to 40 minutes in length.

Programmed Text Instruction in Human Anatomy

In order to provide students with an alternative to traditional text-book study, a series of 40 one-hour linear frame programmed learning texts in anatomy (Metcalf, 1971) were produced. All units employ line diagrams and, where appropriate, clinical applications of anatomy are presented.

Postlethwait Units in Human Anatomy

Because many standard anatomy text-books are deficient in their coverage of the lymphatic system, a series of six mini-courses (Postlethwait-type units [Dusdieker, 1972]) was developed to cover the entire lymphatic system. Each unit consists of schematic diagrams of the lymphatic system and text in cassette format.

Auto-Instructional Program in Living Anatomy

One of the more important components of anatomy education at Nebraska is a series of living anatomy auto-instructional packages (Metcalf, 1974) which are used to supplement living anatomy laboratory instruction. The living anatomy program, which is currently under development, is designed to guide the student through a large number of examinations, each used in clinical physical diagnosis, such as examination of joints and nerves, percussion and auscultation of the heart and lungs, and palpation of abdominal organs, etc.

Clinical Problems in Human Anatomy

The modern medical curriculum demands relevance in the basic sciences. Accordingly, the Nebraska anatomy course is structured to achieve a high degree of clinical relevance. One of a number of devices employed for this purpose is an auto-instructional program based on clinical cases as seen in medical practice. Each unit in the Clinical Problems in Anatomy series is designed to lead the student to the correct diagnosis by application of his anatomical knowledge. For example, one slide-tape unit entitled, 'The Case of the Clumsy Call Girl' deals with thoracic-outlet syndrome in a telephone operator. In this unit, the student is introduced to the anatomy of the thoracic outlet and the symptomatology of neurovascular compression. Since the clinical case contains elements of humour, the student is entertained while he learns.

Auto-Instruction in Histology and Cell Biology

In recent years there has been a trend towards the reduction of traditional histology laboratories in the medical curriculum with greater reliance placed upon the use of coloured atlases and assorted kodachromes as learning aids. In view of these events in medical histology teaching, it was decided to develop a comprehensive histology and cell biology (HCB) auto-instructional teaching program (Bauer, 1975) which could serve as an effective substitute for traditional laboratory activities. Instructional material consists of over 400 kodachrome slides which include photomicrographs, transmission electron micrographs and scanning electron micrographs. Slides are accompanied by scripts in written and audio-cassette forms.

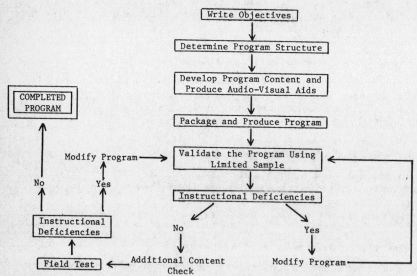

Figure 1. *Algorithm for the development and evaluation of auto-instructional programs in human anatomy*

176

Evaluation

Commitment to evaluation is essential for the maximally successful design and use of a learning system. This is especially true for auto-instructional programs where the focus of student control is transferred from the instructor to the learning system itself. In an auto-instructional system, it is the programmed subject matter that controls the student's behaviour pattern and it is the system that is ultimately responsible for ensuring learner achievement of the objectives. Learner interaction with the system, therefore, must be continuously monitored and evaluated in order that any product deviating from the pre-set standards may be identified and appropriate corrective action taken.

All of the auto-instructional programs employed by the Anatomy Department are continuously evaluated and revised to correct identified deficiencies. As shown in Figure 1, evaluation begins with a validation process utilizing a limited sample of students. Validation is primarily accomplished by measurement of learner gain scores derived from a pre and post-test. A learner gain score is defined as the percentage of the maximum possible attainable gain which, in turn, represents the percentage of success the program had with the learner. The formula $Z = (y-x/100-x)(100)$ is employed, where x = pre-test score, y = post-test score, and Z = percentage of maximum possible attainable gain. Utilization of this formula serves to eliminate the influence of pre-test variability on the data.

The next step in the evaluation scheme depends upon the nature and number of instructional deficiencies identified during the validation process. If there are relatively minor deficiencies, the program is subjected to an additional content check and then field tested. If, however, major instructional flaws are identified, the program is appropriately modified and shunted through a second validation process. Once a program has successfully passed both the validation process and the field test, it is considered a complete program and suitable for implementation.

Implementation

Once an auto-instructional program is evaluated and all identified deficiencies are eliminated, the program is incorporated into the instructional framework of the Nebraska Anatomy Teaching System. It should be emphasized that the volume of subject matter presented in a clinically oriented anatomy course is enormous. In this circumstance, a wide array of both clinical and anatomical teaching aids becomes a necessity. In addition to the previously described auto-instructional programs, the Anatomy Department provides the student with continuous access to clinical movies, anatomical and clinical models, labelled radiographs, teaching transparencies, video-tapes, film loops, and relevant journal articles which present the latest published clinical information on topics of interest.

The immediate availability of the various anatomy teaching aids must be co-ordinated with curriculum structure which is divided into bi-weekly blocks of instruction. All teaching aids are, therefore, divided into bi-weekly sets which are sequentially placed in the Anatomy Department's satellite audio-visual learning centre (Metcalf, 1977). To facilitate usage, a list and description of the bi-weekly sets of teaching aids is posted. At the end of each two-week instructional period, teaching aids relevant to past subject matter are relocated in the medical library and the next set of aids is placed in the audio-visual centre. Students are thus exposed to new teaching aids every two weeks, but may, however, utilize the library at any time for the purpose of review.

Naturally, all auto-instructional aids contain evaluation questionnaires which provide continuous feedback concerning the quality and suitability of a given program. Data thus obtained is periodically summarized and units are, accordingly, updated and/or revised.

Discussion

Undoubtedly the most important characteristic of the Nebraska Anatomy Teaching System is the variety of learning methods the student can use to accomplish the instructional objectives. Students are, therefore, not dependent upon one teaching system such as lectures or laboratory to help them master the subject of anatomy. For example, most students logically rely heavily upon anatomical dissection to learn to identify the various anatomical structures. Students are not, however, totally dependent upon dissection to help them acquire this particular ability. They can also use the Stereoscopic Anatomy Auto-Instructional Program, film loops, movies and video-tapes.

In practice, it has been found that the majority of the students will select a learning method which they feel will best enable them to accomplish a particular series of instructional objectives. Naturally, not all students choose to use the same learning methods and presumably not all available learning methods are equal in terms of instructional efficiency relative to the individual learner. For example, there are 30 programmed texts on the anatomy of the peripheral nervous system. Unit post-test data indicates that these units are extremely effective teaching tools. All 30 programs, however, are not universally used by the medical students. Some students find the programs require too much working time and they are able to learn the peripheral nervous system more quickly by attending lectures, participating in the laboratory and reading the text-book. Other students find it difficult to learn the peripheral nervous system without the aid of the programs. Thus, for some students, the programs are an efficient learning device and for other students, the programs are an inefficient way to learn anatomy. These observations also hold true for the other components of our instructional system. A major objective of the anatomy instructional program, therefore, is to provide the best possible learning methods relative to the individual learner. In this way, Nebraska medical students are able to use their limited time in a more productive manner and, hopefully, acquire a greater degree of knowledge.

References

Bauer, T, Metcalf, W K, Metcalf, N F and Prentice, E D (1976) 'Auto-Instruction in Histology and Cell Biology as a Substitute for Traditional Laboratory Activities' Proc Phys Soc, p 54.

Bloom, B S (1971) 'Mastery Learning' in 'Mastery Learning' Block, J H (ed), Holt, Rinehart, and Winston Inc, New York.

Dusdieker, N (1972) 'The Iowa Experiment VI: Postlethwait Units in Gross Anatomy' Anat Rec, Vol 172, p 438.

Metcalf, N F (1974) 'The Anatomical Approach to Clinical Diagnosis' Anat Rec, Vol 178, p 500.

Metcalf, N F, Prentice, E D, Erickson, D, Povey, C M and Metcalf, W K (1977) 'Experiences of a Basic Science Department in the Development and Operation of a Satellite Audio-Visual Learning Center' Biomedical Comm (in press).

Metcalf, W K, Moffatt, D J, Richardson, G and Versackas, M (1971) 'The Iowa Experiment IV: Programmed Instruction in Medical Gross Anatomy Laboratory' Anat Rec, Vol 169, p 476.

Prentice, E D, Metcalf, W K, Metcalf, N F and Sharp, J G (1974) 'A Multi-Media Approach to Teaching Human Anatomy' Proc Nat Conf Res Technol Higher Educ, pp 125-137.

Prentice, E D, Metcalf, W K, Sharp, J G, Quinn, T H and Holyoke, E A (1975) 'Packaged Anatomical Education I Stereoscopic Gross Anatomy' J Anat Vol 120, pp 628-629.

Prentice, E D, Metcalf, W K, Quinn, T H and Holyoke, E A (1976) 'Replacement of Traditional Anatomical Dissection by a Stereoscopic Slide Based Auto-Instructional Program' Proc AAMC 15th Annual Conf on Res in Med Educ, pp 181-186.

Sharp, J G, Prentice, E D and Metcalf, W K (1975) 'Packaged Anatomical Education: II' 'Radiological Anatomy' Vol 120, p 629.

The Doctor/Patient Interaction or Consultation–Can the Computer Assist in this Dialogue?

C Evans, H C Price

The Problems-Orientated Medical Record — (POMR)

Time is a very scarce commodity in the mass medicine of today wherever it is practised. Hence the patient's medical record or case notes need to be summarized to contain only the minimum of relevant or dynamic functional data obtained by the doctor as a result of his consultation. This he uses for his initial clinical action and he will also use it and rely upon it in his subsequent treatment and care of the patient.

This functional data is the basis of the problem-orientated medical record (POMR). POMR is not yet another redesigned traditional case history. There is the danger that restructuring the old case notes, to provide boxes for the doctor to tick the relevant points or similar procedures, may become even more complicated and bulky than the traditional case notes they are supposed to supersede.

Using POMR requires the re-education of the doctor, in recording key words that describe succinctly those details that move him to clinical action. These key word results, when linked with the key symptoms from the history-taking procedure and the key words describing the abnormal physical signs, enable the doctor to make a value judgement or provisional diagnosis and to take executive or clinical action. Where a large number of medical case notes were carefully analyzed retrospectively in a previous study, the number of key executive words was foun i to be extremely small. These are the key words that need to be stored and recalled when the patient is seen again by any doctor.

Impressions, lateral thoughts, prejudices and idle speculation should be recorded on POMR. Therefore the POMR data collection format must record the key words that describe his value judgement or provisional statement of diagnosis or symptom complex, including the evidence of the testing of this hypothesis by recording the positive results of examination including laboratory procedures, and his executive or clinical decision on treatment disposal and, if necessary, follow-up and final assessment. It should always be available when the doctor sees the patient and updated as required. If another doctor has to take over the care of the patient then he can see simply and clearly the basis of the previous doctor's decision.

A Feasibility Study

In a previous study we investigated the feasibility of using the computer to record the basic functional data generated by the physician at the time of the consultation.

As a result a problem-orientated medical record summary (POMR) was generated using the remote job entry (RJE) mode and linking two general practices and the out-patient physician of the local district general hospital. In this study there was no provision for full summary of the clinical history, the physician's value judgement being defined by the use of key words denoting symptom complex or diagnosis, which he entered into the record himself.

The extent to which a satisfactory diagnosis is achieved depends upon the degree of fit of two profiles, the patient's and the doctor's. Key, lead or 'start' words form the communication links between the two. If we are really to understand the nature of medical interviewing it will be necessary to discover a common word chain that fits both the patient's profile of himself and the doctor's knowledge of disease profiles.

To be realistic about this, it is difficult if not impossible for the busy doctor (especially the general practitioner in winter time) to sort his patients adequately and hence he either takes a short cut through tranquillisers or uses possible 'avoidance' techniques of which the simplest form is referral to the out-patients' department. Thus, written notes are seldom made and if so are seldom referred to. However, as the research study progressed and the doctors became accustomed to using computer summaries, the need for an adequate history slot became apparent.

A New Role for the Computer

The first slot in the Problem-Orientated Medical Record is concerned with the patient's history. For some years we have been experimenting with computer terminals in order to deal with this problem. A computer to help the doctor not to replace him? Interest in the application of computers for on-line interrogation in hospitals and general practice continues to grow and a number of studies have emerged as the result of practical experience in this country (Evans *et al*, 1971; Evans, 1972; Bott *et al*, 1972) and other parts of the world (Mayne *et al*, 1968; Slack, 1968; Slack, 1969; Coombs *et al*, 1970). Many of these studies have achieved unexpected success and the suitably programmed computer has shown itself to be an accurate, acceptable and, in many cases, even preferable alternative to the doctor for routine medical data capture. We have been able to identify with some confidence many of the reasons for this high acceptability and these are discussed elsewhere (Evans, 1972; Bott *et al*, 1972). It is also becoming increasingly clear that the issues raised by studies of this kind throw light not only on the nature of the doctor/patient relationship and the strategy of medical interviewing, but to some extent, the philosophy of medicine itself.

Although previous studies in various hospitals and in various clinical areas have shown consistently high patient and doctor acceptability it has become clear that history-taking programs need to be developed with a strategy and 'mood' tailor-made to the requirements of local hospitals, specific illness and specific types of patient. For example, a program capable of trouble-free administration for, say, dyspepsia in a Scottish urban area could not be guaranteed to work so satisfactorily in, say, a rural part of the south-east of England. Not only are there marked regional differences in terminology and jargon, but there is also some evidence that the optimum 'approach' of a 'computer doctor' might need to be significantly different in the two geographic areas.

This is particularly true in cases where the interrogation is conducted by an automated voice output device such as that developed in the Computer Science Division of the National Physics Laboratory (Evans *et al*, 1972) and which has been successfully employed in the Southern General Hospital in Glasgow. Here there may be enormous preferences or prejudices for different types of voice which may differ markedly in accent, age, or other class labels. For this reason we have retained some caution in interpreting the success of our early studies which were mainly conducted in Glasgow in the case of dyspepsia, and at Guy's in the case of psychiatric interrogation, and have therefore extended our investigations into

HELLO. THIS IS AN EXPERIMENT IN TAKING DETAILS OF MEDICAL SYMPTOMS
BY A COMPUTER. IT IS DESIGNED TO HELP DOCTORS IN THEIR WORK, AND
TO IMPROVE MEDICAL FACILITIES FOR THE PATIENTS AS WELL.

WE WOULD LIKE YOU TO HELP US WITH THIS AND IF YOU ARE PREPARED
TO WOULD YOU PUSH THE BUTTON MARKED 'YES'. IF NOT PRESS THE
BUTTON MARKED 'NO', AND IF YOU DON'T UNDERSTAND PRESS THE '?'
BUTTON.

GO AHEAD AND PUSH ONE OF THE BUTTONS NOW. 0

GOOD, THANKS VERY MUCH. EVERYTHING THAT YOU SAY WILL BE TREATED
IN THE STRICTEST CONFIDENCE AND ONLY DOCTORS AND NURSES WILL MAKE
USE OF THE INFORMATION THAT YOU HAVE GIVEN. ARE YOU QUITE HAPPY
ABOUT THIS? PUSH 'YES' IF YOU ARE, 'NO' IF YOU'RE NOT AND '?'
IF YOU DON'T UNDERSTAND. 0

GOOD. THIS IS A COMPUTER TALKING TO YOU. I CAN ASK YOU QUESTIONS
BUT I CAN ONLY UNDERSTAND SIMPLE ANSWERS, AND YOU GIVE ME THESE
ANSWERS WHEN YOU PUSH ONE OF THE THREE BUTTONS IN FRONT OF YOU.
THEREFORE ALL THE QUESTIONS CAN BE ANSWERED IN THIS WAY. DO YOU
UNDERSTAND EVERYTHING I'VE SAID UP TO NOW? 0

BY THE WAY, IN YOUR JOB DO YOU EVER WORK AT NIGHTS? PRESS ONE
OF THE BUTTONS NOW. 1

OK. NOW I WANT TO ASK YOU SOMETHING ABOUT YOUR CHEST. BEFORE
YOU PUSH ONE OF THE BUTTONS I'D JUST LIKE TO REMIND YOU THAT IF
YOU DON'T QUITE UNDERSTAND WHAT I MEAN BY THE QUESTIONS, THEN
PRESS THE '?' BUTTON. TELL ME, DO YOU USUALLY COUGH FIRST THING
IN THE MORNING IN THE WINTER? PUSH ONE OF THE BUTTONS NOW. 0

DO YOU USUALLY COUGH DURING THE DAY IN WINTER? PUSH ONE OF THE
BUTTONS. 1

DO YOU COUGH LIKE THIS ON MOST DAYS FOR AS MUCH AS THREE MONTHS
EACH YEAR? 0

WOULD YOU SAY THAT WHEN YOU GET A COLD IT GOES DOWN TO YOUR
CHEST? 0

WHEN YOU GET A COLD, HOW LONG DOES IT TAKE TO CLEAR UP. FIRST,
WOULD YOU SAY IT ONLY TOOK THREE OR FOUR DAYS? 1

Figure 1. *Introductory questions typed out by the computer terminal*

NOW I'M GOING TO ASK YOU SOME QUESTIONS ABOUT SMOKING. IT
REALLY IS IMPORTANT THAT YOU TELL ME THE TRUTH ABOUT THIS.
PLEASE BE ABSOLUTELY HONEST ABOUT THIS AND IF YOU NEED TIME TO
THINK BEFORE YOU ANSWER DON'T BE AFRAID TO DO SO, AND READ THE
QUESTIONS AS MANY TIMES AS YOU WANT TO.

NOW DO YOU SMOKE? BY A SMOKER, I MEAN DO YOU SMOKE, FOR EXAMPLE,
ONE CIGARETTE EACH DAY REGULARLY? (IF YOU'RE NOT SURE WHETHER TO
DESCRIBE YOURSELF AS A SMOKER OR NOT, PRESS THE '?' BUTTON) 1
(NO)

TELL ME, HAVE YOU EVER SMOKED AS MUCH AS ONE CIGARETTE A DAY
(OR, SAY, AN OUNCE OF TOBACCO A MONTH) FOR AS LONG AS A YEAR?
THINK CAREFULLY ABOUT THIS AND THEN PRESS YES OR NO. 0
(YES)

NEXT I WANT TO FIND OUT ROUGHLY WHEN YOU FIRST STARTED SMOKING
REGULARLY. OBVIOUSLY ONE CAN'T BE ABSOLUTELY CERTAIN ABOUT THIS,
BUT WOULD YOU SAY THAT YOU STARTED SMOKING REGULARLY BEFORE YOU
WERE 16 YEARS OLD? 1
(NO)

WOULD YOU SAY YOU WERE BETWEEN 16 AND 25 YEARS OLD? 0
(YES)

NOW I WANT TO FIND OUT HOW LONG IT IS SINCE YOU LAST GAVE UP
SMOKING. TELL ME, IS IT LESS THAN A YEAR AGO? 1
(NO)

IS IT BETWEEN 1 AND 2 YEARS AGO? 1
(NO)

IS IT BETWEEN 2 AND 5 YEARS? 1
(NO)

BETWEEN 5 AND 10 YEARS? 1
(NO)

IS IT OVER 10 YEARS AGO? 0
(YES)

GOOD. NOW I NEED TO KNOW WHAT YOU USED TO SMOKE, AND HOW MUCH.
DID YOU SMOKE MANUFACTURED CIGARETTES? 0
(YES)

I SEE. NOW WOULD YOU SAY THAT THE NUMBER OF CIGARETTES YOU SMOKED
EACH DAY WAS REGULARLY LESS THAN 10? 0
(YES)

NOW TO HAND-ROLLED CIGARETTES. DID YOU EVER 'ROLL YOUR OWN'? 1
(NO)

Figure 2. *Routine smoking questions*

various other areas of clinical medicine and regional locations, including an investigatory interrogation of patients with respiratory problems in a London hospital — specifically, the Western Hospital in Fulham (Evans *et al*, 1973; Evans *et al*, 1974).

The computer, in this situation, is unbiased, asexual and patients like its calm relaxed attitude and the patience and ease with which questions can be repeated and embarrassing symptoms discussed in private since the patient is alone with the computer. After our experiment patients were interviewed, and all without exception stated that if given the choice between seeing a real live doctor or the computer doctor they would prefer the latter.

The Experiment Using a Programmed Computer Terminal as 'Interviewer' for Patients with Chest Complaints

As in previous studies the strategy of the medical interview was developed as the result of consultation with physicians working with chest diseases, personal observation of specialists 'in action' and an examination questionnaire developed by the Medical Research Council (1966) which has for some time been used in the out-patients' in the Western and Charing Cross Hospitals, London, as an aid to routine data-gathering. The form of these questions consists of nothing more or less than a checklist which serves as a guide to the doctor in the normal course of events. This questionnaire would be quite unsuitable for administering to the average patient without a doctor or professional interviewer. As with previous experiments we had decided that the program to be developed should be capable of being administered by the computer without any hospital staff in attendance and that the computer should introduce itself, explain its function, conduct the interview and route the patient out at the conclusion without any extraneous intervention.

In line with previous studies, considerable attention was paid to the form of the language employed by the computer when interrogating patients, the aim being to give the simulated doctor a personality which was acceptable to the patient, according to a number of criteria which our past experience has shown to be important. A sample of introductory questions is given in Figure 1. A reproduction of typical questions and answers is given in Figure 2 and the synopsis and summary in Figure 3. The terminal was connected to the Honeywell commercial time-sharing computer via a Post Office telephone and modem. Hospital staff were trained in the signing-on and signing-off procedures.

```
            ** SUMMARY **


    ** COUGHS **   ** CHEST COLD **   ** PHLEGM **
    ** BLOOD **   ** SHORTNESS OF BREATH **
    CATARRH IN WINTER: CHEST OPERATION OR INJURY
    ** OTHER ILLNESSES **   ** EX-SMOKER **
    AFFECTED BY IT.
```

Figure 3. *Summary of medical history at Chest Clinic*

The Interview

The patient who is attending as a routine medical out-patient is seated at the teleprinter by the nurse or clinic clerk and the program signed on. The patient is told to watch as the typescript appears on the typewriter paper and to press the key for 'yes', 'no', 'don't know' or 'please repeat' as necessary. If there is no apparent difficulty experienced in answering the first two questions he is left alone – the computer interview lasting on average about 30 minutes.

Despite the very considerable scope of its investigation the finished program turned out to be essentially simple in form and structure. As with our previous work in other areas of clinical medicine, we found it impossible to prepare a flow diagram to illustrate the structure of the interrogation and this was also uncomplicated, with the exception of the rather elaborate loops that were required when, for example, the patient was interrogated extensively about his smoking habits. In all other respects the development of the program proved to be similar to previous studies, helping to strengthen our suspicion that routine data capture in common areas of general medicine is a simpler and less specialized skill than many medical workers have realized or been prepared to admit.

A further interesting development over our previous systems was that the computer produced a synopsis of the medical history and generated a precise summary on the basis of the answers by the patient.

Results

Some 100 patients, known to have respiratory problems either as the result of previous attendance at the hospital or through referral from their GP were interrogated by the computer. No prior training in the use of the terminal and only minimal explanation of the nature of the experiment were given and the patient was at all times left alone with the terminal. Previous experience, incidentally, has shown that this latter practice, far from arousing anxiety seems actually to alleviate it. The rare failures experienced in computer-patient interrogation seem to have been occasioned by the presence of another human being in the teleprinter room – eg visiting doctors being shown the experiment, the inability of the patient to read because of the absence of reading glasses, etc. After completing the interview the computer printed out a summary which was inspected by the consultant who also took the opportunity to briefly re-examine the patient to assess the validity of the summary.

Our general impression was that the summaries were accurate, concise and effective guides to the patient's condition. The patient was also interrogated by one of the researchers as to his attitude to the interview and the discussion monitored by tape-recorder, concealed from the patient's view. As with previous experiments, a very high degree of patient acceptability was noted with, in sum, the following reasons being given for its acceptability.

Patients stated:

1. They found the computer friendly and polite.
2. Very often that they felt able to be more truthful to it and not withhold details (eg excessive smoking habits).
3. The computer was judged to be clear and understandable.
4. They appreciated being able to 'take their time'. This turned out to be particularly helpful in this area of medicine when many with respiratory problems firstly find it difficult to speak, and secondly tend to have their respiration upset under conditions of stress, such as in the medical interview.

5. Those deaf or hard of hearing particularly appreciate this method of interrogation.
6. They appreciated the fact that the computer acknowledged and indicated that it had 'understood' all their responses, comparing this response favourably with the non-committal approach of many doctors.

A number of negative aspects of the program — mainly ambiguities in some of the questions, or uncertainties about the meanings of some medical terms (eg bronchiectasis) were freely commented upon by patients and the program was modified as necessary. Administration time varied from patient to patient and depended upon such factors as the nature of the patient's previous history, the complexity of his smoking habits and also, of course, the amount of time each individual chose to spend in answering critical questions. It varied, however, from 15 minutes to an upper limit of 45 minutes.

Discussion

Although no attempt was made to quantify the data gathered in this experiment, it is clear that its acceptability and those of parallel studies in other hospitals in different areas of clinical medicine have been confirmed. In addition, observations of the patients in action with the terminal, and a study of the transcriptions of the post-experimental interviews raise a number of questions of an entirely subjective kind which seem to us to be worth commenting on in general terms. These involve, amongst other things, the nature of the doctor/patient relationship.

The interrogation of the patient by a computer even when questions are framed by a doctor raises a number of important problems. What is the purpose of the doctor/patient interaction or consultation? Traditionally this is the time when both patient and doctor assess one another and come to a decision; the patient is satisfied with the doctor's manner and approach and impressed by his apparent erudition and by his degree of interest in his problem. The doctor assesses the patient in a different manner, because of his training, attempting to ascertain the validity of the statements the patient is making and by means of further questions probes other biological systems as well as the one the patient is concerned with and attempts to make a value judgement or provisional diagnosis. The doctor has to judge how to deal most effectively with the provisional diagnosis and comes to an executive decision — to treat or not to treat, to test and treat, to pass to another colleague or admit to hospital under his own or a colleague's care. Each time a doctor sees a patient this routine form of history-taking should be carried out; that is the ideal. However, time, lack of doctors, shortage of facilities for testing, and boredom at repetitive questions in long-term follow-up cases like asthma, bronchitis, rheumatic and cardiac instability mean that this is seldom if ever carried out.

The clinical judgement is normally based on a history-taking procedure and a perusal of the past medical record; however, the history-taking is an essential though time-consuming and repetitive activity, and unfortunately, often has to be shortened because of lack of time and pressure of work. Thus any automatic procedure that can carry out this activity with equal validity and acceptability will be a very valuable tool. This is especially true in sorting out the change in symptoms in those patients who attend regularly with chronic disease and form a large proportion of patients attending general practice and out-patient departments.

There is another question — Is the doctor/patient relationship subject to bias due to the personalities of the two persons concerned? Is the history taken down so laboriously a real objective consideration of the patient's biological imbalance; or only what the patient would like us to think; or the diagnosis we consider most suitable in line with our own specific interests?

Quite apart from the dialogue, however, there is another important factor involved in the doctor/patient relationship — we tend to have been accustomed to consider his as 'all things to all men'. This prompts the question: What of the bias in this relationship? The patient who has decided to use the doctor as a means of off-loading his problems wishes to arouse the interest of the doctor. Frequently the only way he can do this is to attempt to 'turn the doctor on' by using the sort of words that he knows, or assumes the doctor will respond to most readily. The patient has, by seeking advice, already taken the difficult decision to do something about his immediate problem. The possible solution to this problem troubles the patient, who is of course beset with all the confusions of the Cartesian dichotomy between psyche and soma.

As a result he may on further careful investigation exhibit all the interrelated characteristics of the dual-faceted psychosomatic system failure — with psychotic and somatic characteristics arranged stepwise like the interrelated bases on the double helical spiral of the nucleus.

On the other side of the coin, the doctor wishes to use the patient to travel along the verbal diagnostic pathway as quickly as possible to a convenient or currently fashionable taxonomic box, thus enabling him to take appropriate action. However, he reluctantly accepts the fact that a considerable proportion of consultants are asked for because of 'non-physical' reasons.

Incidentally, programs are now being used for the interrogation of patients with suspected gastric ulcers and in ante-natal, psychosexual and marriage guidance clinics. In Charing Cross out-patients' at the present moment a medical follow-up program is being run routinely for the Department of Respirology. Work is well-advanced on a presumptive diagnostic program based on pain as the primary key symptom constructed on a fir-tree pattern; the primary key word 'pain' being linked with secondary, tertiary and quarternary key words to guide the patient through his system pathway. Work has also just commenced on a flow chart for an occupational disease program in conjunction with the same medical unit.

Conclusion

This leads one to an interesting possibility. It may be that the ultimate importance of computers in medicine may not be simply their role in collecting, collating, storing and retrieving data, or routine housekeeping, but their role in facilitating communication. In fact, they could enable the doctor not only to communicate with his patients but also with himself, an extension of his forebrain, whilst at the same time allow patients to participate actively in these procedures.

Perhaps the well-tried father-figure in the age of the family doctor who gave comfort and help when there was no rational treatment should not be completely discarded. It is fair to say that many doctors today consider this entity to be of questionable value when compared with the scientific discipline of statistically significant and rational medicine. Perhaps the father-figure aura can be disembodied and transferred to an inanimate machine? If this new 'rational' machine can be made to work under the aegis of the old medicine, we could find ourselves with a new type of doctor/patient relationship, and one which is much closer to practical reality than the old.

References

Bott, M C, Box, J, Evans, C R and Wilson, J (1972) 'An Investigation of Computer Administration of a Psychological Test to Psychiatric Patients' NPL Report Com 61.

Coombs, G J, Murray, W R and Krahn, D W (1970) 'Automated Medical Histories: Factors Determining Patient Performance' Comps & Biomed Ros 3, 178-181.

Evans, C R (1972) 'An Automated Medical History-Taking Project — a Study in Man-Computer Interaction' NPL Report Com 55.

Evans, C R, Kinehin, C G, Price, H C and Whittle, P B (1974) 'Some Preliminary Experiments in the Use of Programmable Videotape Recorder as an Automated History-Taking Device in a Chest Clinic'.

Evans, C R, Price, H C and Wilson, J (1973) 'Computer Interrogation of Patients with Respiratory Complaints in a London Hospital'.

Evans, C R and Whittle, P B (1970) 'An Inexpensive Mask to Simplify the Layout of Standard Teletype Keyboards for Man-Computer Interaction Studies' NPL TM Com 46.

Evans, C R and Whittle, P B (1972) 'An Inexpensive Commercially Available Tape Recorder Modified as a "Voice Output" Device for Computer-Based Medical Questionnaires' NPL TM Com 67.

Evans, C R, Wilson, J, Card, W I et al (1971) 'A Study of On-Line Interrogation of Hospital Patients by a Time-Sharing Terminal with Computer/Consultant Analysis' NPL Report Com 52.

Mayne, J G, Weksel, W and Scholtz, P N (1968) 'Towards Automating the Medical History' Mayo Clin Proc 43, 1-25.

Medical Research Council (1966) Questionnaire on respiratory symptoms.

Price, H C, MacDonald-Ross, J (1974) 'Hammersmith and Kensington Community Health Information Project — A Study Report' DHSS London.

Slack, W V (1968) 'Patient Reaction to Computer-Based Medical Interviewing' Comps and Blomed Ros 9, 604-621.

Slack, W V (1969) 'Medical Interviewing by Computer' Southern Medical Bulletin, 57, 34-44.

Is Educational Technology Infectious?

I Townsend, J Heath

Maintaining the medical metaphor, this paper will look at the aetiology (history of educational technology in nurse training), the signs and symptoms (an overarching view of the developments that have taken place to date), and the treatment and prognosis for the future of educational technology in the field of nurse education; it will comment briefly on the incubation period.

It is very difficult to answer the question 'Is educational technology infectious?' in a field such as nurse education, and it will be necessary to go to various sources over a nine-year time span to get even an out-of-focus picture.

Aetiology — the History of Educational Technology in Nurse Education

A review of the writings of the most influential nurse educators in this country, the reports of government commissions since the early years of the century, and various reports from the General Nursing Council and the Royal College of Nursing all serve to show that nurse educators and government bodies alike are on the whole unaware of the field of activity encompassed by the term 'educational technology'. (Or at least, if they are aware of it, they have not yet been moved to write about it!)

In 1947, the *Report of the Working Party on the Recruitment and Training of Nurses* (HMSO) wrote that 'special importance attaches to visual aids. These have a unique function as improved teaching media ... Nurse training offers unusual scope to the entire armoury of visual, auditory and other sensory and mechanical aids'.

Fourteen years later, the Royal College of Nursing, in its report *The Nurse Tutor — A New Assessment* (1961) notes the frustration and shortage experienced in the education branch of the nursing service, and identifies possible causes as due to a lack of knowledge about more up-to-date methods in teaching and learning. It drives this home again in 1971, pointing out that 'young people who have been exposed to up-to-date methods of teaching ... are often frustrated and disappointed at the didactic methods too often employed in nurse training' (RCN, 1971). Such comments have gone unanswered for the most part.

The major report of recent years, the *Report of the Committee on Nursing* (Briggs, 1972), although recognising that change is needed in nurse training ('the education of nurses and midwives is a continuous process ... knowledge and the social context are changing') has little to say about educational technology apart from the fact that it 'might be included' as a component in a degree course in nursing and reporting 'with approval the existence of an advisory group on educational technology which coordinates the activities' of the only two units involved in this type of work in the Health Service.

The General Nursing Council has on the whole been more involved with the wider development of nurse education, but it is worth noticing that in 1970 its Education Committee set up an ad hoc group 'to obtain and coordinate information on various audio-visual aids, and consider their use in nurse education' and commented 'there would appear to be a need to provide advice and evaluation, possibly on a national basis, of such equipment and in relation to programmed learning too ...'(GNC, 1972).

The following year the Annual Report summarizes the results of a questionnaire which this ad hoc group sent to nurse training schools 'although many were well equipped, some lacked the basic equipment ... although a reasonable amount of equipment was available this was not always being fully utilized, and that teaching staff needed to be adequately prepared in the use of such equipment' (GNC, 1973).

Annual Reports since then have stressed neither the role of audio-visual equipment nor the concept of educational technology in the teaching process, but it is fair comment to say that for nurse education, this has been a period of severe strain, with major reorganizational upheavals, legislation promised but never arriving, and a quest for self-identify to strive for.

The latest Report gives some hope for the future: a working party is discussing amongst other things, a 'review of the context of basic nursing education ... (the) objectives of units of experience (and) methods of learning/teaching during practical experience'. Another *ad hoc* Committee of the Council, considering the results of a survey of registered tutors and clinical teachers (considered under Signs and Symptoms) highlighted the problems that 'little support has been given to the development of curricula which reflect the truth that the practical experiences are the "core" of the programme' (GNC, 1977).

We mentioned above the chaotic effects of massive reorganisation in the Service. Perhaps this has had a part to play in the history of educational technology in nursing education. A survey of articles on audio-visual aids and educational technology published in the two major nursing weeklies in this country since 1968 hint at this (Figure 1).

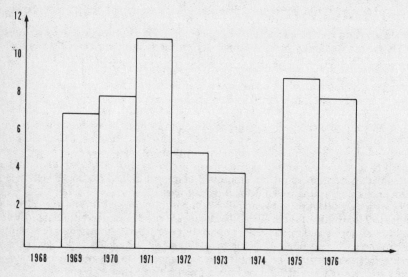

Figure 1. *Articles accessed from nursing weeklies*

The first thing to notice is the small number of articles carried. Each journal averages 10 articles per issue, a rough annual approximation of 1000. It would be an interesting exercise to retrieve figures from the field of general education to

190

compare.

Almost without exception, the majority of the published papers deal with the use of one or other of the aids to teaching, very few with the concept of educational technology as a total approach. In fact, through the nine years surveyed, only two people have devoted themselves to the subject. Mary Wells, writing in an isolated article in 1971, tells us that 'educational technology is ... concerned with the psychology of learning and with the relevant use of audio-visual media for better learning, with curriculum planning, with the production of teaching and learning materials, with the costs and effectiveness of those materials, and with the design of learning spaces' (Wells, 1971). But the history of educational technology, if it can be said to have a history in nurse education (and on the face of it, it is doubtful) is the history of the NHS Learning Resources Unit (Marson & Townsend, 1976a).

In particular, it owes a major debt to the work of one person. Since 1969 Sheila Marson has, initially by herself and latterly as leader of the NHSLRU team, contributed many papers to the Nursing Press. In her *Systems Approach to the Education and Training of Nurses* (1970) she presented a model which is only now being 'rediscovered' in the excitement of nursing acknowledgement of the curriculum development process.

Signs & Symptoms — Is Educational Technology 'Happening'?

The most exciting developments are to be found in these areas: in the work being carried out in the Wessex Region; in the development of learning resource centres by schools of nursing; in the training of nurse tutors; and in 'ground interest' from tutors and nurses themselves.

1. The Wessex Experiment

A paper by Harrison (1969) laid the groundwork for a scheme involving the Universities of Southampton and Hull, and the Wessex Regional Board. These three institutions set up an advisory group on educational technology 'with the intention that it should become a body to which groups interested in the use of visual aids could refer for guidance in planning departments, purchase of equipment and general matters relating to audio-visual education'. It saw itself as covering and coordinating a wide range of services.

This development is unique. True, the trend since the late sixties has been for other universities and institutes of higher education to play in increasingly interested role in the training of nurse tutors and provisioning of services to nurse education — Surrey itself is an example here — but the Wessex Region is the only one to have planned and organized a regional service which incidentally is partly funded from NHS monies.

Colin Coles, writing in *Medical and Biological Illustration* (1977) brings us bang up to date. In 1973 the Teaching Media Centre of Southampton University merged with the regional board's Centre for Medical Illustration and the resultant Department of Teaching Media offers practical advice on 'installation and maintenance of audio-visual equipment ... the making of teaching and learning materials' and it offers 'courses for lecturers on teaching methods and methodology' to 'teaching areas of the University and the Hospitals in the Region'. As he valuably concludes, 'it cannot be said, necessarily, that Teaching Media saves time or money, but it can justifiably be claimed that there is a wider provision of services to many more people than would otherwise have been possible, particularly to colleagues within the Regional Health Authority'.

191

The Wessex Region also operates a Library and Information Service which makes materials and information on the health sciences field available to all hospitals and community-based health workers in the Region. The Regional AV Librarian, Madeleine McKenna, reports that in the library services she is concerned with, the use of media by the nursing profession is very encouraging. One development she cites has enourmous potential: individual tutors can send in lists of topics they intend to teach, and are provided with as wide a variety as possible of non-print material from stock held within the service. She also mentions the existence of a local bibliographic media information service similar to that offered nationally by NHSLRU (McKenna, 1977).

The development of such services shared with other educational establishments is a very healthy sign. It is something which has been raised time and time again in Report after Report — and at long last it looks as if the caring profession is on its way to becoming a sharing profession.

2. Learning Resource Centres

In Marson and Townsend, 1976a, we wrote that 'the last five years have seen the establishment of one or two small Learning Resource Centres' and noted that the General Nursing Council had sanctioned the appointment of a number of audio-visual technicians to schools of nursing. In the 12 months since then the picture (on the surface) has not radically changed. Indeed, learning resource centres are hardly mentioned in Walsh (1975), even though her paper *Keeping Up-to-Date — Libraries in Nursing* appears in a collection dealing with 'basic educational perspectives of teaching and learning'.

A recent literature search (Townsend, 1977c) has identified only eight papers specifically relevant to nurse education, published in this country, and a paucity of 'hard' information for those wishing to draw on research findings (Townsend, 1977a). A national survey carried out by one of us in the Fall of 1976, as part of ongoing work being done as a student with York University Department of Education, has brought up some interesting figures.

All nurse training schools in England and Wales were sampled to find out what, if anything, is happening in the learning resource centre field. 174 institutions (89%) replied, 148 of whom had, or hoped to have, some degree of investment in this particular learning milieu.

Even though this information was given during a period of severe cutback in the Health Service, it is stimulating to note the degree of interest shown in one or more of the stages of a developing resoúrces centre. What is most encouraging is the number of tutors seeing themselves as having a clear role in the development of resource-based learning: even though the post of 'tutor i/c resources' is a nominal one, not formally recognised.

Other straws which may indicate the wind of progress are the slowly increasing number of audio-visual technicians being appointed to nurse training schools, and the fact that one of the major nursing weeklies has published a substantial series on the development of learning resource centres, (Townsend, 1977c) as well as devoting a special issue to the topic (*Nursing Times, 1977*).

3. Nurse Tutor Training

A third development which comments on the spread of educational technology in nursing lies in the context of tutor training courses. Nurses wanting to become tutors (and consequently teachers of trainee nurses) follow either a two-year diploma in nursing course or a one-year course at a technical teacher's college. The former type of course has been available since the 20s, but nurses have (because of the shortage of tutors which became urgent in the mid-60s) been able to follow one-year courses only since 1965, and in most cases, only within the past five years.

The growing interest of tutors in the methods and media of educational technology is probably largely due to their attendance on the one-year course, which is based on the technical teachers' Certificate of Education course. As Dixon and Roberts (1971) have said, 'the introduction of a group of nurses (into a technical teachers' course) was an innovation, but the course they were to follow was not'. The seven institutions now involved in this course were contacted last year, and a crude but informative picture emerges from the five who responded. In this current academic year, some 100 nurses are following the courses, all of which have an element of educational technology (ranging from 20 to 80 hours' experience) in them. College staff involved in the courses themselves attend specialist refresher courses such as those run by the University of London, DES and NAVAC, but their membership of professional bodies is limited to the Association of Programmed Learning and the Network of Programmed Learning Centres.

The content of the educational technology element of the courses is very wide, and it is worth noting that all but two of the institutions have played a very important part in the general development of educational technology in this country.

How do the tutors themselves view their experiences with educational technology?

The GNC in *Teachers of Nursing (1)* (GNC, 1975) surveyed 2923 nurse teachers, 89% of whom declared the 'teaching methods' component of their training 'adequate' (but the Summary of the Report did say that there was 'the general feeling of inadequacy of preparation for the post of tutor').

Nolan, writing in 1973, basing his conclusions on a survey of nurse training schools, showed that schools of nursing vary widely in their provision of the hardware of teaching, and said that 'nurse tutors have a syllabus that leaves teaching methods and content to the individual tutor ... nurse tutors must seek to base their own curriculum design on current trends in biology education if these are more effective than the old methods — provided that they are aware of contemporary thoughts and trends' (Nolan, 1973). He ties up the problem of use of media and methods with the problem of knowing what to use them for.

4. Ground Interest

More and more tutors are coming forward to us with ideas for development, queries to be answered, and our mailing list has increased by one-third over the past year alone. Two of our recent courses were over-subscribed, and the general atmosphere now seems to be recovering somewhat. Several important papers have appeared in 1976 (Bowman on curriculum development, and Lee reiterating many of Marson's ideas from the early years of this decade) although to some people, educational technology still remains 'the term given to the hardware aspect of teaching aids' (Sheahan, 1976).

Finally under this section, the Department of Health and Social Security has set up (in 1975) a National Training Council to promote a coordinated Training Service for the NHS. It has appointed a Working Group on Educational Training Methods and Techniques 'to assist the Council by providing information and advice in ... training technology and methods'.

Treatment & Prognosis — Hope for the Future?

Fundamental contributions to a public debate on the place of the process of

193

educational technology in nurse education have been few and far between over the past decade. The little progress that there has been has had the implicit support of government and statutory nursing bodies, but in the main, advances have come from without rather than within.

We note Nolan's comments on the difficulty which modern developments in biology teaching methods have had in reaching the nurse teacher, but we also note the more positive trends — toward a sharing of resources, increased interest in curriculum development, and a willingness of senior staff to participate in information-gathering activities — which have shown that a need for information on educational technology exists.

The move by universities and other educational establishments to 'help out' in nurse education looks very promising, as do projects mounted by the Council for Educational Technology (CET, 1977) and the Centre for Medical Education, Dundee, to facilitate accessing of audio-visual information.

Certainly, the advent of the NHS National Training Council is promising and will, we hope, bear fruit — eventually.

In Marson, 1976, and Marson & Townsend, 1976b, staff of the NHSLRU suggested various activities which could support nurse tutors: area and regional support services and centres, information services, applied educational research, production of learning resources and in-service training courses for tutors.

The time does seem ripe for development. The signs of *ad hoc*, geographically isolated and institutionally unsupported projects cry out for nationally-planned progress, support and commitment. Grass roots must be stimulated from above if they are not to wither away. It is unfortunate that just when things looked as if they were settling down again (after reorganization) the Health Service has been rocked by loud public dissention, and mooted swingeing re-organization.

The past 10 years have seen the hesitant growth and encouragement of the process of educational technology in nurse education — who can now say what even the next year will bring?

Incubation Period — a Footnote

All well-bred diseases try to creep up unaware on their hosts. Even a superficial reading of the standard works on the institutionalization of innovations (for example, Carlson, 1965; Miles, 1964; Rogers and Shoemaker, 1972) tends to point out that the successful innovations are those that have a lot of things going for them: country-wide support services, massive financial and philosophical commitment. It is unreasonable to expect educational technology to thrive in nurse education at this present time. We believe that the incubation period for this 'disease' in our field will prove to be in the order of decades; that we are just setting foot on the lower slopes of Carlson's curve!

References

Briggs (1972) 'Report of the Committee on Nursing' HMSO.
Bowman, M (1976) 'The Curriculum and the Staff' 'Nursing Mirror' V143 N11 66-68.
Carlson, R (1965) 'Adoption of Educational Innovations' University of Oregon, USA.
CET (1977) 'Annual Report 1975/76' London.
Coles, C (1977) 'In Support of Regional Teaching' Medical & Biological Illustration (in press).
Dixon & Roberts (1971) 'A Course in a College of Education for Nurses Preparing to Become Nurse Tutors in England and Wales' 'International Journal of Nursing Studies' V8, 163-177.
GNC (1971) 'Annual Report 1970-1971' London.
GNC (1973) 'Annual Report 1971-1972' London.

GNC (1975) 'Teachers of Nursing (1)' London.

GNC (1977) 'Annual Report 1975-1976' London.

Harrison, N K (1969) 'An AV Blueprint for the Wessex Regional Hospital Board' 'British Hospital Journal & Social Service Review' 3/1/69, 20-21.

Lee, C (1976) 'The Open University: Self-Instruction in Professional Education' 'Nursing Times' V72 N36 1386—1388.

McKenna, M (1977) 'Personal Communication'.

Marson, S N (1969) 'Progress in Programmed Instruction' 'Nursing Times' 30/10/69, 181-184.

Marson, S N (1970) 'A "Systems Approach" to the Education and Training of Nurses' 'Nursing Times' 9/7/70, 97-99.

Marson, S N (1976) 'Educational Technology in Nurse Education: A Proposal for the Establishment of an Advisory Centre for Educational Technology in Nurse Education' NHSLRU, Sheffield.

Marson & Townsend (1976a) 'Educational Technology ... A Movement for Change: The Future of Educational Technology in British Nurse Education' 'Journal of Advanced Nursing' 1, 155-162.

Marson & Townsend (1976b) 'Individualized Learning in Nurse Education — Past, Present and Future' in 'Aspects of Educational Technology X' 223-228, Kogan Page.

Miles, M B (1964) 'Innovation in Education' Teachers College Press, USA.

Ministry of Health (*et al*) (1947) 'Report of the Working Party on the Recruitment & Training of Nurses' HMSO.

Nolan, R J (1972) 'Development of Teaching Method in Human Biology within Nurse Training Schools' Unpublished M Ed Thesis, University of Manchester Library.

Nursing Times (1977) 'The Learning Resources Centre' V73 No 16 21/5/77, 574-589.

Rogers & Shoemaker (1972) 'Communication of Innovations: A Cross-Cultural Approach' Free Press, Collier-Macmillan.

RCN (1961) 'The Nurse Tutor — A New Assessment' London.

RCN (1971) 'Evidence to the Committee on Nursing' London.

Sheahan, J (1976) 'Education — 6: Teaching Skills and Teaching Aids' 'Nursing Times' V72 N39 1526-1528.

Townsend, I J (1977a) 'The Audio-Visual Revolution: Do We Really Need it? Part 2. Two Innovations Assessed' (in preparation).

Townsend, I J (1977b) 'Sources, Resources, Courses: The Work of the NHS Learning Resources Unit' in 'Proceedings of One-Day Symposium, Achievements, Problems, Possibilities — Education for the Nursing Profession' ed Kilty, J, University of Surrey (in press).

Townsend, I J (1977c) 'Talking about Innovation: A Commentary on the Development of Learning Resource Centres in Nurse Education, parts 1-8' 'Nursing Times' V73, Nos 13, 14, 15, 17, 18, 19, 20, 21.

Walsh, F (1975) 'Keeping Up to Date — Libraries in Nursing' in 'A Guide for Teachers of Nurses' ed Raybould, E, Blackwell Scientific Publications.

Wells, M (1971) 'Educational Technology for Beginners' 'Nursing Times' 30/12/71, 1642-1643.

Systems for Classroom Management

P Waterhouse

Introduction

In spite of the efforts to improve the quality of teaching and learning in the nation's classrooms, results on the whole have been disappointing. We still lack the knowledge or the skill to translate ideas and expectations into effective classroom practice; even when we know what is right we do not seem to know how to do it.

The trouble is that so much of the research, advice, support, development work and in-service education is offered to the teacher piecemeal. Researchers present generalized conclusions about specific aspects of teachers' work. Advisers promote particular ideas on materials and only rarely get the opportunity to do an in-depth study of a teacher's work. Directors of development projects see the classroom as a test-bed for their own ideas, materials and strategies. In-service education presents a supermarket of ideas and techniques. Most of the energy and effort stops short at the classroom door and the teachers are left to sort out the offerings on their own. And there seems to be no body of knowledge or repertoire of techniques and systems upon which they can draw.

The problem is made worse by the confused state of the current debate on education. On the one hand there is the current fashion for clear objectives, sound structures and the setting of performance standards; on the other hand is the liberalizing tradition of the post-war era with its emphasis on the needs of the individual, human values and social realities. Both of these traditions present the teachers with legitimate expectations. But they conspire too to present the teachers with management problems of great complexity which demand highly sophisticated responses.

This paper describes an attempt, still in its infancy, to use a systems approach to the problems of classroom management.

Analysis and Design

The Problem

Society is placing on the teacher demands which are increasing in scale, complexity and inconsistency. The needs of the individual, the desire for social change and reconstruction, the concern for democratic values, the importance of the academic disciplines, the emphasis on compensatory education, the questioning of the validity of the school as an institution, the 'return to the basics', each one has produced in its turn a valid emphasis, and the teachers in the classroom strive to preserve the best of each, while at the same time responding to the declared concerns of the moment. The problem for the teachers in the classroom is to make an intelligent, balanced, purposeful and operational synthesis out of it all.

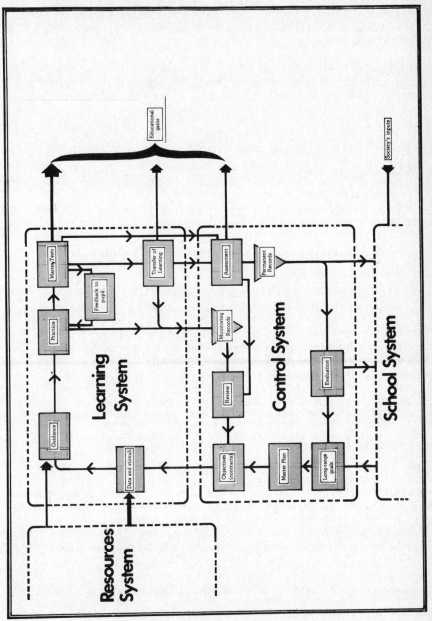

Diagram 1. *A system for classroom management*

The labels within the diagram are:

Educational gains

Society's inputs

Mastery Tests
Transfer of Learning
Assessment
Feedback to pupil
Practice
Permanent Records
Monitoring Records
Guidance
Review

Learning System

Control System

Data and stimuli
Objectives (contracts)
Master Plan
Evaluation
Long-range goals

School System

Resources System

Aims

The systems for classroom management should achieve the following broad aims:

1. Pupils will improve their basic skills in handling language and number.
2. Pupils will develop all their cognitive capabilities: acquire knowledge, develop understanding, develop the higher order intellectual skills of analysis, synthesis and evaluation.
3. Pupils will develop all their affective capabilities: develop awareness and a sense of values.
4. Pupils will grow towards autonomy: independent, but rational, responsible, and authentic.

The Environment

The systems will be for a conventional setting in a maintained secondary school. Assumptions are:

- class size of 30;
- one teacher, unaided;
- conventional classroom with access to school library/resource centre and LEA curriculum support services.

The Components of the Systems

The systems should include:

- routing arrangements for individual or small-group learning;
- provision for stimuli and data, guidance, practice and feedback, either from the learning resources or from the teacher;
- arrangements for storage and retrieval of classroom resources;
- procedures for acquiring resources from beyond the classroom;
- a means of monitoring individual pupils' progress;
- devices for measuring pupils' progress;
- ways of processing information about pupils' progress and achievements;
- arrangements for decision-making, and the planning of pupils' work schedules;
- decisions about possible sequences and mixes of teaching styles and methods.

The Structure of the System

Diagram 1 shows all the components as part of an integrated system. It emphasizes the importance of the control system which is concerned with monitoring, assessment, objectives and evaluation. It emphasizes also the relationships between the various components. No attempt has been made to analyse the components of the two related systems, the school system and the resources system.

Diagram 1 focuses on the concept of individual learning but it is also important to plan the sequences and mixes of teaching styles and methods. Table 1 shows one possible solution.

Management

With the outline of the systems in mind, the tasks of classroom management are to:

- define in more detail the inputs and outputs of the systems;

— develop the organizational structure for planning, directing, and controlling the classroom operations;
— develop the processes and procedures for the classroom activities;
— identify the checkpoints required for efficient monitoring;
— develop the tools required;
— develop techniques to improve teacher efficiency and effectiveness.

Stages	Purposes	Methods and media
1. *Advance organizer*	Stimulation. Motivation. Provide a framework of basic understanding. Provide a means of organizing the learning into a meaningful whole.	Evocative presentation by the teacher. Use of vivid and appealing visual and auditory stimuli. Film.
2. *Development*	Individual (or partners) learning. Own best pace. Independence. Choice. Learner active and self-organizing.	Control by agreed objectives. Direct use of resources — small format booklets, reference books, filmstrip or slides, cassette tapes, simulations and games. Periodic individual consultation with teacher.
3. *Recapitulation*	Review of new learning. Pupil contribution and report back. Development of higher order cognitive skills.	Discussion method. Class recitation. Exhibition. Tape recording. Drama. Simulation.
4. *Assessment*	Measurement of individual pupils' achievements: (a) in relation to potential, and (b) in absolute terms. As an aid to course evaluation.	Objective tests. Written examinations (where appropriate). Course-work assessment.

Table 1.

Clearly, these tasks need to be developed for each activity and method used in the classroom. Much of the complexity of classroom management stems from the fact that substantial modifications need to be made to the basic systems according to the style and method of operation. In the remainder of this article only those activities associated with the development stage of a classroom sequence will be described.

Diagram 2 is a flow chart of pupil activities and information during the development stage. The flow chart reveals the possibilities of various types of tour for the pupil — wholly packaged, semi-independent, wholly independent.

Diagram 3 shows some of the tools required for the system. Details are as follows:

The Contract-Record Card

Stored in conventional card index cabinet, or in visible index unit.
Records details of objectives agreed at each consultation, review observations and assessment information.

Task Cards

Provides packaged guidance to form the basis of (though not the whole of) the contract of objectives. The ideal should contain:

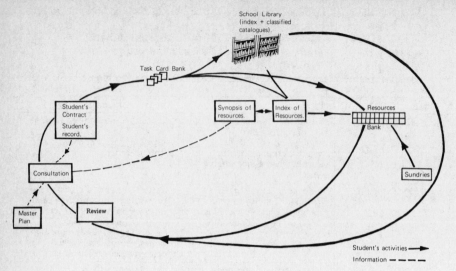

Diagram 2. *A flow chart of student's activities*

- number and title;
- statement of objectives;
- pre-test;
- list of resources required;
- tasks to be performed;
- mastery test.

Index of Resources

An alphabetical subject index of the classroom resources.

Synopsis of Resources

List of the classroom resources in accession number order.

Master Plan

A list of all task cards, a brief synopsis of each, an analysis of each in terms of educational objectives and a number of network diagrams showing possible sequences and choices.

The Learning Resources

Stored in accession number order.

Conclusion

Much work remains to be done. The concepts of classroom management need further study and the practical implications need to be examined in simulations, workshops and in experimental and demonstration classrooms. The techniques of

200

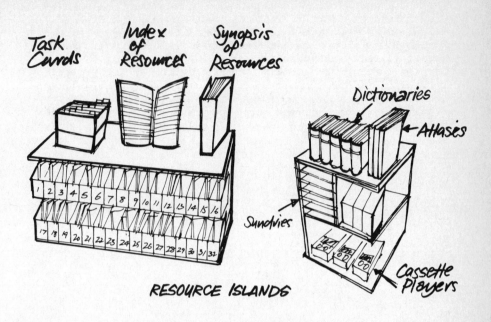

Task Cards

Index of Resources

Synopsis of Resources

Dictionaries

Atlases

| 1 | 2 | 3 | 4 | 5 | 6 | 7 | 8 | 9 | 10 | 11 | 12 | 13 | 14 | 15 | 16 |

| 17 | 18 | 19 | 20 | 21 | 22 | 23 | 24 | 25 | 26 | 27 | 28 | 29 | 30 | 31 | 32 |

Sundries

Cassette Players

RESOURCE ISLANDS

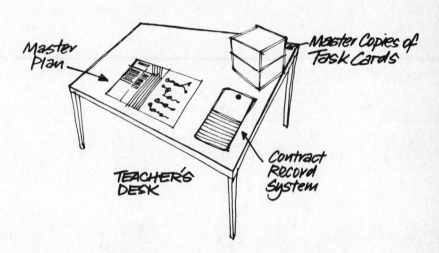

Master Plan

Master Copies of Task Cards

Contract Record System

TEACHER'S DESK

Diagram 3. *The components of the system*

the researcher in classroom observation and in operational research need to be adopted and adapted for the use of teachers who want to improve their efficiency and effectiveness. Possibilities of more delegation by the teachers to sub-professionals need to be re-examined. Possibilities of more co-operation between teachers in the planning, implementation and evaluation of their courses are urgently in need of exploration.

These are imperatives, because without them teachers face the bleak prospect of mounting criticism of their work, and more entrenched attitudes of disillusionment. Some recent reactions among teachers suggest that they are not only aware of the need for systematic classroom management, but are also ready, willing and capable of making a bold leap forward.

Contribution and Appraisal Networking as an Educational Technology

G M Boyd

Introduction

Educational technology cuts across the ordinary conceptual schemes which are used to legitimate most activities and roles in education and training organizations. This mitigates against its acceptance. For example: one Ontario University found itself unable to set up an educational technology department because the courses, projects and topics involved would have trespassed rather heavily on areas which the existing departments of curriculum, instruction and administration considered to be their proper fields of authority.

The problem of unconformability is not confined to universities. Cases occur in business and government training departments where educational technologists schooled in holistic systems approaches to problem analysis and solution find upon investigation that they are frequently being asked to provide instruction merely as a palliative. For example, one airline training director was required by government regulations to provide 32 hours of refresher training on airspace regulations to all pilots once each year. When this educational technologist developed a criterion test on the regulations and argued that pilots who passed this validated test should not have to waste 30 hours 'going through the motions' of being retrained, he ran into difficulties.

In large unionized organizations it is now becoming usual to sidestep the 'merit' evaluation problem by making wage settlements include increments proportional to the number of accredited college courses taken and passed by an employee. This approach leads to apathetic students, and when the college is financed on a per-capita basis, to insubstantial courses. Such 'students' and courses constitute a rather hostile environment for educational technology, which when applied would ensure the students really having to master the objectives set (Boyd, 1976b).

The problem of 'assimilation' provides a further example of the unconformability of an educational technology world-view. Administrators in large organizations gain recognition and advancement by introducing a new project and securing at least some token ouput from it. Such an innovator is then promoted or transferred. His replacement cannot gain enough recognition by merely maintaining and improving the project; he in turn must start his own new project. Educational technology involving appreciable research investment and an extended iterative development process cannot be assimilated in such a 'progressive' environment. In times of austerity it is very difficult to initiate any but cost-cutting projects, and even those often threaten jobs and are resisted. The net result, as pointed out in the third report of the US Federal Fund for the Improvement of Post-secondary Education (1977), is that an America-wide survey of mathematics teaching 'discerned a tendency among many innovative programs to regress to old-fashioned prototypes'.

In all of the above situations educational technologists are rendered partially ineffectual at doing their developmental job largely because they are not influentially linked back into other departments and organizations where decisions are being made which profoundly affect their work. They inhabit what Sir Stafford Beer calls 'esoteric boxes'.

Solutions to the Unconformability Problem

Probably the ideal solution would be to change people's conceptual models and beliefs concerning organizations and the appropriate relationships between division of jobs and division of knowledge, ie in Berger and Luckman's (1966) terms by 'socially reconstructing reality'. This is a tall order. To some extent it has been accomplished in certain areas of the electronics and computer industries where so called 'matrix-organization' (Demaagd, 1970) structures and procedures prevail.

Of course, in another sense it is the success we are having in teaching educational technology students to carry out re-construction of their notions of 'reality' which leads to confrontations, and often to frustration when they are employed, after graduation, in conventional corporations and schools. But clearly it is not possible to supply three years of specialized graduate training for everybody; nor would it be appropriate. The educational technologist can, however, by establishing networks of contacts, greatly increase his opportunities to work effectively at improving education and training.

Definition of 'Contribution and Appraisal Networking'

By 'networking' is meant the formation and maintenance of multiple channels of communication among a number of people who share a common concern or 'mission', in such a way that these people are able to generate effective and efficient strategies to advance their concern or carry out their missions.

The particular way which characterizes 'contribution and appraisal networking' is to send out calls which evoke contributions, then appraise these contributions logically, empirically and in terms of the history of relevance and credibility of the contributor. This basic approach is what Sir Karl Popper refers to as the method of conjectures and refutations (*vide* Lakatos and Musgrave, 1970). This method has much wider application than merely in professional science. Contribution and appraisal networking is a form of 'variety-reducer' which can be used in any large complex process control system. It matches contribution variety against a variety of problem perceptions and what is not cancelled out can then be used for control purposes.

In a sense, such networks are nothing new. Charles II formalized one when he created the Royal Society. However, scientific societies and congresses generally have only one co-ordinating centre. It is the whole complex of journals and societies over the entire world which constitutes the contribution and appraisal network in a given field. That science networks are not merely methods for winnowing knowledge but can also be the basis for the co-ordinated implementation of technology by many disparate organizations and entities, was very clearly demonstrated to the author during his participation in polar communications research projects during the International Geophysical Year and thereafter. Informal networks of private communications resulted in single experiments being supported by assorted government departments, corporations and universities which normally behave as competitive 'esoteric boxes'.

More fashionable examples of contribution and appraisal networking employing computer teleconferencing techniques are to be found in the literature under the title of 'Delphi Conferences'. These are particularly well treated by Turoff and Linstone (1975). Elsewhere (Boyd, 1976a) the author has advanced a 'Relevant Credibility Status Game' model for the process of knowledge development, and currently is attempting to set up two experimental networking projects based on this model.

(The definition of contribution and appraisal networking given above was constructed as the aftermath of participation in an international meeting on 'The Network Alternative' held at Concordia University in the fall of 1976. This was concerned mainly with networking as a basis for creating additional credible 'actors' on the pluralistic political stage. Such actors would give some weight to concerns such as conservation, learning disabilities and environmental aesthetics which are not of central importance to ethnic or politico-geographical 'actors' [*vide* Judge, 1976].)

Modelling the Dynamics of Networks

Directed graph theory and linear network theory would at first sight appear to be the obvious tools for modelling a network. When it is a matter of modelling a contribution and appraisal network, however, one must proceed with caution in using these tools. The communications channels are for the most part bi-directional and if the network is not to degenerate into a mere chain or into an hierarchical structure, there must be a rich parallelism of channels. In other words, there are feedback loops in the network and in graphical terms it will have to be represented by cyclic graphs and, except under idealized conditions, by non-linear control and network theory.

When there are loops in a communications network, they may, if timing and other conditions are right, serve to suppress deviations from goal-oriented behaviour, and under these (negative feedback) conditions the whole loop may be treated as a single entity with known and approximately stable characteristics. This technique is used in signal flow graph theory (for example, see p 98 in Elmaghraby's excellent book on network models in management science, 1970). Unfortunately for the modeller but fortunately for those involved, the loops in a contribution and appraisal network are often deviation-amplifying loops. They act so as to elaborate a small conjecture into a major statement or major strategy. Or such loops may act to reduce mutual credibility to the point where some individuals or groups leave the network altogether. This is grossly non-linear behaviour and is very difficult to model.

One way around some of these problems is to partition out troublesome bits of the network and try to deal with the gross behaviour of the rest. This assumes that the 'vicious' and 'virtuous' circle loops do not involve too many people and that their disruptive behaviour can somehow be bounded. Then if the membership and behaviour of the members is roughly specified it may be possible to use generalized activity network modelling techniques (GANT — Elmaghraby, 1970) to predict the rate at which tasks will be accomplished and to determine the bottlenecks and 'sensitive' variables which limit and shape the networking operation.

Fatal Characteristics

The objective of networking is to enable the educational technologist and those who interact with him in important ways to restructure their reality to forms with greater long-term viability and the greater efficiency and effectiveness which such long-term viability requires. For instance, a network may be used to facilitate assimilation and transfer of an innovation such as computer-assisted learning

A network has fatal characteristics if it inhibits the aim, or attenuates the common concern, which led people to form it. It may exhibit 'vicious' circles of activity which cause part of the network to disperse, or virtuous cycles which form new links and alter the set of aims of its supporters, but these need not be fatal to the network (however difficult they may make analysis).

What can destroy a network's value is a plethora of irrelevant or self-defeating (ie incredible) messages: messages which are effectively 'noise'. Noise from outside is also serious.

Another thing which can render a network worthless is lack of a requisite variety of contributors and contributions with respect to the disturbance-variety which threatens the common concerns uniting the supporters.

These two factors could be summed up together in a single measure of merit: the Relevant Requisite Variety/to noise ratio (RV/N ratio). This variable will take on different values with time and also will vary greatly with the aims which are considered paramount by various supporters of the network. This means that the variety to noise ratio will vary in different parts of the network and consequently cannot provide a unique global measure of viability. Nonetheless, I find it an heuristically useful concept providing that the control objective to which it relates is specified.

In order to ensure that good levels of requisite variety to noise levels are maintained, it is necessary that most of the participants should agree to abide by some simple rules and that some participants should act as score-keepers and some as referees. Such an arrangement is a bit like an intellectual, or at least, serious-problem-oriented equivalent of a football league, the main difference being that players can play for several teams at once, and that teams can as easily be aggregated as eliminated. These characteristics make a contribution and appraisal network resemble somewhat corporate life and the operation of the stock exchange. Consequently, both games theory and some econometric theory may prove useful in modelling networks and estimating their viability and worth. The problem of determining requisite variety to noise ratio is rather like the problem of aggregating utilities in welfare economics. Being more circumscribed, it is hopefully more tractable.

Studies of performance of a number of different types of business organizations are reported in Litterer (1969). The organizations with the best long-term financial performance were those with the highest ratings on both the scale of degree of differentiation of sub-divisions and the scale of degree of integration. Both requisite variety and requisite communications and co-ordination to bring the control variety into appropriate conjunction with the disturbance variety are needed. Networking is a very good way of doing this.

'TOTOs', C & A Networks and Bureaucracies

Contribution and appraisal networks lie somewhere in the middle of a continuum of types of organization extending from what John Warfield (1976) calls task-oriented transient organizations ('TOTOs') on the one hand to fully developed hierarchical bureaucracies on the other.

A network is more permanent than a TOTO but less so than a bureaucracy. A network has a very flat structure; there are contributors and critics at one level and record-keepers and referees at another, and that is all. (Everything else which is needed is provided through other organizations where the network supporters work.) Since network structure is flat and there are many parallel channels of communication and a number of centres of appraisal and record-keeping, it is not possible for the whole network to be dominated by any one group or clique — it would take a very large coalition of subscribers to dominate the telephone network!

Task-oriented transient groups may very well advance ideas and may even conduct pilot projects, but they are not suited to promoting the assimilation of innovations. Under some circumstances bureaucracies may favour the assimilation of innovations. Peter Blau's (1963) studies show that the conditions which must prevail for successful assimilation of innovations in a bureaucracy are:

1. There must be an overall mission which is change or adaptation-oriented. (This is conspicuous by its absence in most schools.)
2. People involved in carrying out development must receive recognition for doing so (must feel their superiors wish development).
3. The people involved must feel confident of their own competence.
4. There must be job security, both in the sense that there will be no serious danger of being fired, and also in the sense that extra people will be taken on to deal with extra work-loads of a continuing nature (ie the maximum commitment requirable by the institution is circumscribed).

Most of these conditions can be provided through networking. Even job security can be enhanced if friends on the network keep one informed of alternate job possibilities, or provide them.

The two syndromes which particularly inhibit innovation and its assimilation in organizations, 'ritualism' and 'legalism', are less likely to find attractive homes in a network based on appraisals related to a common concern of the supporters.

There is, however, the danger that the common concern of many people who might affiliate themselves with a network might be simply a desire to belong. Ritualism, legalism and "affili-itus" are all examples of the human predilection to make means ends, or as Stephen Potter put it: 'The use of useless in the do of doing lies.' In a contribution and appraisal network the best defence against this tendency is for those who are really concerned with major aims to give low appraisals, and to refuse to circulate further contributions which do not advance important aims.

Actual Contribution and Appraisal Networks

Although none are formally organized in precisely the way this paper envisions, there are many contribution and appraisal networks in existence.

The UK Network of Programmed Learning Centres (NPLC, *vide* pp 242-245, Howe and Romiszowski, 1976) which has been closely associated with APLET for a number of years, is a good example of an effective and inexpensive, yet very valuable, interchange network. On a smaller scale, the HELP network to advance physics laboratory teaching (Mr Jon Ogborn, Chelsea College) seems to work well.

A quick and pleasant overview of American networks is provided by a film-strip-audio-cassette learning activity package available from the Association for Educational Communications and Technology (Florida State University, 1975).

In Canada we have an entity called Project Cartier which holds meetings in three cities from time to time to present and appraise ideas and schemes in educational and training technology. The membership is fluid, some supporters and participants are drawn from government agencies, some from industry, some from universities, and the Secretary is with the national head office of the teachers' federation. Project Cartier is 10 years old and still viable. It has led to the establishment of a number of major projects in instructional technology, and it has helped to support their assimilation by providing appropriate contacts when they are needed.

At present one of the projects which was first discussed at Cartier is JOURNET, a computer telecommunications-based conference system designed to produce a refereed journal or yearbook of educational and instructional communications technology. Whether this network, which will depend heavily on existing university computer facilities at a number of universities across the country, and which will probably use DATAPAC communications, will succeed in becoming established is as yet problematical. However, if it does flourish, some of the credit will rest with the Project Cartier network, where it was proposed.

References

Beer. S (1975) 'Platform for Change' J Wiley, London.

Blau, P M (1965) 'The Dynamics of Bureacracy' University of Chicago.

Boyd, G M (1976a) 'Developments in Individualised Instruction at Concordia University' In NRC Canada, 'Proceedings of the Second Canadian Symposium on Instructional Technology' NRC Ottawa p 146-156.

Boyd, G M (1976b) 'Towards a Formalisation of Educational Cybernetics' in Rose, J *et al*, 'Modern Trends in Cybernetics and Systems' Editura Technica, Bucharest p 3-10.

DeMaagd, G R (1970) 'Matrix Management' Datamation 16, 9 p 46-49.

Elmaghraby, S E (1970) 'Some Network Models in Management Science' Springer Verlag, Berlin.

Florida State University (1975) 'Networks for Learning' AECT 1201 16th St W, Washington DC 20036.

Howe, A and Romiszowski, A (1976) 'International Yearbook of Educational and Instructional Technology' Kogan Page, London.

Judge, A and DeLaett, C (eds) (1976) 'Yearbook of World Problems and Human Potential' UIA Publications, Montreal.

Lakatos, I and Musgrave, A (1970) 'Criticism and the Growth of Knowledge' Cambridge University Press.

Linstone, H A and Turoff, M (eds) (1975) 'The Delphi Method' Addison-Wesley, Reading, Mass.

Litterer, J A (1969) 'Organisations' J Wiley, New York.

US Federal Fund for Improvement of Post-secondary Education (1977) 'Report on Teaching No 3' 'Change Magazine' 9, 1 January p 72.

Warfield, J N (1976) 'Societal Systems' Chapter 3, J Wiley, New York.

Electronic Media and Home-Based Learning

V H C Evers, N Hazewindus

Introduction

At present, the facilities available to the home-based adult learner are limited: books, correspondence courses, sometimes records or cassettes, and in a few cases educational radio or television programmes.

More home-based learning is expected to be necessary in future, as changes occur in the way education functions in society. A number of recent technological developments may be used to ease educational problems. It is possible on the one hand that new educational demands will emerge and, on the other hand, that new solutions can be presented. An attempt has been made at our laboratory to obtain more insight into this problem by initiating a 'case-study' round the central question: can electronic equipment help the home-based adult learner to achieve his aims more effectively?

In the past, educational use of technical equipment has created expectations which, however, have not materialized (for a discussion of this point see, for instance, Hooper 1971). A study of this failure indicated the fallacy of thinking from a purely technical point of view. It was therefore decided to widen the scope of our study initially to 'educational system based on electronic equipment', instead of equipment on its own. The selection of suitable educational methods is then the first goal. At a later stage the necessary equipment may be derived from the choice made earlier.

Teaching-Learning Process Design

In the normal book or in the average correspondence course the learning material is the same for all users, though the learner may learn in his own way and often at his own pace. This is because the traditional design of the teaching-learning process in these cases is a non-adaptive one: all students are expected to proceed in more or less the same way through the learning material. The suitability of such a design for the home-based learners may be doubted in view of the unhomogeneity of this group. It seems useful, therefore, to consider the alternative approach of adaptive designs. Here the uniqueness of each learning process is recognized and an attempt is made to organize the teaching-learning process accordingly.

1. The programme-controlled adaptive design, in which learning material is prescribed on the basis of prior knowledge about the learner and also on that of knowledge accumulated throughout the learning process.
2. The learner-controlled adaptive design, where the student himself controls his own learning process to a large extent.

The first task in programme-controlled adaptive design is to arrange the teaching-learning process in such a way that it is optimized for the student's personal situation.

The possibility of adapting the learning material used in the teaching-learning process to the student's personal characteristics is studied in aptitude-treatment-interaction (ATI) research. To date, this type of research seems to have yielded insufficient results on which to base a general prescriptional method. This may, however, be caused by the lack of a suitable methodology, as Heidt (1976) among others, has pointed out. Adaption of learning material to the learner's prior knowledge is often achieved by giving the courseware a modular structure, allowing entry at various levels. The expected variation in learning skills will sometimes require the addition of learning-to-learn material. Adaption to the student's social environment is planned in, for instance, a Dutch 'open school' experiment intended to reach housewives who received insufficient schooling earlier in life.

A second task in programme-controlled adaptive design is the measurement of the student's evolution throughout the learning process and the subsequent adaption of the teaching-learning process. A major problem in this respect stems from the dominant role of motivation in adult learning. The student's initial motivation to start a study can often be derived from his social environment, especially in the case of subjects with a vocational or personal development character. A large variation in initial motivation can be expected in view of similar results of recent research on a relatively homogeneously populated industrial training course (Hulskes, 1977). In addition, the student's motivation to continue the study requires continuous attention, especially when contacts with fellow students are scarce, as may be expected in home-based learning.

In a learner-controlled adaptive design, the student is given the possibility of exercising control over his own learning process. This may be interpreted in a very broad sense. The present discussion, however, is restricted to the application of learner-control principles to courseware design. A basic requirement is that the student has the freedom to choose his own way to gain 'new meaningful understanding', instead of just being flooded with 'new, impressive knowledge' (Northedge, 1976). As a consequence, it seems that electronic media applied in a learner-controlled adaptive design should at least permit the student this 'freedom of choice'.

In programme-controlled designs the student usually is kept actively engaged with the material by an interaction process, which continuously stimulates the learner to find answers to questions (eg in programmed instruction). In that case answers are used to realize the adaption according to a pre-programmed decision strategy. In a learner-controlled situation a similar interaction process should be envisaged, but its function is broader; it should arouse the critical mental activity of the student needed to decide upon the further path to be taken. Some students have the ability to study with (in itself simple) materials such as books. For others, however, electronic media may be used to provide the necessary 'interaction stimuli'.

A drawback of a learner-controlled design may be that the student (and certainly the student at home), missing the coercion of the predescribed step-by-step method, slips away more easily and eventually drops out. Therefore, the material should be attractively designed to arouse the student's curiosity and to stimulate his interest throughout the course. Electronic media especially may have 'entertainment potential', as for instance educational TV series such as *Sesame Street* have demonstrated.

Survey of Media for Home-Based Learning

Electronic media based on extensions and adaptions of television technology, which will be available in the near future, are given in Appendix I. A comparable range of media based on less sophisticated transmission and storage techniques are being developed, some for educational use specially. These are given in Appendix II.

In the survey we also propose to include a number of existing electronic media:

— instructional radio and instructional television (including off-air audio or video-recording;
— telephone tutoring (Turok, 1975);
— audio-cassette;
— dial-up audio learning;
— computer-assisted instruction (CAI) at home.

As we want to rank new and existing electronic media according to the learner-control parameters introduced earlier, it is necessary to include a number of reference learning situations:

— face-to-face tutoring;
— correspondence course study;
— individual study with a normal textbook or a programmed textbook.

These do not use electronic media and are almost universally known, thus allowing a critical appraisal with respect to their relative value of 'freedom of choice', 'interaction stimuli' and 'entertainment potential'.

'Freedom of choice' has been introduced to describe the student's ability to select his own study material. Books certainly provide a maximum of freedom in this respect. At the other end of the scale we placed instructional radio and television. The full range of media ranked on the basis of 'freedom of choice' of the learning material is given in Appendix IIIA.

New media near the upper end of the scale are CAI at home, Viewdata and VLP, all giving considerable freedom of choice. Teletext, with limited content selectability and a relatively large access time, has a lower place.

Closely related to freedom of choice of learning material is the facility for independent scheduling of learning time, in the case of both programme control and learner control. If the same media are ranked for the freedom of the learner to schedule their use, an almost identical arrangement arises.

A completely different order results when the media are ranked for their ability to produce interaction stimuli. Appendix IIIB represents this order and shows that in this case face-to-face tutoring scores highest, followed immediately by three techniques which allow 'live' two-way communication with a teacher.

In this table books move to the opposite end of the scale with instructional TV, radio and Teletext in that order above it. Media that score high on both aspects considered are CAI in the home environment, Viewdata used for educational purpose, the language trainer and VLP.

If we consider the potential for entertainment of the media in individualized learning, we observe that ranking is much more difficult as it involves estimation of the learners' possible affective relation with a medium. Consequently, the ranking in Appendix IIIC is less objective than that of the previous tables.

In this table VLP leads all the other media because of its ease of use, combined with high-quality audio and video presentation. Instructional TV also proves very appealing for the learner.

The electronic keyboard forms an educationally very interesting alternative to the TV type of registration in this respect. The value of good educational books must not be underestimated. We have deliberately ranked face-to-face contact lower than the media just mentioned because we think that adults would often prefer to learn without the personal presence of the teacher.

It is very tempting now to combine the results of the ranking for each aspect into one general conclusion about the use of electronic media for home-based learning. However, we do not want to make any universal conclusions about the 'best' medium for 'all' purposes. We do not think one exists. Instead, attention should be focused on the appropriate use of media combinations, by selecting them for complementary application characteristics.

Utilization of Technical Equipment

Technical equipment is traditionally often used for some form of presentation of learning material: the slide projection in school, televised Open University lessons, etc. Learning, however, is a process that extends beyond this presentation phase.

Four stages of learning may be discerned:

1. The presentation phase, in which the learner accepts the learning material presented to him.
2. The internal integration phase, in which the learner relates the new material to things he already knows. He constructs his own image of the material in association with his existing mental structures.
3. The exercising phase, in which a passive knowledge is transformed into active mastery.
4. The phase of growth to competence, in which the new abilities are integrated into larger patterns of behaviour (see also Glaser, 1976).

Some examples may elucidate this statement. In the case of 'how-to' course materials, technical aids such as VLP might be used effectively in the presentation phase. The internal integration phase may be enhanced by TV lessons aimed at elucidating the mental background of the subject matter. For much mathematical courseware the exercising phase is important, and for this CAI-like systems are useful. Growth to competence is stimulated in computerized simulation, requiring, for instance, management trainees to run a factory in a changing and commercial and social environment.

A careful analysis should be made of the use of technical aids throughout the learning process, relating them to the characteristics of freedom of choice, provision of interaction stimuli and entertainment potential discussed earlier.

At this point it may be appropriate to give some examples of our own work. Starting from an existing book an audio-cassette tape was compiled with stimuli corresponding to the four stages of the learning process. This approach was especially appreciated by adult learners who could otherwise never have contemplated studying this book about the history of the Dutch political system. Appreciation was expressed by students with very different educational results, as it shows that the interactivity of existing material may be increased using relatively modest tools. It substantially widens the range of potential users.

Social and economic factors have not been taken into account in the present discussion, but interaction in small groups has (eg the family has certainly to be considered when designing techniques of courseware for adult study at home). To gather some experience in this direction we are designing a course on video-cassette with practical work to be performed by a small group. We focused our attention on means of getting the members of the group to perform different tasks in the control of the learning situation and on the consequences of the absence of a teacher for the courseware. In addition, we hope to stimulate learning with and from each

212

other in this course.

The costs of courseware generation generally prohibit adapting audio-visual productions to specific audiences.

In this respect the electronic blackboard (see Appendix II) provides a breakthrough as it allows an experienced teacher to generate very specific material without using more time and effort than he would normally require to teach it.

For this reason our laboratory is developing special hardware (writing tableau with recording facility and TV frame memory) suited for educational application.

We are also working on the application of the video-disc, eg by studying the usefulness of electronically-controlled access to each track. This would increase its capacity to provide interaction stimuli.

Future Developments in Adult Learning

In this paper we have tried to replace the usual technological approach to the use of media for education by a more student-centred approach. This led us to the choice of a learner-controlled adaptive design as being suitable for the home-based adult learner. The ensuing discussion of media in terms of the parameters of freedom of choice, interaction stimuli and entertainment potential may provide guidelines for the development of a new generation of equipment for use at home.

The availability of novel equipment is, of course, only a part of the total problem of adult learning. A recurrent education system, for instance, requires a proper institutional framework, a certification system, etc. A mass market hobby and recreation programme raises other problems, such as cost level, standardization and sales outlets.

The development of several courseware components faces various fundamental problems. Two instances:

1. How are 'learning-to-learn' materials to be implemented? Experiments with 'study-advice' (eg Weltner [1977] or Elton and Hodgson [1976]) could provide useful insights.
2. Development of usable diagnostic self-test materials would aid considerably in devising new study methods.

Thorough analysis of such problems of courseware design should be carried out at qualified research centres. It is hoped that this paper will stimulate discussions leading to a wide range of research efforts which might substantially increase the home-based adult learner's chances for successful and rewarding study in many areas of interest.

References

Elton, L R B and Hodgson, V (1976) 'Individualized Learning and Study Advice' 'Aspects of Educational Technology X' Kogan Page, London.

Glaser, R 1976) 'Components of a Psychology of Instruction: Towards a Science of Design' Rev of Ed Res 46, No 1, p 1.

Heidt, E U (1976) 'Medien und Lernprozesse' Beltz Verlag, Weinheim and Basel. See also in 'Aspects of Educational Technology X' p 152, Kogan Page, London.

Hooper, R (1971) In Hooper, R (ed) 'The Curriculum: Context Design and Development' p 411 Oliver and Boyd, Edinburgh.

Hulskes, A G (1977) 'Obsolescence and Motivation for Adult Learning' Philips Social Research Project OMO, in preparation.

Northedge, A (1976) 'Examining our Implicit Analogies for Learning Processes' Progr Learn and Ed Tech 13, p 67.

Turok, B (1975) 'Telephone Conferencing for Teaching and Administration in the Open

University' Brit Journ of Ed Techn 6, No 3, p 63.
Weltner, K (1977) 'The Development of Study Techniques by Integrated Master Programmes'
    Brit Journ of Ed Techn 8, No 1, p 34.

Appendix I. New Media Based on Television Technology

Teletext

In the UK the broadcasting agencies have developed a method for combining
textual information with TV image transmission. A special unit attached to the TV
set at home allows selection of text pages (without sound) broadcast together with
the normal TV programme. The data format adopted makes transmission of simple
coloured diagrams possible. The user will be able to record the information on a
normal cassette recorder.

Viewdata

The British Post Office is running trials with a system which uses the telephone
instead of television transmission to transport information to the TV screen at
home. This system uses the same data format as Teletext, but allows the user to
select from a very large number of pages. The computer which stores this
information may be interrogated 'interactively' by the user.

Videophone

When a suitable network is available the videophone might be used as a more
comprehensive, two-way, closed-circuit TV system on a local scale (our laboratory
is operating an in-house experimental system consisting of a standard 625-line
monitor and a simple camera).

VLP

Philips are to introduce a video long-play system on the United States consumer
market soon. In principle the system allows access to 40,000 individual frames. In
this paper the consumer version is considered which does not have an automatic
random-access facility.

Appendix II. A New Generation of Media for Specific Educational Purposes

The Electronic Blackboard

This is a simple device for the registration on cassette tape of written text or
drawings together with spoken commentary. The cassette is replayed on a recorder
which is connected to a normal TV set via special electronics.

Real-time presentation of drawings and speech is thus obtained. Courseware is
generated and distributed reasonably inexpensively.

Scribophone

Essentially this is the electronic blackboard used via a telephone connection. Use of
such a facility has been considered by the Open University.

The Language Trainer

An audio-cassette recorder with a special facility for dual track use (teacher/
student) enables students to study a language using the audio-active and
comparative (AAC) method. This recorder can also be used for other applications,
eg to enable an amateur musician to record his own playing of an instrument
against the background of a full ensemble.

Electronic Mail

A computer network can be used to improve personal message services. It would

214

enable the student to have written communication with a teacher with a response time not obtainable with ordinary mail services.

Experiments with existing computer networks are being carried out in both the USA and Europe. In the long run it is possible to see home connections permitting the use of these networks for various forms of home-based learning.

Appendix III. Educational Media Ranked on Fundamental Parameters of Learner Control

A. *'freedom of choice'*
1. Books
2. CAI at home
   Viewdata
3. VLP
4. Cassettes
   Language trainer
   Electronic blackboard
5. Dial-up audio
   Electronic mail
   Correspondence course
6. Teletext
7. Face-to-face tutoring
8. Telephone tutoring
   Scribophone
   Videophone
9. Programmed text-books
10. Instructional radio
    Instructional TV

B. *'interaction stimuli'*
1. Face-to-face tutoring
2. Videophone
   Scribophone
   Telephone tutoring
3. CAI at home
   Viewdata
   Programmed text-books
4. Language trainer
5. VLP
6. Electronic blackboard
   Cassettes
7. Dial-up audio
   Electronic mail
   Correspondence course
8. Teletext
9. Instructional radio
   Instructional TV
10. Books

C. *'entertainment potential'*
1. VLP
2. Instructional TV
3. Electronic blackboard

4. Books
5. Face-to-face tutoring
   Videophone
6. Cassettes
   Instructional radio
   Language trainer
7. Programmed textbooks
8. Scribophone
   Telephone tutoring
   Dial-up audio
9. Correspondence course
10. Electronic mail
    CAI at home
    Viewdata
    Teletext.

Programmed Learning Applied to:
(a) Solving a 'Numeracy' Problem
in Training (b) a Group Situation

C M Bateson, P G J Lewis

Introduction

General

The Royal Engineers train their soldiers in a large number of different combat and artisan employments ranging from combat engineers to plumbers and pipefitters. Each soldier has two trades and most of them are trained to work in both a combat and an artisan role. The total number of employments involved is nearly 60 and most of these have three levels of qualification. This means the training requirements involve something in the order of 160 different courses and their associated problems. This paper deals with two of these problems and how programmed learning was used to overcome them.

The first part of the paper deals with a system developed to overcome problems caused in training by the poor standard of numeracy among students. Part Two describes an attempt to enrich a rather mundane learning situation using programmed learning linked to a feedback classroom unit.

Background

Because of the technical nature of the various employments involved, there is considerable requirement for trainees in the Royal Engineers to have specific mathematical abilities. A system is run based on identified mathematical modules required for each course of training. Each soldier has to pass the modules specific to the requirement for his next training course. These modules are used as part of the selection procedure for up-grading courses. It is necessary for qualifications in these modules to be gained in advance of the soldier arriving for training as it is not cost effective to bring soldiers back from all over the world only to have them fail in the first few weeks of their training.

Passes in the modules are obtained by attending courses at education centres near to the soldiers' units. Unfortunately, a problem arose because, due to the frequent need for them to work in their other employment or due to commitments such as Northern Ireland, a number of years may elapse between qualifying and being called forward for upgrading training. On arrival for this training, it was found that many were unable to cope with the 'applied' mathematics on the course. Considerable time was consequently wasted reteaching 'mathematics' and often to little avail. The Training Development Team were invited to look at this problem and suggest a solution to it.

The first half of this paper explains how we set about identifying the exact nature of this problem, providing a possible solution, and the resulting benefits.

Programmed Learning to Solve a Numeracy Problem in Training

Identifying the Problem

The first task was to discover the precise nature of the problem. It was not enough to say that a student's mathematical knowledge was not up to the required standard. We needed to know two things:

1. Why was it not up to standard?
2. In what way was it not up to standard?

There proved to be many reasons why students were not up to the required standard. The most common was that although they had covered the material at some stage in their career, they had now forgotten it. Some arriving for upgrading courses had touched no mathematics for several years.

The second problem (In what way as their knowledge not up to standard?) proved more difficult to solve. Attempts had been made to solve the problem by giving conventional general instruction based on the mathematics required in a particular course. The example we took was plant operator mechanics, part of whose job is to operate earth-moving equipment, and they need to be able to calculate areas and volumes as part of their work. Students arriving for upgrading courses in this employment were tested on areas and volumes and were found to have great difficulty in coping with them. Conventional instruction was given in these topics but it seemed to have little effect.

It occurred to us that the trouble might lie at an earlier stage, so we devised a diagnostic test which consisted of a number of questions, each on a separate topic and spanning the whole range of mathematics required for this particular course, from basic principles, eg fractions and decimals, up to transposition of formulae, areas, volumes etc, up to the standard required. The test is a rather crude one by academic standards but nevertheless it is accurate enough for our purpose. To accompany this test we devised an analysis sheet so that results could be easily and quickly interpreted.

The test was tried with a plant operator mechanic class. It was not marked in the conventional sense, but on a pass/fail basis. Students passed or failed in a particular topic depending on how much of the question they got right and what sort of mistakes they made. The results were analyzed and marked on the analysis sheet. In Figure 1 the shaded squares show where students successfully answered a topic.

The results showed that many students who failed the latter stages of the test, eg areas and volumes, also failed earlier questions such as fractions and decimals. From this we made the assumption that the real problem was one of basic numeracy. For example, many students could remember that the formula for the area of a circle was πr^2, but when faced with using π as $\frac{22}{7}$ or 3.14, they were unable to make accurate calculations. Students who cannot handle simple decimal and vulgar fractions will certainly not be able to cope with more complicated calculations which involve these operations.

An additional complication was the fact that individual weaknesses appeared in different areas. No two students had exactly the same problems. It would have required a one-to-one instructor/student ratio to solve the problem by conventional methods, and this of course was quite impracticable.

Solving the Problem

Programmed learning seemed to offer the only solution. Programs were available for many of the topics covered in the diagnostic test but there were some gaps. We filled the gaps by writing our own programs.

MATHEMATICS DIAGNOSTIC TEST—ANALYSIS SHEET

Test Information	
Date of Test	26/11/75
Time started	0920
Time finished	12.15

Course Designation: PLANT OPERATOR MECHANIC
Course Number: 75/3

Topics

NAMES	01 Fractions	02 Decimals	03 S.I. Units	04 Conversion Imp/Metric	05 Averages	06 Ratio/Proportion	07 Percentages	08 Transposition of Formulae	09 Areas	010 Pythagoras	011 Surface Areas	012 Volumes	013 Logarithms
LOCKE	■	■		■			■	■	■	■			■
MANNING	■	■	■	■		■	■	■	■	■			■
MOFFAT	■	■	■			■	■	■	■	■			■
NICOL	■			■	■		■	■	■	■		■	
PAGE	■	■	■	■	■	■	■	■	■	■		■	■
PHILLIPS	■			■	■	■	■	■		■			
PRICE	■	■	■	■			■						
RODGER	■	■	■				■	■					
SALMON	■	■		■			■	■					
WATKINS	■	■											

REMEDIAL ACTION

	Presentation	Programme
Fractions	Text	
Decimals	Prog. Pack	
The S.I. (Metric) System of Units	"	
The Metric System (Conversion)	"	
Averages	Text	
Proportion	"	
Percentage	"	
Transposition of Formulae	Prog. Pack	
Areas	"	
Pythagoras' Theorem	"	
Surface Areas	"	
Volumes	"	
Logarithms Vol. 1	"	
Logarithms Vol. 2	"	

Figure 1. Mathematics diagnostic test-analysis sheet

The system we adopted was that when the students arrived for a plant operator mechanic upgrading course they were given a mathematics diagnostic test which was appropriate to their course requirements. Areas of weakness were identified and students were given programs appropriate to their individual weaknesses. The programs were given one at a time in ascending order of difficulty. Tests were given at the end of each program so that both student and instructor could monitor progress.

The programs were in two forms. Some were programmed texts, the rest were in paper-pack form suitable for use in a presentation device called the 'Programme Pack' which is basically a plastic binder with a movable mask which conceals the answers to each frame as the student works through the program. Each program is accompanied by a criterion test and marking schedule. All are of the linear type.

Disadvantages

It became apparent that there could be two disadvantages:

1. Students who successfully completed the diagnostic test and needed little or no remedial training were left with nothing to do whilst the rest of the class were working on mathematics.
2. Slow students who were not able to complete the remedial programs they needed in the time allocated.

In the former case the problem was overcome by allowing the students to study privately the technical content of the course. Another possible solution was to give students mathematics programs of a higher standard and so prepare them for further upgrading courses. We have since used both alternatives with considerable success.

In the latter cases the students were encouraged to do extra work in their own time to catch up with the rest of the class. This was not an ideal solution as it tended to put some students who were already under pressure, under still more pressure.

Advantages

The advantage of this system falls into two categories, those general to the technique and those specific to this trial.

The general advantages of the technique were as follows:

1. The individual problems of the student were quickly discovered and (hopefully) remedied. The students were quick to appreciate this and responded to it.
2. Instructors were not forced to work in the dark. At the commencement of a course they could identify the students who were likely to have difficulty with mathematics. They also knew what those difficulties were and could act accordingly.
3. By using teaching programs for the remedial instruction, a number of students could work on different topics under one instructor. Providing that the instructor was familiar with the mathematics involved, he could supervize the class and give help to any individual students who were having difficulty. This of course, is one of the normal benefits of programmed instruction.
4. Remedial programs could be used on a self-help basis, ie students could take them away to work on in their own time.

The specific advantages which we gained from this technique were:

1. The average marks for the earthwork calculations phase of the plant operator mechanics course went up from an average of 61% prior to the introduction of the system to an average of 80% after its introduction. These improvements are indicated in Figure 2(a).
2. On the last five courses which took place prior to the introduction of this system 16% of the students failed this exam and a further 14% had to be re-tested. In the first five courses after its introduction there were no failures and only 3% had to be re-tested. These are shown in Figure 2(b). These failures represented a non-cost-effective wastage of £17,000 per year by filling non-productive training places. On top of this training time was wasted carrying out revision as well as preparing and running re-tests for failures.

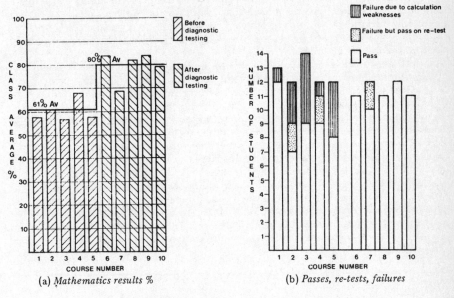

(a) *Mathematics results %*   (b) *Passes, re-tests, failures*

Figure 2. *Plant operator mechanics, class II-I*

A hidden advantage which was subsequently discovered was that instructors had been wasting training time teaching mathematics during instructional periods allocated to other subjects. They were forced to do this in order to assist students to understand technical concepts. The introduction of this diagnostic/remedial technique eliminated this requirement and students were now able to cope with the applied mathematics needed at each stage of their course without difficulty, thus training time was saved.

Conclusions

The system seems to work and is popular with both students and staff. The reduction of the failure rate represents a considerable saving in money.

The system has now been tried with two other employments, ie engine fitters and combat engineers. The results were similar to those obtained with plant operator mechanics. Plans are in hand to introduce it into many other employments.

So far we have only tried this system of diagnostic testing in the field of mathematics, but there seems to be no reason why it should not be extended to the technical knowledge of students coming for upgrading courses, although programmed remedial back-up might present something of a problem at first. This may well be our next step.

Using Programmed Learning in a Group Situation

General

A number of our employments have a need as part of their early training to be taught the basics of the internal combustion engine. In order to try and standardize this training and allow for the differing background knowledge of students, programmed texts were tried out. Unfortunately, as this part of training was at the start of longer courses, the open-ended time factor necessary for normal programmed learning could not be allowed. Similarly, under normal classroom instruction, the weaker students were often being left behind as the instructor had to 'press on' against the clock.

A further problem tended to occur due to the fact that the instructors as experts in the subject found difficulty dealing at the very basic level. Like many experts they often, as a result of student questions, became sidetracked and involved in technical detail outside the requirements of the students. This meant that despite 'lesson' notes, some areas were dealt with out of sequence, some in too much detail and others often barely covered. Further to this, the frequency of these courses meant continual repetition for instructors leading perhaps to a loss of enthusiasm, resulting in bad instruction and student boredom.

At this time we had for trial at the Royal School of Military Engineering a 'Pennant' Response Evaluation Machine and a number of programs prepared on filmstrip for teaching army drivers basic engine principles. Both of these training aids tended to be treated with suspicion by instructors and although one or two separate trials were carried out on each, neither was being used particularly effectively. It was therefore decided to try and combine the two and a pilot scheme was conducted.

Initial Trials and Pilot Scheme

The initial pilot highlighted a number of weaknesses:

1. The filmstrip programs were not particularly convenient to use in our situation.
2. They had insufficient 'question' frames to support the visual material.
3. The instructor was having to add considerably to the text in order to cover the wider objectives required for our training.

The response from the students at the end of the trial was so favourable that we decided it would be beneficial to carry out further trials.

The main problems were related to the fact that programs prepared elsewhere very rarely fit the exact training needs of other establishments. Changes were made therefore to overcome these problems and a second trial was prepared.

The next trial run indicated that the mix of material and questions was about correct. It worked very well with the instructor who had prepared the material, as he kept to the subject of the prepared programs. However, when outside instructors used them they continued to introduce 'red herrings', to teach material covered by later programs out of turn and failed to complete the lessons in the required time. They also forgot to pre-set the answers on the response machine. To overcome the problem of instructor digression, a fairly detailed script was prepared relating to:

1. Exactly what explanation should be given for each picture slide.
2. The question to be asked following it.
3. The correct answer to the question emphasizing the button to press on the control unit.

This being resolved, a further trial was set up using two classes and two control groups. The same two military instructors were used for both the new system and to teach the control groups using conventional classroom instruction.

The System

The system was set up in a normal classroom with the master control unit mounted on the instructor's desk. The program text or script was printed on cards with one frame per card. The cards could be turned over quickly as they were mounted in a ring binder.

Each student had a handset containing four response buttons A, B, C and D. The handsets also had right/wrong lights which gave the student immediate knowledge of results following his response.

The instructor operated the automatic projector to show the picture frame on the screen. He then gave the relevant explanation relating to the picture, emphasizing any special points. The picture was changed to show a multiple-choice question. At the same time, the correct answer master button on his control unit was pressed.

The students were then told to press the button on their handsets corresponding to what they thought was the correct answer. Their responses were shown by lights on the instructor's master panel. In this way he knew immediately which members of the class had chosen the wrong answer. He was then able to take instant remedial action to correct these student errors. The class were then shown a slide containing the correct answer.

When he felt the entire class had understood the correct answer, he proceeded to the next picture frame and the cycle was repeated. Each program contained approximately 50 slides and required about one 40-minute period of instruction. The total package contains nine programs.

Disadvantages

The individual instructor's freedom of delivery is partially restricted once he elects to use this technique, as we maintain there is a real need for fairly tight scripting.

The commercially-produced response evaluation machine is a rather expensive piece of equipment. It has in fact been described by some as an expensive toy which cannot justify its cost by results. This has been overcome by some departments building 'homemade' devices. The cost of these has varied from £5-£30.

Like all programmed material the preparation time for text and visual materials is considerable. This means that any development of the system will require a major effort by training staff in order to prepare programs.

Advantages

Many of the advantages are the same as those found in the normal use of programmed learning. Once again they fall into two categories, those general to the technique, and those specific to the trial.

General advantages of the technique were:

1. Students liked the method as they felt they were taking an active part in the lessons. They themselves pointed out that whereas in normal instruction the instructor can only question one student at a time, the new system allows him to question them all at the same time and be aware of all their answers. When students were unsure of a point in normal class, they hesitated to ask questions and the point would be lost. This is minimized using the feedback system.
2. The learning is in small steps as with normal programmed learning and the next step is not made until the previous one has been learnt and the correct answer understood.
3. The student receives instant knowledge of results, providing reinforcement of correct answers and immediate correction of wrong answers. Similarly, the instructor receives instant feedback on the success of his lesson and is able to take fast remedial action when required. Although restricting the instructions delivery slightly, they themselves liked the system once they had tried it out. In fact, one of our biggest problems was persuading them to instruct control groups by normal methods in order to obtain comparable results.
4. As mentioned in the first part of this paper, one of the disadvantages of programmed learning is the desirability for an open-ended time scale in order to allow the slower students to work at their own pace. Unfortunately, in practice this unlimited time is not always available for reasons beyond control of the trainer. This group approach allows the instructor to have a better control of the time taken to complete each program. He can encourage the slower students, keeping them going with the rest of the class instead of allowing them to work entirely at their own pace.

Advantages specific to the trial were based on the end-of-course multiple-choice objective test. They were:

1. The mean percentage marks for the trial groups were 92% and 88%. Those for the control groups were only 68% and 74%.
2. The range of marks for the trial groups was 76% to 100% whereas that for the control groups was 31% to 92%.
3. The standard deviations for the trial groups were 6.3 and 7.6 compared with 13.4 and 13.0 for the control groups.
4. None of the students in the trial groups would have failed the test but three in the control groups would have failed if the pass mark had been set at 60% (as for other written tests used in the Royal School of Military Engineering). The reliability of the test used is 0.8 calculated by Kuder-Richardson method.

The performance of future courses will continue to be monitored. This is in order to ensure that there is not a drop-off in results due to over-familiarization of students and instructors with the technique.

Conclusions

The overall conclusions on the system were:

1. It appeared to work for this group of students, creating an enriched and more rewarding learning situation which both instructors and students liked.
2. The end-of-course test results for both trials showed an average improvement of 19% for the trial groups over the control groups.
3. Not only were the marks better for the trial groups but the range of marks was far narrower than those for the control groups.

224

4. Three of the students in the control groups would have failed while all those in the trial groups passed.
5. Using the Mann-Whitney U-test the difference between the two groups taking the end of course test was statistically significant beyond the 0.1% level of confidence.

As previously mentioned, other departments are now building their own systems and it is hoped to expand the method into other employment training and run further trials with them.

Systematic Evaluation in a Large Training Organization

J D S Moore

The organization which is the subject of this paper on the development and implementation of systematic evaluation is HMS Collingwood, near Fareham in Hampshire.

HMS Collingwood is the Royal Navy's largest training establishment and its primary purpose is to train personnel of the Weapon Electrical Engineering Branch for eventual employment in the Fleet.

Because of its size, HMS Collingwood is divided into five schools — Common Training, Radio, Ordnance, Control and Digital Systems. The schools run over 270 courses for an annual student throughput of more than 7000.

Courses are divided into Career and Pre-joining Training (PJT) classifications. 22 career courses are run and these provide the general basis of knowledge and skill required at each level in a man's career. The PJT courses offer the specialist knowledge and skill required to maintain equipment fitted in ships of the Fleet.

Although personnel must complete the appropriate career course for each level of their career, they need only undergo PJT training for the equipment that they will be required to maintain in their next job. Thus no one person would ever complete more than a fraction of the 250 or so PJT courses available.

Management decision-making in this large training enterprise is concentrated largely on ensuring that trained men can do their jobs effectively, and on minimizing the human and material costs of such training.

These objective imply two areas in which quality control is essential. However, it has already been mentioned that training involves general (career) courses which are designed to teach broadly relevant principles and skills and also more specific (equipment) courses, which allow specialized training for each man based on the equipment demands of his next ship.

There are significant differences between these two types of courses. The pre-joining training courses tend to be measured in days rather than weeks, have almost nil failure rates (under ½%), small class sizes (averaging about five students) and a high practical content (around 50%). The average score in examinations is nearly 70%. Career courses are longer, with much larger classes, higher failure rates and lower practical content. In view of the different profiles of career and pre-joining training courses, therefore, it was decided to look at quality control in the four areas shown in Figure 1.

	Internal (Establishment)	External (Fleet)
Career courses	1	3
Pre-joining training (PJT) courses	2	4

Figure 1. *Performance Areas*

Systematic evaluation in the Collingwood training context implies the continuous collection of appropriate information (Figure 2) and its processing in such a way that attention can be directed to areas of concern. Decisions to change training in any way (for example, to reduce a high failure rate) can be evaluated using appropriate subsequent feedback.

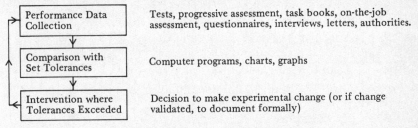

Performance Data Collection	Tests, progressive assessment, task books, on-the-job assessment, questionnaires, interviews, letters, authorities.
Comparison with Set Tolerances	Computer programs, charts, graphs
Intervention where Tolerances Exceeded	Decision to make experimental change (or if change validated, to document formally)

Figure 2. *Systematic Assessment*

Of the four performance areas listed in Figure 1, Area 1 concerns career courses conducted within HMS Collingwood. Each course is considered from three dimensions — student, course and performance characteristics. In a typical case, information is recorded on student general intelligence, literacy and numeracy, on the class perception of the course and on various performance criteria such as scores, times and failure rates. The implication was that, in many instances, variations in interim performance would be paralleled by variations in either student potential or course conduct.

Area 2, pre-joining training courses conducted in HMS Collingwood, presented a different problem in so far as performance criteria were concerned.

The collection of trainee and course data was identical to career course information, but performance data related to 'grading against standard schedules for normal equipments'.

Given factors such as negligible failure rates, small classes and perhaps infrequent courses, a conventional 'exam-style' approach was inappropriate for PJT equipment courses: Given variations due to lack of equipment, malfunctioning of available equipment and externally-imposed time constraints (such as joining routines), the exam or test score, by itself, would mean very little. If, for instance, only theory was examinable in a course one month but theory and practical the next month, then the scores recorded would relate to two entirely different situations.

In these circumstances then, any set of assessment criteria would have to allow for variations in the content and style of testing, in order not only to tell course managers and employers to which a particular score referred, but also to identify the practical strengths and weaknesses to be made good (where possible) by on-the-job training.

Such a profile (Figure 4) was developed and refined so that it applied to the 250 or so different equipment courses. The intention was to add to existing information, to ask for judgements of student competence on virtually a go/no-go basis and to allow for the limitations of individual courses and students to be fed forward to their employers in the Fleet.

Area 4 from Figure 1, external PJT performance, concerns the 'other half' of the PJT assessment profile. In the right-hand column, space is provided for each ship, three months after a man joins it, to give a counter-assessment of his performance against the profile items. This provides:

1. A measure of the validity of internal judgements.

227

NAME .... RATING ....OFFICIAL NO....

CLASS ....PUT COURSE NO. ..... EQUIPMENT ......DATE.....

	PLEASE TICK	
	YES	NO
1. Was your Joining Routine satisfactory?		
2. Was the number of students in your class about right for learning?		
3. Was your previous knowledge satisfactory for beginning this course?		
4. Was the continuity of the Course satisfactory?		
5. Was the Theory content sufficient?		
6. Was the Practical content sufficient?		
7. Was the quality of Practical work adequate?		
8. Were the Theoretical and Practical aspects of the Course well related to each other?		
9. Was the Course length about right?		
10. Did your Instructor(s) stimulate your interest in the subject matter?		
11. Was your Instructor(s) understanding of the subject satisfactory?		
12. Was satisfactory information given about Equipment Documentation?		
13. Did your Examination (or other assessment) cover all major aspects of the Course?		
14. Will you now be able to maintain this Equipment with reasonable confidence?		
15. Did you enjoy the Course?		

ANY OTHER COMMENTS OR SUGGESTIONS

GROUP OFFICER'S COMMENTS

Figure 3. *QC2 – Career Course/PJT Questionnaire*

```
                    PJT ASSESSMENT FORM -
                STAFF-IN-CONFIDENCE WHEN COMPLETED
                                              DATE COURSE
NAME ................ RATING ..... OFFICIAL NO ..... ENDED .......
                                              COURSE MARK(S)
CLASS ...... PJT COURSE NO ...... EQUIPMENT ...... (PER CENT) .....

Key:  * Delete as appropriate
      1. Superior   2. Satisfactory   3. Unsatisfactory
      4. Not assessed    5. Not applicable   6. Not employed
```

	HMS Collingwood		HMS .... (3 months after joining)	
	Grade 1-6		Grade 1-6	
1. Ability to carry out Command Confidence*/ Functional* checks				
2. Ability to carry out Planned Maintenance Routines				
3. Ability to prepare for*/ carry out* Harbour Acceptance Trials				
4. Ability to prepare for*/ carry out* Sea Acceptance Trials				
5. Ability to recognise and diagnose departures from Standard Performance				
6. Ability to repair faults down to Module*/Board*/ Component* level				
7. Ability to use documentation to achieve 1-6 above				
8. Knowledge of Principles and Theory				
9. Is Trainee aware of dangers and safety precautions?	YES* NO*		YES* NO*	
10. Is Trainee aware of Security aspects?	YES* NO*		YES* NO*	

```
GENERAL COMMENTS
```

HMS Collingwood	HMS ....

```
Signed ..........................    Signed ....................

Rank/Rating ......................    Rank/Rating ..............
```

Figure 4. *PJT Assessment Form*

2. An indication of the extent to which a man has been employed in areas not covered by his shore training.

Returns are voluntary but the percentage, which averages about 38%, is an encouraging one.

Area 3, the final performance area, deals with external career course performance (Figure 5). In this case the intention is to measure and facilitate on-the-job training and performance by providing in a Task Book a list of tasks to be carried out in the Fleet to allow a trainee to become fully proficient in his general job area. The distinction between the task areas is so that 'General and General Technical Tasks' will deal with jobs that can be carried out whatever the type of ship, whereas 'Equipment Tasks' will allow for variations from ship to ship.

Collect following data using task books:	For each task record number of trainees:
a. General Tasks	1. Successful first attempt
b. General Technical Tasks	2. Successful final attempt
c. Equipment Tasks	3. Not attempted in time-scale set

Figure 5. *Feedback Area 3 — External Career Course Performance*

The performance information on the right would facilitate the control of shore training decisions in order to refine performance on-the-job. So far the paper has considered the following:

1. The various performance areas in training.
2. The types of information collected.
3. The concept of 'systematic' assessment.

However, the overall evaluation system works as in Figure 6. In the algorithm there is a progression for each course (or course module) from assessment of individual students via classes and courses to whole trainee outputs to the Fleet. If a decision has been made, on the basis of feedback, to change training, then the effects of such a decision (on the original deficiency) are also monitored.

The question of a student being within tolerance is fairly obvious for a career course (either he achieves the pass mark or not) or, in the case of a self-pacing course, he completes his work successfully within the maximum time limit allowed.

In PJT equipment courses however, the trainees continue on to the job whatever their results and the emphasis is on ensuring that the gross, overall quality of performance is maintained.

Going on from the individual student to the class level of quality control, career courses for which a class falls outside set tolerances result in a 'non-standard printout' from the computer system used to store and process the information previously described (Figure 7).

In Figure 7, dealing with the Maths Pre-test for the Basic Electro-technology Course, both the class average percentage score and the failure rate are outside the limits set (paragraph 2).

A comparison in paragraph 3 shows that the intelligence measures for the 'pass' and 'fail' groups within the class are similar, as are the English Language grades (right-hand column under NAMET — Naval Maths and English Test).

However, the maths grades between the two groups are significantly different and probably account for the results falling outside tolerances.

Had no obvious differences in intelligence, maths or English emerged, then

230

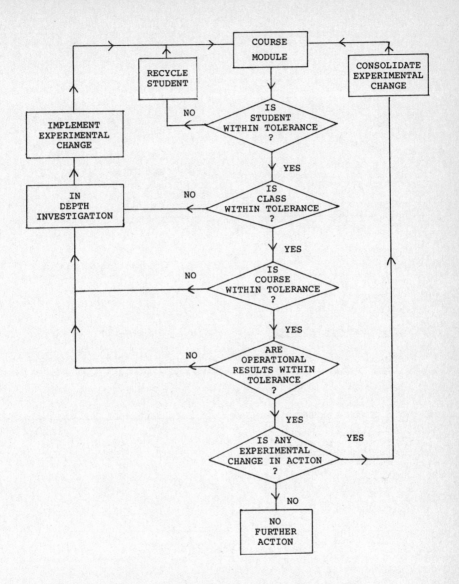

Figure 6. *The Entire Adaptive Training System*

```
QUALITY CONTROL GROUP   -   PRINT OUT OF NON-STANDARD RESULTS FOR
                             WEEK 38 - AUTUMN TERM 1975


1. GENERAL INFORMATION

        CLASS                           MCT       37
        MODULE                          MATHS PRE-TEST
        INSTRUCTOR                      REMN SMITH
        NUMBER OF RN IN CLASS                     12
        NUMBER ON FILE                          1365
        NUMBER OF DIPBACKS IN CLASS     NOT APPLICABLE
        PERCENTAGE PASS MARK                      80


2. RESULTS AND STANDARDS  (NON-STANDARD RESULTS FLAGGED WITH AN X)
                                        UPPER    LOWER
                             ACHIEVED   LIMIT    LIMIT
     X PERCENTAGE SCORE          83       97       85
     X PERCENTAGE FAILURE RATE   41       10
       TIME TAKEN  (DAYS)         O        1        O


3. CLASS/COURSE COMPARISONS
                        T2 SCORE  **NAMET**  PRETEST  SCORE  TIME
        CLASS AVERAGE       84      3  5        O       83     O
        COURSE AVERAGE     102      2  2        O       89     O
        PASS GROUP AVERAGE  85      2  5        O       90     O
        FAIL GROUP AVERAGE  83      4  5        O       73     O


4. QUESTIONNAIRE COMPARISON  -  NO INFORMATION AVAILABLE ON THIS CLASS


5. QUALITY CONTROL COMMENT       GROUP COMMENT       CONCLUSIONS
   ****************************************************************
   *                         *                  *                *
   * ALTHOUGH THIS CLASS HAD A *                 *                *
   * MUCH LOWER T2 THAN AVERAGE, *               *                *
   * A COMPARISON OF PASS AND  *                 *                *
   * FAIL GROUP T2s SHOWS THIS *                 *                *
   * IS NOT THE PRIMARY REASON *                 *                *
   * FOR THE FAILURE.  SUGGEST *                 *                *
   * THE REASON IS SIMPLY LACK *                 *                *
   * OF MATHS ABILITY AS SHOWN *                 *                *
   * BY THE NAMET MATHS.  2 FOR *                *                *
   * PASS GROUP, 4 FOR FAIL    *                 *                *
   * GROUP                     *                 *                *
```

Figure 7. *The Non-Standard Printout*

MODULE. O/CEM WEEK 11	SAMPLE SIZE	MEAN	STD DEV	PASS MARK	FAIL RATE	TIME. (DAY)	INDEX	COMMENTS
PREVIOUS BEST	376	90	7.64	70	1	5.0	193.	PREVIOUS TERMS INDICES, 204. 183. 183. MOST RECENT TERM FIRST.
CURRENT TERM.	76	89	6.23	70	0	5.0	198.	
STANDARD ACHIEVED		UNSAT	SAT		SAT	SAT	SAT	

MODULE. O/CEM WEEK 12	SAMPLE SIZE	MEAN	STD DEV	PASS MARK	FAIL RATE	TIME. (DAY)	INDEX	COMMENTS
PREVIOUS BEST	352	90	7.36	70	0	5.0	198.	PREVIOUS TERMS INDICES, 201. 194. 194. MOST RECENT TERM FIRST.
CURRENT TERM.	61	90	6.80	70	0	5.0	199.	
STANDARD ACHIEVED		SAT	SAT		SAT	SAT	SAT	

MODULE. O/CEM PRACTICAL	SAMPLE SIZE	MEAN	STD DEV	PASS MARK	FAIL RATE	TIME. (DAY)	INDEX	COMMENTS
PREVIOUS BEST	270	95	7.73	70	0	9.1	209.	PREVIOUS TERMS INDICES, 207. 209. 209. MOST RECENT TERM FIRST.
CURRENT TERM.	49	99	2.01	70	0	9.7	218.	
STANDARD ACHIEVED		SAT	SAT		SAT	UNSAT	SAT	

MEAN BEST INDEX = 188.   MEAN TERMS INDEX = 197.

Figure 8. *Termly Course Printout*

233

PERCENTAGE UNSAT TASK PERFORMANCE

TASK		1	2	3	4	5	6	7	8	9	10	11	12	13	14	15	16	TOTAL	EVENTS	%
PERCENTAGE		0	30	90	10	50	10	30	20	20	10	70	30	50	50	30	20			
	A			90				30	20	20		70		50		30	20	330	8	41*
S	B	0		90		50	10			20			30			30	20	250	8	31
U	C			90		50			20				30	50			20	260	6	43*
B	D		30			50			20					50				150	4	38*
	E		30			50			20							30		130	4	33
M	F		30															30	1	30
O	G		30								10					30		70	3	23
D	H			90									30					120	2	60*
U	I			90					20						50			160	3	53*
L	J				10		10											20	2	10
A	K		30		10								30	50		30		150	5	30
R	L			90	10													100	2	50*
	M				10				20									30	2	15
I	N				10				20				30					60	3	20
T	O									20								20	1	20
E	P												30			30		60	2	30
M	Q		30						20				30					80	3	27
	R					50						70						120	2	60*
	S			90		50						70						210	3	70*
																	TOTAL	2350	64	
																			MEAN	37%

STARRED ITEMS ARE THE SUB-MODULAR ITEMS WHICH HAVE THE WORST RECORD

Figure 9. *Task/Sub-Modular Item Matrix*

further investigation would have included evaluation of student perception of the course, and interviews with course staff, if necessary. (It should be noted also that the average class intelligence was well down on that for classes as a whole.)

Moving up to the 'Course' level of quality control, the emphasis is entirely on output criteria (Figure 8). At this level, criteria include mean scores, standard deviations, pass marks, failure rates and times. The intention is to foster either direct or compensating optimization of the criteria. An index has been developed which, for example, allows improvements in some criteria (provided they are sufficiently large) to more than offset deteriorations in other interior levels. The intention is not just to push up mean scores all the time, but in appropriate cases where Fleet performance is satisfactory, to hold standards constant (or slightly reduce them) and minimize course times and resources.

In the bottom of the three examples, the mean score and the standard deviation have improved at the expense of extra time on course. (This is a self-pacing module.)

Finally, a 'theoretical' look at how the external career course quality control might interact with internal assessment. (Some of these procedures are only just being implemented.)

In Figure 9 the horizontal axis refers to the tasks which have been carried out on the job and the percentage of these which have been carried out unsatisfactorily. The vertical axis refers to items within the appropriate course in HMS Collingwood which form part of the whole task performance.

A division of the total percentage unsatisfactory task performances across a particular course item, by the number of tasks involved, gives a measure of the extent to which this item within the HMS Collingwood training has proved deficient in fostering effective on-the-job performance. Remedial action could subsequently be monitored by feedback.

Clearly, the effect of systematic evaluation of the nature described can only be measured progressively over a number of years and this is being done. In the short-term, however, indications are that the system facilitates better communication of the sort of information needed for a large variety of managerial decisions and allows for a greater degree of instructor and student involvement in the information flow. In addition, the policy of 'assessment by exception' has resulted in a saving of over 50% of the original assessment staff.

Educational Technology– Today and Tomorrow

L R B Elton

The Art of Extrapolation

In order to talk about the future it is necessary to extrapolate an activity in time. What one needs for this is some data which show regularity, and also a theory which fits those data and which allows one to extrapolate into the future. Can one then find consistent data and a theory for educational technology?

Mass, Individual and Group

I do not propose to cover the whole area of educational technology but want to confine myself to just one small part, the methods and means of teaching and learning in higher education. Let us look first at the data.

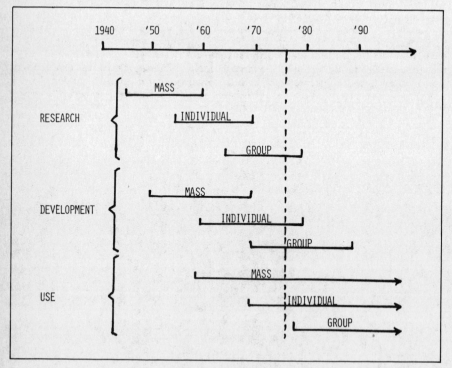

Figure 1. *The data*

Broadly speaking, there has been a change of emphasis from mass instruction via individualized instruction to group learning. Each seems to have followed the classical pattern of development from research through development to use. Furthermore, broadly speaking, in each case the research phase lasts 15 years; development on the whole takes longer, more like 20 years, overlapping research and use comes at a still later stage. Now this is a very broad brush and I have no doubt that if one looks at it more carefully the ends of these lines are not well determined. But by and large this is what happened. The last three lines, the use lines, have not got a bar on the right-hand side but an arrow, because there is no particular reason why the use of a particular area of educational technology should stop. The research and development phases apparently tend to phase out but the use may well continue.

Let me look at what at the moment is an empirical set of data and see whether I can find some justification for them. I want to analyze the three types of teaching, mass teaching, individual teaching and group teaching, to try and find the basis on

	MASS	INDIVIDUAL	GROUP
BASIS	INDUSTRIAL TECHNOLOGY	BEHAVIOURIST PSYCHOLOGY	HUMANISTIC PSYCHOLOGY
MODEL	ECONOMY OF SCALE	STIMULUS – RESPONSE	ENCOUNTER GROUP
METHOD	HARDWARE	SOFTWARE	TECHNIQUES
RESULTS	C.C.T.V. C.A.L. SATELLITES	PROGR. LEARNING KELLER PLAN AUDIO-TUTORIAL	SKILL SESSIONS ABERCROMBIE GROUPS

Figure 2. Data analysis

which educational technology built, the model which it employed, the method that it used and the results achieved.

The first of these was mass instruction. This took its basis in industrial technology; the idea was the economy of scale. The method used was extremely hardware-intensive: closed-circuit television, computer-assisted learning, communication satellites. It was not successful. The next stage was individualized instruction. Here the basic theory was taken to be behavioural psychology and its high-priest was Skinner (Skinner, 1968). His stimulus-response model, that if you provide the right stimulus you get the right response, led to a blossoming of educational software — programmed learning, the Keller Plan, Postlethwaite's audio-tutorial method — a variety of ranges of software all of which were designed to provide individualized learning of a kind where a student is fairly clearly directed through the learning process. Now I myself have used the Keller Plan a great deal and I would deny that the evidence from it is in accord with stimulus-response. There is much that comes out of the Keller Plan that Skinner or Keller did not expect. Indeed, I believe a great deal of individualized learning to constitute enormous progress over the kind of mass instruction which it replaced. However, again there are limits to it and in particular one of the problems about individualized learning is that it is individual and that it makes it difficult for students to interact with each other.

That takes me to the third area, namely group learning. Here the basis is a totally different kind of psychology, namely humanistic psychology, which is particularly associated with Carl Rogers (Rogers, 1969). By the time Rogers wrote his book, a most remarkable woman in England, Jane Abercrombie, had published a book called *The Anatomy of Judgment* (Abercrombie, 1969). This book was to me an eye-opener when I first read it. It showed me how to go about teaching so that people would react to each other. The method that is needed to make people interact with each other requires no special hardware, requires very little software, but it requires techniques of group dynamics. The bottom right-hand corner of the figure refers to two ways in which these have been developed.

Dependence, Independence, Interdependence

I have tried to analyze the three areas in which educational technology has been used and I hope I have produced some systematization. But I have not yet produced a theory. Now let me go off at a tangent and come back in a moment. Education in general follows three stages, dependence, independence, interdependence. As children we obviously start totally dependent. In adolescence we struggle towards independence; we try to achieve it and if we are wise then sooner or later we realize that we cannot be independent — we are surrounded by people, so that the truly developed individual is interdependent, and this is very different from dependent. Interdependent means that you depend on me and I depend on you and I can preserve my independence in this relationship. Now these three stages, dependence, independence, interdependence, are mirrored very closely in the three types of instruction that I have been listing. In mass instruction the student is totally dependent. Students sitting in a lecture are totally dependent on the teacher for any form of learning that takes place. If, however, they are given some materials with which to study, then they become independent of the teacher and have an individualized form of instruction. But not until they work in a group do they become interdependent, and so I maintain that as there is a natural progression in education in this direction, so there is a basic good reason why educational technology moved from mass to individual to group.

In each case the educational technologist started at the beginning. He looked at what was easiest for him. In mass instruction he took the lecturer, put a camera in front of him, recorded him and re-broadcast him. Instead of getting more and more sophisticated in this, he switched to individualized learning and again started at the beginning, writing programmed texts, which mostly satisfied fairly low-level objectives. To achieve higher-level objectives in such methods of teaching as the Keller Plan is not easy. This difficulty of achieving higher-level objectives by any method, is I think behind the switch of method from mass to individual and then to group. Dissatisfied with being stuck at low-level objectives, the educational technologist moved on to the next method and found himself again at a low level, although slightly higher than before. Perhaps educational technology is best at dealing with what is simple and we should be glad that this progress has been followed, instead of our perhaps having been stuck with mass teaching and trying to become more and more sophisticated in this.

We have now got something that resembles perhaps at least an hypothesis, if not a theory, and the next stage should be to test it and see whether we can actually find that it works. We have in England a unique example of educational technology, the Open University, which in the short space of 10 years has gone through those three stages. When it was first discussed in 1964 it was to be called the University of the Air. It was to teach by radio and television and thereby reach the masses. Five years later it was a reality, but it had changed its name to the Open University. By then 'University of the Air' had become a misnomer. It was not true that most of its teaching was taking place by television and broadcasting, by mass instruction. It is now reckoned that about 5%, probably less, takes place that way. 95% of the Open University teaching comes through the letter box, it is individualized material mainly on the printed page. So in five years, merely through the planning stage, before having any real experience, the Open University had moved from mass to individual. Over the next five years it became more and more apparent that there was one thing the students were finding sadly lacking in the Open University, and that was contact with the teacher and contact with each other. Summer schools, local centres, tutorless self-help groups of students sprung up, and for the past three years there have been more and more attempts to bring the human, the group, into the work of the Open University. So I contend that we have indeed got here a text-book example of the way educational technology has moved from mass to individual to group.

Into the Future?

Now let us extrapolate for educational technology in general: what will happen in the next 10 years? What I fear may happen is that many governments have in educational technology what I call 'the Concorde mentality', to go for the big thing that does not pay off. In particular I am horrified by the fact that developing countries are now investing in communication satellites for educational purposes. Why I think that this is wrong is that it replaces the one resource that developing countries have got lots of, namely people, by expensive hardware.

However, teachers need help and now I want to come to what I hope may be the future of educational technology in the three areas of mass, individual and group learning. I divide these into the hardware needs and the software needs. In mass instruction, the crucial thing is to provide hardware to aid the teacher which is cheap, reliable and readily available. As for software, I would like to see a great deal of it used in helping to train the teacher and to help him when he is teaching. In my opinion the best use educational technology can be put to in mass instruction is to make the average teacher a better than average teacher by helping him, not by in any sense replacing him. So it is the teacher that ought to have the

	MASS	INDIVIDUAL	GROUP
HARD WARE	CHEAP AND RELIABLE FOR THE TEACHER (PROJECTORS, PLAYERS).	VIDEODISC CHEAP V.C.R. COLOUR REPROGRAPHY	TELEPHONE TUTORIAL RECORDING OF GROUPS
SOFT WARE	TO TRAIN TEACHER TO HELP TEACHER	TO HELP STUDENT (MIXED MEDIA)	TO FACILITATE GROUP LEARNING

Figure 3. *The next 10 years*

support in mass instruction, and for him then to teach the student, not for the student to have the direct support of educational technology.

The situation is different when we come to individualized instruction. There I feel that we want to have readily accessible and cheap means of video reproduction and cheap colour reprography. The reason for the latter is that far and away the most flexible and cheapest medium that we have is the duplicated printed page, but at the moment it is quite expensive to have colour on that page.

Finally to group learning. Here we are still at the research stage and very little has been done in educational technology to help. As I said, the Open University has found the necessity for it, and they are at the moment experimenting with telephone tutorials. A quite different use of hardware is the recording of groups that are engaged in a learning process. At the moment this is cumbersome and very distracting, but if we are to learn more about how people learn in groups it is essential that we should study recordings of such interactions, and that these should be done in situations in which the people that are engaged in the process should be used to facilitate group learning. It may consist of printed passages, still pictures, sound or videotapes — the cheaper and simpler the better; the real problems here are educational, not technological.

I have tried to give a glimpse into the future, as I see it. It may not look very spectacular, because by and large education is a humdrum activity, but to me it is exciting.

Note Added After the Conference

I have just come across a prediction (McBeath, 1975) that we are moving from mass teaching via group teaching to independent study. We must compare notes in 1987.

References

Abercrombie, M L J (1969) 'The Anatomy of Judgment', Penguin, p 17.
McBeath, R (1975) 'Towards a Definition of Resource-Based Learning', Educational Media International, 4, 4.
Rogers, C (1969) 'Encounter Groups', Penguin, pp 9, 144.
Skinner, B F (1968) 'The Technology of Teaching', Apleton-Century-Crofts, p 61.

Individual Approaches to Problem-Solving

J Cowan

Initial Discussion

The writer has described elsewhere (Cowan, 1975) the opportunities which individualized learning schemes progressively offer in the form of increased freedom in the process of learning. For, once freedom of pace is available, there is no real reason for students to be constrained to work according to the same method as their neighbours, since these neighbours are in any case no longer all at the same point in whatever the learning process happens to be. Similarly, once we have overcome the hurdle of offering some autonomy in the choice of learning method, it is then possible to go on to offer some freedom in the choice of course content. But even before that stage is reached the exercise of autonomy in the choice of study method generates some noteworthy examples of unusual study approaches. The diversity between these strategies is clearly apparent to any interested observer, albeit in terms of superficial detail.

The producer of resource materials may thus be led to give great care, attention and frequent reconsideration to the selection of a form of resource materials which will permit his students to take the greatest possible benefit from the potential of their individuality. The nature of their diversity remains unexplored; the innovator has to be content to rely on the students to take advantage of their freedom by making meaningful decisions and choices (Bingham, 1976). To some extent the offering of freedom then becomes an act of faith, in which the fledgling is eventually trusted to leave the nest for the first time, in the sure knowledge that he will perish if he cannot swiftly learn for himself how to fly. The teacher is more involved in the preparation for freedom than in the difficulties which that freedom will actually bring.

Nevertheless, it is conceivable that the process of education might do better to concern itself with the detailed and highly individual steps which assemble to form a successful or even an unsuccessful problem-solving process. This, of course, would have to be studied in the context of the type of problem which the individual may well face when he has passed beyond the period of his (normally fairly firmly structured) initial training. Nor would it be a worthwhile subject for further study, unless it could also be established at a relatively early stage that the differences between students are significant, are worth studying further, and are not merely the arbitrary result of extraneous circumstances in particular occasions.

The reader is asked to bear these points in mind during the account which follows.

A Conscience is Stirred

In December 1973, the writer attended a short conference for lecturers from his own discipline, where a forceful young man displayed sample items from a test which he had prepared for use with recent graduates. The test problems might well have been included in a final degree examination paper in structures, except for the fact that no values were given. Therefore the candidates could only sketch the shape of the diagram which was the required solution; but they could not calculate magnitudes and obtain the complete diagram by plotting these values.

Those present agreed with enthusiasm that any university graduate who 'understood structural behaviour' should be able to sketch such solutions without great difficulty. They were dismayed to be shown pathetically inept answers which had been provided by graduates from their own departments. Sadly, the writer admitted to himself the relevance of the test, and the importance of the weakness which it would inevitably reveal in the course offered by his own department. Quickly, he decided to make it a top priority to make good this glaring omission in the education of his own undergraduates, starting with those who were already in mid-course.

Pride Goes Before a Fall

The writer was no stranger to the problems presented by remedial teaching. Pre-recorded instruction had proved extremely effective for him in these circumstances, since it allowed a firmly structured learning package to be carefully prepared, thoroughly validated, conscientiously revised, and economically issued and used thereafter.

He also felt no awkwardness in selecting the most appropriate teaching strategy on this particular occasion. Many eminent engineering academics had expressed their opinions on that, and with a fair degree of unanimity. Admittedly the approach which they commended was followed infrequently in British university courses — but was that not perhaps likely to be the origin of the malady which affected the degree of mastery displayed by graduates?

The media and the method were obvious choices — or seemed to be at that time. The materials had only to be carefully prepared and conscientiously run, and then the results (Brohn and Cowan, 1977) could be reviewed with a smug complacency — which was soon shown to be totally unjustified.

Fortunately the first run had only involved a quarter of the total class, so it was possible to introduce revisions before the next run, but these had no effect whatsoever on the performance of the next trial group a week later. It was obviously time for hard rethinking from first principles.

A Straw is Clutched

For no very good reason a small item had been added to the programme for the second trial group. This called on each student to begin to attempt a fairly simple problem for no more than six or seven minutes, while constantly dictating a 'running commentary' of what was in his mind as he went along, and sketching on the pad in front of him if he so wished. The tape and sketch were handed in anonymously, and their author could not be identified afterwards. Nevertheless, the students were far from happy about this innovation. Some suspected it was a means of forcing them to display the depth of their ignorance. Others saw no point in the exercise. A few found it embarrassing to talk to themselves, while there were also some who managed to produce undecipherable recordings, or even no recording at all, despite the fact that they were only required to leave the microphone in front of them and talk naturally.

But from the remaining recordings the writer was about to receive the greatest surprise of his teaching career. Solutions which seemed on a visual examination to be the miserable products of ill-prepared and stupid minds, emerged as commendable records of tortured battlegrounds on which the student, having made one not unreasonable error in his otherwise logical chain of solution, had then struggled on manfully, and ever logically, until he became more and more bogged down through the consequences of that solitary error. And as if this revelation were not enough, the writer was also astounded to discover how many of the students, good and bad alike, chose not to follow the carefully structured and firmly recommended method of solution which had been the basis of the formal instruction.

Perhaps the academic authorities on teaching methods had been wrong? The writer enlisted the assistance of some of his colleagues, who were good enough to talk their way through their own solutions to a problem — though not as simple an example as that offered to the students, since the lecturers would presumably remember easy answers as 'type-solutions'. These trials were hurried and poorly documented; but they confirmed the writer's suspicion that the problems could be, and were, solved in a number of quite different ways, from genuinely dissimilar starting points.

The reader will remember that the overall object of this particular exercise had been to rectify a weakness in an existing curriculum, and will therefore understand that, with two further groups still to use the package, the writer was anxious to effect marked improvements, however empirically. So he decided intuitively (or perhaps out of stark despair) that it would be best to destructure the carefully prepared sequence, and present the raw materials of solution method(s) as individual 'building blocks', to be assembled in any way that the student might choose. When this was done, the improvement in test scores was notable, though not spectacular (Brohn and Cowan, 1977). But at that point our present interest in the development of the learning package rapidly dwindles; for it is with the differences between problem-solving methods that this paper is really concerned.

A Nettle is Left Ungrasped

In the following academic session, the improved package was used once more, and recording sessions were again included in the programme, yielding similar results. The writer was relieved to have 'plugged the gap' in the teaching syllabus, and was sufficiently intrigued by what he had learnt from the recordings to be prepared to talk to other academics about it.

But he could see no way of making any constructive use of this new knowledge, for he could not identify any clear implications from what he had heard on the tapes; indeed, he even found it difficult to describe and classify the method used by any given student in any one particular situation. Furthermore, it must be admitted that the recordings were not particularly satisfactory. It took a long time to listen to them and classify them; many were of very poor quality, and some were virtually incoherent. The students were still suspicious and did not welcome the activity; so it was out of the question to try to obtain and compare a number of recordings from any one student.

The obstacles were discouraging, the way ahead obscure and demanding and the writer untrained for the task in hand. And so the investigation lay stagnant, until eventually commonsense prevailed and demanded further exploration of this strange sphere of individuality. The Scottish Council for Research in Education awarded a modest grant, which provided the necessary incentive to take the study one step further forward.

A Spanner Is Used To Crack The Nut

Student volunteers were recruited from a second-year class who received no instruction whatsoever from the writer in that academic year. They were asked if they would record seven to 10-minute running commentaries on a hand dictaphone, for transcription later by an audio-typist. It was explained that the problems which they would be asked to tackle would not be related to any of the topics in their current curriculum, and that their success or failure in each part-problem was of trivial importance in comparison with the method of attack which they chose to use. Finally, the grant made it possible to recompense the volunteers at the rate of £1 per hour.

All of these features had been felt to be most important if the obstacles in the previous exploration were to be overcome, or at least minimized. The use of the dictaphone, followed by audio-typed transcriptions, was intended to facilitate a confidential and private recording atmosphere. The choice of problems from out-with the current syllabus coverage, and involvement with a lecturer who did not handle any of their classes, should remove the experience from the context of the examinable course and exclude anxiety over the disclosure of weaknesses. But it was the introduction of a form of modest payment which was to prove the most important feature of all, because it established a completely new (and constructive) relationship between the lecturer (who became a researcher) and the student (who became an assistant, with a unique contribution to offer).

Procedure

Having made an appointment, a student subject would call at the office and collect a dictaphone and an examination script book, inside which the problem had been sketched, and all relevant information given in written notes. He or she, (for one subject was a girl) went to a spare staff-room, locked himself in, sat down, switched on the dictaphone and opened the script book. He then talked over his thoughts for the next seven to 10 minutes, stopped the dictaphone whatever his progress, and handed it back to the office, together with the script book which now contained his sketches and doodles.

None of these students had ever tried to do anything at all like this before; consequently their first one or two attempts were somewhat tentative and less productive for the writer than those which followed. The problems which they were given increased somewhat in their level of difficulty as the experiment proceeded, but were never beyond the ability of the student concerned; the writer attempted to match the next problem, to some extent, with the student's performance in the previous one. Recordings were made at roughly a week or 10-day intervals, mainly because of the heavy load which the study was creating for the audio-typing secretary.

The final recording session for each student took the form of an interview, in which the writer presented a number of problems, starting with some which the student had already attempted; in each case he sought immediate reactions to these questions. This proved a far from simple search. The writer found himself torn between the Scylla of forceful leading questioning and the Charybdis of a ponderous silence, during which the student's first reactions would escape from all possibility of recall. The students found that their thoughts were moving so rapidly that they had great difficulty in consciously identifying them, let alone articulating them clearly with all the slowness of the spoken word. Some mutual comfort emerged from the fact that both parties felt far from dominant!

Towards the end of the interview the writer took the student back over the methods he had used, and tried to get him to see a pattern or a favoured strategy to which some descriptive label might be attached. Once this had been identified (and here there was a very grave risk of leading the student), the examples were gone over a second time, to check the accuracy of the diagnosis.

Analyses of Results

The original investigation had led the writer to believe that there were three 'bases' from which student and graduate structural engineers attacked problems concerned with the behaviour of structures. For instance, imagine that the students were given a problem involving a crane lifting a dockside load. Then the 'force-based' man would wish to begin by working out the nature of the reactions which kept the crane in equilibrium and prevented it from overturning. The 'deflection-based' man, on the other hand, would picture the deflection of the crane, and the relative displacement of its parts, and would tend to move towards his solution from there. The 'mathematical' man, even in the absence of values, would tend to label his unknowns with Roman or Greek letters, and seek a solution through manipulation of mathematical relationships and equations.

In most problems it was necessary at some time or another for every problem-solver to make use of each of these classes of approach, to a greater or a lesser extent. But the writer chose to describe the student's base very subjectively — as the point from which he started, to which he tended to return at difficult points in the problem, and around which the other parts of his problem-solving technique were assembled.

Many attempts had been made by the writer to analyze the early recordings in such a way that they clearly demonstrated a student's (apparently obvious) allegiance to one or other base. Even the more successful of these graphical analyses were, to be frank, little more than a manipulation of the facts to make them demonstrate a subjectively chosen diagnosis. Nevertheless, the longer the study went on, the more convinced the writer became that the strategies on which he was eavesdropping were (in many cases) fundamentally different. The reader must interpret for himself the effect of that conviction on the opinions which follow.

The writer, professing himself to be aware of his declared prejudice, approached the final series of transcripts in a rather different manner by trying to identify and classify chosen starting points, non-essential intermediate solutions and the effect of perceived impasses.

Perhaps these cryptic terms should be explained immediately in rather more detail. Starting points were relatively simple to identify, and seemed important; after an initial reconnaissance through the details of the question, it can be argued that the problem-solver is likely to make his first constructive effort from the base which he finds more useful, more familiar, more promising or more natural — because it is the base which he naturally prefers. In the same way it can be argued that, if there are intermediate stages in the solution which he does not find it necessary to pass through, then these omissions are probably an indication of sectors of the subject matter in which his base is not to be located. Finally the writer has already defined the base as something to which the problem-solver will tend to return when he encounters an impasse; in other words, times of difficulty push him back to his favoured base.

The individual solutions were analyzed with these points in mind. Following interviews with the students, some of these conclusions had had to be modified — for various reasons. For instance, the writer now gravely doubts the part-definition of the base as a 'refuge in time of trouble'. Some students would certainly react to an impasse by returning to familiar preferred strategies; but others, perhaps through lack of confidence, or a spirit of adventure, or an ability to change course, or a sense that something is missing in their earlier approach, explain that they would try to change to something different in these circumstances.

Points Arising from the Analysis Process

1. The transcription is a weak version of the spoken commentary, and can never convey the feeling which comes across to the listener when a tape is first replayed. But it is really the only viable basis on which an objective analysis of a large number of records can be based.
2. The students had been told that they should only sketch and scribble on the page before them as they would do for their own purposes when attempting a problem privately; it was emphasized that no explanations should be given solely for the purpose of the exercise. Nevertheless the interviews revealed that, particularly in the simpler problems, the brighter students might immediately remember the solution from an earlier, and very similar problem in their experience — but would then work out and 'dictate' an explanation to justify that solution. Clearly a fair rapport between subject and interviewer must be established if such behaviour is first to be identified and then eliminated without embarrassment in future recordings. Yet until this is done there is good reason for doubting the evidence of the spoken record.
3. It quickly became apparent that it was an oversimplification to classify the problem-solvers in one of three groups; in the present inquiry one student, for instance, seemed to be a 'mathematical/force'-based man, located somewhere between the two bases. But even in such cases the students concerned, together with the writer, felt that there was a basic strategy, however it was to be described, which underlay all their problem-solving in the field of elementary theory of structures.

Doubts and Queries

Despite the readiness of the writer to classify his subjects, and the reasonable willingness of the subjects to accept the basic premise that this was possible, one must be very suspicious of the assumption that students can be crudely divided into groups in this way. Even if a method of problem-solving can be classified, we must ask if any given student will consistently favour a particular method? Would his strategy be identified consistently by different researchers? And will he react differently in favourable and in adverse circumstances? To what extent is he influenced by the strategies which are stressed in his initial instruction and in any worked examples he is shown by his teacher, or finds in a text-book? All these questions have important implications; they must be asked, and they should be answered.

So the decision to proceed with a study in which an engineering lecturer wanders naïvely amongst profound psychological issues is possibly indefensible.

Although the experiment offers many opportunities for destructive criticism, the writer would maintain that all these doubts and queries must surely be set in their proper position and perspective by looking instead to the positive results of this exploration. It is accepted on all sides nowadays that individualized learning is a worthwhile aim; indeed, some would claim that all learning is essentially individual, because it is a purely personal process. If we accept that our students will learn at different rates and in different ways, and will emphasize different aspects of their field of study, then we must also accept that it is at least possible, if not probable, that their final performances in prescribed tasks will differ significantly.

We need to know if they do perform in significantly different ways, as opposed to performing with greater or less competence. We need to know if an appreciation of these differences can help them, and us, to enhance the quality of their learning and subsequent performance. We need to begin to regard the differences between individuals as significant, rather than merely seeing them as a source of scatter in post-test scores, which thereby complicate comparisons between supposedly matched groups. We are not teaching groups — we are helping individuals to learn.

Epilogue

Recently one of my student 'subjects' approached me for assistance: 'Could you spare 10 minutes?' he asked. 'I'm stuck with this problem in second-year structures. Two of the lecturers have been trying to explain it to me, but I don't seem to be able to see it.'

I was glad to have a chance to repay him for his co-operation, so I looked at the problem, and was about to launch into what I hope would have been a neat and carefully presented explanation — when suddenly I remembered our interview session together. We had together labelled him as a 'deflection'-based man, while I was, without doubt, a 'force'-based person.

We agreed that it might be worthwhile if I tried to approach this problem from the consideration of deflections. I felt strange; it took me a little while to put it all together, and my explanations stumbled and faltered. So I soon felt that the effort was a waste of time, especially since the student was in the throes of his final preparation for the exams. 'I see it now', he said, much to my surprise.

Was it the fact that I went slowly, or was it that it was the third explanation in a row which enabled me to 'get through'? I will never be sure; but it encouraged me to discover that the two previous (and unsuccessful) explanations had both been 'force-based'. It made me feel that it is worth while persisting in 'listening-in' to what my students think they are thinking.

References

Bingham, E G (1976) 'Skills for the Occasion' 'Aspects of Educational Technology X', Kogan Page, London.

Brohn, D M and Cowan, J (1977) 'Teaching towards an Improved Understanding of Structural Behaviour' 'Structural Engineer', 55, 1, January 1977.

Cowan, J (1975) 'The Problems and Potential of Individualized Learning', Conference on Independence in Learning, Thames Polytechnic, The Chemical Society, London.

Microteaching—an Aid to Innovation in Developing Countries

A J Trott

Several conferences of a workshop/seminar type have taken place recently in developing countries in Africa and Asia. Microteaching was used at the conferences as the major topic. Many authors have defined and explained microteaching (Allen and Ryan, 1969, Cooper and Allen 1971, McAleese and Unwin 1971, Trott 1976) and so it is not intended to repeat basic information here.

The claims made for microteaching as a method of training or retraining teachers are:

1. Specific skills are identified in a briefing session.
2. Real teaching does take place.
3. Microteaching lessens the complexities and student anxieties of normal classroom teaching.
4. Control can be more effectively maintained — better records and equality in teaching assignments can be ensured.
5. Once it is in operation, microteaching is economical in terms of staff time.
6. Microteaching greatly expands the IKR (Immediate Knowledge of Results) dimension in teaching. Until the advent of the cheap video-recorder, the audio tape-recorder, the light-weight camera, teachers rarely saw or heard themselves teach. Sources of feedback for teachers have never been so devastatingly accurate as they are today.

The teach/reteach cycle (Trott, 1976) would seem to be the basic structure, but the timing of various elements and even the inclusion or exclusion of them varies in different establishments. Other variations can occur in the use or non-use of the supervisor, other feedback agencies, colleagues, peers, participating pupils and either individual or group viewing.

Microteaching has several features which make it a useful way to re-examine the teaching/learning situation.

It is a comparatively recent innovation, easy to implement and if video-tape feedback is avoided, relatively cheap to operate. Perlberg (1975) refers to video-tape as 'a frill that can substantially further the aims of microteaching but should not be viewed as indispensable'.

It has many applications. It has been used to train teachers, lecturers, instructors and interviewers. Plenty of professions from policemen to priests have profited from self-viewing and self-listening. At the present time, research into further applications has been called for (Hargie, 1977) and is beginning. Educationalists are starting to explore microteaching as a technique to train teachers of specific groups of children — very young children and maladjusted children are possible groups.

There exists sometimes the idea that a 'good' teacher is primarily concerned with the transmission of information, the imparting of factual information. Therefore, rote-learning tends to persist, and children and adults are encouraged to repeat after

249

the teacher as an aid to memory. Undoubtedly, one of the functions of a teacher is to impart information, but it would seem that following the work of Ivor Davies (1971) and others, the teacher might be regarded as a manager of the learning environment.

By examining the teacher-pupil relationship in a scaled-down teaching encounter, participants can be encouraged, without overtly concentrating on this aspect, to move from the hierarchical 'guru' model, to a more flexible 'organizer' model. Consequently, the skills of teachers to ask questions, to foster pupil participation, to vary stimuli, to be enthusiastic and so on, can be given detailed scrutiny and analysis.

The idea that perhaps a different way could be as successful as, or more successful than the old, well-tried, traditional method, is sometimes untenable for experienced teachers.

It is only by discussing teaching techniques, training models and the teaching/learning process, that this idea can come to the surface without threatening professional competence. After the discussions, the different technique can be tried and practised in the security of a small group situation.

The normal pattern of teaching practice in Britain and in some other places, is to allocate the trainee to a qualified teacher so that he has a model to copy. This procedure may not be entirely satisfactory (Trott, 1976).

As has been mentioned earlier, there is much more control over the microteaching situation than there is over the conventional teaching practice. When students have to be given a grade, equality of conditions can be ensured, thus avoiding the influence that a particularly good or very bad school can have on the grade.

Theory and practice in an education course sometimes seem to students to be unrelated. Teacher-training courses can contain philosophical, sociological and psychological elements which need to be related to the classroom, illustrated and quickly experienced in practice.

'One of the most important features of microteaching is the feedback element and the resulting self-confrontation. Accurate feedback of behaviour is critical to the improvement of teaching as it helps reinforce desired patterns and creates dissatisfaction with undesirable ones.' (Perlberg, 1975.) Sometimes the supervisor's suggestions and report are not accepted by the student of the in-service teacher and a pantomime situation develops . . . 'Oh, yes you did!' . . . 'Oh, no I didn't.' In the microteaching situation the supervisor can concentrate upon a single aspect if necessary, and all kinds of alternative feedback methods can be used. Rating scales, observer tallies, sign systems, interaction analysis systems and other instruments are available. Pupils and peers can be asked to comment. Audio-tape will give an accurate record of most of the teacher-pupil interaction. Video-tape is not essential, but does record precisely non-verbal teacher behaviour.

In order to offer one possible model to assist educators considering a microteaching workshop, the particulars and an account of a course mounted at the Nakornsawan Teachers' Training College, Thailand are included. It was sponsored by the Thai Government and the British Council. The instructions given to the director of the workshop/seminar were to show as many varieties of microteaching systems and techniques as possible, to mount a 'shop window' so that the assembled teacher trainers and others could select aspects of microteaching which suited their aims and the culture of their country.

Practical limitations placed on the workshop were that it should be devoted mainly to an experiencial study of microteaching, only two experts could be involved, and that it should not exceed 10 days' duration. A CCTV studio, technicians, engineers, audio and audio-visual equipment, simultaneous translation and an abundance of children were available.

After discussion with Thai educationists, it was established that there was a high dependence on information transmission as a principal teacher activity, that some work had been done on microteaching within the country and that students were seldom asked to consider teaching as a set of specific skills.

The main course objectives are given below, further details of some sub-objectives are given in the appendix.

At the end of the workshop/seminar delegates should be able to:

1. Organize microteaching sessions.
2. Use assessment instruments in practical teaching situations.
3. Compare modes of microteaching feedback.
4. Identify and describe teaching skills.
5. Use simulation and gaming techniques.
6. Train others to use the above techniques.

Microteaching and simulation are inter-related, so together they form a package particularly suitable for study in a country where highly traditional methods operate widely. Microteaching and simulation are both concerned with skill training within realistic, safe, practice situations.

A package of 25 papers was prepared and each participant received a complete set. A selected number of documents were sent to Thailand for translation and distribution before the commencement of the workshop. The other documents were distributed at appropriate times, either before or immediately after a related seminar. The papers came from various sources. The author is particularly grateful to the Association for Programmed Learning and Educational Technology for permission to use articles from the journal and occasional papers, and to Dr George Brown for permission to use extracts from his book (Brown, 1975).

The simulation and in-tray exercises written for a similar workshop held in India, were included in the Thai documents. The exercises were translated into Thai and Thai names were substituted. Video-tapes specifically recorded were taken and left in Thailand for future reference and study.

The detailed programme for the seminar is indicated by the following timetable:

Wednesday 14th July
0900-0945	Opening ceremony.
0945-1030	General introduction and outline of the programme.
1030-1045	Break.
1045-1200	Course aims and objectives.
1330-1445	Film or video extract to introduce a general discussion about teaching methods.
1445-1500	Break.
1500-1600	Group discussion on the measurement of teacher effectiveness and on teaching skills.

Thursday 15th July
0830-1030	New methods in teacher education including modular courses, syndicate work, Keller Plan etc.
1030-1045	Break.
1045-1200	Introduction to microteaching — brief history; what is and what is not microteaching.
1330-1445	Introduction to rating instruments — P types, A types, Ryans scales, Stirling lesson sampling instruments.
1445-1500	Break.
1500-1600	Practice using rating instruments by rating video-taped extracts.

Friday 16th July

0830-1030　Teaching skill — varying the stimulus; identification and briefing session.

1030-1045　Break.

1045-1200　Planning session in groups for stimulus variation and practice use of the rating instrument.

1330-1445　Microteaching session. Group A — CCTV + RI Groups B & C — RI only.

1445-1500　Break.

1500-1630　Reteach; group use same feedback modes.

Saturday 17th July

0830-1030　Teaching skill — use of examples.
　　　　　　Identification briefing and planning session.

1030-1045　Break.

1045-1200　Microteaching session. Group B — CCTV + RI Group C — audio-tape + RI, Group A — RI only.

1330-1445　Reteach using the same feedback modes.

1445-1500　Break.

1500-1600　Present thinking and research evidence about the role of the supervisor/tutor.

Monday 19th July

0830-1030　Teaching skills — set induction and closure; identification, briefing and planning session.

1030-1045　Break.

1045-1200　Microteaching session. Group C — CCTV + RI Group A — audio-tape + RI, Group B — RI only. NO reteach for this skill.

1330-1445　Group discussion comparing audio, video and instrumental feedback: also reteach versus no reteach.

1455-1500　Break.

1500-1600　Present thinking and research evidence about the use of models and modelling technique.

Tuesday 20th July

0830-1030　Introduction and historical background to role-playing, simulation and academic gaming.

1030-1045　Break.

1045-1200　Practical session.

1330-1445　Practical session.

1445-1500　Break.

1500-1630　Discussion and start construction of individual simulation exercises.

Wednesday 21st July

0830-1030　Problems of devising measuring instruments; revision of reinforcement theory — groups to identify major components of reinforcement skill and to devise their own measuring instruments.

1030-1045　Break.

1045-1200　Prepare for microteaching.

1330-1445　Microteaching using rating instruments only.

1445-1500　Break.

1500-1630　Reteach using instruments.

Thursday 22nd July

0830-0930　Group discussion on the success or otherwise of the individual rating instruments.

0930-1030　Introduction to Interaction Analysis; FIAC and BIAS.

1030-1045　Break.

1045-1200　Practical experience of the BIAS instrument by rating video-taped material.

1330-1445　Identification and briefing concerning the composite skill of questioning to include redirection, reinforcement, prompting, probing use of the wrong answers etc.

1445-1500　Break.

1500-1630	Planning session.

Friday 23rd July

0830-1030	Microteaching (peer group); teaching skill of questioning.
1030-1045	Break.
1045-1200	Reteach.
1330-1445	Group discussion on pupils versus peers.
1445-1500	Break.
1550-1600	Research evidence concerning self-awareness and implications for the timing of microteaching.

Saturday 24th July

0830-1030	Small group try-outs of simulation exercises.
1030-1045	Break.
1045-1200	Continuation of simulation exercises.
1330-1445	Plenary session.
1445-1500	Break.
1500-1600	Final evaluation and closing ceremony.

In order to allow time for the Thai video-tapes and slides to be shown and discussed, a small number of minor modifications were made to the programme. The participants willingly agreed to extend three or four sessions by up to an hour to accommodate the alterations. Consequently, every item in the original programme was covered although modifications in the timing of some of the items had to be made.

The first two days were devoted to a theory input, and thereafter the practical sessions examined five distinct experiential areas:

1. A comparison of five different types of feedback, experienced singly or in various combinations — rating instrument, audio-tape, peer and supervisor.
2. A comparison between teaching pupil groups and teaching peer groups.
3. A comparison between reteach and no reteach.
4. Identification and practice of teaching skills in simple, complex and paired combinations.
5. Comparison between British-designed, self-designed and other Thai-designed measuring instruments.

The experience given to delegates included teaching, rating and observing mini-lessons, confronting self on video and audio-tape, analysing and modifying their own teaching, manufacturing measuring instruments, comparing measuring instruments with other feedback methods, supervising, analysing teaching into composite skills, teaching a single skill, participating in gaming and simulation exercises and writing simulations and designing games.

If the course were to be run again, modifications would probably be made to the amount of theory included, the early inclusion of a practical experience and the number of support papers issued.

The natural friendliness, courtesy and good humour of the Thai participants helped to create the happy atmosphere in which the seminar was conducted. Although the pace had to be modified from time to time to accommodate the translation from one language to another, the willingness of delegates to learn, compelled the tutors to set a pace which was both exhilarating and exhausting. The evening conferences held between the British and Thai teams at the end of most seminar days indicated that a high level of enthusiasm and motivation was maintained throughout the seminar. This was confirmed when the conference evaluation process had been completed.

Appendix: *Course objectives and sub-objectives*
At the end of this workshop/seminar delegates should be able to:

1. Organize microteaching sessions.
    (a)   Define microteaching.
    (b)   Give a brief history of microteaching.
    (c)   Perceive 'legitimate' variations without departing from the essential features.
    (d)   Define the functions and possible roles of the tutor/supervisor.
    (e)   List priorities in the implementation of a microteaching system.
    (f)   Specify the function of equipment in microteaching.
    (g)   State how modelling techniques should be used.
    (h)   Describe the cosmetic and self-confrontation effects in microteaching and indicate how they might be minimized.

2. Use assessment instruments in practical teaching situations.
    (a)   Define phenomenological and analytical types.
    (b)   Define an interaction analysis system.
    (c)   Use Brown's Interaction Analysis System.
    (d)   State the practical constraints encountered in manufacturing assessment instruments.

3. Compare as methods of microteaching feedback:
    (a)   Pupils;
    (b)   Peers;
    (c)   Measuring instruments;
    (d)   Mechanical — video and audio;
    (e)   Supervising tutors.

4. Identify teaching skills.
    (a)   Specify broad categories.
    (b)   Select teaching skills which can be measured using the feedback methods mentioned above.
    (c)   Use as teaching skills — the six in the programme.

5. Use simulation and gaming techniques.
    (a)   Give a brief historical background.
    (b)   Use simulations, perhaps self-written in their teaching.

6. Train others to use the above techniques.

References

Allen, D W and Ryan, K A (1969) 'Microteaching' Addison-Wesley.

Brown, G A (1975) 'Microteaching — A Programme of Teaching Skills' Methuen.

Cooper, J M and Allen, D W (1971) 'Microteaching: History and Present Status' Microteaching — Selected Papers, ATE Research Bulletin No 9.

Davies, I K (1971) 'The Management of Learning' McGraw-Hill.

Hargie, O D W (1977) 'The Effectiveness of Microteaching: a Selective Review' Educational Review, Birmingham University Monograph.

McAleese, W R and Unwin, D (1971) 'Microteaching — a Selective Survey' Programmed Learning and Educational Technology 8, 10-21.

Perlberg, A (1975) 'Recent Approaches on Microteaching and Allied Techniques Which Can Be Implemented Easily in Developing Countries' UNESCO mimeo.

Trott, A J (1976) 'Microteaching — An Overview' Educational Media International 1976 No 1.

The Development and Evaluation of a Structured Scientific Communication Exercise

F Percival

Introduction

In order to make a conscious effort to develop some of the broader skills associated with science education, some specific exercises (often of a simulation-type) have been produced by the Science Education Group at Glasgow University. These exercises, which have been directed at various levels of secondary and tertiary education, have been developed to fill some of the gaps left by more traditional instructional methods.

This paper discusses one such exercise — 'Proteins as Human Food' — which is a discussion exercise designed to develop lower cognitive, interpersonal, decision-making but, above all, communication skills. The exercise is suitable for use with senior schoolchildren and first-year undergraduates.

Rationale for the Development of a Communication Exercise

Over the past 40 years there has been an increasing concern amongst science educators in considering the desirable skills, habits, attitudes and modes of thinking which science students at various levels should develop, in addition to purely cognitive and psychomotor attainment.

A review of previous writings on objectives in science teaching (Lewis, 1964) highlighted the general trend towards the acknowledgement that science is an essential part of the modern world, resulting in the growing importance of communication skills and the need to relate scientific phenomena to everyday life. Lewis also noted the increasing emphasis on objectives other than the memorization of factual knowledge, but found little evidence of these broader objectives being embodied in science courses.

Broadly speaking, one factor which distinguishes the last decade from previous ones is that the broader objectives of science teaching are gaining wider acceptance and are being incorporated in some courses. There is a growing interest in the concept of education 'through' science rather than education 'in' science (Greenwood, 1972; Holliday, 1973; Rusholme, 1975; Jenkins, 1976).

Secondary school science courses in both England and Scotland now embody objectives which are not of a purely cognitive nature. It should be pointed out, however, that research has indicated that such objectives are not necessarily achieved when traditional teaching methods are employed (Hadden, 1975; Brown, 1975).

At tertiary level, there has been produced a list of 'desired skills' of a science graduate (Maskill, 1971) and similar objectives have been listed elsewhere, sometimes under the separate headings of knowledge, skills and attitudes (Beard, 1973; Billing, 1973; Holliday, 1973; Hughes, Poller and Slade, 1975).

The skills mentioned above have been broadly classified under one or more of the following headings (Percival, 1976):

1. Communication skills — involving the ability to impart clearly to others information in both oral and written form, and to enter into critical discussion with one's peers.
2. Decision-making skills — involving the ability to make balanced decisions on matters where there may be several conflicting views or factors. A decision may have to be made on the basis of ambiguous or incomplete information, but once a decision has been made a student should be able to defend it in the face of a disagreement from his peers.
3. Problem-solving skills — involving the ability to tackle new situations in a scientific fashion. Included in this category are skills in identifying, isolating and controlling variables, so that multivariable situations can be tackled. Another basic aspect is the ability to identify relevant information which may often be included amongst irrelevant data.
4. Library skills — involving the ability to search for and find required information efficiently. Also included are skills in reading and précising scientific papers, discriminating between fact and speculation, and the development of a healthy scepticism towards the written word.
5. Interpersonal skills — involving skills in dealing with other people and the ability to co-operate in a group to work efficiently on a common task.

In addition to the categories given above, a further much-quoted aim of science courses is the 'development of desirable scientific attitudes'.

Traditional methods, at both secondary and tertiary level, appear ill-suited to teaching towards the 'broader' outcomes of a science education discussed above, although it is probable that such skills would be required by a pupil or student long after the detailed scientific facts have been forgotten. It seems obvious, therefore, that alternative teaching methods must be used to teach towards these skills and attitudes which are supposed to be the 'bonus' from a science education, and hence fill the gaps left by more traditional teaching methods (Ellington and Percival, 1977a, b).

It was to fill one such gap in an undergraduate course that the communication exercise entitled 'Protein as Human Food' was developed.

Owing to the large numbers (over 500) taking first-year chemistry at Glasgow University, no formal group tutorials are given because of difficulties in organization. It was to help offset this shortcoming in the course that it was decided to devise an exercise in which the main aims involved the development of communication and inter-personal skills using chemistry and related subjects as the vehicle.

Design of the Exercise

The Style of the Exercise

One problem commonly encountered in group tutorials, even when a skilful tutor is involved and a 'mini-lecture' is avoided, is that some students, possibly through lack of confidence or knowledge, fail to become involved in the discussion, which is often dominated by the tutor and one or two group members. One of the major problems in designing a communication exercise, therefore, is to involve everybody in the group to an approximately equal extent.

Previously-devised communication exercises have taken the form of 'information games' in which the emphasis is laid on communication skills involving delivering and receiving scientific information, in association with problem-solving skills. Examples of such games have been described in which each group member (player) is given one piece of information on a card, which, when considered along with other players' information, leaves the group in a position to solve a given problem (Rae, 1970). This approach has also been used with students of biochemistry (Smith and Jepson, 1972).

In the case of 'Protein as Human Food', in order to ensure the participation of all students in the 'discussion', it was decided to adopt a format in which students in a group were given individual information sheets on a common topic, so that each student had a part to play in communicating relevant information into a central information 'pool' on which other students could draw when considering different aspects of the topic. By using this approach it was hoped that less confident students would feel less inhibited, since they would be in sole possession of information without which parts of the exercise could not be attempted successfully. Considerably more information was given to each student than in previous 'information games' reported.

The broad topic of 'proteins and the world food shortage' was taken as the basis for the exercise for several reasons. Firstly, the topic involved many disciplines, not only chemistry, and students could draw on knowledge without the content of the exercise documents to add to the discussion of certain points. Secondly, it was felt that such a subject was likely to be sufficiently emotive and relevant so that student interest would be high. It was hoped that students would appreciate that chemistry has significance far beyond the text-book, but that chemical considerations often fade in importance when compared to geographical, economic, ethical, social or political factors.

The Strategy

It was decided to involve groups of six students in a structured discussion of the topic in question. Each group of six students consists of one group leader plus five group members. The exercise is designed so that it can be run with the minimum of staff participation.

The group participants receive the following sheets:

Group member	List of objectives
	List of amino-acids and their structures
	Group Member's Guide
	An information sheet
Group leader	List of objectives
	List of amino-acids and their structures
	Group Leader's Guide

The Group Member's Guide introduces the nature of the study to the students and describes how group members are expected to participate.

An individual information sheet is issued to each group member, and the students are given 20 minutes before the exercise to read and digest its content. Each of the five sheets contains information on a different aspect of the topic, which results in the group possessing five 'subject specialists', each with a different area of expertise. The titles of the information sheets are listed below:

1. Chemistry of proteins and amino-acids.
2. Essential amino-acids and protein usability.
3. Conventional sources of protein and their content.
4. Human protein requirements and some novel ways of meeting protein demand.
5. Ecological and economic factors in protein production.

The Group Leader's Guide explains the leader's function in the exercise and contains a brief summary of the contents of each of the five information sheets. The group leader, who does not receive an information sheet, has to act as chairman of the group. The guide contains a series of questions which form the basis of the structured discussion. The leader is not necessarily required to adhere rigidly to the order or content of each question and can ask supplementary questions at his/her discretion. The questions listed in the leader's guide also indicate the information sheet(s) in which relevant information is contained.

The first series of questions in the exercise are purely factual and require an answer from one student at a time in order to build up a pool of information from the five topic areas. As time progresses, the questions often require co-operation from several students for an adequate answer, and students are encouraged to draw on information outside their scripts if necessary. Towards the end of the exercise, the questions posed deal with ethical matters in which moral considerations have to be balanced against scientific, political, economic, geographical, ecological and social factors. The result is that students are forced into the position of making value judgements. At the completion of the exercise each student receives a complete set of information sheets to take away.

It is hoped that students who participate in the exercise gain not only in factual knowledge, but in discussion skills and confidence, in critical thinking and in co-operating with others in trying to solve common problems; in addition, it is hoped that the chemistry involved is seen to have a part in other disciplines, with purely chemical decisions being affected by many other considerations.

The exercise as it stands, although originally designed for first-year undergraduates, is also suitable for use with senior pupils. Including the time allowed for reading and digesting information sheets, the exercise takes between one and a half and two hours to complete.

The basic structure of the exercise is such that the subject matter of the exercises could be modified or changed completely in order to suit variations in student maturity and specialism. The non-cognitive educational objectives would remain largely unchanged. In support of this, it has been claimed that the basic framework of a simulation game, communication exercise, etc is virtually unrelated to its content, and that once a standard form has been established it 'can readily be changed from one subject field to another with the minimum of creative effort' depending on the compatibility of educational objectives in both fields (Cowan, 1974). For example, a simplified and slightly more structured version of 'Proteins as Human Food' has been produced and successfully used with 14-year-old school pupils, while still retaining the major function of developing communication and discussion skills (Reid, 1977).

Evaluation of the Exercise

Assessment Procedures Used

Two general assessment procedures were used.

1. A written assessment involving pre and post-tests was completed by students involved in the exercise. Four basic techniques were involved, namely:
   (a) Multiple-choice objective items based on the cognitive objectives of the exercise.
   (b) Likert-type statements based on the broader objectives. Students were asked to signify their degree of agreement with each statement on a five-point scale. Statements based on communication skills were concerned with the students' confidence in using such skills.

(c)   A rating grid on which students indicated how successful or otherwise the exercise had been in achieving each of the 15 objectives listed. This acted as a check on the assessment methods using objective testing and Likert techniques, and also provided some indication of the attainment of certain objectives which were difficult to test directly.

(d)   Questions based on the semantic differential technique in which students who had completed the exercise rated it in terms such as value, interest and enjoyment.

Procedures (a) and (b) were used in the pre-test to the exercise, while all four procedures were involved in the post-test. In addition, space was provided in the post-test for students to comment on the exercise. A battery of assessment procedures was used in an attempt to reduce any limitations of validity and reliability associated with any one technique.

2. An analysis of tape-recordings of the discussions of several of the groups who participated in the exercise was done in addition to the self-reporting and objective testing techniques. An attempt was made to identify communication patterns and patterns of student involvement during the course of the exercise.

Sample Population

Numbers who have attempted the exercise are, as yet, low, and students from institutions other than Glasgow University have been included in the assessment trials. These students included sixth-formers from a large Scottish comprehensive school, and PGCE students from Liverpool University. In total seven groups (42 students) have been involved in full assessment studies. This does not include the groups who participated in the early trials of the material.

Results of Assessment: Written Assessment

Even with the small number in the sample, the multiple-choice objective items showed several significant differences between pre and post-tests. The items were mainly designed to measure specific cognitive attainments from the exercise. From the results available, it would appear that all the cognitive objectives were being at least partially achieved by the exercise. How much more (or less) efficiently they could be achieved by other, perhaps more traditional, methods is open to question.

All the Likert-type statements indicated some degree of overall change in opinion in the direction indicated by the objectives of the exercise. Although a few changes were significant above the 5% level, larger, unbiased samples would be necessary before statistical analysis would become really meaningful. On the basis of the available data, it would seem that the objectives involved were all partly achieved by the exercise with varying degrees of success. No objective appears to have been, in general, negatively achieved. However, it is interesting that some of the statements which were designed to measure changes in confidence in communication skills indicated a minority of students whose confidence appeared to have decreased as a result of the exercise. This reversal may be a direct result of the exercise having the opposite of its desired effect, but another explanation may be that the student's first estimation of his confidence was too high, and the exercise has involved some self-realization of the student's communication ability.

On the objective rating grid, students were asked to rate, on a five-point scale, how successful the exercise had been in achieving each objective. On the basis of the students' opinions, it would appear that all the objectives have been successfully attained to a varying extent with no objective seen by the students to be entirely without the scope of the exercise. It must be remembered that this method of assessment is crude and gives only an indication of the success of each objective.

The semantic differential part of the assessment indicates that most students found the exercise valuable and enjoyable, and there was a general feeling that the discussion exercise benefited the students' general education in chemistry. Some responses seemed to indicate some attitudinal change towards the problem of world protein shortage. However, more sophisticated testing would be necessary to assess the extent (if any) of any general attitudinal changes towards the subject matter.

The preceding trends from the various assessment procedures would appear encouraging. However, it must be remembered that only 42 students were available, all of whom were volunteers, so that statistical analysis of the results is precarious, quite apart from the fact that the sample is probably biased towards the more enthusiastic and co-operative students.

However, within this small, biased sample the gains which were made in both cognitive and attitudinal areas, allied with the general increase in confidence in communication skills, would appear to be some justification for further trials of exercises such as 'Proteins as Human Food', although it is probable that the beneficial effects of a series of similar communication exercises over a session would probably be greater and more permanent than the effects of such exercises in isolation.

Results of Assessment: Analysis of Tape-Recordings

Tape-recordings were made of the proceedings in the seven groups who participated. On later analysis, general features which emerged included:

1. The total percentage time spent communicating in the exercise as a whole never fell below 10% for any individual. It would appear that the exercise has been successful in its aim of encouraging more reticent students to become involved in the exercise.
2. The average length of the communications in each exercise varied greatly, eg from an average of 6.8 secs in one group to 15.0 secs in another. The length of communications would therefore appear to be controlled more by the individual group members than by the exercise format.
3. A pattern of communication within each group usually takes the form of the discussion being dominated at first by the group leader and those students possessing information sheets one and two. As the exercise proceeds, group members three, four and five are brought in to the discussion to add their specialized information. In the last 20 minutes or so of each exercise, a more general discussion of broader issues involves all students, although the discussion may be dominated by certain students independently of the information sheets provided.
4. The group leader appears to integrate well into the exercise despite being without an information sheet. The group leader also appears to maintain a high level of involvement throughout the exercise. However, in all the analyses, the group leader volunteered, or was selected by a tutor or teacher who had prior knowledge of the student personalities. How well the exercise would proceed with a randomly-selected leader is unknown.

It should be emphasized that the above subject generalizations would need to be confirmed by further analyses of this sort. It may be of interest to study the group interactions in more detail during the course of the exercise by using, for example, some form of interaction analysis procedure.

Conclusion

Due to the reservations expressed above on the generalizing power of the assessment results, very little can be said with absolute conviction about the changes produced in students by the exercise described, or whether any such changes were of a short-term or more permanent duration. However, very few of the assessment results were in a direction opposite from that desired; the short-term general trends being very encouraging in most cases. A further quality of the exercise was the observation, by all involved in its overseeing, of the enthusiasm, motivation and involvement amongst students. Although this is a subjective measure, it would appear an important outcome, but may be coloured by Hawthorne effects. Analysis of the tape-recordings indicated that the exercise had the effect of involving every student in the groups studied to a greater extent than might have been expected using more traditional methods.

It seems obvious, however, that further such communication exercises would be necessary to confirm and develop any non-cognitive gains made in this one exercise.

References

Beard, R M (1973) 'Objective Science Teaching' 'Aims, Methods and Assessment in Advanced Science Education' Billing, D E and Furniss, B S (eds), Heyden, London.

Billing, D E (1973) 'Broad Aims of Chemistry Courses' Chemical Society Curriculum Subject Newsletter No 1, pp 22-23.

Brown, S A (1975) 'Affective Objectives in an Integrated Science Curriculum' PhD Thesis, University of Stirling.

Cowan, J (1974) 'Identification of Standard Game Forms with Definable Objectives' Programmed Learning and Educational Technology Vol 11, pp 192-196.

Ellington, H I and Percival, F (1977a) 'Educating "Through" Science Using Multi-Disciplinary Simulation Games' 'Programmed Learning and Educational Technology' (in press).

Ellington, H I and Percival, F (1977b) 'The Place of Multi-Disciplinary Games in School Science' 'School Science Review' (in press).

Greenwood, N N (1972) 'Education Through Chemistry', 'Education in Chemistry' Vol 9 p 36.

Hadden, R A (1975) 'Affective Objectives in Chemistry', MSc Thesis, University of Glasgow.

Holliday, A K (1973) 'Curriculum Development in Tertiary Chemistry Courses', in 'Aims, Methods and Assessment in Advanced Science Education', Billing, D E and Furniss, B S (eds) Heyden, London.

Hughes, N M, Poller, R C and Slade, R C (1975) 'Aims in Chemistry Teaching', 'Education in Chemistry' Vol 12, p 39.

Jenkins, E W (1976) 'Education Through Chemistry — an Unanswered Challenge', 'Education in Chemistry' Vol 14, pp 84-85.

Lewis, D G (1964) 'Objectives in the Teaching of Science', 'Educational Research' Vol 7, pp 186-199.

Maskill, R (1971) 'The Objectives of Tertiary Chemistry Courses', in 'Chemical Education at the Tertiary Level', British Committee in Chemical Education.

Percival, F (1976) 'A Study of Teaching Methods in Tertiary Chemical Education', PhD Thesis, University of Glasgow.

Rae, J (1970) 'Gaming, Decision Making and Social Skills', in 'Instructional Simulation Systems in Higher Education', Armstrong, R H R and Taylor, J L (eds), Cambridge Institute of Education.

Reid, N (1977) 'Personal Communication'.

Rushole, Lord James of (1975) 'Education "Through" Chemistry', 'Education in Chemistry' Vol 12, pp 108-109.

Smith, A D and Jepson, J B (1972) 'Variation of the "Information Game" ', 'The Lancet' Vol II, pp 585-586.

An Epidemic Model
of the Dissemination of Educational
Technology

P D Mitchell

Introduction

How is knowledge communicated? We are not concerned here with the design of messages, presentation variables, audience characteristics, organizational frameworks or resistance to change. Rather we focus on a macroscopic model of the diffusion of educational technology knowledge that is sufficient to describe the relevant communication process.

The diffusion of knowledge in an area such as educational technology does not occur uniformly. Why do some ideas or practices spread faster than others? Why do some burning issues become glowing embers without being demonstrably less valuable? Is educational technology susceptible to changing fashion?

The plot of the cumulative number of people accepting an innovation over time is characterized by a slow rise initially, followed by a rapid growth. This in turn is followed by a levelling off. What factors determine this growth pattern? Can they be manipulated? Can a growth phase be identified in advance so that resources may be allocated or withheld accordingly?

The Growth of Educational Technology: A Systems View

We usually think of a system as a set of interrelated entities but a system can also be described as a relation between inputs to a process and its outputs. The familiar black box model is just such a system. We know the process that relates inputs to outputs; the exact structure of the system is unknown. Yet we have no difficulty in using such input/output relationships to describe the flow of objects, energy or information through the conjectured system. Consider the process of learning; we can arrange sensory inputs to a student that reliably produce instructional objectives even though we know little about the system that converts these inputs into observable educational outcomes.

Systems technology refers to knowledge of this input/output relationship and the process which produces it. Educational systems technology therefore refers to knowledge of the relation between inputs and outputs of systems which produce educational outcomes. When we consider the spread of educational technology to teachers and trainers, we refer to educational technology as an intellectual and practical pursuit concerned with all aspects of the design and control of systems that contribute to education (Mitchell, 1975). It is this knowledge, not apparatus, which is the fabric of educational technology.

We may understand an input/output relation which produces educational outcomes without knowing very much about the intricate workings of the process itself. This is the essence of a developing technology whereas science is more concerned with understanding the mechanisms that link inputs and outputs. Given

262

the dearth of knowledge about the communication process, can we produce an input/output relation to describe the spread of educational technology?

The Spread of Technology

From a strictly behavioural point of view what matters is that a relatively large number of people are beginning to participate in the activity with which we are concerned. It makes little difference how or why this happened. Acceptance of relevant knowledge or adoption of relevant practice is an output measure of the diffusion process. Thus the spread of educational technology to teachers can be demonstrated by their actions. Similarly the emergence of a new area of research and development is made manifest by demonstrations, contributions to the published literature or papers presented to learned societies.

We assume that educational technology theory and practice spreads as educational technologists pass information to others, mainly through published accounts, and receive information from others. We acknowledge the value of personal contacts at conferences, visits to innovative centres, etc, but these are not well-documented. We must identify publicly observable input/output relations that characterize the communication system.

Growth of Educational Technology Literature

How does the literature of educational technology grow? Consider 'programmed learning'. No entries appear in the *British Education Index* prior to 1962/63 when 12 items were indexed. In 1964/65 there were 32 items; 89 appeared in 1966/67; 54 in 1968/69; and 48 in 1970/71. But in 1972 we find only 10 items, eight in 1973, six in 1974 and nine in 1975. We might speculate that programmed learning research is on the wane (which appears to be the case) and that programmed learning is not spreading (which may not be correct).

The growth of programmed learning is characterized by evolution and differentiation. Thus applications of PL in various fields (eg chemistry, English) are now indexed. (It should be noted that the *British Education Index* does not reflect world trends which may differ markedly from country to country.) Nonetheless the pace of basic research on PL appears to have risen rapidly before tapering off, following an S curve.

A Model of the Communication Process

It is possible to formulate a macroscopic model which describes the communication process by which practitioners became interested in aspects of educational technology, acquired professional capability and contributed to the growth of the subject.

The propagation of educational technology, like the propagation of ideas within other scientific communities, may be modelled and studied as a special case of a more general communication phenomenon. Goffman in 1970 demonstrated that another special case — the spread of infectious diseases — can serve as a model for the spread of ideas. Goffman's generalized theory of epidemics can describe the growth of educational technology and its propagation of potential users.

The Epidemic Model of Communication

As a time-dependent phenomenon, an epidemic is characterized by a set of states (susceptible, infective and removed) amongst which a population is distributed.

Exposure to some event — communicated by an infective — may produce a transition from the susceptible to the infective state. The precise mechanism need not concern us. Similarly, when transition to the removed state occurs, for whatever reason, an infective is no longer in active circulation as a contributor to the subject.

Thus infectives represent active contributors to the theory and practice of educational technology. We operationalize this by asserting that infectives are people who have published at least one paper in a specified area within educational technology; they remain infective until 'removed' as a contributor one year after the time of their last publication on that topic. (Thus someone who published once during the period under review is an infective for one year. Someone who published twice, with a two-year gap, is infective for four years.) Removals are past contributors who no longer participate actively. (This under-estimates the number of infectives insofar as a removal might still be actively engaged in research, development or dissemination and be about to publish after the period being investigated.)

Susceptibles are potential contributors to the relevant literature who have not yet contributed to the topic. It is difficult to delineate this subset of the population in advance. We operationalize the term retrospectively as all those who eventually became contributors.

Exposure to a publication by an infective may produce a transition from the susceptible to the infective state. Whether it requires multiple exposure, personal contacts, etc, is irrelevant to the model. It does not matter that a susceptible may be practising educational technology; if he is not publishing, he is not an infective. Thus the model is not sensitive to the typical teacher's activity. This is consistent with the view that one must distinguish between the activity of a professional educational technologist and that of other professionals.

An epidemic is a positive feedback process that exists when the change in the rate at which the number of infectives accrue is positive. Thus the epidemic process may be in a stable state if change in the rate of increase in infectives is not positive. If the change of rate is not zero the system is unstable (eg either an epidemic or losing infectives and becoming less important).

Note that it is not the number of contributors but the rate of net increase in contributors that characterizes an epidemic state (ie rate of change in $\Delta I/\Delta t$). This is a clue which often can be detected early in the development of a new topic. It is also important to note that a threshold density of susceptibles is a necessary condition to enter the epidemic state; this is analogous to a critical mass.

The Epidemiology of Simulation and Gaming

We illustrate the process using simulation and gaming, a currently popular topic within educational technology.

The data forming the basis for this investigation are found in an extensive bibliography of *Simulation and Gaming in Education, Training and Business* (Tansey & Unwin 1969). This lists more than three times as many items to 1969 as appeared indexed in the *British Education Index* and *ERIC* combined.

The total of 443 references spanned three decades. The total population of contributors or infectives was 274. Using an interval of one year, the first time a contributor appeared he was designated infective and he became a removal one year later unless he published again (as listed in the bibliography).

The distribution of the rate of change in infectives, $\Delta I/\Delta t$, is plotted in Figure 1 for one-year intervals. Rapid fluctuations of the distributions on an annual basis can be ignored.

Inspection of Figure 1 suggests a preliminary epidemic around 1960. Review of

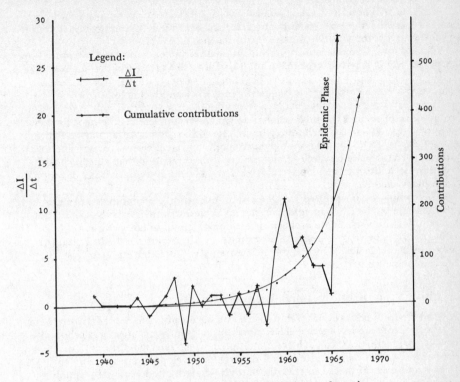

Figure 1. *Epidemic curve for simulation and gaming*

the data suggests an alternative explanation. Most of the references up to this date were drawn from fields outside education. There is a slight overlap of these sources with education sources followed by an emphasis on the literature within education. It is clear that a positive rate of growth in infectives appeared in the education literature about 1964. This is accompanied by a rapid growth in the contributions to the literature on simulation and gaming.

Data were also drawn from the *ERIC* index. References to simulation from 1966 to 1975 were plotted and the cumulative number of items was plotted (not shown here). The slope of these contributions to the literature on simulation is parallel to that plotted from the Tansey and Unwin data. This suggests that the epidemic which began some 15 years ago is still in effect. Thus we have modelled the growth and diffusion of educational technology.

Can Understanding Lead to Prediction?

We suggest, with some reservations, that the epidemic state for contributions to the topic of simulation and gaming could have been predicted from the data available 10 years ago. The probability of an epidemic taking place presumably can be predicted in advance today from analysis of contributions to the literature. One cannot ask, 'What topic is about to reach an epidemic phase?' because analysis is required for each topic. However one can ask, 'Is this topic likely to reach an epidemic phase soon?'

The infective or potential contributor who wants to participate in the early stages of an epidemic process in the literature of educational technology may find it useful to detect the tell-tale positive rate of change in $\Delta I/\Delta t$.

Similarly the administrator of an educational technology unit who is tempted to invest heavily in a certain area may find it useful to determine whether an explosive, positive feedback process is about to begin or, conversely, whether the epidemic process is decaying (as happens frequently in science and technology).

Administrators of educational technology units often find that only a small group of teachers uses the instructional design and media services. Perhaps the key to spreading educational technology lies in establishing and maintaining a positive rate of $\Delta I/\Delta t$. By examining one's own strengths and weaknesses it is possible to prepare a strategy for research, development or dissemination that exploits both existing capability and new opportunities. Thus a leadership position in educational technology might emerge.

The epidemic model shows that a group of educational technologists can have maximum impact only if an epidemic state is achieved in their sphere of operation. Isolated activities should be orchestrated if a small group of co-operating educational technologists hopes to contribute out of proportion to their size. It is also possible to achieve considerable influence by withdrawing one step from the scene of active contribution.

Amplification of Educational Technology

A small group of educational technologists can have a powerful impact by preparing others for professional practice. Thus a handful of faculty members in a school of educational technology can achieve a multiplier effect whereby a research or development idea can generate several research or development projects by students. In principle each of these can contribute to the growth of educational technology theory and practice over a lifetime. In this way the spread of effect can be considerable.

By way of illustration, in my own institution there are nearly 200 students of educational technology at the post-graduate level. More than half are part-time students and are employed in the field. Approximately 25% of the graduates teach at the post-secondary level, a further 25% work in educational technology units at the post-secondary level (eg as instructional designers, media producers, learning consultants) and perhaps 20% are engaged in industrial training. The remainder can be found in all sorts of places (eg broadcasting, ministries of education, school systems, the ministry or consulting). Their impact on personal and cultural development, ie education, is tremendous.

With a flow of some 30 magistral and 30 diploma students into the system each year, the staff of five full-time educational technologists has a profound effect. The regular faculty is augmented by three groups: first, the university's Audio-Visual Department provides considerable support (facilities and staff); part-time faculty have been drawn from, eg the National Film Board of Canada, the Canadian Broadcasting Corporation, private industry and other educational institutions; finally, visiting faculty members are invited to teach courses each summer and occasionally during the regular academic year. These experts supplement the teaching of regular faculty members who are thus enabled to supervise students' research and production activities. This illustration lends support to, but does not depend on, the epidemic model. Future research will test some of its implications.

Conclusion

The theory and models of communication have long formed part of the knowledge resources used by educational technologists. We have examined a macroscopic model of the communication process and have considered its utility in describing and predicting the growth of educational technology. To the extent that the data sources reflect professional activity we can model the spread of educational technology. Theoretical understanding of this process may facilitate its control.

References

Goffman, W (1970) 'An Application of Epidemic Theory to the Growth of Science (Symbolic Logic from Boole to Gode)', p 971, in 'Progress of Cybernetics', Rose, J (Ed), Gordon and Breach, Science Publishers Ltd, London.

Goffman, W and Newill, V A (1967) 'Communication and Epidemic Processes', Proc Roy Soc (London), A, 298, pp 316-334.

Mitchell, P D (1975) 'The Discernible Educational Technologist', 'Programmed Learning and Educational Technology', 12, (5), pp 306-325.

Mitchell, P D (1975) 'Operational Research Models Applicable to Educational Technology for Lifelong Learning' in L Evans and J Leedham (ed) 'Aspects of Educational Technology', Vol X, Evans, L and Leedham, J (Eds), Kogan Page, London.

Rogers, E M (1962) 'Diffusion of Innovations', The Free Press of Glencoe, New York.

Tansey, P J and Unwin, D (1969) 'Simulating and Gaming in Education, Training and Business: A Bibliography', The Education Centre, New University of Ulster, Coleraine.

Acknowledgement

This research was assisted by grants from the Canada Council and the Quebec Minister of Education's 'Programme de formation de chercheurs et d'action concertée'.

Teaching Educational Technology at a Distance

D Butts, J Megarry

In the context of the Jordanhill Diploma course, educational technology is defined as

'the application of scientific method and techniques to the design, implementation and evaluation of courses, with the aim of making the processes of learning more effective and efficient'.

If, as Rowntree (1974) affirms, 'educational technology is what educational technologists do' — in other words, the process of 'educational problem-solving' — in what sense can we claim to be able to teach it, whether at a distance or face to face? Educational technology is not, or should not be, a separate 'subject' within the curriculum. Nor is it merely a collection of rules or selection of techniques that can be applied appropriately to problems as they arise. No one ever became a good educational technologist simply by attending a course or studying a text-book. Nevertheless, a wide range of concepts and skills is involved — the principles of systems planning, the process of course design, the techniques of assessment and evaluation, the characteristics of media, the management of innovation, the production of learning materials. These elements of educational technology lend themselves to direct study as well as to development through practice and may legitimately form the basis of a formal course, at a post-experience level.

However, within the present constraints on educational staffing and expenditure, release for lecturers and teachers to attend long-term residential in-service courses is almost impossible to obtain, at least in Scotland. For the time being, the only practicable formula for all such courses appears to be distance teaching, on an Open University pattern. But can this formula be applied effectively to the teaching of educational technology, if by 'teaching' we imply, not merely feeding students with written material, but a planned process of setting objectives for each part of the course, assessing their achievement and providing remedial support where necessary in the light of such assessment? On the face of it, there would seem to be no reason why a significant proportion of the concepts and skills listed above should not be taught through carefully structured independent learning materials, designed to be studied at base; or why elements of feedback and assessment should not be built into the structure.

Moreover, study at base should facilitate application of ideas, experimenting with innovative techniques, evaluation of learning materials, and so on, more conveniently than long-term residence in a host institution; so that if, indeed, 'educational technology is what educational technologists do', there would seem to be strong arguments in favour of retaining trainees on their home ground. On the other hand, certain essential aspects of a comprehensive educational technology course — demonstration, discussion, acquisition of practical skills in equipment handling and materials making — clearly require the environment and facilities of a central institution. A blend of home cooking and dining out perhaps provides a well-balanced diet, and this is what the Jordanhill Diploma course tries to achieve.

A course on educational technology should logically be constructed on systematic lines. The model shown in Figure 1 symbolizes the concept of the Jordanhill Diploma course as a learning system.

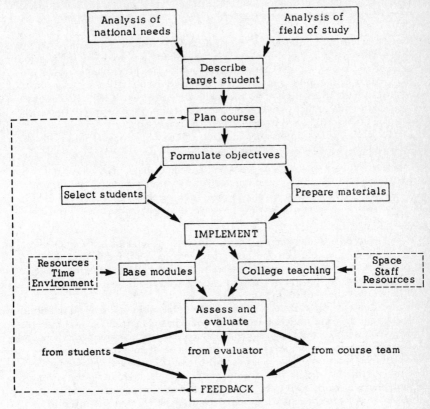

Figure 1. *Jordanhill diploma course as a learning system*

A system of this kind should be responsive to pressures from its environment and internally self-regulating. Planning should take account of current needs, but the course must be more than a succession of *ad hoc* attempts to fill training gaps and meet crises as they occur. To justify study at a diploma level, educational technology should be seen to involve a defined range of knowledge, concepts, skills and approaches. We must retain the right to match students to our course, as well as doing our best to match the details of the course to the requirements and interests of individual students.

The way in which we implement the course is inevitably affected by environmental constraints. For example, we know that students working at home will not have access to VCR equipment and we are thus prevented from incorporating video evidence and illustration in our base modules. Similarly, the organization of our in-college sessions is partly determined by the limitations of space during term time and the demands which other teaching commitments make on departmental staff.

The process of assessment and evaluation is complex, producing a variety of information from students, lecturers and evaluator; information which must be collated, interpreted and fed back into the planning stage of the system. The techniques employed allow for both formative and summative evaluation.

Since a large part of the course-work has to be carried out by members in their own time at their own home base, a decision was taken to parcel up that part of the content into instructional units or 'modules', each of them designed to occupy the student for five to six hours and to be completed in the course of a week. Without this kind of structure as a guide, it was felt that members would find difficulty in pacing their work and that the course team would be faced with an extremely complicated task in keeping track of the progress of each student and in organizing regular assessment. During the periods in college, the student's working day involves five to six hours of contact with tutors, but the time is used flexibly, often with theoretical and practical sessions deliberately interspersed.

The alternating pattern, presently in force, of home-based work and study in college is shown in Figure 2. It will be seen:

1. That the longer spells of college attendance have been placed mainly in vacation periods, so as to minimize disturbance to members' institutions.
2. That members are brought into college for a weekend (normally Friday/ Saturday) once every three or four weeks during the first three terms of the course.

By this procedure a fairly consistent rhythm of work can be built up. As far as possible, each main stage of course content is covered in a three to four-week period, culminating in an assessment exercise. During each weekend in college, members hand in the appropriate assessment exercise and receive the batch of modules to cover the next home study period.

The detailed content of each section of the course and the links and relationships among sections are kept under continuous review in the light of evaluation reports. Achieving coherence and logical sequence in an area of study as complex and wide-ranging as educational technology is inherently difficult; and distance teaching adds to the problem, since only certain aspects of the subject are appropriate to independent study, while all those elements of the course requiring discussion or involving practical work have to be fitted into the brief residential periods.

In its present form the course content falls into three broad and interlinked categories:

— theoretical studies
— management studies
— practical studies.

The first term is occupied with establishing basic concepts and setting educational technology in the context of relevant curriculum and psychological theory. The second term begins with a study of learning systems and moves on to management skills, with particular emphasis on the management of resource centres. The third term is devoted mainly to a consideration of specific management tasks in which the educational technologist is expected to show some expertise. There is thus a broad development from theory to application over the three terms. Concurrently, workshop sessions in practical communication skills are held throughout the year. In the fourth term, members, working in their own institutions, draw together the three strands of theory, management and practice in a curriculum project which requires them to plan, implement, evaluate and report on an exercise in resource-based learning.

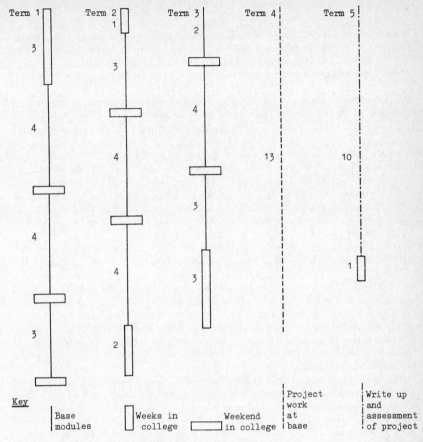

Figure 2. *Diploma course pattern*

Teaching educational technology at a distance creates certain educational and management problems, for both teachers and students, which differ in degree and kind from the problems associated with teaching in a conventional, face-to-face system. For the course teachers, the chief educational problem lies in learning how to communicate effectively through a medium (the learning unit) which denies them the opportunities for interaction, feedback and change of stimulus which are associated with live lecturing and tutoring. Mr X may be a brilliant lecturer; but where, in the index to Mr X's instructional booklet, will the home-based student find the well-modulated voice, the subtle variation of pace, the off-the-cuff joke, the sensitive reaction to loss of the thread? The answer to the problem lies in learning a new craft, since a good 'learning package' differs both from the live lecture and from the well-written text-book. Activity and change of stimulus (perhaps through a blend of print and non-print materials) can be built in; difficulties can be anticipated through careful planning and attention to evidence from the evaluation of previous modules; and, if possible, time must be allowed for validating first drafts before the final version is issued. It has been found essential for the teachers to work as a team, submitting their productions to one another for

271

mutual criticism. This kind of teamwork is a new and testing experience for many lecturers, used to the privacy provided by the four walls of the lecture room, but it pays dividends in terms of anticipating problems of pace, level and duration.

Educational and management problems in distance teaching are closely related, since the course manager must establish a time scale and rhythm of work which makes it possible for the teacher to operate effectively. Again, these factors differ markedly from the conventional course situation. When you give a lecture, a good part of your work is done at the moment of contact. But producing a learning package is like producing a play: all your work has to be completed before the curtain goes up. Moreover, the rhythm of work is uneven. Assuming a three-year life for most of the materials, the major effort will come in the year before the course begins, with perhaps considerable revision, based on evaluation evidence, in preparation for the second year, and a slight reduction of effort thereafter. This wave rhythm must be allowed for in allocating staff and finance to the course. To operate smoothly, a distance teaching course must build up an efficient production line and communication system, to cover the printing, replication, collation and dispatch of learning materials, and the regular collection of evaluation forms, response sheets and assessment exercises from the students. The operation involves a complex network of tasks which must be carefully planned — copyright clearances, for example, should be initiated well in advance of printing dates, and the production schedule for audio-visual materials must allow for duplication as well as processing. Again, a team approach is essential, with particular attention being paid to the quality of secretarial and technical support. New skills and roles may be required. For instance, the efficient compilation and packaging of learning materials is a highly responsible task (imagine the student's frustration if he discovers that he has been sent the wrong set of slides), but the work may not fall within the conventional job description of lecturer, secretary or technician. It is essential to adhere strictly to deadlines, yet vital that the whole operation should conserve the human touch.

Overlapping both educational and managerial considerations is the social problem of overcoming the loneliness of the long-distance learner. The role of the tutor takes on an added significance in this type of course. Without going so far as to offer an educational Nite-line service, the Jordanhill tutors do give their home telephone numbers to their students, so that queries can be dealt with as they occur. Within the constraints of time and finance, students are visited at base throughout the course; in particular, information acquired during the fourth-term visit forms an important element in the assessment of the curriculum project.

The difficulties of home-based study from a student's point of view are well known. Finding time is perhaps the most obvious and pressing problem, and this links to the effort of maintaining initial motivation and enthusiasm, when one is for the most part out of touch with other students. There is a need to feel part of a group, to reassure oneself that the teachers are interested in one's progress. The student requires criteria by which he can assess himself as well as receive judgment from his mentors. In practice, we have been surprised at how quickly and firmly the members of the Jordanhill educational technology course have built up a sense of solidarity among themselves, ringing one another up to discuss problems and paying visits to colleagues' institutions. Perhaps this social effort on their part has helped to keep the number of drop-outs gratifyingly low. So far, from the first two intakes, only two members have withdrawn because they found the going too heavy.

Home-based assessment exercises are currently limited to eight, covering the work of 24 modules. In addition, the students complete two major written assignments, as well as their curriculum project. However, if the learning packages are to be properly validated, we need other means of obtaining evidence on the detail of the students' understanding as they work through each stage of the modules. In this context, assessment is seen as one element in the larger process of evaluation.

A variety of evidence is used for the DET course evaluation; it is summarized in Figure 3. Some types of information are common to the evaluation both of base modules and of in-college sessions (and visits) (numbers 1-5); other techniques are specific to one or the other (numbers 5-9).

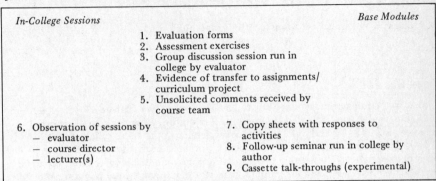

Figure 3. *Sources of data for DET course evaluation*

The various sources of data illustrated in Figure 3 do not all apply invariably, nor do they all receive equal weight in influencing course decisions.

Overall, they may be seen as aimed more at formative than at summative evaluation; the latter would emphasize sources 2 and 4 most, and it is on these that tutors depend especially when drawing up a performance profile of each student at the end of the course. Our preoccupation with formative evaluation perhaps reflects the course's infancy (in April 1977, we are less than halfway through our second course). It also may be related to the origin of our evaluation effort which is from within the course team and stems from a conviction that it will lead to better teaching and learning, rather than from an outside demand for summative evaluation data.

Reference

Rowntree, D (1974) 'Educational Technology in Curriculum Development' Harper and Row, London.

A Strategy for Evaluating University Courses with Reference to Large First-Year Classes in Pure Mathematics

M J Clark, B W Imrie, L C Johnston, W G Malcolm

Introduction

This paper deals with a strategy for the evaluation of two first-year courses in pure mathematics at the Victoria University of Wellington, New Zealand. The two courses, MATH 111 and MATH 112, cover generally the same syllabus, but MATH 112 is designed to cater for students better prepared in mathematics from their school experience. The weekly programme for each course involves four lectures, one tutorial and a written assignment. The strategy involved the planning and the implementation of systematic procedures for evaluating interactions between teacher, subject and student — a triad described by Hyman (1970).

The two courses considered involved eight university teachers (including Professor, Reader, Senior Lecturer, Lecturer and Post-Doctoral Fellow) responsible for the 12 different sections of these first-year courses. MATH 111 and MATH 112 had enrolments of 267 students and 101 students respectively for 1976.

The development of this evaluation project was initiated by Malcolm and, in its formative stages, his leadership was crucial in reconciling some ambivalent attitudes towards evaluation and teaching observation. On this particular point the paper is addressed to heads of departments as well as to others intending to use evaluation.

The teaching group was too large to be expected to meet regularly as a project group. Some form of group development had been identified by Imrie (1974) as having considerable value for such a project, and Clark agreed to join Malcolm, Johnston and Imrie to form a monitoring group. (Clark was responsible for another first year mathematics course and was experienced in educational research.) The development of this group was a vital factor in the development and implementation of the evaluation strategy. The group met regularly each week for an hour, and shared experiences somewhat similar to those advocated by Levine (1974).

It is possible to identify at least eight different types of evaluation when appropriate resources are available.

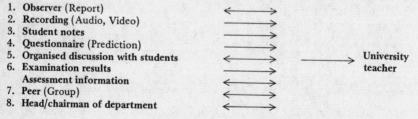

1. **Observer** (Report)
2. **Recording** (Audio, Video)
3. **Student notes**
4. **Questionnaire** (Prediction)
5. **Organised discussion with students**
6. **Examination results**
   Assessment information
7. **Peer** (Group)
8. **Head/chairman of department**

University teacher

Table 1. *Types of evaluation accessible to the university teacher*

Table 1 describes these evaluation procedures, which can provide information to the lecturer so that, as a university teacher, he may:

(a) Increase his professional competence by assessing his performance and by improving his understanding of the triadic interaction;

(b) Begin to move from a relationship with his subject which excludes the student — from defensive lecturing to the enjoyment of engaging the students in a learning experience.

The evaluation strategy used or managed the following techniques or 'accessible sources of information': (1) Lecture Observation and (2) Lecture Recording (Table 1).

It was agreed that three lectures each should be observed — consecutively if possible.

The first observation (01) took place without the prior knowledge of the lecturer. The observer (Imrie) made notes of what appeared to be significant in the presentation of the lecture and in the response/behaviour of the students. A report was then prepared and sent to the lecturer — if possible, before the next observation. If the lecturer wished, the report was discussed with the observer or, indeed, with any colleague, spouse, etc.

The second observation (02, C1) (preferably of the next meeting of the same class) supplemented the observer's notes/report with a cassette-recording. The lecturer could record comments about aims of content and presentation for consideration later. The process of cassette-recording interfered minimally with the lecturer. A second report was prepared.

A third observation (03, C2, TV) again involved the observer and cassette-recording. In addition, 30 minutes of the lecture were recorded on video-tape. The lecture theatres had projection rooms, which minimized the intrusion of operator and equipment. A third report was prepared.

After such a series of observations, the lecturer had available three reports, two cassette-recordings (50 minutes each) and one video-tape recording (30 minutes) — all confidential to the lecturer.

Some considerations are:

(a) The observer's reports are not structured in the form of a check-list. Each report is intended as a record of significant aspects of presentation and of student response. Comments are offered which may stimulate discussion, and the lecturer, for his/her own purposes, is invited to add his/her comments on reading each report, in response to such questions as: 'Did I achieve what I intended?' 'How do I know?' 'What changes (if any) would I make?'

(b) *Student Notes (3)* 'Getting a good set of notes' is usually a major student objective — it may also be an objective of the lecturer. A convenient sample of student notes may be obtained for inspection by borrowing the appropriate notes from a tutorial group (15-17 students) and copying them immediately so that the students are not inconvenienced.

(c) For practical reasons, only 30 minutes of a lecture (50 minutes) were recorded on video-tape. Sometimes this was the first 30 minutes; sometimes the first 10 minutes, a middle section, and then the final 10 minutes. The lecturer could make arrangements to view the video-tape on his own or with someone else.

The video-tape recordings were also used to stimulate group discussion on the lecture and on the tutorial. With the permission of each university teacher, extracts from each recorded observation were compiled for viewing at two lunchtime

University Teacher	Section Topic	Lectures (per week)	Weeks	Observation Weeks 01/02/03	Evaluation Week	N (am/pm) (attendance)	Response %
MATH 111 – Short Form							
Dr P F Rhodes-Robinson*	Calculus 1	15 (2)	1-9	7/8/9	9	(171/68)	88%
Prof W G Malcolm	Vector Geometry	12 (1)	2-16	12/13/14	15	(178/52)	86%
Dr L C Johnston	Linear Algebra	16 (1)	1-20	7/8/9	19	(197/32)	86%
Dr G C Wake*	Calculus 2	9 (2)	12-16	21/22/23	23	(173/36)	78%
		6 (1)	19-24				
Prof W G Malcolm	Number Systems	12 (2)	19-24	–	30	(151/32)	69%
		3 (1)	27-29				
Ms T M H Blithe*	Calculus 3	6 (1)	27-32		–		–
Dr R L Epstein	Calcults 4	10 (2)	27-31	29/30/30	31	(151/24)	66%
MATH 111 – Comprehensive Evaluation	Mid-course				16	(180/46)	85%
	End-course				31	(115)	43%
MATH 112 – Short Form							
Prof W G Malcolm*	Vector Geometry	12 (1)	2-16		15	(71)	70%
Mr D C Harvie*	Calculus 1	10 (2)	1-6	12/13/14	15	(88)	87%
Dr L C Johnston*	Linear Algebra	16 (1)	1-24		23	(90)	89%
Dr J F Harper*	Calculus 2	18 (1)	7-32	21/22/23	30	(100)	99%
Prof W G Malcolm	Number Systems	8 (1)	19-32		31	(89)	88%
		8 (2)	21, 22				
			27, 28				
MATH 112 – Comprehensive Evaluation	Mid-course				16	(73)	72%
	End-course				31	(70)	69%

(*Tutorial Observation during Weeks 21, 22)

Figure 1. *Evaluation of pure mathematics courses (1976)*

meetings. The teaching group shared an experience which compared and contrasted individual teaching styles. University teachers may have some mental pictures of their own different teaching styles. The observer requires some knowledge of the person to be able to interpret the intentions of the lecturer. The video-tape recording provides an opportunity for self-confrontation and, in discussion, for adjustment of any tentative conclusions offered by the observer (cf Axelrod, 1973; Bligh, 1975).

MATH 111/112 Course Section Evaluation

Please give your evaluation of the following aspects of this section of the course, with particular reference to their effect on *your* learning:

Title of Section, eg Vector Geometry

1. Previous knowledge assumed.
2. Material covered in lectures (on average).
3. Explanations given in lectures of subject matter.
4. Average level of *difficulty* of subject matter of lectures.
5. Average *interest* level of subject matter of lectures.
6. (a) Do you own the text-book for this section?
   (b) How often do you use the text-book?
7. The 'helpfulness' of the text-book.
8. The 'helpfulness' of the written assignments for understanding *Vector Geometry*.
9. The difficulty of the written assignments.
10. The 'helpfulness' of the tutorials for understanding *Vector Geometry*.

Figure 2. *The items of the short-form questionnaire*

Questionnaires (4)

Two different types of questionnaire were used, which will be referred to as the Short-Form Questionnaire and the Course Questionnaire.

The Short-Form Questionnaire is shown in Figures 2 and 3. It was used for each topic except one, and usually was administered during the penultimate lecture of that series. The *blank* response sheet was issued to the students, and the UTRC staff member used an overhead projector to reveal each response item in turn. Including final collection of the response sheets, the procedure did not take more than 12 minutes of the lecture time. Some points are:

1. The procedure ensures a very high return — often 100%.
2. The use of the overhead projector 'paces' the student's response, allowing approximately 30 seconds for each item.
3. The control of the procedure by the UTRC allows for interpretation, if necessary, and offers a guarantee of 'confidential neutrality', which has been shown to increase the validity of student evaluation by questionnaire.
4. While the students were completing the response sheet, they knew that the teacher was predicting the majority category of their response for each item. In the example shown in Figure 3, the lecturer has offered a prediction of the 'actual' response and of an 'ideal' response.
5. The systematic, repeated use of this questionnaire, in conjunction with the observation techniques, seemed to give the students a feeling of involvement.
6. The accumulation of results enabled comparisons to be made between the responses to the same topics by the two different groups of students. Also,

277

MATH 111/112 Course Section Evaluation (1976)

Please give *your evaluations* by making a clear tick in the space which *corresponds most closely* with your opinion of the effect of the particular item on your learning progress.

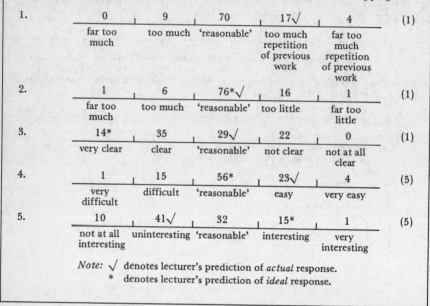

1.

0	9	70	17√	4	(1)
far too much	too much	'reasonable'	too much repetition of previous work	far too much repetition of previous work	

2.

1	6	76*√	16	1	(1)
far too much	too much	'reasonable'	too little	far too little	

3.

14*	35	29√	22	0	(1)
very clear	clear	'reasonable'	not clear	not at all clear	

4.

1	15	56*	23√	4	(5)
very difficult	difficult	'reasonable'	easy	very easy	

5.

10	41√	32	15*	1	(5)
not at all interesting	uninteresting	'reasonable'	interesting	very interesting	

Note: √ denotes lecturer's prediction of *actual* response.
　　　 * denotes lecturer's prediction of *ideal* response.

Figure 3. *The 'blank' response sheet for the short-form questionnaire (% responses added for feed-back — MATH 112 Vector Geometry)*

within the one course, MATH 111, there were comparisons between the two streams — different times for student convenience.

Course Questionnaire

A more comprehensive Mid-Course Questionnaire was administered. Apart from questions on workload and attitudes, students were asked to consider their overall experiences of the course (MATH 111 or MATH 112). Certain items from the Short-Form Questionnaire were included so that responses could be compared.

A similar End-Course Questionnaire was administered. Because of pressure of time (to 'complete' the course), the MATH 111 students were asked to complete the questionnaires in their own time and return them at the next lecture or directly to the UTRC. The resultant 43% response corresponded with the response of 40-60% of other evaluations carried out by take-away questionnaire at the end of the session.

These comprehensive evaluations also invited student comment, and the End-Course Questionnaire was developed (from the Mid-Course Questionnaire) by a working group which included students.

Student Involvement (5)

During Week 20, a lunch-time meeting was held which was attended by 13 members of staff and by 22 students as representatives of the tutorial groups. There were useful exchanges of opinion and information, and students volunteered to join with members of the monitoring group to form a working group:

(a) To consider the information already obtained from the Short-Form Questionnaires and from the Mid-Course Questionnaire;
(b) To produce an End-Course Questionnaire.

At one of the initial meetings of this working group, two interesting points were discussed with reference to student response to the questionnaires. The first point related to the short time allowed for student judgement of response to each item of the Short-Form Questionnaire, and the following question was added for the next administration of the Short-Form Questionnaire:

Please indicate how confident you are that your responses are an accurate indication of your experiences of this section of the course.

(N)	Not at all confident	Not confident	Reasonably confident	Confident	Very confident
(151) MATH 111 (am)	1%	13%	40%	38%	7%
(32) MATH 111 (pm)	0%	19%	47%	22%	13%
(87) MATH 112	2%	16%	21%	48%	13%

Figure 4. *Confidence level of test response to short-form questionnaire*

This response emphasises the importance of not assuming a uniform collective judgement, a point emphasized by Falk and Dow (1971).

The second point relates to what percentage of response to a questionnaire is acceptable as representative of student opinion, and the following question was added to the End-Course Questionnaire:

What *minimum* level of response would you accept as being representative of the opinion of students enrolled for this course?

(N)	%	50-60%	61-70%	71-80%	81-90%	91-100%
(109)	(41%) MATH 111	14%	25%	34%	20%	7%
(67)	(66%) MATH 112	1%	36%	42%	19%	0%

Figure 5. *Questionnaire response acceptable as representative of student opinion*

Two students (from the working group) also attended one of the four three-hour sessions of a review or 'teach-in' which took place over a period of seven days after the final examinations. At the third meeting their individual contributions were very useful as a complement to the aggregate questionnaire responses and to the summaries of student comments obtained by the comprehensive questionnaires. While the written comment can offer insights beyond the constraints of the formal questionnaire items, there is a potential exaggeration of the status of the comment by its selection and presentation (cf Caut, 1972).

The 'teach-in' was designed to involve participants in discussion of:

(a) The information obtained from the evaluation experience;
(b) The problems which could be identified by the group;

(c)   Solutions to these problems; consideration of lecture, tutorial, assignment, text-book and assessment as part of a teaching strategy;

(d)   Desirable, acceptable and feasible changes for short-term and for long-term implementation. (29 points were agreed as proposals for course development.)

While the evaluation data of the project had been considered by individuals during the session and were the focus of the first session, the evaluation experience became more important as discussion moved from analysis to synthesis of the many interdependent considerations of the relationship between teacher, subject and student. The data were still used for reference but the discussion was of greater significance for those involved (cf Cox, 1975, 1976).

Eight to ten university teachers attended these sessions, and one of the teaching group, on study leave at Leeds University, sent his contribution on cassette. The discussions were constructive, considerate and imaginative without being unrealistic.

'Evaluation . . . is a continuing professional responsibility.' Thomas (1974) used these words when concluding a course evaluation study based on end-of-course type evaluation, and Imrie (1975) suggested other implications of professionalism for the university teacher.

It is with such considerations in mind that the strategy described in this paper was developed. In particular, the strategy was considerate of the people involved — the university staff and the students, as Miller (1975) has suggested.

It remains to be seen whether all members of the teaching group of this evaluation will accept all of the proposition (Flood Page, 1974)

'that teachers in higher education should have a reasonable degree of professional competence, should not only know their subject . . . but should also have an adequate idea of the different techniques of imparting and assessing it and should practise those techniques with fully informed awareness of what they are doing.'

Different techniques of evaluation have been described, together with some of the implications. A strategy was used which took into consideration the people involved, the nature of the subject, the level of the course, the type of institution and the resources available. Similar strategies can be developed to meet the needs of different situations.

References

Axelrod, J (1973) 'The University Teacher as Artist', p 15, Jossey-Bass.

Bligh, D (1975) 'Teaching Students', p 212, Exeter University Teaching Services.

CAUT (1972) 'Student Evaluation — An Aspect of Teaching Effectiveness', Report of the Professional Orientation Committee to CAUT Council.

Cox, R (1975) 'The Evaluation of Teaching in Higher Education', in 'Evaluating Teaching in Higher Education', p 27, University of London Teaching Methods Unit 1975.

Cox, R (1976) 'The Evaluation of Teaching', in 'Improving Teaching in Higher Education', p 140, University of London Teaching Methods Unit.

Falk, B and Dow, K L (1971) 'The Assessment of University Teaching', pp 15, 16, SRHE.

Flood Page, C (1974) 'Student Evaluation of Teaching — The American Experience', p 1, SRHE.

Hyman, R T (1970) 'Ways of Teaching', p 13, J B Lippincott Co.

Imrie, B W (1974) 'Managing to Teach as well?', in 'Issues in Staff Development', pp 54-70, University of London Teaching Methods Unit (1975).

Imrie, B W (1975) 'Managing to Teach — Together', in 'Proceedings of the International Conference on Improving University Teaching', pp B19-35, University of Maryland, Heidelberg.

Levine, M (1974) 'Scientific Method and the Adversary Model', 'American Psychologist' Vol 29, No 9, pp 661-677.

Miller, C M L (1975) 'Evaluation of Teaching and the Institutional Context', in 'Evaluating Teaching in Higher Education', p 38, University of London Teaching Methods Unit (1975).

Thomas, I D (1974) 'How Useful Are Course Evaluations?', 'Occasional Paper Number One', University Teaching and Research Centre, Victoria University of Wellington.

Note:

For publication after presentation at ETIC 77, the paper had to be reduced in length by about two-thirds. The complete text, which includes personal statements by the three mathematics teachers (Clark, Johnston and Malcolm) is available* from the University Teaching and Research Centre.

Occasional Paper No 3.

Evaluation of a Keller Plan Innovation in Mathematics Teaching

T M Blithe, L C Johnston

Introduction

From the point of view of a university teacher, many of the important considerations in introducing a new type of course are concerned with how to get it accepted by colleagues and the university administration. Much of the evaluation of such a course must be concerned with points which will persuade colleagues that it is worthwhile using the new method more widely. This is the point of view of the authors of this paper, concerning a course at the University of Wellington, New Zealand.

Design

The tradition of the department in which this course was taught is such that a new type of course must be widely acceptable to most members. After some discussion this acceptance was achieved. There were three main areas of concern of other teachers in the department:

1. The Modular Structure. It was felt by some staff members that breaking a course into modules would destroy the unity of the subject. Mathematics has a logical and often linear development so that breaks may appear to be artificial. However, it was argued that if development is logical and one result depends on preceeding work then mastery of the preceeding work is important; the Keller Plan ensures this.
2. Well-Defined Objectives. Mathematicians are aware of the way they understand mathematics themselves but have not developed good methods of testing understanding at the more abstract levels, nor is it known whether it is reasonable to expect students to achieve these levels. It was believed by some staff members that by the writing of limited behavioural objectives for each module the level of achievement of the best students would also be limited. It was argued by the authors that the students would go beyond the limited objectives stated according to their ability and that for most students it is best to gain mastery at a technical level than to be taught an abstract theory and gain only a hazy understanding of both techniques and abstract concepts.

   The objection that clearly-stated objectives are too limiting was further overcome by designing the course so that a pass was achieved when nine modules were completed but a higher grade would be gained by completing any of a further five modules. The last five modules contained the most abstract material and their tests were designed to test ability as well as mastery.

282

3. Staff time. The staff/student ratio in New Zealand universities is such that most staff would find it quite unacceptable to spend significantly more time on teaching than they do at present. For this reason the teachers of the course gave a personal commitment to spend the necessary time in its first year of operation and this first trial was regarded as experimental. If it took too much time then it was to be dropped the following year.
4. Grades. The University administration works as though all assessment is 'norm referenced' and has given guidelines about what proportion of students should gain A, B and C grade passes. The Keller Plan has 'criterion referenced' assessment and teachers make a commitment to students before the course begins about what they need to do to gain a particular grade. Thus, after the course begins teachers have no control over the proportions of students getting particular kinds of pass grades. This difficulty was overcome by making later modules and tests include more abstract material (as mentioned above) and by combining the Keller Plan 'marks' with the marks of a traditional course, the combination course being called MATH 205. It was not possible to pass either part of MATH 205 separately. Staff were agreed that this assessment procedure would eliminate the danger of having too many A and B grade passes. The course designers hoped, however, that the clarity of objectives and the individualized teaching method would ensure that there would be more C grade passes and less failures.

Implementation

The course organisers were fortunate in having the cooperation of the educational technology centre at the University of Wellington (called the University Teaching and Research Centre). In fact both members of the academic staff at the Centre read the early study guides and course material and made comments and suggestions on them. Although neither had done enough mathematics to fully understand the work, they were able to see the material more from the point of view of students; they were able to see where motivation for new ideas was missing, they often made valuable additions to bare definitions and in particular they were able to point out where procedural instructions were needed for students having difficulty. It appeared that outside readers unfamiliar with the course, particularly those familiar with course design, were able to spot defects missed by those who wrote the course.

Evaluation

As was mentioned earlier, the authors are mathematics teachers rather than educational technologists and consequently were primarily concerned with discovering whether or not the Keller Plan course was an improvement over the traditional course, and persuading colleagues that this particular innovation should be continued and used more widely. Teachers must make judgements about the course before the beginning of the next year so the evaluation was mainly concerned with issues which would help to make good judgements (Falk and Dow, 1971).

Subjective Evaluation

The feelings and beliefs of teachers involved in a Keller Plan course cannot be ignored just because they are subjective. Each teacher was involved with the course for six hours per week and worked closely with many students in this time.

Reactions of the teachers and of the students in talking to the teachers were very positive; in fact from the teachers' point of view, talking to the students and getting honest comments about a course is a new experience if they have been involved only with traditional lecture courses in the past. The closer relationship with students must lead to better understanding of them and better teaching.

A positive feature of the Keller Plan course is that students see it as the first real attempt to reform a system which they see as depersonalized and unjust; it eliminates final examinations without introducing the continual pressure of tests which count towards grading but for which there is no second chance.

Formal Evaluation

Formal evaluation of teaching innovations tends to be resisted by teachers. Their main concern is that students should learn their subject more efficiently and enjoy doing so. It is, however, very difficult to measure whether or not this is being achieved because comparison of a course taught in one year with an innovative course the following year would need a fully criterion-based assessment system in both years and would need control or knowledge of all variations between the two courses, the teachers and the classes involved (Parlett and Hamilton, 1976). The authors were persuaded to carry out a formal evaluation in spite of the difficulty of comparison with the previous year's course, partly to determine what facts they could which would influence the continuance or extension of Keller Plan teaching in the Mathematics Department, and partly to provide a basis on which to build future evaluations when better assessment methods make comparison of courses possible.

Staff Time

One factor which is critical in deciding whether or not Keller Plan teaching can be continued or extended is the amount of staff time used. The preparation of study guides and content material is time-consuming but does not have to be repeated each year. For this reason an analysis has been made of 'teaching time' only. The New Zeland university student's work-load does not allow the possibility of using student proctors, so that all tutoring and testing was done by full-time staff. The total number of man hours per week was 24, and the course was taught at a rate appropriate to a 'six credit course' (about one sixth of a year's work for a full-time student). The initial enrolment was 102 students, so 24 staff hours were used to teach at a rate of 600 student credits/year; this is a rate of 25 student credits per staff hour. This compares unfavourably with the staff time used on the equivalent course before the Keller Plan method was used. Although not so easily measured, this was approximately 30 student credits per staff hour. On the surface, therefore, it would appear impossible to extend the Keller Plan method to all courses as this would increase staff teaching time by 25%.

However, there are two other factors which must be considered. Staff time in a Keller Plan course is clearly proportional to the number of students, since most tutoring and testing is on a one-to-one basis; this is not so for a traditional course, since lecture time is independent of class size. (Of course time spent marking exercises does depend on the size of the class.) Consequently, the comparison between Keller Plan and traditional courses is more favourable to the Keller Plan if the class is smaller.

The other factor is highlighted by the example of a Keller Plan course which is a service course on statistics for a class of 660 students at another New Zealand university. A similar calculation to that given above showed that this course was taught at a rate of 60 student credits per staff hour. The reason for this difference is that in the course at the University of Wellington each module was worth about a quarter of a credit whereas in the course at the other university the value of each module was about half of a credit. Consequently, there is a large difference in the number of tests administered but the marking of tests took a similar amount of time in both courses. A conclusion is that if staff time is to be conserved in a Keller Plan course then modules should be made as large as is possibly compatible with the aims and structure of the course.

Questionnaire Results

The following questionnaire was handed out to the class towards the end of the academic year, ie after much of the traditional part of MATH 205 had been completed and the Keller Plan course had been finished for three months. The questionnaire is short because it was to be completed in a short time before a lecture.

Questions from the Questionnaire:

1. How many modules did you complete?
2. How did you feel about this level of achievement? (Five point scale satisfaction given.)
3. Please estimate the average workload (hours/week) including testing/marking/tutorial time, which you had during this course.
4. Are there any comments which you wish to make comparing and contrasting the Keller Plan course with the traditional course within MATH 205?
5. A Keller Plan course is essentially one which provides a form of personalized instruction for the student. In the light of your experience would you have preferred other forms of teaching contact?
6. Please give your rating of the course as a whole. (Five point scale.)

The results of the questionnaire were generally favourable and some were of particular interest. These are discussed below.

The results shown in the histogram in Figure 1 reflect the expectation of students. They were required to complete seven modules to remain in the course; if only seven modules were completed they had the chance to make up the deficit in the traditional course in the second half-year. Completion of nine modules was the

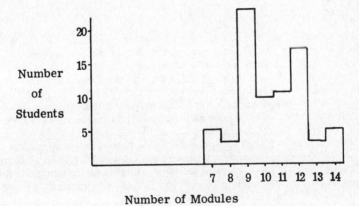

Number of Modules

Figure 1.

pass level; this accounts for the concentration of numbers at that point. The other point of concentration at 12 modules completed is accounted for by the students who wished to go as far as possible but found modules 13 and 14 too difficult.

The general conclusion can be drawn that the achievement of students depends on their own expectation and as has been seen in many Keller Plan evaluations, the clarity with which the pass requirements are expressed almost eliminates the occurrence of students just failing to fulfil them (Boud, Bridge, Willoughby, 1975). The responses to questions 5 and 6 were analyzed in the following way:

0.62 were favourable to the Keller Plan
0.19 were unfavourable to the Keller Plan
0.19 were non-committal.

It is always of interest to a teacher to know what type of student responds unfavourably to a course. If unfavourable responses appear to have no reasonable basis and come from students who perform poorly in all courses, then teachers tend to ignore them. The histogram in Figure 2 shows the Keller Plan mark distribution for those students who responded unfavourably as fractions of the total.

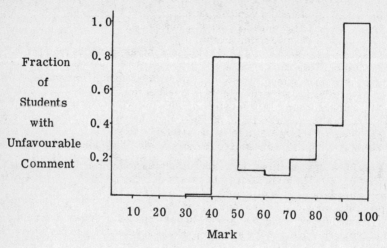

Figure 2.

It is clear that middle-range students are overwhelmingly in favour of the Keller Plan course but a disturbingly large proportion of the best students are not in favour of it, as are a large proportion of the least able students. Detailed comments of these students indicate that the best students find the Keller Plan course uneconomical on their time; they feel that they do not need mastery tests so often and do not need the practice at techniques that the course requires of them. Detailed comments of the least able students indicate simply that they do not feel that they are progressing as they would like to do.

The above analysis in this paper showed how students' relative opinion of Keller Plan v traditional courses depended on their performance and ability in the courses. It is possible also to discover some detail about students who perform well on one type of course and poorly on the other. This is done by drawing a scatter diagram of Keller Plan marks against traditional marks.

In this case the scatter diagram showed that the relationship between the two sets of marks was not quite linear, but it was possible to pick out the 16 students who had done better on one course than the other by the widest margin. Answers to other questions of the questionnaire by these students are summarized as mean scores below:

	Students Better on Keller Plan	Students Better on Traditional
Satisfaction with Keller level	3.5	2.2
Rating of Keller Course	4.0	4.0
Hours of work per week	7.5	5.7

It appears that students gave a rating of the Keller course which was independent of their performance on it. It is natural that students who performed relatively poorly on the Keller Plan course were less satisfied with their performance. The only variable which staff may be able to alter is the work put into the course. Perhaps a tighter control over the students who appear to lie behind their expected level would result in more students being satisfied with their level. This method could give very useful results and would do so if a more searching questionnaire was possible.

Difficulties of Keller Plan Courses in Mathematics

The main organizational difficulty with the Keller Plan courses is that of providing help and testing facilities for students when they want it. The timetable in New Zealand universities is very full for science students and as a result about one-half of the class find one particular time the most convenient. The result is that accommodation is strained so that time and staff resources are barely adequate. There is danger of testing becoming an automatic production-line process instead of being a relaxed discussion between student and tutor. This tendency is resisted but more satisfactory solutions are needed.

Another difficulty is one which related to the nature of mathematics. An advantage of the Keller Plan method of assessment is that the knowledge of the student can be tested verbally as well as by written test. However, one of the skills a mathematician must learn is that of using mathematical language in a clear and precise way. Students are passing Keller Plan tests without practising this skill. A possible solution to the problem is to include at least one question in each test for which a clearly written answer is required, verbal addition being unacceptable. Markers would run the risk of being thought to be pedantic but benefits to students could be considerable.

Conclusions

The Keller Plan course as conducted in 1976 is clearly capable of improvement, but has been successful in that most students found it a better way to learn mathematics and all the staff found it a better way to teach. The evaluation as carried out has shown some areas of possible improvement. No course can be perfect, but the philosophy of the authors is that by making changes which add flexibility to courses and provide a choice of learning methods, improvements can certainly be made. The course is being repeated with modifications in 1977 and it is hoped that a similar evaluation will show that some modifications have been successful.

References

Boud, D J, Bridge, W A, Willoughby, L (1975) 'PSI Now' 'British Journal of Educational Technology' Vol 6, No 2, p15.

Falk, B, Dow, K L (1971) 'The Assessment of University Teaching' SRHE p31.

Parlett, M, Hamilton, D (1976) 'Evaluation as Illumination' 'Evaluation Studies Review Annual' Vol 1, p142, Sage Publications.

Gains and Losses in a Guided-Self-Study Engineering Course: Towards a Problem-Solving Approach

C R Coles

Much of the time university teachers seem to operate on what might be termed a 'drops of wisdom' model of learning. They speak; clouds of wisdom form; the distilled product (knowledge) falls, settles and is absorbed. Unfortunately life isn't that simple!

This study reports a recent evaluation of a first-year BSc engineering course which has been reorganized along the lines suggested by F S Keller (1968). The course tutors had felt for some time that the conventional mode of presentation — lectures and private study — did not accommodate the wide variation in ability of students entering the course. It was argued that a self-paced format would facilitate unconstrained learning by the more able but, at the same time, identify and support those students experiencing difficulties.

The course itself is based on a text-book, which all students are expected to purchase, the content of which has been divided into nine sections, called Blocks, each consisting of two or three chapters. The tutors have supplemented each Block with a duplicated handout covering what they have identified as 'difficult' areas, or parts not fully explained by the text. The notes also include a test to be administered and marked by the students on completion of the Block. The students then present themselves for a tutorial with one of three members of staff during which any difficulties are discussed.

The evaluation of the course can best be described as 'action-research' and rests on an 'inter-active' methodology based on a participant observation model of evaluation rather than the conventional comparative approach. This decision was taken for several reasons, of which two were seen to be crucial.

Firstly, it was felt that evaluation of this nature should be useful and that in order to achieve this the classic distinction between the researcher and researched needs to be blurred. Evaluation is seen to be 'formative' rather than 'summative' and the feedback it provides should lead to improvements during the course rather than after it has ended.

Secondly, in an educational situation such as this, control groups are undesirable, variables difficult to isolate and large samples not possible. Education is essentially local, small-scale, and transient. Yesterday's conditions are rarely repeated today and may not recur tomorrow. (The theoretical and philosophical principles underpinning this form of evaluation have been well documented and recent publications act both as an orientation and a bibliographic source. See, in particular, Stenhouse [1975] and Hamilton [1976].)

The methods of inquiry that were employed were consistent with this methodology. An attempt was made to follow the course through, observing students and staff in action, sitting-in on tutorials and undertaking both formal and informal interviews. The fundamental aim has been firstly, to arrive at an accurate description of the course from the viewpoint of the various participants, followed by a careful analysis based on the issues that appear to be emerging. Fundamentally, this necessitates a deeper review of the assumptions, attitudes, and values underlying both the teaching and learning methods and the nature and structure of the subject matter of the course: that is, its pedagogy and its epistemology.

On the credit side the most striking feature seemed to be that students welcome the opportunity to work at their own speed and in their own time. Many report satisfaction at studying within a structure which allows them to come to grips not only with the subject but also with developing their study methods: in short, the course helped them to work on their own.

Certainly there have been considerable gains, but unfortunately the cost is enormous.

The evaluation soon highlighted the need by most of the 90 students for a considerable amount of tutorial support. Traditionally, the course was allocated 80 hours of contact time per year (approximately 3 three hours a week). In the guided self-study format, this has trebled. It may be argued that this comparison is unfair since, conventionally, the course did not offer tutorial back-up. In the reorganized course with one-to-one tutorials as an important feature, it seems that individual student needs are being recognized and met although at a considerably higher cost. One major focus, then, has been to find out whether the functions of the tutorials might be carried out in another way and so reduce the cost of the course. Naturally this meant first identifying what role the tutorial was fulfilling and this necessitated looking at the subject matter itself.

Now, any course makes assumptions about the nature and structuring of knowledge. However, those underpinning this course required some illumination. The course seemed to many students to be encouraging the acquisition of knowledge specific to that branch of engineering. Certainly this was implicit within the materials used — the text-book and the course notes. Frequently this involved acquiring and applying certain key concepts, some of which were novel to many of the students and caused some learning difficulties. However, in talking with staff it seemed that the overall intention was for students to develop their abilities in problem-solving in that area of engineering, although the tutors had not clearly articulated this intention to the students.

The course, then, was attempting to derive general principles of problem-solving out of the specific knowledge and applications it was teaching. The hope was that the general would somehow 'emerge' out of the specific. How did students cope with this? Some, of course, sailed through: it seemed that they had developed, or perhaps acquired, these principles. They were able effectively and efficiently to solve the problems at the end of Block tests. The average time taken for the completion of a Block by these students, whom we might call the 'generalizers', was about six hours compared with the rest of the students who took between 10 and 20 hours. Very quickly the 'generalizers' became recognized as the 'good' students whilst the 'non-generalizers' became the 'less able'. It will be recalled that the *raison d'être* for the course was to minimize differential student ability on entry. Could it be that the course created the polarization?

One finding was particularly interesting. The 'non-generalizers' were characterized by a unique approach to problem solution. Typically, they requested more 'worked examples' than were provided by the course. In fact this became something of an issue. The students argued that if they could be shown how a number of problems had been solved it would help them in the solution of a novel problem. The argument is common and persuasive. However, the staff were reluctant to submit to these pressures: a stance which gave further evidence that their intention was for students to develop generalized problem-solving skills rather than the application of 'established' solutions.

What, then, actually went on in the tutorials? Tutors seemed to adopt one of two approaches with students in difficulty. One was to ask the student to explain how he was going about tackling the problem and then to point out how to correct the approach. Another way was to demonstrate how to tackle the problem. This appeared to be idiosyncratic and to some extent further confused the student. The investigator then focussed on how staff set about solving problems by asking them to 'talk their way through' a number of different solutions. A common pattern appeared to emerge. Typically, this began with a silence lasting a few seconds followed by some statement by the tutor such as . . .

> 'If you write down the equations to represent these parts of the problem, then it's simple mathematics, isn't it?'

To the student it is simple mathematics at this point, but the solution of the problem is more than just mathematical manipulation. What is not obvious to the student is the thinking behind it: that is, what was going on in the tutor's mind in that few seconds' silence.

From observing a number of tutorials and tutor-solutions, certain generalizations can be made. It appears that the first task is to 'clarify' the problem. This often involves a re-statement of the problem, perhaps involving a reformulation or a visualizing of the problem in another format. An example might be seeing an electronic circuit as a hydraulic model such as a river. This stage quickly leads on to what might be termed searching for the locus of the solution — a hypothesis-generating and testing phase in which guesses, concepts, hunches etc are set up rather like Aunt Sallys, capable of being knocked down. This is rather like the view of science held by Popper (1959, 1963) — hypotheses are generated which are capable of being tested and hence refuted. At this stage the experienced problem-solver seems to be 'narrowing the field'; it is a 'conservative' activity which seems to involve up to three or four informed guesses which are quickly 'checked-out'. The mathematical statements which emerge from this activity are not only the most appropriate but also the most economical way of arriving at the solution.

The whole process is shown in Figure 1.

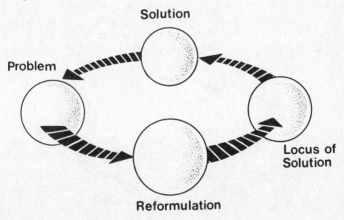

Solution

Problem

Locus of Solution

Reformulation

Figure 1. *The Problem-Solving Process*

Naturally this is a gross oversimplification of a highly complex act, which makes stages occurring almost instantaneously appear to be consecutive and linear: indeed, the arrows only suggest an overall direction — a considerable interaction between the stages must take place. Moreover it is only highly tentative at this stage.

There is some evidence both theoretical and empirical (see, for example, G Polya [1957]) to support this view; indeed it has been suggested that, as a process, it is not unique in engineering. For example, it has been claimed to be the method used by experienced clinicians in arriving at a medical diagnosis (Barrows, 1976, Barrows and Tamblyn). What emerges from these interprofessional studies though is not just the similarity of the process but, more particularly, that generally those who operate in this way are not aware of doing so. Indeed this may yet provide a key to teaching and learning in these areas: if the professional can become aware of the principles on which he unconsciously operates it may be possible to identify and provide a structure through which students might learn (Coles, 1976, 1977).

This engineering course, then, might profit from, as it were, 'being stood on its head'. As was suggested, at present it teaches specifics out of which, it is hoped, general principles are derived by the students. Might it not be better to provide a course which encourages students to develop general principles and for the specific knowledge and skills to be acquired almost incidentally? Certainly Bruner believed this to be possible when he wrote:

'. . . the curriculum of a subject should be determined by the most fundamental understanding that can be achieved of the underlying principles that give structure to that subject' (Bruner, 1960).

Perhaps educational researchers and professional practitioners need to focus more on 'understanding . . . the underlying principles'. Theoretically this seems desirable (Sockett, 1976) and in practice it might be achieved by adopting a more empirical approach: by observing the professional in action and encouraging him to articulate both his cognitive as well as his physical actions.

It might, for example, be possible to identify the principles under which one operates as a learner. One is normally given some information either in its raw state or in the form of a pre-digested learning resource. The first move of the learner is to reorganize the information within some form of 'structure' in order to make more sense of it. Such a structure not only facilitates remembering but, to some extent, reduces the complexity of the learning task. The particular structure generated will be determined by the purpose of the learning as the learner perceives it. The learner

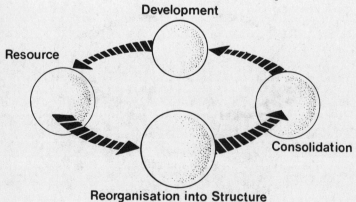

Figure 2. *The Learning Process*

292

then makes use of the structure, applying it to a known or novel situation to see how it relates. For example, information from a new text-book may be structured within one's existing knowledge or it may require a restructuring of it. This leads to a consolidation of that learning and as a result, one is said to have learned something. More particularly, the learner has 'developed' as a result of the structuring/ restructuring process, for out of this process he will have developed a greater capacity for the process itself: he will have generated principles for learning.

Of course this is an idealized picture of an efficient learner (Figure 2): it describes what we might call 'self-directed learning'. But it is a far cry from the concept of 'being taught'.

This apparent diversion into discussing the process of learning was intentional since it suggests a number of similarities between the processes of 'self-directed learning' and 'problem solution'. The first lies in the nature of the stages.

The 'learning resource' relates to the 'problem to be solved' and the 'structuring of the information' to 'reformulating the problem'. 'Consolidating learning' is similar to 'identifying the locus of the solution' and the 'learned outcome' similar to the 'problem solution'.

The second similarity between the processes is that out of each are generated generalized principles aiding, on the one hand, problem-solving and on the other learning (Figure 3).

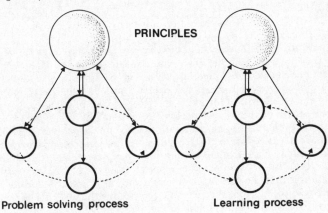

Figure 3. *The Principles of Problem-Solving and Learning*

These, as it were, 'meta-processes' are highly dynamic and fundamentally two-way: the principles help to guide the processes and the processes help to re-formulate the principles. This is not unlike what Ausubel (1968) called 'assimilation' and Piaget 'schema formation' (see Flavel, 1963). The empirical studies reported suggest that understanding this dynamic generation of generalized principles is of crucial importance in efficient professional practice.

The third area is highly speculative: there is more than a mere similarity between these principles of meta-processes — they might be identical (Figure 4).

There is some evidence to suggest that increased awareness of the principles embodied within, say, the professionalism of engineering, transfers to an awareness of the principles of, say, education. Those people called extended professionals by Hoyle (1975) may, indeed, be operating within both professions by applying the same principles. As Bruner (1961) suggests:

'... the more one has to practice, the more likely is one to generalize what one has learnt into a style of problem solving or inquiry that serves for any kind of task one may encounter — or almost any kind of task!'

PRINCIPLES

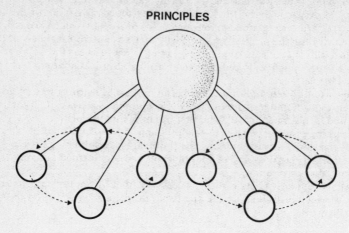

Figure 4. *Generalized Principles of Professionalism*

Finally to return to the course! It has been suggested that it might be reorganized around the principles it embodies. This would mean not hoping they will be derived from specific knowledge but providing a situation in which they would develop. It would seem that the problem-based approach adopted by the course is appropriate and that the guided-self-study format is an effective way of bringing this about. However, the nature of the subject needs to be re-thought as moving from the general to the specific rather than from the specific to the general. In addition, one cautionary note needs to be sounded. Students employing this approach to learning need to establish and clarify the principles that they have acquired. Schmidt (1965) has suggested that this does not always happen automatically in discovery learning. The implication is that the back-up to such an approach is crucial, although it is a rather different tutorial support to the one reported earlier. Rather than showing students how to solve problems, it would involve establishing the principles on which students are arriving at solutions. It is hoped that this role would require substantially less time commitment by staff since much of their former work would become part of the students' routine learning. Moreover it is an activity that might be undertaken by students in pairs or small groups.

It is not new to suggest that the curriculum should be based on fundamental principles embodied within the structure of the subject, nor that there are generalized principles for the solution of problems that could be applied in a number of contexts. However, such a process of curriculum redevelopment does require a clear analysis of the principles involved. It is suggested here that not only is this a task that should be undertaken by curriculum developers but that it only emerges through the inquiry-based approach outlined.

References

Ausubel, D P (1968) 'Educational Psychology: A Cognitive View' New York Holt, Rinehart & Winston.

Barrows, H S (1976) 'Problem-Based Learning in Medicine' in Clarke, J and Leedham, J (eds) 'Aspects of Educational Technology X: Individualized Instruction' London Kogan Page.

Barrows, H S and Tamblyn, R M 'Monograph 1 Guide to the Development of Skills in Problem-Based Learning and Clinical (Diagnostic) Reasoning' McMaster, Ontario. Project for Learning Resources Design, McMaster University, Faculty of Medicine (unpublished).

Bruner, J S (1960) 'The Process of Education' Cambridge, Mass Harvard University Press.

Bruner, J S (1961) 'The Act of Discovery' Harvard Educational Review 31, 1.

Coles, C R (1976) 'Training Lecturers' Correspondence: Times Higher Educational Supplement. 257, 24.9.76.

Coles, C R (1977) 'Acquiring the Principles of Professionalism: a Study of Clinical Competence in a Medical Undergraduate Curriculum' University of Sussex, MA thesis (part) unpublished.

Flavel, J H (1963) 'The Development Psychology of Jean Piaget' London Van Nostrand Reinhold.

Hamilton, D (1976) 'Curriculum Evaluation' London Open Books.

Hoyle, E (1975) 'The Creativity of the School in Britain' in Harris, A, Lawn, M, and Prescott, W (eds) 'Curriculum Innovation' London Croom Helm.

Keller, F S (1968) 'Goodbye, Teacher . . . ' 'Journal of Applied Behaviour Analysis' 1968, 1.

Polya, G (1957) 'How to Solve it' 2nd ed New York, Doubleday Anchor Books.

Popper, K R (1959) 'The Logic of Scientific Discovery' New York Hutchinson.

Popper, K R (1963) 'Conjectives and Refutations: The Growth of Scientific Knowledge' London Routledge, Kegan Paul.

Schmidt, W (1965) 'Processes of Learning in Relation to Different Kinds of Materials to be Learnt' Medical Education in South Africa, Natal University Press of Pietermaritzburg, South Africa.

Sockett, H (1976) 'Designing the Curriculum' London, Open Books.

Stenhouse, L (1975) 'An Introduction to Curriculum Research and Development' London, Heinemann.

Evaluation of Chemical Card Games as Learning Aids

K Vaughan

Introduction

Games based on scientific principles have become a familiar element in the variety of technological aids available to teachers. A recent addition to the range of published chemical games is the activation energy game (Yohe, 1976) which employs dominoes to illustrate the principle of activation energy. A recent innovation in chemical card games is the 'Chemantics' game (Sawyer, 1976), the object of which is to make up correct formulas for compounds using only symbol cards and number cards. A more elaborate game, along similar lines, called ELEMENT CARDS, was devised by Lipson (1972) and later published by Heyden, who also market the organic synthesis game CHEMSYN, devised originally by Eglington and Maxwell (1971). ELEMENT CARDS and CHEMSYN have been discussed, along with several other games, by Megarry (1975) as variations on the theme of Rummy.

This paper describes a study undertaken to evaluate the card games CHEMSYN and ELEMENT CARDS in order to assess their potential as learning aids. Evaluation involved testing students, both before and after their experience with the card games, to determine their ability to carry out the operations used in the games and to test their knowledge of the information provided on the cards. It should be emphasized that one is attempting to evaluate the card games themselves, not using the card games in order to evaluate the student's ability. Furthermore, the test and card game sessions were carried out outside regular class hours and were not an integral part of a course.

CHEMSYN

CHEMSYN was developed in the UK for the benefit of pre-university students of organic chemistry and first-year university students of medicine and engineering. In the experiments at Saint Mary's University, CHEMSYN has been used in tutorial sessions with mixed groups of students taking introductory and intermediate-level organic chemistry. CHEMSYN grew from the idea of using home-made, two-sided 'flash' cards to learn the names and classes of organic compounds, and has evolved into a sophisticated, but simple, method of learning the rudiments of organic synthesis. The game is played with 50 cards, each card representing an organic compound, and the cards are laid down, picture side up, in such a way that adjacent cards must represent interconvertible compounds.

Students playing CHEMSYN for the first time had difficulty in fitting compounds into a sequence for synthesis, particularly in connecting aliphatic and aromatic compounds; most, however, were stimulated to learn from the game and began to enjoy the exercise after several 'hands'. Although only 50 compounds are represented in a CHEMSYN pack, each new game produces a different synthetic sequence, presenting a challenge to even the most accomplished students. After a few hours playing group CHEMSYN with a tutor, students can confidently take on SOLO CHEMSYN in their own time, an advantage of CHEMSYN not entirely shared by ELEMENT CARDS.

ELEMENT CARDS

The ELEMENT CARDS game is more adaptable to a variety of games, which include rummy, cribbage and solitaire. The games are designed to teach familiarity with element names and symbols, oxidation states, trends in valence, physical properties of elements, isotopes, electron configurations and chemical combinations. The ELEMENT CARDS game is suitable for tutorial use with students taking first-year university general chemistry at Saint Mary's University (equivalent to A level in the UK). In ELEMENT RUMMY elements are grouped into (a) same valence sets, eg H, Li, K or (b) valence-run sets, eg Cu, Cr, Pt or (c) premium sets (valence-run sets with atomic numbers also in sequence) eg Ne, Na, Mg. A serious disadvantage of this game is the tendency for students to associate cards solely by the numbers displayed on the cards, ignoring the names and symbols. Consequently the game may not help students to associate elements into valence groups (families) when given only the names and/or symbols of the elements.

ELEMENT SOLITAIRE is played as the common form of solitaire (Klondike), with the noble gases assuming the role of Kings and Aces being replaced by a set of base elements (H, Li, Na, K, Cu, Ru and Ag). This game is particularly useful for making students aware of the variations in the outer-shell electrons of elements, and thus facilitates the association of elements into families. Another excellent feature of this game is the frequency with which elements with two outer-shell electrons turn up and become largely redundant, illustrating the relative abundance of transition elements, most of which have two electrons in the outer shell.

Another game which may be played solo, or in groups, is ELEMENT CONCENTRATION, the object of which is to match pairs of elements that have some property in common. A useful extension of this game is COMPOUND CONCENTRATION, in which pairs of elements that can form binary compounds, are selected, thus introducing the players to chemical combination.

Evaluation: Tests and Results

As an integral part of this project, tests were devised that would reveal the students' knowledge of card game material and operations. The CHEMSYN tests contained questions on preparation methods, class reactions, nomenclature, physical properties, molecular geometry, one-step conversions, named reactions and synthesis. The first CHEMSYN test revealed particular weakness in nomenclature, named reactions and synthesis; significantly, the students from the more advanced organic course (Group B) performed only marginally better than those from the introductory course (Group A). See Table 1.

After several card sessions, during which the total playing time per student varied from two to 10 hours, the surviving students (Group C) were retested. In the second test, the synthesis question was modified to the form of an actual CHEMSYN game, with several formulae omitted, the object being to fill in the gaps; in other respects, the second test was of the same model as the first, but with different examples chosen.

Although the number of students retested was small, all but one showed a

	Average mark on 1st test (%)			Average mark on retest (%)
Question	Group A(24)	Group B(8)	Group C(5)	Group C(5)
1. Preparation	52	51	60	60
2. Reactions	30	40	44	58
3. Nomenclature	24	17	44	80
4. Phys. props.	44	48	50	76
5. Stereochem.	40	63	60	90
6. Conversions	57	58	50	56
7. Named Rns.	23	43	32	18
8. Solubility	52	42	50	60
9. Synthesis	27	23	23	30
Total (Avge)	39%	43%	47%	54%

Note:　Group A – Students from introductory Organic course
Group B – Students from intermediate Organic course
Group C – Students (from groups A & B) who sat the 1st test and the retest
The numbers in parentheses indicate the number of students in each group.

Table 1. *CHEMSYN Test Results*

significant improvement of 10 to 12% in overall performance. With respect to individual performance on specific questions, considerable variation was noticed. Much improvement was seen with respect to the synthesis question. The latter observation, relating as it does to the main objective of CHEMSYN, is disturbing but requires further elaboration. The only question that showed a decline on the second test was that concerning named reactions, for which there is no obvious explanation.

The ELEMENT CARDS tests covered the topics: element names and symbols, principle valence, binary compounds, physical properties of elements and isotopes.

	Average mark on 1st test (%)		Average mark on retest (%)
Question	Group D(15)	Group E(4)	Group E(4)
1. Element names	55	37	59
2. Principle valence	43	37	87
3. Symbols	93	100	45
4. Binary compounds	40	35	27
5. Element properties	38	31	53
6. Isotopes	24	21	45
Total (Avge)	46%	38%	54%

Note:　Group D – Students from 1st year General Chemistry
Group E – Students in group D who sat the 1st test and the retest.

Table 2. *ELEMENT CARDS Test Results*

Although the questions on names and symbols were well done, the first test revealed weakness in knowledge of physical properties, valence and binary combination, and almost total ignorance of the concept of isotopes (see Table 2, Group D). The number of students that persevered, through approximately six hours of card games, to the second test was again small, but the results of the retest (Table 2, Group E) show a significant overall improvement when compared to the results obtained by the same students in the first test. Satisfactory improvement was seen in specific questions on the weaker topics, such as isotopes and physical properties. The drastic drop in the marks obtained in the question on symbols can only be attributed to a particularly easy choice of symbols on the first test.

Conclusions

The card games used in this study certainly succeed in arousing interest in specific aspects of chemistry, once the student is sufficiently motivated to participate in the games. However, the objective of the exercise can easily decline into playing the game for its own sake, rather than for learning the chemical principles underlying the game. The results of the tests and retests do show that the games improved knowledge of those specific chemical principles, but further evaluations are necessary to enlarge the size of the group tested and to establish the statistical significance of these observations. A slight modification in future evaluations might be to retest a control group of students who have not played the game, to establish if performance is increased simply by familiarity with the test model.

The tests themselves seem to be particularly useful for identifying the specific aspects of chemistry that are strengthened by playing the games, eg, CHEMSYN appeared to improve knowledge of nomenclature and physical properties, rather than adeptness at synthesis, for which it was devised. Some students were evidently unaware of certain aspects of chemistry until confronted with a question on a test, but were consequently acutely aware of these aspects while playing the games. This was certainly true of the question on isotopes in the ELEMENT test, and the improvement on this question in the retest is possibly a reflection of this increased awareness.

Postscript

During the course of play with ELEMENT CARDS, a new game, not previously described, was devised, which we have christened PERIODIC ELEMENT CARDS. The game requires a large-scale periodic table plan (or grid), with a space for each element card, but with all symbols, numbers, etc, omitted as in Figure 1.

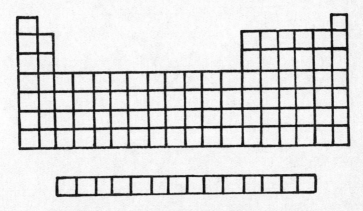

Figure 1. *Grid for PERIODIC ELEMENT CARDS*
(actual size approx 3' x 4')

The object of the game is to place each element, given only the name, in its correct place on the periodic table grid. The element cards are divided equally between the players, being kept face down. The first player looks at the first card in his hand and reads the name of the element to the next player, who must then indicate the position of this element in the periodic table (without seeing the face of the card). If he succeeds, the card is placed on the grid and he continues the game by offering the element on his top card to the third player. On the other hand, if the second player fails to put the element in the right place, he must accept the element card in question, place it at the bottom of his hand, and then offer his top card to the third player . . . A player who never finds the correct position for an element will always have the same number of cards in his hand, whereas the player who is always right will soon have no cards left and win the game. Although simple in conception and operation, this game proved to be a very effective way of learning the periodic table and also assisted tremendously with association of elements into families.

Acknowledgement

I would like to express my sincere thanks to all the students at Saint Mary's University who participated in this projcct. I am also grateful to Heyden and Son Ltd for permission to reproduce the Figures in this paper.

References

Eglington, G and Maxwell, J R (1971) 'Chemsyn — Chemical Card Game 1' 'Education in Chemistry' 88 p 142–144.

Lipson, J I (1972) 'Element Cards' Heyden and Son Ltd, Illinois

Megarry, J (1975) 'A Review of Science Games — Variations on a Theme of Rummy' 'Simulation and Games' p 423–437.

Sawyer, A K (1976) 'Chemantics — A New Chemical Educational Card Game' 'Journal of Chemical Education' 53 p 780.

Yohe, G R (1976) 'Dominoes — and Activation Energy' Chemistry 49 p 8–9.

Course-Work Assessment: Computer-Aided Decision Making

J Hartley, A Branthwaite

The argument in this paper is that computers can be programmed to aid decision-making in choosing between different patterns of assessment. Two investigations are reported.

Study 1

In the first investigation the effects of including course-work assessment in determining the end-of-year grades for a subsidiary psychology course were examined by comparing the end-of-year results obtained without course-work assessment (in 1973—74) with those obtained with course-work assessment (in 1974—75 and 1975—76). The course-work assessment score was derived from the marks obtained for three essays written during the year — one per term. The results are shown in Table 1.

Year		Essay	Paper I	Paper II	Overall
1973—4	$\bar{x}$	—	51.5	53.4	52.7
(N=75)	s.d.	—	8.5	8.5	7.7
1974—5	$\bar{x}$	62.2	50.3	52.4	55.0
(N=85)	s.d.	6.3	8.1	7.2	5.6
1975—6	$\bar{x}$	60.5	50.0	55.4	55.4
(N=85)	s.d.	7.6	9.7	6.4	7.8

Table 1. *The exam scores, essay scores and overall grades (expressed as percentages) for 1973—4, 1974—5 and 1975—6*

In these courses the essay assessment was given a weighting of one-third of the overall mark. Computer simulations were then run with these data in order to assess the effects of other different weightings. These simulations provided *post hoc* evidence to support the initial arbitrary decision of a weight of 33% (see Table 2).

Study 2

In the second investigation the effects of introducing various patterns of course-work assessment into a student's final degree classification were assessed — again by means of computer simulation. The initial base-line data are shown in Table 3.

With these basic data before us, we then used the computer to answer a number of questions about the effects of including various patterns of course-work assessment on the final degree results. These questions, and the answers, are given below. In each case the 1976 data are given in the left-hand column for comparison purposes.

Essay Weighting	Average Overall grade with that Weighting		Number of Failures		Significance of the difference between tutorial groups in the overall grades (F values)	
	1974—5	1975—6	1974—5	1975—6	1974—5	1975—6
%	%	%				
10	52.4	53.6	10	10	1.60	0.21
20	53.5	54.4	7	8	1.85	0.18
30	54.6	55.1	5	5	2.13	0.20
40	55.7	55.9	3	4	2.45*	0.27
50	56.8	56.7	1	3	2.77*	0.40
60	57.8	57.4	1	3	3.06*	0.56
70	58.9	58.2	1	3	3.30*	0.76
80	60.0	58.9	1	2	3.46*	0.96
90	61.1	59.7	1	3	3.54*	1.14
100	62.2	60.5	1	3	3.55*	1.31

* statistically significant at 5%

Table 2. *The effects of different weighting for the essay contribution to the overall results 1974—5 and 1975—6*

Exam Papers	Mean	Standard Deviation
Paper 1 (Essay)	64.3	4.73
Paper 2 (P2 work*)	60.5	6.18
Paper 3 (General)	61.7	7.14
Paper 4 (Option)	59.9	7.40
Paper 5 (Project)	63.3	8.45

The distribution of students in terms of the degree classes awarded in 1976 (based on the examination papers only) was as follows:

	Frequency
First	0
2:i	20
2:ii	35
3rd	5
Pass	0

P2 Written work*	Mean	Standard Deviation
Best Essay/Project	72.4	5.00
Best 2 Essays/Projects	70.4	5.93
Best 3 Essays/Projects	68.0	9.66
Best 4 Essays/Projects	65.8	11.93
Best 5 Essays/Projects	63.2	14.55
All 6 Essays/Projects	58.7	20.06
P2 End of Year Assessment	63.3	8.13

P2 = Principal Year Two. (At Keele there is a four-year course — a Foundation Year, followed by three principal years, P1, P2 and P3. Each student is examined in two principal subjects.)

Table 3. *The initial baseline data*

Question 1 What would happen to the distribution of grades if we simply dropped one paper?

	1976	−Paper 1	−Paper 2	−Paper 3	−Paper 4	−Paper 5
First	0	0	0	0	0	0
2:i	20	20	22	22	23	17
2:ii	35	33	33	32	32	39
3rd	5	7	5	6	5	4
Pass	0	0	0	0	0	0

Conclusion: Dropping papers 2, 3 or 4 would lead to slightly higher grades. Dropping papers 1 or 5 would lead to slightly lower grades.

Question 2 What would happen to the distribution of grades if we simply added in last year's P2 end-of-year assessment with the weight of one paper?

	1976	+P2 end of year assessment
First	0	0
2:i	20	22
2:ii	35	33
3rd	5	5
Pass	0	0

Conclusion: Adding in the P2 end-of-year assessment slightly increases the number of 2:i degrees. This has the same result as dropping Paper 2 which is mainly concerned with P2 work.

Question 3 What would happen to the distribution of grades if we counted in a certain number of best pieces of written work with the weight of one paper?

	1976	+1	+2	+3	+4	+5	+6 best pieces
First	0	0	0	0	0	0	0
2:i	20	24	23	22	22	22	20
2:ii	35	33	33	34	34	32	32
3rd	5	3	4	4	4	6	8
Pass	0	0	0	0	0	0	0

Conclusion: Adding in the single best piece of work would lead to the highest grades: adding in written work would improve final results, up to the fifth piece. Adding in three (as originally envisaged) leads to almost the same effect as adding in the P2 end-of-year assessment — but it might be seen as preferable by students.

Question 4 What would happen if we deleted one paper and added in P2 end-of-year assessment with weight of one paper?

	1976	−Paper 1 +ass.	−Paper 2 +ass.	−Paper 3 +ass.	−Paper 4 +ass.	−Paper 5 +ass.
First	0	0	0	0	0	0
2:i	20	20	23	23	21	19
2:ii	35	32	33	30	34	35
3rd	5	8	4	7	5	6
Pass	0	0	0	0	0	0

Conclusion: Omitting Paper 2 (or 3) and adding in P2 overall assessment leads to the highest grades. There is a certain logic to replacing Paper 2 by the P2 assessment.

Question 5 What would happen if (a) we deleted one paper, and (b) counted in a certain number of best pieces of written work with the weight of one paper?

Minus Paper 1

	1976	+1	+2	+3	+4	+5	+6 pieces
First	0	0	0	0	0	0	0
2:i	20	24	22	22	22	22	18
2:ii	35	32	33	33	32	29	32
3rd	5	4	5	5	5	8	9
Pass	0	0	0	0	1	1	1

Minus Paper 2

	1976	+1	+2	+3	+4	+5	+6 pieces
First	0	0	0	0	0	0	0
2:i	20	29	27	24	21	21	20
2:ii	35	28	30	32	35	34	33
3rd	5	3	3	4	4	5	7
Pass	0	0	0	0	0	0	0

Minus Paper 3

	1976	+1	+2	+3	+4	+5	+6 pieces
First	0	0	0	0	0	0	0
2:i	20	26	26	25	23	23	21
2:ii	35	32	32	32	32	29	30
3rd	5	2	2	3	5	8	9
Pass	0	0	0	0	0	0	0

Minus Paper 4

	1976	1	+2	+3	+4	+5	+6 pieces
First	0	0	0	0	0	0	0
2:i	20	28	26	25	24	23	18
2:ii	35	29	31	32	31	32	36
3rd	5	3	3	3	5	5	6
Pass	0	0	0	0	0	0	0

Minus Paper 5

	1976	+1	+2	+3	+4	+5	+6 pieces
First	0	0	0	0	0	0	0
2:i	20	26	23	21	21	20	17
2:ii	35	31	34	36	35	33	36
3rd	5	3	3	3	4	6	5
Pass	0	0	0	0	0	1	1

Conclusion: Omitting Paper 2 and adding in one or two best pieces of written work leads to the highest grades. With three pieces it makes little difference whether one drops Paper 2, 3 or 4. Omitting Paper 2 and incorporating five pieces almost maintains the status quo.

Question 6 What would happen if we gave degree results based on course work only?

	1976		P3 project + P2 end of year assessment	P3 project + P2 course work					
				+1	+2	+3	+4	+5	+6 pieces
First	0	1		9	6	4	, 3	3	1
2:i	20	30		36	35	32	29	28	24
2:ii	35	21		14	16	19	21	22	22
3rd	5	8		1	3	5	6	5	9
Pass	0	0		0	0	0	1	2	4

Question 7 What would happen if we gave degree results based on P2 end-of-year assessment (with right of challenge and no-one challenged!)

1976 P2 end-of-year result reclassified as a degree result

First	0	1
2:i	20	30
2:ii	35	21
3rd	5	6
Pass	0	2

Questions 6 and 7 were really non-starters because of current institutional requirements. We may note here, however, that using course-work assessment alone to produce the final grades would lead to higher grades being awarded to many of our students. It was, in fact, the only procedure that produced firsts!

Students and staff completed the following questionnaire:

Suppose in 1976 the average overall mark for the five papers (ie four written papers and one P3 project) was 60%. What do you predict the mark would be if we:	Student Estimate (N=78)	Staff Estimate (N=9)	Simulated Data
1. Added in, as an extra paper, the student's P2 end-of-year assessment.	61.4	60.6	60.2
2. Added in, as an extra paper, each student's one best piece of P2 written work.	65.7***	62.5	61.7
3. Added in, as an extra paper, each student's three best pieces of P2 written work.	64.2**	62.2*	60.9
4. Replaced Paper 2 (which examines P2 work) by the P2 end-of-year assessment.	62.7**	60.9	60.5
5. Replaced Paper 2 (which examines P2 work) by the three best pieces of written work done in P2 with the weight of one paper	65.4***	61.8	61.4
Difference between estimates and simulated data significant at:		* $p < .05$ ** $p < .01$ *** $p < .001$	

Table 4. *The questionnaire results*

These results indicate that many of the changes possible lead to little real change in the pattern of results, although some results were unexpected (ie in some cases

Students were asked to indicate which of the options numbered 1—5 in the questionnaire they preferred, and to say why.

% Choosing

Option No.	P2 Students	Final Year Students	Typical reasons for choice:
1	18	2	— Fairest method: most representative of the students' work.
2	18	20	— The highest overall mark is obtainable by this method — Not all work is good, so the best piece shows what a student can do.
3	0	7	— The less exams the better. — Gives a more balanced view — disasters can be rectified.
4	26	18	— A fairer way of assessing P2 work. — Has the greatest amount of course-work assessment and the smallest number of exam papers.
5	29	48	— Takes the pressure off P3. — Would encourage greater effort and concentration. — A fairer appraisal of P2 work. — One less exam paper.
No clear preference	9	5	

Table 5. *Student preferences*

students do worse with course-work assessment included). Only drastic changes — such as totally replacing examinations with course-work assessment — seem likely to alter radically the distribution of grades.

Such computer simulations provide data which can aid subsequent decision-making. We have further data to show that without such simulations there may be a tendency to over-estimate the impact that inclusion of course-work assessment will make to the final grades (see Tables 4 and 5). Such an over-estimation may produce an overly cautious approach to innovation.

Reference

Hartley, J and Branthwaite, J A (1976) 'All This for Two Percent: the Contribution of Course-Work Assessment to the Final Grade' 'Durham Research Review' Vol VIII, No 37, pp 14—20.

Footnote

This paper presents a considerably shortened version of the paper presented at the Conference. A full treatment of the issues involved can be found in the original paper, copies of which are available from the authors on request.

An Evaluation of the Use of Self-Instructional Materials in the Library

N D C Harris, S Kirkhope

Introduction

Evaluation is a measure of the 'worth' of something (Popham 1975). At the University of Bath there has been a rapid escalation in the use of independent learning materials beyond books and journals. The figures for material in the library show two particular areas of expansion:

	Number in Use		
	1975	1976	1977
video-cartridges	13	147	250
study packs	210	720	899

In addition there are nearly 1000 microfiche resources (excluding the library catalogue), 20 synchronised tape-slide sequences and six audio-cassettes with printed materials.

In spite of the large increase little information was available in terms of uses, learning efficiency and cost effectiveness. This is a report on the start which has been made in evaluating these materials.

Little work appears to have been carried out on the evaluation of non-book media as independent learning materials in libraries. Much of the evaluation work in non-book resources has been based at the Open University (for example Bates, 1973, McIntosh, 1974). The development of illuminative evaluation techniques (Parlett and Hamilton 1972) has brought in the necessity of looking at rationale, evaluation, operations, achievements and difficulties. This approach has much in common with the model proposed by Eraut (1972) and emphasizes that evaluation is idiosyncratic to a particular course or innovation. The generalizations may be realized for techniques and methodology, but the conclusions may not be generalizable.

The Library Situation

The self-instructional materials are in a variety of formats, as already outlined. Within one format considerable variations also occur. For example the study packs vary from a collection of off-prints to sets of small circulation materials or government papers. Students are required to read the contents of a study pack in preparation for a written assignment or for a seminar.

The study packs are part of a short-term loan collection available at the library issue desk. The library assistants find the packs from shelves labelled by the name of the lecturer. Some lecturers have as many as 50 packs each with a separate title making the extraction of the manilla files or wallets quite tedious. The short-loan collection permits students to have the materials for four hours during the morning,

307

four hours during the afternoon or overnight.

The video-cartridges are on open access on a self-help basis with the video-cartridge machines and associated receivers nearby. A similar room is available for synchronized tape-slide sequences.

The Aims of the Investigation

Within the constraints of finance, which only allowed part-time assistance to collect and collate data, the investigation intended to answer some of the following questions:

Who uses the materials and when?
How are the materials used and where?
How do the materials relate to the student's course and assessment?
What is the main purpose of the materials?
What is the cost of assembling and administering the materials?
How much cognitive learning takes place when using or having used the materials?

It should be clear that with a part-time research assistant it was necessary to reduce the scope. The last question has been made the basis of a separate investigation.

The Methods

The methods being used are:

Observation
Questionnaires
Interviews with students (i) individually
                        (ii) in groups
Costing

Observation includes checking study packs for content and for number of uses. The packs are date stamped (this includes information on the time of loan: morning, afternoon or overnight). In addition the time to assemble a study pack and to issue a study pack can be collected to provide a basis for costing. The students using video-cartridges can be watched from a distance to identify whether the recording is stopped and/or rewound before reaching the end (ie do students use a video-recorder's facilities to assist their learning or do they just sit and watch television?).

The interviews are of two types:

(a) with students in the library immediately before or after using a study pack, video-cartridge or other materials;
(b) with groups of students who have used specific materials.

The costing exercise will attempt to find how much materials cost when put together, in using and in maintenance. The methods used will be developed from previous published works (Layard, 1973, Haller, 1974, Laidlaw and Layard, 1974).

The Pilot Study

This paper is based on data collected during the pilot study in autumn 1976. Most information has been collected using observation, interviews with individual students and questionnaires. Some initial work has also been carried out on costing.

Basis of Responses

Up to 10th December 1976 124 questionnaires had been received and 57 interviews conducted. These sampled 18/70 lecturers' materials in study-pack form, 11/26 in video-cartridge form, 3/15 in tape-slide form and one microfiche.

Observation

The data collected by observation were primarily in relation to the times of use of the study-packs. The date stamps were still in many packs from 1975/6 which gave an expected use. The actual use for the autumn term 1976 is shown in Figure 1. The distribution in this term is remarkably similar to that for the autumn term in the previous year.

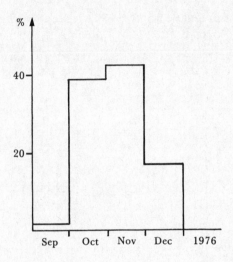

Figure 1. *Number of Uses of Study Packs during Autumn Term 1976*

Obviously the use varies from pack to pack, but from an issue point of view the global information is the important one. The distribution from school to school is consistent. The number of packs for the schools in the university is shown in Table 1. The distribution of uses during the day is shown in Figure 2.

When compared with last year there has been an increase in the morning use of study packs, mainly associated with a group of mature students studying on a taught master's course. The overnight use obviously has the advantage of an extended time period. The distribution is consistent over most schools.

Readings have been collected on the time taken to issue a study pack, and the time taken to put a study pack together. Where lecturers have used their own material, copying and collating times have also been samples. There is insufficient data available at present to draw any conclusions, except to note that a study pack has a cumulative cost because each issue and return has a labour implication. The video-cartridges only have labour implications when the equipment has a fault, although the initial cost of the resource is obviously much higher.

The video-cartridge use has been derived from both observation and interview.

School	Number of study packs	
	1975/6	1976/7
Humanities and Social Sciences	448	494
Management	145	273
Education	33	30
Pharmacy and Pharmacology	32	30
Biological Sciences	22	21
Modern Languages	14	15
Materials Science	10	12
Mathematics	8	8
Electrical Engineering	–	6
Physics	3	3
Engineering	3	3
Chemistry	2	2
Chemical Engineering	1	1
Centre for European Industrial Studies	–	1
TOTAL	721	899

Table 1. *Distribution of Study Packs between the Schools in the University*

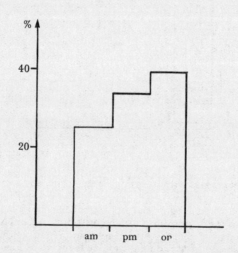

Figure 2. *Distribution of Uses during the Day Autumn Term 1976*

The viewing is often carried out by groups of students who discuss the contents both during the programme (often whilst it is still playing) and afterwards. No other information was collected by observation which differed from that collected by interview.

No system has been installed to keep a full check on the use of video-cartridges. It has been clear that there are parts of the term when little use occurs and other parts when a slight queueing has occurred for the two machines available. The maximum possible uses would be 240 each week; our estimate is a maximum of 50 uses a week, based on limited sampling.

Questionnaires

The questionnaires used four basic categories: student data; material data; scales for interest, difficulty, clarity, each with associated comments; and open questions.

Questionnaires were placed in every study pack, at the issue desk in the library and in the rooms where the audio-visual materials were available. The study-pack response rate was very poor (3.1%) but more questionnaires were returned for video-cartridges than study packs, suggesting a much better response rate.

Based on the limited response students' answers to questions were as follows:

Did you find this material interesting?
1. Very interesting.   2. Fairly interesting.   3. Not very interesting.   4. Not interesting at all.   5. Don't know.
n = number of students

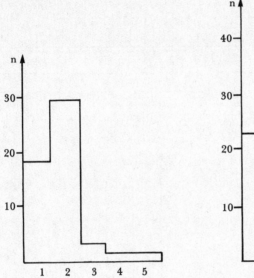

Figure 3. *Study Packs*

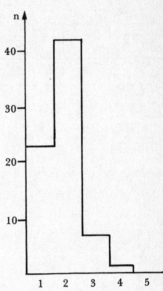

Figure 4. *Video-cartridges*

When asked if any parts of the material were boring, comments ranged from 'none' to most of it.

How difficult did you find this material?
1. Very difficult.   2. Difficult.   3. Just right.   4. Easy.   5. Very easy.
6. Don't know.

How clearly do you think this material put its main points over?
1. Very clearly.   2. Fairly clearly.   3. Not very clearly.   4. Not clearly at all.   5. Don't know.

Another question asked: *What do you think were the main points of this material?*

In some cases the lecturer's and students' answers were almost identical, for example the video-cartridge series on Fortran had a unanimous response, 'It is our course'. Sometimes the discrepancy was wider.

From the question: *How does this material relate to your course?* came such

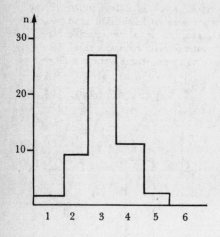

Figure 5. *Study Packs*

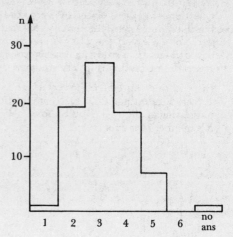

Figure 6. *Video-cartridges*

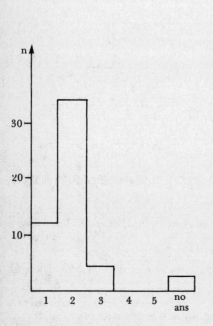

Figure 7. *Study Pack*

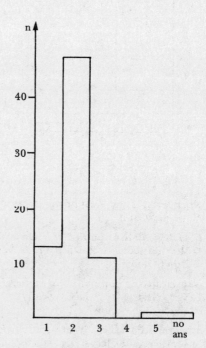

Figure 8. *Video-cartridges*

responses as:

Study Packs	Video-cartridges
Part of an assignment	Told in lectures
Preparation for seminar	Revision
Background reading	Audio-visual clarification

Interviews

A similar pattern was used in relation to student and material data, but students were first asked, 'What is your reaction to this study pack/video-cartridge?' Some resulting answers to this and subsequent questions are given below.

General Reactions

Answers included: 'very good, very useful'; 'from a convenience point of view, very useful'; 'a great saving of time as documents are collected together' (study pack).

Source of Information

Where students identified the source of their knowledge of the presence of the material in the library these were:

from the lecturer	31 (22 study packs, 9 video-cartridges)
from other students	3 (3 video-cartridges)
from library staff	3 (2 study packs, 1 video-cartridge)

In addition some students found material by browsing (video-cartridges): 'Tape (video) viewed for personal interest — a lot was learned' (OU video-recording); 'material was personal interest rather than course-orientated' (OU video-recording).

Use of Study Packs in Relation to Course

Where responses were given, 36 students were required to read study packs in preparation for seminars (five schools, 13 lecturers covered) and 10 students had to prepare an assignment or an essay based on the study pack (two schools, four lecturers).

The type of comments from students on seminars were: 'presenting a seminar on Monday'; 'specific reading for a group discussion'; 'discussion for next lecture'; 'have to make notes followed by discussion groups'; 'must read before seminar next week'.

Student comments on assignments and essays: 'will read and make notes for an essay'; 'will use for assignment and write essay'; 'usually associated with assignment'; 'particular interest for an essay I am doing'; 'material directly related to two essay titles and seminar'.

Handouts were sometimes used in association with study packs: 'handout very useful, what was good was (a) the summary and (b) the references'; 'the handout wasn't an information handout, but suggested various ideas in the article that should be thought about'.

Use of Video-Cartridges in Relation to Course

The commonest responses were 'part of course'; 'as pre-lecture material'; 'aid to understanding theory'; 'clarification of lecture'. In most cases it did not appear that the material was as well integrated into the course as the study packs. However,

313

some lecturers used other materials such as handouts or booklets in association with the video-cartridges: 'it helps very much to clarify the film'; 'notes very useful'.

It is also clear that some lecturers do not know or do not wish students to know about recordings available: 'used last year — found when doing work for another lecturer; not told by lecturer'.

How Used

1. Study Packs

Very few students have any evidence of being at all systematic or selective in reading and using the material: 'selected papers for week-end — seven appropriate — take notes'; 'one section useful, made notes'.

Most students gave no information on selection save comments such as 'take notes, if several papers just flog through, no selection'; 'if too long to read either photocopy or borrow again'; 'thought it necessary to read it all thoroughly'.

Students varied on their methods from 'read and made notes' (10 responses) to 'just read, did not take notes' (two responses). Several students incorporated comments on preferring to use overnight or at weekends: 'prefer to read it leisurely', whilst others photocopied as mentioned above.

2. Video-cartridges

Again a spectrum from 'run right through' (eight responses) without notes to 'stopped when not able to understand, rewound, replay; make some notes' (two responses).

Work Pressure

Many students commented on the problems of using study packs effectively in the four-hour loan period allowed during the day on the short-term loan: 'short loan period not long enough' (11 students). In some cases this was reversed to: 'the pack was too long to cope with in four hours'. One student was obviously well acquainted with the problems: 'came during vacation . . . extended loan period: two days, . . . four hours doesn't give time and under pressure'.

Where Used (Study Packs)

Where the response was definite:

    16 in the library
     8 at home
     4 sometimes one, sometimes the other.

Library Staff

All comments were complimentary: 'helpful', 'very helpful', 'very kind'.
    One student suggested two irritations:

(a) study packs are issued to students who have not reserved them when others have;
(b) late returns need dealing with.

A final comment by one student, a plea from the heart: 'never abolish study packs'.

Conclusion

Two reports have been sent to lecturers with material in the library giving both the general results of the evaluation and information specific to their materials when we have had any.

The pilot project has given us some insights into problems. The poor response to the questionnaires in the study packs was disappointing. A contributing factor may be that the study packs are frequently linked to assignments or seminars as discussed above, and constitute a heavy work load in a limited period of time. Students perhaps intending to fill in the form forget in the pressure of returning the pack on time. A second problem is that we have only been sampling users and not finding out why others have not used the materials.

At present we are interviewing groups of students (six to eight) from particular courses who have used materials; where possible these groups include users and non-users. Those who do not come to discuss the materials are asked to write their reactions. The lecturer is also being interviewed to provide comparative data on expectations.

The costing exercise is also presenting us with more problems than anticipated. Where do you draw the line on what is included? The economic climate has changed considerably in higher education since the proposal was put forward; this in turn has changed the base line for calculations of this kind.

Acknowledgements

We are grateful to the Nuffield Foundation for providing a small grant to support this investigation and to lecturers within the university who have given us assistance.

We would also like to thank the librarian and his staff for their co-operation.

References

Bates, A W (1973) 'An Evaluation of the Effect of Basing an Assignment on Broadcast Material in a Multi-Media Course' 'Programmed Learning and Educational Technology' 10, 348–359

Eraut, M (1972) 'Strategies for the Evaluation of Curriculum Materials' in Austwick, K and Harris, N D C (ed) 'Aspects of Educational Technology VI' London, Pitmans.

Haller, E J (1974) 'Cost Analysis for Educational Program Analysis in Popham, W J (ed) 'Evaluation in Education' Berkeley (Calif), McCutchan Publishing.

McIntosh, N (1974) 'Evaluation of Multi-Media Educational Systems — Some Problems' 'British Journal of Educational Technology' 5, 43–59.

Parlett, M and Hamilton, D (1972) 'Evaluation as Illumination: A New Approach to the Study of Innovatory Programs' Edinburgh: Centre for Research in the Educational Sciences (Occasional Paper No 9).

Scientific Discovery at the Elementary Level

E E Green, O O McKay

Many commercial publishing houses are interested in serving a wide variety of needs for all levels of education. They are concerned with mass audiences but nonetheless try to cater as much as possible for individual differences within the materials they produce. Most often a potential market is identified, materials are produced, and then it is hoped that the market will purchase the materials. The educationist, however, generally looks at the specific needs of an individual or a group of individuals and then tailors an instructional system to meet those particular needs. He then implements and refines the resulting products to make sure that the needs are met.

Both of these reasons for project initiation were included within the investigation of the scientific discovery process at the primary level recently by the David O McKay Institute of Education and Motion Picture Studio at Brigham Young University. The producers at the Motion Picture Studio were interested in covering a wide market in order to pay for the costs of distributing material on 'dinosaurs' to capitalize upon the recent finds of one of the BYU faculty members in the Dry Mesa Quarry in Colorado. They contacted the David O McKay Institute of Education requesting that a needs assessment be conducted and that instructional intents be given to a proposed set of materials being considered by the Motion Picture Studio.

This paper will describe subsequent efforts to produce the unit 'Dinosaur Dynasty' which resulted from the needs assessment. The explanation will be given within the following categories:

- ☐ Determination of the need for a unit of instruction in scientific discovery and inquiry at the primary level
- ☐ Clarification of the needs, goals, and objectives for the resulting project recommended in the Needs Statement
- ☐ Instructional design
- ☐ Prototype testing
- ☐ Revisions
- ☐ Production
- ☐ Distribution

Determination of Need

A team of developer-evaluators was organized to interview local school district personnel at the administrative, teaching and student levels to determine the need for materials in this area. A report was submitted to the producers outlining the discrepancies between the school personnel objectives and the producer objectives. We found as a result of a Q-sort that the objectives the producers had indicated high

Higher on list than producers' objectives:
- ☐ Understand characteristics and habits of dinosaurs.
- ☐ Desire to learn more about dinosaurs.
- ☐ Become excited about discovery.
- ☐ Causes of dinosaur extinction.
- ☐ Appreciate size and structure.
- ☐ Environment of the dinosaur.

PRODUCER OBJECTIVES

Higher than teachers':
- ☐ Curious about the past.
- ☐ Desire to preserve the past.
- ☐ Importance of not disturbing fossil bones.
- ☐ Theories about dinosaurs.
- ☐ Appreciate patience required in dinosaur discovery.

Figure 1

on their list were low on the list of the school personnel objectives, and those that were high on the school personnel objective lists were low on the producer's list, as indicated in Figure 1. The decision was made to cater more to the school personnel objective list than to the producer list.

Clarification of Needs and Objectives

It was generally decided as a result of the initial investigation that the following general aims were appropriate for the student:

1. To understand that scientific investigation is systematic and orderly.
2. To understand the size, structure and environment of dinosaurs.
3. To understand how scientists classify.
4. To understand how scientists make conclusions based upon observations.
5. To know how scientists make discoveries involving long preparation, planning, and hard work.
6. To understand that scientists study and search for dinosaur bones in order to study and preserve the past.

It was felt that if data could show that these aims were reached, then both the producers and the users of the materials would be satisfied.

Design

It was decided that a two to three-week unit of instruction would be more appropriate than a set of seven filmstrips which was initially suggested by the producers. Instructional designers met for several days and decided upon the following recommended components of instruction: a set of three filmstrips outlining the major activities usually involved in dinosaur exploration. These filmstrips would be an integral part of the instructional aims and would provide more than increased effect for students. They would be co-ordinated on a conceptual level with the content outline agreed upon by the subject matter experts and school personnel.

1. Filmstrip 1 is entitled *Dinosaurs, the Terrible Lizards* and contains a general overview and definition list in a story form so that children could associate

with it and be able to remember the terms as they confronted them during the unit of instruction, and hopefully afterwards continued their interest in scientific discovery and exploration. It included a dinosaur classification list with examples and questions about extinction, and covered the problems of the systematic nature of scientific investigation which include analysis, comparison, and classification. The basic student objectives for this filmstrip were as follows:

(a) Define in writing and give examples of the following items:
(i) palaeontologist, (ii) reptile, (iii) fossil, (iv) dinosaur, (v) classification, and (vi) extinction.
(b) Distinguish reptiles from mammals.
(c) List four possible reasons given by scientists why dinosaurs became extinct.
(d) Describe the probable environment in which dinosaurs lived.
(e) List six different examples of classification systems found in everyday life.

2. Filmstrip 2 is entitled *Dinosaur Detectives at Work*. Its purpose was to cover the general scientific process of inference to include inductive and deductive reasoning and hopefully to encourage curiosity and open-mindedness on the part of the student. Specifically, it discusses the similarities between the way palaeontologists and detectives work and how they arrive at particular conclusions; specific dinosaur details such as how dinosaur bones are deposited, fossilized, and uncovered; characteristics of reptile bones; and dinosaur size, weight, diet, intelligence and appearance. The objectives for Filmstrip 2 were as follows:

(a) List the steps by which a bone becomes petrified.
(b) Define in writing the term 'inference'.
(c) Name four different bone characteristics from which the palaeontologist can make inferences about the size and shape of a dinosaur.

3. Filmstrip 3 is entitled *Dinosaur Jim Finds the Big One*. It was generally intended to explore the process of scientific discovery and show the results of constant effort and work and the pay-off that typically results. Specifically, it covered the excavation for fossil remains and how the discovery and preserving process took place with Dinosaur Jim's big find in Colorado. Its specific objectives were the following:

(a) List the steps in excavating and preserving a dinosaur bone.
(b) List the steps involved in the process of discovery.
(c) Relate the experiences of three persons who made important discoveries.

The basic instructional characteristics of the filmstrips generally followed this pattern:

1. From general principles and concepts to specific concepts.
2. From a simple to complex level of difficulty.
3. The narrative contained an introduction, subject matter and review.
4. Segments are small enough for a child's span of attention yet large enough to enable him to 'connect' several together.
5. New concepts are related to what the child already knows.
6. The tone and delivery is appealing.
7. 'So what?' or 'Why study this material?' is given consideration.
8. The presentation form is: concept presentation → examples → questions.
9. Integrated with a unit of instruction.

STATEMENT SUMMARIZING RESULTS OF "THE DINOSAUR DYNASTY"

EVALUATION STUDY

The unit on dinosaurs entitled "The Dinosaur Dynasty" consisting of a teacher's handbook, three filmstrips and the movie, "The Great Dinosaur Discovery," was field tested in the fall of 1975. Three different combinations of the unit materials (the materials including the movie, the materials without the movie and the movie alone) were compared in terms of student and teacher affect, and student cognitive gains at grade levels 3, 4, and 6.

Twelve teachers and 292 students in two schools of the Alpine School District, located near Brigham Young University, Provo, Utah, were involved in the study. The following summary briefly presents the results:

This is a good, solid product! It has at least the following characteristics:

The unit consisting of the teacher handbook and the filmstrips provides the teacher with a viable vehicle for teaching about dinosaurs. Much cognitive information is learned. The average gain score for students in classrooms using the materials was 57.2 compared to 31.8 for students in classrooms not using the materials. The teacher is helped greatly in the performance of her duties by these materials. As an additional tool for teaching, the movie provides a fine summary or introduction to the other materials in the unit. The movie results in considerable positive effect toward the overall activities associated with the unit.

Teachers can use the materials successfully at various grade levels depending on how the materials are used. A variety of units on dinosaurs can be organized around the filmstrips and movie by choosing appropriate learning activities and instructional aids from the teacher handbook.

In conclusion, the materials form a solid, high-affect core around which teachers of various grade levels can build their units on dinosaurs.

Adrian P. Van Mondfrans, Ph. D.
Professor of Educational Psychology
Director:
Department of Instructional Evaluation and Testing
Brigham Young University

Figure 2.

When used with supplementary introductory and review materials the filmstrip evaluation data showed reasonable cognitive gains (see Figure 2).

In addition to the three filmstrips there are a set of supplementary transparencies and bulletin board ideas which could be used to introduce the concepts in the filmstrips and for the unit of study as well as suggested games, references, field trips, etc which could be made available to students. A complete day-by-day recommended guide for the utilization of all of these materials was provided to show how the total system could possibly operate.

The prototype materials were produced and tried out on a pilot effort with 12 teachers and 292 students in two schools in the Alpine School District located near Brigham Young University, Provo, Utah. A statement summarizing the results of this study can be found in Figure 2. This type of evaluative statement is now required by several states before public funds can be expended for marketed instructional products.

After the evaluation results were in, revisions were made and the packaging effort began. The resulting set of materials is entitled *The Dinosaur Dynasty* and is available from the Motion Picture Marketing Division, Brigham Young University, Provo, Utah.

This project assisted not only in the refinement of the development aspects but also resulted in the recouping of a financial investment by the Motion Picture Studio. It may also, as the market expands to Canada and other areas, provide money for other development work to take place in areas of need at the primary and secondary levels.

Individual Instruction for Scientific Laboratory Technicians

M J Frazer, D F Herbert, F J Webb

Introduction

Each year some 30 school-leavers are recruited to work as laboratory technicians at Harwell. They start with an eight-week initial training course in the Education Centre, before they disperse to 30 different laboratories distributed around the Harwell site. While the tuition of such a small group might be considered a highly specialized field, of interest to a relatively small number of large organizations undertaking scientific research, these young people are representative of all who leave school with a minimum of four O levels, a considerable fraction of the output of schools. It is suggested that the techniques we are applying to the scientific training of our new entrants would have equal success in training other school-leavers for their first jobs, and perhaps also in their general education.

The Initial Training Course

The initial training course is an intensive course, required to achieve certain definite aims. It must be seen to be effective in achieving these aims because it is so costly — the cost in students' salaries alone is around £9000. Perhaps the most important function of the course is to act as a buffer between school and work, between a situation expressly designed for the benefit of the pupil, with continual careful supervision and guidance through an orderly curriculum, and a situation where the technician is a means to an end, the success of a scientific project, where supervision may be intermittent and the daily routine dictated by the work in hand.

In one sense the initial training is a survival course, continually emphasizing the basis of safe behaviour in the unfamiliar and often potentially hazardous environment of a research laboratory. In addition the course revises and reinforces (and rectifies) what has been learnt at school, and provides instruction in techniques which would rarely be taught at school, such as computer programming, vacuum techniques, laboratory instrumentation. The syllabus includes workshop practice, vacuum technique, electricity, laboratory instrumentation, chemical laboratory practice, computing, nuclear physics and data handling. These diverse topics are considered essential to render a student useful in a working laboratory. In short, we aim in eight weeks to convert school-children into scientists, with some appreciation of the importance of accurate observation and scientific integrity.

Problems with Conventional Instruction

The aims of the course are ambitious enough without added complications which must be familiar to many working in an industrial environment rather than an educational establishment. The 30 new entrants are not a homogeneous class; their ages range from 16 to 20 or more, they come from different backgrounds, from different types of schools; they have differing interests, abilities, experience and qualifications, ranging from the minimum four O levels to a year or more at university. They arrive hoping to specialize as physicists, chemists, mathematicians or perhaps metallurgists, chemical engineers or electronic engineers. Most arrive a day early in September, but a few are always a week or two late. On arrival they continue their general scientific education by attendance on courses at local colleges. If we are fortunate, we have a complete class present on one day of the week.

In this situation conventional class teaching has always presented problems, involving repeating lectures each week and difficulties in reconciling simultaneously the needs of the more able and the less able. It is quite natural to suggest that some form of individual instruction might be appropriate. For this reason the two of us from the University of East Anglia were commissioned to investigate the existing initial training course, with a view to improving its effectiveness. The existing course consisted basically of lectures to present theory, with laboratory work for practical instruction and an examination at the end. The examination was intended ostensibly to check the students' grasp of their training, but served also to make them revise their lecture notes. It was felt that this training strategy might be improved!

The main results of the investigation were already obvious. The students enjoyed the practical work and gained useful experience, but they sat passively through the lectures, and within experimental error learned nothing from them. Detailed questioning of the students yielded two somewhat more surprising complaints: they failed to recognize the relevance of many topics in their training, and were worried by the lack of assessment. These two points illustrate the value of an external investigator: the students would never have admitted such criticisms to a member of the staff. Indeed the instructors themselves maintained that they always took great pains to demonstrate the relevance of the training, and carefully assessed each individual student.

A Scheme of Individual Instruction

To combat the failings of our existing teaching techniques, we experimented with a number of forms of structured individual instruction. In all cases it was individual instruction, rather than self-instruction, for we assumed the availability of an instructor when necessary to give advice or additional tuition, or to modify the programme to suit any individual. For this reason we restricted ourselves to linear programmes, leaving the instructor to insert any necessary branches.

In view of our students' previous experience of, and reaction to, school teaching, we relied as little as possible on written material. In view of their comments about our earlier methods of instruction, we explicitly explained the relevance of topics whenever possible, and included continuous assessment as an integral part of the instruction.

The subjects to which we have applied individual instruction are nuclear physics, materials science, vacuum techniques, data handling and computer appreciation. A knowledge of nuclear physics was considered essential for young people starting work at Harwell, since many would be handling radio-active materials and working with reactors, and all needed a basic understanding of atomic energy. This course was completely converted from a series of formal lectures to 10 units of individual instruction. Each unit had the same basic structure.

1. *An introductory sheet* listing the objectives of the unit, the components of

the unit, and the technical terms introduced in the unit.

2. *Tape-slide programmes*, each containing 36 slides, the magazine capacity of the Hitachi Sound Slide projector, incidentally a very salutary limit to the author's visual exuberance. Each commentary lasted between 10 and 20 minutes (not more); the cassette was pulsed with inaudible pulses for synchronized slide advance and automatic stop.

3. *Notes for the student* summarizing the main points presented in the unit. The intention was to free the student from the distraction of taking notes during the programme, though in practice we found many jotted additional comments and information on the printed sheets of notes.

4. *Assessment questions* — up to 20 multiple-choice questions, testing mainly comprehension. A good student should with care have scored 100%.

The instructor checked the answers (any necessary was laid out for rapid checking) and gave any necessary tutorial assistance, sending the student back to repeat any section he had not understood. Having ultimately answered all the questions correctly, the student proceeded to the next unit.

At the end of the course the student had accumulated a complete set of notes which he kept for future reference.

The tape-slide programmes were designed to present concise frames of information with clarity, and in an attractive fashion. Having a technical illustrator on the staff we were able to employ as wide a range of graphic techniques as desired.

In addition to one or two tape-slide programmes, some units contained booklets from which the students had to abstract information. In one unit the students had to refer to the Chart of the Nuclides to answer the assessment questions.

We gained evidence that few students read the introductory sheet of notes! However, it served a useful purpose in forcing the author to put his thoughts in logical order at the outset, and to prune out irrelevant information.

Some of our programmes proceeded without a break, straightforward presentations of strictly limited pieces of information. But whenever appropriate the programme stopped to involve the student in an active response — working out an example, drawing a graph, answering questions or hunting for information. Stops were used sparingly to avoid breaking the flow of the argument.

The materials science course was an equally tightly structured course, but audio-visual aids were replaced by practical work. Some of the experiments were brief investigations of specific scientific points: crystal growth, work hardening, various corrosion mechanisms. Other experiments involved the use of metallurgical equipment: a hot-mounting press, polishing wheels, a metallurgical microscope.

One vacuum techniques course was based essentially on each student building up a straightforward vacuum system and making it work. Background information was presented by detailed notes, with tape-slide programmes to explain pressure units, and the functioning of vacuum gauges. Four video-cassettes are planned to augment this course. A final simple assessment test served to show the instructor any topics the students had failed to grasp so that he could clear up misconceptions. A second vacuum techniques course was based on seven unorthodox vacuum systems, each illustrating a particular point concerning the performance of vacuum equipment. In addition to printed data sheets and operating instructions, each system was accompanied by a tape-slide programme setting out the object of the experiment and the method of operating the equipment. Students found these tape-slide programmes of great value, enabling them to appreciate the experiment much more quickly and surely than by reading the written instructions.

Three tape-slide programmes were concerned with numerical manipulation of data and the calculation of experimental error. Five tape-slide programmes, with accompanying notes and assessment questions, replaced two lectures on computer appreciation, which preceded a week's tutorial instruction in Fortran programming.

Practical Aspects

For individual instruction activities the 30 students were split into three groups of 10, the groups coinciding as far as possible with day-release groups. Two rooms were employed. The library, 3.8 by 7.8 metres, was used by students for reading, writing, answering assessment questions, for the tutorials, and for storing the programmes and notes. An adjacent room, 2.6 by 7.8 metres, was divided by temporary screens 1.5 metres high into five cubicles, each with a small desk. Five Hitachi projectors, each with two pairs of headphones, were mounted on shelves, to leave the desk tops free for writing. A sixth projector was situated in a small room nearby as a reserve.

The students started the course in pairs, but the pairs often became broken up after a few units. Each group worked at individual instruction for one hour a day, three days a week, for seven weeks. At the end of this time they still accepted the method without complaint; the only complaints came from students for some reason tied to machines for more than one hour at a time.

Each unit of the nuclear physics course was designed to take about one hour. Some students completed the course in less than 10 hours, others took up to 15 hours. Some were unable to finish all the units, but all the vital basic information was in the first seven. It was essential that they grasped the fundamentals, not that they completed the course.

Choice of Visual Aids

The aim of the visual aids was to present information quickly and concisely, in a manner attractive to students not of the highest academic calibre, and to maintain their interest throughout a concentrated eight-week course. The tape-slide method was chosen for several reasons.

1. Material is relatively easy to prepare and to revise.
2. Definition and colour are good.
3. The equipment is robust, easy to service, and readily portable.
4. The automatic stop facility enables insertion of examples or activities to relieve the student's purely passive role.

The tape-slide method has, however, a number of definite limitations. A single projector is admirable for presenting single, discrete frames of static information. It cannot portray movement, nor even the growth of a continuous argument. A further limitation is that the student's eyes are glued to the screen; he cannot operate equipment or refer to written material without diverting his attention.

This latter drawback is no problem with an audio-tape; the student's eyes and hands (and imagination) are free to attend to models or apparatus, or to follow text or complicated plans and diagrams. We have used an audio-tape in the materials science course to guide the student through the assembly of crystal models from polystyrene balls, with the aid of diagrams.

The video-cassette permits the portrayal of movement, which may be vital to the demonstration of equipment, technical operations and the like. We have employed it for a demonstration of leak detection in vacuum systems, where the speed of response of the leak detector to the probe gas is an important feature.

In our early trials we were concerned lest a continual diet of tape-slide programmes should prove indigestible for our students. To remedy this we made one nuclear physics unit as a video-cassette, alternating excerpts from a suitable film with a series of static shots. Our early tape-slide programmes were accepted without comment, but the students immediately criticised the video-cassette on the ground that it did not move! Video-cassette, of course, invites immediate comparison with professional television.

Assessment of Individual Instruction

We have attempted no rigorous quantitative evaluation of individual instruction, with control groups and direct comparison of results before and after. However, a statistical analysis of the assessment questions was performed to identify any faulty questions or failure to convey particular items of information. By observation, by questionnaires, and by informal discussion we attempted a qualitative evaluation of our innovations.

Individual instruction in general, and tape-slide programmes in particular, were accepted by the students without question. Indeed, it was difficult to get them to voice any criticism at all, except concerning points of detail. This was in sharp contrast to their earlier unenthusiastic response to identical material presented in lecture form.

On completion of the nuclear physics course, all students were presented without warning with a final test of 40 multiple-choice questions, based on the information in the first half of the course. In 1975, and again in 1976, the mean score was 75%, in sharp contrast to the execrable result in the final examination in earlier years.

These qualitative results support our belief that we have developed a method of instruction acceptable to this group of students and efficient in conveying information. From the instructor's point of view the method obviated repeating basic lectures, so that he could spend all his time in solving particular problems of individual students. The students appreciated the concise presentation of information and learnt more. They recognised the relevance of the closely defined objectives to their future work, and were encouraged by the continuous assessment.

On the other hand, less information is conveyed altogether in the 10 to 15 hours of the present nuclear physics course than was previously presented in four or five hours of lectures. Some of the marked improvement in student performance may reflect the careful setting of realistic objectives, the pruning of inessential material, and the increased time devoted to the subject, rather than the precise method of presentation adopted.

We have conducted other trials of tape-slide material with older technical staff. They have received them very happily, welcoming the carefully prepared units of information, which they could assimilate at their own speed, no longer dependent on keeping pace with a class, nor on immediately following the galloping train of thought of an enthusiastic lecturer. However, we have been less successful in persuading line management of the efficiency of individual instruction. Sending a man to attend a series of lectures is proper training; audio-visual material is light relief!

Conclusions

We have invested a considerable amount of time and effort (and hence money) in the production of individual instruction schemes and material. It has not achieved an appreciable saving of staff time, for instructors now spend their time tutoring instead of lecturing. It appears to have achieved an improvement in conveying factual information to our students, and enabling them to carry out certain basic scientific calculations and operations. In the economy of a working research laboratory such an improvement outweighs the additional effort demanded. Failure in a laboratory may well be more serious than failure in an examination.

Our laboratory technicians are representative of many schoolchildren, who are often intensely interested in particular subjects, in this case scientific and technological subjects, but never seem to achieve their potential in their examination marks. Since tape-slide programmes have been so successful in our environment, similar material may be equally appropriate to education in other subjects for young people not destined for high academic achievement.

British Gas Corporation Product Knowledge Training Package

J Green, J Smith, D M Clifford

British Gas has some 940 showrooms within its 12 regions. These showrooms generate a considerable amount of business for the industry, and although their role is primarily concerned with selling appliances it also embraces service inquiries, accounts payments and general customer relations work. They are highly successful operating units staffed by both male and female employees in full-time and part-time capacities. Traditionally, the training given to such staff has consisted of supervised showroom experience supplemented by attendance at an off-the-job course covering basic product knowledge, selling and customer relations skills. This approach was established in order to cope with a regular recruitment pattern in most regions.

The Problem

During the past few years there has been a gradual reduction in staff turnover resulting in more sporadic recruitment of showroom staff. At the same time a higher proportion of part-time showroom staff has been employed, in many cases married women who were returning to work after bringing up families, the 'married women returners'. The work pattern of such employees is varied and depends on local circumstances. These circumstances change from time to time and this creates problems in planning and implementing accepted approaches to training.

The main problem was the extended delays between recruitment and attendance at an off-the-job course. In some regions several months might elapse before such a course could become viable if staff turnover were very low for a period. In these circumstances supervisors and showroom managers were key figures in that they had to take responsibility for the initial job training of their new staff. Although many of the supervisors had been trained in the skills of training, inevitably the techniques and materials they used varied quite considerably. This meant that the effectiveness of new staff could be limited for a considerable period after recruitment.

During early discussions about these problems it became apparent that although different systems and patterns of work existed in many regions the prime aim of the initial training was to give new starters sufficient information to enable them to deal confidently with the majority of customers they would meet. This aim related to full-time and part-time staff since both categories have the same responsibilities, the only difference between them being in the hours worked.

It became clear that the existing pattern of training should be supplemented by a system which could impart common core information to new entrant sales staff as soon as possible after joining. Supervisors needed a common framework on which to base their follow-up on-the-job training and planned experience. The problem was thus defined and was undoubtedly similar to those encountered by many other large organizations.

The Decision-Making Process

Having defined the nature of the problem it was clearly necessary to go further and state the learning objectives as precisely as possible. Newly-appointed showroom staff would need fundamental knowledge of gas as well as outline knowledge of appliances if they were to be able to deal confidently with customers. Thus the defined outline objectives covered knowledge of gas as a fuel, how it burns, the principles of ignition, burners, flame failure devices and gas controls as well as knowledge of appliances such as gas cookers and gas fires.

From the outset it was recognized that an investment of time, effort and money had to be made if a learning system to meet these objectives were to be produced. Whichever approach was adopted had necessarily to take account of cost and estimated benefit. It was thought likely that the annual intake of new staff would be about 100, and that if the subject matter were general rather than specific (ie to particular appliances) it would probably have a useful life of five years. These assumptions were part of the basis for further decision-making.

Deciding 'where to go' was easier than deciding 'how to get there' and the next step, therefore, was to relate the objectives to the target population and to the range of alternative learning systems which could be used. First, on the newly-appointed staff, our target population, some general statements could be made. They would include:

- Many youngsters of both sexes;
- A large number of women, including 'married women returners';
- Full and part-timers;
- People who are literate and intelligent, but not academic;
- Staff recruited at irregular intervals;
- People who are motivated to learn.

Against this background the available learning systems could be considered. Those involving off-the-job courses; either full-time at a training centre or by part-time attendance at classes, could not be applied in the short term because of the number of part-timers and because of the irregular intervals at which staff are recruited.

Of the on-the-job training possibilities, coaching by managers and supervisors seemed promising but would have involved training supervisory staff as on-the-job trainers and monitoring training would have been difficult. The study of text-books, CCTV programmes, tape and slide presentations also seemed to offer possibilities, but would only be acceptable if provision could be made for trainee responses and feedback.

Our criteria for selecting a learning system for this purpose demanded that the system should:

- Consist of easily portable materials and equipment, since it would be used in several locations, moved frequently and handled by female as well as male staff.
- Have visual and audio facilities so that the senses of sight and hearing could be applied to the learning.
- Have a trainee response/participation facility.
- Be robust, easy to use and reasonably priced.
- Contain a facility for progress checking/error recording.

An important issue was whether a projected image as opposed to a photograph or printed diagram was an essential ingredient of the input. It was recognized that

328

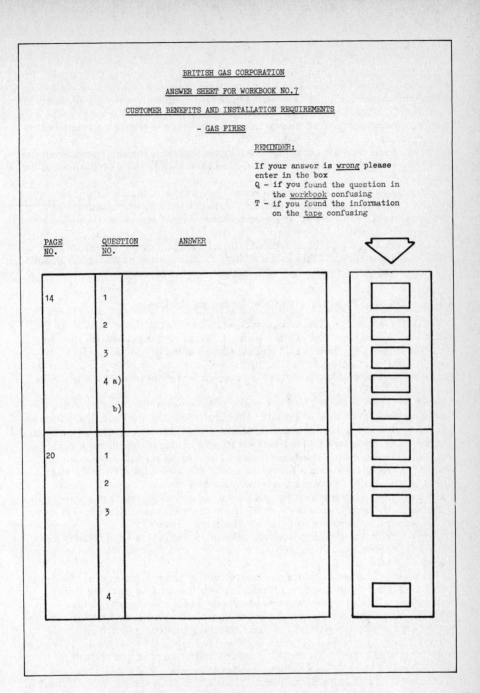

Figure 1. *A British Gas Corporation answer sheet*

some additional impact could be expected from a projected image, but that the extra cost of projection equipment, risks of breakdown, additional handling, transportation and storage problems, more than off-set any probable advantage.

It was, therefore, decided that a training package for use on-the-job should be produced and that it should be designed to cover the objectives already outlined. The input should be provided by tape recordings, supplemented by workbooks containing the visuals and additional information. Progress should be monitored by objective questions included in the workbook at the end of each short learning sequence. It was estimated that nine learning sessions each lasting about 40 minutes would be necessary. Separate cassette tapes and workbooks should be produced for each.

In order to train showroom managers and supervisors in the use of the package and at the same time give them practical experience in using the medium, an additional 'on-the-job trainers' session consisting of cassette tape and workbook was also to be produced.

The solution to the problem seemed rational enough, but there remained the problem of translating the idea into a reality. The production of between 400 and 500 minutes of programmed material seemed a daunting prospect.

The Design and Production of the Learning Package

For various reasons, programmed instruction had not been widely used in the gas industry and from the onset of the scheme it was realized that most sales training staff would have only limited skill and experience in the production of learning package material. Consequently, five British Gas sales trainers were selected to attend the normal mid-May eight-day programme writers' workshop at Middlesex Polytechnic in 1975.

This workshop is divided into two parts, a five-day session with a three-day follow-up some four to six weeks later. During the first five days the newly formed team were able to reach understanding on the overall aims of the learning package and agreement on detailed objectives for each of the nine planned sessions. This facilitated the writing of criterion questions which in turn led to some rapid progress in drafting the scripts for the tapes and the visuals for the workbooks.

At the end of this first week the training officers returned to their regional training centres to resume their normal duties. No special arrangements were made to deal with the additional workload, but managers were made aware of it and had agreed to give consideration to these additional commitments.

Also at the end of this first week an action plan was generated and target dates for five fundamental activities were set to coincide with the three-day follow-up session timed for early July.

These main activities included the completion of a comprehensive list of objectives for all the planned sessions; a set of practical tests to ascertain what the student could do after he had studied the whole package and the first drafts of the programmed scripts and workbooks which would, where possible, be tried out on a few selected showroom staff so that their reactions could be noted. This would provide a basis for discussions on the style and format of the workbooks. Estimates could then be obtained from graphic designers and printers so that realistic decisions could be made on production times and costs.

Almost all the deadline dates were met, but to maintain the momentum another two-day briefing session was arranged for late August at Goldicote House, the Management Training Centre of West Midlands Gas at which progress was reviewed.

As the target dates for the main activities had been realized, the first half of this session was devoted to discussion on the format of the workbook, arranging a

Please complete this short questionnaire and hand it to ....

Session No. .... Time taken in minutes ....

Please tick <u>one</u> of the alternative answer boxes for each of the following questions:

1. Did you find the illustrations and drawings were:

very helpful	helpful	not very helpful	confusing	very confusing

2. Did you find the written information was:

very helpful	helpful	not very helpful	confusing	very confusing

3. Did you find the information on the cassette was:

all new	nearly all new	partly new	mostly known	already known

4. Did you find understanding the cassette was:

easy	fairly easy	just right	difficult	very difficult

5. Did you find learning by this method was:

too easy	easy	moderately easy	difficult	very difficult

6. Apart from ease or difficulty I found learning by this method was:-

pleasing	fairly pleasant	not bad	somewhat tedious	boring

7. Are you satisfied with the progress made in this session?

Yes	No

If 'no' please say why ....
....

Please state briefly any suggestions you have for improving this session:
....
....
....
....

Figure 2. *Trainee's assessment sheet*

provisional but realistic timetable for the production of master copies of the tapes, which were to be recorded within British Gas, and making detailed arrangements for the completion and distribution of the learning package.

In the second part of this meeting final decisions were made on how the validation of the learning material itself and the evaluation of the pilot scheme as a whole should be undertaken. As this would involve managers as well as trainees, questionnaires and answer sheets were provided for the trainees and special briefing instructions for managers were produced to supplement the tape workbook session for on-the-job trainers. It was important that managers should understand the order in which trainees should tackle the sessions and the procedure for dealing with tests and answer sheets.

Validation and Evaluation

As this was a new training development for British Gas it was essential that there was sufficient feedback built into the process to indicate whether learning was taking place and to identify any problem areas within the material.

As part of the programmed basis for the workbook, question pages to test understanding had been incorporated at appropriate intervals. The answers to these questions were recorded by trainees on individual answer sheets provided with the package. Each answer sheet related to a particular session and the answer spaces were tailored for each question. On completion of a page of questions the trainee would then switch the cassette on again and listen to the correct answers. He could then check whether he had made correct responses or not. Where his own answer differed from that given on the cassette he was asked to write in a code letter on the answer sheet indicating why he thought he made the mistake. Two alternatives were offered — one to indicate that the information given during the session was inadequate, and the other to indicate that the question itself was confusing. The reason for providing separate answer sheets was that the workbooks were part of a package which was to be used on many occasions by different trainees, and therefore should not be marked in any way.

At the end of each session the trainee was asked to return to his supervisor or showroom manager to discuss any areas of difficulty and to clarify any parts of the subject matter which were still not understood.

The trainee was also asked to complete an assessment sheet at the end of each session expressing his feelings about the learning experience he had just undergone. This was a simple tick assessment along several rating scales.

At the end of a series of sessions covering a particular product group, eg cookers, a practical test was included. This test was an attempt to get the trainees to transfer their learning into the working situation. In the initial package there were two tests and the trainees normally worked through the questions with the supervisor or showroom manager as the assessor. These practical tests also allowed for the inclusion of additional questions if required.

As a final form of feedback a supervisors' assessment was incorporated to find out their views on the reactions of new staff to the total package and the relevance of the material.

The package was launched on a pilot basis during the first half of 1976 and during this phase, answer sheets, assessment sheets and practical test forms were returned to British Gas headquarters so that overall reaction throughout the industry could be gauged. During the pilot phase 40 new entrants worked through the package and the error rates for each question were calculated as an indicator of package quality and success.

Since then some regions have continued to provide detailed feedback as part of an ongoing monitoring exercise. Apparent faults in some of the visuals have been discovered and some parts of the text were also identified as in need of improvement. The revision of all sessions is now under way, although several will only need minor alteration since faults appear to be in matters of detail only. However, one session contains some major design faults and the information sequence may need to be substantially amended to make it completely effective. These amendments are being made by a small headquarters design team.

The cost of this package approach to training up to the trial stage was some £2600, and this included the cost of the tape cassette players, the artwork for each workbook, the costs of the training workshop, the carrying case within which the package material is contained and the recording and copying costs of the cassette tapes, but excludes the salaries of British Gas training staff engaged on the project.

Originally 14 complete packages were produced but the number now in use is nearer 20 even though all the amendments have still to be made to the final version.

It is impossible at this stage to state the exact cost of the revision, and the additional cost of amending all existing copies. Some artwork, re-recording and printing will be involved, but the volume is not great and the total bill will probably be less than £400. It is not expected that substantial alterations will need to be made again once this initial material revision is completed and, therefore, additional complete packages could be produced for about £80 each.

The life of these packages is probably in line with our original estimate of five years and even with recruitment levels for sales staff being irregular there could be about 100 new entrants making use of the packages each year. However, even if only 300 trainees use the package and the final figure is likely to be much higher than that, the cost per trainee/usage would be about £10.

It is difficult to give a precise figure in terms of the cost-benefit to the industry as a whole and to individuals who have used the package for their own training. However, it is clear that the crucial gap between recruitment and systematic off-the-job training has been bridged with a flexible, easy to use and acceptable method of basic product knowledge training. Indeed the response from trainees, from their supervisors and from top management has been enthusiastic. Training staff too have seen the contribution that such an approach can make to the total training of new showroom staff. From the outset it has never been seen as a panacea for the training problems of sales staff, but as a supplement to other effective forms of training. It is not expected that the package will be added to after the current series of sessions under preparation has been completed. The aim is to produce a self-contained package which could have possible additional application in other parts of the gas industry's training operations. From the information available on its use and potential so far this aim will undoubtedly be achieved.

The Application of Educational Technology for In-Factory Training in the Printing and Packaging Industries

E J Pritchard

For the last 20 years the printing industry in the UK has been faced with rising manpower costs and diminishing profits. One of the ways of improving the situation is to maximize the human resources, to increase the output per head and decrease the wastage of materials. This is particularly important when large capital expenditure has been incurred in introducing a new technology.

Training can be given by courses of lectures and demonstrations, practical work on the equipment to be used, and by training packages. To provide the most effective training, we must know the numbers and groups of persons requiring training, the level of education and pre-knowledge within each group, and the availability of the groups. The availability of the groups is particularly important in determining the forms that training can take. For example, there is usually a limit to the number of pressmen that can be released at one time without serious interference with production.

It is self-evident that training must be planned to be as effective as possible, to minimize both the time trainees spend away from their work and the time taken by instructors or supervisors in training them. Firms are becoming more and more reluctant to send personnel on long day-release courses at schools or colleges, and are looking for ways of implementing the training in-factory in a shorter time period.

We will illustrate the way we have assisted in the development of in-factory training by describing some examples of the use of various types of training packages, and their integration into modular training schemes.

Example 1. A Modular Re-Training System for the Total Personnel of a Newspaper Plant

Since 1964 provincial newspapers have been converting from the old-established letterpress processes to the newer technology of web-offset. This has produced a vast training requirement.

Management

Management will have a need prior to conversion. This group will have to decide whether to convert fully, or only for colour; whether to go over to photo-typesetting or to retain hot metal; what kind of press to buy; what kind of plates to use; and make many other decisions of this nature. They need to know the alternatives open to them in each area, and the implications of each decision on the total system. The data for decision-making is usually obtained from the literature, from visits to other plants, and from suppliers. Data collection can be accelerated, and decision-making improved, by an orientation course.

ORIENTATION TO WEB OFFSET FOR MANAGEMENT

Subjects: principles of lithography; photocomposing; applications of computers to typesetting; conversion systems and page make-up; copy requirements; monochrome and colour reproduction; registration systems; platemaking; blankets, ink and paper; the press; web tension control.

Coverage: underlying principles; equipment and systems; sequence of steps; quality control points and devices; interdependence of operations; implications of systems on other areas.

Operations are demonstrated, and practical work and syndicate exercises performed where appropriate.

Personnel Training

The training of other personnel cannot really begin until the management decisions on systems and equipment have been made, since the training, to be effective, must be based on the systems that are to be used in the plant.

The first step in preparing the training programme is to spend a day or two in the plant, to see the procedures and equipment being used, to find out what people do and which of them will have to be re-trained for new jobs, and to ascertain what the new systems and equipments will be.

Personnel can be divided roughly into two main groups — editorial and advertising, and production — as follows:

Editors	Composing
Journalists	Stereo
Advertising staff	Reproduction
Photographers	Platemaking
	Press room
(Administration buyers)	Works management

We must then determine from the data collected what each group needs to know, what it would be nice for them to know, and whether there is any information needed that is common to some or all groups.

It is self-evident that all personnel should understand the basic principles of offset lithography and the main ways in which it differs from letterpress. One of the major differences that affects almost all areas of the plant is the need for flat copy for a single unit plate. The other main change for most newspapers is the use of colour. Thus, we can say that all personnel need instruction in the basic principles of offset lithography, how copy and illustrations are dealt with and combined together to make a single unit plate, and the basic principles of colour reproduction.

We can also say that it would be interesting for them to have details of the equipment to be used for production, why it had been chosen, and the benefits envisaged from the changeover.

Editorial and advertising all deal with the copy and artwork that will be combined together on the printing plate. We can treat them as one group, and define their needs as follows:

Copy evaluation; the production requirements of all flat copy, artwork and transparencies;

The effects of unsuitable artwork and transparencies on production and quality;

The requirements of editorial layout sheets;

The difficulty of correction on a unit plate;

The need for exact copy; the influence of bad copy on production;

The best use of colour and page layout.

As the work of editorial and advertising can affect production speed and quality, so the production groups interact with one another. Each group, therefore, needs to appreciate the operations of other groups. We can therefore list areas of information for which they can be treated as one group as follows:

Phototypesetting: methods and equipments.

Page make-up: an appreciation of good quality.

Paste-up: the effects of bad paste-up on production and quality.

Principles of platemaking: how plates should be treated and handled.

We have now defined the coverage of four 'knowledge content' courses. The management course can be done externally, but the other three need to be in-plant, and repeated over a number of days to avoid a complete halt in production.

Module 1   Orientation course for management, two-week course at Pira.
Module 2   All personnel.
Module 3   Editorial and Advertising.
Module 4   Production workers.

	DAY 1	DAY 2	DAY 3	DAY 4
AM	Module 2	Module 2	Module 2	Module 2
PM	Module 3	Module 4	Module 3	Module 4

Editorial and advertising, together with administration and buyers were split into two groups; one group attended on day 1, the other group on day 3. Administration and buyers attended mornings only. Production workers did a similar exercise on days 2 and 4.

Apart from knowledge content, each production group needed practical instruction in their own particular area. These requirements were dependent on the system being adopted, and on whether experienced workers were being brought in, or existing staff re-trained for other work. For example, if photosetting was being introduced, then keyboard operators would have to be either hired or trained. It is usual whenever possible to re-train existing staff; composing room staff are usually re-trained to handle paste-up operation; stereo workers may be re-trained as platemakers. The needs for particular manual skills were isolated, and arrangements for these to be acquired were made by management, often in conjunction with equipment suppliers.

Pressmen

Within the area of manual skills, pressmen are a special case. These men are usually letterpress men, used to running webs of paper on rotary presses, but with no experience of lithography. They need a greater in-depth knowledge of the total process, as well as practical instruction on press. Further, they usually work on a shift system, so that it is difficult to gather them together for group instruction for long periods without serious interference with production. In cases like this, the knowledge content can be provided most successfully by self-instruction training packages, either in the form of teaching machines programmes or programmed texts. A man experiences stress in learning a new job and so is unwilling to train for a new occupation. But many features of teaching machines contribute to reducing this stress, which makes them eminently suitable for older workers, particularly when they have had little formal education. The instruction is individual and self-paced, with the accent on carefully arranged sequences of small steps designed to teach in the clearest possible manner. Accordingly, we set out to provide teaching machine programmes to fulfil this need.

A lithographic pressman must be capable of producing quality lithographic prints of a consistent standard in the shortest possible time. To do this, he must:

1. Be capable of setting up and running a press.
2. Be able to decide, and to take, whatever remedial action is necessary if print quality deviates from an accepted standard.

The programmes were not intended to teach the manual skills involved in press operating, nor to deal with the detailed running of any particular press, but only to teach the principles and procedures common to all presses. To determine the exact nature of these principles, a detailed job analysis was performed. This fell into two parts:

1. A straightforward job specification to determine what the pressman must know to be able to set up and a run a press.
2. An analysis of print faults to determine what enables him to make decisions and take action to maintain print quality.

This analysis was established in teaching areas, which were then grouped under the following headings:

Image and non-image areas
Plates
Fountain solutions
Damping systems
Ink
Inking systems
Paper
Pressure, blankets and register.

Each of these headings formed one unit of instruction. Although all the factual information could be grouped under the above eight headings, a further three units were devised for the complete programme.

Introduction: to outline the process and give a basic framework, so that the pressman is not given detailed information in isolation.

Running a press: to relate the information given in the other units to the job of running a press; to teach the order of events for setting up a press.

Maintaining print quality: to create a system of applying the previously acquired knowledge to fault correction.

Thus the complete programme consisted of 11 units. Before the programme could be written, it was important to know to what level the various subjects had to be dealt with. For example, how much does the pressman need to know about the viscosity of ink? Is he concerned with molecular forces, or is it enough for him to know that some inks flow more easily than others? Reference to the job analysis showed the depth of knowledge required for each teaching area.

Knowing the teaching areas and the depth to which they must be taught, it was possible to write the behavioural objectives of the programme. This was documented by stating the desired terminal behaviour for each section. The list of teaching areas and the terminal behaviour gives a very accurate description of what the programme must teach. The material to be taught was then broken down into a series of very small steps (teaching points) which were carefully checked for technical accuracy and arranged into a logical sequence.

When the first draft was complete, it was presented to a sample of the target population to test their reactions. Observations were carefully noted, and the draft re-written and presented to another group, until all areas of possible misunderstanding had been eliminated. This developmental testing assists in obtaining the correct language level, in getting the terminology right, in improving illustrations and pinpointing concepts that are difficult to understand.

Branching programmes were written, with multi-choice questions for an ESL AutoTutor teaching machine.

Since the programmes taught factual information, it was a relatively simple matter to test the acquisition of these facts. Straightforward written tests were prepared, based directly on the terminal behaviour for each part of the programme. These tests were administered immediately before, and again after the trainee had worked through each section on the teaching machine. Each man could be taken off work for an hour at a time to work through a section of the programme, without serious interference to production.

Practical Training

These programmes should not be used in isolation. They teach basic principles which must be followed up by practical training on a press. For practical training, we were fortunate in having a web-offset press made available to us by the Vickers Printing Machinery and Supplies Group; Pira instructors gave a five-day course of on-press instruction to groups of pressmen, with one instructor to each group of three, so that each man could perform each operation himself.

PROGRAMME OF ON-PRESS INSTRUCTION

Day 1. Basic principles of offset lithography; press design and cylinder layout of web-offset presses; introduction to Spearhead press.

Day 2. Blanket make-up, fitting, packing and maintenance; plate bending, fitting, packing; care of plates and surface treatments; web tension control; inspection of reels for web-offset paper requirements; introduction to folder and settings.

Day 3. Roller and damper settings; care and maintenance; duct setting; fountain solutions; webbing up; web leads; press start-up procedures; damper/inker sequence; on-run press settings (running on one web all day).

Day 4. Press running; instructors giving distant supervision, allowing pressmen full control (one web only); running two web leads, giving pressmen opportunity to control colour; press stations; reel stands and folder controlled by instructors; pressmen to concentrate on inker and damper settings, maintaining colour and ink/water balance.

Day 5. Fault recognition and remedies; web-offset problems on plates, inkers, blankets, reel-stands and folders; causes and defects and how to overcome them; press wash-up.

The Spearhead press is not in general production, but is a very open press, ideal for instruction. Details of the actual press on which the men would work were obtained, and the areas in which this differed from the Spearhead were explained during the course.

Teaching machine programmes have also been produced for three MGD presses, the Metro, Surburban and Urbanite. These are press familiarization programmes, aiming to make the pressman feel 'at home' with the actual press, so that he is not overawed or confused by it, and enabling him to identify the units and controls. It is not in any way an alternative to an on-press instruction, but complementary to it.

We now have Modules 5, 6 and 7 for pressmen.

Module 5 Teaching machine programmes on offset lithography.

Module 6 On-press instruction, five-day course.

Module 7 Press familiarization; teaching machine programmes.

Group Training Needs

Apart from the orientation course for management, the training needs of other groups have been defined in terms of their areas of work. Further needs become apparent when they are classified within the vertical structure of the organization. For example, middle management and supervisors need a greater in-depth knowledge of the process as a whole then one can be given in the introductory modules, in order to appreciate the way in which the requirements from their own departments will be altered, and how the alterations in other departments will impinge upon them.

Lastly, once conversion has taken place, general managers have to take decisions to ensure that volume and quality of production are optimized for the least possible cost. To do this, they must be able to appreciate the causes of shortcomings in terms of quality, output or cost.

The needs of supervisory staff and general management can be covered by courses, as shown in Modules 8 and 9.

Module 8   Web-offset for middle management and supervisory staff five-day course.

Day 1. Line and halftone photography; transparency evaluation; colour separation photography.

Day 2. Page make-up and pin register systems; lithographic plates and platemaking.

Day 3. Ink and paper; offset blankets; web-tension control.

Day 4. On-press instruction.

Day 5. On-press instruction; general discussion on control procedures and fault-finding.

Each session of lectures is followed by practical work, so that supervisors can see what is involved in each operation. Evening discussion sessions are run on the topics of each day.

A photograph taken of the group on arrival is processed through all stages by the trainees, emerging on the last day as a print in a complete newspaper.

Module 9   Control of web-offset for general management, five-day course.

The topics are the same as for Module 8, starting at the hard copy stage and following through to the final printed newspaper.

Each subject is covered by an introductory lecture, practical work and a discussion group. Introductory lectures cover: principle of operation; equipment and materials; steps in operation; methods of control and control equipment; interdependence of operations.

Discussion sessions on each topic are led by an instructor down the following channels:

1. Implications of control:
   (a)   cost and time versus quality and wastage;
   (b)   influence on subsequent operations.
2. Economic aspects of the various systems and equipments.
3. Minimizing waste.

Speakers with considerable experience in web-offset production are brought in to contribute to these discussion sessions.

Conversion from letterpress to web-offset requires a considerable amount of re-training throughout the plant, over a long period of time. It must be considered by the management when the decision to convert is taken, if the right training is to be provided at the right time. Most of the basic needs can be covered by nine modules of training.

Module 1   Orientation for management.

Module 2   All personnel.

Module 3   Editorial and advertising.
Module 4   Production staff.
Module 5   Pressmen; teaching machine programmes.
Module 6   Pressmen; on-press instruction.
Module 7   Pressmen; press familiarization; teaching machines.
Module 8   Middle management and supervisors.
Module 9   General management; control of web-offset.
Additional training will be needed in particular skills.

Nowhere is the interdependence of operations so apparent as in the reprographic department. Here they are dependent at one end on the quality of the transparencies sent to them, and at the other on the paper/ink/machine interaction. This is stressed throughout the training courses, but the actual matching of the repro work to the specific papers and inks to be used on the press should perhaps be considered as a consultancy service rather than direct training.

The effectiveness of courses can be improved and the burden on lecturers lightened, by the pre-preparation of training packages containing good visual material. So far, this had been done in three areas — introduction to offset lithography, page make-up, and the selection of transparencies for graphic reproduction. The latter package has been prepared as self-instruction material, so can be used by editorial and advertising personnel unable to attend a course. If used by print buyers and agency staff, it can assist the printer by ensuring that he at least starts off on the right foot with good quality, suitable materials.

Effective training depends on identifying the needs of each group, usually by means of job analysis, and then providing the training in the most suitable form for each group, bearing in mind the availability of groups and the effect of absence on external courses on production.

Example 2. Development of Self-Instruction Packages

Teaching machine programmes were used successfully as part of the programme for Example 1. They had some disadvantages, not the least of which was the unreliability of the machines, which needed constant servicing, and the cost of producing the programmes.

Consequently, we decided to convert the material into a set of manuals, with line diagrams and a set of colour slides to be viewed by the trainee in a small hand or table viewer.

We had not experienced much success with straight programming, in which trainees had to fill in blanks in the text — all our programmes were branching, in which the trainee could not proceed until he had demonstrated that he had understood by getting the question right. If he answered wrongly, he was branched round a remedial loop.

This technique is more difficult to operate in a textual format. Tutorial texts solve the problem by referring the trainees to answers on pages at random, so they may have to turn from page 40 to 20 then on to 45, back to 33, and so on. We found this proved an irritation to trainees, who did not want to be bothered with it.

We solved the problem by ordering the material so that the trainee could proceed in one direction through the manual, turning to different pages according to his answer choice. If he wished, he could of course, get the right answer accidentally, or by cheating. We allowed for this by providing the remedial instruction on the correct answer pages as well as on the incorrect ones, thus, although the system is not completely foolproof, it is well liked, and has validated equally as well as the teaching machine programmes.

Example 3. Induction Training for Safety

Here we have an ideal situation for self-instruction. New staff arrive in ones or twos, rather than in large groups. It is usually too costly to employ an instructor to train one or two people, consequently, what usually happens is that apart from a chat from the personnel officer, and perhaps a company booklet on safety to read, a new entrant is turned loose in a factory environment, perhaps for the first time, until such time as sufficient persons have accumulated to warrant a training session.

When designing the format of the package, we took note of the Department of Employment statement following an investigation of training needs in one industry — 'that too much safety training was focused on the mechanisms of safety, and too much material was produced as films or given in a passive lecture situation that had little or no effect on the recipients'. It suggested that emphasis should be placed on inducing an awareness of hazards and safety consciousness by using more modern techniques in which the trainees could participate more actively.

Initially, we prepared a set of objectives, and produced material in two forms — a straight text and a programmed text, both with illustrations and coloured slides. The first half of both packages was given to persons in the target population group to study, with the instruction that we wanted them to vet it for us, and tell us which they liked best. The programmed texts were brought back very rapidly, with requests for the rest of it, because it was interesting. We never managed to get the straight texts read after a few pages. It was pronounced to be 'like the start of some dull old book'.

We have found this reaction throughout to programmed text. In the contexts in which we have used it, it has been well liked, created interest, and done a good training job.

Following the success of these packages, we have produced similar formats for other packages, the last of the series being to train packaging machinery mechanics in the machine/product/materials interaction in cartoning machines, with the objective of improving their ability for logical fault-finding.

There are many other situations where self-learning packages can be effective. The supervisor in charge of a routine testing laboratory often spends a great deal of time training new entrants in how to carry out standard tests. Girls can teach themselves how to prepare the samples, do the tests and record the results with training packages that can be used alongside the test instruments, thus saving the time of the supervisor for more important tasks. The material can be slide-text or slide-tape, with earphones. We have demonstrated that a girl can learn to do a quite complex series of manual operations in about two hours by this method. In some companies new entrants learn by 'sitting by Nellie', a system likely to lead quite rapidly to non-standard methods being employed. With a training package, one can be sure that each girl is taught to do the test, or any other simple manual operation, in exactly the same standard way.

Currently, more diverse packages are being prepared for top management and supervisors on safety training. It is envisaged that the supervisory material will contain both straight and programmed texts, leaflets, pamphlets, work books and hazard spotting cards.

Validation

When discussing validation, we must differentiate between self-instructional material and material for group instruction. Self-instructional material is validated by preparing written tests based directly on the specified terminal behaviour, and administering them immediately before and again after the student has worked through the package.

Examples of results on four packages are shown below . No1 was written specifically for pressmen, but was thought to be applicable to other persons in editorial and sales departments who needed induction material, so was validated on both groups.

	Mean pre-test	Mean pre-test
No 1 (pressmen)		
79 trainees	49.2%	84.4%
No 1 (editorial, sales)		
53 trainees	48.8%	88.0%
No 2		
31 trainees	62.4%	92.4%
No 3		
30 trainees	40.4%	95.6%
No 4		
32 trainees	47.2%	91.2%

A student's 't' test was done on the scores on No 1. This was significant at the 0.001% level, ie there is only one chance in a thousand of these results occurring by chance. Since the programme was written primarily for pressmen, the other group should not show a significantly greater improvement. This hypothesis was tested using Snedecor's F test which showed that the difference in improvement between the two groups was not significant.

We have not found a good method of validating packages prepared for group instruction. Firstly, there is an interaction between the instructor, the students and the material. Secondly, the target population is not specified so closely, as the instructor is expected to suit the presentation to the particular student group. Presumably some attempt could be made by pre and post-testing after presentations by a number of different instructors, but this would be time-consuming and we have not felt it to be worth the effort. We have relied on feedback from experienced training officers and instructors who have used the packages in industry.

Self-instruction packages must be written for defined target populations to clearly stated objectives, in such a way that the teaching can be guaranteed to be successful without any outside intervention. Training packages that are envisaged as group instruction material are really aids to a lecturer, and can rarely be used for self-instruction. They can only be used if the student is of the requisite educational level and the package is a completely self-contained entity. If, during group instruction, the lecturer has to provide additional material, or points need clarification by discussion, then this same package cannot be suitable for self-instruction by the self-same group of students.

In conclusion, we think that for a teaching package to be successful, it must persuade the student that it has been produced expecially for him, and is not simply projecting information for anyone who happens to pick it up. It must begin in a way that will catch his interest, so that he can appreciate its relevance to his work situation, and motivate him to want to learn. Once his interest has been captured, it must be sustained by keeping the material well within his grasp, so that he feels his learning is successful, yet just difficult enough to offer a challenge to which he can respond constructively. Lastly, whenever possible the material must be structured so that he can participate actively in it, rather than be a passive target.

The packages described may appear to be rather simple in format, considering the wide range of hardware now available for training. We have tried to concentrate on the production of high quality software at minimum cost, that can be widely used in factories without incurring a high expenditure on hardware. We have produced twin-projector slide-tape programmes using varying rates of fade for particular purposes, but in an industry where the majority of firms do not possess a projector, the use of complex and costly packages would be severely limited.

Investigation of New Techniques for Teaching and Learning using Laser Holography

J A Bellamy

It is generally recognized that visual communication is one of the most vital parts of effective teaching, giving far better retention of information than the spoken word by itself. The increasing use and the improvement in the quality of visual aids stem from this fact, and pupils at all levels of education have come to expect that visual displays will be of a high standard, whether photographs, colour slides, overhead projector, cine-film or television.

However, all these visual aids have one limitation in common, that is they represent the real, three-dimensional world in two-dimensional form. For many purposes, this is satisfactory. Artists have long been aware of the rules of perspective and clues to depth which can be built into a picture, and since people are so accustomed to looking at two-dimensional illustrations, they are rarely aware of the amount of information which these do not convey. In effect, the understanding of a three-dimensional scene shown in two-dimensional form relies upon the past experience of the observer of similar scenes seen in reality, and therefore serious problems of perception and communication of ideas can arise when the scene portrayed is not familiar, or is not related to objects which are understood. It is a common experience that when examining an unfamiliar object, people look around it, to observe it from different viewpoints in order to appreciate the structure, and to relate the mental imagery of views from front, side, above, and so on. It is this ability to look around an object which is not available with two-dimensional representations.

There have been various attempts at creating three-dimensional images, each with its own particular features and limitations. One method of relatively recent origin is that of holography. (The word stems from the Greek 'holos', referring to 'the whole picture'.) The theory of holography as a method of recording three-dimensional scenes in encoded form on photographic plates or film was developed in 1948 by Denis Gabor, but as suitable light sources did not then exist, the making of realistic holograms only became a possibility in the early 1960s with the advent of practical lasers. The hologram has since become widely known and included as a standard component in laser accessory kits for schools, but it is generally regarded as something of a gimmick, producing low-quality images; in practice, most of the serious applications of holography have been in the field of engineering meteorology and data processing.

The potential of holography as a three-dimensional visual aid was brought to the attention of the Leicestershire Education Authority, and in September 1974 a physics teacher, John Bellamy, was seconded to Loughborough University to undertake research into the educational applications of holography, under the direction of Professor J N Butters of the Mechanical Engineering Department. Since it is a common experience of teachers, lecturers and trainers that pupils and students (in a wide age range) have difficulties in fully appreciating the three-dimensional layout of objects portrayed in pictures or blackboard diagrams, or of components shown in engineering drawings, it was proposed to test the hypothesis that holography could assist in such situations.

Preliminary Investigations

An early part of the project was to find what existing work had been done on the need for three-dimensional display for effective learning, and on the educational psychology of reaction to viewing three-dimensional images. It was found that there is well-detailed knowledge of the development of spatial ability, and also of the way in which clues to depth, or the third dimension, may be presented in two-dimensional images (and, significantly, that tests of spatial ability and understanding of three-dimensional layouts are based purely on two-dimensional test sheets and questions); but the search for work relating to the use of and reaction to actual three-dimensional images was in vain. Hence it has been necessary to build up a core of experience from teachers and pupils as this project progressed.

A similar survey was carried out on the use of holography for display or for teaching, and again it was found that there has been virtually no such use, apart from large demonstration holograms made in some centres of holographic work and used to demonstrate the principles of hologram making, before progressing to the engineering applications of the subject.

The third aspect of study at this stage was to discuss with teachers what areas of the curriculum presented problems in communicating three-dimensional concepts, and to select the most suitable topics for holographic treatment to use for initial trials. Molecular structures, geometrical models, design exercises, relief maps and biological specimens are typical examples, together with an unexpected interest from psychologists in the use of holograms for perception trials.

Necessary Technological Developments

General Considerations

Before any trials of holographic educational material could be considered, or valid comparisons made with other methods of three-dimensional viewing, or even any convincing demonstrations given of classroom display holography, it was necessary to make significant advances in the technology involved. Many early holograms show poor-quality images which are frequently difficult to locate, and more than one physics teacher has known pupils to be reluctant to admit that they could not find the image which they had been told they would see in the space behind a hologram. Further, whilst a laser is the essential tool for making holograms, lasers had also been necessary for viewing the holographic image if any reasonable quality was to be achieved. These factors are probably foremost in accounting for the earlier lack of use of holograms for teaching or regular display.

It was considered essential to avoid the use of lasers for the classroom viewing of holograms; safety regulations would not permit the normal use in schools of lasers of greater power than 1/3 mW, but this low power would be quite useless for illuminating a display hologram of any acceptable size, even in a room with a good blackout. Apart from the safety aspects, we anticipated some difficulty in getting schools to purchase, say, 20 mW lasers purely for illuminating holograms, at a cost of around £1700 each! Our project has aimed at low cost and convenience for the user, and looked to the ultimate goal of obtaining bright, high-quality holographic images without the need for blackout, whilst using inexpensive and readily available light sources.

Laser Improvements and Hologram Processing

Several factors contribute to our present ability to make holograms which give good-quality images when using non-laser sources for viewing. Improvements in laser technology in recent years have made available lasers with a narrower frequency band-width and longer coherence length, producing a better defined interference pattern to be recorded by the holographic plate and also allowing the recording of larger scenes. Loughborough University has been the centre of significant improvements in the chemistry of the photographic processing of holograms, and in this field we are delighted to acknowledge the work of Mr N J Phillips of the Physics Department. The developing process has been changed to avoid the production of coarse-grained silver which was responsible for excessive noise in the final image, and yet at the same time improving the contrast and tonal gradation. The fixing process was found to cause surface reticulation of the gelatin when hardening chemicals were present in the fixer, and this may also now be avoided. Perhaps the greatest advance has been in the bleaching process, however. It is well known that the brightness and efficiency of a hologram is improved if an amplitude hologram is converted to a phase hologram by bleaching the image after the developing process. Unfortunately, this bleaching action was found to damage the gelatin, producing noise and flare in the final result, and the work at Loughborough has been able to produce a new bleaching process giving ultra-high-efficiency holograms without damaging the gelatin of the photographic emulsion, and at the same time producing a tonally accurate flare-free result. The improved image quality and reduced noise has meant that much larger image volumes can be recorded in the holograms. It has been encouraging to hear visitors to the university assure us that our holograms are 'better than anything seen in America'.

Light Sources and Viewers

With these improvements in the creation of holograms, acceptable-quality image reconstruction is possible with non-laser light sources, provided that the layout of the object and optical components have been arranged with this requirement in mind. The full coherence of the laser light, necessary for recording, is not essential for viewing, and other sources which approximate to monochromatic point sources may be used; our work has been centred on sodium and mercury lamps, and also quartz iodine bulbs.

The sodium lamp is cheap and convenient; the lamp and choke may be bought for around £16, for a user who is prepared to mount and wire them himself. Otherwise, it may be bought from an educational supplier, ready mounted, boxed, and wired, for around £66. The two sodium D lines are too close to be separable by filter, causing slight blurring of the image, and, depending on the aperture of the source, a compromise must be reached between clarity and brightness: the larger the aperture, the brighter the image, the smaller the aperture, the better defined the image.

Better image quality may be obtained by using a mercury source: since the lines in the mercury spectrum are well separated, it is simple to extract one line, usually the green, by a filter. An inexpensive 'street lamp' type bulb may be used at a cost little more than for sodium, with the advantage of long lamp life, or alternatively a point-source laboratory mercury lamp will further improve the result obtained, but at the cost of shorter lamp life and higher expense (around £200 complete for a laboratory point-source mercury lamp).

Under certain circumstances, particularly with the 'real image' or 'projection' type of hologram, discussed later, a slide-projector fitted with a quartz halogen bulb and with a suitable filter in the slide holder can give acceptable results, but this is best reserved for holograms in which the image is located close to the plane of the plate.

Our present experience indicates that for good quality and brightness, we would recommend the mercury source; for cheapness where near blackout is available, the sodium; and for specialist applications where the finest detail has to be read, and partial blackout is available, then a small laser in a self-contained viewer box would be the answer. (One may obtain a 2 mW laser for such applications for around £200.)

We are also investigating the possibility of developing a self-contained viewer, in which source and hologram may be mounted in the same small box, as an alternative to the use of separate lamp and free-standing 'holoscreen' to support the hologram and provide a non-distracting black surround. It appears, however, that with presently available lamps, to bring the viewer down to acceptable size for portability and desk-top use might involve the use of unacceptably expensive optics.

The size of hologram used is another variable: the alternative to display holograms of 15 by 12 inch or even larger, viewed by groups of people, is to set a lamp in a corner of a room, and give each individual a small hologram, say three inch square.

Holography for Display and as a Visual Aid

Comparison with Other Three-Dimensional Methods

Whilst our intention has been to make hologram viewing simple, inexpensive and convenient for the user, we would not deny that the making of holograms is a complex technology, requiring the services of a specialist laboratory. (For example, most of our display holograms are made with a 4 watt argon ion laser or a one joule ruby pulse laser, costing around £16,000 and £25,000 respectively.)

In view of the complexities and the capital cost of the equipment for making holograms, one may well ask what are the advantages which holography offers compared with the other methods of three-dimensional viewing.

Stereoscopic pictures are well known, and can be made in colour if necessary, but the information they convey is little better than that obtained from two photographs. If the observer moves his head, he does not obtain a different view; he cannot look around the object; he cannot place a pointer through parts of the image, or locate them by a non-parallax method, and he cannot easily measure distance between points apparently at different distances from him. Furthermore, the necessity for observing through some kind of spectacles can be distracting and give a sense of falseness.

Lenticular screens vary widely in quality and cost but they are subject to the same limitations as stereoscopy, and show the 'stepping-back' effect as the observer moves continuously. The possible depth which may be shown with any reality is severely limited also.

Stereoscopy and lenticular screens, however, both have the telling advantage that they do not require special light sources for illumination.

Another type of three-dimensional presentation, if not usually thought of as such, is to use the real object or its model. Naturally this is the obvious course where the object or model is available, but many objects are too large or expensive or fragile to be brought to the classroom, and good models can be very costly. Large selections of models deteriorate and present storage problems; one box of holograms can store the equivalent of several shelves of models. Once a single model has been made, as many holograms as are desired may easily be made from it.

347

Present Display Potential and Features

Most holograms are of the virtual image kind, in which the observer looks through the plate and sees the image behind it. He can look around the object within the limits of the aperture of the plate, and when large plates are used, several people may view the image simultaneously. The hologram is the only three-dimensional method to give a truly spatial image; a teacher can point out features inside the image, and accurately measure distances between points contained in the image; the hologram presents an infinite number of three-dimensional images, seen from the infinite number of possible viewpoints.

The conventional or 'virtual image' hologram may be used in a second process to make a 'real image' or 'projection' hologram, in which the observer, still looking towards the plate, sees the image either partly behind and partly in front of the plate, or alternatively formed completely in front of the plate.

It has been found that this kind of hologram has tremendous 'impact' and some useful features, including a higher tolerance of the lower coherence of non-laser sources than the pure virtual image hologram, so that filtered quartz iodine illumination may readily be used, but unfortunately we are working at the limits of the available technology here, and there are severe constraints upon the size of scene which can be portrayed, and on the number of people who can simultaneously observe the image without severe distortion. We anticipate significant improvements in this particular field in the near future.

Multiple-exposure holograms permit the recording of more than one image on the plate, and these may be viewed separately. This enables a three-dimensional scene to be built up in stages; or front and rear views of objects to be quickly compared; or the superimposition of section planes lying through solid objects; or the insides of components seen through outer casings. In these ways holograms can show features not generally available with a model. It is also possible to insert a pointer through the image to reach parts that would be inaccessible with the real thing. Many of the developments necessary to achieve high quality holograms of this nature have still to be carried out, since there has been very little effort in this particular field of holographic technology so far.

Emerging and Future Possibilities

We are aware that the technology is still in its infancy, and that limitations remain to be overcome, for example, full-colour holograms have yet to be developed beyond the crude prototype stage, and the present necessity with conventional holograms to show objects at approximately their real size means that the easiest way of making a hologram of a building, for example, is to make a model first, and make the hologram of the model. Methods are beginning to emerge, however, in which this problem may be overcome; these include the multiplex hologram, which by using a cine-film as an intermediate stage between objects and hologram, enables a reduction in scale of large objects and also the viewing of the resulting hologram in white light. We would eventually hope to see the production of improved light sources, and possibly a printing process for mass-producing holograms. One experiment of this kind has been carried out successfully in America, but if it became commercially practicable, a dramatic reduction in hologram costs would follow.

Trials, Reactions and Projects

At present, we feel in something of a 'chicken-and-egg' situation; teachers would be the more ready to use holograms in teaching trials and see their full potential if they were readily available in large variety and at low cost, and rather more convenient for classroom use, whereas manufacturers would make the necessary investment and development if they were convinced of the scale of the demand.

Many demonstrations have been given to teachers and pupils in Leicestershire, and to other institutions, and at a seminar in London to representatives of many Industrial Training Boards. A high level of interest and enthusiasm has been aroused, but naturally the evolvement of teaching trials of this new medium with the associated curriculum development work is slower to take place. Reactions so far indicate that the greatest value of holography as a visual aid may lie in the more sophisticated applications which exploit its unique features, such as the multiple-exposure type, or holograms displaying statistical data in three-dimensional space, or showing 3D vector force fields, or sections through a solid object; and the example in the new project described below to assist the understanding of the relations between two-dimensional engineering drawings and the three-dimensional objects they represent. Sixth form projects are being established in several Leicestershire schools in subject areas including physical and biological sciences, craft and design, geography and mathematics, to give students and teachers active involvement not only in the development of materials for holographic display, but also experience of the production of sets of holograms for use in teaching. A wide variety of holograms have already been made in the project for demonstration or loan to schools to illustrate the applications of holography to many areas of the curriculum, for example, to aid the teaching of three-dimensional geometry, molecular structures, complex mechanisms and so on. Since the number of students who can view a single hologram at once is limited, we are not overlooking the potential of holography as an aid in courses of individualized learning or revision.

Training Services Agency Project

One of the most pleasing aspects of the work has been the association between the Leicestershire educational project at Loughborough University and the Training Services Agency, who have seen our developments in holography, and have felt that here is a potential training aid which should be given a realistic trial.

The Agency is to finance a controlled feasibility study to test the effectiveness of holography, and believes that it could prove to have a wide potential in many different industries. Already a number of organizations, apart from those involved in the feasibility study, have expressed interest in the technique and its possible applications, particularly where trainees find difficulty in learning with existing media which are not capable of accurately representing three-dimensional subjects. The pilot study will use holograms as an aid to the syllabus for the training of foundry technicians at the West Bromwich College of Commerce and Technology. The study will be rigorously monitored by using balanced control and experimental groups of students on the TEC course at the college. Production of the holograms to be used in the experimental course will be taking place during the summer of 1977, and the pilot study will take place during the 1977/78 academic year. Examples of topics to be taught with the aid of holography include the appreciation of engineering drawings, the relation of inside and outside shapes of castings and moulds, and changes in shape and dimension of metals as they cool during casting. We look forward to the results of this pilot project with interest and enthusiasm.

With the developments that have taken place during the lifetime of this project, and the newly emerging applications and trials, we feel that holography is now poised to take its place as a valuable educational aid in addition to its role as a tool for the engineer and a curiosity for the many.

The Work of the Educational Techniques Subject Group of The Chemical Society in the Spread of Educational Technology to Teachers and Trainers

P J Hills, R B Moyes

The Educational Techniques Subject Group is one of the three subject groups associated with the Education Division of The Chemical Society. It was set up with two main aims:

1. To provide up-to-date information to teachers and trainers on the methods, techniques and materials available for chemical education;
2. To originate new materials for use in chemical education.

In this short paper we should like to describe how the Group has tried to fulfil these aims to date and to indicate some of its plans for the future. This is not an account of a theoretical study, but rather an account of the way in which a subject group of a learned society has worked in a very practical way until it has become a recognised forum for chemical educators at all levels.

The first of our aims, to provide up-to-date information, has been carried out by organizing national and regional meetings which have provided an opportunity not only to listen to new (and old) ideas, but also to discuss their use in schools, universities and colleges. The proceedings of several of these have been published, for example, *Alternatives to the Lecture* (Haynes *et al*, 1973), *Independent Learning in Tertiary Science Education* (Furniss and Parsonage, 1976) and *Educational Techniques in the Teaching of Chemistry* (Hills, 1976).

An increasing emphasis on the student as central to the learning process has led to the development of learning aids laboratories, of which there are now about 15 in chemistry departments throughout the country, and to a demand from both students and lecturers for more resource material suitable for independent and guided use by students. The Educational Techniques Subject Group has initiated a programme of work in chemistry which attempts to explore the present situation, obtain information on existing material and develop learning materials both at sixth-form and university levels.

Following an initial meeting at the University of Aston in 1976, a one-day symposium and exhibition on learning aids laboratories and resource centres was organized as part of The Chemical Society Autumn Meeting in Sheffield. This meeting showed clearly the considerable and increasing range of interest in this area. One central theme emerging from the meeting was the need for an exchange of information on material already produced and a mechanism whereby existing materials can be made readily available to potential users.

One possible solution to some of these problems is being pursued by the Educational Techniques Subject Group's Media Exchange Project, which has been given a small grant from The Chemical Society's Appeal Fund to set up a pilot scheme for the exchange of unpublished resource materials between univeristy and polytechnic chemistry departments. A considerable range of such material has been produced in chemistry departments, and these are often made available to students in departmental learning aids laboratories or resource centres. The production of such materials is expensive in terms of both time and resources and this has a number of consequences:

1. the production of all the desired material usually cannot be carried out within one department;
2. the production of identical, or very similar, material in several different departments should be avoided if possible to avoid wasteful duplication of effort;
3. the location of existing material should be more widely known.

A previous publication of the Group, *Catalogue of Unpublished Teaching Materials in Chemistry* (Moyes, 1972), edited by Dr R B Moyes, Chemistry Department, University of Hull, has already contributed to this aim. A primary aim of the project is that existing material should be readily available without the initial substantial expenditure of time required for production. The co-ordinators of the project, Dr B S Furniss and Dr C R McHugh of the School of Chemistry, Thames Polytechnic, would therefore like to hear from lecturers who have produced material which might be suitable for inclusion in the collection, and also from those who have a need for resource material.

The Group's interest in resources and resource centres also links in with its second aim, to produce materials for use in chemical education. Here there are two main developments.

The first of these, described in the leaflet *A New Voice in Chemistry*, copies of which could be found on our exhibition stand in the member's exhibition, is concerned with the production of a series of audio-tapes with accompanying booklets called Chemistry Cassettes. Copies of these can be obtained from the General Editor of the series, P D Groves, Chemistry Department, University of Aston in Birmingham.

These cassettes present authoritative accounts of various aspects of chemistry, prepared and spoken by distinguished chemists. The titles at present available are:

CC1: *Heavy Metals as Contaminants of the Human Environment* By Derek Bryce-Smith, Professor of Organic Chemistry, University of Reading.
CC2: *Some Aspects of the Electrochemistry of Solutions* By Graham Hills, Professor of Physical Chemistry, University of Southampton.
CC3: *Some Organic Reaction Pathways* By Peter Sykes, Fellow and Director of Studies, Christ's College, Cambridge.
CC4: *Symmetry in Chemistry* By Sidney Kettle, Professor of Inorganic and Theoretical Chemistry, University of East Anglia.

Each tape is accompanied by a booklet containing diagrams, equations and other material discussed by the speaker.

The second development in the preparation of materials for chemical education is a project concerned to prepare a series of resource boxes in chemistry. Modern teaching techniques draw increasingly on a variety of resources and media. However, a teacher in a school or a college or university lecturer may find it very difficult to locate and subsequently assemble the wide range of materials that are currently available for teaching a particular topic. A resource box can help to overcome this and can contain a variety of resources and information on a topic.

Our first chemistry resource box is on 'plastics'. This contains the following:

1. (a) A labelled collection of common plastic objects;
   (b) Labelled specimens of raw materials;
   (c) Flow diagrams on the production of synthetic fibres and plastics.

2. Photostats of some original papers on the development of plastics and synthetic fibres.
3. Some suggested experiments, eg for identification of common plastics and synthetic fibres.
4. A comprehensive list of readily available audio-visual aids on plastics and synthetic fibres.
5. Where to go to obtain further information on plastics and synthetic fibres.
6. A bibliography on plastics.
7. A guide (for the student using the box for individual study) on order, to obtain the maximum benefit from it.

It is our intention to develop a series of chemistry resource boxes. At present boxes on chemical kinetics, crystal structures, proteins and surface chemistry are in preparation. A number of 'plastics' boxes are currently undergoing trials in a number of institutions.

We would be most interested to hear from anyone who would either like to help us to prepare a box or to evaluate one. Please write to Monica Seeley, Learning Aids Laboratory, Chemistry Department, Queen Elizabeth College, Campden Hill, London W8 7AH.

We hope that this short account has given you some indication of the work of the Educational Techniques Subject Group in the spread of educational technology to teachers and trainers. There has not been time to talk in detail about the projects described, especially in regard to the evaluation of some of the work. If anyone has a particular interest in any of these areas we hope that they will contact either the people mentioned or will write directly to us. Incidentally, some indication of the spread of the work of our Group is provided by the list of countries where our chemistry cassettes are now in use. These include: Australia, Austria, Belgium, Canada, Denmark, Fiji, France, Germany, Greece, Holland, Hong Kong, India, Eire, Italy, Japan, New Zealand, Norway, Singapore, South Africa, Spain, Sweden, Switzerland, Turkey, UK, USA, Venezuela and Zambia.

References

Furniss, B S and Parsonage, J R (eds) (1976) 'Independent Learning in Tertiary Science Education' The Chemical Society, London.
Haynes, L J, Hills, P J, Palmer, C R and Trickey, D S (eds) (1973) 'Alternatives to the Lecture in Chemistry' The Chemical Society, London.
Hills, P J (ed) (1976) 'Educational Techniques in the Teaching of Chemistry and Other Sciences' The Chemical Society, London.
Moyes, R B (ed) (1972) 'A Catalogue of Unpublished Teaching Resource Material in Chemistry' The Chemical Society, London.

The Roles of Tertiary Teaching Units in Australian Universities

W C Hall

Almost all Australian universities and many colleges of advanced education now have tertiary teaching units. Australia leads the world in this area of educational technology. The formation of the units resulted from three main pressures: politics; students' associations; and a minority of academic staff. A variety of organizational structures has been used in their formation and it is possible to identify six organizational models which will be discussed in the paper. The history of the development of the units and a detailed analysis of the first three years of one of them, the Advisory Centre for University Education, are covered in the paper. Examples of the work of the Centre, including its roles in curriculum development and curriculum evaluation, are given.

Although each unit reflects the interests and skills of its staff (but, particularly, of its director) common aims can be identified. These include assisting with the improving of teaching and learning within the institution, conducting applied educational research, offering an audio-visual production service, offering confidential advice on teaching to individuals and to departments, running in-service courses for members of staff and conducting surveys.

The Development of Teaching Units

The first two teaching units to be established in Australia were those at the University of Melbourne and at the University of New South Wales. Both were formed in 1961. (Four years later the University Teaching Methods Unit of the Department of Higher Education at the University of London was set up with a grant from the Leverhulme Trust.)

Other units were quickly established in Australia at Macquarie University (1967), Monash University (1969), The University of Western Australia (1968) and Queensland University (1973). Now 12 of Australia's 19 universities have tertiary teaching units; those without are the smallest institutions with one surprising exception: the University of Sydney has yet to form one.

The Australian Vice-Chancellor's Committee produced guidelines for the formation of tertiary teaching units in 1973 (AVCC, 1973). Their report justifies the formation of the units in the following way:

'In Australian universities, as in those of many other countries, there is considerable concern about the effectiveness of educational programmes and processes.
'There is now, more than ever before, pressure on administrators to examine their institution critically — its objectives and processes — and to effect changes where these are deemed necessary. There is pressure on teachers to improve their courses of study; to develop effective ways of facilitating students' learning; and to evaluate their own performance as well as that of their students. The present concern is in response to conditions which challenge universities everywhere; conditions such as:

(i)   the increased number and diversity of students;

(ii)   the critical and often articulate student body;

(iii)   the explosion of knowlege;

(iv)   the changing community values and expectations;

(v)   the changing requirements of professions, of employers of graduates, and of governments;

(vi)   the institutional characteristics of some universities, their size and emphasis on activities other than teaching.

'In response to these and other emerging conditions, universities have begun to study themselves, applying the processes of scientific inquiry to their own institutions — to the input, process and output of universities. To assist in this process a number of universities have set up special centres, specifically charged with the responsibility of carrying out institutional research and development, with the objective of improving our understanding of institutional characteristics, and facilitating change or improvements. A special task of these centres has been to initiate improvements in instruction to improve the quality of the teaching/learning process.'

The Vice Chancellor's Report suggested three guidelines for the setting up of the units:

1. units should be distinct and autonomous;
2. staff should be accorded normal academic status;
3. units should be organizationally linked to instructional service units (ie audio-visual media).

Although I believe that the second guideline is not contentious, the other two are debatable and will depend upon the particular model which is used by the institution when setting up the unit.

Models for Tertiary Teaching Units

A detailed discussion of the six models which can be identified has been described (Hall, 1977) and so a summary only will be given here. I have labelled the models as follows:

1. independent model (units are independent of all other departments and of the university's administration);
2. departmental model (units are part of a larger department, usually the Department of Education);
3. co-ordinator model (units are divided into three separate functions: audio-visual, training and advisory, research and development);
4. committee model (a committee runs courses and directs research);
5. faculty member model (educationalists are seeded throughout the university in different faculties);
6. central administration model (courses and research are centrally administered).

The independent model is favoured by the Australian Vice-Chancellor's Committee and is the most common in Australia. A detailed description of the model in action has been prepared by the author (Hall, 1975).

The University of Melbourne teaching unit is part of the Faculty of Education. It has adopted the departmental model.

The University of New England has not got a teaching unit and so has adopted the committee model. Newcastle University has recently appointed a medical educationalist to the Medical Faculty and so this could be the start of the faculty member model at that institution. The co-ordinator and central administration models cannot be found in Australia although the latter has been adopted by Swedish Universities.

Functions of Tertiary Teaching Units

I have described the functions of units in another paper (Hall, 1977) and so a list will suffice here:

1. running courses for members of staff;
2. assisting with curriculum development and evaluation;
3. doing applied research;
4. giving advice to individuals, departments and faculties;
5. providing an audio-visual media service;
6. operating an objective testing service;
7. supplying information;
8. facilitating communication between various sections of the university population;
9. acting as an educational catalyst;
10. serving as a link between institutions and the educational community at large.

All of these tasks are undertaken by my own unit, the Advisory Centre for University Education at the University of Adelaide and examples of (1) and (2) to illustrate this are given below.

During 1976 we ran 11 courses and conducted 15 seminars. Over 600 enrolments (about 400 different people) were received for these activities. 24 of these people attended our one-year course in tertiary curriculum which has two main aims:

1. To consider research evidence relevant to tertiary curriculum studies (including teaching and assessment).
2. To learn and to practise skills which are relevant to university teaching.

The content of the course is as follows:

Unit 1 The Curriculum Process

Models of the curriculum process.
Ways of teaching: learning models (a).
Ways of teaching: learning models (b).
Individualized learning.
Motivation; creativity.
The organizing of content.
Taxonomies of educational objectives.
Curriculum process: practical constraints.

Unit 2 Practical Techniques

Small group teaching.
Small group teaching; demonstrating.
The lecture.
Lecture techniques: microteaching workshop (a).
Lecture techniques: microteaching workshop (b).
Using audio-visual media.
Audio-visual workshop (a).
Audio-visual workshop (b).

Unit 3 Evaluation and Assessment

Assessment as a part of the educative process.
Methods of assessment.
Assessment workshop.
An introduction to educational statistics (a).
Evaluating university courses.
Questionnaire design.
An introduction to educational statistics (b).
The curriculum process: case studies of curriculum development and evaluation.

The main text for the course is one of our publications, *University Teaching* (Hall and Cannon, 1975).

Another of our publications, *Evaluating Courses* (Hall, 1977) describes our approach to curriculum evaluation. This is summarized below in terms of the five main stages we pass through and a brief description of our activity as independent evaluators.

Stage	Evaluator's possible actions
1. Determining the questions that need answering about a course.	Interviewing staff. Interviewing students who have completed the course. Reading departmental literature. Direct observation.
2. Evaluation schedule	Departmental meeting.
3. Applying techniques to obtain preliminary answers to questions.	Administering general questionnaires to students and/or to staff. Discussions with groups of students and/or with staff. Direct observation.
4. Applying further techniques to obtain more specific answers.	Sound or video recordings. Specific questionnaires administered. (Questionnaires at this stage are usually open-ended.) Interviewing groups of carefully selected students. 'Living' with an average student. Interviewing staff. Direct observation.
5. Descriptive report	Departmental meeting.

We have undertaken 15 full-scale curriculum evaluations since our formation at the end of 1973 and a further three are being carried out this year.

The Australian Experience: a Critical Review

In work that depends so much on personalities, on the ability to communicate clearly with non-educationalists, and on the skill of unit staff to break down some of the preconceived ideas of their academic colleagues in other departments, it is not surprising that the Australian tertiary teaching units have met with a mixed reception. A few have antagonized staff with their dogmatic approach to educational technology, some have reinforced the prejudices of colleagues, and (as in every subject area) there has also been a degree of incompetence. Units have become departments of higher education research, neglecting their advisory roles in some instances.

In the majority of cases the apparent influence on a campus has been negligible. Indeed, the time is ripe for an evaluation of the units — a suggestion bitterly opposed by the majority who attended a recent meeting of unit directors, which is, in itself, probably significant.

Not surprisingly, I would claim that the Advisory Centre for University Education at the University of Adelaide has become one of the successful units. The reasons for this would probably be better discussed at a theological conference than this one! Nevertheless, an attempt will be made to summarize our first three years.

Firstly, the personality of all of our staff has been of paramount importance. Patience, willingness to undertake the most mundane task (eg demonstrating the use of an overhead projector) and the ability to respect the confidence of those who seek advice are essential characteristics.

All of our courses have been of practical use to participants. Examples have been drawn from tertiary education (even in such courses as 'Learning Theory') and there has been an emphasis on participant involvement. Also, we have attempted to make our courses a model (not the model!) of course design.

In curriculum development we have adopted the stance that rarely is there a best way to do anything in education. We have never interfered with the decision-making process; our role has been to raise fundamental questions for consideration by course planners. Many of these questions are listed and discussed in two of our publications (Hall, 1976; Hall and Cannon, 1977).

Our research is never esoteric; it is always practical and usually problem-solving. Being a university department, we publish like any other academics. Our aim is to help people to help themselves, never to pose as the tertiary education experts in which the whole truth resides but acquainting people with alternatives, helping them to be aware of research in the field and offering to assist with development and evaluation.

Every university department has now been in contact with us, and so we think that our approach is one that seems to work.

References

AVCC (1973) 'A Report on Australian University Centres for Higher Education Research and Development by the Directors of the Existing Centres' Australian Vice-Chancellors' Committee, Canberra, Australia.

Hall, W C (1975) 'Pretending Not to be an Educational Technologist' in 'Programmed Learning & Educational Technology' November.

Hall, W C (1976) 'Course Planning' Advisory Centre for University Education, The University of Adelaide.

Hall, W C (1977) 'Models for Tertiary Teaching Units' Australian Journal of Education (in print).

Hall, W C (1977) 'Evaluating Courses' Advisory Centre for University Education, The University of Adelaide.

Hall, W C and Cannon, R A (1975) 'University Teaching' Advisory Centre for University Education, The University of Adelaide.

Hall, W C and Cannon, R A (1977) 'University Curricula' Advisory Centre for University Education, The University of Adelaide.

Staff Resources and Innovation–
Open Learning for Polytechnic
Teachers

I J Winfield

What's in a Name

If you set out to design an in-service staff resources programme whose general brief is to promote the development of training of lecturing staff, you are faced with choosing a set of strategies from any number of attractive and well-tried alternatives.

For example, a recent survey of the content of in-service courses offered for polytechnic teachers (Harding, 1974) found that no single topic was considered in more than half of them. High on the league-table of contents were found: the promotion of the use of audio-visual aids; topics concerned with the role of the teacher; topics concerned with the specification of educational objectives and with methods of student assessment.

Even, however, before selecting objectives, a programme must select for itself a name.

A polytechnic programme to promote staff resources, starting 'from scratch' such as the example discussed in this paper should, at the beginning, select for itself a calculatedly non-alienating title. Cantrell (1972) found that teaching staff objected to centralized units having the words 'training' or 'staff development' included in their titles.

At the North Staffordshire Polytechnic an Open Working Party was formed to debate the issue of developing staff resources. The Working Party commenced life as an open forum for discussion, but ultimately found itself implementing and monitoring the progress of a specific tool designed both to enhance staff resources and to promote innovation among polytechnic staff — the Staff Resources Directory.

This paper explains the history and reasons for the choice of a directory and examines the progress in achieving these goals.

The Evolution of Objectives of the Working Party

Many tertiary education establishments find themselves with both teaching and material resources spread over a wide geographical area. The North Staffordshire Polytechnic is no exception to this, finding itself on a split site where main buildings are located some 16 miles apart; as well as possessing the familiar scattering of annexes, satellite institutions and the like.

Uppermost in the initial deliberations of the Working Party were preoccupations with not only the content of the programme to be offered, but also the form. For example:

1. If a programme of staff development were designed with services offered in some central location, what proportion of staff could realistically be

358

expected to use such facilities?

2. Alternatively, could a programme be physically taken to staff concerned — designed, that is, on a dispersed model? In this case could the Working Party muster the necessary technological resources to meet potential demand?

Often, in the early discussion about the content of the programme, the issue of media resources was brought up. The ensuing discussion had a familiar sound. The constraints operating against individual staff adopting an experimental and innovative approach to teaching techniques and/or, media were frequently mentioned. This is a feature documented, for instance, by Zeckhauser (1972) who noted that perhaps certain features may characterize educational institutions in general. Zeckhauser observes:

'The education system itself has not been overly responsive to the media or its untapped potential. Innovative practices are discussed at educational conventions and in professional journals; seldom are they readily adopted. This unresponsiveness to media innovation (and not only to media) may be explained by both the inertia of the educational system and by the attitudinal bias of those within it.'

The debate often centred on the features of academic life felt to operate against individual innovation, for instance the organization of educational establishments into departments. It was noted that departments can develop into independent and relatively segregated sub-units within educational institutions, becoming themselves resistant to change (a point, in fact, noted by Evans, Hopper and Littlejohn, 1971). Likewise it was observed that membership of a particular department could contribute directly to staff attitudes towards new techniques and media (the relationship between department and attitudes to programmed instruction was examined by Hopper, Evans and Littlejohn, 1974).

Objectives as Defined

The overall objective to emerge from the deliberations of the Working Party was to promote in staff despite the observed constraints, the personal willingness to innovate and gain wider experience in four defined areas of staff resources. The Working Party defined four discrete areas.

1. The area of administrative experience/course promotion.
2. The area of educational media and technology.
3. The area of methods of student assessment.
4. The area of different forms of teaching/lecturing.

It was maintained that the individual decision to adopt an innovative approach to teaching or to try new media was not itself a single event. It was, it was felt, a process characterized by a number of distinct stages. Clearly 'awareness' and 'mild interest' in a technique or media must be experienced by an individual before he or she is able to 'evaluate' its worth, or to 'try' it for a period.

Considering this multi-stage process prompted questions about how the diffusion of new forms of teaching and educational technology take place within educational institutions in general.

A medium of some importance was felt to be formal and informal conversations among members of staff. It was speculated that the social network of conversations might be the vehicle that carried staff through the stages of the decision-process mentioned above. In support of the importance of conversations to academics the research of Halsey and Trow (1971) was cited. Halsey and Trow found, when documenting the process of diffusion of subject-knowledge among academics in British universities, that conversations with colleagues were ranked as second in importance to formal academic journals.

The objectives of the Working Party were finally defined in the following way:

'Given the constraints of geographical dispersal of staff and the organizational
constraints of departmental partisanship, conversations among staff members on any or
all of the four topics areas will be fostered in such a way as to promote personal
innovation and experimentation.'

Skill Exchange

The objectives of the Working Party once defined, then they involved members in
discussion about the nature of expertise or experience-sharing among staff. The
system whereby individuals who wish to acquire skills or expertise in a defined
field, gain appropriate contact with acknowledged experts or skill models
prepared to instruct them, has been termed a 'skill exchange' (Illich 1971).
According to the speculations of Illich, if such a system could be set up the
resultant learning would be decentralized, under the control of learners and 'skill
models', and would be non-hierarchical in form. Individuals would identify their
own learning needs and seek out a person from whom they could learn the skill in
question. Illich argues that such a system of skill-transfer and learning can be
workable only to the degree that the participants, in non-coercive manner, want to
make it work. Illich (1973) maintains that the participative spirit of such a system
for the free exchange of skills be termed 'convivial':

'I choose the term "conviviality" to designate the opposite of industrial productivity. I
intend it to mean autonomous and creative intercourse among persons, and the
intercourse of persons with their environment . . . I consider conviviality to be individual
freedom realized in personal inter-dependence and, as such, an intrinsic ethical value. I
believe that, in any society, as conviviality is reduced below a certain level, no amount of
industrial productivity can effectively satisfy the needs it creates among society's
members.'

But What of Polytechnic Teachers?

Could elements of this somewhat idealized system be directly employed by the
Working Party? Could staff be asked to name their experience and teaching skills
and other staff, in need of these skills, be placed in contact with them? Could the
more meaningful flow of ideas and the willingness to innovate be prompted by
developing such a learning system?

These questions could only be answered by constructing and circulating a Staff
Resources Directory.

The Staff Resources Directory — A Retooling of Resources?

A directory, it was envisaged, could become a tool, the stock-in-trade of the
individual lecturer in the same way that administrative handbooks or directories of
hardware are considered as tools. The difference, of course, lay in the nature of
access to the resources detailed by the directory, for each member of staff was to
be seen as a resource to be of potential use to another member. A list of equipment
or material resources, broadly speaking, allows us access at our bidding. A person,
however, can become a skill resource of potential value to others only when he
consents to do so.

An introductory letter (Figure 1) was circulated to all full-time teaching staff
(425) in June 1976.

Staff Resources Questionnaire

Working on a brief from the Academic Board Resources Sub-Committee an Open Working Party is now considering ways of promoting staff development. One area examined is that of the pressing problem of communication of individual teaching expertise and the knowledge of particular teaching methods from lecturer to lecturer — the often arbitrary contacts of staff room, course acquaintance etc, are all that we currently possess.

A catalogue is now being compiled locating staff that have experience, however limited, with various categories of teaching method which they would be willing to talk about and share with other interested staff, on an informal basis. This is the objective of the questionnaire (Figure 2).

It is intended to 'pool' returned questionnaires which will then be re-circulated to all staff in booklet form for easy reference.

Finally, if sufficient demand warrants it, the working party could arrange short talks, or demonstrations of different methods and media, for interested staff.

Figure 1.

Overleaf was printed the Staff Resources Questionnaire (Figure 2).

After a follow-up reminder 157 completed returns were obtained. The frequency of the responses are displayed in Figure 3.

Results of Staff Resources Questionnaire

Recorded experience, and staff wishing to know more about certain techniques and media, (Figure 3) bear similarities to the results of a survey of the use of training techniques and media by 550 firms, (Romiszowski and Ellis, 1974).

The polytechnic survey reveals, perhaps, the technological and vocational bias of many of the college courses. From Figure 3 can also be seen several areas of high current staff interest. These will serve as targets for the provision of seminars and workshops by the Open Working Party.

The Directory Circulation: Does it Work?

A further questionnaire was distributed to participating staff prior to the circulation of the directory. This sampled the frequency of conversations about techniques and media amongst staff; the specific educational topics discussed; the number of persons involved, and the length of the conversations. After the directory has been in circulation the exercise will be repeated at the appropriate time. A measure of gross behavioural change as a direct function of the directory may then be revealed by the comparison of aggregate statistics.

Finally, it is intended to monitor the actual mode of use of the directory, as well as the evolution of any possible reward system for the dissemination of experience, by participant observation of the network system in action.

The author is grateful for the assistance given by staff and students of the Department of Graphic Design and Printing, North Staffordshire Polytechnic.

References

Cantrell, E G (1972) 'Attitudes of Junior Medical School Staff towards a Proposed Course in Teaching' Report to the Social Science Research Council. Mimeo 64pp.

Administration Experience	Please tick if you have any experience of these	Please tick if you would like to know more
Arranging educational visits, transport etc, eg art exhibitions, theatre visits		
Arranging student residential periods		
Arranging field work periods eg geography, mining		
Arranging sandwich periods eg industrial placements		
Educational Media		
Audio-tape		
Slides		
Tape-slide synchronisation unit		
Film: integration of films into teaching eg 'saftey' films		
manufacture of films		
TV and Video-tape: manufacture of video-tapes eg in-service training		
use of pre-recorded programmes		
Overhead projector transparencies, animation, etc		
Computer-assisted games		
Computer graphics terminals		
Computer-assisted programmed learning		
Programmed materials eg texts, workbooks		
Methods of Assessment		
Open-book examinations		
Continuous assessment		
'Seen' examinations		
Projects		
Objective tests eg multiple choice		
Methods of promoting class participation		
Case Study		
Rôle-Play		
Gaming simulation		
Brain-storming, synectics, buzz groups, syndicate work		
Others		
Language Laboratory		
Writing behavioural objectives		

Please indicate any other experience you have had:

Figure 2. *Staff Resources Questionnaire*

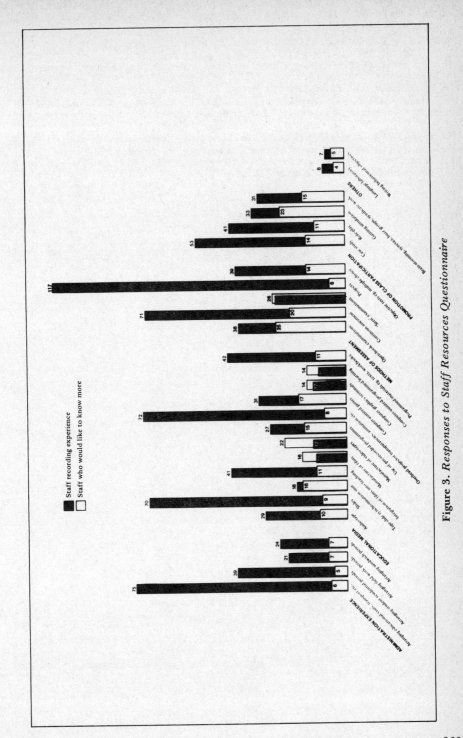

Figure 3. Responses to Staff Resources Questionnaire

Staff recording experience

Staff who would like to know more

363

Evans, J, Hopper, E, and Littlejohn G (1971) 'Possibilities for Instruction Innovation in Higher Education' Visual Education, December.

Halsey, A H and Trow, M (1971) 'The British Academics' Faber, London.

Harding, A G (1974) 'The Training of Polytechnic Teachers' Society for Research in Higher Education.

Hopper, E, Evans J, and Littlejohn G (1974) 'Staff Attitudes to Instructional Innovation in Higher Education' Programmed Learning and Educational Technology', 11, 3, 140–155.

Illich, I D (1971) 'Deschooling Society' Calder & Boyars, London.

Illich, I D (1973) 'Tools for Conviviality' Calder & Boyars, London.

Romiszowski, A J and Ellis, P (1974) 'The Use of Innovative Techniques and Media in Industrial Training' 'Programmed Learning and Educational Technology 11, 1, 39–50.

Zeckhauser, S H (1972) 'A look at the Media in Higher Education' 'Programmed Learning and Educational Technology', 9, 6, 312–323.

Educational Technology–Persuading the Teachers

C R McHugh, J R Parsonage

Since 1971 the School of Chemistry at Thames Polytechnic has offered a fellowship in chemical education which has been held successively by the authors.

The fellowship is postdoctoral and the holders came to it directly on completion of a research degree in chemistry. This fact, and the association of teaching duties with the fellowship, has allowed us to work in an integrated and accepted fashion within the School and to act as a bridge between academic staff and external educational developments (Furniss, McHugh and Parsonage, 1976).

It has also enabled us to hold wide-ranging, structured discussions with the lecturers (N=20) of the School and we report here on their views concerning educational technology and the way in which it is communicated to them.

Commonsense and our own experience suggest that our School is not greatly different from physical science departments throughout Britain in the age-range, background and experience of its staff. We see this small-scale exercise as providing useful information as well as laying the groundwork for further studies.

In this paper we use the terms 'educational technology' and 'educational development' rather freely, because to most academics either can be taken to mean the range of educational equipment, techniques and organizational methods which are available to teachers at present. We also refer to 'educational research', meaning those parts of this activity which seek to provide some theoretical or empirical basis for making changes in current educational practice.

To set the results of the investigation in context, it is necessary to give something of the history of formalized educational development at Thames Polytechnic.

The growing use of audio-visual aids in the polytechnic and the possibly wasteful duplication of equipment and specialists in different departments led to the establishment in 1968 of a Central Service Unit (CSU) for the whole college. In this unit were concentrated most of the hardware, photographers, graphic artists and television technicians.

This move was in accordance with the Brynmor Jones report on the use of audio-visual aids in higher scientific education in the UK (Brynmore Jones Committee, 1965).

One of the recommendations of this report was that a person should be appointed to direct each of these audio-visual centres and that 'to ensure that each unit has proper academic status, directors should receive immediately or attain later, a rank equivalent to that of senior lecturer . . .' (paragraph 471).

Obviously the committee intended central service unit heads to be more than mere technicians!

Paragraph 425 of the report says that 'information, consultation and instruction should be regarded as possibly the most useful and therefore the most important functions of the central service unit'.

As a result, in our college, the CSU found itself charged (according to the college prospectus of 1976) with the 'development of teaching methods and the production of audio-visual aids'.

Thus an attempt to rationalize the purchase and care of audio-visual equipment has created a unit which has also acquired the entirely different and vastly more difficult function of educational development.

Thames Polytechnic was not unique in its interpretation of the Brynmor Jones report. Confining ourselves to polytechnics alone we find numerous titles such as Media Resources Unit, Programmed Instruction Centre, Learning Resources Department and so forth. Scrutiny of the respective prospectuses reveals that all of these units have educational development as one of their functions, although in each case the title suggests that the unit was conceived for a different, specific purpose. Some polytechnics, such as North East London with its Centre for Curricular Development, have attempted to put audio-visual aids under the umbrella of educational development rather than vice versa.

This tacking on of educational development to the provision of audio-visual aids and programmed texts was facilitated by the way in which committees generally operate in educational institutions. A committee responsible for setting up a CSU within a college will inevitably contain committee 'educationalists' as well as more traditional academics. Its final recommendations for action will have to satisfy everyone to some degree and, in the nature of things, the duties and responsibilities of the new director will be only vaguely delimited. Thus the exact role of the unit will depend greatly on the interests of the person appointed to run it.

Initially the unit's role will be largely determined by the status within the college of the director. If, ignoring the Brynmor Jones report, it were decided to have a technician in charge of the unit, then the college would probably look for someone with a sound knowledge of the specification and maintenance of audio-visual equipment. As an additional qualification an applicant might have an enthusiastic, even missionary, interest in the very latest lecture theatre technology.

However, if a college decided to appoint an academic to such a post they would expect him, besides having some technical knowledge of audio-visual aids, to show a commitment to change in teaching methods. An academic may find it difficult to limit his view of change in teaching methods to a purely audio-visual one. Having been a teacher he will have views about teaching.

Once appointed, an educational developer having academic status can decide to play an active, missionary role or a passive, consultant role. The consultant role, if carried to extremes of passivity, depends for its success entirely on the motivation of the college academics towards changing their teaching methods. The missionary role, if pushed too far, can easily antagonize. It is important to note that an academic trying to cause teachers to change some fundamental part of their teaching will encounter much greater resistance than a technician trying to bring about the introduction of a new audio-visual technique. This is not only because the former change may be more profound but because academics resent other academics telling them what to do.

An obvious compromise is for the director to stick at first to the provision of audio-visual aids and to use the contact with teachers which this allows to further educational development tactfully.

This is by no means an easy task. In our case the centralization of audio-visual aids meant that some departments within the college initially lost, for example, their photographic facilities. It took time before the new unit could provide services as good as those the teachers had enjoyed before. To this extent, teachers were not likely to feel favourably disposed towards the new unit and the demands it made on space and resources in the college.

366

This rendered even more difficult the unit director's strategy of introducing discussion of educational factors; from the teachers' point of view here was someone who was forcing them into involved appraisals of their teaching when all that was asked for was a set of slides.

At the time of our interviews the educational development aspect had been divorced from the audio-visual aids provision and was now the responsibility of the Teaching, Research and Staff Development Committee, a sub-committee of the Academic Council.

The audio-visual aids service was working well by this time and there were no complaints about the slides, tapes, video-tapes and artwork being produced. One lecturer in fact maintained that the quality of this work was higher than that needed for educational purposes.

This historical background goes some way towards explaining why our lecturers were generally against any attempt to set up an educational development service. This rejection is summarized in Figure 1.

For	4
Consider it a waste of resources	12
Don't know	4
Total	20

Figure 1. *Views of the lecturers about setting up a polytechnic educational development service*

We defined an educational development service as being at least one full-time person with the responsibility for bringing general developments in teaching and learning methods to the attention of lecturers.

A frequently given reason for the low priority which our lecturers assigned to such a service was the impossibility of transforming educational developments in one subject into a useful basis for change in the teaching/learning of another. The underlying assumption in most cases seemed to be that there are no fundamental and applicable new facts about teaching being discovered. Perhaps it is a lot to expect that chemistry lecturers should have faith in educational research when so much questioning of the bases of this activity is being voiced by educational researchers themselves (Kempa, 1976).

Given that there was some subtle improvement in business administration teaching which could usefully be applied to chemistry teaching, doubts were expressed as to whether anybody would be in a position to notice it. Indeed, very few people would have the time and the interdisciplinary awareness usefully to keep such a vigil.

These views were accompanied by those attitudes best summarized by quotations such as:

'People on the educational technology bandwagon are generally not very impressive intellectually'

and

'There is a tendency among educational technologists to try to tell us how to teach'.

Yet changes do occur in the teaching/learning methods used by a school such as ours. Some of those that have occurred over the last five years are listed in Figure 2.

1. Short answer sections in examinations.
2. Modularization of courses.
3. Complementary studies.
4. Learning aids laboratories.
5. Science for humanities students.
6. Increased use of A/V aids in tutorials.

Figure 2. *Some changes in the teaching/learning of the School of Chemistry since 1972*

The question therefore arose how new ideas did enter the school, given the absence of an operational educational development service.

A channel mentioned independently by 11 of the 20 lecturers was their colleagues in the department. Further questioning (since the ideas had to reach these colleagues by some means) revealed the picture presented in Figure 3.

Conferences and courses	Colleagues
Reading	
Professional bodies	
Personal experience	
Own ideas	Self

Figure 3. *How academics see the manner in which new developments in chemistry teaching reach them*

The presence of a research fellow in education in the School, as well as that of one or two 'educationist' lecturers was pointed to many times as the right and proper catalyst for educational development. These individuals were seen as important channels through which new ideas could enter the school by 16 out of the 20 lecturers.

Returning to Figure 2 (our list of recent changes in the School) it can be said that of these changes the first three were due to pressures not entirely within the control of the members of the School. This cannot be said of the last three, however, and these occurred in precisely the manner perceived by the lecturers: a small nucleus was interested in chemical education, tried some changes and these were adopted to varying extents by the School as a whole. The importance of nuclei such as this was stressed by a recent report from the Nuffield Foundation (Nuffield Foundation Group, 1976).

Before looking more critically at this view of educational development we should mention some other opinions expressed by our lecturers on the role of centralized (that is non-departmental) educational development.

Four lecturers were in favour of a polytechnic-wide educational development service. One of these saw the main use of such a service as the training of new lecturers — who are often reticent about consulting older colleagues. Another saw the circulation of literature on education as an important function. The remaining two proponents of a central service saw it contributing also to the design of courses.

On being asked to do so, 10 of the 16 remaining lecturers made suggestions as to how the flow of information about educational research and development might be improved. These included an educational news sheet, to be organized by the library, an annual review lecture on teaching methods and the free circulation of the educational journals. (Some of these methods had been tried unsuccessfully in the polytechnic within the last five years.)

We have already stated that colleagues within the School play a major part in educational development — according to the model perceived by the lecturers themselves.

There are two limitations inherent in this model. One of these is the placing of the responsibility for the investigation of innovations on a small section of the academic community. In effect the majority of teachers are saying (again, direct quotations are appropriate):

'If someone is interested in pursuing educational development, let him.'

or

'People who want the information will get it.'

We found that the more administrative responsibility (and consequently the less involvement in teaching) that a person held within the School, the more inclined he was to state that every teacher has a duty, that it is part of his job to keep up-to-date on the available teaching and learning methods.

Our sample is insufficiently large for us to state that this is a definite trend, but if it is then the teacher tends to leave educational development to his colleagues while the administrator sees educational development as the duty of the teacher. In many cases administrators above departmental level see themselves as providers of finance for teachers to attend courses and conferences, rather than as initiators of change.

The second limitation is the fundamental irresponsibility of the role being assigned to colleague-innovators. A group of teachers within a school who have the unofficial duty of providing the lively counterpoint to the stolid flow of 'traditional' teaching are likely to adopt a certain approach to educational development. We shall call this the 'innovative' approach — it consists of examining the current literature in educational research and development and trying to find ideas which can be tried out in the innovators' own situation. This approach is not irresponsible in the context of the generation of new ideas — it is in fact an essential part of the development of education — but it is entirely inappropriate when one seeks to develop a strategy for informed change which will involve the majority of teachers in an institution.

An obvious approach to the improvement of the educational process is to identify problems experienced by teachers and learners. In attempting to solve recognized problems the services of educational technologists and others might be enlisted by teachers and institutions.

This model is the more attractive because it recognizes the fact that large-scale changes are known to take place when problems generate sufficient pressure (Collier, 1974).

However, to adopt such an approach deliberately, to try to identify and solve educational problems, demands a radical change in the attitudes of teacher and administrator.

The former would need to be prepared to assess the teaching/learning opportunities he provides — actually (in his present view) to create problems for himself. The latter would need to assign priority to this assessment.

Until these changes in attitude occur the educational technologist will continue to be in the position of offering something which the customer doesn't want.

References

Brynmor Jones Committee (1961) 'Audiovisual Aids in Higher Scientific Education' HMSO, London.

Collier, K G (ed) (1974) 'Innovation in Higher Education' NFER, Windsor.

Furniss, B S, McHugh, C R and Parsonage, J R (1976) 'An Efficient Strategy For the Production of Self-Instructional Materials' in 'Aspects of Educational Technology X' Kogan Page, London.

Furniss, B S and Parsonage, J R (1975) 'Independent Learning in Tertiary Science Education' The Chemical Society, London.

Kempa, R F (1976) 'Science Education Research: Some Thoughts and Observations' in 'Studies in Science Education 2' University of Leeds.

Nuffield Foundation Group (1976) 'Making the Best of It' in 'Times Higher Education Supplement'.

Educational Media Implementation: Strategies for Initiating Change in Formal Learning Environments

G O Coldevin

In the second half of the 20th century 'innovation' has become synonomous with the world of business and communication technology and a corollary standard of success has evolved into an ability to incorporate technological advances. For a variety of reasons, the formal school environment has remained one of the more resistant institutions in this process, except for a brief flurry of activity during the 1960s. As Goodlad (Goodlad, 1969) summarized, during the period 'innovation and revolution were used interchangeably in discussing the changes taking place in schools'. Like the weather, however, in retrospect while innovations such as the implementation of new educational media were much talked about, the basic format of traditionalism and status quo still characterizes the majority of North American school environments. The preponderance of equipment and software gathering dust in storage closets is a striking example of the success of the revolutionary decade.

The purpose of this paper is to provide a rationale for innovation facilitation with emphasis on newer educational media and the salient factors which may contribute toward success or failure in their implementation. In outlining a framework for analysis, basic elements of innovation diffusion developed from advertizing and social marketing research are reviewed and applied to an educational setting. Within this framework an innovation is defined as an 'idea, object or practice, the application of which is perceived as novel by an individual or group of individuals'.

Elements in the Diffusion of Innovations

Types of Innovation

In developing a taxonomy of simple to complex types of innovation, a useful overview is provided by Meierhenry (Meierhenry, 1966). Although the grid he proposes is related to innovation in general, the examples given here relate to education specifically.

1. ABORTIVE ATTEMPTS
A new practice is advanced and is advocated by a few practitioners, but for a variety of reasons disappears after a time. The early teaching machine developed by Pressey is often cited as a classic example of this type of innovation which never got off the ground.

2. SUBSTITUTION
Types of material or hardware in use are replaced by similar types of material or hardware. Other relations which pertain to the system remain fundamentally

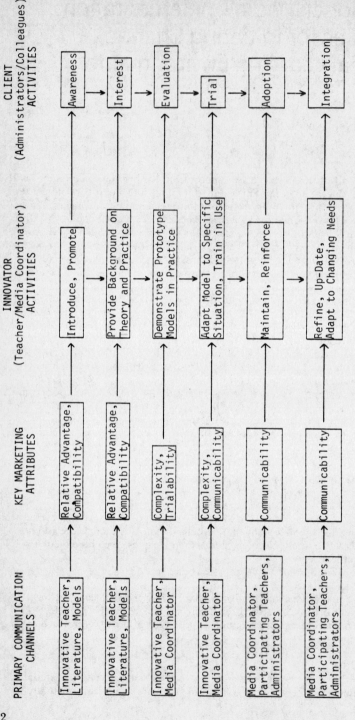

Figure 1. *A Model for Facilitating Educational Media Implementation*

PRIMARY COMMUNICATION CHANNELS	KEY MARKETING ATTRIBUTES	INNOVATOR (Teacher/Media Coordinator) ACTIVITIES	CLIENT (Administrators/Colleagues) ACTIVITIES
Innovative Teacher, Literature, Models	Relative Advantage, Compatibility	Introduce, Promote	Awareness
Innovative Teacher, Literature, Models	Relative Advantage, Compatibility	Provide Background on Theory and Practice	Interest
Innovative Teacher, Media Coordinator	Complexity, Trialability	Demonstrate Prototype Models in Practice	Evaluation
Innovative Teacher, Media Coordinator	Complexity, Communicability	Adapt Model to Specific Situation, Train in Use	Trial
Media Coordinator, Participating Teachers, Administrators	Communicability	Maintain, Reinforce	Adoption
Media Coordinator, Participating Teachers, Administrators	Communicability	Refine, Up-Date, Adapt to Changing Needs	Integration

unchanged. The replacement of sound motion pictures for silent, colour for black and white, and the early use of overhead projectors as a replacement for chalkboard activities are pertinent to this category.

3. PERTURBATION AND VARIATION
Events in society or changes in philosophy emerging from a culture produce different emphases in education although the major direction remains unchanged. In the United States the launching of the Russian Sputnik produced pressures on school systems to increase the attention being given to mathematics and sciences.

4. RESTRUCTURING
Basic social changes are required in order for a new practice to become acceptable and permanent. The teaching of foreign languages at the elementary level for example reflects the philosophy that younger children can and should learn at least one additional language.

5. VALUE REORIENTATION
Major shifts are required in a society's basic value system to allow the innovation to proceed. The desegregation of schools in the United States is a notable example of this type of change.

6. CREATION OF A NEW STRUCTURE
Entirely new structures must be created prior to the implementation of the innovation. Open learning systems, massive reliance on computer-assisted learning and performance contracting[1] are examples of this more complex type of innovation.

In general, the more complex the innovation, the larger the number of variables that must be brought into consideration. The implementation of newer educational media, as can be noted, for the most part (with the exception of computer-assisted learning) fall within the second and third levels. Within the third level, 'perturbation and variation' in this context may stem from the influence of mass media upon contemporary students and the wide-spread failure of educational institutions to incorporate technological advances into formal learning environments. The type of innovation we are discussing is therefore relatively simple and essentially the substitution of one or a combination of mediating agents for another. Within this framework teachers become high-lighted as competing mediating agents with good or poor qualities for specific instructional contexts in the same way as other educational media.

Stages in Innovation Adoption

Rogers and Shoemaker (1971) have suggested that the process through which an individual or group of individuals proceed from first knowledge of an innovation to a decision of adoption or rejection involves five levels:

---

1. Performance contracting involves the engaging of an outside firm by a school, usually to accelerate development of student skills in areas such as mathematics and reading. The firm is reimbursed according to student performance as measured by achievement tests. A detailed discussion with examples of this type of 'pay for results' arrangement is provided by Blaschke (Blaschke, 1972).

1. Awareness that the innovation exists;
2. Interest in seeking additional information about it;
3. Evaluation of the utility of the innovation in present and future anticipated situations;
4. Trial where the innovation is adopted on a small-scale or trial basis; and
5. Decision where the individual decides to adopt or reject an innovation.

A sixth factor which is necessary to maintain and provide for additions or up-dating of the innovation once the adoption level has been satisfied is termed 'integration' (Havelock, 1970). Research has consistently indicated that each of these stages must be satisfied before complete adoption behaviour may be encouraged. The failure of too rapid innovation-adoption behaviour may be encouraged. The failure of many rapid innovation-adoptions for example may be traced to proceeding directly from the interest level to adoption without paying careful attention to the evaluation and trial stages.

Marketing of Innovations

Eichholz and Rogers (1964) after analyzing teacher opinions for innovation failure propose the following list of typical reasons for rejection.

1. Rejection through ignorance — an innovation was unknown or its complexity led to misunderstanding;
2. Rejection through default — admitting a knowledge of the innovation without any interest in its use;
3. Rejection by maintaining the status quo — an innovation was not accepted because it had not been used in the past;
4. Rejection through social mores — teachers thought that society would not find the innovation acceptable and therefore would not use it;
5. Rejection through interpersonal relationships — colleagues do not use the innovation or find the school innovation acceptable and therefore the others will not use it;
6. Rejection through erroneous logic — the use of rational but unfounded reasons for the rejection of proven innovations;
7. Rejection through substitution — using one practice over another practice requiring the use of the innovation;
8. Rejection through fulfilment — the teacher knows the 'best' and 'only' way to teach, making any innovation completely unnecessary;
9. Rejection through experience — discussing with others the failure of some innovations.

In collapsing the above rejection factors, the mental set of the intended adopter(s) appears to be one of either lack of awareness or interest, adherence to the status quo, conflict or dissonance. Each of these in turn is essentially a non-decision or avoidance of decision behaviour. Conflict is defined as 'a condition of equivalence between objects or practices when a discrepancy between them is desired'. Dissonance on the other hand refers to 'a perceived cognitive discrepancy when a condition of balance or equivalence is desired'. Two types are possible. A post-decision state of cognitive dissonance occurs when the reasons for the original decision are no longer perceived as viable (eg built-in obsolescence features of the innovation or spiralling software costs render its further use to be impracticable). Dissonance may also be 'pre-decision' and anticipatory of a dissonant state should a decision be made. The individual then becomes immobilized in a non-decision state.

In reducing status quo adherence, conflict and dissonance toward promoting adoption behaviours, innovations should ideally be marketed through consideration of the following attributes (Rogers and Shoemaker, 1971).

1. RELATIVE ADVANTAGE
The degree to which the innovation is better than the object or practice it is intended to supercede. The degree of relative advantage is often expressed in economic terms. Prestige, convenience and instructional impact are important corollary components.

2. COMPATIBILITY
The degree to which the innovation is consistent with existing values and past experience of the intended adopter(s). Integrated teacher/media roles are prime considerations for successful marketing of this attribute.

3. TRIALABILITY
The degree to which an innovation may be tried on a limited basis. This attribute is especially important in 'demystifying' roles and operation of educational media.

4. COMPLEXITY
The degree to which an innovation is relatively difficult to understand and use. Major innovations such as CAL require sustained attention to this attribute.

5. COMMUNICABILITY
The degree to which the results of an innovation may be communicated to other potential adopters. Prototype media/instructional models in close proximity to adopter situations are particularly appropriate to this marketing strategy.

Consistent with our earlier assumption regarding the importance of satisfying each of the adoption stages, it is hypothesized that the failure of many innovations has been due to incomplete marketing strategies and consideration of the broad range of attributes the foregoing model incorporates. It should also be noted that the simpler the innovation (such as most educational media) the easier will be its marketing and ultimate chance for successful adoption and integration.

Educational Innovation Diffusion

In the light of the factors to be considered within the general framework of innovation diffusion, the following discussion is centred around a brief historical overview of the receptiveness of educational institutions toward change. A revised mandate is then suggested for teacher-training institutions in challenging the problems which exist in educational media implementation and a new role for teachers as educational technology change agents is advocated.

The Lag in Educational Innovation

Mort (Mort, 1964) in reviewing studies of the time-lag in innovations in American educational institutions notes that a half century elapses between the identification of a need and the development of a solution which may be accepted. Another 15 years is required to diffuse the innovation among 3% of the nation's schools followed by a 20-year period of rapid diffusion where the innovation reaches most but not all of the remaining schools. For general acceptance of a proven innovation the lag is noteworthy when considering that television sets were at a saturation level in American homes during the same period.

Potential Role of Teacher-Training Institutions

In assessing the reasons for failure in the widespread use of media in formal education, the available evidence points in large part to the orientation of teacher-training institutions. Tobias (1966, 1968) for example found a lack of knowledge combined with fear of automation to be primary correlates of teachers' attitudes toward educational media. Fear of mechanization and reduction of self-importance were also reported by Handleman (1960) as negative barriers to teacher's use of instructional television. On the more positive side, Knowlton and Hawes (1963) and Midson (1975) attributed increased use of audio-visual materials after course work in educational media to improved information; and Aquino (1968) found that teacher attitudes toward educational media improved significantly after formal studies in the area. Similar results were reported by Guba and Snyder (1964) when media were used in actual teaching situations.

The sequence of the foregoing research suggests that if teachers, and subsequently the environment in which they operate, are to change, they must be exposed to models of what they are to change to. Teacher programmes primarily based on a paradigm of verbal communication have increasingly limited utility. Goodlad (1970) amplifies this point when he intimates that 'teachers are trained for and in yesterday's classroom'. In McLuhan terminology, teachers are trained to march backward into the future. If stimulus generalization or transfer is to occur from teacher colleges to the operating classroom it follows that the training model should parallel as closely as possible the desired teaching situation. Siegel (1967) notes that 'the real significance of the possibilities for minimizing the teacher's role as a dispenser of facts will be lost unless teacher-training institutes come to grips with what teachers ought to be doing and unless schools make appropriate curriculum revisions'. The initial reorientation accordingly must take place in the universities if the lag in educational media implementation is to be significantly altered.

A minimal requirement for all potential 'classroom managers' should be an overview of developments and applications of educational media. Torkelson (1970, p 48) projects a more comprehensive view: 'A change from traditional training will require a thorough knowledge of modern methods of communication and, equally important, an understanding of learning objectives, processes and learner characteristics as these influence the applications of instructional technology to learning problems.' It is further suggested that teachers must be prepared to initiate change and in doing so to cope with a potentially hostile environment for the introduction of educational media. Their training should therefore include exposure to factors involved in facilitating change and strategies for dealing with typical educational environments.

The above remarks are particularly appropriate to the pattern of teacher training in Canada. Gillet (1973) for example quotes a national survey conducted by the Canadian Teachers' Federation in 1970 which found that one quarter of English-speaking universities did not offer regular courses in 'understanding educational technology' and 'equipment operation'. Gillet estimates that at least half the teachers entering Canadian schools in 1973 had no opportunity to take even one course in educational technology. The situation was compounded for those already in schools. An up-dated survey by Midson (1975) showed that conditions had improved slightly but at least one-third of newly-qualified teachers had no exposure to either the development or application of audio-visual materials. It is also a fair assumption that virtually no training was received in the techniques of innovation implementation.

Rowntree (1974) poses the question, 'Can we teach people to innovate?'. This

376

paper suggests an affirmative response and further implies that if universities do not encourage 'change agent' activities in their graduates, the future of educational media implementation is likely to remain haphazard.

The Teacher as Educational Media Change Agent

Having advanced the need for teacher training in both a thorough grounding in educational media and exposure to principles of innovation diffusion, a tentative model is proposed for:

1. promoting the adoption of educational media; and
2. a supporting environment to sustain various educational media utilization once they are acquired (Figure 1).

In applying the model it is stressed that the change agent or teacher/media co-ordinator in this case should have initially undergone the same type of activities as those intended for the client, ie he must be convinced of the value of an innovation or adaptation thereof within his particular situation and those of his colleagues. Usually this will take the form of an operational evaluation which may be readily communicated.

Given the plethora of untested materials commercially available, the 'proven' value approach is particularly important. Komosky (1974) notes that of the 300,000 available commercial instructional materials in the United States, only about 1% have been empirically tested. Similar figures are advanced by Gilkey (1976). According to these reports 99% of all instructional materials being sold to American schools (around which in turn at least 75% and in some cases 99% of the students' instructional time is centred) have not been systematically validated and then revised or improved on the basis of testing. Where commercial materials are advocated a pre-requisite for successful innovation diffusion therefore would seem to indicate evaluation of the materials in the actual setting in which they are to be used prior to promoting the innovation to other members in the system. The value of this type of evaluation base has also been suggested by Klasek (1976) for administrators' successful introduction of ITV to American schools.

The model further suggests that the primary innovative thrust must be provided by the teacher (or group of teachers) to dispel the negative connotations inherent in an approach by an agent 'outside' the profession. The media co-ordinator's role on the other hand should be one of substantial support during the trial, adoption and integration stages. The integration stage is particularly crucial to media co-ordinator functions to maintain a climate for successful use of the innovation once it is installed and to provide for up-dating, possibly through in-service training, as improved versions of the innovation appear.

Finally, it should be noted that the model is primarily intended for future professionals, with clients referring to administrators and teachers whose training preceded either the growth and availability of a variety of educational media or the opportunity for formal course exposure. In-service training and consistent up-grading in this circumstance should be part of the systematic development of teachers committed to merging technology and education.

Post-Script

From the studies generated regarding teachers' exposure to and use of newer educational media it is apparent that training institutions have failed to come to grips with the availability of and training for a variety of mediated instructional formats. The education industry has been and is a highly institutionalized organization and accordingly resistant to change. Paradoxically, as Meierhenry (1966) observes, teaching and learning consists of trying to bring about behaviour changes and the purpose of education is to develop individuals who are adaptive and creative. The reluctance on the part of educationalists to deal with relatively simple levels of innovation such as the incorporation of educational media into instructional settings therefore represents a perplexing question.

It is suggested that the failure of principles and applications of educational technology to become firmly entrenched in formal learning environments is due to the inertia of universities in familiarizing students with the potential role of educational technology and in further preparing future teachers for initiating planned change in schools. A parallel problem has been the lack of awareness of educational technology by school administrators. The model proposed in this paper is one attempt to redress this imbalance.

Educating the television generation with 19th century technology seems to be an increasingly frustrating experience for both teachers and students. Providing stimulating learning environments is one of the major challenges to be mastered if the school is to remain a dominant force in children's education. A gap of 35 years between the emergence of a proven innovation and general acceptance is no longer acceptable nor indeed tolerable. Torkelson (1970) writes that 'the test of an educated person in the future may be his ability to adapt to change'. The test of a successful educator should be no less.

References

Aquino, C C (1968) 'A Study to Determine Educators' Attitudes Toward Audio-visual Instruction Following Study in That Area' Ph D dissertation, Syracuse University.

Blaschke, C (1972) 'Performance Contracting: Who Profits Most?' Phi Delta Kappa, Bloomington.

DuMolin, J R (1971) 'Instructional Television Utilization in the United States' ERIC (Ed 055 427).

Eichholz, G and Rogers, E (1964) 'Resistance to the Adoption of Audio-Visual Aids by Elementary School-Teachers: Contrasts and similarities to agricultural innovation' in 'Innovation in Education' Miles, M B (ed) Teachers College Press, New York.

Gilkey, R (1976) 'Evaluation of Materials' ECT Newsletter, 7 3 November.

Gillet, M (1973) 'Educational Technology: Toward Demystification' Prentice Hall, Toronto.

Goodlad, J I (1969) 'The Schools v Education' Saturday Review April 19.

Goodlad, J I (1970) 'The Reconstruction of Teacher Education' Teachers College Record 72 1 September.

Guba, E and Synder, C (1964) 'Instructional Television and the Classroom Teacher' Ohio State University, Columbus.

Handleman, S (1960) 'A Comparative Study of Teacher Attitudes Toward Teaching by CCTV' Ph D dissertation New York University.

Havelock, R G (1970) 'A Guide to Innovation in Education' University of Michigan, Ann Arbor.

Klasek, C B (1976) 'ITV and the School Principal' Educational Broadcasting 9 5 October.

Knowlton, J and Hawes, E (1962) 'Attitude: Helpful Predictor of Audio-Visual Usage?' AV Communication Review 10 3 Fall.

Komoski, P K (1974) 'An Imbalance of Product Quantity and Instructional Quality: The Imperative of Empiricism' AV Communication Review 22 4 Winter.

Meierhenry, W C (1966) 'Innovation Education and Media' AV Communication Review 14 4 Winter.

Midson, T (1975) 'Teacher Education in Audio-Visual Techniques' National Film Board of Canada, Montreal.

Mort, P R (1964) 'Studies in Educational Innovation from the Institute of Administrative Research: An Overview' in 'Innovation in Education' Miles, M B (ed) Teachers College Press, New York.

Rogers, E M and Shoemaker, F F (1971) 'Communication of Innovations' Free Press, New York.

Rowntree, D (1974) 'Educational Technology in Curriculum Development' Harper and Row, London.

Siegel, L (1967) 'Instruction: Some Contemporary Viewpoints' Chandler, San Francisco.

Tobias, S (1966) 'Lack of Knowledge and Fear of Automation as Factors in Teachers' Attitudes Toward Programmed Instruction and Other Media' AV Communication Review 14 1 Spring.

Tobias, S (1968) 'Dimensions of Teachers' Attitudes Toward Instructional Media' American Educational Research Journal 5 1.

Torkelson, G M (1971) 'Education/Industry Cooperation — Instructional Technology in Teacher Education' Audio-visual instruction 16 3 March.

Institutional Transfer
and Adaptation of a Content-Free
Computer-Managed Learning
(CML) System

N J Rushby, H F McMahon

The major content-free CML system currently operational in the United Kingdom is that developed by the CAMOL (Computer-Assisted Management of Learning) project, which had its origins in the early days of the United Kingdom's National Development Programme in Computer-Assisted Learning. It became clear in the summer of 1973 that there were a number of institutions interested in developing various applications of computer-managed learning, and it seemed that it could be a waste of resources to fund educational and computing staff in each institution to design individual CML systems, tailored to specific content areas, when there was apparently a high degree of similarity in the individual users' requirements, certainly from a computing, if not from an educational point of view. The goal of developing a CML system which could be applied to a wide range of content areas, to different age levels and in support of a variety of instructional modes seemed to be worth pursuing. Discussions were held between interested people drawn from a range of educational institutions and from the British computer industry. These discussions culminated in July 1974 with the publication of an outline for a CML system called CAMOL. Although designed by a committee and therefore an obvious butt for witty comments on its origins, it appeared to provide most of the facilities required by most of the people most of the time.

Throughout the next two years the group of individuals which defined CAMOL was transformed into a consortium of active developers either using or writing CAMOL (Rushby *et al* 1976). The consortium now comprises: The New University of Ulster (NUU) in association with the Methodist College, Belfast and Ulster College; Brighton Polytechnic; Bradford College with Keighley Technical College and Shipley College of Further Education; and the Trade Training School, Catterick. The considerable problems of co-ordination of effort and communication of ideas throughout the consortium were eased by the establishment of a Steering Committee and a Project Co-ordinator.

Built-in Transferability

Two major objectives of all development work in the National Programme are institutionalization in the home environment, and transfer and adaptation to other institutional environments of the innovative teaching system and the developed computer package. These two are closely linked, for institutionalization, moving projects onto local budgets at the end of external funding, is much easier if the costs are kept down. This can be helped by the sharing of expertise and the transfer of materials between institutions, which spreads the initial investment and reduces the unit cost. However, such economic gains may have to be traded off against the educational cost of producing a package which imposes untoward constraints on its disparate users, each having to accommodate individual or institutional ideals to the realities imposed through definition of common ground.

To be applicable to a wide range of educational and training environments, a CML system should set out to be not only content-free, that is independent of subject material, but also context-free, so that it is not circumscribed by a particular model of the teaching/learning process. Ideally CAMOL should be a value-free system that will support the teacher and his students by reducing the administrative and clerical load, without imposing its own conditions or rigid model. In practice it is very difficult to produce a CML system which is truly adaptable — supporting but not imposing — to its users. Nevertheless, the objective of generality provided a bonus in that it gave a framework for content and context-free discussions about CML, a lingua franca which in principle could be dissociated from specific applications of specific CML systems.

So from the outset CAMOL had transferability built into it. This also implied adaptability. By making the system very general and providing a plethora of facilities, it was possible to envisage that most of the users would be satisfied most of the time; but different institutions have very different needs and furthermore their needs are constantly changing. It is difficult to hit such a moving target continually. CAMOL was therefore considered as a starting-point from which each institution could, with relatively little effort, develop a system to meet its own unique requirements, and from which it could subsequently tailor new systems as its requirements evolved. The educational development in the eight project institutions would complement the program development, feeding back ideas and experiences to the programming team. These eight institutions were deliberately chosen to give a wide spread of environments — university, polytechnic, further education, secondary school and military training, and subject area — curriculum studies in teacher education, physics, mathematics, technician training and general administration. Each of the institutions would use and develop those features of the system most fitted to its own needs, and the end result would be a combined wealth of expertise in the various facets of computer-managed learning. It is pleasing to note that as the end of the transferability project draws nigh, this aspiration has been largely realized.

There are two aspects to the transfer and adaptation of computer-assisted learning materials. In addition to the educational problems of carrying out local curriculum development, or of transferring curriculum materials and overcoming the consequent 'not invented here' syndrome, there are the problems of running the computer programs in different environments. Experience within the National Programme has shown that, with some exceptions, the problems of moving the programs are less than the problems of developing or moving the educational materials. Nevertheless, the computing aspects cannot be overlooked.

The transfer of computer programs is largely a mechanical process which may be easy or difficult, depending on the similarity of a new computer system to the old. Within the CAMOL project consortium, this problem has been avoided at one level because all the institutions are using ICL computers, on which the programs can run interchangeably. But a CML system consists of much more than the computer itself, encompassing as it does manual procedures, methods for preparing input data for the machine and most important — people. Of all the components of a CML system the people are — happily — the most difficult to get right. Relatively speaking, the transfer of the computing components of a CML system is easy.

However, at another level the computer program transferability problem has not been avoided, or solved. While transfer of CML out of the ICL CAMOL consortium is enhanced by the availability of back-up from experienced educational and computing developers, this applies only to customers who want to implement on ICL machines. The potential customer may find it difficult to get the people 'right', and the consortium can help on that, but for CAMOL he also has to have the right machine.

Some features to facilitate adaptation of the system can be built into the computer programs themselves. A technique called 'structured programming' results in programs which can easily be understood by other programmers and can be altered with less risk of introducing errors.

Computing staff need a comprehensive description of the system and the way in which it works before they can adapt it with any confidence. It is unusual for such full documentation, which may run to many thousands of pages for a large system, to be available to the users of a commercial system such as CAMOL, but in its absence it may prove impossible to modify the system. This systematic approach to engineering a CML system also leads to fewer errors and greater reliability. On these qualities rests the users' confidence in the system, and hence its acceptability. There is a useful parallel here with that simpler educational technology, the overhead projector, which is accepted as long as it works, but is rejected when the standby lamp blows too!

Transfer of CML systems to other institutions and their successful adaptation and use of them requires computing support as well as educational support from the donor institution. Where the computer programs have been produced by an academic institution, it is often difficult to provide adequate resources to support the software. In the CAMOL project, this problem has been overcome by the involvement of ICL who, having produced the computer package are now marketing it commercially. Hence the documentation, support and maintenance of the system are assured, albeit for a charge to the user. It remains to be seen whether the distinct advantages of a professionally-engineered package, which is reliable, adaptable and supported by good program documentation and educational expertise, outweigh the disadvantages of having to pay for the product.

Major Adaptations

It was anticipated from the beginning that a development project lasting several years and spread across several institutions was bound to throw up a range of instances where local adaptation of the centrally-produced package would be necessary. To date there have been upwards of 20 such adaptations ranging from simple changes costing man-hours of programming, through intermediate program developments costing man-weeks, to very major changes involving policy decisions to deploy systems design and programming effort in terms of man-months or man-years.

This paper examines three examples of the third level of adaptation, where the system and program changes involved have considerably influenced the shape of the total CAMOL package and its use in educational terms. These are firstly, the development of test analysis facilities in CAMOL, secondly, the adaptation of CAMOL to meet the needs of students exhibiting different study styles, and thirdly the appearance within the consortium of macro-CAMOL, a major adaptation which shifts the application of CAMOL from the management of learning within courses to the management of courses across institutions.

Test Analysis

The design and implementation of the test analysis facilities in CAMOL was carried out at Brighton Polytechnic as a preliminary to their use of the CAMOL system.

Although the test analysis sub-system is now an integral part of CAMOL, its production, by a user rather than by ICL, was in many ways a prototype adaptation. The design of test analysis drew heavily on a number of sources. The original Systems Outline provided a basis which was modified in the light of Brighton's experience with their own objective testing system. Useful contributions were made by NUU who also had their own analysis program, and by the National Foundation for Educational Research. Talks with the study staff at TTS Catterick identifield significant differences in the assessment process between education and training environments.

The timing of an adaptation clearly has major effects on the relative efficiency with which the adaptation is carried out. In this case the test analysis facilities in CAMOL became an extension of those specified in the Systems Outline, and as such were more closely related to the needs of actual and potential users. In addition they were developed at a time when the design of the main CAMOL suite had not hardened and the inter-face problem could be handled more flexibly. On the other hand, because the adaptation was carried out before the main system was completed and documented, various problems of communication resulted directly from the lack of adequate documentation.

A general point illustrated by this experience is that if adaptations are to be widely transferred, then they too must be supported by good documentation and maintenance. Substantial adaptations like test analysis need substantial maintenance commitments, a problem which was resolved in this case by arranging that the test analysis sub-system should become an integral part of the ICL CAMOL system, marketed, maintained and supported as a part of that system. It is hoped that similar arrangements can be made to incorporate other adaptations.

Accommodation to Study Styles

The original specification of CAMOL assumed that there would be four basic stages in the student's cycle of study:

1. The student works through a multi-media learning module.
2. He takes an end-of-module diagnostic test.
3. The test is marked by computer and the student is provided with 'corrective comments' on each individual test item.
4. The computer applies a routing algorithm via a decision table and the student is provided with a summary analysis of his full test results and is routed to the next appropriate learning module.

Flexibility was built into the system by providing a powerful generalized test marking system and a facility for writing routing algorithms at each end-of-module decision point where the routing decisions could be made on any combination of information drawn from a student history file, the student's latest diagnostic test results and subjective performance data entered by the tutor.

These assumptions were shown to be applicable only to a sub-set of students who followed a simulated CAMOL managed course at NUU during the autumn of 1974. The evaluation study of this simulation (Hutchinson, 1975; McMahon et al, 1977) indicated that only 42% of the students followed the four stages of study as outlined above, completing one cycle before moving on in a serialist way along the recommended route to start the next cycle. Given the opportunity to use the. learning modules in whatever way they chose, 25% of the students followed all four stages but did not wait until the end of the first cycle before starting the second. These students used what might be described as a holist approach, exploring the field as a whole and studying the materials in sequences other than those

383

anticipated by the course designer, often submitting the diagnostic tests in batches. The remaining students made use of the learning packages but ceased using the diagnostic tests after only one or two cycles.

This evidence of student behaviour became available in early 1975 at a time when the design characteristics of the main CAMOL could still be altered. As a result of this adaptation the system can now accommodate to the learners' preferred study style, the assumption no longer being made that students necessarily need or will accept prescription of routing within a serialist mode of learning.

It is perhaps symptomatic of the pressures experienced in the hurly-burly of development that it was the tenuous evidence from a rather scrambled simulation exercise carried out with the consortium, rather than the results of research studies on learning style available in the literature, which had the stronger influence on adaptation of the design characteristics of the system.

A detailed analysis of the effects of this major adaptation on course development and teaching roles in the CML system at NUU is presented by McMahon and Anderson (McMahon and Anderson, 1977).

The Emergence of Macro-CAMOL

The major adaptations described above arose either from needs identified by the users who could not see a CML system operating without an effective test analysis suite, or from needs arising during simulation where students made it clear that they would not be confined within the learning system as originally conceived. Macro-CAMOL was different, in that its conception arose more from coincidence than from the rational analysis of operating or simulated CML systems.

During the first simulation of CAMOL at NUU in 1974/75 one of the main tasks was the construction of routing algorithms and decision tables which governed the in-course routing of students on an individualized basis through a sequence of modularized learning packages. This work was carried out by McMahon, who by coincidence was undertaking at the same time a comprehensive review of the unit structure of the Education Centre as a whole. The spark which generated the idea of macro-CAMOL was the realization that in principle the systems which were being used to route students through a 12-week course unit consisting of multi-media packages, and diagnostic tests could also be used to collect and analyze routine cumulative assessment and formal examination results across many course units, and to route students through the institutional course structure according to rules which expressed the institution's standard course construction and examination regulations.

Even though the idea emerged in the autumn of 1974 and rapidly gained the interest and support of individuals inside and outside the consortium, it was not until the summer of 1976 that a clear specification for macro-CAMOL and a secure environment for its development were established. Macro-CAMOL development is now in train at Ulster College, the Northern Ireland Polytechnic, under the direction of the Academic Registrar. Again, the design strategies described earlier for built-in transferability are being used to produce a system which will be reliable, adaptable and supported by documentation meeting ICL's standards. Early results from simulation studies currently running at the Polytechnic and at NUU suggest that the system is likely to further enhance the transferability potential of CAMOL in that the macro-CAMOL adaptation allows the CML system to be used to maintain and effectively exploit a data-base which consists of historical and current data concerning students' academic progress, already processed by an amalgam of computing and clerical methods by universities and polytechnics. Using

384

macro-CAMOL can greatly enhance the information service provided to students, advisers of studies, course committees, external examiners and subject tutors without the additional curriculum development load that CML support of an in-course individualized learning system normally involves.

Predicting Transferability Potential

Despite the diversity of practical experience in CML which has been an emerging characteristic of the CAMOL consortium, and despite our strong commitment to transferability and the analysis thereof, we do not feel able to propose a general model for predicting transferability potential of a content-free CML system, except in the most tentative way.

The model which follows (Figure 1) draws on a similar one developed by Dr David Satterley of the University of Bristol (Rushby, 1977). It is little more than a summary of a number of dimensions which we feel have prima facie relevance to the prediction of the success of CML system applications. It would of course be a task for empirical inquiry to examine the inter-relationship of these dimensions in practice, through examination of CML systems in operation.

Dimension	Characteristics of CML applications with high transferability potential		Characteristics of CML applications with low transferability potential
Subject Matter	Sciences	Social Sciences	Humanities
Form of Presentation of Learning Materials	Modular/linear		Generic/stellar
Chief Function	Record-keeping	Testing	Routing
Prime Beneficiary of Information	Administrator	Teacher	Student
Purpose of Routing Algorithms	Application of existing across-course regulations		Development of in-course diagnostics
Locus of Control of Learning	Teacher		Student

Figure 1.

Our experience in the CAMOL consortium would suggest that the greater the number of dimensions which cluster towards the pole on the left, the greater the transferability potential of any particular application of CAMOL. In contrast, the more a CAMOL application attempts to move to the right, the more it seems to challenge the established pedagogical assumptions of institutions in secondary and tertiary education in the United Kingdom, and the greater is the educational and computing resource input required to make the innovation stick.

The transferability potential of a content and context-free CML system such as CAMOL is enhanced to the extent to which it can accommodate applications at each end of the spectrum represented by these dimensions. In the CAMOL consortium we are implementing adaptations which increasingly provide experience and understanding of the development problems encountered at each end of the spectrum.

References

Hutchinson, L (1975) 'Student Responses and Reactions to Individualized Learning in ED 204' Unpublished report CAMOL Project, New University of Ulster.

McMahon, H *et al* (1977) 'Student Responses to Differentiated Learning Tasks in CML' 'Programmed Learning and Educational Technology' (May 1977) (in press).

McMahon, H and Anderson, J S A (1977) 'Implementing a CML Package — the Tutor's Role in Course Development and Teaching' in 'Aspects of Educational Technology Vol XI' Hills, P, and Gilbert, J (eds) Kogan Page, London.

Rushby, N *et al* (1976) 'Computer-Assisted Management in Learning — the CAMOL Project' in 'Aspects of Educational Technology Vol X' Clarke, J and Leedham, J (eds) Kogan Page, London.

Rushby, N (ed) (1977) 'Computer-Manager Learning in the 1980s' Technical Report No 16 National Development Programme in Computer-Assisted Learning, London.

Development of Science Programmes for Rural Children under the Project Satellite for Instructional Television Experiment

M M Chaudhri

Introduction

The Applicational Technology Satellite, ATS—6, launched by the USA on 30 May, 1975, was loaned to India for a period of one year starting August 1, 1975. This project was called SITE — Satellite Instructional Television Experiment. The ground segment responsibilities in India were with the Indian Space Research Organization (ISRO) and All India Radio (AIR) (Krishnamurthy, 1976). Amongst the various hardware responsibilities in terms of installation and maintenance of the earth stations, the TV receivers etc, ISRO was also responsible for developing research tools and designs for evaluation along with a large segment of science programmes for rural children. The most sophisticated communications technology was thus utilized to reach about 2340 remote villages in 20 districts (or countries) spread over clusters in the six states with a population of nearly 45 million.

The general objectives of the experiment were to gain experience in the development, testing and management of the satellite-based instructional television system, particularly in rural areas. SITE proposed to focus on upgrading education to suit the changing requirements of the country (Chandler, Karnik, 1976). It was used to emphasize the need for population control, communicate about health, nutrition and the new agricultural methods and to create scientific awareness amongst the people. SITE had been designed for villages located in different linguistic, cultural, climatic and agricultural regions of the country. This diverse selection of villages meant four different Indian languages — Hindi, Oriya, Kannada and Telegu for the six SITE states. Broadcasts were in two sessions: the educational one in the morning was meant for schoolchildren between the ages of five and 12 and the evening broadcast was mainly for adults. During school vacation (twice in the SITE year) nearly 48,000 teachers were to get in-service training through a multi-media package consisting of TV, radio, print material, experiments and resource persons.

SITE became a challenge in communication for the programmers who knew little about the audience which had a diversity of sub-culture and ethos. For producers of science programmes it meant coming into conflict with the old beliefs of the rural way of life. The process of science ran counter to the traditional values held for centuries, such as rote learning from Vedas, superstition, rituals and the adage that one does not question mother, father, teacher and one's God.

---

* This work was carried out at the Television Centre, Indian Institute of Technology, Kanpur, India by the author under a project from Space Applications Centre (SAC), ISRO.

** The author, now Professor and Head of the Department of Teaching Aids, was till 1976 Head of the TV Centre at IIT Kanpur.

The work reported in this paper relates to a joint project between IIT, Kanpur and SAC. It concerned itself with survey, research design, development of scripts on science for children, production of half-inch videotapes, assessment and final recording for transmission on one-inch VTR. The programmes were made in Hindi and later dubbed into three languages by SAC and AIR for broadcasting purposes. This project was only one segment of the total science programmes produced by SAC with the involvement of scientists, film-makers, teachers, educationalists and others.

Objectives of this Project

1. To develop 12 prototype half-inch videotape programmes which have been tested and assessed for their utility and which could provide guidelines for large-scale production of science programmes for rural children. Later on six programmes were also recorded on one-inch VTR for transmission in four languages to SITE clusters.
2. To provide a documented basis for the generation of innovative ideas and intuitive judgements that have gone into the making of the programme.
3. To record the basis for understanding the process of communication in basic science for rural children through the medium of television.

Methodology

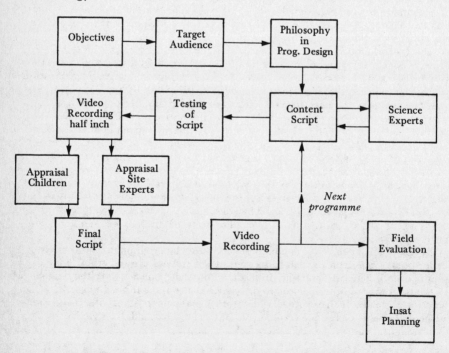

Target Audience

The target audience of the programmes for children in SITE was defined to be between the ages of six and 11. However, the project team after some initial work felt that the ideal target range for such programmes would be between eight and 11. The children below eight years had very little comprehension of language, visuals and science in general.

Because of the large distance (about 200 miles) between the nearest cluster (in Rajasthan) and IIT Kanpur, we chose two villages (Devisahainagar and Nankari) at the outskirts of the Institute as our target audience. These villages were not in the SITE clusters. Though many of the villages worked at IIT or in the city, their way of life was very rural. The school condition and environment spoke little of modernization. Having studied these two villages in another project (Chaudhri, 1974) related to education, it was easier for our team to communicate with its people.

Devisahainagar (No 1) school had about 80 children and four teachers and Nankari (No 2) 120 children and six teachers. No 2 school functioned better than No 1 and the response also turned out to be more helpful towards the project. It therefore became easier to plan programmes with them as time went by.

The teachers went about their tasks without much enthusiasm. Their method of teaching could hardly be said to be scientific. The authoritarian approach of the teacher with emphasis on rote learning had virtually suppressed the sense of inquiry amongst the children. Perhaps the teacher carried on with the traditional rote learning because of the importance attached to the scriptures learnt by heart. Asking a question in the class was considered impertinent.

Teachers were called to the TV Centre and shown programmes made earlier by the Centre. The research associates (RA), both females, went twice a week to teach in the classes in order to build up an informal relationship and rapport with the village children. The research associates selected those topics for teaching which offered the widest scope for using pictures, maps and visualization. The children had initial difficulty in comprehending this style since they were not used to it, but gradually they adjusted to it. This experience in turn helped the RAs to work out scripts taking account of the children's level of understanding, language and comprehension. We had earlier thought of involving the school-teachers in scripting and production. This could not succeed because the medium was totally new to them and they had very little time to work with us. Their work schedule included responsibilities other than teaching. For example, the teachers took up private tuition to supplement their low income from school.

The interaction with schoolchildren also took place at the TV Centre where they were brought and shown in batches a number of videotapes and films made earlier. This was done to get them used to the medium and the new surroundings. Later on, these children became the primary source of feedback on our successive productions. To achieve this it was considered essential to place the children and the teachers in different rooms. This arrangement helped children to open up and feel relaxed with RAs for the communication we wanted to establish.

Selection of Topics

The selection of the first five topics was based on the children's curiosity and their syllabus. These were:

1. The Earth.
2. Day and Night.
3. Rain.
4. What is Electricity?
5. Mirror.

The later seven topics were chosen according to the SAC programme briefs and their basic outlines.

Philosophy in Programme Design

During the interaction with children certain guidelines for scripting and production emerged. They were as follows:

1. The script should relate to the child's rural environment and develop from the known to the unknown.
2. It was understood that the actual TV viewing conditions in the SITE villages might be far from ideal — 100 to 200 children of different ages sitting and watching on one set. Therefore, the programme should have a certain entertainment value in addition to the teaching of science. This entertainment could be in terms of folk music and puppets to keep them amused.
3. There should only be two or three concepts in the 12-minute production in simple but correct language and the concepts should be repeated in different ways.
4. The idea of learning science by doing experiments could be highlighted in the TV programme in a simple way so that the village teachers might also be motivated to carry them out in their own classes.
5. To produce a series of science programmes which were also independent of each other so that a child who missed one programme would still be able to understand the concepts.

Scripting and Production Aspects

1. The scripts were developed without the teacher image 'on camera'. It was felt that a good TV teacher might tend to become a threat to the conservative school-teacher in the village.
2. We would have liked to use children as subjects in our programmes, but in our initial experimentation we found that children who were available were hard pressed for time and appeared frozen when participating in a scripted programme.
3. The first few programmes started with puppets introducing the topic through a story, riddle or questions. Later, we changed this format to a puppet, looking like an eight-year-old child, which featured in all our programmes. This was done with the view that children would tend to identify themselves with him. Thus the child puppet by his own speech could also create the illusion of a one-way medium, TV that is, appearing as a two-way medium. He could become the source of humour and entertainment.
4. The script was written in consultation with the science experts in the Institute and was first tested on a sample of children other than the village schoolchildren. This was done by reading out the script to them informally and getting their reaction to words, visuals, complexity of concepts and their treatment. It also gave us an idea of the element of humour to be built into the TV programme.
5. Quite often the proper scientific terms are not used in the village. Therefore, we made a deliberate attempt to introduce and use them along with the equivalent familiar ones. This, when repeated in the programme, could add to the vocabulary of the children.
6. Overall, while scriptwriting, we maintained the belief that the reality of science is sufficiently fascinating in itself to hold attention. The scientific

phenomena should not be presented as if they were magic (Rose Mukherjee 1970).

7. Our first programme 'The Earth' had a commentary given by a female voice which suited the story type of programme production. The rest of the programmes were a dialogue between an adult male voice and a child's voice on puppet. There was a very definite reason for keeping the adult voice as that of male and not of female. Hardly any female teachers exist in rural schools in India. Women teachers are essentially an urban concept.

8. All the programmes were recorded on SONY half-inch at the studios of IIT, Kanpur. There were no editing facilities. Neither did we have any professional crew. The students who had learnt CCTV production as part of their extra-curricular activities acted as crew members for all the production work, which mostly had to be done after dinner.

9. Owing to lack of time, the male voice and child's voice were pre-recorded and then played back for rehearsals and videotaping.

Assessment

A deliberate and conscious effort is made here not to use the term evaluation, even though we had earlier thought we could do so. The evaluation of our work was qualitative because of several parameters not quite under the control of the research team. Hence it is more appropriate to call it assessment or appraisal. This was done with the help of two different sets of groups:

1. In one case it was the *children* of our school under study from whom feedback was obtained in an indirect way. Firstly, by formally giving them 'pre' and 'post' objective type of tests. The children, like the medium itself, were first exposed to the model tests designed on the pattern used in the appraisal. The written tests dealt more with content and less with visuals, pace, voice, music, treatment etc. These aspects were verbally discussed with the children. The scoring of the entire class was averaged out. The difference between the 'pre and 'post' test served as an index for gain in learning from each programme. Though the gain in learning was not the sole objective of appraisal, it nevertheless served to provide us along with the informal chat, with the feedback we wanted. It is, therefore, not important to give numbers, but only the broad pointers. These were as follows:

    (a) The data suggests that the contents of the videotape were ideally suited for grade III, who from low scoring in 'pre-test' achieved high in the 'post-test'. On the other hand, grade IV and V students scored well in the 'pre-test' and then improved only very slightly in the 'post-test'. It is possible that the grade III students 'learnt' the concept through TV, whereas for grade IV and V it may have been the process of unlearning the concept first and then learning. The latter is always more difficult.

    (b) The second viewing, which took place after a week, made a significant difference in learning. It is safe to assume that many kinds of interaction such as student-student and teacher-student interaction may have taken place in between the two viewings to improve this learning. Teachers never felt at ease with tests, and in spite of our repeated assurances, had the suspicion that this testing was in some way going to reveal their poor teaching in the classroom. To overcome this, the teachers often coached the children in advance, thereby disturbing our appraisal. If, however, this interaction was not significant then the case for a repeat playback was all the more convincing.

391

(c) Ideally speaking, the pre-testing or validity of questions should have also been done, but because of certain factors it was not possible. Another weakness in our testing design was that we gave the same test to grade III, IV and V children, knowing very well that the comprehension of III and V was quite different.

(d) One was not too sure if the puppet style of beginning was better at capturing their attention in the science concepts. If it was too good, it could very well become distracting for the science treatment to come later.

2. The other sources for appraisal were experts in TV programming, communication and psychology who were shown the earlier programes. Their comments were direct such as:

(a) The programme became serious and heavy after the captivating light beginning. They could become more interesting if the humour and drama element could be kept all through the programme.

(b) Script and visuals should be closer to the rural child's environment.

Based on these observations, the puppet child was introduced as an element to replace the story in the beginning. It became, in our later six programmes, the central figure around which revolved the science concepts. There was nothing so very special about the puppet. What made it popular amongst the children was its mannerisms, humour, and the music it played. The children love to see their traditional form of entertainment. It made them relax and to some extent also made them forget the awe and wonder of the sophisticated medium.

All the production materials were transported to Bombay to record the latter six proprammes in SAC TV studios. These were meant for SITE broadcast in four languages.

Conclusions

India is a country with extreme diversity. From the extreme modernity in the urban areas one can see villages which have not been touched by any of the conveniences of the 20th century. The communicators, film or television producers, all happened to be very urbane persons and SITE clusters consisted of villages which represented a totally different culture. For communication to be effective it was necessary to know the target audiences in great depth. It was not merely a question of giving information to the rural child. The problem was to show him or her images and sound so that he or she could comprehend the reasoning and processes of science.

The project was significant because it brought together diverse kinds of people with the primary objective of communicating. In our case the project leader and producer was a physicist who had become a communicator. Then the group had a child psychologist, evaluator, science experts, school-teachers and young engineering students working towards their bachelors' degree. All of these persons had been very remote from the milieu in which the rural child lived. The programme developed from being crudely rural to being somewhat realistic for the rural audience.

It is difficult to estimate the impact of SITE on the rural child, for in many villages he was not only exposed to television, but a lot of supporting facilities in his surroundings. In the case of the communicators, educational producers, it can be said that the challenge of making television programmes for children brought a great deal of awareness amongst them. It created a culture totally new to the country in terms of media, its application in the rural setting and above all the significance of doing it. It was a pity that just when we began to understand somewhat the nuances of TV communication for rural India this project as well as SITE came to an end.

References

Krishnamurthy, P V (1976) 'A Report — Satellite Instructional Television Experiment'.
Chander, R and Karnik, K (1976) 'Planning for Satellite Broadcasting', UNESCO Report No 78 on Mass Communication.
Chaudhri, M M (1974) 'A Feasibility Report on Utilization of Media in Rural Schools'.
Mukherjee, Rose, (1970) 'Television Guidelines for Early Childhood Education' A Report Prepared for National Instructional Television, USA.

The Nuffield 'Working with Science' Project and its Evaluation

J K Gilbert

During the early 1960s only the most academically inclined 16-year-old students took O Levels before going on to the A Level course. The introduction of the CSE broadened the band of students who were awarded a paper qualification at 16. Also, students began to stay on in full-time education without taking a full A Level programme. The Schools Council estimated this group as being 25% of the total in 1970. This figure is certainly no smaller in 1977.

Typically, these students return to school, or go full-time to a college of further education for one year, to repeat, or take additional subjects at, O Level or CSE, or to 'convert' a CSE into an O Level. Their time-table may well contain a large number of private study periods. They stay on for a variety of reasons: because their parents want them to do so, because they want more time or more qualifications before getting a job, or because they are not old enough to start in their chosen career, or because of the difficulty of getting a job. The majority of these students regard science as difficult and unrelated to their lives. The need for appropriate science-based materials became evident.

Preliminary work on the production of modular units of science-orientated work started in 1972. Activity gradually expanded, with the evolution of working parties in various parts of the country, and the Project Team, including an evaluator, was established in 1974 and is to continue to function until September 1977 at least.

Some facets of the development may be picked out for comment:

1. The writing team consisted mainly of teachers, over 100, in daily contact with the students for whom the materials were being developed. They included people often from outside teaching, who had special knowledge of the topic being developed.
2. Of the Organizing Team, only the organizer is full-time (being a science adviser on secondment).
3. The emphasis of the materials produced is on involving students in the way of science. They stress the method, skills and attitudes of science through topics related to the aspirations and interests of the students.

The materials, which are being published in three batches of about 13 units, starting in April 1977, by Longman's Resources Unit at York, cover a wide range of content area, eg brewing, noise, questioning prejudice and superstition, fire, psychology, keeping the heat in.

The key features to 'Working with Science' are given below:

Self-Programming

The materials have taken the form of a wide choice of self-programmed units. So, with a range of topics available to the students and several units normally in simultaneous use within a class, it follows that the student guides, addressed directly to the student, are the essential requirement. The units are intended to be used by individuals or small groups and the teacher's role is likely to be that of giving support and encouragement, questioning assumptions and developing scientific method, rather than trying to be a source of all knowledge. The aims of each unit are made clear to the student and self-evaluation devices are built in.

Support Material

For each unit a student's guide has been provided, giving objectives, ideas for investigation and background information. In most cases a set of teacher's notes have been written to supplement the student's guide. Slides, tapes, film-strips or packs of photographs were produced during the trials to support some of the units.

Choice

During trials, teachers in a school or college were asked to choose a bank of about a dozen titles. Students then made a choice of three or four units from the bank. There is considerable flexibility within each unit as most of them have a compulsory core with a number of options. Furthermore, students can generate their own investigations from a starting point suggested in a unit.

Relevance

The units are designed to be relevant to the needs and potential of the post-16 student and, therefore, are geared to the hobbies, vocations and any issues likely to be of interest to the students. They are asked to investigate real problems concerned with the real world.

Science

A broad view of science is taken and students apply the skills, methods and attitudes of the scientist to a wide range of topics.

Decision-Making

In several units students are invited to consider the factors which are (or should be) taken into account when taking decisions and to anticipate the social and economic consequences of them.

Time Allocation

The schools and colleges involved in trials were asked to provide about three hours per week.

Most units were designed to be about a half-term's work, experience showing that it is usually difficult to sustain student interest for longer than this. The units are divided into sections of which four or five were frequently found to give sufficient work on one topic.

The short 'mini-units' are designed to last two or three weeks. They were developed in response to suggestions that some units were too long and that shorter ones were needed to broaden the area of study or to provide work where a few weeks only were available. It was also suggested that short units were a useful start to the Project, giving both the teacher and the students and opportunity to establish the new pattern of working before beginning a major topic.

Community Involvement

In addition to involvement in the writing of several units, other members of the community have responded to questionnaires, given interviews and generally provided information.

Student Reports

The units encourage students to communicate their findings, conclusions, suggestions and ideas to anybody likely to be interested in their work. Reports may include an 8 mm film for a particular audience, a tape-slide set, display material for an exhibition or science fair, a local radio programme, a newspaper article and models or equipment which have been made. These end products are usually supported by a 'Project File' containing day-to-day records, cuttings, essays, questionnaires and test results.

Assessment

One means of assessment involves the mounting of an exhibition of student reports which is seen, and commented upon, by fellow students, teachers and visitors. This form imposes a minimum of constraint on the use of the Project materials.

During the trials it has become clear that some students expect a tangible reward for their efforts. Authors agreed that the units should be written and presented in such a way that assessment for the purpose of awarding a certificate was not excluded. The Schools Council has been conducting feasibility trials towards the introduction of the Certificate of Extended Education (CEE) intended to serve one-year subject-centred post-CSE courses. Many trials' teachers have used 'Working with Science' materials to support CEE syllabuses, often of the Mode III variety (teacher-designed and teacher-examined). The majority of such submissions include a good proportion of continuous assessment provision.

The evaluation of the project had three overall aims: to examine the scope and limitations of the novel aspects that were included, to assist in the development of the materials themselves, and to throw some light on the general educational concerns associated with the Project.

There are several novel features to this Project. Firstly, the material was almost exclusively written by serving science teachers. How well did this procedure work out? What sort of things did they produce? What 'view of science' is shown therein? Secondly, the materials were written for a rather ill-defined (and definable) group of students. Who are the 'New Sixth'? What are their achievements, ambitions, strengths and weaknesses? How do these materials relate to their needs, whether personal or externally imposed? How did they get on with the rather novel way of working? Thirdly, how do the teachers like the 'way of working' and, in some instances, novel approach and content of units? Did they approve of the view of science presented? Fourthly, how do the schools react to 'the New Sixth Former', particularly in the science education context?

Three threads were seen to the formative side of the evaluation. To monitor the trials, seeing where the materials were used, by whom and to what effect. To estimate the extent to which the trials materials met the declared aims of the Project, both within individual units and overall. Lastly, to identify constraints on the use of the materials by students, teachers and schools.

The general concerns are extremely broad, but likely to become increasingly pressing in the future. Namely, what is involved, for all concerned, in the establishing of independent learning in secondary school science and what are the educational needs, especially in relation to science, for this group of students?

The evaluation used two main tools: the questionnaire and the personal visit to the school. Questionnaires were used to collect factual information and overall opinions. They were designed at the outset of the formal trials (in 1974) and were based on the declared aims of the Project and classroom experience during the experience of the preliminary trials (1972-74). When a group of teachers, assembled at Buxton in 1974 for a writing conference, were asked, 'What questionnaires will teachers and students actually fill in for this Project?', the answer led to a battery of five one-page inquiries.

The main approach to the evaluation was by visits. The evaluator visited 12 (out of 40) schools in 1974 and 24 (out of 72) in 1975-76, the selection normally being on the recommendation of an area co-ordinator on a variety of criteria. Teachers were questioned, alone, on the background to the class, the reactions to individual units, the problems associated with choice and independent learning and on assessment. Students were met, either individually or in natural working groups, in the absence of the teacher, to inquire into their previous academic history, reactions to the units, problems with the independent learning format, and on their view of science. As a result of each visit, a report, based on the taping of the above interviews, was prepared.

The outcome of all this diverse activity was numerous and only a small part can be presented here. One major fact was the production of an evaluation report on each unit immediately after its designated trial period. Each report contained: an analysis of all questionnaire data; a collection of all written comments on questionnaires, analyzed into categories; the relevant sections of all visits' reports and a commentary on how the unit was received, with observations on apparent weaknesses and recommendations for rewriting. These reports, together with all crude data available, were sent to the respective rewriting sub-editors. They were discussed with the original writers of the units and formed the basis for the reconsiderations of each unit.

Some of the observations of the evaluation, on the non formative side, are as follows:

1. The typical trials school was a large, mixed, 11-18 comprehensive. Very few further education colleges were involved in the trials, perhaps because of their different organizational traditions.
2. The majority of students intended to remain at school for one further year (ie 16 to 17). Although a comparatively high proportion (15%) declared themselves 'undecided' as to future jobs, the majority intended to take 'non-science' jobs, eg footballer, shop assistant.
3. The spectrum of students who used the materials was extremely broad, from three A Level candidates to five CSE candidates. On the whole, the 'target population' was reached.
4. Discussion with teachers and students revealed the following 'view of science':
   (a) Science seen as a process, as a framework of procedures. These included observation, recording, analyzing, hypothesis formation, the priority largely being unquestioned.
   (b) Science seen as relevant content, eg how to analyze vitamin C, how to insulate a house.
   (c) Science seen as being buried underneath materials, ie seen in terms of subject content, eg the chemistry in 'crime detection', the idea of models in 'paper aeroplanes'.

(d)   Science seen as an investigation into the consequence of acts by individuals.

5. The idea of 'the image of a scientist' was a recurrent theme. Seeing a scientist as a person who knows all the answers is a totally different framework in which to use 'Working with Science' from seeing the scientist as a person who asks the questions. Perhaps the best manifestation of this theme occurred where many, particularly those with extensive experience in the physical sciences, found difficulty in handling the imprecise results obtained from experiments involving the responses of people. The association of 'the scientist' with 'producing a unique current answer' proved very strong in a society where the concepts of chance are not part of the formally taught, cultural background.

6. It became apparent that teachers, to get best use from the materials, ought to work only with students who were volunteers and about whose background and aspirations they know a good deal; be able to appreciate the difference in role implied; have a definite idea of the role of practical work.

These latter points indicate the need for in-service work to precede the use of these materials.

The Use of Simulation Games in Schools–a Case Study

H I Ellington, N H Langton, M Smythe

Introduction

During the last 10 years, educational games have become an established part of the school curriculum in a number of subject areas, particularly geography, modern studies and the various social sciences. Until recently, however, there has been a comparative shortage of good science-based games, especially at a level suitable for use in the upper forms of secondary schools. It was in an attempt to help fill this gap that 'The Power Station Game' and the other simulation exercises described in this paper were developed.

Section 1. The Development of 'The Power Station Game'

Initiation of the Project

In 1973, Professor N H Langton, Head of the School of Physics at Robert Gordon's Institute of Technology, Aberdeen, was asked by the Scottish Central Committee on Science (the body that advises the Scottish Education Department on matters relating to the science curriculum) to look into the possibility of developing a physics-based simulation exercise suitable for use in Scottish schools in the somewhat slack period following the end of the 'Higher' grade examinations. Professor Langton set up a working party comprising himself, Dr H I Ellington (Head of the Educational Technology Unit at RGIT) and HMI Mr H MacLaren. This subsequently prepared a report outlining the structure and format of a possible game based on the planning of a new power station for a hypothetical area ('The Power Station Game'), suggesting what its educational aims and objectives might be, and giving details of a possible programme for its development.

As a result of this report, the Scottish Central Committee on Science set up an official sub-committee in order to develop 'The Power Station Game'. This comprised the members of the working party together with the principal physics teachers of four local comprehensive schools (Mr T Carnie, Inverurie Academy, Mr A Garrow, Kincorth Academy, Mr K Jackson, Bankhead Academy and Mr I Muckersie, Hazlehead Academy) and Mr J Graham, Senior Depute Director of Education, Grampian Region.

Development and Field Testing of Game

Work on the development of the first version of 'The Power Station Game' was completed between February and May 1974, and two full-scale pilot runs of the game were held in June 1974 — the first in Inverurie Academy and the second in

Hazlehead Academy. A paper describing the progress of the project to date was subsequently presented at the 1974 SAGSET Conference (Ellington and Langton, 1975a).

The pilot runs held in June 1974 showed that 'The Power Station Game' was a viable and worthwhile educational exercise that achieved all its educational aims and objectives at least in part, and that no major alterations to its organization or structure appeared to be necessary. There were, however, a number of ways in which the detailed organization and presentation of the game could be improved, so it was decided to carry out a complete re-write of the game package with a view to holding a second series of pilot runs in the summer term of the 1974/75 session. Following completion of this work, three highly-successful pilot runs of the game were held in local schools in May-June 1975 (in Inverurie Academy, Cults Academy and Rubislaw Academy) and a one-day seminar incorporating a complete run-through of the game was held for local teachers. A paper on the game and a two-part article presenting the data on the physics of power stations contained therein was subsequently published in *Physics Education* (Ellington and Langton, 1975b, c, d).

The highly-successful series of pilot runs that was held in May-June 1975 showed that 'The Power Station Game' required only a few minor modifications to its organization and structure in order to make it a suitable exercise for use in schools. It was, however, decided to carry out another complete re-write of the game, since the form of the game package that had been used in all the pilot runs was not suitable for mass production. Work on this final re-write of the game, in which the various documents were re-designed to incorporate a completely new set of diagrams and photographs (the latter supplied by the CEGB photographic library, whose co-operation is gratefully acknowledged), was completed by the end of September 1975.

Publication of Game

In 1974, the Scottish Central Committee on Science waived all claim to copyright in respect of 'The Power Station Game' and vested same in the members of the organizing Sub-committee. The Sub-committee was also authorized to investigate ways in which the game package could be mass produced and made available for general use in schools and colleges.

During the summer of 1975, Professor Langton and Dr Ellington carried out preliminary negotiations with two publishing firms and Dr Ellington made an approach to the Institution of Electrical Engineers with a view to their sponsoring publication of the game. Subsequently, the IEE offered to undertake publication of the game and to meet all the associated expenses.

During the following two months, the final form of the game package was worked out by Dr Ellington and Mr M Smythe, whom the IEE had placed in overall charge of the Power Station Game project. Preparation of the game documents was completed by the end of January 1976 and the game was launched in February.

To date (January 1977), the game has been purchased by over 100 schools, local authority resource centres, colleges of education, technical colleges, polytechnics and universities in all parts of Britain as well as by over 20 educational establishments in other parts of the world, including Australia, Canada, France, Norway, South Africa and New Zealand. In addition, it has been purchased by a number of other bodies such as the Central Electricity Generating Board, Fawley Power Station and the Fast Reactor Centre at Dounreay, where it is being used in staff training. All feedback received so far (including that from a number of full-scale field tests of the final game package held in the Aberdeen area in June

1976) has been extremely encouraging, indicating that the game package is now satisfactory in all respects and that the game itself is an extremely valuable addition to our educational armoury.

Section 2. Description of 'The Power Station Game'

General Description of Game

'The Power Station Game' is concerned with the many factors which must be taken into account before a decision can be reached to build a certain type of power station at a particular site. The starting point of the game is the hypothesis that an Electricity Generating Board has decided to build a 2000 MW station in a certain area, and has selected a number of sites on which it may be built. The object of the game is to reach a decision as to the type of station (which may be coal-fired, oil-fired or nuclear) and the site. The participating pupils are divided into three equal groups, each of which has to make as strong a case as possible for building one particular type of station.

Educational Aims and Objectives

Apart from the obvious aim of teaching the citizens of tomorrow something about the technology and economics of the electricity generation industry, 'The Power Station Game' has been designed to achieve a number of well-defined educational aims and objectives. The most important of these are: to provide practical experience of the handling, interpretation and analysis of data; to provide an opportunity of working with others on a common problem; and to show that the process of decision-making can be extremely complex.

Note that the primary function of the game is not to teach the participants hard facts, although they undoubtedly learn a great deal about physics and electrical engineering as well as other subjects such as geography, economics and environmental studies. Rather, it is to demonstrate that physics is not a dull, rather difficult academic subject that is of no great importance except to scientists, but an interesting and far-ranging field of study that has important applications in areas that affect the everyday lives of us all; and also to act as a vehicle for cultivating the various ancillary skills and desirable attitudinal traits that are generally considered to 'rub off' on pupils who undertake a science education. The important role that exercises such as 'The Power Station Game' can play in fostering such 'bonus' skills (eg decision-making, problem-solving, communication and interpersonal skills) and attitudinal traits (eg willingness to appreciate the points of view of others) is discussed in detail elsewhere (Ellington and Percival, 1977a, b).

Contents of Game Package

'The Power Station Game' is designed to be played by 18 pupils (although it can easily be adapted for higher or lower numbers) and the game package contains all the material needed to play the game with this number. The package consists of:

1. 20 copies of an Introductory Booklet providing a general introduction to the process by which electricity is generated and distributed; the booklet is fully illustrated with photographs of power stations and their associated plant.
2. 3 copies each of a Coal Station Booklet, an Oil Station Booklet and a Nuclear Station Booklet. These contain comprehensive technical and financial data on the three types of station and are fully illustrated with photographs and specially-prepared diagrams.

3. 3 copies of a Project Group Booklet providing the pupils in each group with detailed instructions relating to the various stages of the game, comprehensive geographical information about the area in which the station is to be sited and a file of reference material for use in the later stages of the game.
4. A set of role cards for use in the Public Inquiry that forms the final stage of the game.
5. A Teacher's Guide containing detailed instructions regarding all aspects of the organization and running of the game, specimen solutions to all the technical and financial calculations and a guide to the solution of the siting problem for each type of station.

The Game Schedule

'The Power Station Game' is designed to be played over a continuous two-day period, with the final stage (the Public Inquiry) taking place a few days later. The various stages of the game are described below.

STAGE 1

Roughly a week before the game is due to take place, each of the pupils involved is issued with a copy of the Introductory Booklet. Any remedial or preliminary work thought necessary by the teacher-in-charge is also carried out at this time.

STAGE 2

At the start of the game proper, the pupils are introduced to the game by the teacher-in-charge. This takes roughly 15 minutes.

STAGE 3

The pupils are now divided into three teams, each team representing a group of 'experts' on one type of station and having the task of trying to ensure that their particular station is the one finally built. The teams are issued with all three copies of their Station Booklet and with a copy of the Project Group Booklet, and, after familiarizing themselves with their contents, carry out the technical calculations for their station. These involve working out the energy losses at each stage of the generation process, calculating the fuel and cooling water requirements and finding the rates at which waste products are produced. Stage 3 takes roughly three hours.

STAGE 4

When the technical calculations have been completed, each group retains one copy of its Station Booklet and hands one copy to each of the other teams. Each of the three teams is then further subdivided into three subgroups (hence the reason why 18 pupils is the optimum number for the game).

The first of these subgroups carries out the costing calculations for their station, making use of the data in their Station Booklet to calculate both the capital cost and present and future running costs for the station.

The second subgroup has the task of determining the best site for their station using the information contained in their Station Booklet and in the Project Group Booklet.

The third subgroup — the survey subgroup — has the task of examining the cases likely to be made for the other two stations. This subgroup is able to obtain from the teacher-in-charge any information relating to the other two stations that it may deem necessary, although it is not, of course, provided with information about the group's own station. The survey subgroup is necessary in order to enable an informed discussion to take place in the plenary session that constitutes the penultimate stage of the game.

STAGE 5

After the completion of Stage 4 of the game (which takes roughly two and a half hours), the various subgroups in each team re-combine in order to prepare a report on their proposed scheme for presentation at the plenary session. Any visual aid materials that they require are also made available. Stage 5 takes roughly two hours.

STAGE 6

The plenary session at which spokesmen from the three competing teams present their reports forms the climax of the main section of 'The Power Station Game'. Order of presentation is determined by drawing lots, each team being allocated 15 to 20 minutes to present its case and answer questions on its proposed scheme. An open discussion then follows, at the end of which a decision is reached as to which scheme should be adopted by the Generating Board. The plenary session is chaired by the teacher-in-charge, an independent assessor (or panel of assessors) being present to adjudicate as to which group has put forward the best case.

STAGE 7

The final stage of 'The Power Station Game' consists of a Public Inquiry into the proposed scheme. It is recommended that this be held a few days after the plenary session in order to give the pupils time to identify with their new roles and prepare their cases by making use of the Public Inquiry Reference File. Three of the pupils from the winning team are given the task of defending their proposed scheme against possible objections, the remaining members of the team being assigned roles supporting the scheme. The members of the two losing teams are given roles of objectors. The Public Inquiry is chaired by the teacher-in-charge, a new independent assessor being present in order to deliver the final verdict on the proposed scheme.

Potential Uses of the Game

The original brief of the team that developed 'The Power Station Game' was to produce an educational game that could be used with post-Higher physics pupils in Scottish secondary schools. The level of the game was therefore pitched accordingly, the physics content being roughly 'A' level in standard; this means that the game is also ideally suited for use in the sixth form of English secondary schools.

By suitable modification, however, the game can also be used with younger or less able pupils and with students at tertiary level. With the former, the teacher-in-charge can provide the participants with the answers to some or all of the technical and costing calculations, thus allowing them to concentrate on the more qualitative aspects of the game. With the latter some of the technical data and instructions can be withheld, thus putting a greater onus on the participants. Nor is the game limited to physics pupils, since it is sufficiently broad in its scope to enable it to be used as a teaching tool in other subject areas. The parts of the game concerned with the siting of the station, for example, can be used with geography pupils, and by omitting the technical calculations, the game can easily be adapted for use by modern studies pupils.

The game is also sufficiently realistic and sophisticated to enable it to be used as a staff training exercise by various branches of the electrical engineering industry, local authorities, and (as we have seen in 'Publication of Game') Atomic Energy Authority establishments. It can also be used for training purposes by bodies such as the Institution of Electrical Engineers; indeed, this was one of the reasons why the IEE decided to sponsor the project.

Section 3. Projects Generated by 'The Power Station Game'

General Review

During the last three years, a number of further simulation exercises designed for use in schools have been developed as a direct result of the Power Station Game project, and work on a number of other projects is currently in progress. These are described below.

Point Fields Public Inquiry

As shown in 'The Game Schedule', the final stage of 'The Power Station Game' consists of a Public Inquiry, and the great success of this during pilot runs of the game led three members of the organizing sub-committee (Dr Ellington, Mr Garrow and Mr Muckersie) to the conclusion that a simulated Public Inquiry would constitute a viable and extremely worthwhile educational exercise in its own right. 'Point Fields Public Inquiry' (a simulated public inquiry into the siting of a large petrochemical complex) was subsequently developed, receiving its first (highly successful) field test at the 1976 SAGSET Conference. The game (which is now commercially available — see footnote) is described in detail elsewhere (Ellington, Garrow and Muckersie, 1977; Ellington and Percival, 1977b).

Hydropower 77 and the Pumped-Storage Multi-Project Pack

Another direct outcome of 'The Power Station Game' is the 'Hydropower 77' competition being run by the North of Scotland Hydro-Electric Board during the winter of 1976-77 for secondary schools in their area. This is a competitive multi-disciplinary design project that makes use of the same basic concept as 'The Power Station Game', namely, the planning of a new power station (this time a hydro-electric pumped storage scheme) for a hypothetical area, and embodies many of the ideas used in the latter (overall maps of the area, detailed maps of potential sites, calculations based on realistic technical and economic data, etc). The project was devised by Dr Ellington in collaboration with Dr E Addinall (also of RGIT) and is described in detail elsewhere (Ellington and Addinall, 1976).

The material developed for use in 'Hydropower 77' has itself been used as the basis of a further exercise — the 'Pumped-Storage Multi-Project Pack'. This is a completely new type of educational package that exploits the same basic set of resource materials in a variety of projects designed for use in the teaching of a wide range of subjects (geography, modern studies, economics, physics and engineering). The six basic projects included in the pack are primarily designed for use in secondary schools with pupils of roughly O level standard, but are all sufficiently flexible and open-ended to enable them to be used with more advanced pupils or to be adapted for use at tertiary level. The package (which is now commercially available — see footnote) is described in detail elsewhere (Ellington and Addinall, 1977).

The Broadcasting Game Project

Because of the success of 'The Power Station Game', the Institution of Electrical Engineers and Robert Gordon's Institute of Technology decided (in mid-1976) to collaborate in the development and publication of a successor. This is to be based on the establishment of a broadcasting system in a developing country, and will probably take the same form as the 'Pumped-Storage Multi-Project Pack' described in the previous section. A joint RGIT/IEE Committee has been formed to develop

404

the game, which is hoped to be available towards the end of 1978.

The Central Heating Game Project

Another direct by-product of 'The Power Station Game' is the 'Central Heating Game' currently being developed by staff of Robert Gordon's Institute of Technology. This will be based on the central heating of a house, and will also probably take the form of a multi-disciplinary multi-project pack. It is hoped that the package (which will be primarily designed for use in the upper forms of secondary schools) will be available late in 1977.

Conclusion

The main lessons learned from the Power Station Game project are as follows:

1. Given proper central co-ordination, it is perfectly feasible for a number of separate bodies or organizations to collaborate successfully in the initiation, development and exploitation of a large-scale educational exercise such as 'The Power Station Game'.

2. Large-scale science-based simulation-games such as 'The Power Station Game' appear to be capable of fulfilling an extremely worthwhile and important educational role; their main strengths, however, are in cultivating skills peripheral to or associated with the teaching of a subject and not in the main-line teaching of the cognitive content of the subject.

3. Such exercises, however, suffer from one major disadvantage in that their length makes them difficult to fit into the normal curriculum of a school or college (the main body of 'The Power Station Game' occupies two complete days); this virtually limits their use to the slack time after examinations or at the end of a term or session. (The various exercises that have been and are being developed as a result of 'The Power Station Game' should not suffer from this restriction on their use, being designed to fit easily into the normal curriculum.)

4. The experience gained by working on a major project of this type is extremely valuable to all concerned, making it much easier for subsequent projects of a similar or related nature to be conceived and carried through.

References

Ellington, H I and Langton, N H (1975a) 'The Power Station Game' 'SAGSET Journal' 5,1 p 31-35.

Ellington, H I and Langton, N H (1975b) 'The Power Station Game — a Simulation Exercise for Sixth-Form Physics Pupils' 'Physics Education' September p 445-447.

Langton, N H and Ellington, H I (1975c) 'The Physics of Power Stations' Part 1: Fossil-Fuelled Power Stations 'Physics Education' September p 448-452.

Ellington, H I and Langton, N H (1975d) 'The Physics of Power Stations' Part 2: Nuclear Power Stations 'Physics Education' November p 504-508.

Ellington, H I and Addinall, E (1976) 'Hydropower 77' Bulletin of Scottish Centre for Mathematics, Science and Technical Education (Dundee College of Education) 9 p 9-10.

Ellington, H I and Addinall, E (1977) 'The Multi-Disciplinary Multi-Project Pack — a New Concept in Simulation-Gaming' Programmed Learning and Educational Technology (in press).

Ellington, H I, Garrow, A G and Muckersie, J M (1977) 'Point Fields Public Enquiry — a New Science-Based Simulation Game for Use in Schools and Colleges' Bulletin of Scottish Centre for Mathematics, Science and Technical Education (Dundee College of Education) (in press).

Ellington, H I and Percival, F (1977a) 'The Place of Multi-Disciplinary Games in School Science'

Schools Science Review (in press).

Ellington, H I and Percival, F (1977b) 'Educating "through" Science Using Multi-Disciplinary Simulation Games' Programmed Learning and Educational Technology (in press).

Footnote

'The Power Station Game' and the 'Pumped-Storage Multi-Project Pack' are available from the IEE, Station House, Nightingale Road, Hitchin, Hertfordshire, SG5 1RJ.

'Point Fields Public Inquiry' is available from The Scottish Centre for Mathematics, Science and Technical Education, Dundee College of Education, Gardyne Road, Broughty Ferry, Dundee, DD5 1NY.

Language Games
for Reading Progress

E Hunter

There is no single formula by use of which all children can be taught to read. Four basic methods, used more or less concurrently, are generally accepted as valuable. I believe that the learner should be exposed to all four, with some emphasis on the ones to which he responds best.

First, there is the language-experience approach. Ideally the pupil is 'caught' during or immediately following some pleasant activity — for example drawing or painting.

'I like that. Tell me about it', says the teacher.
'It's my mum hanging out the washing', replies the child.

On a strip of paper attached for the purpose to the child's drawing, or on a facing page, the teacher prints in lower case letters:

'This is my mum hanging out the washing.'

and now there exists an entry in a personalized reading book, to which more entries may be added. Children usually take pleasure in reading and re-reading their own dictated words, and books of this kind can be regularly read to the teacher and to other pupils.

In the case of an older pupil, the dictated words should relate to a topic of interest, for example,

'My big brother bought a second-hand motor bike on Saturday.'

or

'Stan Bowles won the match for Queens Park Rangers last week by scoring the only goal.'

Cut-out magazine or newspaper photographs can accompany these statements to provide picture 'cues' for future reading sessions as the personal reading book grows.

Motivation is the most important single feature of the language-experience method. Through familiarity with his own spoken words, the pupil is enabled to 'read' them, and this can be wonderfully encouraging to a pupil who has hitherto failed in his attempts to decode written language. Of course he may well be memorizing more than he is actually reading, particulary in the initial stages, but I do not believe that this in any way invalidates the language-experience method. Pupils begin to read and to recognize individual words by being asked to do so:

'Can you point to the word "Saturday"?'
'Show me the word "only"'

The recognition of individual words is best achieved by keeping them in the context of the original meaningful prose. It is not very important that the pupil should be able to recognize words which have been listed as isolated words out of context. But it is important that he should have frequent practice in the reading of his 'book', and a great deal of praise and encouragement for achievement.

The second method is an ongoing strategy by which pupils should be helped to make meaning of printed prose and hence to read it. This is often called the psycho-linguistic guessing game method; 'psycho-linguistic' because it is derived from psychological and linguistic theory, 'guessing game' because this is how we hope that the pupil will come to see and enjoy the task. Psychology tells us that we have an instinctive desire to make meaning, and from linguistics comes the theory that it is familiarity with the patterns and rhythms of their native tongue which helps children to make meaning of printed prose. When the pupil encounters an unfamiliar word in a sentence, the teacher should always give him plenty of time to solve this problem for himself. Pressure of time inclines the teacher towards supplying the unknown word so that the pupil may continue as quickly as possible. But in the long term it is much more valuable to provide the pupil with a strategy by which he himself can deal with the problem. In a situation where a child is confronted by an unknown word, he should be given plenty of time, in a relaxed atmosphere, to establish its meaning. When it becomes evident that he is unlikely to do this, the teacher should help him by asking him to

'Read what comes before that word once again. Now, leave the word for a minute, and see if you can read what comes after it.'

If the pupil can do this, he is now asked to 'have a guess' at what the unknown word might be:

'What do you think it might be?'

If the guess is an intelligent one which shows that the pupil has understood the passage, he should be given praise for the guess, even if it is inaccurate. With a build-up of confidence and plenty of practice, accuracy will be achieved at a later stage in the learning process. If the task of reading is seen as that of deriving meaning from the printed text, then an occasional word can often be altered without affecting the meaning. A child may read the sentence,

'When it began to rain, Susan went to Sandra's home to play.'

as

'When it began to rain, Susan went to Sandra's house to play.'

Understanding and reading this sentence may represent a great deal of progress of a highly motivating kind, and it could be inhibiting and counterproductive at this stage to refuse to accept the word 'house' for 'home', and to attempt to engage the pupil in phonics analysis and synthesis after which the meaningful 'flow' of the sentence could be lost. Where and when to insist on accuracy is a matter for the teacher's judgment, and a teacher who understands the principles of this method is unlikely to lack sensitivity in using it. Competent fluent adult readers use the psycho-linguistic 'guessing game' method when meeting an occasional unfamiliar word. They derive its meaning from the context in which they find it. In training children to do this we are helping them to become intelligent adult readers. Finding classroom time is the problem when one wants to use this method. Individual reading sessions are difficult to accomplish in a busy classroom, and it is probably advisable to help children privately in 10-minute periods immediately before or after school.

Older children can be given practice in the use of the psycho-linguistic method by working on close procedure exercises. A passage of appropriate difficulty is typed, and every fifth word is replaced by a gap or a line. Working individually, or collaborating in groups of two or three, the pupils are asked to supply the missing words. This is a valuable way of occupying groups of children productively without continuous teacher involvement.

The third method on my list is the phonics method by which the pupil's attention is drawn to the individual sounds and blends of sounds represented within each word. These sounds are then synthesized to form the word. The method is slow, and lacks motivation for many children, but some knowledge of phonics is an essential component of reading 'equipment'. Children should know the sounds which the letters of the alphabet are likely to represent, despite the fact that there are so many exceptions to the rules; for example 's' does not sound like the usual 'hissy snake' in the 'sugar'. But these exceptions will gradually be accepted as experience grows. Knowledge of letter sounds provide children (and older backward readers) with what is called 'word attack skill' — a strategy for attacking the problem of decoding. Common blends, like 'ing' or 'est' endings should be learned. Used together with the psycho-linguistic guessing game method, a knowledge of phonics can help to change an intelligent guess into one which is also accurate. There are theorists who regard these two methods as dichotomous, or almost mutually exclusive, but I see them as complementary. The problem surrounding phonics is the question of degree. To what extent should written language be analyzed into parts of words which have to be sounded out before being put together again? The degree of phonics teaching depends upon the needs and responses of individual pupils, and this can only be determined by the teacher's judgment. It is like balancing the ingredients of a recipe to achieve the index mix for the individual. I believe that some phonics teaching is essential for all pupils, but clearly no pupil should have his progress slowed down by an emphasis on phonics which, for him, is undesirable.

The fourth method is whole word recognition or 'look and say' as it is often called. Pupils are asked to recognize and remember whole words, often presented to classes or groups of children on flash cards. A limited number of these words is then used to produce texts which are often both repetitious and artificial. Some of the most commonly used reading schemes are based on this method, and the strictly controlled vocabulary results in reading matter which often lacks interest and meaning. Moreover it can be argued that the task of learning words in isolation is more difficult than learning the same words in a meaningful context. If a child is attempting to differentiate between the words shoulder and shelter presented on flash cards, the task may be confusing, even if a knowledge of phonics is used for extra cues. But it is less likely that the words will be confused if they are presented in meaningful sentences, for example:

'Tom fell down from the tree and hurt his shoulder.'
'When it started to rain Tom ran for shelter.'

Pupils will often use whole word recognition quite naturally, because certain words in a story are longer than others, or because some words have unusual 'shapes'. They rarely hesitate over words like 'aeroplane', 'elephant', 'Cinderella' — while words like 'was' and 'saw' often prove to be confusing. Whole word recognition should certainly be encouraged when children are reading meaningful language, but it is doubtful if there is anything to be gained by reversing the process — that is, by isolating words and teaching them in advance of their use in meaningful context. Similarly it is of doubtful value to list words at the end of a story to find out if children can read them out of context after they have read the story. If the words are kept in context for this revision exercise the pupil has some cues available to help him to decode the individual words. He is much more likely to arrive at the meaning of the word by processes involving intelligence and reasoning.

Successful blending of these four teaching methods is an individual matter and is likely to depend upon the teacher's philosophy concerning the nature of the reading task. If reading is seen as being essentially the matching of sound to written symbol, then phonics and 'look and say' will be given emphasis. But if reading is viewed as deriving meaning from the text, if comprehension is felt to be the object of the exercise, then phonics and 'look and say' will be used as ancillary methods, and emphasis will be given to the language-experience and the psycho-linguistic 'guessing game' methods.

Reading is inextricably interwoven with the other communication skills of listening, speaking and writing. Use of the language-experience and psycho-linguistic approaches highlights the importance of spoken language upon which these methods depend. Children whose spoken language skills are well developed are more likely to be able to make good use of prediction in the process of reading. If this is so, there are two corollaries. Firstly, the reading materials which we offer to young readers should be as similar to spoken language as possible, and secondly, in our attempts to improve the reading skills of our pupils we should endeavour to develop and extend their skills in spoken language. Improving children's ability to use speech is clearly a worthwhile educational aim in its own right. The improvement of reading skills provides, however, an extra reason for giving pupils as much practice as possible in listening and speaking. The Bullock Report, *A Language for Life* (1975) lists the following objectives for language development on page 67:

'5.30 We advocate, in short, planned intervention in the child's language development. At the level at present being discussed this will mean that the teacher recognizes the need for the child to include in his experience the following uses of language, and that she will then keep an effective record of his progress in them:
Reporting on present and recalled experiences.
Collaborating towards agreed ends.
Projecting into the future; anticipating and predicting.
Projecting and comparing possible alternatives.
Perceiving casual and dependent relationships.
Giving explanations of how and why things happen.
Expressing and recognizing tentativeness.
Dealing with problems in the imagination and seeing possible solutions.
Creating experiences through the use of imagination.
Justifying behaviour.
Reflecting on feelings, their own and other people's.'

How does a teacher set about the task of helping her pupils to achieve objectives of this kind? Clearly, by using every opportunity to foster conversation with her pupils, and among them. The teacher should exploit classroom methods which necessitate group work — co-operative and collaborative learning situations. Children should be expected to discuss their ideas, and to listen to the opinions of others. Discussions relating to real situations which interest the pupils are the most desirable kind. These are likely to be meaningful and stimulating: the planning of a class excursion, the production of a play, the creation of a new recipe for cooking. Together with real situations there is ample scope for the use of games which stimulate conversation. It is noteworthy that the Bullock Report recommendation quoted above exhorts the teacher to give the child experience in various uses of language and also to

'keep an effective record of his progress in them.'

Together with the recommendations relating to the need for a school policy which is both 'organized' and 'systematic', this points to the desirability of having sets of materials and schemes or systems of games in a school resources bank by use of which individual progress can be assessed and monitored. It is not suggested that the use of games should replace real discussion in the classroom, only that it should augment and complement it.

As for the nature of the games, they should serve as far as possible to enable children to achieve objectives of the kind quoted. They should help to promote confidence in the use of language — in articulation. They should involve children in situations which demand listening skills, clarity of thought and precision of language — situations which will effectively help children to extend their vocabularies and to become increasingly confident and sophisticated in language usage generally. Dennis and Georgina Gahagan, in their book *Talk Reform*, describe 11 language games which they used in a research project in London infant schools. These games provide a useful basis for the development of a system of games for children of primary age. The Inner London Education Authority's Media Resources Centre has published a series of language games which were devised and piloted by London teachers. The games are valuable in their original form, but they become even more valuable if they are adapted to meet the specific needs of individual pupils and groups of pupils.

Ideally, language games should be planned to require teacher intervention rather than continuous teacher supervision or involvement. Nevertheless games must be taught. The quality of the pupils' language 'output' will depend upon the teacher's initial 'input' when useful vocabulary is introduced and explored. Grading into appropriate levels of difficulty and the subsequent drawing up of individual record sheets is discussed in some detail in a recent publication by the Council for Educational Technology, *Reading Skills: A Systematic Approach* (Hunter, 1977).

Devising, adapting, producing, grading and organizing a resource bank of language games represents a formidable amount of work. Administrators and heads of schools who wish to implement the recommendations of the Bullock Report will give suitable priority to this task, and arrange for some working time allocation within school hours to reduce the extra time required. Success will depend upon the degree of commitment of the team of teachers whose combined efforts are necessary to create and implement a language policy for a school or a group of schools.

References

Gahagan, D M and G A (1970) 'Talk Reform' Routledge and Kegan Paul, London.
Hunter, E (1977) 'Reading Skills: A Systematic Approach' CET Guidelines 3. Councils and Education Press Ltd, London.
HMSO (1975) 'A Language for Life' Report of the Committee of Inquiry appointed by the Secretary of State for Education and Science under the Chairmanship of Sir Alan Bullock, London.
ILEA Media Resources Centre, London.

Individualized Learning Centres: a Pragmatic Approach to the Development of a Cost-Effective and Flexible Way to Provide Remedial Help

M Needham, W J K Davies, S Leevers

Introduction

The use of a systems approach to the provision of remedial work in reading was a natural response to the demand for this service at the County Programmed Learning Centre in St Albans. The approach is completely individualized and based on prescriptive teaching using structured materials following diagnostic testing. This paper describes the system used in St Albans and also discusses a number of forms in which the system has been 'exported' so that experience gained could be more evenly spread over the county of Hertfordshire. The export of this system involved training teachers to use educational technology in the classroom situation by working within a system thus using educational innovation rather than initiating it. This was achieved by a basically mathetical approach using backward chaining: a situation was set up by the Centre; school-teachers were encouraged to send children and then to come themselves to see what was happening and thereafter gradually to take over operation of the system. This prevented the dichotomy between theory and classroom practice which often occurs when training courses are organized separately from the ongoing work in the classroom.

Remedial Reading at the Programmed Learning Centre, St Albans

In 1968 when certain college craft students were using basic mathematics learning programs, a group of students was identified as needing remedial work in reading. Applying a systems approach to the problem led to the development of an individualized materials-based system designed to meet the needs of young adults. The selection of structured materials, the design and production of further programmed materials, the selection and use of suitable diagnostic tests and the design of methods of recording resulted in a flexible individualized system which can equally well be used with secondary schoolchildren and with adults so that the viable age range was extended from 11 to 60-plus.

The development of reading by systematic progression within a structured framework as described by Potts (1976) is an efficient and effective way to the mastery of the hierarchy of skills involved. Where remedial reading is concerned, it is also important, at the outset, to measure current attainment and to identify any underlying problems. By using suitable tests, the starting point can be identified and the problems diagnosed, and thus the selection and use of suitable materials ensures that the chain of failure is broken. The structured materials used for teaching reading were programmed to ensure constant student involvement, immediate knowledge of results, step by step development and constant review in mechanical reading, subskills area, comprehension, writing and spelling.

A carefully structured system of phonic exercises (IRMA, 1973) was developed for adults and secondary schoolchildren and later a phonic scheme (Signpost Word Families, 1976) which included comprehension work and word games was developed for use with junior schoolchildren. As the work progressed, a very wide range of commercially produced structured materials was assembled and used. Where areas of deficiency were identified, structured materials were developed to fill the gaps (eg Resources Charts; Visual Perception Exercises, 1976; Cursive Writing Programme, 1977). The Programmed Learning Centre, as a county display unit for programmed and structured materials, collects, develops and uses the majority of available materials for teaching reading. These materials, together with a variety of books at various reading levels, are currently used to teach about 150 adults and children during 13 sessions each week. This teaching load is maintained to ensure that experience at the coalface continues and the identification of areas of need occurs at first hand. See Table 1 for a summary of the system used.

Exporting the Systems Approach to Literacy Work

As a Centre responsible for the development of programmed learning in schools throughout Hertfordshire, the geographical location of the Centre in the south west of the county led us to consider how the systems approach to literacy work could be exported so that there would be more even provision throughout the county. This approach involved selecting and assembling a suitable collection of materials and training the teachers in diagnostic testing and prescriptive teaching. Various methods of training teachers to use the systems approach were considered and four contrasting schemes of training were tried out. Each scheme has been applied in more than one type of situation and the results from these are evaluated. The four different approaches to training are described below.

1. *In-service courses:* Many courses for teachers on the various skills involved including diagnostic testing, design of structured materials, organization and use of individualized learning materials, etc, have been organized. These varied in length from two days to two years on a one meeting per week basis. The courses were held in various locations — local colleges, teachers' centres, colleges of education, individual schools, etc. Although the professional expertise of the teachers involved was improved, the effect in the classroom situation appeared to be very small.

2. *Distance learning:* This took the form of a manual (Leevers, 1973) designed for secondary school teachers who were inexperienced in remedial literacy work to be able to:
   (a) use diagnostic tests to identify reading and spelling standards and difficulties;
   (b) select suitable materials from the collection suggested as the minimum necessary to cover most eventualities;
   (c) use appropriate materials and techniques to improve the reading ages of the pupils involved.
   This manual was originally monitored in use in two totally different secondary comprehensive school situations:
   (i) In a school where the children in need of remedial help were formed into a class for all subject teaching at first-year entry and continued in this class until suitable standards of work enabled them to be transferred.
   (ii) In a school where remedial teaching was provided at the teacher's request by withdrawal from any class in any year.
   A second form of the manual was developed as the *Voluntary Tutors Manual*

Summary of Prescriptive Teaching

Skill Areas	Specific Skills	Examples of Tests	Examples of Techniques	Examples of Materials
	reading aloud	—	—	Books and reading laboratories at appropriate levels
	phonics	Daniels & Diack 7 Aston Index 12	one sound at a time – check for complete mastery before moving on	IRMA/Signposts Moseley SRA Schoolhouse
	structural analysis	Daniels & Diack 7 Aston Index 12	work at each level of development – recurrent theme	Material scattered throughout workbooks, workshops, etc.
Reading	comprehension/ use of context	Daniels & Diack 12	cloze procedure group prediction exercises comprehension cards	Reading laboratories Workshops Home-made materials
	auditory discrimination	Wepman Aston Index 11, 14 Daniels & Diack 5	taped materials and work cards	Concept 7-9 Moseley
	visual discrimination and memory	Daniels & Diack 2, 3 and 4 Aston Index 8, 10, 13 and 15	visual discrimination exercises in variety work cards	Moseley Visual discrimination materials LDA materials
	phonics	Daniels & Diack 11	see phonics above	see above

414

Spelling	rules ⎤ rote learning ⎦	Daniels & Diack 11 extended test Daniels & Diack 11	if wanted by student and based on known words a very systematic approach and work on strengthening visual recall, if necessary	Various workbooks especially *Spellbound, Spell of Words* Blackwells
	auditory discrimination and memory	Wepman Aston Index 11, 14 Daniels & Diack 5	taped materials and work cards	Concept 7-9 Moseley
	visual discrimination and memory	Daniels & Diack 2, 3 and 4 Aston Index 8, 10, 13 and 15	visual discrimination exercises in variety work cards	Concept 7-9 Moseley
	handwriting ⎤ sentence awareness ⎦	none known, therefore based on observation	over learn tape at first stage, clauses to modify, sentence beginnings to complete	Cursive writing programme Patterns
Writing	functional writing ⎤ creative writing ⎦	Aston Index 9 and observation Aston Index 9 and observation	work at each level of development — recurrent theme tape at first stage, then aim to cover broad types — description, narrative, poem, essay	Material scattered throughout various workbooks and cards Usual English content

Table 1.

415

(Leevers, 1976) which was produced for volunteer tutors in the Adult Literacy Scheme in Hertfordshire. It was used as training course support and also as a vade-mecum for use on the job.

Evaluation of the effect of these manuals on the teaching/learning situation is very difficult. Feedback indicates that the teachers have found them extremely useful.

3. *Reading clinics:* These consisted of a weekly session of consultation and demonstration of teaching and materials held at various teachers' centres in the county. A member of the Programmed Learning Centre staff, together with a supply of diagnostic tests and a small collection of structured learning materials, spent two to three hours at the teachers' centre during which time teachers brought along children whose progress in reading was causing them concern. After testing, the children, whose ages ranged from seven to 16 years, were matched to suitable learning materials and thus the visiting teachers could see the approach in use. In some cases the tutor involved simply tested the child and then advised the teacher on suitable approaches and materials. These clinics have been organized in three different teachers' centres. One has developed into a teacher-advice session only. One was used as a remedial centre with very little teacher consultation or involvement. The third has managed to keep the balance between teaching and consultation as originally intended. One explanation of the varied developments is differing local needs. In each case the number of children helped was large compared to the tutor time involved. This approach clearly affected the way in which some teachers worked with certain children in their own classrooms but for others the main effect was to provide a remedial service outside the school. In addition, these clinics proved to be a practical way of disseminating information about available materials and resources.

4. *Fading agencies:* This method of exporting the system has been undertaken in four different school situations at widely separated locations in the county:
   (i)   As a co-operative venture between three middle schools.
   (ii)   As a co-operative venture between a lower, middle and upper school.
   (iii) To provide a remedial service in a single large grammar school in the throes of becoming all-ability. This has developed into a co-operative venture for feeder primary and other secondary schools.
   (iv)   As a co-operative venture between three upper schools which have now drawn in one of the feeder primary schools.

The essential features of the fading agency are:
   (a)   The financing of an initial bank of structured materials and equipment. This is paid for by the schools involved over a two-year period; thus no one school has too heavy a cost to bear in one financial year. When the payment is completed the original sum of money is once more available to finance a collection for the next co-operative venture.
   (b)   The provision of staff from the Programmed Learning Centre to work alongside the staff of the schools involved so that training occurs on the job as well as through short courses which the Centre staff organize on specific topics as the work proceeds. As the skills of the school staff develop, the Centre staff are gradually withdrawn until PLC involvement is reduced to attendance at management committee meeting and/or termly visits.

In this way, the staff become involved in educational innovation without having to initiate it. The effects in the classroom are apparent and appear to resist decay.

Evaluation

The different approaches to training have been evaluated by reference to four criteria.

1. *Effectiveness of the teaching/learning* as indicated by the improvement in reading skills measured with standard reading tests. Table 2 shows average increases in the reading ages over a finite period. On the whole, progress has been encouraging. Some of the children showed remarkably large gains whereas others, particularly those near the upper limit measured by the test, progressed more slowly. Similar measurable improvements occur in spelling, writing and reading experience. It is interesting to note that improvement rarely occurred simultaneously in all aspects. Typically, students would make substantial advances in reading or spelling and then reverse this at a later stage. In addition to these measurable achievements, there are observable improvements in the attitudes to work and the ability to concentrate. The factors responsible for these improvements arise directly from the nature of the individualized work; students inevitably take responsibility for their own progress, complete the work assigned, check it and ask for help if problems occur. When the competitive element is removed and the risk of failure reduced by the use of carefully structured materials, students feel free to work to their own standards.

2. *Cost effectiveness* in terms of materials, teacher/pupil ratio and training time. The co-operative ventures are particularly economical in the provision of materials. It would be difficult for an individual school to justify either the initial outlay or the level of use achieved. In all cases, the cost per child is remarkably low except for the PLC itself, where a comprehensive display is important. The individualized attention possible via this structured prescriptive teaching enables effectively one-to-one teaching to occur with a student/staff ratio varying between 5/1 to 14/1. This compares very favourably with most conventional remedial situations. Trainer time is long in the fading agency situation but the trainer is also teaching and his/her presence is reflected in the staff/student ratios. Thus the training element cannot be said to occupy the whole time the trainer is present at the Centre. It is difficult to make an accurate estimate, but trainer time on courses is also considerable and less effective for the transfer of skills. Trainer time in distance teaching is low. Similarly, it is difficult to isolate the training element in reading clinics.

3. *Effectiveness of innovation* — has change occurred? The fading agency approach certainly has the most impact in this field. Without doubt the ability to be in the midst of a new system immediately rather than attempting to build it up gradually has a great halo effect. The other systems are also effective but to a different degree. In some cases, the innovation emerges in a different form, for example, distance teaching has emerged as a remedial resources and teaching unit in a school.

4. *Effectiveness of training* is best judged in those situations where PLC support has been withdrawn. Where this has happened there is every sign that the learning system has been maintained and developed. There is far less decay in the fading agency than in other situations.

In conclusion, the most effective methods of bringing about innovation would seem to be the fading agency on the large scale and the reading clinics on a smaller scale. These methods involve the marrying of theory with practice so that relevance

Summary of Different Types of Provision

Centre	Approx. cost of materials	Number of sessions per week	Number of students per week	Attendances per student per week	Teacher/ student ratio	Average increase in reading age over 6 months as example of attainment
Programmed Learning Centre	£3,000	13	150	1	1/11	1.2 years
Distance learning						
1.	£150	5	24	5	1/24	0.7 years
2.	£200	5	30	1	1/6	0.6 years
Reading Clinics						
1.	£100	1	18	1	1/9	1.0 years
2.	£100	1	18	1	1/9	0.9 years
3.	£150	1	16	1	1/8	1.2 years
Fading Agencies						
1.	£100	4	62	1	1/14	1.2 years
2.	£300	8	90	1	1/5	1.1 years
3.	£400	8	74	1	1/6	1.1 years
4.	£450	7	102	1	1/6 (Not yet faded)	1.1 years

Table 2.

and use are constantly demonstrated. This would appear to be a powerful method of ensuring that a very complex skill such as managing a learning system is able to be put into practice. See Table 2 for a summary.

References

Daniels, J and Hunter, D (1973) 'Standard Reading Tests' Chatto & Windus.

Kay, K (1977) 'Cursive Writing Programme' PLC, St Albans.

Leevers, S (1973) 'IRMA Integrated Remedial Reading Materials for Adults and Adolescents' PLC, St Albans.

Leevers, S (1974) 'Teachers' Manual' PLC, St Albans.

Leevers, S (1976) 'Voluntary Tutors' Manual' PLC, St Albans.

Newton, M and Thomson, M (1976) 'Aston Index' Learning Development Aids.

Potts, J (1976) 'Beyond Initial Reading' Union Educational Books.

PLC (ed) (1976) 'Visual Perception Materials' PLC, St Albans.

Wepman, J M (1958) 'Auditory Discrimination Test' Language Research Association.

Westrope, A, Tross, H (1976) 'Signpost Word Families' PLC, St Albans.

Youngs, D (1975) 'Group Reading Test' University of London Press.

The Training of Student Teachers in the Field of Educational Technology in Malaysia

Chan Geok Oon

Introduction

The rapid rate of population increase in Malaysia is posing many problems to its educational system. The high birth rate has created a 'population explosion' among the school age-group. This is accompanied by a shortage of facilities (such as classrooms, furniture, equipment) and of teachers to cope efficiently with the influx of students. A vast majority of the schools in the country are operating on a two-shift and occasionally three-shift basis, with mainly primary schools using premises in the morning, secondary schools in the afternoon, and special form five and form six classes in the evening. Hence a tremendous amount of inconvenience, disturbances and distractions are created for the classes scheduled at the transitional times. The over-crowded, noisy environment is most unconducive to effective teaching and learning. Moreover, in the face of competition from other communication media outside the school, the traditional classes and teaching methods themselves are no longer able to hold the interest of a large proportion of the student population. Evidently, the lack of motivation, as well as other constraints, is a factor contributing towards the problems of truancy and high drop-out rates.

It is time that teachers and educators seriously considered ways and means of gearing the teaching techniques and strategies to match the constraints and changing mode of learning by our students in this modern age of technology. A widespread use of the systems approach to instructional and educational planning should be promoted. In addition, a wide range of educational resources and facilities must be made available for group instruction and individualized learning in the schools. In short, there is a need for a new technological approach to education in Malaysia.

It can be seen that the problems of formal education in Malaysia are many and varied, like all other countries in the world, and there is no one solution. But it is strongly felt that when the use of educational technology is fully supported financially, administratively and in all other respects, it can go a long way towards contributing to the urgent task of improving teaching and learning in the Malaysian schools. Without pretending that educational technology is the panacea for all ills, I would like to stress that the careful harnessing of the systems approach and the resources of modern technology, found effective and indispensable in the world of science and technology, commerce and industry, can play a vital role in helping to solve some of Malaysia's educational problems.

Unfortunately, in Malaysia the full use of modern technology has been relatively slow to take root, especially in the realm of education. Nonetheless, this does not mean that various aspects of the field of educational technology are totally out of Malaysia's educational picture. There has been for a long time some interest at the

420

national level in the use of audio-visual aids for classroom instruction. In fact the government's interest in the use of media for educational purposes showed itself as early as 1958, when the Audio-Visual Department was set up in the Ministry of Education. In the mid-sixties, a special one-year programme was established at the Specialist Teachers' Training Institute to train experienced teachers in the area of audio-visual education. This special programme lasted for three years, and was recently revived in 1975. Then came the introduction of radio broadcasting to the schools in 1966. This was followed by the launching of educational television in June 1972. Thus the educational scene of Malaysia has been coloured by developments in the field of educational media since the 1950s.

The Educational Media Service Division of the Ministry of Education, which co-ordinates the three services of audio-visual aids, educational radio and educational television, is carrying out its share of training teachers in the proper use of educational mass media through the State Educational Media Service Officers. Since the one-day utilization training programme was launched in 1972, as many as 10,000 teachers have benefited from it. However, there is also a crying need for non-mass-media utilization training, which unfortunately up to the present has been given very little attention. The proper use of the systems approach and effective low-cost media in instruction can make learning more interesting and meaningful. In fact, the need for motivation in the classroom is great in the face of competition from the various media outside formal education. Teachers have to be trained in large numbers to harness the resources of educational technology to bring about more effective teaching on their part and efficient learning on the part of the students. Malaysia can certainly do with large scale in-service and pre-service training of her teachers in this field.

It is pre-service training that this paper will focus on. As the title of the paper suggests, it is the training of student teachers that it is mainly concerned with. The term 'student teachers' means students undergoing training in an institution to be teachers in the primary or secondary schools. This naturally implies pre-service training in contrast to in-service training, which is also being carried out in various forms and by different institutions, as well as by the Ministry of Education.

In Malaysia, the preparation of teachers is done at two different levels, and by two different types of institution: (a) the teachers' training colleges and (b) the universities. The teachers' training colleges under the Ministry of Education prepare trainees for a teaching profession in the primary and lower secondary schools, while the universities train graduates for service in the upper secondary schools, including the sixth-form classes (which prepare students for the Cambridge Higher School Certificate Examination).

Teachers' Training College Level

All the teachers' training colleges, being under the direct control of the Ministry of Education, share a common curriculum geared at producing teachers for the primary and lower secondary schools. Within the curriculum is a subject called 'audio-visual education' which was introduced in 1973. The general course objectives as stated in the present syllabus are as follows:

'This course is intended to prepare student teachers with the necessary knowledge, skills and attitudes concerning the application of basic communication principles and the utilization of instructional resource materials to (a) promote qualitative teaching (b) enhance efficient learning and (c) solve quantitative problems in teaching.'

The specific objectives are given below:

1. Analyze teaching-learning activities in the classroom from the viewpoint of human communication.
2. Employ basic communication principles for the planning of effective instruction.
3. Be aware of the values and limitations of the wide range of educational resource materials for instructional purposes.
4. Locate, select and use relevant instructional resource materials for overcoming pedagogical problems encountered in day-to-day teaching.
5. Design, produce and/or improvise simple aids for specific instructional needs.
6. Carry out simple evaluation concerning the instructional effectiveness of ready-made and/or self-produced resource materials for teaching.
7. Display a sense of responsibility in the care and maintenance of expensive teaching materials.
8. Develop an awareness of the importance of keeping abreast with trends and developments in audio-visual education.

The content of the course is presented over a period of two years, with one hour of lectures per fortnight during the first year, and one hour per week in the second year, giving a total of about 45 teaching hours for the whole course. In most cases teaching is carried on in a normal classroom which holds about 30 to 35 students. But when the lecturer-student ratio is high and there are rooms which have high seating capacity, then each class session may have more than 30 students ... and may be as many as 70 or more. Because of the shortage of teaching staff in the field the lecturers have to teach many sessions, as many as 15 classes per week. Other constraints are the lack of proper facilities and the shortage of both hardware and software.

A number of college administrators are sympathetic towards the idea of providing the proper teaching facilities and the necessary equipment and materials for effective instruction of the audio-visual education course. The Teachers' Training Division of the Ministry of Education is also considering the provision of a media or audio-visual room in each of the new buildings that are coming up under the Third Malaysia Plan.

University Level

Besides the teachers' training colleges the universities also train teachers. In fact, all the five universities in Malaysia have a teacher-training programme of one kind or another. Of these five, only two have included educational technology courses in their curriculum. They are Universiti Sains Malaysia, Penang and University of Malaya, Kuala Lumpur. In the case of the University of Malaya there is at present no compulsory educational technology course, although optional courses or elective courses may be offered from time to time, depending on the availability of lectures. At present, two elective educational technology courses are listed in its 1976/77 Educational Faculty Handbook, namely, teaching instruction and educational technology and educational technology in language education. It must be mentioned that the Faculty of Education, being in the oldest and most established university in the country, is quite well equipped with facilities such as graphic and photographic facilities, and the resource centre which serves the academic staff as well as the students.

Universiti Sains Malaysia

This is the only university which provides some basic training in this field to all its education students. Because it takes the lead in the area of educational technology training, a large portion of this section of the paper will be devoted to a discussion of its training programmes. The Centre for Educational Studies of the university has realized the importance of giving a certain amount of basic training to all its teacher trainees even before they go on their first teaching practice.

Basic Course in Educational Resources (BACER)

It was found that a few sessions in the methods courses on the use and preparation of teaching aids were insufficient to do justice to the fundamental aspects of educational technology. Hence a course in educational technology is being offered. This course, entitled, 'Basic Course in Educational Resources' exposes second-year education students to the basic principles of educational technology. The course also considers a wide range of educational resources, their characteristics and utilization, varying from very simple improvised materials to more sophisticated, commercially-produced software and hardware. The students are also provided with laboratory experience in the operation of audio-visual equipment, as well as the organization and use of a variety of media resources to solve a particular teaching-learning problem. As far as possible, an attempt is made to teach the course in the most conducive environment available. Most of the teaching is conducted in a large room equipped with carrels along three side walls, and a large octagonal table in the centre with electrical outlets. Around this table about 24 students can sit comfortably facing one another. The main idea of keeping the class small and using a more or less circular seating arrangement is primarily to provide a suitable environment for the discussion and sharing of ideas, as well as to show them from first-hand experience that learning can take place outside the traditional classroom seating arrangement.

The course lasts for 14 weeks and consists of two-hour weekly sessions giving a total of 28 hours for the whole course. An average of about 100 students go through the course per term. Instruction is carried out by three lecturers on a team-teaching basis, and by means of a series of lectures, demonstrations, seminars and practical laboratory sessions. It is hoped that those who have taken the course will eventually assume the role of change agents in the schools where they teach, difficult though it might be under the present general circumstances of shortage of equipment and materials as well as the lack of strong support from the administrators and teachers. One whole class session is devoted to 'the problems of innovations'. This session discusses, amongst other aspects, the role, strategies and problems of change agents in the field of educational technology. The underlying aim of the course is to motivate them, and indirectly their colleagues, to use the systems approach and a wide range of media resources to up-grade their teaching and to facilitate the learning process.

Principles and Techniques in the Production of Learning Materials

In addition to the above, there is a second course entitled: 'Basic Principles and Techniques in the Production of Learning Materials'. This is an optional course for the final-year students, but under the new unit system, it will be offered to third-year students who have the prerequisites of a basic educational technology course, and at least one teaching-practice exercise. This particular aspect of the field of educational technology is chosen amongst others because the knowledge and skill of being able to communicate visually and effectively, and of being able to prepare simple but effective instructional materials using systems approach, are fundamental tools for teachers and hence are given top priority. The aim of the course is to provide the students with some basic knowledge and skill in simple learning materials production so that they will be able to use them in the preparation of their own teaching aids, as well as to help their colleagues make theirs, thus widening the influence and fostering the dissemination process. The course structure has two sections:

1. Basic principles and techniques in illustration, preservation, lettering, photography and duplicating.
2. The principles of systems approach to media and instructional development.

For their projects, they are given the opportunity to show their ability to select, plan, produce and evaluate media systematically, and integrate the various photographic skills they have acquired from the first part of the course. One of the assignments given is the production of a tape-slide set. A major group project requires them to produce materials for teaching a particular topic to pupils in school. The students have to go through the whole media development process systematically, beginning with the identification of objectives, analyzing the audience and content, the design and preparation of the media and ending up with field testing and writing the evaluation report. Below is a list of the general course objectives:

1. To introduce students to the basic principles of graphics communication.
2. To familiarize them with the principles and techniques of illustration, lettering, preservation, photography and duplication.
3. To provide them with the background knowledge that will enable them to make wise decisions regarding the selection of types of lettering and duplicating processes for certain specific functions.
4. To enable them to develop skills in applying the principles and techniques as given in (2) above.
5. To help them towards an understanding of systems design to media and instructional development.
6. To provide them with the opportunity to acquire the ability to apply systems approach and the basic principles and techniques of production in the development of materials for the teaching of a unit of instruction.

Because there is a fair demand on equipment and facilities such as wash basin, large work-table, dry-mounting press, light box/table, paper guillotine, and graphics and photographic equipment, the course is conducted in the workroom where these facilities are either available or readily accessible from the equipment room which is located just across the hallway.

Supporting Facilities

It must be pointed out that the teaching of the two basic educational technology courses at Universiti Sains Malaysia is facilitated by the availability of both human and non-human resources existing in the educational technology unit. Up to the present, the BACER class size has been kept at the optimum level of around 20 to 24 because of the availability of a sufficient number of staff to teach the course. From the equipment loan service, all types of hardware, ranging from portable cassette tape-recorders to 16mm film projectors and cameras, can be used for teaching purposes as well as for loan to the student. The educational technology unit also supplies the students with consumable materials such as cardboards, OHP transparencies, tapes, coloured paper, plasticine, styrofoam boards etc required for their course projects, and for teaching practice. Thus opportunities are given for them to try out and put into practice what they have learnt. The two most useful supports are the equipment loan service and the materials loan service from which students can borrow hardware and software for use during their teaching practice. Other facilities available include the carpentry workshop and the audio-recording facilities. Utilization of these resources is facilitated by the fact that they are well serviced and centralized within one building.

The possibility of offering another optional course in educational technology for the education students is under consideration.

Another Educational Technology Course

Besides the two undergraduate courses in educational technology, Universiti Sains Malaysia also offers a two-year masters-level programme in educational technology. Courses such as principles and practice of media development, communication theories, systems design and management of educational resource centres, programmed instruction, microteaching and educational broadcasting etc are included. This programme was launched in 1976 and is available to experienced graduate teachers and officers from the Ministry of Education. In addition, there is also a one-year educational broadcasting training programme organized to meet the Ministry's need for well trained and qualified producers of educational television and educational radio programmes. Included in this curriculum is a course entitled 'Introduction to Educational Technology'.

Conclusion

Bearing in mind the theme of the Conference, and to put the role of training in the proper perspective, I would like to mention that educational technology training of student teachers alone can do very little to bring about innovation in Malaysian schools, or any other schools system in the world for that matter. It has to be stressed that for a widespread use of educational technology to take root, the training of student teachers in the field must be backed up with adequate provision of facilities, resources, technical know-how and a conducive attitudinal climate in the school environment. Until and unless these are prevalent, there will be little opportunity and incentive to apply whatever educational technology training is obtained from the universities and colleges. Moreover, the zeal and enthusiasm of the new teachers soon die off when they are left to struggle alone and unaided. In other words, for training in the field of educational technology to achieve its full impact, it must of necessity be well supported by the appropriate infrastructure within the entire educational system and in particular within the schools themselves. Other things being equal, extensive in-service training of teachers in the schools to provide the know-how must be carried out. This naturally involves money and energy. Since funds come from above, it is vital that the full sympathy of the higher authorities must be obtained. A supportive administration at the higher level is most desirable. In a nutshell, what is required for effectively disseminating the innovative ideas is a three-pronged attack, ie at three different levels, as clearly illustrated in Figure 1. Dissemination of ideas has to take place at all levels — from the top administrative structure, to the teacher-training institutions and down to the grassroot level of the school system. There is a need to deal with the situation as a whole. Only then will there be an effective spread, with the resources of educational technology fully harnessed to facilitate the teaching-learning process.

Moreover, when this 'global' approach to the problem is adopted, it will undoubtedly provide more of an incentive and contribute towards a more concerted effort on the part of the teacher-educators, particularly those who are involved in the field of educational technology.

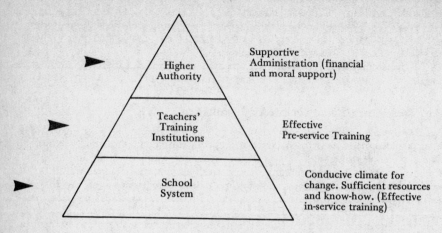

Figure 1.

It must be mentioned that notwithstanding the teething problems of growth, the training of student teachers in the field is forging ahead. It is encouraging to note that there is a growing awareness of, and an interest in, the potential of educational technology in Malaysia. For this reason, I am optimistic about the future prospects for the development, spread and use of the resources of the field of educational technology in Malaysia.

The Application of a Modified Operational Research Technique in the Design of Curricula Systematic Curriculum Design (SCUD) Technique

B W Vaughan

The need for structuring the curriculum has been widely discussed (Leith, 1966; Gagné, 1968; Bloom, 1956; Skemp, 1971. See Figure 1) and more recently in regard to teaching or reading. (Strang, 1972; Southgate, 1972). While there are variations in detail there is a measure of common ground which may be considered when designing a curriculum. The need for logical planning of the curriculum and adequate record-keeping has been emphasized (Bennett, 1976; Bullock, 1975).

The process of learning may be seen as a spiral of experiences starting at the level of simple discriminations.

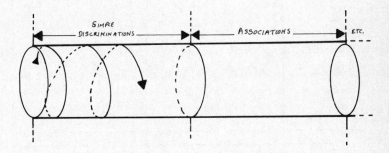

Figure 2. *A model to show path of pupil through hierarchies of learning*

If, for example, mathematical concepts are introduced it would resemble Figure 4.

In his spiral of progress the pupil will need a number of graded experiences in each of the concepts. These have been shown as lettered ovals.

If this model is seen as a cylinder which is then cut from end to end and laid out flat, the result would be as in Figures 6 and 7.

The way in which a network analysis of a curriculum can be of value has been explained (Wood and Wyant, 1970; Wyant, 1972 and 1973; Vaughan, 1972). An extended description of the application of a network analysis to the design of a mathematics curriculum, and the manner in which an integrated individualized scheme was built upon this design has been given (Vaughan, 1974 and 1975).

Individualized Mathematics Scheme Based on a Network Analysis

Summary

1. Network analysis of the curriculum.
2. Design and implementation of a storage and retrieval system.

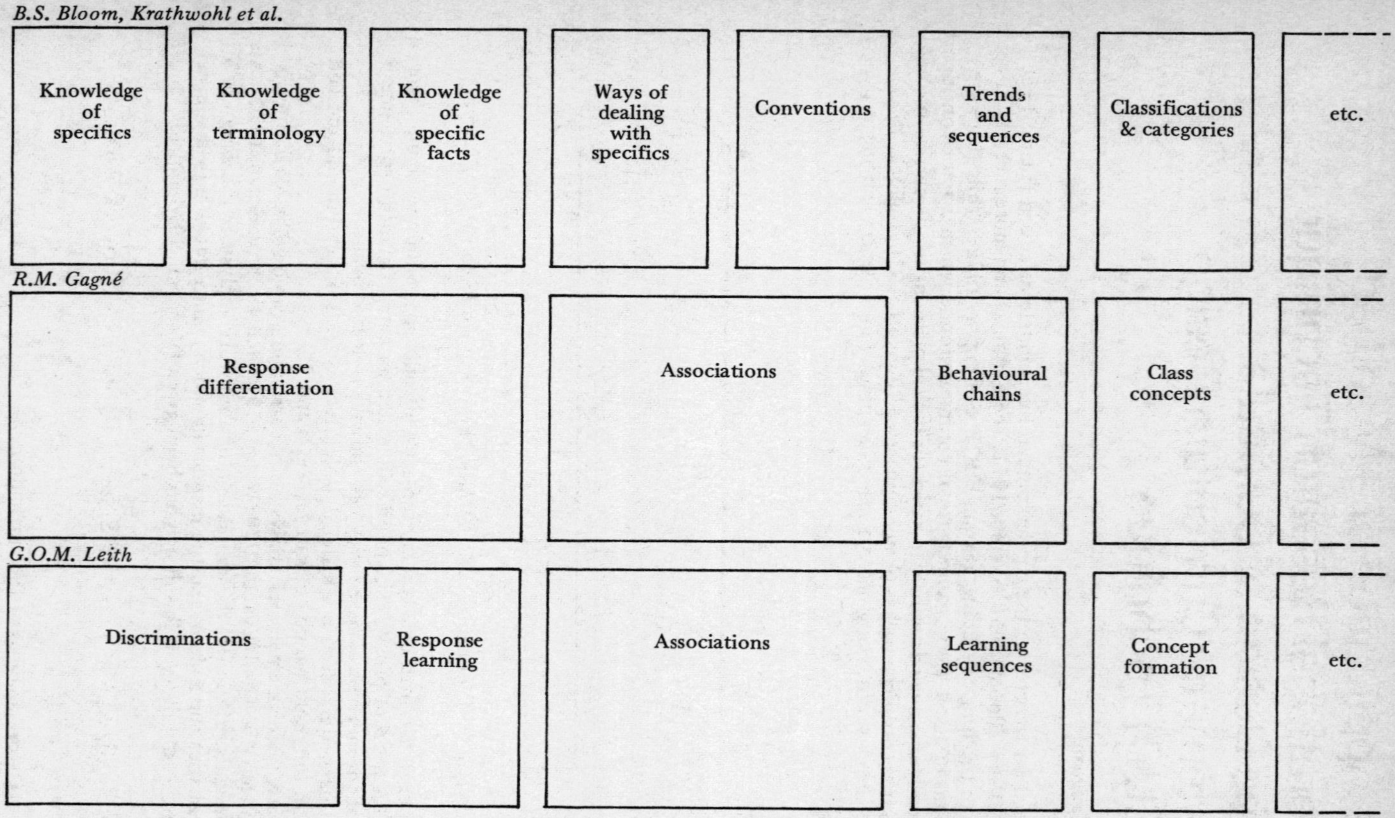

Figure 1. *A comparison of hierarchies of learning postulated by different educational psychologists*

3. Design of record cards based on network numbering.
4. Design and use of assessment tests at each stage.
5. Deployment of variety of teaching materials.
6. Training pupils to work as individuals pursuing courses suited to their needs.

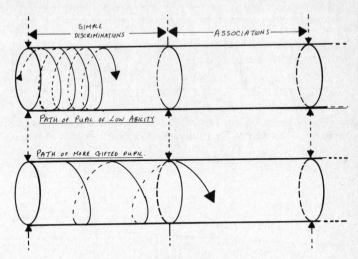

Figure 3. *A comparison of models of learning experiences of high and low ability pupils*

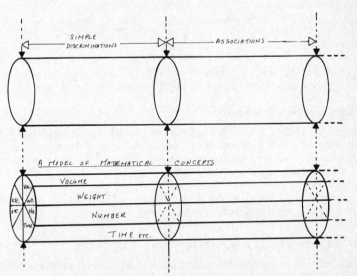

Figure 4. *Combination of a model of hierarchies of learning and mathematical concepts*

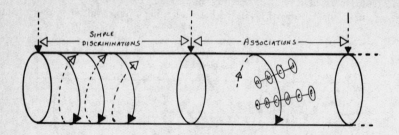

Figure 5. *A combination of the model of spiral of experiences of a pupil in a hierarchy of learning & the gradation of experiences at each stage*

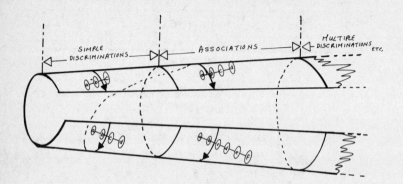

Figure 6. *The alteration of three dimensional cylindrical model to a flat representation of path of pupil through the curriculum*

The Technique of Network Analysis

The accepted method of designing a network is for each activity arrow to have two numbers, one at the start of the activity, another at the completion.

Elongated nodes are used to show a stage beyond which one may not proceed until activities leading into it are completed.

Thus, none of the activities 3—4, 3—7 and 3—5 may commence until activity 1—3 is completed. As a result, a record card based on a similar network would require two identifying numbers for each activity.

The Modified Network Analysis Technique

In this case only the number in the node on the activity arrow on the left is required.

There are no elongated nodes. These are replaced by vertical lines which serve the same purpose.

This makes the design of record cards much simpler as only one number is

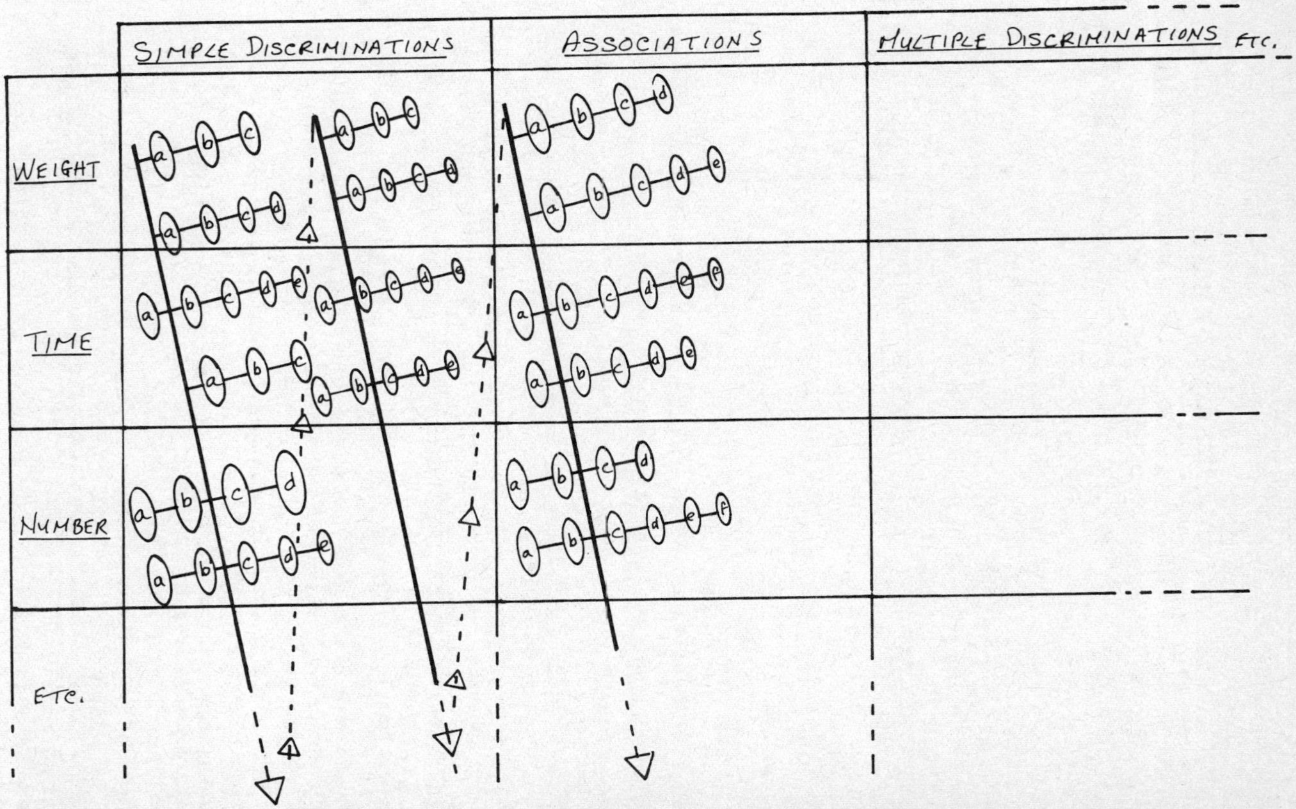

Figure 7. Flat representation of graded educational experiences at each stage of hierarchies of learning in mathematics

needed to indicate an activity.

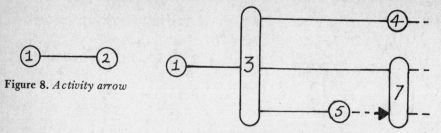

Figure 8. *Activity arrow*

Figure 9. *Section of network*

Figure 10. *Section of network and record card*

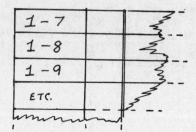

Figure 11. *Record card based on network in Figure 10*

Once the modified network analysis of the curriculum is completed the activities can be arranged in columns which comprise those activities at a similar level of learning, called in this case, units.

In each of these units are a series of activities of graded difficulty for each of the concepts being developed in that particular curriculum. It is envisaged that at the end of each unit there will be an assessment test.

A Modified Network Analysis of an Early Science Curriculum

In this small section of the whole curriculum it can be seen that the pupil starts by examining his own body, and from that starting point explores his environment.

This sorting and classifying will lead on to the formation of scientific concepts which later are used in abstract form. Each activity has a unique number and so the design of record cards is simple, and so is the deployment of teaching materials.

Although it is not so clear cut, there is a progression of complexity, and the skills required in early art and craft work.

Here the early stages involve simple operations and crude skills which lead on to more skilled work, and greater artistic discrimination. This is a small section of the modified network which includes experiences with woven materials, wood, metal, solid and liquid colours and a variety of other media. The record card based on the numbering system is simple and ensures that each individual pupil has a variety of activities which gradually increase in the complexity and skill required. Similar networks have been designed using this modified network analysis technique for English, history and geography (Vaughan, 1977).

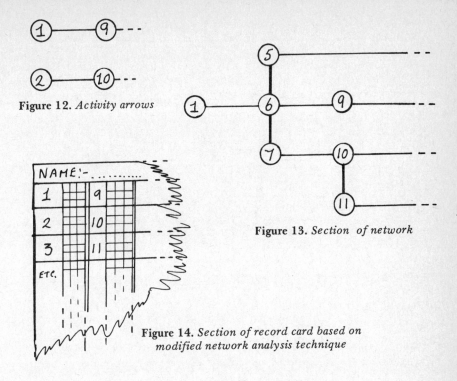

Figure 12. *Activity arrows*

Figure 13. *Section of network*

Figure 14. *Section of record card based on modified network analysis technique*

Subject Interdependencies

A problem in our education system is that subject specialists need to have a clear idea what their colleagues are doing in other subjects so that any interdependencies may be taken into account. In Figure 18, three such interdependencies are shown where science teaching is dependent upon prior teaching of mathematical concepts.

The science teacher should ensure that his pupils have an understanding of weight before they engage in activity 406, and understand the making and uses of graphs before starting activity 650 in science. This is shown as a numbered node on the science network with a dotted arrow leading to an activity which depends upon it. The number in the node is that on the mathematics network. On the mathematics network a dotted arrow is shown leading to the node with the science network number on it. Mathematical network numbers 234 and 676 lead by dotted arrows into, respectively, activities 406 and 650 on the science network. In this way both mathematics and science teachers can easily be altered to these interdependencies (Vaughan, 1977).

References

Bennett, N (1976) 'Teaching Styles and Pupil Progress' Open Books.
Bloom, B *et al* (1956) 'Taxonomy of Educational Objectives. Cognitive Domain' Longmans Green.
Bullock, A (1975) 'A Language for Life' HMSO.
Gagné, R M (1968) 'Psychological Review' 75, 177.

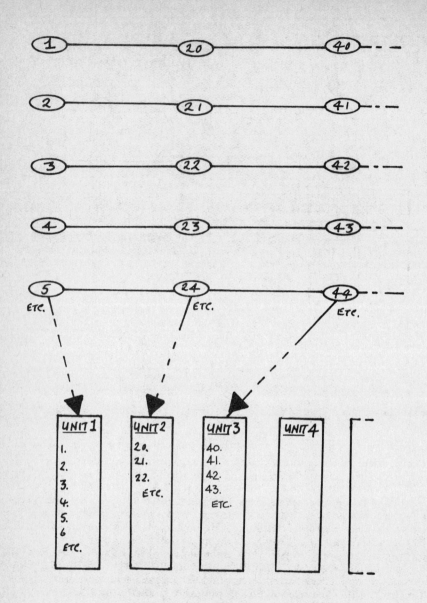

Figure 15. *Section of modified network analysis showing division of curriculum into units*

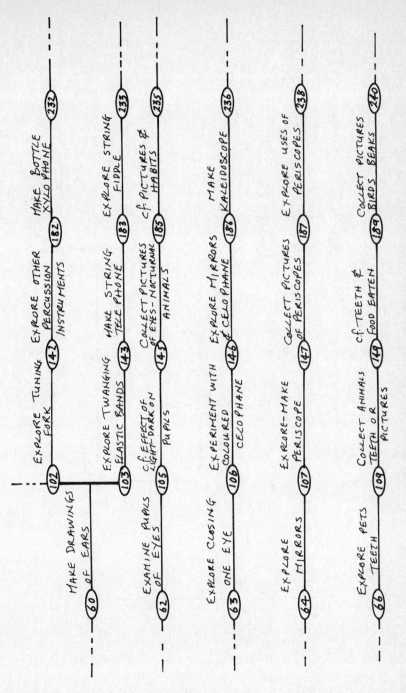

Figure 16. *A small section of modified network analysis of primary science curriculum*

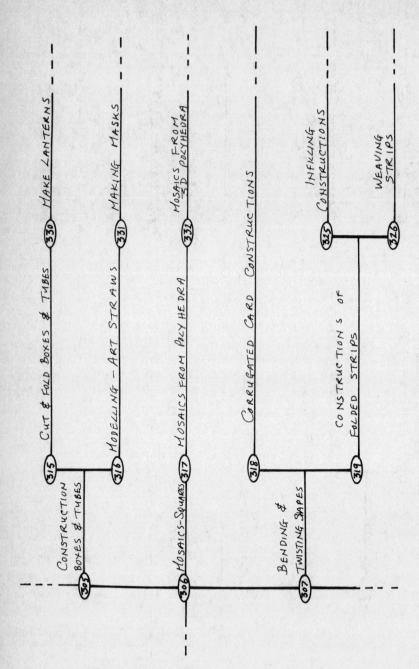

Figure 17. *Paper & card section of modified network diagram of primary/infant art & craft curriculum*

305 Construction Boxes & Tubes
315 Cut & Fold Boxes & Tubes
330 Make Lanterns
316 Modelling – Art Straws
331 Making Masks
306 Mosaics-Squares
317 Mosaics from Polyhedra
332 Mosaics from 3D Polyhedra
318 Corrugated Card Constructions
307 Bending & Twisting Shapes
319 Constructions of Folded Strips
325 Inruing Constructions
326 Weaving Strips

436

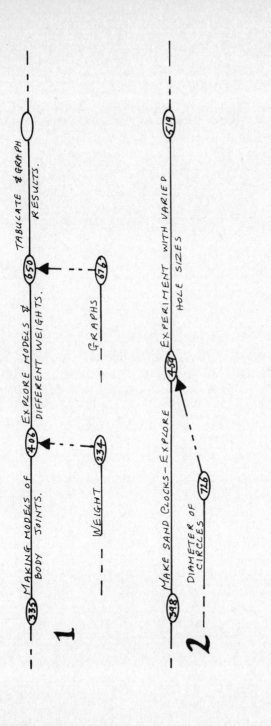

Figure 18. *Three dependencies of science upon prior mathematics teaching, emphasizing need for identification of these interdependencies*

Leith, G O M (1966) 'Visual Education' March.

Skemp, R R (1971) 'The Psychology of Learning Mathematics' Penguin.

Southgate, V (1972) 'The Reading Curriculum' eds Melnik, A and Merrit, J, University of London Press.

Strang, R (1972) in 'Reading Today and Tomorrow' eds Melnik, A and Merrit, J, University of London Press.

Vaughan, B W (1972) in 'Aspects of Educational Technology VI' Pitman.

Vaughan, B W (1974) in 'Mathematics in School,' 3, 3 June.

Vaughan, B W (1975) in 'Mathematics in School' 4, 1, 2 & 3.

Vaughan, B W (1977) in 'Mathematics in School' 6, 1 January.

Vaughan, B W (1977) 'Curriculum Design and Educational Organisation' Cambridge University Press.

Evolvement of an Instructional Strategy for Teaching Educational Evaluation

M S Yadav, R Govinda

Instruction is an organized system of activities which works towards the realization of certain specific goals. The system, here, involves different components which, although distinct in their nature and operation, function in a co-ordinated manner contributing to the achievement of common goals. In an instructional situation, the components of the system are input learning material and various techniques and media of presentation such as lecture, discussion, programmed learning, seminar, practical work, library work, radio, TV, tape-recorder, film projectors, etc. An instructional strategy is taken, here, to mean the organization of suitable instructional components with their functions specified in relation to the specific goals to be achieved. These components, as in any 'system', have to appear in the final form of the instructional strategy in an integrated fashion.

Evolvement of such an instructional strategy has, therefore, to be carried out in different phases. The first phase consists of analysis and identification of specific objectives to be realized through the instructional strategy. In the second phase, suitable learning material for achieving the pre-specified objectives is to be prepared. The third phase relates to the empirical validation of the individual components of the strategy. The fourth phase involves integrating the different components to form the instructional strategy and studying its effectiveness and efficiency in realizing the pre-specified objectives. An instructional strategy developed through these phases will have two important characteristics. One is that it will have specificity with regard to the goals which are to be realized through the individual components. Secondly, the different components of the strategy are empirically tested and integrated to contribute towards common goals in such a manner that the strategy will possess the characteristic of reproducibility in similar conditions.

The present paper attempts to describe the developmental process followed in evolving an instructional strategy for teaching educational evaluation to B Ed students of the M S University of Baroda. The project does not have the aim of arriving at any set of findings that are theoretical in nature; rather, it has been executed to evolve an alternative instructional strategy, duly evaluated, that can be adopted for regular instructional work in the faculty.

Educational evaluation is included as a compulsory course in the B Ed programme at the M S University of Baroda. Instruction in the course is provided for one full semester. The course has two broad objectives, viz:

1. Imparting basic knowledge about educational evaluation under the heads: educational evaluation and measurement; characteristics of a good instrument of evaluation; major tools of evaluation and their uses; teacher-made achievement tests; and elementary statistics in education.
2. Developing certain skills of evaluation, eg stating objectives in behavioural terms, preparing blue-prints for tests, developing unit tests, etc. Evaluation

scheme for the course consists of periodical tests during the semester, and a comprehensive test at the end.

On a logical consideration of the broad objectives of the course, an appropriate instructional strategy may be conceived to involve the use of techniques of programmed learning, discussion, library work and practical work in proper combination. Basic knowledge related to different concepts in the course would be given through programmed learning material (PLM). Knowledge through the PLM would be augmented by organizing library work. Practical work would be organized to develop various skills needed by a teacher to carry out educational evaluation in a school. The purpose of discussion would be to provide a forum for the exchange of ideas, and to seek clarification of concepts covered. It may be noted that the instructional strategy suggested seeks to utilize human media for presentation of software material. Use of any hardware equipment for this purpose has been deliberately avoided. The main consideration for such a decision has been the feasibility aspect of the strategy. As such, the university has an adequate faculty to organize the programme of instruction for the course. The purpose of developing an alternative instructional strategy is to increase the effectiveness and efficiency of the instructional work, and not to replace the teacher. Further, utilization of hardware does not seem to be economically viable considering the availability of resources. Apart from the feasibility aspect, the authors have presumed that non-utilization of hardware media in this instructional strategy may not seriously jeopardize the efficiency and effectiveness of instructional work.

Phase I

An analysis of the course content prescribed and the broad objectives specified was carried out. Based on this analysis, the course was divided into six instructional units. For each unit, specific objectives were stated in behavioural terms. Flow charts were prepared for these units to determine the proper sequence of presenting different content points.

Phase II

This phase relates to the development of the PLM which forms the major software component of the strategy. The PLM was developed following the usual steps prescribed for preparing a valid programme. The programme has been developed in linear form, although it is not a linear programme of the traditional Skinnerian type. For instance, the frames are not always very small; the frames often include open questions; the correct answers are frequently followed by further explanation before going to the next frame. No special entering behaviour has been pre-supposed on the part of the learners in respect of the content, as the entrants to the B Ed course are graduates from various streams. All that is presumed is the basic ability to read and understand simple English, and the skills of performing fundamental operations of arithmetic involving decimals.

The first draft of the PLM was edited by an expert from the point of view of content and language, as well as programming principles. Along with the PLM, the criterion test prepared for each unit was also scrutinized by the expert.

The edited PLM was then tried out on a group of ten B Ed students. It was made clear to these students beforehand that for this particular course they should read only the PLM and not any other text. At the end of each unit the corresponding criterion test was administered. Performance on these criterion tests constituted periodical assessment for these students. Difficulties encountered by the students regarding language, frame-sequence and the like were noted. The six units of the course were covered in one full semester. Errors committed by the students on the programme frames and on the criterion tests were analyzed. Based on these error analyses and on the suggestions offered by the students regarding the language, frame-sequence, etc, the programme was revised for use under Phase III.

Phase III

This phase relates to the validation of the PLM, studying its feasibility aspect as regular instructional material. The nature, extent and sequencing of other components of the strategy, viz, discussion, library work and practical work are to be determined on the results of the validation study. Validation experiment here involves the comparison of results of learning through the PLM and the lecture method. However, the purpose of comparison is not to establish the superiority or otherwise of any of these methods. It is only to see whether the PLM developed can produce learning effects comparable to those produced by the lecture method which is, normally, the method of instruction adopted.

Total sample for the validation experiment consisted of 69 B Ed students of the M S University of Baroda. The sample was divided into two groups matched on the basis of academic qualification and teaching experience. The experimental group had 35 students and the control group had 34 students. Experimental group students learnt through PLM. The control group was taught using the lecture method. But proper controls were introduced so that there would be no discrepancy in the content input and the total instructional time for the two groups.

Students in the experimental group studied the PLM for each unit in scheduled class hours for the estimated length of time. The average time required for completing each unit was estimated based on try-out study. A few students who could not complete the unit within the prescribed time were allowed to study the remaining part at home. After each unit was completed, students were given the PLM for the unit. Students were administered the corresponding criterion test at the end of each unit. Feedback sessions were organized to discuss the performance of students on each test.

Elements of structuring and interaction were introduced in the lecture method adopted for teaching students in the control group. Structuring was done by providing the teacher as well as the students with booklets containing the course content, organized in the sequence in which the teacher would deal with it while lecturing. Six booklets were prepared to cover the six units of the course. These booklets and the six units of the PLM were developed based on common task analysis of the course. It was explained to the students that the booklets were not to be taken to replace teachers' lectures in the class, but were meant only to help them recall in an organized manner what was delivered through the lectures. A booklet for each unit was given to the students after it was taught in the class. Although the content to be delivered through the lecture was preplanned and put in the booklet, the course of the lecture was made flexible enough to provide for intermittent interaction. At the end of each unit, the criterion test for that unit was administered which was the same as the one administered to the experimental group. Feedback sessions were organized to discuss the performance of students on each test.

Effectiveness of the PLM was studied unitwise by comparing the criterion test scores of the two groups. Mean differences were tested for significance by using students' t-test. The results obtained are presented in Table 1.

For studying the effectiveness of the PLM as a whole, two indices, viz, mean performance on the comprehensive test, and the mean of combined scores

	Group		M	S.D.	t-value	Significance
Unit I	Experimental	(N=34)	17.40	5.79	1.64	Not significant
	Control	(N=34)	14.85	6.84		
Unit II	Experimental	(N=35)	23.51	3.24	3.63	Significant at .01 level
	Control	(N=34)	19.39	5.33		
Unit III	Experimental	(N=35)	29.37	3.25	2.74	Significant at .01 level
	Control	(N=34)	25.97	6.36		
Unit IV	Experimental	(N=35)	21.46	4.33	0.39	Not significant
	Control	(N=34)	21.00	5.13		
Unit V	Experimental	(N=35)	17.49	3.24	0.21	Not significant
	Control	(N=34)	17.68	4.17		
Unit VI	Experimental	(N=34)	12.94	3.73	0.61	Not significant
	Control	(N=33)	12.39	3.57		

Table 1. *Mean Achievement Scores on Criterion Tests*

representing the performance on the six criterion tests, were obtained. Comparisons were made after adjusting these mean scores by analysis of covariance for intelligence of the subjects measured using Raven's Standard Progressive Matrices. The adjusted means for the two groups are presented in Table 2. Differences in the adjusted means were tested for significance using t-test.

	Group	Mean	S.D.	t-value
Comprehensive Test Scores	Experimental (N=34)	62.64	9.93	0.168
	Control (N=34)	63.42	10.37	
Combined Criterion Test Scores	Experimental (N=34)	73.99	10.09	1.901
	Control (N=34)	68.28	12.23	

Table 2. *Mean Achievement Scores Adjusted for Intelligence*

It may be observed that neither of the differences is significant, showing that achievement through the PLM and through the lecture does not differ. These results indicate that the PLM as instructional material for B Ed students is as effective as the lecture method adopted for the control group, suggesting that the PLM may be used in the regular instructional work of the faculty for providing instruction to B Ed students in the course on educational evaluation. It should be noted that the 'lecture method' adopted for providing instruction to the control group is not just the same as the method by which instruction is provided in the usual course. The lectures, here, are highly structured which, in fact, ensures that all the necessary content points are delivered, with proper emphasis, by the lecturer. The course of each lecture, that is, the sequencing of materials, is pre-specified on the basis of scientific task analysis of the course content and the objectives. Enough provision is made for interaction between students and the lecturer. The booklets provided to the students serve as guides for their reference and help them remember what they have learnt, in an organized way. Contrary to these procedures, in lectures in the usual course, decisions regarding specific emphasis to be laid on different content points, sequencing of instructional points, time to be devoted to teaching different points, etc, are left to the vagaries of the individual lecturer. It may not be too wrong to assume here, that a well planned and structured lecture of the type adopted in the experiment is not the method usually adopted by the lecturers; and also that this method would be more effective than that of the usually adopted unstructured lectures.

In order to obtain empirical evidence regarding the comparative effectiveness of the structured lecture and the conventional lecture method, comparisons were made of the performance of the group taught by structured lecture (control group of the validation experiment referred to above) with that of a group taught by the conventional lecture method. The group which received instruction through conventional method consisted of 57 students. Distribution of students into different groups was done on the following lines. All the 126 students studying in the B Ed class were divided into two divisions on the basis of the subject offered by the students for practising teaching. Both groups included an approximately equal number of students offering the different subjects for practising in teaching. One of the divisions was further divided into two groups, GA_1 (experimental group of the validation study referred to earlier) and GA_2 (control group which was taught through structured lecture). GA_1 consisted of 35 students and GA_2 of 34 students. The other division GB which was taught through conventional lecture method consisted of 57 students. Comparison was made of the performance of the groups GA_2 and GB. It may be stated that the two groups GA_2 and GB could not be matched on any specified criterion. This sacrifice of matching had to be made because of certain practical organizational difficulties. Group GB was taught by three members of the faculty staff who had been teaching that course in earlier years. There was no restriction placed on these teachers to follow any specific plan for teaching this group. They distributed among themselves the units to be covered according to their convenience. Performances of the two groups GA_2 and GB were compared in terms of the mean scores obtained in a common comprehensive test conducted at the end of the course. These means are presented in Table 3.

Group	Mean	S.D.	N	t	Significance
GA_2 (Structural Lecture)	62.62	22.42	34	2.185	at 0.05 level
GB (Conventional Lecture)	52.67	19.74	57		

Table 3. *Mean Performance on Comprehensive Test*

From Table 3, it may be noted that the mean performance of GA_2 is significantly better than that of GB. This indicates that the structured lecture is more effective than the conventional lecture. This point is further substantiated by the trends in scores at different percentile points for the two groups presented in Table 4.

Percentile points	GA_2	GB
P_{10}	33.00	27.33
P_{20}	41.50	33.50
P_{30}	49.83	38.68
P_{40}	55.50	46.36
P_{50}	61.50	53.39
P_{60}	68.30	59.72
P_{70}	78.83	66.05
P_{80}	87.50	72.75
P_{90}	93.63	80.10

Table 4. *Percentile Points for Comprehensive Test Scores*

From Table 4, it may be observed that the trend in scores of the groups GA_2 at different percentile points is definitely in favour of the structured lecture method. This, along with the mean difference, demonstrates the increase in effectiveness of the lecture method due to the introduction of structuring. Findings of this comparison lead us to accept the hypothesis that the structured lecture adopted in the validation experiment is more effective than the usually adopted unstructured lecture. This finding further strengthens the conclusion that the PLM whose effectiveness was found comparable to the structured lecture adopted in the validation experiment is effective enough to be utilized as instructional material for the particular course.

Error analysis of students' performance on criterion tests was carried out. On the basis of this analysis and in consultation with the faculty members involved, decisions were taken regarding the details of other components of the instructional strategy. It was considered that the deficits in learning indicated by performance on criterion tests could be made up by enriching the instructional process with the use of techniques of discussion, practical work and library work. Sequencing of these different components was decided in consultation with the concerned faculty members. The first step in the sequence of instructional work for each unit would be that students read the PLM; the students would, then, do the library work based on references provided to them; the third step would be that the students do the practical work under the supervision of the teacher; this would then be followed by a discussion session.

Phase IV

This phase relates to the integration of the four components, viz, PLM, discussion, library work and practical work to form the instructional strategy and study its effectiveness for providing instruction. Effectiveness of the strategy would be measured in terms of students' performance on tests. Procedural details about the organization of instructional work for studying effectiveness are given in the following.

All the 168 students of the B Ed class were considered as subjects for this phase of the study. However, to facilitate proper organization of the instructional work, the class was divided into three groups. Three faculty members were put in charge of the three groups. An orientation was given to the students at the beginning of the session regarding the procedure for studying the course. Instructional work in relation to different components was carried out as under:

Programmed Learning

Students read the PLM during regular class hours. The concerned faculty member remained present during these hours. If some students could not complete the unit within specified hours, they did so outside class hours. The PLM for each unit was given to students at the beginning of the particular unit, and it remained with them for their reference.

Library Work

Books for references with necessary details were given to students for each unit. They were instructed to refer to these books after they had read PLM for that unit and before they came for the discussion period. Library work was done independently by students at their convenience. It was suggested to students that they maintain records of their library work.

Practical Work

Practical work sessions were organized for each unit. Details of the work to be carried out in these sessions were decided in consideration of the specific objectives of the units, and in consultation with the faculty members involved in the instructional work. These details were made available to the members in charge. Practical work was done under the direct guidance and supervision of the member in charge. One or two class hours were devoted to each unit for this purpose.

Discussion Session

A discussion session for each unit was organized after the completion of the practical work for that unit. Discussions were based on the contents of the respective units. Certain points for discussion were specified based on the analysis of students' performance in criterion tests conducted during the previous phase. In addition to the discussion around these points students were free to raise points for clarification. Discussions were guided by the faculty members in charge.

Scheme of Evaluation

Evaluation included unit tests, feedback sessions, practical work assignments and a comprehensive test. A unit test was organized after discussion for that unit was completed. Students' performance on the test was discussed in a feedback session after each unit test. In such sessions the teacher in charge discussed and clarified the points which were not clear to students as indicated by their performance on unit tests. Work done in practical sessions was evaluated based on records of practical work submitted by students. At the end of the course a comprehensive test was organized.

For the purpose of evaluating the effectiveness of the strategy, the total system consisting of different components has been considered as the unit. And the effectivenesss of the total system has been studied against the same criteria which were developed for Phase III. Contribution of individual components and their interaction has not been considered in this study. Effectiveness of the instructional strategy was studied by computing the means, standard deviations, and percentiles on the six unit tests and the comprehensive test. Results have been presented in Table 5.

	Unit I	Unit II	Unit III	Unit IV	Unit V	Unit VI	Comprehensive
Mean	17.72	20.08	19.56	19.56	19.01	14.71	70.60
Standard Deviation	5.10	4.02	4.53	4.83	3.27	4.98	20.60
Percentile10	9.35	14.17	12.71	11.00	13.48	6.86	40.20
P20	13.20	16.73	15.79	15.62	15.51	9.91	50.71
P30	14.70	18.68	17.93	17.50	17.12	12.32	58.44
P40	17.26	19.82	19.50	19.10	18.61	14.64	66.18
P50	18.57	20.96	20.86	20.38	19.60	16.42	74.32
P60	20.50	21.91	21.90	21.64	20.59	17.77	76.73
P70	21.52	22.69	22.65	22.71	21.58	18.45	86.05
P80	22.84	23.49	23.40	23.78	22.58	19.13	90.38
P90	23.91	24.26	24.15	25.00	23.57	19.82	95.43

Table 5. Mean, S D and Percentiles on Various Tests*

*Maximum score for unit tests I—V is 25; and it is 20 for test VI. Maximum score for comprehensive test is 100.

	P10	P20	P30	P40	P50	P60	P70	P80	P90
Phase III (Experimental)	33.25	45.50	52.00	58.67	67.83	73.79	78.79	84.50	90.73
Phase IV	40.20	50.71	58.44	66.18	74.32	76.73	86.05	90.38	95.43

Table 6. Percentiles on Comprehensive Tests under Phase III & IV

From Table 5, it may be observed that nearly 50% of students have scored 75% and above on the comprehensive tests, which is generally considered as performance with distinction. Only less than 10% of students have scored 40% and below; and 20% of them have scored above 90%. A closely similar trend can be noticed on each unit test. Under Phase III students in the experimental group learnt solely through the PLM; the other components of the strategy were completely absent. Therefore, comparison of performance of the students on the comprehensive test in the Phase IV and that of students in the experimental group during Phase III should reveal the effectiveness of instructional strategy adopted in Phase IV. It may be recalled here that the project was carried out over a period of two years. As a consequence, the subjects of Phase III and Phase IV belong to groups which took the B Ed course in two different academic sessions. Thus for obvious practical reasons the two groups — experimental group of Phase III and Phase IV group — could not be matched on any specific criterion. However, it may be noted that the admission requirements and procedures remained the same for both the years. Therefore, it was assumed that the two groups were similar in nature, and their performance on a common comprehensive test could be compared. By observing the results presented in Tables 2 and 5, it becomes clear that there have been considerable differences in the mean performance of students in favour of the Phase IV group. Percentiles for the two groups presented in Table 6 give a more detailed comparative picture of the students' performance on the comprehensive test. Results presented in Table 6 strengthen the conclusion drawn earlier regarding the effectiveness of the instructional strategy. It clearly indicates that the enrichment brought into the instructional work under Phase IV by including the components, library works, practical work and discussion, and integrating them with the use of the PLM, has positively influenced the achievement of students.

Conclusion

The instructional strategy has been evolved through continuous experimentation over a period of two years. The main motive behind this study has been to modernize instructional work with a view to increasing its effectiveness and efficiency. In the present case, an attempt has been made to achieve this with maximum utilization of available human resources and with total exclusion of any hardware equipment. This has made the strategy an economically viable one for wider implementation in colleges of education. Another important feature of the strategy relates to the conditions under which it has been evolved. When experiments are conducted in special extra class situations they do not suggest any practical strategy for implementing the new approach. However, it might be observed that in the present case, the experiments have been conducted strictly within the regular schedules of instructional work specified by the faculty. This points to the administrative feasibility of utilizing the strategy for instructional purposes.

The authors are grateful to Dr G R Sudame, Mr B R Panchal and Dr (Miss) M S Padma of the Faculty of Education and Psychology, M S University for rendering academic help at various stages of this project.

447

A Pragmatic Approach to Initiating a Computer-Assisted Instruction Service and Some Problems Involved

M Leiblum

Introduction

Computer-Assisted Instructional (CAI) has been part of the educational and computing environment at the Katholieke Universiteit, Nijmegen, Netherlands (KUN) since about 1973. From that time, the medium has undergone a number of 'growing pains' concomitant with its informal introduction and implementation as an instructional resource. This paper describes the current status of CAI at KUN and briefly describes several ongoing projects. Attention is directed to the problems that can be resolved through the use of CAI. The author also presents a rationale for selecting or justifying CAI usage today.

CAI at KUN

Getting Started

The CAI group evolved from an earlier special interest group that was formed in late 1970. Informal selection of a CAI system began in late 1971 with the support of the university computing centre. A preliminary version of the currently used PLANIT (Programming Language for Inter-Active Teaching) Instructors' Computer Utility was received in late 1972, but many improvements and modifications had to be made. In 1973 development continued with additional support from an education research institute. At no time were more than one or two people committed to work on a full-time basis, thus progress was slow. In reality all group members had other tasks to perform. A proposal was then put forth requesting that a 'formal' CAI Project should be created, but not controlled by the computing centre (who felt that CAI was not one of its service functions). Finally, in late 1974, the university's governing council recommended that a project be formed and placed under the administrative umbrella of an educational research institute; however, a separate budget was granted as well as the affirmation that all policy and operational decisions should rest within the CAI Project itself.

The pilot project was given a two-year trial period. The staff would consist of one full-time educational technologist, one full-time system programmer, one half-time educational psychologist, and one half-time instructional programmer. In actuality all staff members perform a wide range of activities not indicated by their titles. One or two part-time student assistants have also been associated with the project.

The PLANIT System

The CAI system was initially developed in the United States under a grant from the National Science Foundation (NSF). It can be obtained from its distributing agency

(Frye, C, 1975). The language is machine transferable and has been implemented on a number of different computers with varying degrees of success. Its source code consists of about 15,000 FORTRAN statements. A separate input/output interface program must be written by the host computer installation (requiring about two to four man-months of study and coding). The language provides most of the necessary author and student features for CAI work (see Leiblum, 1974) and includes a built-in calculation mode. It is, however, not terribly efficient (from a computer system specialist's point of view), requires a large memory and disc space, and lacks computer graphics facilities. With the co-operation of the University of Freiburg (West Germany), we obtained and improved the system.

Our Computer Environment

The PLANIT system is running on our IBM 370/158 under VS2R1, with TSO and HASP. Our primary hardware expenses were for terminals and other AV devices. We have 'priority' rights on five terminals (shared by non-CAI users), and occasionally make use of some of the other 26 terminals on campus. Since our project was 'experimental', we were granted free computer time, though this may change shortly. The computing centre services a student population of about 14,000, and handles about 6000 jobs weekly.

Putting it Together

Our approach has been to fit CAI into an existing computing framework, to make minimal demands and not to promise that CAI is the 'cure-all' for all educational ailments. It is of necessity a low-keyed effort with sensitivity to the traditional conservatism of educational institutions. The approach is based on the belief that students can and do learn through CAI, that there is a decrease in learning time requirements when CAI is compared against traditional instruction, and that almost every curriculum area can use the medium. The problem is to use it effectively. We can show that students respond favourably to the medium, that faculty members are willing to become involved in CAI work, and that it can be used to supplement, and under certain conditions, supplant traditional instruction. Our primary concern was not with the research aspects of CAI (learning about learning), but to gain operational experience, to become familiar with the problems of CAI, and to discover where and how its capabilities could be wisely utilized. We tried to select appropriate conditions under which CAI would 'work'. Thus, our approach was to uncover an existing instructional problem (defined by an instructor), and to use CAI to help that problem.

The Applications: Problems and Proposed Solutions

Rather than going into great detail about the instructional contents or CAI strategies used, one can identify the specific problems that we hoped CAI could resolve.

PROBLEM 1
A decision reached by a curriculum committee changed the amount of 'hours' made available to a botany instructor for scheduled lectures and work-sessions (practicums). Due to the drastically-shortened period, the instructor was faced with the problem of compressing much of the basic material from his 'live' lectures without endangering the quality of instruction. At the same time that the scheduled practicum sessions were reduced, the student load doubled (from 50-60 to 120).

The instructor placed a high value on giving individual student assistance and feared that the new schedule and increased class size would prevent this. The number of student-assistants did not increase (frequently only one year ahead of the class they were helping), and they could hardly provide the insights and expertise given by the instructor. Lectures, on theoretical foundations needed for the practicums, were sometimes inadvertently scheduled (by other faculty members) to conflict with the practicums, forcing students to miss one or the other. *Proposed CAI solution:* Several tutorial-type programs providing a combination of theory and exercises to replace the 'lost' lecture and practicum time. Slides and syllabus to support the programs which can be executed at the student's convenience (day or evenings). The instructor gains more time to provide individual help, the students progress at their own pace, at convenient times. The computer system receives greater 'non-prime time' usage.

PROBLEM 2

The computing centre offers a course on 'Job Control Language' twice yearly. Users of the computer cannot always wait for these 'live' courses, and those that do sometimes find that conflicting schedules prevent attendance. Handbooks and reference manuals are available, but do not always suffice. The entry-level experience of many students differs greatly, putting a strain on the teacher covering the materials. Some basic remedial instruction is frequently required. The programming advice and teaching staff of the computing centre are repeatedly asked similar questions which could be answered through automated means. The operating system is regularly altered, forcing continuous changes/revisions to existing documentation related to JCL. The usage of time-sharing and of interactive video-terminals has also grown, forcing users to gain 'live' terminal experience. The limited terminal facilities makes the scheduling of large classes impossible, so a more individualized approach is needed.
Proposed CAI solution: Tutorial-type instructional programs providing information on basic computer concepts, and preparation for better understanding of JCL (terminology, descriptive information on statements and exercises). Students gain actual terminal experience through CAI that is transferred to other time-sharing work. Instructional material can be easily modified to reflect current system status. Scheduling flexibility makes student usage easier. Those requiring remedial work (ie those without any computer experience) can get it and are thus better prepared for the shortened 'live' course or self-study.

PROBLEM 3

The mathematical-statistical advice department provides regular instruction (traditional lectures) plus individual help to 'clients' of many faculties. Some of these clients have previously followed statistics, or research design courses, but the time-lapse between learning and the actual application can be long. The statistical advisors also find it time-consuming, and sometimes annoying, to help re-establish the basic concepts. In another case, the traditional lectures of the statistics instructor are accompanied by practicums (exercise sessions). There is a limit to the individual help he can offer students in these practicums. Another instructor finds it difficult to handle certain statistical concepts (confidence limits, normal distributions, etc) in a classroom without real computational facilities. The teacher of statistics for linguistic students wants his students to lose their fear of computers, to learn some computer concepts without having first to learn a computer language, and to have access to an easily-learned calculation utility.
Proposed CAI solution: Development of CAI problem-solving exercises on statistics and probability containing generous remediation and guidance assistance. Also

development of short tutorial programs describing the use of the 'CALC' features of the PLANIT system and other 'calculation' topics. Students taking the problem-solving program are capable of solving more problems in a shorter time because of built-in prompting cues, references, and can make use of the calculation facility. The 'linguistic' students learn about computing concepts through CAI (rounding, accuracy, library functions, hierarchies) and need not first learn FORTRAN. Students can also execute tutorial programs on statistical concepts at convenient times, and can then report to an 'advisor' for other guidance.

Justifying CAI Today

A First Warning

The decision to enter CAI now must be tempered by the reality of the present economic crunch in education. CAI is expensive both in the consumption of program development time and in money. If cost reduction is a priority far outweighing the improving of instructional effectiveness or the seeking of unique solutions to instructional problems, then resorting to CAI now is foolhardy. It is possible to juggle data, minimize reported expenses or to forget about those extra months of development time. Upon closer scrutiny, one will usually find that CAI is not cheaper than traditional instruction. This may change over the coming years. Clearly the trend is for cheaper computer hardware and software costs. Consider CAI now only if you are in an environment that already has a respectable computer and time-sharing system plus terminals. Dedicated computer systems for CAI exist (in Europe), but are a rarity. If an in-house computer is not available, then joining an existing CAI 'network' is possible and cheaper but often means a loss of control. On the other hand 'networking' allows the user to share resources not possessed locally. It enables both teacher and student to have access to program libraries (courses) and support programs developed elsewhere. Seidel (1973) also states that networking on a national scale allows you to 'pool your resources and create critical masses of personnel resources and facilities to further curriculum reform' (p 615).

The following reasons for justifying CAI are therefore conditionally based on easy access to an existing computer system (networked or otherwise).

Rationale

The decision to use CAI can be based on three broad rationalizations: theoretical factors, practicality, experimental study.

THEORETICAL FACTORS

CAI, just like films, text-books, live lectures etc is an instructional medium. A medium can be selected based on theoretical factors. Instruction, no matter what its form, involves: (1) a display of stimulus materials; (2) the scheduling of responses; and in some cases, (3) feedback messages to the students. If a learning situation calls for a student to repair the gears of his bicycle, then selecting the medium of an audio-cassette containing instructions would be improper and probably highly frustrating. It is possible for a study of stimulus and response requisites, from an analysis of the learning situation, to select the 'best' media to carry an instructional strategy. Gropper (1976) and Rockart, Morton (1976) provide excellent frameworks for making such decisions. Gropper divides media into two main classes, eg active and passive, with CAI fitting into the 'active' because it provides for the three components mentioned earlier (with stress on overt or active response). Rockart and Morton present a model for matching technology to learning, and specify a set of attributes for learning mechanisms. Included among these attributes are content-related items (ability to telescope time, to present structure, provision of rich environment, flexibility for adding new materials, etc), user-related items (degree of learner control, adjustment to individual needs, ease of usage), communication-related items (sensory impact, degree of learner feedback, etc), and economics (low cost per data item or concept; decentralized availability). The authors provide a ranking scheme of the various media versus 16 learning attributes.

Now unfortunately the real-life situation demands that decisions concerning media selection are based on financial, logistical, attitudinal, or just practical grounds, and not just on whether it is theoretically preferable.

PRACTICALITY

Computer-based learning can be selected as a medium if it offers a unique solution to an existing instructional problem. For instance, it might be better (from a learning theory viewpoint) for a student to actually perform a chemistry experiment with explosive constituents, but the accompanying dangers (blowing up a laboratory) would indicate this was not practical. If in addition, the local chemistry lab contained only 20 experimental situations for the 100 students in the course, then those stations would have to be used very efficiently. A CAI 'simulated experiment' program might solve both problems. A program allowing students to design and perform simulated experiments (eg describing set-up procedures, allowing students to vary types and quantities of chemicals, analyzing faults, performing equation balancing etc) would be a unique and practical solution. The simulation program would reduce the danger of bodily harm. At the same time the student could complete the other 'live' experiments in a more efficient way, having prepared for them through the CAI program (resulting in a more effective use of existing facilities).

Another extremely practical use of CAI is for drill and practice exercises and for remediation. The well known D&P arithmetic programs developed by Suppes have shown that the computer can play the role of a patient drill-master. Students receive randomly-generated arithmetic exercises based on their ability level, are given immediate feedback and reinforcement for desired behaviour, and can progress at their own pace. The only alternative to this approach would be to hire an army of live tutors.

In an earlier section, a number of 'problems' were identified which resulted in our selecting CAI as the medium to solve them. A broad range of applications can be found which makes use of the 'practicality' rationale.

EXPERIMENTAL STUDY

CAI can be used as a research tool to study how people learn. Proper analysis of automatically collected student performance data can provide insights into the learning process. The work of Landa, Pask, and other artificial intelligence scientists are sure to influence CAI. Computer learning models (created by AI experts) can be tested and verified through CAI. The literature is full of studies reporting investigations of learner-controlled instruction, of inductive versus deductive approaches, of the analysis of student performance under specified conditions, and many of these studies can be questioned. The fact is, this kind of work must be continued. Experimental study is needed to establish guidelines for the future. The responsibility falls on current researchers to help pave the way for innovative and effective uses of instructional computing. CAI can now be justified to provide the real experience necessary to keep the state-of-the-art advancing. It is not enough to leave this job to a few rich universities in rich countries. Modest computer-based-instruction systems can be implemented making use of small computers and limited personnel.

References

Frye, C (1975) 'Information Regarding the Availability of PLANIT' Northwest Regional Educational Laboratory, 710 S W Second Avenue, Portland, Oregon 97204.

Gropper, G (1976) 'A Behavioural Perspective on Media Selection' 'Audio-Visual Communications Review' Vol 24, No 2, pp 157-86.

Leiblum, M (1974) 'An Analytical and Comparative Study of CAI Programming Languages, Their Characteristics and Usage' Katholieke Universiteit, Nijmegen, Netherlands.

Rockart, Morton (1976) 'Computers and the Learning Process in Higher Education' McGraw-Hill, New York.

Seidel, R (1973) 'Hardware from a User's Point of View' 'The Physiologist' Vol 16, No 4, November 1973.

The Use of Computer-Assisted Testing in an Introductory Course of Educational Psychology

J L Derevensky, G F Cartwright

Educators and psychologists have become increasingly aware of the multitude of problems inherent in traditional classroom instruction and evaluation. The development and construction of examinations is a task many instructors often find difficult and requiring a great amount of time and energy. Taking this into consideration, many publishers have attempted to ease the burden of preparing examinations by providing an instructor's guide with numerous essays, short-answer and multiple-choice questions for many introductory texts. Thus, an instructor need only consult the appropriate guide, and employ both an efficient typist and a capable printer to produce the required number of examination papers. The evaluation of the papers, however, is not quite as easy. With essay or short-answer examinations, an instructor may be required to spend countless hours reading students' responses. In many universities this task is often assigned to graduate assistants or departmental readers. Instructors without access to such help often opt for multiple-choice examinations.

The multiple-choice format is perceived to be advantageous because scoring is more objective than subjective, and may be done by a machine. Once the test is prepared, students respond by filling in the appropriate area on a mark-sense sheet or answer card. Later, the answer card is scored by the computer and the students' scores and relevant statistical data concerning the test are printed. While this system has several advantages, there remain the problems of constructing large numbers of items (if these are not provided by the publisher), selecting the appropriate items for a particular test, and printing the items in an error-free format. Fortunately, in addition to scoring, the computer can also be used to solve some of these problems. This form of computer-assisted testing (CAT) is often referred to as computer-assisted test construction (CATC). It is a system designed to assist the instructor by selecting items with particular attributes, assembling them into a test, and printing the test in an error-free format (Cartwright, 1975). Such programs have been used in traditional courses (Ansfield, 1973; Brown, 1973; Dudley, 1973) and for student-paced courses (Cohen and Cohen, 1973).

While computer-constructed examinations can provide an efficient, low-cost procedure for evaluating performance, and can generate equivalent forms of examinations, there is often a significant delay between the writing of a test and the return of the results. This lack of immediate feedback, often referred to as knowledge of correct results (KCR), is thought to be essential for optimal learning (cf Skinner, 1968). Since CATC systems traditionally have centred on test production and item analysis, students have no direct contact with the computer and therefore no immediate KCR.

However, there exists an alternative method of CAT which provides for immediate KCR by allowing the computer to administer the test and provide feedback immediately after each test item. Such a system requires on-line computational facilities and because of its interactive nature is known as interactive computer-assisted testing (ICAT) (Cartwright & Derevensky, 1976b). ICAT has numerous advantages over CATC in that it can be effective for teaching and learning as well as for evaluation (Cartwright & Derevensky, 1976a).

One of our first attempts to implement ICAT was in 1970 in an introductory psychology course taught at McGill University. Previously it had been determined that testing would consist of a series of six multiple-choice examinations using items provided by the textbook publisher. The question remained whether or not it would be feasible to present the test items by computer. The biggest problem at that time was to code the items in a computer-assisted instruction (CAI) author language known as MULE (McGill University Language of Education). The task was given to the 60 students in the course, each of whom programmed approximately 14 questions to produce an item bank of over 800 items. The project was regarded as highly successful, and since the students appeared to benefit from the addition of ICAT to the course (Cartwright, 1971), consideration was given to further developing and improving the ICAT system.

In 1973, work began on coding the items for a course in introductory educational psychology. The questions were provided by the publisher, but the items were somewhat unique in that along with our addition of immediate KCR, each had an elaborate feedback paragraph associated with it. These feedback paragraphs indicated to the student the correct answer, why alternative answers were incorrect, and contained page numbers in the text for further reference. The items were coded in a somewhat more powerful CAI author language known as CAN-6 (Cartwright and Tessler, 1975), and were presented by an IBM 370 series computer on 10 teletype terminals which were later replaced by cathode-ray tube (CRT) terminals.

Five quizzes were developed based on specific chapters of the text-book (Biehler, 1971; 1974). Recently, students requested that a sixth quiz be implemented to sample questions from the entire text. This is now in operation. Each of the quizzes consists of 20 items based on specific text-book chapters, selected at random from the item bank. After each item immediate KCR is provided and the student is given the opportunity of requesting the feedback paragraph. In addition, a utility function was developed to allow students to communicate with their instructor, to use the computer as a desk calculator, or to check their current score file.

Each student may take a quiz as often as he likes but must attain the criterion score in order to receive credit for that quiz. During the initial phase of the quiz development, the criterion was set at 70% but was later raised to 80%.

The quizzes are adjunctive in the sense that students must still attend lectures and are responsible for studying their text. The fact that the quizzes are closely keyed to the text acts as an incentive for further study. In one of our studies, it was found that students' attitudes towards the quizzes changed markedly during the course of the year. At the beginning of the year they tended to see the quizzes as strictly evaluation sessions. Towards the end of the year, however, they came to view the quizzes as more of a learning than an evaluative tool. It is possible that the existence of the feedback paragraphs contributed to this changed perception (Cartwright and Derevensky, 1976b). The amount of learning that actually takes place as a result of the quizzes is not yet clear but data are currently being collected in an attempt to answer this question.

Evolution

In the last few years the quizzes have evolved significantly. The first three revisions dealt exclusively with developing and improving the questions, revising them for a second edition of the text, modifying the format of the items, adapting them for use with CRT terminals, and adding upper/lower print for easier readability. Subsequent revisions were primarily structural and involved a number of technical improvements, many of which are transparent to the students. For example, the items themselves were separated from the random selection and scoring routines. This allowed the development of various kinds of independent 'question pickers' which act in different ways on the same bank of items. While careful planning may have brought us to this point somewhat earlier, it must be remembered that originally each quiz had been programmed as if it had been a conventional CAI lesson with answer processing built into each item. Next, a separate answer processing routine was established to evaluate student responses for each item. This resulted in a large saving in disc storage and allowed the answer processing and scoring to be easily changed for all items simply by changing that routine. The answer processor also contains provision for selecting different feedback statements for each item to provide some variety in the responses given by the computer. Finally, with the quizzes modularized in this way, provision was made to introduce experimental conditions easily to the quizzes. For example, one of the quizzes is now operating with three variations to determine the differential effects of scoring on learning and test reliability. What is interesting here is not so much the fact that a number of treatments are possible, but that the computer is used to assign each student at random automatically to a particular treatment. In this way the computer manages the experiment itself.

To some extent the development of ICAT at McGill has been influenced by a great many outside factors. First, the decision to use ICAT at all might never have been made if test items had not been readily available from the text publisher. Second, it was decided to use a CAI author language to code the question items rather than to develop a special program specifically to select and present test items. Some new operation codes had to be added to the language to accommodate the random selection of quiz items easily. Third, student behaviour helped initiate changes in the system. For example, when it was found that a student could sign on to a number of terminals simultaneously and by running from terminal to terminal attempt to complete several quizzes at once, a change was made to the language to ensure that no student could sign on to more than one terminal at a time. It was also found that several students would spend as many as six consecutive hours in front of the terminal, repeating quiz after quiz. Since this was believed to be counter-productive in that time could be better spent in studying the text before attempting to repeat a quiz, facilities were developed to control the number of sign-ons per day, the hours of the day, and the days of the week when access to the quizzes was permitted.

Now that most of the techniques have been refined in the ICAT system, work has continued to adapt to ICAT over 700 items based on a different text. These items have no feedback paragraphs associated with them, but the larger bank of questions together with immediate KCR yields additional possibilities for research.

It is readily apparent that ICAT has several advantages over CATC, the chief one being immediate feedback and the possible provision for elaborate feedback paragraphs. While the chief disadvantage is one of high cost (Lippey, 1977), this may be justified on the grounds that ICAT is also an instructional system as well as an evaluative technique. That students can learn from adjunctive auto-instruction is nothing new (Pressey, 1926) and it can be pointed out that the costs of such systems are falling dramatically.

The use of ICAT as an adjunct to traditional methods in an introductory course in educational psychology at McGill has been perceived by both students and staff to be advantageous. Its use is now well beyond the experimental stage and has expanded to several other departments outside the Faculty of Education, including social work and classics. It is anticipated that with further development and research in the area, ICAT will be even more widely used in the future.

References

Ansfield, P J (1973) 'A User-Oriented Computing Procedure for Compiling and Generating Examinations' 'Educational Technology' 13, p12-13.

Biehler, R F (1971) 'Psychology Applied to Teaching' Houghton Mifflin, Boston.

Biehler, R F (1974) 'Psychology Applied to Teaching' (2nd edition) Houghton Mifflin, Boston.

Brown, W A (1973) 'A Computer Examination Compositor for the IBM 360/40' 'Educational Technology' 13, p 15-16.

Cartwright, G F (1971) 'Social Factors in Computer-Assisted Testing' Proceedings of the McGill University Conference on University Teaching and Learning, McGill University, Montreal.

Cartwright, G F (1975) 'A Promising Innovation: Computer-Assisted Test Construction' 'Learning and Development' 6, p 1-3.

Cartwright, G F and Derevensky, J L (1976a) 'Interactive Computer-Assisted Testing: a Feasibility Study' Paper presented at the annual conference of the Canadian Educational Research Association, Laval University, Quebec City.

Cartwright, G F and Derevensky, J L (1976b) 'An Attitudinal Study of Computer-Assisted Testing as a Learning Method' 'Psychology in the Schools' 13, p 317-321.

Cartwright, G and Tessler, F (1975) 'Course Author's Guide to Computer-Assisted Instruction Using CAN VI' Centre for Learning and Development, McGill University, Montreal.

Cohen, P S and Cohen, C R (1975) 'Computer Generated Tests for a Student Paced Course' 'Educational Technology' 13, p 18-19.

Dudley, J J (1973) 'How the Computer Assists in Pacing and Testing Student Progress' 'Educational Technology' 13, p 21-23.

Lippey, G (1977) 'Observations' 'CATC Digest' 1, p 3.

Pressey, S L (1926) 'A Simple Apparatus Which Gives Tests and Scores — and Teaches' 'School and Society' 23, p 373-376.

Skinner, B F (1968) 'The Technology of Teaching' Appelton-Century Crofts, New York.

A Study of Some Results of an Educational Media Course Within a Teacher Preparation Program

W E McCavitt

Introduction

Accountability seems to be the name of the game in higher education today, at least in the United States. In the public schools, parents are asking why education is costing more, in terms of tax dollars, and yet Johnny does not know the basics such as reading, writing and arithmetic. In higher education we find some professors expounding information that is outdated and no longer relevant in our modern society. And even more frightening, there are cases where students are suing universities because they claim that they gained nothing from a course.

Procedure

With this in mind I undertook a research project to try and determine the on-the-job behaviour of a sample of secondary public school teachers in two curriculum areas (physical and behavioural sciences). The study broke these teachers down further into teachers with one year's teaching experience and teachers with five years of teaching experience. The sample included teachers from both urban and rural areas.

These teachers had all taken an audio-visual course at the same institution as part of their teacher preparation curriculum. The point of the research was to attempt to determine if the objectives as outlines in the course actually carried over into the classes being taught by the teacher sample.

Figure 1 shows a simple model designed as a beginning for output evaluation for higher education (Lawrence, 1970).

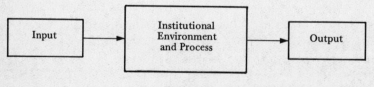

Figure 1.

Input passes through the environment to become output. The objective of higher education is to add value to the input (students) via instructional process as it passes through the environment (college). Relating this model to this study it would look like the following (see Figure 2).

In order to measure programme outputs a means of determining desired outputs as opposed to unwanted outputs must be devised.

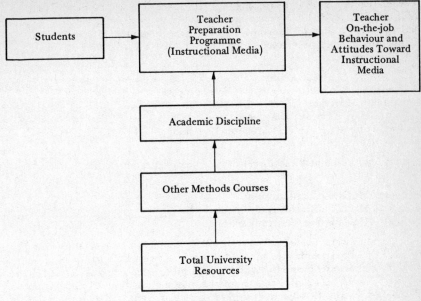

Figure 2.

The basis of the instrument used in this study is the behavioural objectives written for the basic instructional media course. After the objectives are articulated and implemented the question remains, does the output reflect the fulfilment of these objectives?

This research sought to determine this through the use of a LIKERT-type scale designed to determine attitudes and behaviour of in-service teachers toward the use of instructional media in the classroom, in student assignments, and in student evaluation. Schematically the research design looked like this:

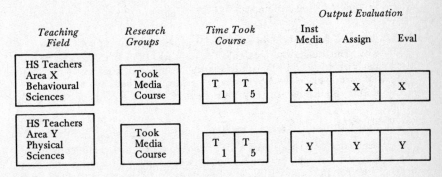

Figure 3.

The process followed in developing this questionnaire began by dividing the objectives that had previously been established for the media course into cognitive, affective and psychomotor domains. Once this was completed, questions were developed that related to selected objectives in these six general areas of instructional media:

1. Theoretical Considerations.
2. Management of Instructional and Systems Design.
3. Equipment Usage.
4. Selection of Learning Resources.
5. Development of Visual Production Techniques.
6. Emergent Technology.

The questions in each of these areas were then reorganized into the following categories:

1. Use of Media in the Classroom.
2. Use of Media in Student Assignments.
3. Use of Media in Student Evaluations.

These categories were divided into an attitude section and a behaviour section, the purpose being to determine attitudes of the teachers toward the use of media in the classroom, in assignments and in student evaluations. Behaviour was defined as the use of media in the classroom, in assignments, and in evaluation. Each question related back to a specific objective within a particular domain, determining the existence of an attitude or behaviour in the three areas of use, assignment and evaluation.

The sample consisted of 100 first-year teachers in the behavioural sciences, 100 first-year teachers in the physical sciences, 100 fifth-year teachers in the behavioural sciences, and 100 fifth-year teachers in the physical sciences. These two areas for the purpose of this study are defined as follows:

Behavioural Science:	Social Science
	Language
	Art
	English
Physical Sciences:	Mathematics
	Sciences

The data collected was run through a computer program entitled TESTAT to determine means and standard deviations. The data was then analyzed using a two-way analysis of variance by means of another computer program (AVAR23). The analysis of variance was used to determine significance between observed differences among the means of the various teachers' scores.

Summary and Conclusions

Among teachers who have completed a pre-service instructional media course one year ago as against those who had such a course five years ago, there was no significant difference in their attitude and behaviour in all three tested areas: uses of instructional media in the classroom, in student assignment and use of instructional media in evaluation.

Among teachers in the behavioural sciences as against those in the physical sciences, there was a significant difference, with physical science teachers scoring much higher in both attitude and behaviour toward the use of instructional media in the classroom, and also in their use of instructional media in student evaluation.

460

There was no statistically significant difference between academic discipline and how recently the instructional media course had been taken in terms of attitudes or use.

The teachers taking part in the study agreed that an instructional media course was a valuable experience in their preparation to become teachers. It should be pointed out, however, that first-year teachers, according to their mean scores, were slightly higher in attitude toward the use of instructional media in the classroom than fifth-year teachers. This attitude may change as they continue in their teaching experience as is reflected in the fifth-year mean scores. The norms of the world of work gradually tend to displace the learning and values of the professional preparation programmes. It may also reflect the fact that the first-year teachers are younger and have literally grown up with a transistor radio in their ear, a portable television set in front of them while they sit in a drive-in movie watching a motion picture film.

It became apparent also that the physical science students are learning the basic media course with a better attitude toward, and a willingness to use, instructional media. This may be due to the nature of science and their science instruction rather than to the instructional media course.

Based on the raw scores of the instrument used, it would seem that there is room for improvement in providing a basic instructional media course for teachers preparing to be secondary teachers. It is a historical fact that the attitudes of teachers toward technology in education get more negative as we go up the educational ladder. We may be seeing the effect of this attitude toward instructional media in the results of this study. It is possible, for instance, that due to the manipulative and material dimensions of the sciences, those physical science students enter the instructional media course with an appreciation of the visualization of concepts. This appreciation may have been nurtured by professors in their major fields who use instructional media extensively in their teaching.

On the other hand, it is possible that behavioural science students are not willing to accept instructional media in education due to the lack of use by professors in their major fields of study.

Recommendations

1. The basic instructional media course be structured to deal better with the different needs of secondary students in the behavioural and physical sciences.
2. The basic instructional media course could better serve students in each academic area if divided into two courses. One dealing with the theoretical aspects of instructional media (learning theory and management of instruction), systems design, and instructional development, while the other course would emphasize production and use of materials.
3. Teaching the operation of various types of instructional media equipment (projectors, tape recorders, etc) should be conducted on a self-instruction basis (automated laboratories).
4. Follow-up studies such as this one should be conducted on the graduates of other educational methods courses.
5. Additional research should be conducted using the procedures used in this study, but using elementary school teachers as the sample.

Technology in education is here to stay. True, it has not progressed as rapidly as its champions had predicted, but as James Koerner suggests:

'History suggests that new technologies are often overrated in the short run but vindicate their prophets in the long run.' (Koerner, 1973.)

References

Lawrence, G W and Patterson, V W (eds) 'Outputs of Higher Education: Their Identification, Measurement, and Evaluation' 1970, Boulder, Colorado, Western Interstate Commission for Higher Education.
Koerner, J 'Educational Technology, Does it Have a Future in the Classroom?' 'Saturday Review of Education' 1, 4, April 14th 1973, pp 43–46.

Practice Teaching and Teacher Training at the Thai-German Technical Teacher College, King Mongkut's Institute of Technology, Bangkok, Thailand

C Kasipar, S Thaitrong, T G Wyant

The college (the Faculty of Technical Education and Science) was established in 1969 as part of the aid programme given to Thailand by the Federal Republic of Germany.

In addition to supplying the necessary educational resources, the West German Government also supplies teams of technical and educational experts to assist in the setting up and running of the college.

Each expert is allotted a Thai counterpart, and as each expert fulfils his contract and returns to Germany, his Thai counterpart takes over his position. Benefiting from the experience gained, the Thai educational teachers have further developed the original ideas and concepts taught to them and adapted them to suit the needs of a developing country.

One of the main problems in Thailand has been the lack of teachers in vocational schools, together with a shortage of teaching/learning materials in the Thai language.

The solution to these problems was to take technicians who have completed the two-year technician course and train them to be teachers. We offer four full-time teacher-training courses (bachelor degree level); two classes in the Mechanical Engineering Department and two classes in the Electrical Engineering Department.

The syllabus for our teacher students covers four main areas of study and work:

1. Educational subjects;
2. Advanced technical studies;
3. Practical workshop/laboratory training;
4. Microteaching and classroom teaching practice.

Our main emphasis in all areas is practical application of the subjects taught, and to impress on our teacher students the need for application in their own teaching sessions. This paper is mainly concerned with the fourth area, teaching practice.

Subjects Taught

Teacher students are expected to be able to carry out a wide spectrum of teaching activities. When teaching specialized topics and subjects, some of which may require a great deal of practical application whilst others may be totally abstract, the teacher is expected to be able to analyze the subject matter and use the best method of teaching it. With this requirement in mind, tutors select lesson topics for the students that cover the whole range of teaching skills.

Systems Approach to Teaching Practice

The teaching practice programme follows a systems approach to ensure that the teacher is fully trained by the end of his period in the college. Teacher students are in the college for four semesters (two years) and their progress is carefully monitored through the two main stages of teaching practice, these are:

1. Microteaching (first semester).
2. Classroom teaching practice (second, third and fourth semesters).

1. Microteaching

In the first stage, which we call microteaching, the teacher student is given a choice of topics that he can teach (the topics having already been written in objective terms by the tutor). The teacher student then has to prepare his own teaching aids and give the lesson to his own colleagues and his tutor. After the lesson the student is allowed to give his version of the success or failure of the lesson. It is then discussed by his colleagues and the tutor. The tutor provides comments and advice and awards a grade, which is made known to the whole class.

2. Classroom Teaching Practice

In the second stage the students are required to teach in front of a class of technician or skilled worker students, either from our institute or those of neighbouring colleges. The student is now given more responsibility for the lesson; he has to write the lesson objectives, worksheets and test sheets. A diagram will help to illustrate how we use a systems approach.

TASKS / Semester	INFORM-ATION SHEET	CHALK BOARD LAYOUT	TEACH-ING AID	LESSON PLAN	TEST ANALY-SIS	WORK SHEET	TEST SHEET	OBJECT-IVES
1								
2								
3	STUDENTS' WORK					TUTOR'S WORK		
4								

Figure 1. *Work distribution*

In the first semester (microteaching), the tutor provides the teacher student with lesson plan, work and test sheets, and the objectives.

In the second semester when the actual classroom teaching practice sessions start, the teacher student is responsible for the lesson plan, chalkboard layout, teaching aids, information sheets and test analysis.

In the third semester, he gets the added responsibility for designing and producing work sheets.

In the fourth semester he is also made responsible for the test sheets and the objectives. (We find with our teacher students that the writing of objectives is one of the hardest skills to learn). Each teaching practice session that the teacher student takes is divided into five distinct phases:

1. Preparation Seminar.
2. Rehearsal lesson.
3. Actual lesson.
4. Discussion.
5. Report.

The preparation seminar is handled by the tutor who outlines the subject matter to be taught, explains and develops the objectives, proposes a selection of teaching methods that can be used, discusses effective teaching aids, demonstrates common faults or errors made by students, establishes the pre-knowledge requirements and agrees the evaluation procedure to be used.

In the rehearsal lesson the teacher student will show his fellow colleagues and tutor how and what he proposes to teach: this is based on the previous preparation seminar that was given by the tutor. Thus any mistakes can be remedied before the student teacher goes in front of the actual class. The teacher student can also revise his teaching methods if he agrees with the suggestions made by his colleagues and tutor. We find that with this type of organization it encourages interaction between group members. During the actual lesson phase the student is given complete responsibility, with no interference from his tutor or colleagues who sit at the back of the class and record, on special observation sheets that we have developed, what happens during the lesson.

The discussion which takes place immediately after the end of the class has many advantages such as: immediate feedback, no loss of information, correction of factual or technical mistakes, boosts confidence and encourages teacher students to be self-critical and their colleagues to give constructive criticisms.

Finally, the teacher student has to produce a report on the lesson that he has given, making comments and suggestions for improvement and compiling the statistics from the observation sheets that were supplied by his colleagues.

Systems Thinking Approach

In our teaching practice system there are four levels of people concerned: tutors, regular teachers (the teacher who would normally teach the class our students take), teacher students and demonstration students.

Each of them has a role to play. For example, Tutor No 1 is responsible for students when they are in the preparation and rehearsal stage, whilst Tutor No 2 takes care of the students in their actual teaching practice sessions, student observation periods, discussion and evaluation seminars. The regular teacher co-operates with the two tutors with regard to course development, students' progress and any other problems that may arise.

The skilled worker students who acquire knowledge and information from our teacher students have to apply them during the actual lesson by completing worksheets and tests sheets in the classroom. The evaluation at the end of the lesson takes about 10 minutes, and the results are given to the students before they leave the classroom. Students are tested at the end of the semester. After the lesson — which in most cases will have been video-taped — the teacher student and his colleagues discuss the lesson with the tutor. After the discussion the teacher student

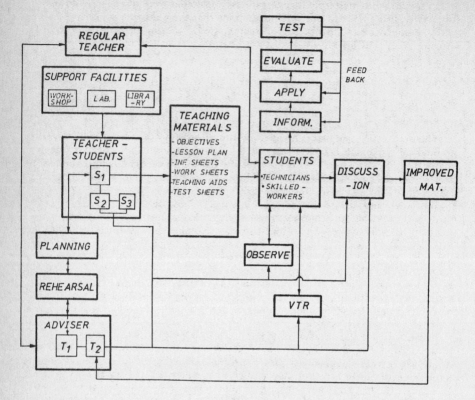

Figure 2. *System diagram of classroom teaching practice*

is awarded a grade by the tutor.

The teacher student, as a post-lesson assignment, must produce a short report containing an analysis of the test results, suggestions for improvements, revised objectives and worksheets etc.

The final grade awarded to the teacher student for his teaching practice is confirmed by a board of tutors before being passed to the registrar.

Course Organization and Numbers

The number of students on each course is limited to 16. The 16 are divided, after the first semester of microteaching, into four groups of four for the second semester. The small group of four are given the maximum amount of assistance by their tutor and they are also encouraged to help each other, as a team, when preparing lessons and materials.

The splitting of the class into four groups allows us to run four parallel classes, all of which are held on the same floor of the building, all teaching the same topic at the same time. This is of considerable advantage in many respects; it allows tutors to see what other teacher students are doing, teacher student observers can

466

move from class to class and observe the different methods and rates of progress, it encourages friendly competition and co-operation between the four groups and it helps to provide a much wider range of discussion topics.

Our teaching practice supervision is situated in the college itself, to obtain the best possible use of resources, close supervision of our teacher students, maximum use of tutors' time, minimum amount of travelling, and the efficient running of our systems approach method.

In the third and fourth semesters the groups are further reduced in size to four groups of three and one group of four. This further split is necessary to ensure that the students get the maximum amount of teaching practice. The total hours of classroom teaching practice, per student, is in the region of 325 hours, over the four semesters.

Teaching Aid Production

Apart from the classroom teaching sessions, teacher students have two semesters where they have to produce teaching and learning aids concerned with technical and educational subjects. Students are given topics by the tutor and are then expected to design and produce aids that can be used by subject teachers.

Students are given teaching/learning special projects to be completed before they leave the college. The tutor provides the topic only, the teacher student is then expected to devise, design and produce teaching aids. The teaching aid, which must be demonstrated, must be supported by a report that gives details of construction, design, various uses and evaluation of its actual use in the classroom. Teacher students are taught to use a systematic approach to this assignment.

Summary

The faculty trains technicians to become technical teachers and provides them with the technical and educational background required. The main emphasis is on practical skills, whether in the cognitive or psycho-motor domain or not.

The whole scheme of technical teacher training is based on a systems approach, which enables us to keep a close control of the progress to be maintained, and a ready evaluation can be made at any time.

Reviews of Workshops

J K Gilbert

Eleven workshops were organized during the course of the conference and a summary is given in Figure 1.

A Digest of Workshops

Organizer	*Title of Workshop*
B Smith	Applications of the Stereo-Cassette Recorder in Secondary Schools
S Edwards D Laurillard	Computer-Assisted Learning in Undergraduate Science
N J Rushby	The Spread of Use of Computer-Managed Learning: The Next Fifteen Years
J C Clay G Moult	Programmed Learning in Airline Marketing Training
W H Dowdeswell	Teaching Biology Through Decision-Taking: The Rid-Pest File
P Willetts J S Wild	Role-Playing Used to Teach International Relations
J S Wild	The Teaching of International Relations Using a Simulation of an International Community
L F Evans N R Winterburn	Peripheral Pick-up or 'Doing Good by Stealth'
J P Bond	The Introduction of an Assessment Case Study into a Training Management Course
R E Wroot	A System for Training Programme Development
A J Trott	Plotting Possibilities in an Educational Technology

Figure 1.

They divided roughly into three groups: four were concerned with the use of particular techniques in educational technology; five were concerned with the use of simulations and games; and two were concerned with broader aspects of the integration and use of facets to the educational technology approach.

Within the area of the use of particular techniques, B Smith demonstrated the use of the stereo-cassette recorder in the secondary school, eg to train debaters and to stimulate interest in sound technology. Susan Edwards and Diana Laurillard provided an introduction to the use of teaching packages for use with interactive graphic terminals, in the use of computers in undergraduate physical science courses. N J Rushby discussed the role of computer-managed learning during the 1980s, whilst Jennifer Coutts Clay and Gerry Moult demonstrated the use of a broad package of techniques, including computer-assisted instruction, programmed texts and video-tapes, in training schemes for British Airways staff.

The difficulties in differentiating between 'simulations' and 'games' became apparent in reviewing the five workshops in this area. W A Dowdeswell presented the 'rid-pest file', a thoroughly tested system, using paper, audio-tape and filmstrip, of teaching biological themes, eg the use of pesticides, by decision-making exercises to 13 to 16-year-olds. Willets and Wild organized a game in which the principles of international relations are taught by reference to the Southern Africa situation. J S Wild also presented an example of 'simulation gaming' (thereby easing the reviewer's problems of interpretation) as used in the systems and management degree at City University. The use of simulated role play was demonstrated by J P Bond's contribution on the problems of reinforcing the concept of the assessment function in a Royal Navy training management course. The use of such techniques to change attitudes in an almost subliminal way was presented by Evans and Winterburn, who suggested the use of an educational technology approach whilst 'doing good by stealth' at City University.

On a broader canvas, R E Wroot from Canada presented a system for the development of training programmes which rests firmly on the base of occupational analysis. The workshop that I personally found of greatest interest, in my search for an explanation of what educational technology actually is, was that by A J Trott, who bravely attempted to draw thought-provoking maps of the area.

Although the attendance at workshops was not what it might have been, and organizers reported a certain preference on the part of participants to listen rather than do, the broad spectrum and detailed preparation of those arranged demonstrates that the format is of great interest in the educational technology field.

Post-Deadline Papers and Delegates Forum

A J Trott

Conference proceedings which include a report of post-deadline papers usually manage to indicate that the standard of paper varied; some seemed excellent and were after the deadline simply because the writers were working on the research right up to the last moment, others were less than excellent because they lacked preparation and were, in fact, after-thoughts. The Guildford Conference might well be remembered by the absence of any 'after-thoughts'. The post-deadline papers were, without exception, of a high standard, and seemed to form a mini-conference of their own.

An examination of the authors involved gives the clue. With such eminent educational technologists as James Hartley, Chris Buckle, Eddie Phillips, Ron Clements, Alex Romiszowski and W D Clarke contributing, the listener was assured of variety, logical reasoning, good presentation, entertainment and up-to-date thinking. It is indeed unfortunate that these papers could not be published in full.

In a paper entitled *Minimum Requirements for a Mental Models Approach to Learning*, M J Coombs and J L Alty of Liverpool University discussed a 'mental models' approach to information processing, the requirements for theory development, and found some interesting conclusions. They examined the suitability of interactive problem-solving situations in the advisory service and found that some advisers looked for specific attributes in order to clarify the extent of the user's knowledge first, whilst not all advisers sought the same information. They also found that personal attempts at problem-solving displayed marked individual differences in the degree to which individuals would continue to maintain an hypothesis in the face of conflicting evidence. Their first conclusion was that it should prove possible to explore questions of representation in relation to different types of previous experience, problem-solving skills and personality factors. Their second conclusion was that in order to study factors affecting correction and transition it may be necessary to use constructed experimental situations. As a third conclusion they suggested that research should be continued on two fronts, one aimed at the establishment of a mental model paradigm, the other a study of the development of problem-solving skills longitudinally.

Chris Buckle in his paper *Programmed Learning and Adolescent Judgements about Careers* also examined thinking and problem-solving. He reported three levels of thought, a restricted level about the age (mental) of 11, a circumstantial level about 13, and an imaginative level about the mental age of 15. He had made use of the problems used by Professor E A Peel in studies of adolescent thinking, and so this work will be of interest to the many educational technologists who have studied at Birmingham. Buckle reported that the research data was still being analyzed, but that the results to date indicated that the choice of a career was probably programmable. And, as Chris Buckle said, 'the most important choice we ask a child to make at school is that of a career'.

James Hartley and Ivor Davies critically examined research evidence on note-taking in lectures. The authors suggested that note-taking could be considered as an example of analysis which involved three separate but related activities:

1. Identifying and discriminating between *elements* (distinguishing the parts).
2. Identifying and discriminating between *relationships* between the elements (determining the structure of the material).
3. Identifying the *organizing principle* (determining the plan which determines structure for this material).

They were able to proffer a set of guidelines for teachers and learners as summarized below.

Guidelines for Teachers

It would seem helpful to the process of note-taking by learners if teachers could do some of the following:

1. Instruct learners in the skills of note-taking.
2. Make clear the organizing principle.
3. Consider the role of advance organizers, summaries, behavioural objectives or even pre-tests as a way of making clearer to the learner what is to follow.
4. Provide lecture handouts during lectures.
5. Use verbal signposts in a lecture or text so as to convey its structure and, in a lecture, provide cues as to when note-taking is important.
6. Counteract fatigue by using these same devices, by humour and by 'buzz' sessions.
7. Make arrangements for the tasks of listening and note-taking to be separated as these tasks interfere with one another.
8. When collecting feedback from students, ask specific questions about the lecture in terms of ease of note-taking.
9. Encourage students to take notes, and suggest how their note-taking might be improved.

Guidelines for the Learner

Learners might like to try some of the following activities:

1. Use layout techniques to display the notes as they are taken.
2. Note key words or concepts in a diagrammatic format.
3. Record ideas that have personal meaning, and give personal insights into the material.
4. Rewrite abbreviated/unstructured notes taken in class into a separate notebook using layout techniques to convey structure.
5. Leave space at the beginning of any such notebook for contents/index pages.
6. Leave space for making additions to notes.
7. Use a system for denoting points of importance.
8. Give full references to notes made from any supplementary reading.
9. Consolidate learning by reviewing the notes.
10. Try to create a master framework with a set of notes from a lecture series or from several text-books so that the notes become a meaningful whole.
11. Finally, try to consider notes as something meaningful to an individual — something which will transcend simple regurgitation for examination purposes. The method of recording information for later recall can profoundly influence the long-term direction of knowledge development.

A modified Keller Plan course used since 1972 to teach organic chemistry to first-year undergraduates was the research topic used by T M Poole of the University of Surrey. The development of this course was funded by a two-year grant, and within this time the course had to be used without prejudicing the students and evaluated so as to be accepted or rejected by the faculty. In the third term students sit an internal three-hour examination, which is thus an independent measure of the student's mastery of the course. T M Poole found a significant correlation between examination marks and the number of Keller Plan units completed, which seemed to indicate that the modified plan as used at Guildford improved the learning of organic chemistry. Also, this modified plan seems very suitable for first-year undergraduates doing foundation courses which require memorizing of considerable material, as well as understanding fundamental principles. It was suggested that the more advanced aims in the teaching of science — perception, creativity and inventiveness, problem-solving and so on, were not likely to be achieved through the Keller Plan programme. But it did encourage regular study, gave immediate feedback, and was well received by most students. This research and development project is to continue, and to expand to inorganic and physical chemistry teaching.

So often, we hear the criticism of educational technologists that they do not employ the audio-visual techniques they recommend to others. Eddie Phillips of the Post Office Corporation produced an excellent example of how to present a paper using audio-visual techniques, an answer to the critics. He examined techniques used in management and supervisory training and suggested that these could be used for basic training just as effectively. He illustrated his suggestion with examples from the initial training course for Post Office counter clerks. The techniques discussed were guided discovery learning, team learning, the construct lesson plan, work aids and transactional analysis. The paper concluded that:

> 'The use of a variety of training techniques in a course of long duration can be justified on the grounds of trainee motivation alone. If at the same time we are able to imbue our trainees with a sense of partial responsibility for their own learning and development and total responsibility for their own behaviour, we will have killed a number of birds with one stone.'

The second paper mentioning transactional analysis theory was read by Ron Clements of the Wellcome Foundation Limited. After an examination of the basic principles of transactional analysis, he went on to explain how he had solved the seeming incompatability between the need for a self-paced programme and the need for a seminar containing involvement and interaction for the learner.

In his package of four audio-cassettes with accompanying work-books, trainees are routed through a highly structured sequence aimed at covering important transactional analysis knowledge and skills, thus improving communication effectiveness. Early experience shows the package to be effective. After about 10 to 12 working hours, the trainee finishes with a detailed analysis of his own communication style and patterns of behaviour, thus having an action plan for behavioural change.

Dr Keith Barker in his paper entitled *A Self-Paced Integrated Audio-Visual and Computer-Based Course in Combination Logic*, started by answering the question, 'Why do it?' Next he considered the course format, how the course had been integrated with the co-operation of other departmental members and students, the considerable cost and computer assessment. He concluded that it is difficult, exacting work to produce self-learning material and to administer it efficiently. However, it can be rewarding and an effective vehicle for improving staff/student relationships and proving that members of staff are on the side of the students. He stated that audio-visual material can be, at least, of equal value to other methods in helping students to learn and can provide acceptable variety. He found that some students prefer the freedom of self-paced instruction, but others prefer the structure and discipline of routine lectures and tutorials. His final conclusion was that there was no substitute for personal contact and that the student in difficulty must have access to the lecturer.

Dr W D Clarke began his presentation by examining his title . . . *Advertising and Education — Alternative Approaches to Patient Education* and suggested that it should be treated in the same way as the old man's advice to the young man on choosing a wife . . . 'Don't judge the chocolates by the wrappings on the box!' He suggested that the subject matter of health education was defined, but the principles and techniques of educational technology had not been applied to this subject matter. From his study he found that generally, intuition, the 'school-teacher' approach, authoritarian pulpit thunder and a diluted form of the medical school curriculum had all contributed to present practice. Therefore, he had attempted to research a model based upon communication as practised in the world of advertising.

The research was a sequel to that reported in *Aspects of Educational Technology IX*, and used a poster-changing machine containing cartoons accompanied by short messages. The research demonstrated that using a machine of this type, in this way, could be an effective way of promoting health education, and gave support to the advertising model. Further exploration on a pre-retirement project is being conducted by the British Life Assurance Trust.

Evaluation: A Taxonomy of Concepts and Procedures was the title chosen by Dr Richard Lincoln. He examined the concept of evaluation, on one hand as held by instructors, who generally agreed upon the significance of the concept, placing it equally with the specification of instructional objectives, sequencing etc; and on the other hand the many ways in which the term evaluation is used. Analysis of evaluative activities indicates that they all have two factors in common:

1. They involve a comparison, judgement or appraisal phase and,
2. They assume that a relevant decision, based on objective or subjective data, can be made.

The author proposed that a useful distinction can be made between validation, assessing the extent to which the unit possesses the desirable characteristics of instruction; and vindication (a new concept) determining the effect of the instruction on the performance problem caused by a skill/knowledge deficiency.

An attempt to define educational technology to include teaching and training was the introduction of the paper read by Pat Noble of Garnett College. Existing published sources of information were reviewed in detail. The methodology of a pilot study was reported together with a framework for presenting survey data. Problems of reporting capabilities in educational technology were discussed and these seemed related to problems of demarcation over the exact boundaries of what was educational technology, what was management, organizational development, consultancy and audio-visual construction and advice. It was reported that some centres of educational technology activity were so committed that they could scarcely envisage any wider responsibility for information provision unless they were specifically funded for this purpose.

The paper presented by Stan Gilmore of Stirling University reported the validation of a competency-based teacher education module designed to extend the repertoire of student-teachers' reacting behaviour.

The results indicated that the module increased the competency of student teachers in extending their use of discourse structures of elicitation—

response—reaction and that there was an association between the type of structure used by the student teachers and the ability of the pupils to infer implicit meanings from the reading passage.

I quote the implications presented in the paper:

'The study of teaching is a complex of knowledge and teaching skills. Teaching competencies, therefore, can only be adequately assessed by multiple and multi-levelled observation over an extended period. The evidence of small-scale research, in which a singular univariate examination of teacher competency is related to a dependent variable of pupil achievement, leads to an isolated, over-simplified explanation of teacher-pupil interaction. Yet such studies show the presence of common patterns of teacher-pupil talk. There does seem a connection between the communication patterns of the teachers and the pupils' learning. Whether some patterns are more enabling than others to maximize pupil achievement ought to be the focus of further research in this area of teacher competency. As Douglas Barnes (1976) argues:

"A child's participation in lessons does not arise solely from his individual characteristics — his 'intelligence'. 'articulateness' or 'confidence' — but includes the effects of his attempts to understand the teacher and the teacher's attempts to understand him."

'A crucial determinant of the pupil's ability to elicit meaning from the on-going activity of classroom teaching must surely lie in the patterns of discourse which the teacher employs in verbal interaction.

'The teacher whose discourse structures are formed in order to relate and use contributions made by the pupils is not simply adopting one verbal strategy as against another but is setting up a particular social context or communication system which determines the pupils' learning.'

Acknowledgements

I do not have space to mention in detail all the papers and so apologize to those who have not been specifically mentioned. I would thank all who took part, and who helped to make this mini-conference so enjoyable, worthwhile and interesting. I name them hereunder.

Minimum Requirements for a Model of Higher Learning *M J Coombs, J L Alty*
A Study of Educational Technology Centres in the United Kingdom *P Noble*
Individualization of Mathematics — Who Makes the Decisions? *A J Romiszowski*
Evaluation of a Self-Paced Course in Organic Chemistry *T Poole*
The Development of Course Models for Adult Education *E W Anderson*
Evaluation: A Taxonomy of Concepts and Procedures *R E Lincoln*
A Self-Paced Integrated Audio-Visual and Computer-Based Course in Combinational Logic *K Barker*
Automatic Monitoring of Student Use of a Computer *P H Blundell*
The Evaluation of a Performance-Based Module in an Inferential Reading Comprehension Skill. A Study in a Teacher Education Context *S Gilmore*
Programmed Learning and Adolescent Judgement about Careers *C Buckle*
The Use and Evaluation of Computer-Simulations to Help Teach Genetics *G Carmody*
Film 'Atoms' Followed by Discussion *M M Chaudhri*
I am Responsible for Me *E Phillips*
Advertising and Education. Alternative Approaches to Patient Communication *W D Clark*
Using Educational Technology to Teach Transactional Analysis *R Clements*
Note-Taking in Lectures *J Hartley, I Davies*